GURPS

BASIC SET

game design by steve jackson • third edition, revised

COVER BY JEFF KOKE
ILLUSTRATED BY DAN SMITH

Philip Reed, Chief Executive Officer
Sam Mitschke, Chief Creative Officer
Susan Bueno, Chief Operating Officer
Miranda Horner, Executive Editor
Sean Punch, *GURPS* Line Editor • Jason "PK" Levine, Assistant *GURPS* Line Editor
Steven Marsh, *GURPS* Project Manager
Page Layout and Typography by Jeff Koke
Interior and Color Production by Jeff Koke
Proofreading by Susan Pinsonneault and Bob Apthorpe
Art Direction by Bruce Popky and Lillian Butler
Rhea Friesen, Marketing Director
Ross Jepson, Sales Manager
Vicky "Molokh" Kolenko, *GURPS* FAQ Maintainer

Editorial Assistance: Norman Banduch, Mike Hurst, Jeff Koke, Sharleen Lambard, C. Mara Lee,
Charles Oines, Ravi Rai, Lisa A. Smith, Melinda Spray, Monica Stephens, Loyd Blankenship

Additional Material: Steve Beeman, Craig Brown, Jerry Epperson, Jeff George, Scott Haring, Mike Hurst, Stefan Jones, Jim Kennedy,
David Ladyman, Jeff Lease, Walter Milliken, Steffan O'Sullivan, Ravi Rai, W. Dow Rieder, Art Samuels, Curtis Scott, Scorpia

Playtest: Norman Banduch, Jeb Boyt, Keith Carter, Caroline Chase, James Crouchet, Jim Gould, Scott Haring,
Rob Kirk, David Ladyman, Martha Ladyman, Creede Lambard, Sharleen Lambard, C. Mara Lee, Mike Lopez,
Michael Moe, David Noel, Susan Poelma, Warren Spector, Gerald Swick, Allen Varney, Dan Willems

Blindtest: Aaron Allston, Mark Babik, Sean Barrett, Bill Barton, Vicki Barton, James D. Bergman, David Castro, Bruce Coleman,
Jerry Epperson, Jeff Flowers, Dave Franz, Cheryl Freedman, Jeff George, Kevin Gona, Kevin Heacox, Carl Leatherman,
Alexis Mirsky, Guy McLimore, Joseph G. Paul, Greg Poehlein, Greg Porter, Randy Porter, Mark Redigan, Glenn Spicer,
John Sullivan, Rick Swan, Kirk Tate, David Tepool, Bob Traynor, Alexander von Thorn, and many others

Reality Checking: Warren Spector, Monica Stephens, Allen Varney, Jim Gould, David Noel, Rob Kirk

Research Assistance: Mike Hurst, Jeffrey K. Greason, Walter Milliken

Computer Simulation: Jim Gould, Norman Banduch

Helpful Comments: many of the above, plus Tim Carroll, Nick Christenson, Jim Duncan, David Dyche, Ron Findling, Mike Ford,
Steve Maurer, John Meyer, Ken Rolston, Dave Seagraves, Bill Seurer, Brett Slocum, Gus Smedstad, Karl Wu, and Phil Yanov

Many thanks to everyone above — and for all the others I couldn't list. And special thanks to everyone who enjoyed the first two editions and said so!

Softcover: stock # 01-6017 • ISBN 978-1-55634-826-6 • PDF: stock # 30-6031 • Version 8.0 – February 2018

STEVE JACKSON GAMES

CONTENTS

INTRODUCTION

GURPS stands for "Generic Universal RolePlaying System." The name was originally a joke . . . a code-word to describe the game while we looked for a "real" name. Years went by – literally! – as the game developed. We never found a better name. *GURPS* may sound strange, but it really fits.

"Generic." Some people like quick, fast-moving games, where the referee makes lots of decisions to keep things moving. Others want ultimate detail, with rules for every contingency. Most of us fall somewhere in between. *GURPS* starts with simple rules, and – especially in the combat system – builds up to as much *optional* detail as you like. But it's still the same game. You may all use it differently, but your campaigns will all be compatible.

"Universal." The basic rule system emphasizes realism. Therefore, it can fit *any* situation – fantasy or historical, past, present or future. I've always thought it was silly for game companies to publish one set of rules for fantasy, another one for Old West, another one for science fiction and another one for super-powers. *GURPS* is *one* set of rules that's comprehensive enough to let you use *any* background. There are world-books and supplements that "fine-tune" the generic system for any game-world you want. But they *are* still compatible. If you want to take your Wild West gunslinger and your WWII commando and go fortune-hunting in Renaissance Italy . . . go for it!

"RolePlaying." This is not just a hack-and-slash game. The rules are written to make true roleplaying possible – and, in fact, to encourage it. *GURPS* is a game in which you take on the persona of another character – and pretend, for a little while, to *be* that character.

"System." It really is. Most other RPGs are *not* "systems" – they started out as a simple set of rules, and then were patched and modified, ad infinitum. That makes them hard to play. *GURPS* is a unified whole. We've gone to a great deal of effort to make sure that it all works together, and it all *works*. *GURPS* will let you create any character you can imagine, and do anything you can think of . . . and it all makes sense.

I've wanted to do this game for a long, long time. Several years ago, I designed my first fantasy roleplaying system.* It was good, but it had flaws. For one thing, like other RPGs, it "grew" from a simple set of rules, and had many inconsistencies. And, though it had the potential to be a universal system, it was never developed past the basic "fantasy" game-world. When the publisher went out of business, the game went out of print. I was disappointed . . . but it motivated me to start on a new and better system.

I've never tried to design in a vacuum; every game builds on the ones that came before. We learn from our successes – and from the successes of others. I think the best games are those that are simple, clear and easy to read, and I've tried hard to make *GURPS* "friendly." One important influence was Hero Games' *Champions,* for the flexibility of its character-creation system. Another was Flying Buffalo's *Tunnels & Trolls,* for its appeal to solitaire gamers. Finally, M.A.R. Barker's *Empire of the Petal Throne* is noteworthy for the detail and richness of its alien game world.

But there's more to *GURPS* than trying to repeat past success. The failures of earlier game systems are important, too. In *GURPS*, I've tried to achieve several things I think earlier designs missed.

*The Fantasy Trip (Metagaming), comprising several products released from 1977 to 1980.

How to Learn GURPS

Most of you have some experience with roleplaying games already. You should find *GURPS* easy to pick up. But if this is your first RPG, you'll have a little more to learn. Relax; if you got this far, you'll be fine.

Don't be alarmed by the thickness of the book. There's a lot of material here – 250,000 words, more or less – but we've done our best to make it easy to use. Both the Table of Contents and the Index are as detailed as we could manage.

Several features have been designed specifically to make the rules easier to learn. These include:

The Quick-Start section (p. 9). This is a one-page description of the basic *GURPS* game mechanics.

The Glossary (p. 250). This is a listing of definitions of the terms used in the game, along with page references.

"All In A Night's Work," the introductory solo adventure, which starts on p. 218. This adventure is designed for one player (no Game Master is needed). You can play it as one of the pre-generated characters (pp. 214-217), even if you don't yet know the rules. It's written to help you learn as you go; it can also be used by an experienced GM to teach the game to friends.

Here's a good way to learn *GURPS:* Start by skimming through this book, just to get the flavor of the game. Don't worry about the details yet.

Then read the *Quick-Start* section to understand the basic game mechanics. After that, read through the *Characters* section, just to get an idea of the different things characters can do.

Then play *All In A Night's Work.* Any time something is unclear, use the *Glossary* or *Index* to find the rule sections you need.

Then try creating your own character, and play again. Try to design a 100-point character that can best survive the adventure.

Finally, read the rest of the rules in detail, including Chapter 21, *Game Mastering.* Now you can be the GM and run a few of your friends through the solo adventure . . . either one at a time, or all cooperating at once to play the thief! You'll find that you already know enough to get along, and you'll learn fast. These rules were designed to fade into the background and let you play the way *you* want to.

Now you're ready to invent your own adventures – see Chapter 23. You can do whatever you want . . . that's the whole point of the system.

Have fun!

Materials Needed for Play

The *GURPS Basic Set* is a 256-page book; its major sections, after the introductory material, are *Characters, Adventuring, Game Mastering* and *Charts and Tables*, plus the adventure.

Also included is a 16-page section in the back of the book; feel free to copy it for personal use. First is the "Instant Characters" play aid, a reference for you to use in creating characters. Also supplied are two blank character sheets.

There is a two-sided 11"×17" map with a hex grid (you'll have to tape two pages together to form the map). One side of the completed map represents a building interior; the other side shows an outdoor area. Each hex on the map is a yard across. Blank hex paper is also provided in two sizes.

Three forms for the GM to use are also provided. They are explained in more detail in the chapter on *Game Mastering*.

You will also need:

Photocopies of the Character Record Sheet, and the other planning and record sheets, for player use. Make as many copies as you need (for your own use only – not for resale) before you start to play. Likewise, you may copy the various charts and tables, and the *Random Characters* section, for your own use.

Three six-sided dice.

Pencils and scratch paper.

Removable tape – to hold the maps down on the table (optional).

The GM will need his maps, notes, etc., for the adventure you're going to play.

About the Author

Steve Jackson has been playing games for entirely too many years, and designing professionally since 1977. His other game design credits include *Ogre* and *G.E.V.*, the award-winning *Illuminati*, the best-selling *Car Wars* and many others. He has served as secretary of the Game Manufacturers Association, and is the youngest person ever inducted into the Origins "Hall of Fame."

He is the founder of Steve Jackson Games, in Austin, Texas.

Steve is an active member of the Science Fiction Writers of America. He is also an active science fiction *fan*, and wastes a great deal of time writing for various zines and attending (or helping to run) conventions.

When he's not at a game or science fiction convention, his hobbies include BBSing, beekeeping, gardening (especially water lilies) and tropical fish.

First and foremost, of course, is the *flexibility* of a "universal" system. Others have tried this, but have fallen into the twin traps of watered-down combat (where a lightning bolt is just like a .45 pistol) or incompatibility (where players have to learn so many alternate rules for each new game that they might as well be learning a new game, and characters don't easily cross over). I think that *GURPS* presents a single, unified system that allows for great diversity without losing its coherence. This Third Edition includes several complete sections (*Magic, Psionics, Modern and Futuristic Weapons* and more) that were originally parts of separate worldbooks. They seemed important enough to bring into the Basic Set – so here they are.

Second, and almost as important, is *organization*. Any realistic RPG has a lot of detail. After all, *life* has a lot of detail! So RPGs should be well-organized. But few are. Every gamer has had the experience of hunting frantically through one book after another, looking for a rule . . . and not finding it. *GURPS* is extensively cross-referenced, with Table of Contents, Index and a Glossary of terms used in the game. I hope this helps.

Third is *ease of play*. In *GURPS*, most of the detailed calculations are done before you start play . . . they are entered on the character sheet, and saved until you need them. Once play actually begins, it should not be complex. I've tried to make *GURPS* as fast-moving yet realistic as possible. It's up to you to decide whether I succeeded.

Most roleplaying systems depend for their success on a continual flow of "official" supplements and adventures. *GURPS* is different. True, we've released a lot of material already, and we plan to do much more; a totally universal system offers great leeway, and we've got a supplement list as long as your arm. See the next page for details.

But *GURPS* is designed to be as compatible as possible with supplements written for *different* games. The reason? Simple. Suppose that you're a *GURPS* player. You're at the hobby shop, and you see a really interesting supplement package. But it's by another publisher, for another game.

So what?

The *GURPS* system breaks everything down into plain English and simple numbers. Distances are given in feet and miles, rather than arbitrary units; times are given in minutes and seconds. That's what makes it generic. That also makes it easy to translate. If you see an interesting supplement for another game, go right ahead and get it. You can use it as a sourcebook for *GURPS*.

Likewise, if you really insist on playing another game once in a while (sigh) . . . you can still use your *GURPS* adventures. As long as that other game uses units that you can translate into feet, minutes and other plain-English terms, you can use your *GURPS* adventures in that system.

To be honest, we hope *GURPS* will become the "standard" roleplaying system. But we don't expect to do that by driving everyone else out of the market, or even by forcing them to conform to us. Instead, *we* are conforming to *them* – by producing a system that will work with *any* clearly-written adventure.

At any rate, here it is. I'm satisfied that *GURPS* is the most realistic, flexible and "universal" system ever developed. It was five years in the making, and this Third Edition is the product of another two years of development and player comment after the initial release. I hope you like it.

– Steve Jackson

MORE FOR GURPS

This book is all you need to play *GURPS* . . . everything else is optional. But if you'd like more detail about a particular background, we've got almost everything you could possibly dream of.

We currently have over 160 different *GURPS* worldbooks, source-books, and adventure collections available, full of backgrounds, gadgets, and character-creation rules for various genres.

System Expansions

GURPS Compendium I covers hundreds of new advantages, disadvantages, skills, and other character-creation options that have been added to the system since 1986. And *GURPS Compendium II* offers optional rules for everything from bad weather to combat to physical feats, a complete mass-combat system, advice for Game Masters, and more. *GURPS Vehicles* gives players the ability to duplicate any conveyance imaginable, from a rowboat to a space station.

Fantasy

GURPS Magic and *GURPS Grimoire* expand on the magic system presented in this book, with hundreds of new spells and rules for potions and other new ways to do magic. Other fantasy sourcebooks include *GURPS Magic Items 1*, *Magic Items 2*, and *Magic Items 3*, as well as *Fantasy Bestiary*, *Faerie*, *Shapeshifters*, and *Low-Tech*.

Science Fiction

GURPS Ultra-Tech and *Ultra-Tech 2* are the sourcebooks for science-fiction gadgets, from near future to near-magical. *GURPS Space* depicts the future, with rules for starships and aliens. Other sourcebooks include *GURPS Robots* and *Psionics*. *GURPS Bio-Tech* explores human upgrades and modifications, and *GURPS Mars* features the latest scientific data plus three different campaign worlds.

Time Travel and Historical

GURPS Time Travel is designed to support either a parallel-worlds campaign or actual adventures through history. *Steampunk* is a complete sourcebook of steam-powered roleplaying in an alternate Industrial Age, while *Cliffhangers* captures all the action of 1930s pulp adventures.

Historical worldbooks can be used as part of a *Time Travel* campaign or on their own. Our background books include *Age of Napoleon*, *Arabian Nights*, *Celtic Myth*, *Imperial Rome*, *Japan*, *Middle Ages I*, *Old West*, and *Vikings*.

Modern Day: Horror, Spies, Strangeness, and Reality

GURPS Illuminati describes the world as it might be today if every conspiracy theory and tabloid story were true. *Horror, Undead, Spirits, Cabal, Monsters, Blood Types*, and *Creatures of the Night* bring your worst nightmares to life. Other "strange" worldbooks include *Warehouse 23* (a collection of strange items from all over), *Black Ops* (modern-day secret agents taking on the forces of darkness), *Y2K* (millennial madness), and *IOU* (Illuminati University, a light-hearted inter-dimensional nexus and seat of learning), as well as a *GURPS* version of our angels-and-demons *In Nomine* roleplaying game.

And if you're looking for modern-day adventures taken right off the front page of the newspaper, check out *Cops, Covert Ops, High-Tech, Modern Firepower, Special Ops*, and *SWAT*.

"Powered by GURPS"

While most of our sourcebooks are supplements for *GURPS* – they require the *GURPS Basic Set* to play – some are complete roleplaying games in and of themselves. We call those games "Powered by *GURPS*."

GURPS WWII is a complete line covering all the aspects of Mankind's Greatest Conflict. *Transhuman Space* is a near-future science-fiction gameworld as alien as any galaxy-spanning space opera. Advances in genetics, bio-tech, nanotech, computing, and more make the early days of the 22nd century an exciting time. The *Transhuman Space* line has nearly a dozen supplements, covering all the regions of the solar system, and life from the most glittering space station to the darkest Third World slum.

And More . . .

Steve Jackson Games is committed to full support of GURPS players. We can be reached by e-mail: **info@sjgames.com**. Our address is SJ Games, P.O. Box 18957, Austin, TX 78760. Resources include:

Supplements and adventures. *GURPS* continues to grow – see what's available for Third Edition and what's new for Fourth Edition at **gurps.sjgames.com**.

Warehouse 23. Our online store offers *GURPS* print items, adventures, play aids, and support. You can also get digital copies of our books in PDF form, and exclusive material available only on Warehouse 23! Just head over to **warehouse23.com**.

Pyramid (**pyramid.sjgames.com**). Our monthly PDF magazine includes new rules and articles for *GURPS*. It features systemless locations, adventures, and much more. Look for each themed issue from Warehouse 23!

Internet. To discuss *GURPS* with our staff and your fellow gamers, visit our forums at **forums.sjgames.com**. You can also join us at **facebook.com/sjgames** or **twitter.com/sjgames**. Share your campaign teaser in 140 characters or fewer with #GURPShook on Twitter. Or explore that hashtag for ideas to add to your own game! The *GURPS Basic Set, Third Edition, Revised* web page can be found at **gurps.sjgames.com/books/Basic/3e**.

Gamer and Store Finder (**gamerfinder.sjgames.com**): Connect with other people and places playing our games. Add yourself to our database so they can find you as well!

Bibliographies. Bibliographies are a great resource for finding more of what you love! We've added them to many *GURPS* book web pages, with links to help you find the next perfect element for your game.

Errata. Everyone makes mistakes, including us – but we do our best to fix our errors. Errata pages for *GURPS* releases are available at **sjgames.com/errata/gurps**.

WHAT IS ROLEPLAYING?

A roleplaying game is a game in which each player takes the part of a "character," participating in a fictional adventure. The nature of the adventure is set by a referee, called the Game Master (GM, for short). The GM determines the background and plays the part of the other people the characters meet during their adventure.

No gameboard is necessary for a roleplaying game (though some systems, including *GURPS,* include optional "boardgame" rules for combat situations). Instead, the game is played *verbally.* The GM describes the situation, and tells the players what their characters see and hear. The players then describe what they are doing to meet the challenge. The GM describes the results of these actions . . . and so on. Depending on the situation, the GM may determine what happens arbitrarily (for the best possible story), or by referring to specific game rules (to decide what is realistically possible), or by rolling dice (to give an interesting random result).

Part of the object of a roleplaying game is to have each player meet the situation as the *character* would. A roleplaying game can let a player take the part of a stern Japanese samurai, a medieval jester, a wise priest, a stowaway gutter kid on her first star-trip . . . or absolutely anyone else. In a given situation, all those characters would react differently. And that's what roleplaying is about!

Thus, good roleplaying teaches cooperation among the players, and broadens their viewpoints. But it's not purely educational. It's also one of the most creative possible entertainments. The major difference between roleplaying and other types of entertainment is this: Most entertainment is passive. The audience just sits and watches, without taking part in the creative process.

But in roleplaying, the "audience" joins in the creation. While the GM is the chief storyteller, the players are responsible for creating their own characters. And if they want something to happen in the story, they *make* it happen, because they're in the story.

So, while other types of media are mass-produced to please the widest possible audience, each roleplaying adventure is an individual gem, crafted by the people who take part in it. The GM (or the original adventure author) provides the raw material . . . but the final polish comes from the players themselves.

The other important thing about roleplaying is this: It doesn't have to be competitive. In most roleplaying situations, the party will succeed or fail as a group, depending on how well they cooperate. And, just as in real life, the most important rewards of good roleplaying come in *character development.* The more successfully a player portrays his character (as judged by the GM) the more that character will gain in ability.

A roleplaying adventure may have a fixed objective . . . save the Princess, find the treasure, stop the invasion. Or it may be open-ended, as the characters move from one escapade to the next. It's all up to the GM and the players. A roleplaying "campaign" can be open-ended, lasting for years, as characters (and players) come and go.

When it's all said and done, the GM and the players will have created a story . . . the story of how the characters met, learned to work together, encountered a challenge, and (we hope) triumphed!

metric conversions

All *GURPS* books use the old imperial units of measurement, rather than metric, because most of our readers are Americans who use the old system. But not all! Every year, more and more people in the rest of the world start *GURPS* campaigns. And outside the U.S., people think in metric.

Our authorized French, Spanish, Portuguese, etc., translations use metric units. But many people want the English versions. And we can't afford to do two editions of everything. So . . . here's a conversion table.

Note that there are two conversion columns. The first column is an approximation, easy to do in your head, and plenty good enough for gaming. The second column is the *real* metric equivalent, just in case you ever need to be exact.

Imperial	Game Metric	Real Metric
1 foot (ft.)	30 cm	30.48 cm
1 yard (yd.)	1 meter	.914 meters
1 mile (mi.)	1.5 km	1.609 km
1 inch (in.)	2.5 cm	2.54 cm
1 pound (lb.)	½ kg	.453 kg
1 ton	1 metric ton	.907 metric tons
1 gallon (gal.)	4 liters	3.785 liters
1 quart (qt.)	1 liter	.946 liters
1 ounce (oz.)	30 grams	31.103 grams
1 cubic inch (ci)	16 cu. cm	16.387 cu. cm
1 cubic yard (cy)	.75 cubic m	.765 cubic m

Temperature: When dealing with changes in temperature, one Fahrenheit degree is 5/9 the size of a degree Celsius. So a change of 45° F is equal to a change of 25° C. To convert actual thermometer readings, subtract 32 from the Fahrenheit temperature and multiply the result by 5/9. So 95° F is 5/9 of (95-32), or 5/9 of 63, or 35° C.

QUICK START

Read this first!

This section is a one-page guide to the whole **GURPS** game system. Although the **Basic Set** is over 250 pages long, most of it is detail, "color," and special cases. The game system is actually *easy*.

GURPS is designed to be "friendly," both for the player and the Game Master. A glossary of important terms is on p. 250. The rulebook includes a lot of detail, but it's indexed and cross-referenced to make things easy to find. And all the detail is optional – use it only when it makes the game more fun.

There are only three basic "game mechanics" in **GURPS**. Learn these and you can start to play. (A good beginning is the solo adventure, *All In A Night's Work,* on p. 218. It will teach you the game as you go along.)

The three basic rules are:

(1) *Success Rolls.* A "success roll" is a die roll made when you need to "test" one of your skills or abilities. For instance, you might test, or *roll against,* your Strength to stop a heavy door from closing, or against your Naturalist skill to identify a strange animal by hearing its cry.

The only dice used in this game are six-sided ones. Roll 3 dice for a success roll. If your roll is *less than* or *equal to* the skill or ability you are testing, you succeeded. Otherwise, you failed. For example, if you are rolling against Strength, and your ST level is 12, a roll of 12 or less succeeds.

Sometimes you will have *modifiers* to a roll. For instance, if you were trying to stop a *very heavy* door from closing, you might have to roll against Strength at a -2 (or ST-2, for short). In that case, with a Strength of 12, you would need to roll a 10 or less to succeed. Rolling a 10 or less is harder than rolling a 12 or less, just as stopping a heavy door is harder than stopping an ordinary one.

For an especially easy task, you would get a *bonus* to your attempt. You might roll "Animal Handling+4" to make friends with a very friendly dog. If your skill was 12, a roll of 16 or less would succeed. Making a roll of 16 or less is easier than making the base skill roll of 12 or less, because a friendly dog is easy to deal with.

For details on success rolls, see p. 86.

(2) *Reaction Rolls.* A "reaction roll" is a roll made by the Game Master (or GM) to determine how his non-player characters (NPCs) react to the player characters. This roll is always optional; the GM may predetermine reactions. But (at least some of the time) it's more fun to let the dice control the reactions.

To check reactions, the GM rolls 3 dice and consults the *Reaction Table* (pp. 204-205). The higher his roll, the better the NPCs will react, and the better treatment they will give the players.

Many player characters have *reaction modifiers* that add to (or subtract from) the reaction roll. If you have a +2 reaction due to your good looks, the GM will add 2 to any reaction roll made by someone who can see you. This is likely to improve the way they behave toward you!

For details on reaction rolls, see p. 180 and the *Reaction Table*, pp. 204-205.

(3) *Damage Rolls.* A "damage roll" is a roll made in a fight, to see how much harm you did to your foe. Damage rolls use the "dice plus adds" system (see the box below).

Many things can affect the final damage done by an injury. Armor protects the wearer; cutting and impaling weapons, and some bullets, can do extra damage if they get through the armor. "Critical hits" can do extra damage. All these things are explained in the combat rules, starting on p. 95. But the combat system is "modular"; you can use all the rules for a complex, detailed, realistic combat simulation – or just the Basic Combat System for a quick game.

There's another important system – but you don't need to know it to start with. It's the *character creation* system. Each character starts with 100 points to spend. High levels of Strength, Dexterity, etc., cost points; so do special advantages. "Disadvantages" like Greed and Berserk are also available; these give you *extra* points.

This is described in the *Characters* section, on the next page. These rules let you do all your calculations *before* play starts, and enter them on the Character Sheet (p. 12). That way, you don't have to bother with calculations during play!

But you don't need to know this to start; you can pick one of the pregenerated character sheets, pp. 214-217, for your first adventures.

Got all that? Good. Now you can play **GURPS.** The rest is just detail. Have fun.

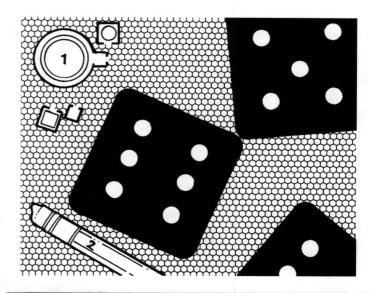

a note on dice

GURPS uses six-sided dice only. All "success rolls," and most other rolls, require 3 dice to be thrown at once.

To figure combat damage, and for many other things, the "dice+adds" system is used. If a weapon does "4d+2" damage, this is shorthand for "roll 4 dice and add 2 to the total." Likewise, 3d-3 means "roll 3 dice and subtract 3 from the total."

If you see just "2d," that means to roll two dice. So if an adventure says "The base is guarded by 5d human soldiers and 2d+1 robots," that's short for "Roll five dice for the number of human guards at the base. Then roll two dice, and add 1, for the number of robots."

For really huge numbers, dice can be multiplied. "2d×10" would mean "roll 2 dice and multiply by 10."

Character Types

There are no "character classes" in *GURPS*. Any character can learn any sort of ability or combination of abilities. The restrictions are those of realism and point totals, not artificial "classes."

However, the characters of heroic fiction do fall into a number of distinct types. If you need inspiration when you're creating a character, consider some of these:

Warrior. Whatever the time period or game-world, he (or she!) knows several weapon skills, and possibly one unarmed-combat skill. Strategy or Tactics skills can also help. ST and DX are most important, though high HT is always useful, too. Useful advantages could include Toughness, High Pain Threshold, Combat Reflexes, Ambidexterity, Peripheral Vision, and Rapid Healing.

Thief or Spy. Needs a high IQ and DX. Any of the skills in the Thief/Spy section (p. 65) will be useful – especially Stealth! Spies will probably know more than one language.

Wizard. IQ and/or Magical Aptitude are vital; DX is useful. This character is most common in generally-magical worlds, of course. But in low-mana worlds, where magic is rare, the "surprise value" of a mage can make up for his increased cost and lowered effectiveness. Magical ability can be combined with any other character type: you can have a wizard-warrior, wizard-thief, wizard-ranger, et cetera.

Cleric. This character type is most effective in worlds where gods are a "real" force and magic works. A cleric can use Theology, Diplomacy and all sorts of medical skills. Honesty and Pacifism are obvious choices for disadvantages – though some clerics are also warriors. Specific religions can require specific skills – Naturalist for Druids, for instance.

Soldier of Fortune. IQ and DX are most important. He is a many-skilled hero, with weapon abilities, unarmed-combat ability, and other specialized talents (Acrobatics and Sex Appeal are often handy). He may be a mercenary, bush pilot, newspaper reporter, or even trader – in which case Merchant skill is valuable.

Tinkerer. An expert with machines – whatever the tech level allows. IQ is most important; DX is also useful. Any and all craft and engineering skills fit this sort of character.

Ranger. A woods-runner. All attributes are equally important. Animal Empathy is a useful advantage; valuable skills include Survival, Naturalist, Tracking, and all animal-related skills.

Expert. A scientist, naturalist, or professor. This character is most useful if he has many scientific skills, possibly with *incredible* expertise in one or two skills. IQ is the important attribute here; Eidetic Memory can be useful.

You can create your character with *any* combination of skills – these are merely some common types.

CREATING A CHARACTER

This is the first part of the game, and one of the most important. The whole idea of roleplaying is to take the part of another person – a "character" that you create. *GURPS* lets you decide exactly what kind of hero you will become.

There are two ways to create a character. The fastest way involves random die-rolling. It is explained on page 84. The other way (and the usual way to create a character) is to *design* him, just as though he were a character in a story you were writing.

First, you should decide what type of person you want to be. Warrior? Spy? Adventurer? Rogue? You can take your inspiration from a fictional hero or heroine – or create your new "self" from the ground up. Either way, start with some idea of the sort of person you want to play. Then bring that character to life!

When you create a character, you start with 100 *character points* to "spend" for your new character's abilities. The greater you want your strength to be, for instance, the more points it will cost. You will also be able to "buy" special abilities called *advantages*. If you want more than 100 points' worth of abilities, you can get extra points by taking lower-than-average scores in some of your basic attributes, or by taking *disadvantages* – specific handicaps such as bad vision or fear of heights.

Start with a **Character Sheet** (see p. 12). Blank forms are in your *Instant Characters* booklet. Fill it in as you go along, keeping track of the points you spend. You may make as many copies of this form as you like, but only for personal use.

Four sample characters, with complete Character Sheets already filled in, are included on pp. 214-217. You may use these characters for the adventure included in this set. The character of Dai Blackthorn (p. 214) has also been used for the examples throughout this section; you may want to find this character sheet now and use it for reference as you read on.

INDIVIDUALIZING YOUR CHARACTER

Character creation starts with four basic *attributes* – Strength, Dexterity, Intelligence and Health. These four basic attributes are explained on the next page. They are very important . . . but they are also very "generic."

Several other things make your character an individual: *Physical Appearance, Wealth and Status, Advantages, Disadvantages, Quirks* and *Skills*. It doesn't matter what order you take them in . . . start with the one most important to you, and work from there. Skills and advantages cost points. Disadvantages, if you choose to take them, give you *extra* points to spend elsewhere. Personal appearance, unless it is especially good or bad, does not affect your point total. It's just a matter of deciding what your character looks like.

The next page shows a Character Sheet for the sample character we will create. Each section of the sheet is keyed to the chapter that explains it.

One thing should be understood before you go on. This system of creating a character is designed to give a *balanced* individual, whose strengths and weaknesses more or less cancel each other out. In real life, of course, being super-strong doesn't necessarily mean you have to give up something else. And being weak in body (like Dai Blackthorn – see p. 214) doesn't mean you'll automatically be good at something else.

A totally realistic system would be one in which a character's strength (for instance) was determined randomly, with no relationship to anything else . . . and so on for each attribute and every other facet of his personality. In fact, such a system is presented later in these rules – see *Random Characters*, p. 84.

But such random choices aren't really satisfactory for your personal player characters. The luck of the dice may bring you a superman . . . or a weak, stupid, boring clod. You avoid people like that in real life; why would you want to become one, even for a minute, in a game?

The *GURPS* system is balanced. All 100-point characters start off "equivalent," though not the same. But you can design the type of character you want while leaving room for growth and improvement.

When you create a character, you start with a fixed number of "character points" to spend on abilities. For most campaigns, we suggest that beginning characters be "built" on 100 points. This is intended to allow them to be *above-average* people . . . the stuff from which heroes are made. With 100 points, they can have an interesting number of useful skills and abilities, without being so powerful that they waltz through the opposition!

If you insist on starting with "average" people for your adventures, take 25 points and go ahead . . . but average people tend to die quickly in dangerous situations.

For GMs who want to run different sorts of games, and as a guideline for creating NPCs, here is a range of point totals for different "levels" of characters:

Below-average	15 points or less
Average	25 points
Above-average	50 points
Experienced	75 points
Hero material	100 points
Full-fledged hero	150 points
Truly outstanding	200 points
Superhuman	300 points or more

Game World Adaptations and Nonhuman Races

The character-creation information here is "generic." For the most part, it applies to any character anywhere – though of course not all skills are available in every game world! Each specific game world may have its own skills to be learned, special advantages available to characters born there, etc. If your game world comes from a *GURPS* supplement, all that information will be supplied. If you are inventing your own game-world, give some thought to the things that make its people different and special!

Other races – that is, nonhuman characters – can also be created. This would include elves, dwarves, orcs, etc. (covered in our *Fantasy Folk* source book); alien races from your favorite science fiction epic; mutant strains of human; and anything else you can think of.

Most nonhuman characters are "built" the same way that a human character is, with modifications to reflect the special strengths and weaknesses of their race. An example:

Elves

To create a character who is an *elf*, add 1 point to his final DX and 1 to IQ. Subtract 1 from ST. An elf weighs 15 lbs. less than a human on the average. All elves get the Combat Reflexes advantage, and one level of Magical Aptitude automatically. The cost to be an elf is 40 character points.

See p. 80
See p. 15
See p. 134
See p. 126
See p. 74
See p. 11
See p. 95
See p. 81
See Chapter 7 (p. 42)

GURPS®
CHARACTER SHEET

Name DAI BLACKTHORN Player _____
Appearance 5'6", 110 lbs., FAIR SKIN, DARK HAIR and EYES
Character Story STREET KID, THIEF

Date Created	Sequence
Unspent Points	Point Total 100

Pt. Cost			FATIGUE
-15	**ST**	8	

			BASIC DAMAGE
60	**DX**	15	Thrust: 1d-3
20	**IQ**	12	Swing: 1d-2
20	**HT**	12	HITS TAKEN

Mvmt	BASIC SPEED 6.75 (HT+DX)/4	MOVE 6 Basic – Enc.

ENCUMBRANCE
None (0) = 2×ST	16	
Light (1) = 4×ST	32	
Med (2) = 6×ST	48	
Hvy (3) = 12×ST	96	
X-hvy (4) = 20×ST	160	

PASSIVE DEFENSE
Armor: 1
Shield: ___
TOTAL 1

REACTION +/– NONE

ACTIVE DEFENSES
DODGE	PARRY	BLOCK
6 = Move	7 KNIFE Weapon/2	5 Shield/2

DAMAGE RESISTANCE
Armor JACKET : 1
___ : ___
___ : ___
TOTAL 1

ADVANTAGES, DISADVANTAGES, QUIRKS
Pt. Cost	
5	ABSOLUTE DIRECTION
10	ACUTE HEARING (+5)
	Hears on 17
5	DOUBLE-JOINTED
15	DANGER SENSE
-15	ENEMY: Thieves' Guild
	roll of 6 or less
-10	OVERCONFIDENCE
-15	POOR
-1	SENSITIVE ABOUT HEIGHT
-1	AFRAID of DROWNING/dislikes lakes
-1	LOVES HIGH PLACES
-1	NO DRUGS OR ALCOHOL
-1	FLAMBOYANT SHOWOFF
0	CANNOT READ

WEAPONS AND POSSESSIONS
Item	Damage Type Amt.	Skill Level	$	Wt.
SMALL KNIFE	cut 1d-5	17	30	½
	imp 1d-4			
DAGGER	imp 1d-4	17	20	¼
LOCKPICKS			30	–
CLOTHES (low-class)			10	1
SHOES			40	2
LEATHER JACKET			50	4
RING			20	–
SILVER $			10	–

Totals: $ 200   Lbs. 7¾

WEAPON RANGES
Weapon	SS	ACC	½ DMG	MAX
KNIFE	11	0	3	8
DAGGER	12	0	3	8

SKILLS
	Pt. Cost	Level
AREA KNOWLEDGE	2	13
CLIMBING	–	13
FAST-TALK	2	12
KNIFE	4	17
KNIFE THROWING	½	14
LOCKPICKING	4	13
PICKPOCKET	4	15
SHORTSWORD	4	16
STEALTH	2	15
STREETWISE	2	12
TRAPS (from lockpicking)	½	11

SUMMARY
	Point Total
Attributes	85
Advantages	35
Disadvantages	-40
Quirks	-5
Skills	25
TOTAL	100

See p. 13
See p. 14
See p. 77
See p. 76
See p. 99
See pp. 15, 180
See pp. 79, 98
See Chapter 8 (p. 71) and the Equipment Lists (pp. 212-213)
See p. 79
See Chapter 4 (p. 19) Chapter 5 (p. 26) Chapter 6 (p. 41)
See p. 16
See p. 79
See p. 75 and the Ranged Weapon Table
Illustration: See p. 80

1 BASIC ATTRIBUTES

Four numbers called "attributes" are used to define your basic abilities. These are:

STRENGTH (ST), a measure of "brawn" or physical muscle.

DEXTERITY (DX), a measure of agility and coordination.

INTELLIGENCE (IQ), a measure of brainpower, alertness, adaptability and general background experience.

HEALTH (HT), a measure of energy and vitality. HT also stands for "hits" – the amount of physical damage a character can take. When you have taken "hits" equal to your Health score, you soon fall unconscious. Further injury can kill you. Death is not permanent in all game-worlds, but it's inconvenient.

The four attributes are considered equally valuable. Getting a Strength of 12 will "cost" just as many points as a Health, Dexterity or IQ of 12. The point cost for beginning attributes is given in the table below. Note that a score of 10 in any attribute is *free*, since 10 is "average." Scores below 10 have a negative cost – for instance, if you take a Dexterity of 8, the cost is -15. By making your character somewhat clumsy, you have "earned" an extra 15 points that can be applied elsewhere.

The scores below range from 1 to 20. 1 is the lowest score permitted for a human. There is NO upper limit to any score – however, very high scores are impossible for beginning characters. For each attribute, a score of 10 represents the human average; anything from 8 to 12 is in the range considered "normal." Scores above 16 are definitely unusual; scores above 20 are superhuman!

This table is intended for (physically) *adult* characters – 15 years old and older. For a younger character, follow the rules given for children on page 14.

beginning attribute levels and their meanings

Level	Point Cost	Strength (ST)	Dexterity (DX)	Intelligence (IQ)	Health (HT)
1	-80		Infant	Vegetable	Barely awake
2	-70	Cannot walk	Cannot walk	Insect	
3	-60	3-year-old		Reptile	Very sickly
4	-50	4-year-old	Ludicrous	Horse	
5	-40	6-year-old		Dog	Sickly
6	-30	8-year-old		Chimpanzee	
7	-20	10-year-old	Clumsy	Child	Weak
8	-15	13-year-old		Dull	
9	-10			Dull average	
10	0	Average	Average	Average	Average
11	10			Average +	
12	20	Weekend athlete	Graceful	Bright average	
13	30			Bright	Energetic
14	45	Athlete		Very bright	
15	60			Genius-minus	
16	80	Weightlifter	Very nimble	Genius	Very healthy
17	100			Genius-plus	
18	125	Circus strongman			
19	150			Nobel Prize	
20	175	Olympic wtlifter	Incredibly agile		Perfect health

Each additional point in any attribute costs another 25 character points. Any score over 20 is superhuman!

How to Select Basic Attributes

The basic attributes you select will determine your abilities – your strengths and weaknesses – throughout the game. Choose wisely.

Strength is in some ways the *least* important of the attributes – unless you are a warrior in a primitive world, in which case it is very important indeed. A high strength (ST) lets you do more damage with bare hands or hand weapons. It also lets you climb well, move and throw heavy things, move more quickly with a load, etc.

Dexterity controls your basic untrained (or *default*) ability at most physical skills. A high DX is very important to any warrior (primitive or modern), craftsman, athlete or machine-operator. DX also helps determine your Speed score – how fast you run.

Intelligence represents both native intellectual ability and general experience. It rules your default ability at all "mental" skills – languages, sciences, magic and so on. Any wizard, scientist or gadgeteer needs a high IQ first of all. A warrior can get along without much intelligence, especially if he has smart friends.

Health represents endurance, resistance to poison, radiation and wounds, and basic "grit." The higher your HT, the more physical damage you can take, and the less likely you are to succumb to illness, injury, etc. A high HT is good for *anyone* – but for low-tech warriors it is vital. However, do not let a high HT blind you to the importance of armor. A battle-axe will cut a healthy man in two just as easily as it will an invalid!

Handedness

Decide whether you are right- or left-handed. These rules assume you are right-handed unless you decide otherwise or pay the points to be ambidextrous. If you decide to be left-handed, and combat damage is rolled to your right hand, it happens to your left instead. There is no point bonus or penalty for being left-handed.

Whenever you try to do anything significant – swing a sword, forge a letter, etc. – with your "off" hand, you will be at a -4 penalty. This does not apply to things you *normally* do with your off hand, like shield use.

Example of Character Creation

Dai Blackthorn is a beginning character. He has a Health of 12 (20 points); a Strength of 8 (-15 points); a Dexterity of 15 (60 points); and an IQ of 12 (20 points). This adds up to only 85 points, out of the 100 that Dai gets to start with. We'll get back to the other 15 points in a minute. We'll need them!

What do his four attribute scores tell us about Dai Blackthorn? Well, he's fairly bright, and he's *very* graceful and well-coordinated. He's also healthier than average. But he's not strong; almost any adult can lift more weight than Dai. He's fast, though; 12 (HT) plus 15 (DX) is 27, divided by 4 gives a Speed of 6.75 – unencumbered, he runs 6 yards per second.

You can easily picture him . . . a tough, wiry little fellow, smart and nimble, who leaves the heavy work to others.

As for handedness, we don't care. He might as well be right-handed.

But that's all we know so far. His background and history, knowledge and skills, likes and dislikes, even the world he lives in . . . we haven't filled those in yet. Dai Blackthorn could be a wizard's apprentice, a 17th-century swashbuckler, a 20th-century secret agent, or a 23rd-century Free Trader in outer space. If he lives long enough, he may be *all* these things . . . someday. But he has to start somewhere.

We'll develop Dai's character as we go through the chapters on Physical Appearance, Wealth and Status, Advantages, Disadvantages, Quirks and Skills.

Pt. Cost	ST	8	FATIGUE	
-15				
60	DX	15	BASIC DAMAGE	
			Thrust:	1-3
20	IQ	12	Swing:	1-2
20	HT	12	HITS TAKEN	
	Mvmt	BASIC SPEED 6.75	MOVE	
		(HT+DX)/4	Basic - Enc.	

Listing Attributes on Your Character Sheet

As shown on Dai's Character Sheet (p. 12 and 214), the four attributes are listed in the boxes in the upper left corner. *Point cost* for each attribute goes in the blanks to the side, to help keep track of the total number of points you have spent.

Your Speed Score

Speed (how fast you run) is another important factor. However, your Speed score is figured from your HT and DX attributes, and shows how fast you can run *without encumbrance*. An average person has a Speed of 5, meaning that, without any encumbrance, he can run about 5 yards per second – though he can go a little faster if he sprints in a straight line (see p. 108).

Add your HT and DX together. Divide the total by 4. The result is your Basic Speed Score – enter it on your Character Sheet. *Do not round it off*. If (for instance) your Basic Speed is 5.25, your unencumbered movement is 5 hexes. But there will be times when a Speed of 5.25 is better than a 5!

Leave the *Move* box blank for now. This will show how far you can move each turn when carrying your weapons, armor, loot, etc. You will fill it in later, after you choose your equipment and determine how much it weighs.

CHILDREN

The table of attributes given on p. 13 is intended for adult (or near-adult) human beings. Children will have different "average" levels in each attribute. If you want a character under 15 years old (usually as an NPC), you can use these average levels for each age:

average attributes for children

Age	ST	DX	IQ	HT
0-1	1	1	3	1
2	2	3	4	2
3	3	4	6	3
4	4	5	6	4
5	4	6	7	5
6-7	5	7	7	6
8-9	6	8	8	7
10-11	7	9	8	8
12-13	8	10	9	9
14	9	10	9	10

A character 15, 16 or 17 years old is created on the regular table, but must take the Youth disadvantage.

If you want to create an *unusual* child – one whose attributes are different from the average – you may do so. The point cost (or bonus) is the same as for an adult, based on the difference between the desired attribute level and the average level for the child's age. *Example:* You want a 9-year-old child with an IQ of 15. Average IQ for that age is 8. The difference is 7 points. On the Attribute Table, we see that the cost for an adult to have an IQ of 17 (7 more than adult average) is 100 points. So it will cost 100 character points to give a 9-year-old child an IQ of 15.

Note that the lower IQ score for children does not correlate with the type of IQ measured by a test. IQ in this game is *both* intelligence and general experience. A child may be bright, but is not likely to have as much general experience as an adult. And note that a beginning character may not put more than (2 × age) points into skills; a 12-year-old child could have a maximum of 24 points in skills.

As a rule, children should be created with 50 points or less. To make up for this, when a child stays in the game for a long time, keep track of his birthday! For instance, when a child turns 10 years old, his ST, DX and HT all go up one (IQ stays the same). This increase is absolutely free.

2 PHYSICAL APPEARANCE

You are free to set the physical appearance of your character in any way you like. Or you may randomly choose hair color, skin color and so on; see p. 84.

However, outstanding good (or bad) looks are considered *advantages* (or *disadvantages*). Good looks cost points; bad looks give you bonus points to spend elsewhere.

Hideous Appearance: May be any sort of disgusting looks the player specifies: hunchback, severe skin disease, wall-eye . . . preferably several things at once. The character is -4 on any reaction roll except by totally alien creatures (who don't care) or by people who cannot see him or her (who will be very surprised when they finally meet the character, and may have to make another reaction roll at the GM's discretion). *-20 points.*

Ugly Appearance: As above, but not so bad – maybe only stringy hair and snaggle teeth. -2 on reaction rolls, except as above. *-10 points.*

Unattractive Appearance: Nothing you can put your finger on – the character just looks vaguely unappealing. -1 on reaction rolls by members of his/her own race, but no penalty for other races – this problem is too subtle for them to notice. *-5 points.*

Average Appearance: No bonuses or penalties of any type; this person can blend easily into a crowd. A viewer's impression of his/her looks will depend on behavior. An "average" person who smiles and acts friendly will be pleasant-looking; one who frowns and mutters will be remembered as unattractive. No point cost or bonus.

Attractive Appearance: This person doesn't enter beauty contests, but is definitely good-looking. +1 on all reaction rolls by his/her own race. *5 points.*

Handsome (or Beautiful) Appearance: This person *could* enter beauty contests. +2 on all reaction rolls made by the same sex; +4 by opposite sex – as long as races are same or similar. *15 points.*

Very Handsome (or Beautiful) Appearance: Enters beauty contests and wins regularly. +2 on reaction rolls made by the same sex. +6 (!) on reaction rolls by opposite sex. *Exception:* If members of your own sex already had reason to dislike you (more than 4 points of negative reaction modifiers, regardless of positive modifiers), then they will *resent* your good looks, and instead of a +2 you will have a -2. This problem will appear at the GM's discretion. A further difficulty: You may be bothered by talent scouts, friendly drunks, slave traders and other nuisances, depending on where you are. *25 points.*

Height and Weight

Players are free to select height and weight for their characters, within reason (whatever they think that is). This can be important for several reasons. Not only is it good to have a definite idea what your character looks like, but height and weight can determine whether you can impersonate an enemy, fit into that suit of armor you found, make it into that narrow hole, reach that window ledge . . .

The tables in the sidebar can be used to determine "average" height and weight, and to provide a slight random variation if desired. Average height is based on your ST score. Weight, in turn, is based on your height.

Height/Weight Tables

ST	Height	Weight
–	5'2" or less	120 lbs.
–	5'3"	130 lbs.
5 or below	5'4"	130 lbs.
6	5'5"	135 lbs.
7	5'6"	135 lbs.
8	5'7"	140 lbs.
9	5'8"	145 lbs.
10	5'9"	150 lbs.
11	5'10"	155 lbs.
12	5'11"	160 lbs.
13	6 feet	165 lbs.
14	6'1"	170 lbs.
15	6'2"	180 lbs.
16 or more	6'3"	190 lbs.

For each inch of height over 6'3", add 10 lbs. to average weight.

Modifications

If you don't want average height and weight, roll 3 dice and consult the following table for a modifier to height. Find modified (i.e., true) height, *then* find average weight based on true height, and use the table again to find true weight. Note that, even with this table, most people will have a fairly average build . . . but (for instance) you *could* come out very tall but skinny! Anyone with a better-than-average appearance should have a weight within 20% of "average" for his height.

Die roll	Modification
3	-6" or -40 lbs.
4	-5" or -30 lbs.
5	-4" or -20 lbs.
6	-3" or -10 lbs.
7	-2" or -5 lbs.
8	-1" or -5 lbs.
9-11	no modifications
12	+1" or +5 lbs.
13	+2" or +5 lbs.
14	+3" or +10 lbs.
15	+4" or +20 lbs.
16	+5" or +30 lbs.
17	+6" or +40 lbs.
18	+6" or +50 lbs.

These tables are based on 20th-century males. For a female, subtract 2" from average height and 10 lbs. from average weight). For a historically accurate pre-19th-century character, subtract 3" from average height. Weight is always determined *after* height.

Dai Blackthorn's Appearance

So Dai will blend into the crowd, we give him average looks. We want him to be small; rather than roll dice, we choose the appearance shown on his character sheet.

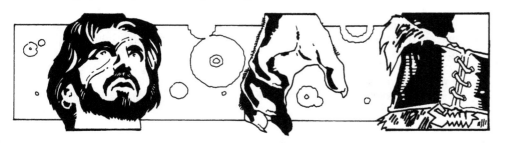

3 WEALTH AND STATUS

Starting Wealth

"Starting wealth" covers both money and property. Start with the amount of money your "wealth level" entitles you to for your world. Buy the possessions you want to start with (using the shopping list in the appropriate worldbook). Any unspent money is your "bank account."

Realistically, characters with a "settled" lifestyle should put 80% of their starting wealth into home, clothing, etc., leaving only 20% for "adventuring" gear. For wanderers, or anyone Poor or worse (pioneers, knights-errant, hoboes, Free Traders), the GM may allow all starting wealth to be used for movable possessions. This is most appropriate if the PCs live in their ship/wagon/balloon as they travel.

Characters should not be allowed to provide bankrolls for their dead-broke friends. Otherwise, the disadvantages of poverty become meaningless. GMs may enforce this by any means, reasonable or otherwise. The GM can allow rich characters to HIRE poor ones, if he wishes.

A PC who needs a *little* extra money may spend character points for it, either at the time of creation, or later. Cash equivalent to one month's job earnings costs 1 character point. Note that it is not "cost-effective" to spend more than a few points this way when a character is created; it is better to buy a higher level of Wealth.

Standard Starting Wealth

Standard starting wealth depends on the game world. In the 20th century, inflation reduces the value of the dollar so much that equivalent starting wealths change rapidly over a few decades. Some suggestions:

Fantasy/medieval worlds: $1,000 (that is, 1,000 copper farthings).
Late 19th century: $750 (£150 British).
Early 1900s ("Roaring 20s"): $750.
Mid-20th century (WWII era): $5,000.
Modern (late 20th century): $15,000.
Interstellar campaign: $15,000.

Later Earnings

A character can depend on his adventures to bring in money . . . or he can get a job (see *Jobs*, p. 192). Remember that in many worlds, unemployment is cause for grave suspicion and bad reaction rolls.

If a poor PC becomes wealthy, or if a dead-broke PC wants a job, the GM should require the disadvantage to be "bought off" with character points – see p. 82.

The next thing to determine is your character's social background. How much money does he have? What is his position in society? Does he have a reputation? How do other people react to him? Like the rest of your character conception, this is very important to roleplaying.

WEALTH

Wealth and poverty are relative. A middle-class American lives in more luxury than a medieval king, though he may have fewer gold coins in his basement. It depends on the game world – see the sidebar.

All characters get the "standard" starting wealth for their world, unless they paid extra character points for Wealth, or took the disadvantage of Poverty. In most worlds, the range of standard starting wealth and income is relatively great, and your skills will determine your job and income.

Several levels of wealth are presented below. See *Economics* (p. 189) for more information. The precise meaning of each wealth level will be defined, for a particular game world, in that world's book.

Wealth governs:
(a) how much money you start play with;
(b) how much money you earn per game month (though this depends on your specific job, too);
(c) how much time you must spend earning your living.

Wealth Levels

Dead Broke: You have no job, no source of income, no money, and no property other than the clothes you are wearing. You are either unable to work, or there are no jobs to be found. *-25 points.*

Poor: Your starting wealth is only ¹⁄₅ "average" for your society. You spend 50 hours per week at your job. Some jobs are not available to you, and no job you find will pay you very well. *-15 points.*

Struggling: Your starting wealth is only ¹⁄₂ "average" for your society. You spend 40 hours per week at your job. Any job is open to you (you can be a struggling doctor, or a struggling movie actor), but you don't earn much. This is appropriate if you are (for instance) a 20th-century student. *-10 points.*

Average: You have exactly the average starting wealth for your society. You spend 40 hours per week at your job, and support an average lifestyle. *No points.*

Comfortable: You work for a living, but your lifestyle is better than average. You spend 40 hours per week at your job. Your starting wealth is twice the average. *10 points.*

Wealthy: Your starting wealth is five times average; you live very well indeed. Your job takes only 20 hours per week. (In a badly-paid job, such as "servant," you don't make any more than anyone else, but you still have your high initial wealth, and you still work only 20 hours a week.) *20 points.*

Very Wealthy: Your starting wealth is 20 times the average. You spend only 10 hours a week looking after business (this is hardly a "job"). *30 points.*

Filthy Rich: Your starting wealth is 100 times average. You spend 10 hours a week on business pursuits. You can buy almost anything you want without considering the cost. *50 points.*

REPUTATION

Some characters are so well-known that their reputation actually becomes an advantage or a disadvantage. For game purposes, reputation affects the *reaction rolls* made by NPCs (see p. 180). The details of your reputation are entirely up to you; you can be known for bravery, ferocity, eating green snakes, or whatever you want. If you have a reputation, either your name or your face will be enough to trigger a "reputation roll" to see if the people you meet have heard of you. Roll once for each person or small group you meet. For a large group, the GM may roll more than once if he likes.

There are three components to your reputation: Type of Reputation, People Affected, and Frequency of Recognition.

Type of Reputation affects the reaction roll modifier (see p. 180) that you get from people who recognize you. For every +1 bonus to a reaction roll (up to +4), the cost is 5 points. For every -1 penalty (up to -4), the cost is -5.

People Affected modifies the value of your reputation. The larger the "affected class" – the people who might have heard of you – the more your reputation is worth, as follows:

Everyone you will meet in your campaign: use listed value.

Large class of people (all people of a particular faith, all mercenaries, all tradesmen, all autoduelling fans, etc.): 1/2 value (round down).

Small class of people (all priests of Wazoo, all literate people in 12th-century England, all mages in modern Alabama): 1/3 value (round down).

If the class of people affected is so small that, in the GM's opinion, you would not meet even one in the average adventure, your reputation doesn't count at all. This is entirely based on your own campaign; for instance, mercenary soldiers will be very rare in some game worlds, and very common in others.

Frequency of Recognition also modifies the value of your reputation. The more often you are recognized by members of the "affected class," the more important that reputation is, as follows:

All the time: no modifier.

Sometimes (roll of 10 or less): 1/2 value, rounded down.

Occasionally (roll of 7 or less): 1/3 value, rounded down.

Example: Sir Anacreon has a reputation for fearless monster-slaying – which earns him a +2 reaction from those who recognize him. Everyone has heard of him (no modifier); he is sometimes recognized (1/2 value). This is a 5-point advantage.

Example: Snake Scarsdale is a cheap crook and part-time stoolie. His name is good for a -3 reaction (-15 points). He is only recognized occasionally (1/3 value). And he is known to a fairly large group (the underworld – 1/2 value). 15 ×1/2 ×1/3 is 2.5 – rounding down to a big 2-point disadvantage.

Note that it is possible to have more than one reputation. For instance, a crimefighter might be well-known, earning a +4 from honest citizens and a -4 from the underworld. In terms of point value, this would cancel out. But if you want to record it on your sheet and play it . . . more power to you! If you have overlapping reputations (especially if one is good and one is bad), the GM should check each one before determining how an NPC reacts to you.

Of course, your reputation extends only within a certain area. If a character travels far enough away, the GM may require him to "buy off" the disadvantage points that he took for a bad reputation. (There is no corresponding bonus for losing a good reputation.)

Literacy

Literacy – the ability to read – is in real life a *skill*. But it is an unusual skill, and its value varies widely from one game world to the next. Therefore, it warrants special treatment!

In high-tech game worlds (anything at or above TL5, which is the Industrial Revolution period), many people can read (at least enough for street signs and the evening paper) and illiteracy is a handicap. Any character in such a game world is assumed to be literate unless you specify otherwise. Therefore, being *illiterate* is a disadvantage, worth -10 points.

In primitive game worlds (anything at or below TL4, which is the Renaissance/Colonial period), few people can read, and it is quite possible to get by all your life without *needing* to read. Any character created in a primitive world is assumed to be illiterate unless you specify otherwise. Being *literate* is an *advantage*, which costs 10 points.

If you, as a GM, create a game world where the printed word does not matter at all, then literacy would be of no account, and literacy would not be an advantage *or* illiteracy a disadvantage. However, we could not think of any Terran examples past the Bronze Age . . . The printing press (developed at TL4, and common by TL5) has had a tremendous effect on culture.

GMs, remember: If you are dealing with illiterate characters (in *any* sort of game world) – *they really can't read!* Enforce this. Notes, signs, scrolls, books, and the names on maps (though not the maps themselves) are only for those who can read! The *player* may still pass secret notes, if necessary, and you may pass the player notes to tell him things the other players don't know – but the *character* cannot read *anything.*

Let's go back to Dai Blackthorn, the character we started on page 14, and fill in a few more things. Currently, Dai has 15 unspent character points.

Wealth: We're going to make Dai poor. He will start with only ¹/₅ the "standard" wealth for his game world. In a fantasy game world, the standard starting wealth is $1,000 (i.e., 1,000 copper farthings) – so Dai starts with $200. Price information is given in the tables on pp. 206-213. We'll equip Dai later, after we know more about him.

Poverty is a disadvantage worth -15 character points, so Dai now has 30 character points to spend.

Reputation: To Dai's chagrin, very few people outside his immediate circle have ever heard of him. He has no Reputation.

Status: Dai is definitely a "questionable" sort, so we could certainly give him a -1 (criminal) status if we wanted to. In this particular case, we choose not to. We justify that by saying that in his home area, everybody is a bit ragged, and there's no way to recognize him as an underworlder just by looking. So he has Status 0: ordinary citizen, worth no points either way.

Literacy: Dai can't read, but since his is a low-tech fantasy world, this is no disadvantage. It would cost him 10 character points to be able to read. He can get along without it . . . we hope!

STATUS

Status is much like reputation, except that it reflects your social standing rather than your personal popularity. Anyone can determine your status by looking at you, your dress, and your bearing. If you have very high status, your *face* may be easily recognized – or perhaps the gaggle of servants that surrounds you will get the message across. (If you disguise yourself successfully, you can change your apparent status, but this is a good way to get into a lot of trouble!)

Status is measured in "social levels," ranging from -4 (worthless scum) to 8 (you are considered literally divine). For a sample chart of social levels, see p. 191. The point cost is 5 points per "level" of status. So a status of 5 costs 25 points, and a status of -3 is a *disadvantage* worth -15.

Status also costs money to maintain. For more on this, see *Social Level and Cost of Living*, p. 191.

High Status

High status means that you are a member of the ruling class in your original culture. Your family may be hereditary nobles (e.g., Plantagenet, Windsor), successful businessmen and/or politicians (Rockefeller, Kennedy), or some other type of big shots. Or you may have achieved status by your own efforts. As a result, others *in your culture only* will defer to you, giving you a bonus on all reaction rolls. Your Savoir-Faire skill (see p. 64) for your own culture defaults to your IQ+2; for other cultures, it defaults to your IQ.

High status carries various privileges, different in every game world. If you are not using a specific game world book, these are up to the GM. Because of the common relationship between status and wealth, a wealth level of Wealthy or above lets you pay 5 fewer points for high status. In effect, you get one level of status free. But note that any high-status person is a likely target for kidnappers and status-seeking nuisances, and some criminal types *hate* "the ruling class."

Low Status

You are a servant, criminal or slave. Note that this is not the same thing as the disadvantage of Social Stigma (p. 27). In medieval Japan, for instance, a female could have very high Status (and the associated cost of living), but still get a -1 on reactions due to the Social Stigma of being female.

The interaction of Status, Social Stigma and Reputation can give interesting results. For instance, a person who is obviously from a lower social class, or even a disdained minority group, might earn such a reputation as a hero that others react well to him.

Status as a Reaction Modifier

When a *reaction roll* (p. 180) is made, the relative status of the characters involved can affect the reaction. The GM can roleplay his non-player characters as he likes, of course, but some general guidelines would be:

Higher status usually gives you a reaction bonus. If you have status 3, for instance, those of status 1 would react to you at a +2, and those of status 0 would react to you at a +3. (Except, of course, for criminals who resent status.)

Negative status usually gives a penalty. If your status is so low that it's negative, those of higher status will react badly to you. Take the difference between your status and the NPC's as a reaction penalty, but no worse than -4.

Lower status may give a penalty. If you are dealing with an NPC who is basically friendly, your status won't matter (as long as it's positive). After all, the king has a far higher status than his knights, but he reacts well to them . . . most of the time. But if the NPC is neutral or already angry, lower status makes it worse. "How dare you, a mere knight, tell me my battle plan is foolish?"

These are character traits that are innate abilities. With few exceptions, a character may only be given these advantages when he is first created. After that, there is no way to gain or "earn" them. (But note that magic or high technology may give a character the artificial equivalent of an advantage like Acute Hearing!) Each advantage has a *cost* in character points. A character may have as many advantages as he can afford.

For some advantages, the cost is fixed. Others (e.g., Acute Vision) can be bought at any level, at a certain point cost for each level. For instance, Acute Vision costs 2 points for each +1 bonus. If you want a +6 Acute Vision bonus, it will cost 12 points.

For a complete list of all advantages, see the *Instant Characters* play aid included with this book.

Absolute Direction   5 points

You always know which way is north, and you can always re-trace a path you have followed within the past month, no matter how faint or confusing it may be. This ability does not work in environments such as interstellar space, the limbo of the astral plane, etc., but it *does* work underground, underwater, and on other planets. Also gives a +3 bonus on your Navigator skill.

Absolute Timing   5 points

You have an accurate mental clock. Unless you have been knocked unconscious, hypnotized, or otherwise interfered with, you always know what time it is, down to the second. You can also measure any elapsed time with equal accuracy. Sleep does not interfere with this (and you can wake up at a predetermined time if you choose). Changes of time zone also have no effect. Time travel *will* confuse you until you find out what the "new" time is.

Acute Hearing   2 points/level

You get a bonus on your Hearing roll (see p. 92) whenever you must roll to hear something, or when the GM rolls against IQ to see if you noticed a sound. Cost: 2 points for every +1 bonus to your roll.

Acute Taste and Smell   2 points/level

You get a bonus on any Taste or Smell roll (see p. 92). For instance, the GM might roll to see if you noticed the taste or smell of poison in your drink. Cost: 2 points for every +1 bonus to your roll.

Acute Vision   2 points/level

You get a bonus on any Vision roll – that is, when you roll to look for something, or whenever the GM rolls against IQ to see if you noticed something. Cost: 2 points for every +1 bonus to your roll.

Alertness   5 points/level

A general bonus you get on *any* Sense roll, or when the GM rolls against your IQ to see if you notice something. This advantage *can* be combined with any or all of the acute senses. Cost: 5 points for each +1 bonus to your roll.

Ambidexterity   10 points

You can use both hands with equal skill. You do not suffer the -4 DX penalty for using an "off hand" (see *Handedness,* p. 13), and can fight (or act) with either hand, or (in an All-Out Attack) with both hands at once. Should some accident befall one of your arms or hands, assume it is the left one.

Animal Empathy   5 points

You understand animals and like them, and they like you. You get a +2 on any reaction roll by a wild animal, and a +4 on any reaction from a tame animal. You also get a +4 bonus on any "animal" skill roll (Animal Handling, Riding, Vet, etc.). However, you may never kill an animal without a very good reason, and you should try to prevent others from doing so. Note that killing for food is perfectly acceptable, and in a hunting situation you will get a +3 bonus to find game.

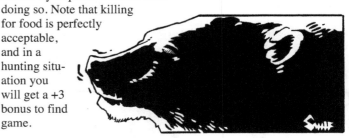

Attractiveness
Variable (see p. 15)

Charisma   5 points/level

This is the natural ability to impress and lead others. Anyone can acquire a semblance of charisma by good looks, good manners and intelligence – but *real* charisma works independently of these things, and you either have it or you don't. It affects any reaction roll made by any intelligent creature. Cost: 5 points for each +1 bonus.

Clerical Investment   5 or more points, GM's discretion

You have been ordained as a minister of some religion. A cleric has a number of powers and privileges that a layman lacks, including a +1 reaction bonus from co-religionists and those who respect his faith. He or she will be addressed by a title – Father, Sister, Reverend, Shaman – and can perform such ceremonies as Confirmation, Marriage and Exorcism.

Remember that not all clerics are nuns or rabbis. Aka'Ar, high priest of the unholy Cult of Set, is a vested priest as well, and the blessings and marriages he performs will be just as meaningful to his own flock as are those of a vicar to his parish. And, if Set so wills, Aka'Ar will be able to perform exorcisms as potent as those of a Christian minister, if not more so. Aka'Ar will have a better working knowledge of demons . . .

The GM should determine whether clerics, in his campaign, can call upon active aid from Beyond. If so, and if clerics are *known* to be able to get such aid, Clerical Investment will be worth 10 points or more. If Investment is merely (as far as the players know) a "social" advantage, it costs 5 points.

ADVANTAGES

Combat Reflexes   15 points

You have extraordinary reactions and are very rarely surprised for more than a moment. You get a +1 to any Active Defense in combat. You also get a +1 on any Fast-Draw skill, and +2 to any Fright Check (p. 93). And you never "freeze" (see p. 122).

Furthermore, your *side* gets +1 on initiative rolls to avoid a surprise attack, or +2 if you are the leader. You, personally, get a +6 on any IQ roll to wake up or to recover from surprise or a mental "stun."

Common Sense   10 points

Any time you start to do something that the GM feels is *STUPID*, he rolls against your IQ. A successful roll means he must warn you, "Hadn't you better think about that?" This advantage allows an impulsive *player* to take the part of a thoughtful character.

Danger Sense   15 points

You can't depend on it, but sometimes you get this prickly feeling right at the back of your neck, and you know something's wrong . . . If you have Danger Sense, the GM rolls once against your IQ, secretly, in any situation involving an ambush, impending disaster, or similar hazard. A successful roll means you get a warning that something's wrong. A roll of 3 or 4 means you get a little detail as to the nature of the danger.

Note: In a campaign that uses psi powers, this can be an ESP ability! See Psionics, Chapter 20.

Double-Jointed   5 points

Your body is unusually flexible. You have a +3 on any Climbing roll, on any roll to escape from ropes, handcuffs or other restraints, or on any Mechanic roll (to reach into an engine, of course!).

Eidetic Memory   30/60 points

You remember everything you see or hear. This talent comes in two levels.

At the first level, you remember the general sense of everything you concentrate on. Thus, all points you put into "regular" mental skills count double (there is no bonus for psi skills). You get a +1 on magic spells. Also: whenever you need to remember a detail of something you have been told, the GM rolls against your IQ. A successful roll means he must give you the information! Cost: 30 points.

The second level is true "photographic memory." You remember everything that has ever happened to you! All points you put into "regular" mental skills count *quadruple*. You get a +2 bonus on magic spells. Furthermore, any time you (as the *player*) forget a detail your character has seen or heard, the GM or other players must remind you – truthfully! Cost: 60 points.

Empathy   15 points

You have a "feeling" for people. When you first meet someone, or when you are reunited after an absence, you may request the GM to roll against your IQ. He will then tell you what you "feel" about that person. (Note that a failed roll means the GM may lie to you.) This talent, when it works, is excellent for spotting imposters, ghostly possession, etc., and determining the true loyalties of NPCs. You can also use it to determine whether someone is lying . . . not what the truth really is, but just whether they are being honest with you.

Note: In a campaign that uses psi powers, this can be a Psi ability! See Psionics, Chapter 20.

High Pain Threshold   10 points

You are as susceptible to injury as anyone else, but you don't *feel* it as much. If you are hurt in combat, you are not stunned and do not have the normal DX penalty on your next turn (exception: a head blow or critical hit will still stun you). If you are tortured physically, you are at a +3 to resist. The GM may let you roll at Will +3 to ignore pain in other situations.

Immunity to Disease   10 points

Your body naturally resists all disease organisms. You will never catch any infection or disease "naturally." If you are forcibly injected with a disease organism, your body will throw it off immediately. Virus and fungus invasions are also considered "disease," though larger parasites (e.g., a tapeworm) are not. You may not take this advantage unless you also start with a HT of 12 or better. However, the immunity will remain, even if HT is reduced below 12.

Intuition   15 points

You usually guess right. When you are faced with a number of alternatives, and no logical way to choose between them, you can use your intuition as follows: The GM adds your IQ to the number of "right" choices, subtracts the number of possible "wrong" choices, and rolls against the resulting number. A successful roll means he steers you to a good choice; a roll of 3 or 4 means he tells you the *best* choice. A failed roll means you are given no information. A critical failure means he steers you toward a bad choice . . . your intuition failed you. The GM can modify this system as he sees fit for other situations in which intuition might logically help.

Only one roll per question is allowed. Note also: The GM cannot let this advantage be used to short-circuit adventures – by letting the intuitive detective walk into a room, slap the cuffs on the guilty party, and close the case. At the most, intuition would point the detective in the direction of a good clue. GMs who don't think they can control this advantage should not allow it at all.

Language Talent   2 points/level

You pick up languages quickly. This talent *is* cumulative with others; if you have Eidetic Memory and Language Talent, you will probably be speaking 20 languages before long. Whenever you learn any language, add your level of Language Talent to your IQ. Example: Your IQ is 10; your Language Talent is 2. You learn languages as though your IQ were 12! You get the same bonus on Linguistics skill. See *Language Skills*, p. 54. Cost: 2 points for each +1 bonus.

Legal Enforcement Powers   5, 10 or 15 points

You are an officer of the law, with all the accompanying rights, powers and restrictions. In some times and places, this amounts to a license to kill; in others, it's little more than the right to carry a badge and write parking tickets.

The point cost is determined by the rights and privileges of the character's branch of law enforcement. Generally, a policeman with local jurisdiction, the ability to arrest suspected criminals, the right to perform searches with an appropriate warrant, and *possibly* the right to carry a concealed weapon, has 5 points' worth of Legal Enforcement Powers. Examples would be a Victorian bobby or a modern policeman.

Someone with national or international jurisdiction, *or* not obligated to respect the civil rights of others, *or* free to engage in covert investigations, *or* able to kill with relative impunity, must pay 10 points for his powers. Examples would be a modern FBI agent or a medieval Royal Guardsman.

An officer with three or more of the above abilities has 15 points of Legal Enforcement Powers. An example might be a top agent of the CIA, KGB, or MI-5.

Legal Enforcement Powers usually go hand-in-hand with an appropriate Duty disadvantage, and with a Reputation which may be an advantage, a disadvantage, or both.

Lightning Calculator   5 points

You have the ability to do math in your head, instantly. If you have this talent, then you (the *player*) may use a calculator at any time, to figure anything you want – even if your character is fleeing for his life at the time! Alternatively, for simple math problems, the GM may just say the character knows the answer.

Literacy   0 or 10 points

Although in real life this is a skill, it is treated as an advantage for reasons which are explained on p. 17. In general, you are assumed to be literate if your world is mostly literate, and illiterate if your world is mostly illiterate (TL4 and below). Being literate in a world where most people cannot read is an advantage worth 10 points. Being illiterate in a world where most people can read is a *disadvantage*, worth -10 points.

Longevity   5 points

Your lifespan is naturally very long. You will fail aging rolls (see p. 83) only on a natural 17 or 18. A character with this advantage gets no points by taking Age as a disadvantage!

Luck   15 or 30 points

Some people are just born lucky. Once per every hour of *play*, you may make up to three rolls for some one thing, and then take the best one! If the GM is rolling (e.g., to see whether a certain NPC arrives, or to see if you notice something), you tell him you are using your luck, and he must roll three times and give you the best result. You can use this advantage after the dice are rolled the first time to get two more attempts. Cost: 15 points.

Extraordinary Luck works the same way, but it is usable every 30 minutes, instead of every hour. Cost: 30 points.

Your luck only applies on rolls for your character to try to do something, OR on outside events that affect you or your whole party, OR when you are being attacked (in which case you may make the attacker roll three times and take the *worst* roll!).

Luck cannot be shared. If Strong Sam is trying to kick open a door, Lucky Lou can't stand behind him and transfer his luck. He'll have to kick that door himself.

Once you use your Luck, you must wait an hour (or 30 minutes for Extraordinary Luck) before using it again. You cannot use Luck at 11:58, and then again at 12:01. Note also that Luck cannot be saved up. You cannot play for hours without using Luck and then use it several times in a row!

Magical Aptitude (Magery)   15 points for first level
10 points/level afterward

You have a bonus to learn any magic spell. Of course, if you are from a non-magical culture you will not start with any spells, but you can still learn them more easily if you ever find an opportunity. And when you enter a magical world, those who can detect your aura (p. 162) will recognize you as a potentially powerful, though untrained, magic-user. They may want to teach you – or kill you.

When you learn any spell, you learn it as though your IQ were equal to (IQ + aptitude). *Example:* You have an IQ of 14 and a Magical Aptitude of 3. You learn spells as though your IQ was 17!

In addition, the GM will roll vs. your (IQ + aptitude) when you first *see* any magic object, and again when you first *touch* it. If the roll succeeds, you will know intuitively that it is magical. A roll of 3 or 4 will also tell you whether the magic is helpful or dangerous, and about how strong it is. *Example:* If you have IQ 13 and 3 levels of aptitude, you will recognize a magic item on a 16 or less. If the GM misses the roll, he will simply tell you nothing. Note that use of this advantage becomes tricky for a character from a non-magical background – like 20th-century Earth. Such a character will still have the ability to sense magic, though until he gains experience with magic the GM should not say, "That idol is magical," but "That idol looks very strange to you, very sinister. You sense there is something special about it." Characters without Magical Aptitude don't get *any* roll to sense magical objects.

Cost: 15 points for the first level of Magery; 10 points for each subsequent level up to a maximum of 3 levels.

Magic Resistance   2 points/level

You are less likely to be affected by magic of most kinds. Note that this advantage *cannot* be combined with Magical Aptitude. You cannot be both magically apt and magically resistant. Indeed, if you have Magic Resistance, you can't cast spells at all (though you can still use magic weapons). Also, you cannot "turn it off" to let friendly spells be cast on you.

Magic Resistance, and its precise level, can be recognized by any mage who looks at your aura, or by anyone who casts a spell against you. The level of your Magic Resistance is subtracted from the caster's skill with the spell. If you have a Magic Resistance of 3, and the caster has skill 15, his effective skill is 12. Magic Resistance also adds to resistance against elixirs (see ***GURPS Magic,*** pp. 98-100).

ADVANTAGES

Your Magic Resistance also adds to your ordinary resistance against spells that *can* be resisted.

Your Magic Resistance thus protects you from having a spell thrown directly on you. It does not defend you against (a) missile spells; (b) attacks by magical weapons; (c) information-gathering spells in which the spell is not thrown directly on you, like Aura.

Magic Resistance has no effect on psionic attacks.

Mathematical Ability   10 points

This gives you a +3 on any math or computer skill except Computer Operation, and a +2 to any Engineering skill at Tech Level 6+.

Military Rank   5 points/level of rank

Just as Status (p. 16) reflects your position in society, Military Rank (also called "grade") reflects your position in a military or paramilitary organization. Each rank has authority over those of lower ranks – regardless of personal ability. Cost: 5 points per rank, up to Rank 8.

Titles of ranks vary between organizations. Typical examples:

Rank 8: Corps-level command or higher (Lieutenant General, General or Admiral)
Rank 7: Division-level command (Brigadier or Major General)
Rank 6: Brigade/group/regimental command (Colonel) or Captain of a capital ship
Rank 5: Battalion command (Lieutenant Colonel)
Rank 4: Company command (Captain or Major)
Rank 3: Platoon command (Lieutenant or Warrant Officer)
Rank 2: Non-commissioned officer (NCO) associated with platoon, company, or battalion commands (Sergeant 1st Class, First Sergeant or Sergeant-Major)
Rank 1: Squad/platoon NCO (Sergeant or Staff Sergeant)
Rank 0: Enlisted man (Private, Airman or Ordinary Seaman)

In good professional armies, field-grade officers (Rank 5 or 6) must have a Leadership skill of at least 12; general officers (Rank 7+) must have a Leadership skill of at least 13. This prerequisite *can* be satisfied by its default of ST-5. Incompetence in the higher ranks is not tolerated under any circumstances. (But in many less-professional or politically-dominated forces, incompetent officers are common.)

It is strongly recommended that no PC be allowed to start the game with a Military Rank above 5, since high rank is normally bestowed only on leaders of *proven* ability.

Military Rank, unlike social status, costs no money to maintain. But insubordination, extreme cowardice, or stupidity can cause a permanent or temporary loss in rank, depending upon your superior's reaction (as played by the GM).

Brevet ranks are given by superior officers (usually of Rank 6 or higher) to *temporarily* increase your rank for a predetermined amount of time – until the end of a battle, campaign, or the like. To keep a brevet rank, you must meet the requirements of that rank as well as pay the point cost (see p. 81).

In some armies, rank may be purchased for money. In such a case, a PC who is Wealthy or better gets Rank 3 automatically if desired. Higher levels still cost character points as well as cash. A Wealth level of Average or less *doubles* the point cost to start with a Military Rank from 1 to 6. Once a character has been created, rank can be bought for the normal *point* cost, if the *cash* cost for the campaign is met.

In many lands, Military Rank carries some automatic Social Status, which need *not* be paid for separately and has no cash cost

to maintain. The "default" here is one level of Status for every 3 of Rank, rounding to the closest number. Where this varies, it will be mentioned in society descriptions.

Military Rank is almost always accompanied by a significant Duty (see p. 39).

Musical Ability   1 point/level

You have a natural talent with music and musical instruments. Your level of musical ability is a bonus when you study Singing or a musical instrument. That is, when you learn a musical skill, learn it as though your IQ were equal to (IQ + Musical Ability). This bonus also adds to HT for the Singing skill. Cost: 1 point for each +1 bonus.

Night Vision   10 points

Your eyes adapt rapidly to the darkness. You cannot see in total dark – but if you have *any* light at all, you can see fairly well. Whenever the GM exacts a penalty because of darkness, *except for total darkness*, this penalty does not apply to you.

Peripheral Vision   15 points

You have an unusually wide field of vision. Whenever something dangerous or interesting happens "behind your back," the GM rolls against your IQ. A successful roll means you saw it, or saw enough to alert you in case of an attack.

If you are playing with a game map, you can attack into your right and left hexes as well as front hexes. (Note that with a one-handed weapon, an attack to the left is clumsy and is still considered a "wild swing" – see p. 105.)

If you are attacked from the right or left hex, you defend without penalty. Your active defense is at only -2 against attacks from the rear. You still cannot attack a foe directly behind you (without a wild swing).

Furthermore, you have a wider "arc of vision" for ranged attacks. The figure below shows the arc of vision for a normal character (white) and for someone with Peripheral Vision (gray plus white).

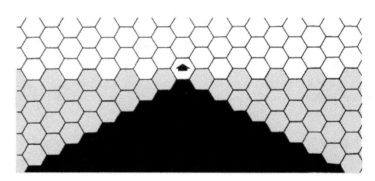

Psionic Resistance   2 points/level

Psionic Resistance interferes with *all* uses of psionic powers against you, friendly or hostile, against or *by* the subject. It can never be turned off!

If you have Psionic Resistance, the level of your resistance is subtracted from the effective skill of any psionic attempt where you are the subject – even psychokinesis and clairvoyance. It is also subtracted from *your* effective skill with any psi ability. Therefore if you have a high Psionic Resistance, it will be hard for you to develop any significant abilities of your own.

Rapid Healing   5 points

This advantage is only available if your basic HT is 10 or above. You recover rapidly from all kinds of wounds. Whenever you roll to recover lost HT, *or* when you roll to see if you can get over a crippling injury, add 5 to your effective HT. This ability does not help you get over being stunned, etc.

Reputation   Variable

A good reputation counts as an advantage. See p. 17.

Status   Variable

High social status is an advantage. See p. 18.

Strong Will   4 points/level

You have much more "willpower" than the average person. Your level of Will is added to your IQ when you make a Will Roll for any reason, including any attempt to affect you by Diplomacy, Fast-Talk, Sex Appeal, Interrogation (with or without torture), Hypnotism, or psionic or magical attempts to take over your mind. Strong Will adds to your resistance when you want to resist a magic spell (p. 150). However, this advantage does not help against combat shock, and so on. In questionable cases, the GM's ruling is law.

Example: You have 3 levels of Strong Will. An enemy spy is trying to seduce you. The GM rolls a Contest of Skills: the spy's Sex Appeal vs. your IQ. But you have a +3 in the contest, because of your willpower.

Cost: 4 points per +1 bonus.

Toughness   10/25 points

Your skin and flesh are tougher than the average human's. Your body itself has a Damage Resistance score. This DR is treated just like the DR from armor: you subtract it from the damage done by any blow, *before* you multiply the damage done by a cutting or impaling weapon. Toughness does not make you any *harder* to hit – it just lets you survive more injury.

Toughness does not let your skin "turn" weapons. They still break the skin – they may even draw blood. But you're not *hurt*.

However, if a poisoned weapon breaks your skin, the poison will do its normal damage. Note also that your *eyes* are not tough! A hit there will do normal damage.

Cost: 10 points for DR 1, or 25 points for DR 2. Higher bodily DRs are not possible to a "natural" human. But some creatures have natural Toughness, or even natural armor that can stop weapons.

Unusual Background   10 or more points

This is a "catch-all" advantage that can be used whenever it is needed. For instance, if your parents were traveling merchants, you could reasonably claim to have two or three "native" languages. But that is clearly an unusual background, which costs points.

Similarly, if you have access to skills not available to the people around you, that is Unusual. In general, any time a player comes up with a "character story" that would *reasonably* give him some special benefit, the GM should allow this, but require Unusual Background to cover it.

The GM may charge extra points if he rules the background is *very* unusual. "Raised by aliens" or "trained from birth by a mysterious ninja cult" might be considered "very unusual" in most gameworlds. Psi-users, supers or wizards are Very Unusual if they appear in a game world where their special talents are unique.

Voice   10 points

You have a naturally clear, resonant and attractive voice. You get a permanent +2 bonus on all the following skills: Bard, Diplomacy, Performance, Politician, Savoir-Faire, Sex Appeal and Singing. You also get a +2 on any reaction roll made by someone who can hear your voice.

Wealth   Variable

Wealth can be a truly wonderful advantage. See p. 16 for the point cost for different levels of wealth. Remember that wealth is relative, and determined by the game world you start in. The precise meaning of each level will be defined, for each game world, in that world's book.

ALLIES

Many fictional heroes have partners – loyal comrades, faithful sidekicks or life-long friends – who accompany them on adventures. These partners are Allies. Having an Ally is an advantage.

In one sense, the other PCs who adventure with you are allies. But they can be unreliable allies indeed. Often they are chance acquaintances, first encountered at a roadside tavern only hours ago. They have their own hidden goals, ethics and motives, which may or may not coincide with your own.

An NPC Ally, on the other hand, is wholly reliable. Perhaps you fought side-by-side in an extended campaign, trained under the same master, or grew up in the same village. The two of you trust each other implicitly. You travel together, fight back-to-back, share rations in hard times, trade watches through the night.

The point cost for an Ally is determined by his point value and frequency of appearance.

Ally's Power

An Ally built on 75 or fewer points is actually a Dependent (see p. 38).

An Ally built on 76 to 100 points costs 5 points.

An Ally built on 101 to 150 points costs 10 points.

An Ally built on 151 to 200 points costs 15 points, etc.

An Ally built on over 50 points more than his PC is actually a Patron (p. 24).

An Ally having special abilities – magic powers in a non-magical world, equipment far beyond the world's TL – costs an extra 5 to 10 points, at the GM's discretion.

Frequency of Appearance

To determine whether your Ally appears in a given play session, the GM rolls 3 dice. If the number rolled is within the range for the ally (see below), then the ally will be with you for that adventure.

Ally appears almost all the time (roll of 15 or less): triple cost.

Ally appears quite often (roll of 12 or less): double cost.

Ally appears fairly often (roll of 9 or less): listed cost.

Ally appears rarely (roll of 6 or less): half cost (round up).

ADVANTAGES

Creating an Ally

An Ally character is created just as though he were a PC. An NPC Ally can have disadvantages totaling no more than 40 points, or one disadvantage of any value. A GM may allow occasional exceptions to this guideline, however, just as he might for a PC.

NPC Allies must all pay the points to have their PC as an Ally. For a normal, 100-point PC, this will cost 5 points.

When selecting skills, advantages and disadvantages for an Ally, remember that most Allies share a common background with their PCs. Soldiers will usually have fighters for Allies, thieves will have other underworld types, priests will have clerics or holy knights, etc. A player should come up with an excellent rationale if he wants his PC to have an Ally from a wildly different background.

Neither an NPC Ally or his PC may receive points for a disadvantage such as Sense of Duty or Oath to his comrade. The point cost to have an Ally already takes this bond into account.

GMing the Ally

An Ally is a non-player character, and should be played as such. While Allies are usually agreeable to the suggestions of their PCs, they are not puppets. They will disagree with their friends from time to time. An Ally may try to dissuade a PC from a plan that seems foolish to him; if he can't talk his friend out of the plan, he may refuse to cooperate. An Ally may even cause problems for his PC, picking fights, landing in jail, insulting a high noble . . . Of course, the Ally will also try to bail his friend out when *he* makes similar mistakes.

A PC should receive no character points for any play session in which he betrays, attacks or unnecessarily endangers his NPC Ally. If the betrayal is particularly blatant, prolonged or severe, the trust between the PC and his Ally will be broken; the ally is lost, but the points are not recovered.

If, on the other hand, an Ally dies through no fault of his PC friend, the PC should not be penalized. Let the PC form a relationship with another Ally. This relationship should develop gradually – no one gains a true Ally overnight.

Since Allies are NPCs, they don't automatically earn character points. However, the GM may choose to give them more points over a period of time, as they gain experience. The GM, not the player, decides how these points are spent. (If the Ally increases in value – e.g., from 100 to 101 points – the PC must pay more for the advantage of the more powerful Ally.)

PATRONS

A Patron is a non-player character, created initially by the player but controlled by the GM. A Patron can be a big help, as friend, advisor, protector or employer. (You can have a job without having a Patron – see *Jobs*, p. 192. A Patron is more than an ordinary boss.)

The GM may limit or prohibit Patrons if they would disrupt the flow of the campaign.

The point cost of a Patron is determined (a) by his/her/its power, and (b) by the frequency with which that Patron appears to help you. *Power is a GM determination; the scales below are examples, and some Patrons won't fit neatly on them.*

Power of Patron

If the Patron is a single powerful individual (created with at least 150 points), and/or a group with assets of at least 1,000 times starting wealth for the world: 10 points.

If the Patron is an extremely powerful individual (created with at least 200 points) or a reasonably powerful organization (assets equivalent to at least 10,000 times starting wealth): 15 points. *Example:* The Los Angeles police department.

If the Patron is a very powerful organization (assets equivalent to at least a million times starting wealth): 25 points. *Example:* a large corporation or very small nation.

If the Patron is a national government or giant multi-national organization (net worth basically incalculable): 30 points.

Equipment and Patrons

If a Patron supplies useful equipment, that increases its point value *only if* the character can use the equipment for his own purposes, while other characters in the same campaign have to buy it. So, in an Illuminati campaign, the Network is a costly Patron because it supplies computer equipment. But a soldier in a military campaign doesn't pay character points for his weapons; if he goes off duty, he can't take them along.

In most cases, this adds 5 points to a Patron's cost. If the equipment is worth more than the standard starting wealth of the campaign, it adds 10 points.

Special Qualities of Patron

Referees may adapt point values if necessary. For example, if a player's Patron is an extra-dimensional creature with demonic powers, or a super, or the Governor of New York, the Patron should cost 20 to 25 points – because, even though the Patron is a single individual, he wields great power.

Extra-special abilities should add 5 or 10 points – GM's discretion. Some examples:

Patron can use magic in a generally non-magical world.

Patron has technology much better than the world's norm.

Patron has unusual reach in time or space.

Frequency of Patron's Appearance

The point cost of a Patron is modified by the frequency with which he appears. Use the Frequency of Appearance modifiers described for *Ally*, above.

The GM rolls at the beginning of each adventure. If several players have the same Patron, they only get *one* roll! If the number rolled is within the range for the Patron, then the GM *may* design the adventure to include an assignment, or just aid, from the Patron. He may also choose to leave them out. However, if the GM determined that the Patron could have appeared, and if you try to contact them during the adventure (for help, advice or whatever), then the contact is likely to be successful, and help may be offered. (Be reasonable. If you're locked in a dungeon without a radio or other means of communication, you're not likely to be contacting *anybody*.) You will not know whether your Patron is "available" on a given adventure until you try to reach him, and, as a rule, you should only be able to reach your Patron for help once per adventure.

Some possible Patron/character relationships for a continuing campaign:

A powerful wizard as Patron to warriors (or young wizards) whom he sends to find magical items or slay foes.

A crimelord as Patron to freelance thieves or assassins.

ADVANTAGES

A minor deity as Patron to a traveling Righter of Wrongs.

A local police department as Patron to a private detective. They may resent him, but he helps them out, and vice versa.

A local ruler (in any world) as Patron to an adventurer.

A large company as Patron to a troubleshooter or spy.

A super-crimefighter or politician as Patron to a news reporter.

Any intelligence organization as occasional Patron to a freelance operative, or full-time Patron to its own agents. (The difference between this and ordinary jobs is that you can't quit . . .)

The GM is the final authority on the cost of a Patron. The GM may also simply reject a proposed Patron if he feels that he/she/it is unworkable within the frame of the campaign, or just too silly.

It will often prove useful to have several characters share the same Patron (they are all agents of the same government, servants of the same cult, etc.). This is an advantage to the players, too; if the Patron appears for one of them to give an assignment or offer help, the GM will usually find it reasonable to assume that the Patron is available for the other characters as well, regardless of their rolls at the beginning of the adventure. However, the cost of the Patron is *not* split; each character pays full price.

Players and GMs should both remember that a powerful Patron can be helpful without actually intervening! A Chicago hood who can say, "I'm from Big Eddie," or a crimefighter who can flash a Q-clearance card, may carry some extra weight in a tough spot.

Drawbacks of Patrons

If your Patron is an employer, feudal lord, etc., you may owe him a *duty*. This is considered a disadvantage – see p. 39. A sizable duty can cut the cost of a Patron considerably, and turn him from a benefit to a considerable liability!

A Patron may have powerful foes who are now *your* foes, too. This can give you the *Enemy* disadvantage – see p. 39.

Employers and Patrons

Not every employer is a Patron. If your employer can be depended on to get you out of trouble (at least sometimes), then that might really be a Patron. Otherwise, it's just a job. For example, a small police department is a 10-point Patron if, as most do, it takes care of its own. But the U.S. Army, though powerful, is not a likely Patron, at least for an ordinary trooper. You *could* say, "The Colonel takes care of his men." But you could just as easily say, "I'm on my own if I get in trouble," and be a soldier character who pays no points for a Patron.

New Advantages

The GM (no doubt with the enthusiastic advice of the players) is free to add as many new advantages as he can think of. It will be necessary to balance the costs of these new advantages to make them comparable to the existing ones. Don't add picky, complicated advantages unless you are willing to put up with the increased bookkeeping.

Mental "psi" powers are also considered advantages. They are listed in the chapter on *Psionics,* p. 165.

EXAMPLE OF ADVANTAGE SELECTION

Dai Blackthorn, at the moment, has 30 character points to spend. Let's see what inborn advantages we want to give him.

At this point, we need to think about what sort of career Dai is going to take up. He has far more intelligence and coordination than he does strength. Since we want to start him off in a fantasy world with low (medieval) technology, we have a couple of logical choices. He could be a wizard-in-training . . . or a thief. How about it, Dai? Got a preference?

Magic is hard work. But 'thief' is such a low-class term. How about 'rogue' or 'gentleman adventurer'?

Okay, Dai. Rogue it is. So . . . looking back through the list of advantages, we immediately see Absolute Direction. That could be very handy for someone exploring where he doesn't belong, and it's only 5 points.

Acute Hearing looks attractive, too. We don't want Dai to be taken by surprise. It costs 2 points for each +1 bonus. Dai's regular Hearing roll is based on his IQ, which is 12. That's already pretty good. Raise that by 5 and he'll have a 17 – which means he'll almost *always* hear ordinary sounds, and will be likely to catch even faint ones. That's another 10 character points.

Being Double-Jointed could be useful, since it gives a +3 bonus for climbing and escaping from bonds. It's only 5 points. We'll take it.

"High Status" doesn't seem appropriate here, so we pass it by. Likewise, "Patron" doesn't seem right for an independent spirit like Dai. "Rich" is right out! Similarly, we rule out most of the other advantages as inappropriate or not useful.

But "Danger Sense" looks like it would be useful to a thief. The only problem is . . . it costs 15 points. That's very expensive, but it's also useful. We'll take it, and stop; that ought to be enough advantages.

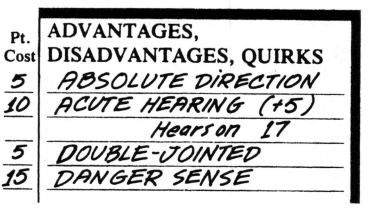

Pt. Cost	ADVANTAGES, DISADVANTAGES, QUIRKS
5	ABSOLUTE DIRECTION
10	ACUTE HEARING (+5) Hears on 17
5	DOUBLE-JOINTED
15	DANGER SENSE

At this point, Dai has advantages worth a total of 35 points. He started this section with only 30 to spend, so right now his total is -5. It looks like Dai will need some *disadvantages* before he's through, to balance his point totals. We'll get to those in the next chapter.

5 DISADVANTAGES

These are problems acquired before the character first comes into play. As a rule, a character may only be given disadvantages when he is first created.

You are probably wondering, "Why would I want to give my character disadvantages?" There's a reason. Each disadvantage has a *negative* cost in character points – the worse the disadvantage, the higher this cost. Thus, disadvantages give you extra character points, which will let you improve your character in other ways. Besides, an imperfection or two makes your character more interesting and realistic, and adds to the fun of roleplaying.

It is possible to "buy off" certain disadvantages and get rid of them. But if a character eliminates a disadvantage without spending the points to "buy off" that disadvantage, the GM may assign a replacement disadvantage. *Example:* You kill your blood-enemy. Unless you spend the points to buy off the *Enemy* disadvantage, the GM will give you a new foe!

"Good" Disadvantages

It may seem strange that virtues such as Truthfulness and Sense of Duty are listed as "disadvantages." In most senses, such traits are advantages! Nevertheless, these virtues limit your freedom of action. For instance, a Truthful person will have trouble lying, even for a good cause.

Therefore, within the framework of the game, several virtues are treated as "disadvantages." This has one very worthwhile benefit; if you want to create a wholly heroic character, you don't have to take any "character flaws" at all. You can get points by choosing only those disadvantages that are actually virtuous!

Limiting Disadvantages

Game Masters should be careful how many disadvantages they allow players to take. This problem is often self-correcting; someone who spends a couple of hours playing a one-eyed, berserk, deaf hunchback who is afraid of the dark will either (a) kill the poor fellow off to be rid of him, or (b) have so much fun that nobody else will mind. But too many disadvantages can turn your game into a circus.

A suggested limit: Disadvantages should not total more than -40 points. However, if only a single severe disadvantage (e.g., blindness) is taken, it may have any cost. Poverty, ugliness, bad reputation and attributes of 7 or less count as disadvantages.

In a campaign where *all* characters, or at least all PCs, have a certain disadvantage, it *does* count for points, but should *not* count against the 40-point limit. In an espionage campaign, for instance, all the PCs could have 40 points of disadvantages in addition to their "required" Duty to the Agency.

But GMs should set their own limits and guidelines, as appropriate for each campaign. Keep it fun.

SOCIAL DISADVANTAGES

Odious Personal Habits   -5, -10, -15 points

You behave, some or all of the time, in a fashion repugnant to others. The worse your behavior, the more bonus points. You may specify the behavior when the character is first created, and work the bonus out with the GM. Some samples: Body odor, constant scratching or tuneless humming might be worth -5 points apiece. Constant bad puns or spitting on the floor would be worth -10 points apiece. -15-point habits are possible, but are left to the imagination of those depraved enough to want them.

For each -5 points your habit is worth, subtract 1 from all reaction rolls made by someone in a position to notice your problem. *Example:* Ragnar Foulbreath, who has halitosis worth -10 character points, suffers an automatic -2 on reaction from anyone who comes face-to-face with him.

Note that certain sorts of disgusting behavior will not bother non-humans. A person with a constant drool will irritate other humans, but a Martian would not even notice, and a troll might think it was cute. The reaction penalty for an odious personal habit is for members of your own race; it is up to the GM to handle differing reactions from other races.

Poverty   Variable

You were born poor, relative to the norm of your culture, or lost your money somehow. You start with only a fraction of the money normal for a beginning character, and your income is limited. The various degrees of poverty are discussed under *Wealth* (p. 16).

Primitive   -5 points per tech level

You are from a culture with a lower TL than that of the campaign. You have no knowledge (or default skill) relating to equipment above your own tech level. You can start only with skills or equipment from your local culture. (To play a character of a primitive race *without* this disadvantage, assume he is from an area near "civilization.")

The value of this disadvantage is 5 points for each TL by which your native TL is less than that of the campaign. If the ruling race or culture looks down on your people, that is a separate Social Stigma disadvantage.

You may not acquire Mental skills relating to high-tech equipment until you buy off this disadvantage. Physical skills (driving, weaponry, etc.) may be acquired at no penalty if you find a teacher.

SOCIAL DISADVANTAGES

Reputation   Variable (see p. 17)

Social Stigma   -5, -10, -15, -20 points

You are of a race, class or sex that your culture considers inferior. The "stigma" must be obvious to anyone who sees you; otherwise, it is merely a bad reputation (p. 17). The point bonus depends on the reaction penalty:

Second-class citizen (e.g., a woman in 19th-century America, or members of some religions): -5 points. -1 on all reaction rolls except from others of your own kind.

Valuable property (e.g., a woman in 18th-century America or 16th-century Japan): -10 points. GMs and players may work out the details for each case – it usually takes the form of limited freedom and/or lack of intellectual respect.

Minority group (at GM's discretion): -10 points. -2 on all reaction rolls made by anyone except your own kind, but +2 on rolls made by your own kind.

Outsider, outlaw, or barbarian (e.g., a 19th-century American Indian in white man's territory, a Goth in Imperial Rome, or an Untouchable in India): -15 points. (Note that there is no bonus for a "barbarian" created and played within his own culture, for there he is not a barbarian at all. This requires judgment on the part of the GM.) You also get -3 on all reaction rolls, but +3 from your own kind when met outside your home culture.

In all cases, a character who takes a Social Stigma disadvantage must be bound by it. For example, a medieval Japanese lady must pay for her 10-point bonus by giving up her freedom of movement in many cases, and must defer to older male relatives when they are present. And a black slave in the 19th century will be allowed to learn very little, can own almost no property, and will have little freedom of any kind unless he manages to escape north. (If he does escape, he will have traded off his Social Stigma disadvantage for a powerful Enemy!)

Status   Variable (see p. 18)

PHYSICAL DISADVANTAGES

These are physical handicaps that a character starts with. In most cases they are permanent, though sometimes magic or high technology can rid you of a physical disadvantage. If that happens, you must either pay enough earned character points to "buy off" that disadvantage, or take a new disadvantage worth the same number of points.

You may also acquire a physical disadvantage during play. This may be a replacement for another disadvantage, as described above, or it may be a "natural" result of accident or combat. In either case, you will immediately acquire all the bad effects of that disadvantage. However, physical handicaps acquired as a result of combat or accident do *not* give you more points with which to buy abilities. If you start out blind, you start with an extra 50 points . . . but if you're blinded by an explosion during the game, you're just blind, and that's that. You *should* reduce the point total for your character by 50 points to reflect his new disadvantage. You *may not* keep the same point total and take 50 compensating points of advantages!

Age   -3 points per year over 50

Your character is over 50 years old when created. Thus, you will have to roll a number of times (see *Age and Aging*, p. 83) for possible loss of attribute points due to old age. Note that creating a very old character will be self-defeating: a character created 70 years old would get 60 bonus points (!!) but would have to roll 20 times for each of his attributes, chancing loss of points each time, and would already be near the end of his life.

Albinism   -10 points

You have no natural body pigment; your hair and skin are pink-white, and your eyes are pink. An albino may seem attractive or ugly, but "average" appearance is impossible when choosing Physical Appearance. An albino will always be remembered, and can never blend into a crowd. Albinos must avoid direct sun, as they have no resistance to sunburn; you will take 1 point of damage for every 30 minutes of ordinary direct sunlight you are exposed to, or every 15 minutes of hot summer or desert sun. You are also at -2 for every Vision roll, or ranged weapon attack, made in direct sunlight.

Bad Sight   -10/-25 points

You may be either nearsighted or farsighted – your choice. If you are nearsighted, you cannot read small print, etc., more than a foot away, or road signs, etc., at more than about 10 yards. When using a hand weapon, you are at -2 to your skill rolls. When using a thrown or missile weapon, use the modifier appropriate to *double* the actual distance to the target.

If you are farsighted, you cannot read a book except with great difficulty (triple the normal time), and you are at -3 DX on any close manual labor.

Any character at TL5 or higher can acquire glasses which will compensate totally for bad sight *while they are worn;* in the 20th century, contact lenses are available. Remember that accidents or head blows may knock glasses off, enemies may take them, etc.

For anyone starting at a tech level in which vision can be corrected, Bad Sight is worth only -10 points. For a character from a time in which vision cannot be corrected, Bad Sight is worth -25 points.

Blindness   -50 points

You cannot see at all. As partial compensation, you may start with Acute Hearing and/or Acute Taste and Smell at only half cost. Furthermore, you suffer no extra penalties of any kind when operating in the dark! In unfamiliar territory, you must travel slowly and carefully or be led by a companion or guide animal. Many actions and abilities – too many to list – are impossible to the blind; GMs should use common sense.

A blind character is at -6 on any combat skill. He *can* use hand weapons, but *cannot* aim a blow at any particular part of a foe's body, and *cannot* fire a missile weapon (except randomly, or at something so close he can hear it). This all assumes that the character is accustomed to blindness. Someone who suddenly loses his eyesight will fight at a -10, as though in the dark.

In civilized countries, a blind person will receive a +1 on reaction rolls.

As an option, the GM may ask the player of a blind character to wear a blindfold during play; this will give some slight appreciation of the problems facing the blind, *and* of the many things a person can accomplish without sight!

PHYSICAL DISADVANTAGES

Color Blindness   -10 points

You cannot see any colors at all (this is total color-blindness). In everyday life, this is merely a nuisance. In any situation requiring color identification (gem buying, livery identification, or pushing the red button to start the motor), the GM should give you appropriate difficulties.

Certain skills will always be harder for you. In particular, you are at a -1 penalty for any Driving, Piloting, Chemistry, Merchant or Tracking roll.

Deafness   -20 points

You can hear nothing. Any information you receive must be communicated in writing (if you are literate) or through sign language. You also have a -3 penalty to IQ when learning any language but your own. However, you get a +3 on any Gesture or Sign Language (p. 55) or Lip Reading (p. 66) skill roll.

As an option, the player of a deaf character may wear earplugs to force the other players to write notes or use sign language. This is not too practical (good earplugs are hard to find) but can be interesting. Note that the GM may talk to the player whenever he wants.

Dwarfism   -15 points

You are a genetic dwarf – abnormally small for your species. Determine your height normally (p. 15) and then reduce it to 60% of that. You may not have an "average" Physical Appearance – you will either be thought "cute and charming" or noticeably unappealing. Anyone attacking you with a thrown or missile weapon will be at a -1 – you are a hard target! In combat, you are automatically 2 feet below a normal-sized human foe. Certain things are impossible to a dwarf because of size; others are much easier. The GM must use his imagination!

Dwarfism is a condition found in all species. A genetic dwarf is *not* the same as a member of the race called Dwarves (though it is possible to be a dwarf Dwarf . . .).

A dwarf's strength and health are determined normally; many dwarfs are strong for their size. However, dwarfs have a -1 to their Move, and jump as though their ST were 4 less.

Epilepsy   -30 points

You are subject to seizures, during which your limbs tremble uncontrollably and you cannot speak or think clearly. (This represents a *severe* form of the ailment.) Whenever you are in a very stressful situation (especially if your life or the life of a friend is threatened), you must roll 3 dice against your basic HT. A failed roll will bring on a seizure lasting for 1d minutes. Needless to say, you can do *nothing* while the seizure goes on, and you take 1 die of fatigue damage as well. If you have any sort of phobia, exposure to the object of fear is automatically a stressful situation; roll vs. HT once every 10 minutes.

By concentrating, you may attempt to induce a seizure through autohypnosis. This requires one minute and a successful IQ roll. A seizure in a high-mana (magical) area will produce visions, which may at the GM's option be true or even prophetic.

Primitives, not understanding "fits," are sometimes awed by them, and may think your seizure shows a communication from the gods. Make a reaction roll at +1. Very good results indicate worship! Poor results will cause the savages to flee – never to attack.

Eunuch   -5 points

You (male characters only) have lost your manhood, either through accident or hostile action. You are immune to seduction, and cannot seduce others. Anyone aware of your condition will have a -1 on reaction rolls.

Fat   -10/-20 points

You are unusually obese for your race. (A character may also be just *Overweight;* this is listed separately, below.)

For -10 points, determine weight normally from ST (p. 15) and then increase it by 50%. This gives -1 on all reaction rolls; HT may not be greater than 15. For -20 points, determine weight normally and *double* it; this gives -2 on all reaction rolls; HT may not be greater than 13. In either case, the extra weight counts as extra encumbrance (see p. 76), which you cannot get rid of. (Exception: fat encumbrance does not count against you when swimming.)

Normal clothes and armor will not fit you. You will also be at -3 to Disguise, or to Shadowing if you are trying to follow someone in a crowd.

As a rule, fat people have many small problems, which the GM should interpret creatively. However, there are a few small advantages. For instance, fat people get +5 to their Swimming roll, and are very hard to dislodge if they choose to pin you down by sitting on you . . . If you are fat, you also get +2 to your ST when you make (or resist) any Slam attack.

Gigantism   -10 points

You are a genetic giant – abnormally large for your species. Determine your height normally (p. 15), and then increase it by 20%; if you are still less than 7 feet tall (for humans), increase your height to that minimum. Minimum size for giants in other races is left up to the GM. Weight is in proportion to height, as listed on the tables. Strength and health are unaffected. You suffer a -2 on reaction rolls except in potential combat situations, where you receive a +1 from either potential allies or enemies. You are considered to be a foot above normal-sized foes, automatically.

Since giants live in an undersized world, they have many small problems . . . clothes, chairs, etc., simply don't fit them. However, this is not an especially disastrous disadvantage.

Hard of Hearing   -10 points

You are not deaf, but you have some hearing loss. You are at -4 to IQ on any Hearing roll (so your roll is IQ-4, rather than IQ). You are at -4 to your language skill roll for any situation where you must understand someone (if you are the one talking, this disadvantage doesn't affect you).

Hemophilia   -30 points

You are a "bleeder." Even a small wound, unless well bandaged, will not heal – and you may bleed to death. Any untreated wound will bleed at a rate equal to its original damage every minute. For instance, an untreated 3-point hit will do another 3 hits of damage after the first minute, and so on until staunched. A hemophiliac may not have a basic HT over 10.

First Aid will be satisfactory to treat most wounds. However, any impaling wound to the torso will cause slow internal bleeding. Such a wound will do damage as above until it receives First Aid. It will *continue* to do damage equal to its original damage once per *day* until properly treated. Only a Surgeon, or magical/psychic healing, can cure this injury or restore the HT lost to internal bleeding. If proper treatment is not available – you die.

Lame   -15, -25, or -35 points

You have some degree of impaired mobility. The point bonus depends on the damage, as follows:

Crippled leg: You have one bad leg; your Move and Dodge are reduced by 3. You suffer a -3 penalty to use any physical skill that requires walking or running. This definitely includes all hand-weapon skills and all martial arts (missile weapon ability is unimpaired). *-15 points.*

One leg: You have lost a leg. You are at a -6 penalty to use any physical skill that requires the use of your legs. You cannot run; using crutches or a peg leg, you have a maximum Move of 2. (Otherwise, you cannot walk at all.) If you have access to TL6 (20th-century) prosthetics, you can reduce the effect to that of a crippled leg, but you must buy off the point difference in some way. (TL8+ technology could replace the leg, possibly with one that was better than the original, but then it's no longer a disadvantage.) *-25 points.*

Legless or paraplegic: You are confined to a wheelchair or wheeled platform. If you power it with your own hands, its Speed is 1/4 your ST, rounded down. Alternately, you may be carried piggy-back or on a stretcher. The GM should assess all reasonable penalties for this handicap. Examples: you cannot pass through narrow doors, navigate staircases or steep curbs, travel except in specially-equipped vehicles, fight effectively (except with guns or crossbow), etc. If you have to fight with a sword, etc., you will be at a -6. *-35 points.*

Low Pain Threshold   -10 points

You are very sensitive to pain of all kinds. Double the "shock effect" of any injury – e.g., if you take 3 points of damage, DX is at -6 on your next turn. You always roll at -4 to resist physical torture. Whenever you take a wound that does more than 1 hit of damage, you must make a Will roll to avoid crying out (possibly giving away your presence). Barbarians, soldiers, thugs and so on will react to you at -1 if they know you have this disadvantage.

Mute   -25 points

You cannot speak. All your communications with others (and the *player's* communication with other players!) must be in writing, or with sign language. (It is all right for the GM and the player to go into a separate room, if necessary, and talk about what the character is *doing*.) A mute character gets a +3 on any Gesture or Sign Language skill roll (see p. 55). However, no roll is required (or allowed!) when you try to communicate with other player characters who don't know your sign language; roleplay this on your own!

No Sense of Smell/Taste (Anosmia)
                                          -5 points

This is a rare affliction . . . you can smell and taste nothing. Thus, you are unable to detect certain hazards that ordinary people spot quickly. However, the disability has its advantages . . . an anosmic character never worries about skunks, and can always eat what is set before him.

One Arm   -20 points

You have lost an arm (or you were born without it). It is assumed that you lost the left arm if you were right-handed, or vice versa. You cannot use sword and shield simultaneously, or any two-handed weapon, or do anything requiring two arms – GM's ruling is final in case of argument. Anything requiring only one hand can be done without penalty. In borderline cases, it is best to allow the character to attempt the action at a -4 DX penalty, or to try a quick reality check if possible!

One Eye   -15 points

You have only one good eye; you may wear a glass eye, or cover the missing eye with a patch. You suffer a -1 DX penalty on combat, and on anything involving hand-eye coordination, and a -3 on anything involving missile weapons, thrown objects, or driving any vehicle faster than a horse and buggy. You will also suffer a -1 on any reaction roll except with utterly alien creatures. Exception: If you have Charisma, or are Handsome or Very Handsome, the patch just looks romantic, and does not affect reaction rolls.

One Hand   -15 points

You have lost a hand; it may be replaced by an appropriate pros-thetic (hook, mechanical grabber or bionic hand). A fully bionic replacement (TL8 or higher) is just as good as the original, and is therefore worth no bonus points. An obviously mechanical replace-ment will cost you -1 on all reaction rolls, and -2 DX (for a mechanical grabber) or -4 DX (for a claw). However, a hook or claw counts as an undroppable large knife in combat (use Knife skill). This can be very intimidating if waved at the foe.

One Leg   See Lame, above

Overweight   -5 points

You are not truly fat – just somewhat heavy for your race. Determine weight normally for ST, and then increase it by 30%; this adds to encumbrance as for Fat (p. 28). Overweight characters get a +2 bonus to their Swimming roll.

Being overweight carries a reaction penalty of -1 among health-conscious societies – like that of the 1980s yuppies – and in areas where food is in especially short supply – such as among the dregs of Autoduel America.

There are no other bonuses or penalties; you can easily get clothes, and blend into a crowd, because many people are overweight.

Skinny   -5 points

You are notably underweight. After figuring your height, take "average" weight for that height (see p. 15) and cut it by 1/3. You may not take Handsome or Very Handsome appearance, and your HT may not be more than 14.

Normal clothes and armor will not fit you. You will also be at -2 to your ST when you make (or resist) any Slam attack, and -2 to Disguise, or to Shadowing if you are trying to follow someone in a crowd.

Stuttering   -10 points

You suffer from a stammer or other speech impediment, which the GM may require the player to act out. -2 on all reaction rolls where conversation is required, and certain occupations and skills (e.g., Diplomacy, Fast-Talk, Public Speaking, interpreting, news-casting) are impossible.

Youth   -2 to -6 points

You are underage by your culture's standards: 1 to 3 full years underage, at -2 points per year. You suffer a -2 reaction roll when-ever you try to deal with others as an adult; they may like you, but they do not fully respect you. You may also be barred from night-clubs, vehicle operation, war parties, guild membership, etc., depending on the culture and game world. You *must* keep track of time, and "buy off" this disability when you reach "legal age" (usu-ally 18) for your time and place.

MENTAL DISADVANTAGES

*Note to the GM: Many mental disadvantages permit the afflicted character to make IQ or Will rolls (p. 93) to avoid the bad effects. In these cases, any roll of 14 or over **still fails.** Otherwise, very smart or strong-willed people would be almost immune to their own bad habits – which isn't the way life works!*

Absent-Mindedness   -15 points

The classic disadvantage for eccentric geniuses. You have difficulty paying attention to anything not of immediate interest. An absent-minded person suffers a -5 penalty on any IQ roll except those for a task he is currently interested in and concentrating upon. If no engaging task or topic presents itself, his attention will drift to more interesting matters in five minutes; he will ignore his immediate surroundings until something catches his attention and brings him back. Once adrift in his own thoughts, an absent-minded character must roll against IQ-5 in order to *notice* any event short of personal physical injury.

The absent-minded person may attempt to rivet his attention on a boring topic through sheer strength of will. To do so, he must make a Will-5 roll once every five minutes. "Boring topics" include guard duty, small talk or other forms of meaningless conversation, repetitive manual tasks, driving on an empty highway . . .

Absent-minded individuals also tend to forget trivial tasks (like paying the bills) and items (like car keys and checkbooks). Whenever it becomes important that an absent-minded character have performed such a task or brought such an item, the GM should call for a roll against IQ-2. On a failed roll, this detail slipped his attention. For example, an absent-minded detective is in a shootout. He has been involved in gunplay earlier today, in which he fired four rounds, so the GM calls for an IQ-2 roll. The detective fails the roll, discovering too late that he forgot to reload his weapon, so his revolver only has two bullets left!

Addiction   Variable

You are addicted to a drug, which you must use daily or suffer the penalties of withdrawal (see below). The bonus for this disadvantage depends on the nature of the drug addiction, as follows:

If each daily dose costs $20 or less: -5 points.
If each daily dose costs $21-$100: -10 points.
If each daily dose costs over $100: -20 points.
If the drug is incapacitating or hallucinogenic: -10 points.
If the drug is highly addictive (-5 on withdrawal roll): -5 points.
If the drug is totally addictive (-10 on withdrawal roll): -10 points.
If the drug is *legal* in your original game world: *plus* 5 points!

Examples: Tobacco is cheap, highly addictive, and legal; a chain-smoker has a -5-point addiction. Heroin is very expensive, incapacitating, illegal and totally addictive; a heroin addict has a -40-point disadvantage.

Effects of Drugs. An *incapacitating* drug will render its user unconscious (or blissfully, uselessly drowsy) for about two hours (four hours for characters with ST below 10, one hour for those with ST over 15). A *stimulating* drug will affect its user for the same period of time: the user thinks he is smarter, but in fact is temporarily at IQ-1. However, he *does* have a +1 bonus to Speed. A *hallucinogenic* drug renders its users useless for work or combat, though they may be active and talkative. Some drugs (e.g., tobacco) have none of these effects, and some drugs have unique effects. Side effects are also possible; GMs are free to look up (or invent) side effects for real or imaginary drugs!

Withdrawal. Sometimes, voluntarily or otherwise, a drug user must try to give up his addiction. This may happen if he is imprisoned, if he travels to a place where his drug is not available, or just because he can't afford it. Withdrawal is a painful process requiring two weeks (14 days) of successful HT rolls (the GM may vary this time as he thinks appropriate for a particular drug).

Each day, the addict rolls against HT, plus or minus Will. A successful roll puts him one day closer to shaking off the addiction. A failed roll means the addict must (if his drug is available) give in to the craving and take a dose of the drug. He must then start withdrawal all over again if he still wants to try. If the drug is *not* available, the addict takes 1 hit of damage and may continue to try to withdraw . . . but that day doesn't count toward the 14 successful rolls needed to withdraw. HT losses caused by withdrawal cannot be cured (by any "normal" means, that is) until the withdrawal has succeeded or been abandoned.

Remember that you must "buy off" the disadvantage of addiction before you voluntarily withdraw, or immediately after forced withdrawal; see p. 82.

Alcoholism   -15 or -20 points

You are an alcohol addict. Alcoholism is treated as an addiction (see above); it is inexpensive, incapacitating, and (usually) legal, so it would normally be a -10-point addiction. But alcohol is insidious, because it is different from most addictions. Therefore, it is worth 15 points, or 20 if it is illegal.

An alcoholic may, under normal circumstances, confine his drinking to the evenings, and therefore be able to function (for game purposes) normally. However, *any time* an alcoholic is in the presence of alcohol, he must roll vs. Will to avoid partaking. A failed roll means he goes on a "binge" lasting 2d hours, followed by a hangover twice as long, during which all stats are at -3. Alcoholics on a binge are characterized by sudden swings of mood – from extreme friendliness to extreme hostility – and may attack their friends, talk too freely, or make other mistakes.

The other drawback of alcoholism is that it is hard to get rid of. Should an alcoholic character successfully "withdraw," he no longer needs to drink daily . . . but he must still make a Will roll, at +4, whenever in the presence of alcohol. A failed roll does not reinstate the addiction, but does set off a binge. (Three binges in a week *will* reinstate the addiction.) Thus, there is no normal way that this disadvantage can ever be "bought off."

An alcoholic must roll yearly against (HT+2), until he withdraws. A failed roll means the alcoholic must lose one point from one of his four basic attributes – roll randomly to determine which.

Bad Temper   -10 points

You are not in full control of your emotions. In any stressful situation, you must make a Will roll. A failed roll means you lose your temper, and must insult, attack or otherwise act against the cause of the stress.

Berserk   -15 points

Like Bad Temper, but worse. You tend to lose control of yourself under stress, making frenzied attacks against whoever or whatever you see as the cause of the trouble. (You cannot take both Bad Temper and Berserk.)

Any time you take more than 3 hits in one turn, you *must* roll vs. Will. A failed roll means you go berserk. Other conditions of extreme stress (GM's option) may also require a Will roll to avoid berserking. A berserker may *deliberately* go berserk by taking the "Concentrate" maneuver and making a *successful* Will roll.

While berserk, you must make an All-Out Attack each turn a foe is in range, and Move as close as possible to a foe if none is in range. Or, if the enemy is more than 20 yards away, a berserker may attack with ranged weapons – but he may not take time to aim.

High-tech berserk: If an experienced gunman goes berserk, he will fire as many shots as he can every turn, until his gun is empty. He will not reload unless he has a Fast-Draw skill for reloading, letting him reload "without thought." When his gun is empty, he will attack with his hands or another weapon. He may never aim.

While berserk, you cannot be stunned, and injuries cause no penalty to your Move score or attack rolls. All rolls to remain conscious or alive are made at a +4 bonus to HT; if you don't fail any rolls, you remain alive and madly attacking until your HT reaches (-5×HT). Then you fall dead!

When a berserker downs his foe, he may (at the player's discretion) roll vs. Will to snap out of the berserk state. If he fails the roll (or does not roll), he continues berserk and attacks the next foe. Any friend attempting to restrain the berserker will be treated as a foe! The berserker gets one Will roll each time he downs a foe, and one extra roll when the last foe is downed. If he is still berserk, he will start attacking his friends . . .

If you snap out of the berserk state, all your wounds immediately affect you; roll at normal HT, to see whether you remain conscious and alive.

Bloodlust   -10 points

You want to see your foes *dead*. You will go for killing blows in a battle, put in an extra shot to make sure of a downed foe, attack guards you could have avoided, and so on. A Will roll is necessary to accept a surrender, or even to take a prisoner under orders. Even in a non-combat situation, you will never forget that a foe is a foe.

This may seem a truly evil trait, but many fictional heroes suffer from it. The character is not a fiend or sadist; his animosity is limited to "legitimate" enemies, whether they are criminals, enemy soldiers, feuding clansmen, or tavern scum. Often he has a very good reason for feeling as he does. And, in an ordinary tavern brawl, he would use his fists like anyone else.

On the other hand, a gladiator or duellist with this disadvantage would be very unpopular, and a policeman would soon be up on charges.

Bully   -10 points

You like to push people around whenever you can get away with it. Depending on your personality and position, this may take the form of physical attacks, intellectual harassment or social "cutting." Make a Will roll to avoid *gross* bullying when you know you shouldn't – but to roleplay your character properly, you should bully anybody you can. Since nobody likes a bully, others react to you at a -2.

Code of Honor   -5 to -15 points

You take pride in a set of principles which you follow at all times. Codes of honor differ, but all require (by their own standards) "brave," "manly," and "honorable" behavior. A Code of Honor may also be called "pride," "machismo," or "face." Under any name, it is the willingness to risk death rather than be thought dishonorable . . . whatever that means.

In any culture, there are those who pretend to have honor but have none, and those who truly try to follow the code but often fail to live up to it. But only one who truly follows the code may get points for it as a disadvantage.

A Code of Honor is a disadvantage because it will often require dangerous (if not reckless) behavior. Furthermore, an honorable person can often be forced into unfair situations, because his foes know he is honorable.

This is not the same as a Duty or Sense of Duty. A samurai or British grenadier will march into battle against fearful odds out of duty, not for his personal honor (though of course he would lose honor by fleeing). The risks a person takes for his honor are solely on his own account.

The point value of a specific Code varies, depending on just how much trouble it gets its followers into, and how arbitrary and irrational its requirements are. Some examples:

Pirate's Code of Honor: Always avenge an insult, regardless of the danger; your buddy's foe is your own; never attack a fellow-crewman or buddy except in a fair, open duel. Anything else goes. This code of honor is also suitable for brigands, motorcycle gangs, and so on. *-5 points.*

Gentleman's Code of Honor: Never break your word. Never ignore an insult to yourself, to a lady, or to your flag; insults may only be wiped out by apology or a duel (*not* necessarily to the death!). Never take advantage of an opponent in any way; weapons and circumstances must be equal (except, of course, in open war). This code of honor is especially appropriate for the swashbuckling period, whether British, European or Colonial. Note that it only applies between gentlemen; a discourtesy from anyone of Social Status 0 or less calls for a whipping, not a duel! *-10 points.*

Chivalric Code of Honor: As above, except that flags haven't been invented; you must resent any insult to your liege-lord or to your faith. In addition, you must protect any lady and anyone weaker than yourself. You must accept any challenge to arms from anyone of greater or equal rank. Even in open war, sides and weapons must be equal *if* the foe is also noble and chivalric. *-15 points.*

MENTAL DISADVANTAGES

Combat Paralysis   -15 points

This is the opposite of Combat Reflexes; you tend to "freeze up" in a combat situation. It is not Cowardice; you don't have to roleplay fear. You may be brave, but your body betrays you.

In any situation in which personal harm seems imminent, roll against HT (*not* IQ). Any roll over 13 is a failure, even if you have high HT. You do not roll until the instant when you need to fight, run, pull the trigger and so on.

A successful roll means you can act normally. A failed roll means you are mentally Stunned (see p. 122). You must roll every turn, at +1 to your effective HT each turn, to break the freeze. A quick slap from a friend will give +1 to your cumulative roll.

Once you unfreeze, you will not freeze again until the immediate danger is over. Then, in the next dangerous situation, you may freeze once again.

Compulsive Behavior   -5 to -15 points

You have a habit (usually, but not always, a vice) which you feel compelled to indulge on a daily basis. You waste a good deal of your time indulging your habit.

Examples of compulsive behavior include gambling, attraction to another person, arguing (or even fighting).

In general, a Will roll is required if the player wants his character to avoid the compulsion in a specific instance (or for a specific day). Note that it is very bad roleplaying to attempt to avoid the compulsion often!

The specific point value of the disadvantage depends on what the behavior is, how much it costs, and how much trouble it is likely to get the PC into. The GM is the final judge. Compulsive Lying, below, is one example; see **GURPS Compendium I** for more examples.

Compulsive Lying   -15 points

You lie constantly, for no reason other than the joy of telling the tale. A compulsive liar delights in inventing stories about his deeds, lineage, wealth – whatever might impress his audience. Even when exposed as a liar, he will cling tenaciously to his stories, calling his accuser a liar and a scoundrel.

In order to tell the pure, unvarnished truth, a compulsive liar must roll against Will-4. A charitable GM might allow a liar to tell a slightly-fractured version of the truth if he narrowly fails this roll. When a PC liar makes a roll to tell the truth to his fellow party members, he should roll out of sight of the other players. Thus, they can never be sure that they are getting accurate information from their comrade.

Cowardice   -10 points

You are extremely careful about your physical well-being. Any time you are called on to risk physical danger, you must roll against Will. If there is a risk of death, the roll is at a -5. If you fail the roll, you must refuse to endanger yourself unless you are threatened with *greater* danger! Soldiers, police, etc., will react to you at -2 once they know you are a coward.

Delusions   -1, -5, -10 or -15 points

You believe something (or several things) that are simply not true. This may cause others to consider you insane. They may be right. If you suffer from a delusion, you *must* roleplay your delusionary belief at all times. The point value of the delusion depends on its nature; you may not get more than 40 points from delusions, regardless of how insane you really are.

Quirk. -1 point. Any or all of your five Quirks may be a trivial delusion that does not affect your everyday behavior, and is not likely to be noticed by a casual acquaintance. *Examples:* "The Earth is flat." "The Pentagon controls the Boy Scouts and the health food stores." "Socks cause disease of the feet."

Minor delusion. -5 points. This delusion affects your behavior, and is likely to be noticed quickly by anyone around you, but it does not keep you from functioning more or less normally. *Examples:* "Squirrels are messengers from God." "The Illuminati are watching me constantly – but only to *protect* me." "I am the rightful Duke of Fnordia, stolen at birth by gypsies and doomed to live among commoners." Strangers who notice your delusion react at -1.

Major delusion. -10 points. This delusion affects your behavior *strongly*, but does not keep you from living a fairly normal life. *Examples:* "The government has *all* phones tapped." "I have Eidetic Memory and Absolute Direction." Others will react to you at -2.

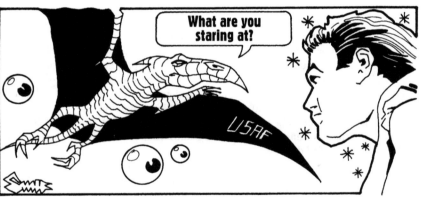

Severe delusion. -15 points. This delusion affects your behavior so much that it may keep you from functioning in the everyday world. *Examples:* "I am Napoleon." "I am immortal." "Ice cream makes machines work better, especially computers. Spoon it right in." Others will react to you at -3, though they are more likely to fear or pity you than to attack. GMs should limit this sort of delusion carefully, or the character may not be able to participate meaningfully in the campaign.

Note that the character's *behavior* is the important thing. Depending on behavior, the same delusion could be any level from quirk to severe. Suppose you believe that "Everything colored purple is alive." If you pat purple things and say hello, that's a quirk. If you won't discuss serious matters with purple things in the room, it's a minor delusion. If you picket the Capitol demanding Civil Rights For Purple Things, that's major. If you attack purple things on sight, that's severe!

A GM who wants to shake up his players can make a delusion be *true*. Not all delusions are suitable for this. Of those listed above, for instance, the ones about squirrels, ice cream and Napoleon seem unlikely. The one about socks isn't too interesting. But the Earth might really *be* flat in your game-world, or the Illuminati might really exist, or the gypsies might really have stolen the heir to the throne of Fnordia . . . Have fun.

If a delusion turns out to be true, it does *not* have to be "bought off" until the other players realize that it's true. (And remember: the player should *not* be told that his character is not really crazy. Somebody can be right and *still* be crazy . . .)

Dyslexia   -5 or -15 points

You have a *severe* reading disability. (Minor forms of dyslexia are common, not crippling, and not significant in game terms, except possibly as a quirk.) You can never learn to read or write; even simple maps and road signs are beyond you. You can learn any skill at normal speed *if* you have a teacher. If you try to learn a mental skill without a teacher, you will learn at only 1/4 speed, and only if it can be self-taught without books (GMs may vary this for special circumstances). You also cannot learn magic (you cannot handle the symbolism required) though you can still use magical items.

The value of this disadvantage depends upon the type of culture the character is originally from, as follows:

Primitive or medieval (Tech Level 4 and below): -5 points. Most people around you can't read, either.

Post-printing-press (Tech Level 5 and above): -15 points. This handicap will cause you problems every day. You are automatically illiterate, but you get no extra points for it.

Fanaticism   -15 points

You believe very strongly in one country, religion, et cetera. It is more important to you than anything. You might not die for it (depending on your degree of personal bravery), but you will put it ahead of everything else. If your country/religion/whatever requires obedience to a certain code of behavior, you will follow that code rigidly. If it requires obedience to a leader, you will follow that leader with total loyalty. You *must* roleplay your fanaticism.

Note that fanatics do not have to be either mindless or evil. A glaring priest of Set, brandishing his bloody dagger, is a fanatic. So is a kamikaze pilot, exchanging himself for an aircraft carrier. So is a patriot who says, "Give me liberty or give me death!" Fanaticism is a state of mind; it is *what* you are fanatic about that makes the difference.

Gluttony   -5 points

You are overfond of good food and drink. Given the chance, you must always burden yourself with extra provisions. You should never willingly miss a meal. Presented with a tempting morsel or good wine which, for some reason, you should resist, you must make a successful Will roll to do so. Gluttony is not a terrible weakness, but by its nature it will soon be obvious to everyone who meets you.

Greed   -15 points

You lust for wealth. Any time riches are offered – as payment for fair work, gains from adventure, spoils of crime, or just bait – you must make a Will roll to avoid temptation. The GM may modify this roll if the money involved is small relative to your own wealth. Small amounts of money will not tempt a rich character (much), but a *poor* character will have to roll at -5 or even more if a rich prize is in the offing. *Honest* characters (see below) roll at +5 to resist a shady deal and +10 to resist outright crime. However, almost any greedy character will eventually do something illegal.

Gullibility   -10 points

There's one born every minute, and you're it. A gullible person naturally believes everything he hears; he'll swallow even the most ridiculous story, if it's told with conviction.

In order to *not* believe a lie – or an improbable truth, for that matter – you must roll against IQ, modified by the plausibility of the story. A lie well-told, or involving something the character has no familiarity with – "My father is the chief of police in this town, and he won't stand for this!" – calls for a -6 penalty to IQ. A lie concerning a topic the gullible character is familiar with – "Didn't you know they bred ducks in your village, Torg?" – calls for a -3 to the roll; and even a totally outlandish tale – "Of course the Eskimos are descended from Spanish conquistadors; everyone knows that!" – will be believed if the victim fails a roll against unmodified IQ.

Furthermore, a gullible character suffers a -3 penalty on any Merchant skill roll, or in any situation in which his credulity might be exploited. A gullible person can *never* learn the Detect Lies skill.

Honesty   -10 points

You MUST obey the law, and do your best to get others to do so as well. You are compulsive about it; this is essentially another type of Code of Honor (see above).

In an area with little or no law, you will not "go wild" – you will act as though the laws of your own home were in force. This is a disadvantage, because it will often limit your options! Faced with unreasonable laws, you must roll against IQ to see the "need" to break them, and against Will to avoid turning yourself in afterward! If you ever behave dishonestly, the GM may penalize you for bad roleplaying.

You *may* fight (or even start a fight, if you do it in a legal way). You may even kill in a legal duel, or in self-defense – but you may never *murder*. You may steal if there is great need, but only as a last resort, and you must attempt to pay your victims back later. If you are jailed for a crime you did not commit, but treated fairly and assured of a trial, you will not try to escape.

You will always keep your word. (In a war, you may act "dishonestly" against the enemy, but you will not be happy about it!) You will also assume others are honest unless you *know* otherwise (make an IQ roll to realize someone may be dishonest if you haven't seen proof).

Honesty has its rewards, of course. If you stay alive and in one place long enough for your honesty to become known, GMs should allow you a +1 on any non-combat reaction roll, or a +3 if a question of trust or honor is actually involved. This is essentially a free "reputation" reaction bonus.

You *are* allowed to lie if it does not involve breaking the law. Truthfulness (p. 37) is a separate disadvantage.

Illiteracy   0 or -10 points

This is the normal condition in a low-tech culture, and gives no bonus in such cases. In a TL5 or later culture, where the printing press is common, it is a disadvantage. See p. 17.

Impulsiveness   -10 points

You hate talk and debate. You prefer action! When you are alone, you will act first and think later. In a group, when your friends want to stop and discuss something, you should put in your two cents' worth quickly – if at all – and then do *something*. Roleplay it! If it is absolutely necessary to wait and ponder, you must make a Will roll to do so.

Mental Disadvantages

Intolerance -5/-10 points

You dislike and distrust some (or all) people who are different from you. A thoroughly intolerant character (-10 points) has a -3 reaction against *anyone* not of his own race and/or class. On a "good" reaction, he will tolerate the person and be as civil as possible (but will be stiff and cold toward him); on a "neutral" reaction he will still tolerate him, but make it plain in words and deeds he doesn't care to be around him and considers him inferior and/or offensive; on a worse reaction, he may attack or refuse to associate with the victim at all.

Intolerance directed at only one *specific* race or class is worth from -5 for a commonly-encountered victim, to -1 (just a nasty quirk) for a rare victim.

Members of a disliked group will sense intolerance, and will normally react to the intolerant person at -1 to -5.

Intolerance may manifest itself in other ways as well. *Religious* intolerance may take the form of a -3 reaction against those of a particular faith (-5 points) or to anyone not of your own faith (-10 points). On a "neutral" reaction or better, an intolerant person will attempt to convert unbelievers to his own faith.

Jealousy -10 points

You have an automatic bad reaction toward anyone who seems smarter, more attractive, or better-off than you! You will resist any plan proposed by a "rival," and will *hate* it if someone else is in the limelight. (This disadvantage goes well with Megalomania.) If an NPC is Jealous, the GM will subtract 2 to 4 points from his reaction to the victim(s) of his jealousy.

Kleptomania -15 points

You are compelled to steal – not necessarily things of value, but anything you can get away with. Whenever you are presented with a chance to steal, you must make a Will roll, at up to -3 if the item is especially interesting to you (not necessarily *valuable* unless you are poor or Greedy, just "interesting"). If you fail the roll, you must try to steal it. Stolen items may be kept or sold, but not returned or discarded.

Laziness -10 points

You are violently averse to physical labor. Your chances of getting a raise or promotion in *any* job are halved. If you are self-employed, your weekly income is halved. You must avoid work – especially hard work – at all costs. Roleplay it!

Lecherousness -15 points

You suffer from an unusually strong desire for romance. Whenever in more than the briefest contact with an attractive member of the opposite sex, you must roll vs. Will (at a -5 if the other person is Beautiful, or a -10 if Very Beautiful). A failed roll means you must make a "pass," using whatever wiles or skills you can bring to bear. You must then suffer the consequences of your actions, successful or not . . . physical retribution, jail, communicable disease, or (possibly) an adoring new friend.

Unless the object of your affection is Very Handsome or Beautiful, you need not roll more than once a day to avoid making a pass. If a specific character turns you down very firmly (e.g., a black eye, or an arrest for sexual harassment) the GM may allow you a bonus on further rolls . . .

Note also that a Lecherous person may change his or her standards of attractiveness if no truly attractive members of the opposite sex are available!

Megalomania -10 points

You believe that you are a superman, or that you have been chosen for some great task, or that you are destined to conquer. You must start by taking the Fanatic disadvantage – but you are fanatic for yourself! You must choose some great goal – usually either conquest or the completion of some fantastic task. You may let nothing stand between you and this goal. You may attract followers who are also Fanatics; nobody else will enjoy hearing you talk about your brilliance and your great plans. Young or naive characters, and Fanatics looking for a new cause, will react to you at +2. Others will have a -2. This is a better disadvantage for NPCs than it is for player characters.

Miserliness -10 points

Like Greed (p. 33), except that you are more concerned with holding on to what you already have. You may be both greedy *and* miserly! You must make a Will roll any time you are called on to spend money, and you must always hunt for the best deal possible. If the expenditure is large, the Will roll may be at a -5 (or even greater) penalty. A failed roll means you will refuse to spend the money – or, if the money absolutely *must* be spent, you should haggle and complain interminably.

Overconfidence -10 points

You feel yourself to be far more powerful, intelligent and/or competent than you really are, and you should behave that way. Any time (in the GM's opinion) you show an unreasonable degree of caution, you must roll against your IQ. A failed roll means you may not be cautious, but must go ahead as though you were able to handle the situation. An overconfident character will receive +2 on all reaction rolls from young or naive individuals (they believe he is as good as he says he is), but -2 on reactions from experienced NPCs.

This is like Megalomania (above) but on a smaller scale. Robin Hood was overconfident – he challenged strangers to quarterstaff duels. Hitler was a megalomaniac – he invaded Russia! Heroes are rarely megalomaniacal but often overconfident.

This characteristic requires roleplaying. An overconfident character may be proud and boastful, or just quietly determined – but play it up!

Pacifism   -15 or -30 points

You are opposed to violence. This opposition can take three forms, each with its own point value.

Total nonviolence is just that: you will not lift a hand against another intelligent creature, for any reason. You must do your non-violent best to discourage violent behavior in others, too. You are free to defend yourself against attacks by animals, mosquitoes, etc. *-30 points.*

Self-defense only means that you will only fight to defend yourself or those in your care, using only as much force as may be necessary (no pre-emptive strikes allowed!). You must do your best to discourage others from starting fights. *-15 points.*

Cannot kill means that you may fight freely, and even *start* a fight, but you may never do anything that seems likely to kill another. This includes abandoning a wounded foe to die "on his own"! You must do your best to keep your companions from killing, too. If you *do* kill someone (or feel yourself responsible for a death), you immediately suffer a nervous breakdown. Roll 3 dice and be totally morose and useless (roleplay it!) for that many days. During this time, you must make a Will roll to offer any sort of violence toward *anyone*, for *any* reason. *-15 points.*

Paranoia   -10 points

You are out of touch with reality. Specifically, you think that everyone is plotting against you. You will never trust anyone except old friends . . . and you keep an eye on them, too, just in case. Other characters, understandably, react to paranoids at -2. A paranoid NPC has an automatic -4 reaction against *any* stranger, and any "legitimate" reaction penalty (e.g., unfriendly race or nationality) is *doubled*. This goes very well with Delusions, which of course have their own disadvantage value!

Phobias   Variable

A "phobia" is a fear of a specific item, creature, or circumstance. Many fears are reasonable, but a phobia is an unreasonable, unreasoning, morbid fear.

The more common an object or situation, the greater the point value of a phobia against it. Fear of darkness is far more troublesome than fear of left-handed plumbers. Phobias may be mild or severe; the severe version is worth twice as much.

If you have a *mild* phobia, you may master it by a successful Will roll. This is also called a "Fright Check" – see p. 93. For example, if you have acrophobia (fear of heights), you may still go onto the roof of a tall building if you can first make your Will roll. However, the fear persists. If you successfully master a mild phobia, you will be at -2 IQ and -2 DX while the cause of your fear persists, and you must roll again every ten minutes to see if the fear overcomes you. If it does (that is, if you fail your Fright Check) you will react badly, rolling on the table on p. 94.

If you suffer from a *severe* phobia (worth double points), you are deathly afraid. Under normal circumstances, you must simply refuse contact with the feared situation. If forced into contact with the object of your fear, roll a Fright Check . . . at -4 to Will! You will be at -3 IQ and -3 DX while the cause of your fear persists, rolling again every 10 minutes.

If a phobia victim is *threatened* with the feared object, he must immediately make a Fright Check at +4 to Will (whether the phobia is mild or severe). If enemies actually inflict the feared object on him, he must make the normal Fright Check (as above). If the roll is failed, the victim breaks down, but does not necessarily talk – see the Interrogation skill. Some people can

panic and fall apart but will still refuse to talk, just as some people will not talk under torture.

A phobic situation is, by definition, stressful. Anyone who is prone to personality shifts, berserking, etc., is likely to have these reactions when he encounters something he fears and fails his Fright Check.

Some common phobias:

Crowds (demophobia): Any group of over a dozen people sets off this fear unless they are all well-known to you. Roll at -1 for over 25 people, -2 for a crowd of 100 or more, -3 for 1,000, -4 for 10,000, and so on. *-15/-30 points.*

Darkness (scotophobia): A common fear, but crippling. You should avoid being underground if possible; if something happens to your flashlight or torch, you may well lose your mind before you can relight it. *-15/-30 points.*

Death and the dead (necrophobia): You are terrified by the idea of death. A Will roll is required in the presence of any dead body (animals, etc., don't count, but portions of bodies do). This roll is at -4 if the body is that of someone you know, or -6 if the body is unnaturally animated in some way. A ghost (or apparent ghost) will also require a roll at -6. *-10/-20 points.*

Dirt (rupophobia): You are deathly afraid of infection, or just of dirt and filth. You must make a Will roll before you can do anything that might get you dirty; you must roll at -5 to eat any unaccustomed food. You should act as "finicky" as possible. *-10/-20 points.*

Enclosed spaces (claustrophobia): Another common, crippling fear. You are uncomfortable any time you can't see the sky – or at least a very high ceiling. In a small room or vehicle, you feel the walls closing in on you . . . You need *air*! A dangerous fear for someone who plans to go underground. *-15/-30 points.*

Heights (acrophobia): You may not voluntarily go more than 15 feet above ground, unless you are inside a building and away from windows. If there is some chance of an actual fall, all Will rolls are at an extra -5. *-10/-20 points.*

MENTAL DISADVANTAGES

Insects (entomophobia): You are afraid of all "bugs." Large or poisonous ones subtract 3 from the self-control roll. Very large ones, or large numbers, subtract 6. Avoid hills of giant ants. *-10/-20 points*.

Loud noises (brontophobia): You will avoid any situation where loud noises are likely. A sudden loud noise will require a Will roll immediately, or panic will ensue. Thunderstorms are traumatic experiences. *-10/-20 points*.

Machinery (technophobia): You can never learn to repair any sort of machine, and you will refuse to learn to use anything more complicated than a crossbow or bicycle. Any highly technological environment will call for a control roll; dealings with robots or computers will require a roll at -3, and hostility from intelligent machines will require a roll at -6. *-15/-30 points in a culture of TL5 or better; -5/-10 below TL5*.

Magic (manaphobia): You can never learn to use magic, and you react badly to any user of magic. You must make a self-control roll whenever you are in the presence of magic. This roll is at -3 if you are to be the target of friendly magic, and -6 if you are the target of hostile magic. (The magic does not have to be real, if YOU believe in it!) *-15/-30 points in a culture where magic is common, -10/-20 if it is known but uncommon, -5/-10 if "real" magic is essentially unknown*.

Monsters (teratophobia): Any "unnatural" creature will set off this fear – at a -1 to -4 penalty if the monster seems very large or dangerous, or if there are a lot of them. Note that the definition of "monster" depends on experience. An American Indian would consider an elephant monstrous, while an African pygmy would not! *-15/-30 points*.

Squeamishness (no technical name): You are afraid of "yucky stuff." You are upset by little bugs and crawly things, blood and dead bodies, slime and the like. But this is *not* just a combination of the standard fears of insects, reptiles, dirt and the dead. Huge bugs or reptiles don't bother you unduly; neither does ordinary "clean" dirt; neither do ghosts. But nasty creepy things, filth, and bits of grue will get to you. Mild squeamishness, as a "dislike," is a common quirk that is fun to roleplay. *-10/-20 points*.

Strange and unknown things (xenophobia): You are upset by any sort of strange circumstances, and particularly by strange *people*. You must make a Will roll when surrounded by people of another race or nationality; this roll will be at -3 if the people are not human. A xenophobe who loses control may very well attack strangers, simply out of fear. *-15/-30 points*.

Weapons (hoplophobia): Any sort of weaponry upsets you; the presence of weaponry is stressful, and *using* any weapon, or being threatened with one, would require a Will roll at -2. *-20/-40 points*.

Dislikes

To give your character depth, you may take any of the above phobias, in a *very mild* form, as "dislikes." These are quirks, worth -1 point each, and have *no* specific penalties; they are merely an opportunity for roleplaying. Or, if you suffer from a real phobia, you may try to pass it off as a mere dislike – until the crunch comes and you fail a Will roll! The GM may be requested to make your rolls in secret, to help conceal your phobia as long as possible. See *Quirks*, p. 41.

Number 13 (triskadekaphobia): You must make a self-control roll in order to do anything with a 13 in it – visit the 13th floor, buy something for $13.00, et cetera. This roll is at -5 if Friday the 13th is involved! *-5/-10 points*.

Oceans (thalassophobia): You are afraid of any large body of water. Ocean travel, or air travel over the ocean, will be basically impossible, and encounters with aquatic monsters will also be upsetting. *-10/-20 points*.

Open spaces (agoraphobia): You are uncomfortable whenever you are outside, and become actually frightened when there are no walls within 50 feet. *-10/-20 points*.

Reptiles (ophiophobia): You come unglued at the thought of reptiles, amphibians and similar scaly-slimies. A very large reptile, or a poisonous one, would require a roll at -2; a horde of reptiles (such as a snake pit) would require a roll at -4. *-10/-20 points*.

Sharp things (aichmophobia): You are afraid of anything pointed. Swords, spears, knives and hypodermic needles all give you fits. Trying to use a sharp weapon, or being threatened with one, would require a Will roll at -2. *-15/-30 points at TL5 and below; -10/-20 points above TL5*.

Pyromania   -5 points

You like fires! You like setting fires, too. For good roleplaying, you must never miss a chance to set a fire, or to appreciate one you encounter. When absolutely necessary, make a Will roll to override your love of flame.

Sadism   -15 points

You delight in cruelty . . . mental, physical, or both. (This is a particularly "evil" trait, more appropriate to NPC villains than to heroic characters.) The GM may completely prohibit this disadvantage (or any other advantage or disadvantage) if he does not want anyone roleplaying it in his campaign.

People react to a known sadist at -3, unless they are from cultures holding life in little esteem. When a sadistic character has an opportunity to indulge his desires, but knows he shouldn't (e.g., because the prisoner is one that should be released unharmed), he must make a successful Will roll to restrain himself. Note that it is possible, though despicable, to be both a bully *and* a sadist.

Sense of Duty   -5, -10, -15, -20 points

See p. 39.

Shyness   -5, -10, -15 points

You are uncomfortable around strangers. This disadvantage comes in three grades: Mild, Severe and Crippling. You must role-play your shyness! This disadvantage can be "bought off" one level at a time.

Mild Shyness: Somewhat uncomfortable around strangers, especially assertive or attractive ones. -1 on any skill that requires you to deal with the public – in particular, Acting, Bard, Carousing, Diplomacy, Fast-Talk, Leadership, Merchant, Politics, Savoir-Faire, Sex Appeal, Streetwise and Teaching. *-5 points.*

Severe Shyness: Very uncomfortable around strangers, and tends to be quiet even among friends. -2 on any skill that requires you to deal with the public. *-10 points.*

Crippling Shyness: Avoids strangers whenever possible. Incapable of public speaking. May not learn any skill that involves dealing with the public; -4 on default rolls on such skills. *-15 points.*

Split Personality   -10 or -15 points

You have two or more distinct personalities, each of which may have its own set of mental problems or behavior patterns. This allows you to have mental disadvantages that would otherwise be incompatible (e.g., Pacifism and Berserk, or Paranoia and Lecherousness).

Each personality should have his or her own character sheet. There should be at least 50 points' worth of differences. Even their basic stats may vary somewhat (ST, DX, and HT being artificially lowered for personalities that "think" they're weak, clumsy or sickly). IQ and skills may be different, and personality traits can be totally different. The personalities' character point values should *average* to 100 when you start, but they need not be the same! Distribution of earned character points between the personalities is up to the GM.

In any stress situation, the GM rolls against your IQ; a failed roll means a switch to another personality. No more than one roll per hour (game time) is required.

Any NPC who is aware of this problem will feel (possibly with justification) that you are a dangerous nutcase, and will react at -3 to you.

If your personalities are facets of a single "individual," this is a -10-point disadvantage. If the personalities are largely unaware of each other, interpret their memories differently, and have different names, it is a -15-point disadvantage.

Stubbornness   -5 points

You always want your own way. Make yourself generally hard to get along with – roleplay it! Your friends may have to make a lot of Fast-Talk rolls to get you to go along with perfectly reasonable plans. Others react to you at -1.

Truthfulness   -5 points

You hate to tell a lie – or you are just very bad at it. In order to keep silent about an uncomfortable truth (lying by omission), you must make your Will roll. To actually *tell* a falsehood, you must make your Will roll at a -5 penalty! A failed roll means you blurt out the truth, or stumble so much that your lie is obvious. (If someone is using Detect Lies on you, you are also at a -5 penalty.)

Unluckiness   -10 points

You just have bad luck. Things go wrong for you – and usually at the worst possible time. Once per play session, the GM will arbitrarily and maliciously make something go wrong for you. You will miss a vital die roll, or the enemy will (against all odds) show up at the worst possible time. If the plot of the adventure calls for something bad to happen to someone, you're the one.

The GM may *not* kill a character outright with "bad luck," but anything less than that is fine.

Vow   -1 to -15 points

You have sworn an oath to do (or not to do) something. This disadvantage is especially appropriate for knights, holy men and fanatics. Note that, whatever the oath, you take it seriously. If you didn't, it would not be a disadvantage. The precise value of a vow is up to the GM, but should be directly related to the inconvenience it causes the character. Some examples:

Trivial Vow: -1 point (a quirk). Always wear red; never drink alcohol; treat all ladies with courtesy; pay 10% of your income to your church.

Minor Vow: -5 points. Vow of silence during daylight hours; vegetarianism; chastity. (Yes, for game purposes, this is *minor*).

Major Vow: -10 points. Use no edged weapons; keep silence at all times; never sleep indoors; own no more than your horse can carry.

Great Vow: -15 points. Never refuse any request for aid; always fight with the wrong hand; hunt a given foe until you destroy him; challenge every knight you meet to combat.

If you make a "vow of poverty," you may not also take points for being dead broke. Neither may you make a vow not to kill and then take points for Cannot Kill pacifism . . . and so on.

Most vows end after a specified period of time. You must buy off a vow's point value when it ends. Vows for a period of less than a year are frivolous! If a character wants to end a vow before its stated time, the GM may exact a penalty; in a medieval world, for instance, a quest or other penance would be appropriate. (A quest can itself be a vow, too.)

Weak Will   -8 points/level

You are easily persuaded, frightened, bullied, coerced, tempted and so on. For every level taken, your IQ is effectively reduced by 1 whenever you make a Will roll, including attempts to resist Diplomacy, Fast-Talk, Sex Appeal, Interrogation, Hypnotism, or magical or psionic attempts to take over, read, or affect your mind. Weak Will also affects all attempts to master phobias, to resist hostile magic, to make Fright Checks (see p. 93), and to avoid giving in to Addictions, Berserk behavior, and the like. A character cannot have both Strong and Weak Will.

Dependents

A dependent is a non-player character for whom you are responsible – e.g., your child, younger brother or spouse. Dependents can be a problem: you have to take care of them, and your foes can strike at *you* through them! Therefore, a dependent is a disadvantage, worth negative character points. The point value of a dependent is set by his or her competence, importance in your life, and frequency of appearance, as shown below.

The GM may restrict the dependents allowed in a campaign, or even forbid them entirely, if they would unduly disrupt the flow of the adventure.

Competence of Dependent

The dependent is created just like any other character, but instead of the 100 points used to create a player character, you use 50 points or less. The more character points you use to "build" your dependents, the more competent they will be and the *fewer* points they will be worth as a bonus to you.

A dependent built with over 50 points is not helpless enough to be worth any bonus points. Indeed, a "dependent" built on 51-75 points may be capable enough to be helpful . . . in essence, an Ally (p. 23) who costs no character points. The only drawback to such a "competent dependent" is that you *must* still look after him or her.

Dependent built with 26-50 points: Slightly more competent than average. *-6 points*.

Dependent built with 1-25 points: Average. *-12 points*.

Dependent built with 0 or fewer points: Possibly a young child or feeble older person. *-16 points*.

Importance of Dependent

The more important the dependent is to you, the more you multiply his or her intrinsic "nuisance value" and worth in points.

Employer or acquaintance: You feel a responsibility toward this person, but you may weigh risks to them in a rational fashion. Use half the listed value.

Friend: You must always try to protect this person; you may only risk harm to him or her if something very important (such as the safety of many other people) is at stake. Use the listed value.

Loved one: The dependent is a relative or lover. You may not put *anything* before the safety of this dependent. Double the listed value.

Frequency of Appearance

The more often a dependent shows up, the more bonus points he is worth. Pick a frequency of appearance that fits the "story" behind the dependent. If the dependent is your infant child, for instance, it would be odd for him to appear "quite rarely"!

Dependent appears almost all the time (roll of 15 or less): triple the listed value.

Dependent appears quite often (roll of 12 or less): double the listed value.

Dependent appears fairly often (roll of 9 or less): use the listed value.

Dependent appears quite rarely (roll of 6 or less): use half the listed value.

Example: Marshal Jack O'Rourke is in love with the town's pretty schoolmarm. She is a better-than-average character, created with 50 points (a 6-point bonus for O'Rourke). He is in love with her (double her value to 12). And she's around almost all the time (triple her value to 36). The net result: -36 character points for Marshal Jack. But he'll spend a lot of his time rescuing that schoolmarm from rustlers, Indians and train robbers.

If your dependent is kidnapped or otherwise mislaid during play, you *must* go to the rescue as soon as you can. (If a powerful enemy and a dependent are both "rolled up" at the beginning of an adventure, the GM can start off by letting the enemy kidnap the dependent and go on from there!) If your dependent is in trouble and you don't go to his aid immediately, the GM can deny you bonus character points for "acting out of character." Furthermore, you can *never* get any character points for a play session in which your dependent is killed or badly hurt. So . . . if you have dependents, take good care of them!

If your dependent is lost (killed, or so seriously injured that the GM decides he is effectively out of the campaign), you *must* make up the bonus points you got for them. There are three ways to do this: "buy off" the amount by spending points earned during your adventures, take a new disadvantage, or get a new dependent. New dependents are usually inappropriate, but a mental disability brought on by the loss is a good solution. (Ever since the octopus got Amy, you've been afraid of the ocean . . .)

No character may ever earn points for more than two dependents at once. However, GMs may interpret this rule creatively. For instance, a crimefighter who is a schoolteacher in his mundane identity could have "generic dependents" – all pupils. They are young (12 points) and around quite often (double value, for 24 points each). They count only as "friends" – but, even so, the two-dependent limit allows that character 48 points' worth of dependents. (And if one gets hurt, there will always be others.)

Some good dependents . . . For anyone: elderly relatives, teachers, friends, children, young brothers or sisters, lovers, husbands, or wives. For crimefighters: young sidekicks, reporters, or wards. For wizards: apprentices. For ship captains (ocean- or space-going): ensigns or cabin boys. For soldiers: orphans, new recruits. For criminals or mad scientists: incompetent henchmen.

You have a significant responsibility toward others, and you are personally committed to that responsibility. Duties may come from an arduous job, a feudal responsibility, or elsewhere. (Duty toward dependents doesn't count separately.) By definition, a duty is imposed from outside. A wholly "self-imposed" feeling of duty is "Sense of Duty" (see below.)

The GM rolls at the beginning of each adventure to see if each character will be "called to duty" in that adventure. The point cost of a duty depends on the frequency with which it is demanded:

Almost all the time (roll of 15 or less): *-15 points*. For a Duty of this level, the GM may always rule that the character is on duty, without rolling.

Quite often (roll of 12 or less): *-10 points*.

Fairly often (roll of 9 or less): *-5 points*.

Occasionally (roll of 6 or less): *-2 points*.

To be significant, a duty should be dangerous. An ordinary job is *not* a "duty." If a duty does not require you to risk your life, at least occasionally, reduce its value by 5, which negates those less frequent than "quite often."

Some examples of duties: Feudal responsibility toward one's liege-lord. A good military officer's responsibility to his men and his superiors. A loyal spy's duty to the Agency.

The GM can make good use of duties (by "fixing" the die-rolls, if necessary) to send characters on adventures or interesting side-trips. A character who tries to avoid such a situation should be penalized for bad roleplaying. However, the GM may restrict the duties allowed in a campaign, or even forbid them entirely, if they would unduly disrupt the flow of the adventure.

Sense of Duty   -5, -10, -15, -20 points

This is different from a *real* Duty (see above). A real Duty can be enforced upon you. A Sense of Duty comes from within.

It is not the same as Honesty (see p. 33). A dishonest person may still have a sense of duty. Robin Hood was dishonest; he stole! But he felt a strong sense of duty, both toward his men and toward the poor folk he met.

If you feel a sense of duty toward someone, you will never betray them, abandon them when they're in trouble, or even let them suffer or go hungry if you can help. If you are known to have a sense of duty, others will react to you at a +2 to trust you in a dangerous situation. If you have a sense of duty, and go against it by acting against the interests of those you are supposed to feel duty toward, the GM will penalize you for bad roleplaying.

The player defines the group to which the character will feel the sense of duty, and the GM sets its point value. Examples: only toward close friends and companions (*-5 points*); toward a nation or other large group (*-10 points*); toward everyone you know personally (*-10 points*); toward all humanity (*-15 points*); or toward every living being (*-20 points* . . . and you are a saint, and very hard to tolerate).

ENEMIES

You have an enemy (or enemies) that may enter some or all of your adventures, to work against you or just to try to kill you! The point value of an enemy is governed by his (or its) strength, plus the likelihood that it will show up in any given adventure. Enemies will be NPCs or Adversary Characters (see p. 180).

The GM may restrict the enemies allowed in a campaign, or even forbid them entirely, if they would unduly disrupt the flow of the adventure.

Power

The more powerful your enemy, the more points he, she or it is worth as a disadvantage. The GM sets this value. Some guidelines:

A single above-average individual (created with 50 points): *-5 points*.

A single very formidable individual (created with 100 points) or a group of 3 to 5 "normal" or "average" 25-point people: *-10 points. Examples:* A mad scientist, or the four brothers of the man you killed in a duel.

A medium-sized group (6 to 20 people): *-20 points*. Examples would be a small gang of criminals, or a city police department (which numbers in the hundreds, but they're not all after you at once).

A large group (20 to 1,000 people), or a medium-sized group which includes some formidable or superhuman individuals: *-30 points*. Examples would be the FBI and the Mafia.

An entire government, a whole guild of powerful wizards, the Space Patrol, an organization of supers, or some other utterly formidable group: *-40 points*.

Frequency of Appearance

At the beginning of each adventure, or each session of a continuing adventure, the GM rolls 3 dice for each enemy to see if he appears.

If the enemy appears almost all the time (roll of 15 or less): triple the listed value.

If the enemy appears quite often (roll of 12 or less): double the listed value.

If the enemy appears fairly often (roll of 9 or less): use the listed value.

If the enemy appears quite rarely (roll of 6 or less): halve the listed value (round up).

You are responsible for determining the nature of your enemy when you first create your character; you should explain to the GM why this enemy is after you. However, the GM should feel free to fill in the details – because the enemies, once created, are *his* characters. Whenever the GM determines that an enemy should show up, he must decide how and where he will become involved. If an enemy is very powerful, or if several characters' enemies show up at the same time, the whole adventure may be influenced.

If you take a very powerful enemy, you are likely to be jailed or killed before long. So it goes. You can get a 60-point bonus by taking the FBI as a "quite often" enemy, but your every adventure will be that of a hunted criminal, and even with the extra 60 points, your career may be short.

On the other hand, if you start with a weak enemy or play cleverly, you may manage to kill or eliminate your foe, or permanently change his attitude toward you. But there ain't no such thing as a free lunch! When you eliminate an enemy this way, you have three choices:

(a) Pay enough character points to "buy off" the original bonus you got for that enemy.

(b) Take a mental or physical disadvantage to make up for the point bonus. For instance, you might have been kicked in the head during the final battle, leaving you partially deaf. Or you might have been attacked by a giant spider, leaving you with a phobia about bugs. The new disadvantage should have the same point cost that the enemy did (or less, if you want to buy off *part* of the disadvantage). If you cannot think of a good substitute disadvantage, the GM should supply one.

(c) Take another enemy of the same type and start over. You may have destroyed the fiendish Dr. Scorpion – but his brother is continuing his evil work.

Since too many enemies can disrupt a game, no character may take more than two enemies, or total more than 60 points bonus from enemies. (If the whole U.S. Government is out to get you, the fact that your old college professor has lost his mind, and is *also* after you, will pale to insignificance.)

The GM *always* has the right to veto a player's choice of enemy, if it seems silly or if it will be too hard to fit into the campaign.

Notes on Disadvantages

Negating Disadvantages. GMs should never allow players to take a disadvantage (or a quirk) that is negated by an advantage! For instance, no one may take both Hard of Hearing and Acute Hearing.

Dramatic Villains. Some disadvantages – Sadism, for instance – are not at all suitable to a "heroic" player character. But they are often found in the more fiendish villains of adventure fiction. So, in the interest of good NPC creation, they are included.

Tragic Heroes. Many of the greatest heroes of history and literature had a "tragic flaw." Alcoholism, great ugliness, missing limbs, and even drug addiction – all are found in the *heroes* of fact and fiction. So don't assume that your heroes have to be perfect . . . try giving them a significant problem to overcome.

New Disadvantages

GMs (and players, with GM approval) are welcome to develop new disadvantages. The only constraints are:

(1) If the character is not penalized in some way, it's not a disadvantage!

(2) Make sure that the point bonus allowed is fair with regard to the existing disadvantages! Suppose you want to introduce "allergies" as a new physical disadvantage. It would be ridiculous to make an allergy a 20-point disadvantage! The exact level of disadvantage would depend on the physical effect of an allergy, but 5 points, or 10 for a really crippling one, would be more reasonable.

(3) Make sure that the disadvantage isn't just another kind of Odious Personal Habit, easily covered by a reaction penalty.

Example of Disadvantage Selection

We know that Dai Blackthorn will need some disadvantages. When we left him on p. 25, after selecting his advantages, he was at -5 character points. He will need to take some disadvantages . . . because he still needs character points to gain some skills.

We are limited to 40 points of disadvantages. (We *could* take a single massive disadvantage, worth more than 40 points, but we don't want to do that – it would make Dai too unusual.) Our quirks do not count toward these totals.

Poverty is a natural social disadvantage for a thief or rogue. We already decided to take "poor" back on page 18; it was good for -15 points, which we've already counted into our point total for the character.

Most of the physical disadvantages seem crippling, and we picture Dai as being healthy and of average appearance. So our second disadvantage will be another social disadvantage . . . an *enemy*. We've already decided that Dai is a thief. Let's say that he's a freelance operator, not affiliated with the local Thieves' Guild. Naturally, they object! The guild is a very powerful organization – normally a 30-point enemy. But Dai is a trivial nuisance by their standards, and they don't often bother with him; they will intrude in a given adventure only on a roll of 6 or less. That halves their value, making this a 15-point disadvantage.

Mental disadvantages are a lot of fun; there's a lot of roleplaying potential here. Greed? Too obvious. Honesty? Contradictory. Cowardice? Doesn't go with the character conception. How about *overconfidence?* That goes well with Dai as we see him. It's good for another -10 points.

That makes up our limit of 40 points worth of "bonuses." We'd already counted 15 of them. The other 25 add to our current total of -5, to bring Dai back up to 20 points.

Pt. Cost	ADVANTAGES, DISADVANTAGES, QUIRKS
5	ABSOLUTE DIRECTION
10	ACUTE HEARING (+5)
	Hears on 17
5	DOUBLE-JOINTED
15	DANGER SENSE
-15	ENEMY: Thieves' Guild
	roll of 6 or less
-10	OVERCONFIDENCE
-15	POOR

6 QUIRKS

A "quirk" is a minor personality trait. It is not an advantage, and is not necessarily a disadvantage – it is just something unique about your character. For instance, a major trait like Greed is a disadvantage. But if you insist on being paid in gold, that's a quirk.

You may take up to five "quirks" at -1 point each . . . so, if you do, you will have 5 more points to spend on advantages or skills. These do *not* count against the maximum number of disadvantage points allowed in your campaign.

The only drawback to a quirk is this: you *must* roleplay it. If you take the quirk "dislike of heights," but blithely climb trees and cliffs whenever you need to, the GM will penalize you for bad roleplaying. The points you lose this way will cost you much more than you earned for taking the quirk. So don't choose a quirk you aren't willing to play!

A quirk can also be "bought off" later by paying one character point. But as a rule, you shouldn't do that. The quirks are a big part of what makes your character seem "real."

You may *change* quirks (with GM approval) if something happens to justify a change in your personality. You may also leave two or three quirks "open" when you first create your character, and fill them in after the first couple of play sessions – letting your character design himself!

Some examples of quirks:

Beliefs and goals. If a belief or goal is strongly held, important and/or irrational, it may be an important disadvantage. Religious fervor, greed and lust are examples of important goals. But a minor belief or goal makes a good quirk. *Examples:* Your life objective is to get just enough money to buy a farm (or boat, or spaceship, or castle) of your own. Or you insist on exhibiting "gentlemanly" behavior to all females. Or you insist on spurning "chauvinistic" behavior from all males. Or anything else you can think of!

Dislikes. Anything on the Phobia list (pp. 35-36) can be taken as a mere dislike. If you dislike something, you must avoid it whenever possible, though it does not actually *harm* you as a phobia would. But dislikes don't *have* to come from the phobia list. There is a whole world full of things to dislike: carrots, cats, neckties, the opposite sex, violence, telephones, income tax . . .

Likes. Pick anything you can think of. If you like something, you will seek it out whenever possible. This is not a compulsion – just a preference. Gadgets, kittens, shiny knives, ceramic owls, fine art . . . whatever.

Habits or expressions. Saying "Jehoshaphat!" or "Bless my collar-button" constantly, for instance . . . or carrying a silver piece that you flip into the air . . . or never sitting with your back to the door. (If you push one of these too far, the GM may decree that it has developed into an Odious Personal Habit – see p. 26 – that causes others to react badly. So don't overdo it.)

Anything else that you can think of that will make your character into a "real person"! Peculiarities of dress . . . choice of friends . . . unrequited love . . . hobbies (perhaps backed up by a few points in a hobby skill) . . . favorite entertainment . . . it's up to you.

Example of Character Creation

Let's go back to Dai Blackthorn, the character we started on page 14, and fill in a few more things. Currently, Dai has 20 unspent character points.

We decide to take the full five points of quirks, to make Dai more interesting. We settle on these:

a) He's sensitive about his small stature;

b) He dislikes large bodies of water;

c) He *loves* heights and high places;

d) He refuses all drugs, even alcohol (very unusual in his culture);

e) He is flamboyant and a show-off.

The quirks are listed at the bottom of the Advantages/Disadvantages/Quirks section of the Character Sheet.

We now have a lot more meat for roleplaying – and we *must* roleplay these quirks, or the GM will penalize Dai. Each quirk was worth a point, so Dai now has 25 character points unspent. That's how many we will have available to use in the next, and last, phase of character creation: Skills.

Pt. Cost	ADVANTAGES, DISADVANTAGES, QUIRKS
5	ABSOLUTE DIRECTION
10	ACUTE HEARING (+5)
	Hears on 17
5	DOUBLE-JOINTED
15	DANGER SENSE
-15	ENEMY: Thieves' Guild
	roll of 6 or less
-10	OVERCONFIDENCE
-15	POOR
-1	SENSITIVE ABOUT HEIGHT
-1	AFRAID of DROWNING/dislikes lakes
-1	LOVES HIGH PLACES
-1	NO DRUGS OR ALCOHOL
-1	FLAMBOYANT SHOWOFF
0	CANNOT READ

7 KILLS

Improving Your Skills

Once you have created a character, you can increase your skills in two ways. First, the bonus points you receive for successful adventuring can be used for skill improvement. You may also spend game-time in *study,* to improve your skills or learn new ones. See *Character Development,* p. 81.

Free Increases in Skills

There is one way to increase several skills at once: pay the character points (see *Character Development*) to raise an attribute. If you do this, *all* your skills based on that attribute will go up by one. For instance, if you raise your DX, all your DX-based skills – weapons, skiing, etc. – go up by one point. (A skill with two possible defaults – like Climbing – goes up only if you had originally based it on the attribute you're raising.) Further increases due to study are based on the new DX value.

Skills can also be based on defaults from other skills, and if the basic skill is increased, the advanced skill might be increased as well. For details on this, see *Defaulting to Other Skills*, p. 44.

A "skill" is a particular kind of knowledge. Judo, nuclear physics, swordsmanship, auto mechanics, death spells and the English language are all skills. Every skill is separate, though some skills help you to learn others.

Each of your skills is represented by a number – for instance, "Shortsword-17" means a skill level of 17 with the shortsword. The higher the number, the greater the skill. When you try to do something, you (or the GM) will roll 3 dice against the appropriate skill, modified as the GM sees fit for that particular situation – see *Success Rolls,* p. 86. If the number you roll is *less than or equal to* your (modified) score for that skill, you succeed! But a roll of 17 or 18 is an automatic failure.

Certain skills are different at different *technological* levels ("tech level" or "TL" for short). Such skills are designated by /TL. For instance, the Shortsword skill is the same everywhere, but Surgery/TL4 (cut his arm off with an axe) is very different from Surgery/TL9 (graft on a replacement arm from his clone). See *Technological Levels* (p. 185).

Just as in real life, you start your career with some skills, and you can learn more if you spend time training.

LEARNING SKILLS

In order to learn or improve a skill, you must spend character points. The cost of a skill depends on its type and difficulty. Smart characters will have an advantage when learning mental skills; dextrous characters will have an advantage with most physical skills.

When you spend points for a skill, you are getting training to bring that skill up to a useful level. Skills are easy to learn at first – a little training goes a long way! But added improvement costs more, as shown on the tables below.

The *Skill Tables* (p. 44) show the character point cost to study each skill. Skills are divided into two types – mental (based on IQ) and physical (usually based on DX). The harder a skill, the more points you must spend to improve it.

Choosing Your Beginning Skills

When you first create a new character, you use character points to "buy" skills (see the *Instant Characters* sheet for a complete list). The *maximum* number of character points a starting character can use for skills is equal to twice his age. For instance, an 18-year-old character could apply no more than 36 points to skills. Reason: This represents about the maximum amount of training that you would have been able to pack into your lifetime up to the point at which you entered play. This limit does *not* apply to skills added after a character is created.

No cash expenditure is needed for the skills a character starts with.

The GM may forbid you to start with any skills he feels are not appropriate for your character. For instance, a stone-age hunter could not be an expert jet pilot, and a Renaissance swordsman could not know scuba. And a gentleman in Victorian London would need a *very* good explanation (and probably the Unusual Background advantage) if he wished to start out as a skilled sorcerer!

Likewise, adventurers in futuristic universes may have some difficulty finding training in Survival and "archaic" weapon and vehicle skills (a military background will help).

As a rule, the GM should allow greater leeway in skill choice for a character who is wealthy or has high status.

Prerequisites

Some skills have *prerequisites* – usually other skills. This happens when a more advanced skill is based on, and is in some ways an outgrowth of, a basic one. You must know the prerequisite skill at level 12 or better before you can study the higher skill. For instance, you must have the Mechanic skill at a level of 12 or better before you can study (vehicle-type) Engineering skill. Mathematics is a prerequisite for Nuclear Physics – and so on. Actual study of the prerequisite is required; a high default won't do.

POINT COSTS FOR SKILLS

The following table shows the character point cost to learn the two types of skill (physical and mental) at each level. For a detailed example of skill selection, see p. 70.

The first column shows the skill level you are trying to attain, *relative to the controlling ability* – DX for physical skills, IQ for mental ones. If your DX is 12, then a level of "DX-1" would be 11, "DX" would be 12, "DX+1" would be 13, and so on.

The next columns show the point costs to learn skills of different difficulties – *Easy, Average, Hard,* and *Very Hard* – at that level. Harder skills take longer – that is, cost more character points – to learn!

Specializing

Required Specialization

Some skills – Engineering, Armoury, Piloting, Survival and several others – are very wide-ranging. Anyone learning the skill *must* "specialize." Each "specialty" is considered a separate skill. You may learn the skill any number of times, each with a different specialty, because each specialty is a different skill.

The various Driving skills (for instance) default to each other at -4. If you have skill 18 in Driving (Automobiles), you have a default skill of 14 in Driving (Heavy Equipment), Driving (Trucks), and so on.

Optional Specialization

Other skills – the sciences, for instance – allow *optional* specialization. In such a case, you *may* pick a specialty within the field. For instance, an astronomer might specialize in comets. A specialist has a +5 on any problem relating to his specialty, but a -1 on any question outside it, or -2 if he has two specialties. You are only allowed two optional specialties within any one particular field. The GM may reject any proposed "specialty."

Familiarity

Many skills – Driving (Automobiles), Beam Weapons, and many more – have a penalty when the user is faced with an unfamiliar *type* of item. For instance, if a Star Ranger was trained on the Fisher blaster, the Hamill model will be "unfamiliar." Use of an unfamiliar type of item is at a -2 to all skill rolls.

As a rule, if you have the general skill to deal with a piece of equipment, you are considered *familiar* with a new make or model of gear after you have had eight hours of practice with it. There is no limit to the number of types of gun, car, plane, etc. you can become familiar with. If you are familiar with at least 6 types, the GM may roll against your skill when you pick up a new type; on a successful roll, you are already familiar with something similar and may use the new device at no penalty.

The GM may always rule that an item is so similar to a known one that it is familiar – for instance, two similar models of Colt revolver should be considered identical.

Familiarity for Beginning Characters

Note that both specialization and familiarity come into play with many skills. For instance, with the Driving skill, you *must* pick a specialization (say, Automobiles.) You can then start with one vehicle type (probably your own) with which you are familiar. You may pick one added familiarity for each point of skill over 14.

Skill Defaults: Using Skills You Don't Know

Many skills have a "default level." This is the level at which you perform the skill *without training*. A skill has a default level if it is something that everybody can do . . . a little bit.

As a general rule: any Easy skill has a default of DX-4 (if physical) or IQ-4 (if mental). Average skills default to DX (or IQ)-5; Hard skills default to DX (or IQ)-6. There are exceptions to this, but not many.

For instance, the "default" for Lockpicking is IQ-5. If your IQ is 11, and you have to pick a lock without any training, you need a roll of 6 or less. 11 minus 5 is 6, your "default" skill at Lockpicking.

Default levels in skills do not carry any of the skills' special benefits with them, such as damage bonuses, dodge bonuses, 2/3-skill parry, unpenalized off-hand use, and so on.

Some skills have *no* default level. Karate, Nuclear Physics and Lasso, for example, are complex enough that nobody can do them *at all* without training.

The GM should change (or forbid) defaults to avoid silly results. For instance, a medieval knight, transported to the 20th century, would not get a default roll to use scuba gear the first time he saw it! The Scuba default assumes that most people would have some idea (if only from TV) what to do with scuba gear.

Maximum Default

If a skill defaults to a basic attribute that is higher than 20, treat that attribute as 20 when figuring default skill. Superhuman characters get *good* defaults, but not *super* ones.

Defaulting to Other Skills

Some skills default to *another skill*. This can get a bit more complicated, but bear with us; it's worth it.

For example: Broadsword defaults to DX-5 *or* Shortsword-2, because the two skills are very similar. If you have studied Shortsword, you already know something about Broadsword use.

Suppose you have a Shortsword skill of 13. Broadsword defaults to Shortsword-2. So, without study, you have a "default" Broadsword skill of 11. Now, if you *study* Broadsword, you will have the advantage of your Shortsword training. You start learning at your current level of 11. Each added level of skill requires as much training as though you had started learning the normal way and worked your way up.

(In other words, your training in a related skill gives you a head start – but you *can't* add more skill levels with a few hours' training. Only a beginner can learn that fast, and you're no beginner.)

Continued on next page . . .

physical skills

	Difficulty of Skill		
Your Final Skill Level	**Easy**	**Average**	**Hard**
DX-3	–	–	½ point
DX-2	–	½ point	1 point
DX-1	½ point	1 point	2 points
DX	1 point	2 points	4 points
DX+1	2 points	4 points	8 points
DX+2	4 points	8 points	16 points
DX+3	8 points	16 points	24 points
DX+4	16 points	24 points	32 points
DX+5	24 points	32 points	40 points

mental skills

	Difficulty of Skill			
Your Final Skill Level	**Easy**	**Average**	**Hard**	**Very Hard**
IQ-4	–	–	–	½ point
IQ-3	–	–	½ point	1 point
IQ-2	–	½ point	1 point	2 points
IQ-1	½ point	1 point	2 points	4 points
IQ	1 point	2 points	4 points	8 points
IQ+1	2 points	4 points	6 points	12 points
IQ+2	4 points	6 points	8 points	16 points
IQ+3	6 points	8 points	10 points	20 points
IQ+4	8 points	10 points	12 points	24 points
IQ+5	10 points	12 points	14 points	28 points

Further increases follow the same progressions: 8 additional points per level for physical skills, 4 per level for very hard mental skills, 2 per level for other mental skills. There is no limit (except lifespan) to the amount of improvement possible with any skill. But the useful maximum for most skills is in the 20 to 30 range, since problems to challenge a greater skill may not be common.

Explanation of Skill Tables

Physical skills are based on DX (or, for a few skills, HT or ST – but the chart is read in the same way). They are easy to learn at first, but you rapidly reach a "plateau." After that, further improvement is very time-consuming. Examples would be climbing; cycling; driving most vehicles; all weapon skills. With a physical skill, you reach the "point of diminishing returns" at a level of DX+3 to DX+5. Further study is a sign of great dedication!

Mental skills are based on IQ (except for Sex Appeal, which is based on HT). Once you get the basic grounding in a subject, training proceeds at a steady rate, and indefinite improvement is possible. Examples of mental skills include simple craft skills; sciences; magic spells; psionic skills; languages. Study of these skills "levels off" relatively quickly; further improvement requires only 2 character points per skill level (4 for Very Hard mental skills).

Note that, at high levels, physical skills are harder to improve than even the toughest mental disciplines. This is realistic. A master swordsman, striving for further improvement, must discipline both mind and body. A student or scientist need only discipline the mind – and of the two, the body's limits are far more confining!

MEANING OF SKILL LEVELS

So you have a skill of 9 in Geology, 13 in Shortsword and 22 in the French language. What does that *mean*? What is good, bad and indifferent? That's very important when you create a character. It's also important if you're converting characters from another system into **GURPS,** or vice versa.

To use a skill, you must make a "success roll" against your skill level – see p. 86. Success rolls are made on 3 dice. For instance, if your skill is 13, you must roll a 13 or less on 3 dice to succeed with that skill. Skill levels can be over 18, and often are . . . but a roll of 17 or 18 always fails. And modifiers for difficult tasks or unfavorable situations will usually adjust your "effective" skill to a number under 18.

The *probability* of success at each skill level is shown below. If you have a skill of 10 (defined as an "average" level of skill), you will fail exactly half the time. Obviously, "average" is not really very good in many cases! Note that a roll of 17 or 18 is automatically a failure, so nobody succeeds 100% of the time.

This table should be used to judge overall competence at most skills. A special table for languages is found on p. 55.

Skill Level	Probability of Success	Skill Level	Probability of Success
3 – Abysmal	0.5%	10 – Average	50.0%
4 –	1.9%	11 –	62.5%
5 –	4.6%	12 – Rather skilled	74.1%
6 – Inept	9.3%	13 –	83.8%
7 –	16.2%	14 – Well-trained	90.7%
8 – Mediocre	25.9%	15 –	95.4%
9 –	37.5%	16 or above – Expert	98.1%

These figures give the probability of succeeding on the first try at a task of *average* difficulty – whatever that is. Remember that your roll for a difficult task will be *modified* by the GM. If you have a Lockpicking skill of 18, you will get most ordinary locks on the first try. But a tough lock – -8 to open – gives you an *effective* skill of only 10, and your chance to open it drops to 50%!

Note that once your skill reaches a level of 14 or so, your chance of succeeding doesn't really go up very much with each added point of skill. Furthermore, learning those added points of skill gets harder and harder. It isn't pointless, though. For instance, suppose you have a Lockpicking skill of 23. Ordinary locks are no easier for you – you can't have better than a 98% chance, no matter what. But that hard lock, which was -8 to open, adjusts your skill down to 15 – which still gives you a 95% chance to open it the first try!

For weapon skills, the usual range of useful levels is 10 to 16. A "real-world" comparison of weapon skill levels:

3: Astoundingly bad. You will never hit a foe except by luck.
6: Clumsy. An average man using an easy weapon for the first time.
9: Unskilled. A rookie in his first month of basic training.
12: Novice. An average man after a little study, or a talented beginner.
15: Veteran. A good, experienced fighter. You rarely miss.
18: Expert. You have a *lot* of experience.
20: Master. You could train others, and train them well.
25: Wizard. You could fight blindfolded.

Defaulting to Other Skills (Continued)

Because of your Shortsword training, you have a default Broadsword skill of 11. Assume your DX is 12. Your skill of 11 is equal to your DX-1. This would have cost 1 point had you bought it originally. The next level (DX) costs 2 points. The difference is 1. So, if you pay 1 character point, you can raise your Broadsword skill from its default level of 11 to (DX), or 12.

Double Defaults: If Skill A defaults to Skill B-5, and B defaults to IQ-5, does A default to IQ-10? No. A skill can't default to another skill known only by default.

Improving Skills with Defaults

Suppose that you increase a skill (for example, Shortsword) on which you had based another skill (Broadsword). Your default Broadsword skill goes up. But if you started learning Broadsword with your default from Shortsword, and then put more points into it, improving Shortsword won't necessarily improve your Broadsword skill further.

In the example above, suppose you spend the 1 point to raise Broadsword to 12 (DX). Now you spend 4 more points in Shortsword, improving that skill to a 14 (from DX+1 to DX+2). Does your Broadsword skill also go up a level? No. Your new default from Shortsword is now 12 (Shortsword at 14, minus 2), but to go from level 12 to level 13 (from DX to DX+1) with Broadsword costs 2 points, and you've only spent 1 on Broadsword. Keep track of that point, though, and when you spend 1 more on Broadsword, it goes up by a level, as well.

If you study *Broadsword* until it is better than your Shortsword, it might be best to switch the defaults, so your Shortsword now defaults from Broadsword. But you may *never* decrease either level – you must have enough unspent points available to keep each at its current level.

Keeping Shortsword at 14, you've spent 39 total points on Broadsword, improving your skill to 18 (DX+6). You'd like to default Shortsword from Broadsword now, rather than vice versa. You must first spend the extra point on Broadsword that you saved when you first defaulted Broadsword from Shortsword. You can now default Shortsword from Broadsword. That default level is 16 (Broadsword-2). And you've spent 8 total points on Shortsword (getting it to 14, earlier) – that 8 points is now enough to improve your Shortsword skill to 17.

This feels like an abstract number shuffle, but it works. You're no better off than if you had started with Broadsword skill, and you aren't being penalized for learning Shortsword first.

LIST OF SKILLS

Skills are listed alphabetically within categories. The listing for each skill gives the following information:

Name of the skill. If the skill is one which varies at different tech levels, this will be shown – e.g., "Blacksmith/TL."

Type. The variety of skill (mental or physical) and its difficulty (easy, average, hard or very hard).

Defaults. The basic attribute(s) or other skill(s) to which use of the skill defaults if the skill itself is not known. If there is more than one possible default, the skill defaults to whatever will give the user the most advantage. Some skills (foreign languages, for instance) have no defaults. You *cannot* attempt to use these skills unless you have actually studied them.

Prerequisites. Other skills which must be known at level 12 or better before this skill can be learned. Most skills have no prerequisites.

Description. A brief explanation of the way the skill works.

Modifiers. A list of common bonuses and penalties for use of the skill. It is always *entirely* up to the GM to decide whether a given modifier should apply or not.

New Skills

Game Masters and players are free to come up with other skills as needed. Defaults, learning time, et cetera, should be assigned by comparison with the skills listed here. Keep in mind that many so-called "new" skills will really just be specialties within existing skills.

ANIMAL SKILLS

These skills can easily be learned in any low-tech culture – or in farm and ranch country in any culture at all. A "city kid" might have trouble finding a teacher unless he is wealthy.

Any of these skills can be learned with an optional specialization in one general type of animal (e.g., horses, cats, raptor birds).

Animal Handling (Mental/Hard)   Defaults to IQ-6

This is the ability to train and work with all types of animals. To *train* an animal, the Animal Handler must make his success roll once per day of training. A failed roll means the animal learned nothing; a badly-failed roll means the Handler was attacked. The time it takes to train an animal depends on the animal's intelligence and tractability – see *Animals,* p. 140.

When working with a trained animal, the animal handler rolls against his skill for each task he sets the animal. Modifiers: -5 if the animal is not familiar with the handler, -5 if the circumstances are stressful to the animal, -3 or more if the task is a complex one.

This talent can also (sometimes) be used to quiet a wild, danger-ous or untrained animal. Modifiers: -5 if the creature is wild or very frightened, -10 if it is a man-eater or man-killer.

Finally, this talent gives an advantage in combat against ani-mals. If you have this skill at level 15 or better, any animal's attack and defense rolls are at -1 against you, because you can predict its behavior. If you are an expert (skill 20 or better), the animal's rolls are at -2.

Falconry (Mental/Average)   Defaults to IQ-5

This is the skill of "hawking" – hunting small game with a trained hawk. A good falconer will know hunting and training tech-niques, as well as how to care for a falcon (see sidebar, p. 142).

Finding a wild falcon's nest in spring requires a week of search and a successful Falconry roll; a nest will have 1d-3 chicks.

Packing (Mental/Hard)   Defaults to Animal Handling-6 or IQ-6
Prerequisite: Animal Handling

This is the ability to efficiently and speedily get loads on and off of pack animals. It includes the skill of getting the best performance from the beasts, judging them before purchase, and selecting the best routes for pack trains.

A skilled packer will be in demand in any commercial area before TL6, and will earn as much as a sergeant of mercenaries. A caravan must have at least one master packer (skill 15+), or its speed is reduced by 20%. The U.S. Army used thousands of pack

animals in WWII, and would have used many more, but couldn't find enough skilled packers – and four years of war was not enough time to train them!

At higher tech levels, this is replaced by the professional skill of Freight Handling – which is less complex (Mental/Average) because it requires no knowledge of beasts.

Riding (any type) (Physical/Average)   Defaults to Animal Handling-3 or DX-5

This ability is different for each animal type (in other words, you must pick an animal to "specialize" in). If you encounter an unfamiliar riding animal, default to the closest Riding skill you have. For instance, if you know how to ride a horse, you would be at -3 for a camel, -6 for a dolphin, and no penalty for a mule.

You must make your Riding roll when you first try to mount a riding animal, and again each time something happens to frighten or challenge the creature (e.g., a jump). Modifiers: +5 if the animal knows and likes you; -10 if the animal is not an "ordinary" riding creature and/or has not been trained for riding.

Teamster (Mental/Average)
Defaults to Animal Handling-4 or Riding-2
Prerequisite: Animal Handling

This is the skill of driving teams of animals, such as wagon or gun teams. It includes the skills of harnessing the animals, caring for them and judging them for quality before purchase. Driving more than four animals, or driving a team of unfamiliar animals, is -2 to skill. Each *species* of animal requires a different skill; these default to each other at -3. Horses and mules are covered by the same skill.

When a wagon or other load (such as a gun) is moved at a gallop (over 20 mph, or 10 hexes per turn), the driver must roll against his Teamster skill every ten seconds, at a penalty of up to -5 for bad terrain. A failed roll spills the wagon. This is equivalent to a 5-yard fall (5d-10 damage) for each man and animal involved. Animal Handling rolls will be required to calm the beasts. Also, roll 2 dice for each horse; on a 12, a leg is broken! Time required to reload the cargo depends on the load, the terrain, and the weather.

Veterinary/TL (Mental/Hard)
Defaults to any appropriate Medical skill-5, or Animal Handling-5

This is the ability to care for a sick or wounded animal. It is a Medical skill (see p. 56). Modifiers: +5 if the animal knows and trusts you; -2 or worse if the animal is of an unfamiliar type. An optional specialization (p. 43) is allowed.

Musical Instrument (Mental/Hard)
Defaults to any similar instrument-3

Each musical instrument is a separate talent. A successful use of the talent will allow you to perform competently on the instrument in question. Roll again for each new performance.

Photography/TL (Mental/Average)
Defaults to IQ-5

This is the ability to use a camera competently, use a darkroom, et cetera, and to produce recognizable and attractive photos. A default roll is allowed to use a camera, but not to develop film or prints in a darkroom. Modifiers: -3 for an unfamiliar camera; -3 for a motion-picture camera.

These skills may be learned anywhere, any time, as long as the skill is known to the character's culture. Many people seem to have "inborn" artistic aptitude. For simplicity, all artistic ability is treated as a skill rather than an advantage – but to balance this, assume that you can start with any level of artistic skill regardless of your age or availability of a teacher.

Artist (Mental/Hard)
Defaults to IQ-6

This is the ability to draw and paint with both accuracy and beauty. A successful roll against this skill would let you (for instance) draw a recognizable picture of someone to help identify him; draw a map that would be easy to follow; or even paint a picture good enough to trade for a meal. (Note that, for the last case, the GM should not allow a default roll. Intelligence can let you draw an accurate picture but not a beautiful one.)

Bard (Mental/Average)
Defaults to IQ-5 or Performance-2

This is the ability to tell stories and to speak extemporaneously. Successful use of this talent would (for instance) let you give a good political speech; entertain a group around a campfire; incite (or calm) a riot; or put on a successful "court jester" act. Modifiers: +2 if you have the Voice advantage; any Charisma bonus.

If you try to perform in a language other than your native tongue, subtract 1 from your skill for every point below 12 in your skill with that language – e.g., if you are performing in French, and your skill with French is only 8, you have a -4 penalty on your Bard skill.

Calligraphy (Physical/Average)
Defaults to Artist-2 or DX-5
Prerequisite: Literacy

This is the art of beautiful and decorative handwriting. It is of use primarily to earn a living.

Dancing (Physical/Average)
Defaults to DX-5

This is the ability to perform dances appropriate to your own culture, and to learn new dances quickly. Modifiers: -5 if the dance is unfamiliar. Once you have successfully performed a dance three times, it is familiar. Note that certain physical handicaps make this skill effectively impossible!

Poetry (Mental/Average)
Defaults to IQ-5 or Language-5

This is the ability to compose "good" poetry of any type native to your culture, in any language you speak. A successful Poetry roll lets you write one good poem, in an appropriate amount of time (GM's decision). A failed roll means you couldn't come up with good rhymes, or (for whatever reason) your audience just didn't care for your work. Modifiers: -3 (or worse) if you are under unreasonable time pressure; +3 (or better) if you have a lot of time; foreign language penalties as for Bard (above).

Sculpting (Physical/Average) Defaults to DX-5 or IQ-5

This is the ability to fashion a reasonable likeness of a person or object, using clay, wood, stone, ivory or whatever comes to hand. A metalsmithing skill is also required to produce a metal sculpture.

Time required is up to the GM. Sculpting is primarily of use in earning a living, but can have useful applications for an adventurer. Modifiers: -5 if the appropriate tools are not available; -5 if the medium is unfamiliar; -5 if the medium is difficult (e.g., marble).

ARTISTIC SKILLS

Singing (Physical/Easy) — *Defaults to HT-4*

Study of this skill is based on HT, not DX. This is the ability to sing in a pleasing fashion. A successful roll means the audience liked your song. Modifiers: -2 if the audience does not understand the language; +2 if you have the Voice advantage.

Writing (Mental/Average) — *Defaults to IQ-5 or Language-5*

This is the ability to write in a clear and/or entertaining manner. A successful roll means the work is readable and accurate. Modifiers: -3 if you were rushed; +3 if you had a generous amount of time; -5 if you are writing about an unfamiliar subject. This ability is of most use to earn a living and/or write for *GURPS,* but can sometimes be of use on adventures . . . or after them. The report of a spy, military man or private investigator will be far more useful if it is well-written!

ATHLETIC SKILLS

Acrobatics (Physical/Hard) — *Defaults to DX-6*

This is the ability to perform acrobatic and gymnastic stunts, roll, take falls and so on. A separate skill roll is required for each trick. This can be handy on an adventure; tightrope walking, human pyramids and trapeze swinging all have useful applications.

An Acrobatics roll may be substituted for a DX roll in any attempt to jump, roll, avoid Knockback and so on.

A character trying to Dodge a blow may attempt an Acrobatic Dodge (see p. 108), a jump or roll which avoids the attack in a flashy way. A successful Acrobatics roll will also reduce the effective distance of any fall by five yards (see p. 131).

The GM may apply penalties as he sees fit for an especially difficult trick.

Bicycling — *See Vehicle Skills, p. 68*

Breath Control (Mental/Very Hard) — *No default*

This is the ability to breathe at maximum efficiency. On a successful skill roll, the user can triple the time the breath is held for any reason (e.g., underwater). A successful skill roll will also allow a point of fatigue to be regained in only two minutes (this cannot be combined with magic spells which restore fatigue).

This skill is not normally known outside Oriental cultures; the GM might make it available in a futuristic scenario.

Free Fall/TL (Physical/Average) — *Defaults to DX-5 or HT-5*

This is the ability to handle yourself in a free-fall (zero-gravity) environment. One roll is necessary when you first go into free fall; a failed roll means you become spacesick, and a further roll against

HT is required to avoid choking! Treat this as drowning (see *Swimming,* p. 91). A further roll would be required each time you try to perform some complex action in free-fall. Failure does not make you spacesick – your attempted action just fails.

Jumping (Physical/Easy) — *No default See Jumping, p. 88*

This is the trained ability to use your strength to its best advantage when you jump. When you attempt a difficult jump, you may substitute your Jumping skill for your ST or DX.

Parachuting (Physical/Easy) *Defaults to DX-4 or IQ-6*

This is the ability to survive a parachute jump. A failed roll could mean anything from a slight drift off course to panic that makes you drop your gear – GM's option. A critical failure means the chute did not open, or was fatally fouled (see *Falling,* p. 130). For a jump under bad conditions, a roll on landing may be required as well . . . for instance, to survive an "ankle-breaker" landing without injury, or to dodge trees on the way down.

Riding — *See Animal Skills, p. 46*

Running (Physical/Hard) — *No default*

This skill is based on HT, not DX. It represents training in sprints and long-distance running. If you have *studied* this skill, divide your skill level by 8 (don't round down) and add the result to your Speed for the purpose of calculating your Move score for the purposes of using the Move manuever on land (it does not affect Dodge!). For instance, if you have a Running skill of 18, your Speed is increased by 2.25 before calculating your Move. See *Running,* p. 88.

Scuba (Mental/Average) — *Defaults to IQ-5 or Swimming-5*

This is the ability to use an underwater breathing apparatus. One roll is required when you first go in the water, and one every further 30 minutes, to avoid inhaling water, with a loss of 1 ST and a risk of drowning (see *Swimming,* p. 91). A successful roll (no defaults allowed) will also let you spot problems with the equipment if you check before putting it on.

Skiing (Physical/Hard)   Defaults to DX-6

This is the ability to ski. A roll is required when you start down any but an easy slope, and another every 30 minutes (or every hazardous situation). A failed roll means you fall. On a critical failure, take 1d-1 damage to a randomly chosen limb, and suffer through the appropriate Crippling damage until you heal. If you roll 5 points of damage, the limb was actually broken.

Sports (many types) (Physical/Average)   Varies

Every sport is a different skill. Most default to DX-5. Those putting a premium on strength (e.g., football, rugby) default to ST-5 as well. These skills are mostly useful in building a good character background and/or earning a living, but a clever player or GM can make a sports background useful on an adventure.

Swimming (Physical/Easy)   Defaults to ST-5 or DX-4

This skill is used both for swimming (on purpose, or to keep afloat in emergencies) and for saving a drowning victim. See Swimming, p. 91, for full rules on swimming, drowning, and life-saving.

Throwing (Physical/Hard)   No default

This is the general ability to throw whatever you can pick up. It helps both accuracy (roll against your Throwing skill to throw anything you can lift) and distance (add 1/6 of Throwing skill to ST when determining distance). See Throwing Things, p. 90. There is little point to learning a Thrown Weapon skill in addition to Throwing. Learn the weapon skill instead if you want to specialize without spending too much time in practice.

If you do not have this skill, you roll against DX-3 when throwing something at a target, or DX to lob it into a general area. If you're throwing something for which there's a specific skill, use that skill.

Weapon skill   See Combat/Weapon Skills, below

COMBAT/WEAPON SKILLS

Anyone interested in a combat skill can usually find teachers, if the skill is known in his culture. The best way to learn is to have a military, mercenary or police background.

Special terms used in the descriptions of these skills are explained in Chapters 13 and 14, and the Glossary. Note also that several skills are listed here but not mentioned elsewhere. They are covered in other releases, and are listed here only for completeness.

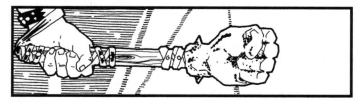

Axe/Mace (Physical/Average)   Defaults to DX-5

Ability to use any short or middle-sized unbalanced weapon, such as an axe, hatchet, mace, pick, etc.

Axe Throwing (Physical/Easy)   Defaults to DX-4

Ability to throw any sort of balanced throwing axe – but not an unbalanced battleaxe!

Battlesuit/TL (Physical/Average)   Defaults to IQ-5, DX-5, Exoskeleton-2, or Vacc Suit-3

This is the ability to use a suit of powered armor, including its integral weaponry. Designed for use under great stress, most battlesuits are very user-friendly. A battlesuit in good shape can actually be operated by a novice, if the novice is smart and lucky. A damaged battlesuit is another matter; the details are up to the GM.

Beam Weapons/TL (Physical/Easy)   Defaults to DX-4 or (other Beam Weapons skill)-4

This is the ability to use beam-type weapons, including blaster, laser, stunner, etc. It requires specialization – see p. 43. It covers both handguns and long-arms, since beam weapons are essentially recoilless. Add 1 to your skill for an IQ of 10 or 11, and 2 for an IQ of 12 or better. Modifiers are as per Guns, p. 51.

Blackjack (Physical/Easy)   Defaults to DX-4

Ability to use a blackjack or sap. This weapon is good only in close combat, and is most often used for surprise attacks. It does very little basic damage, which is why it is used against the head. Special note: If it is desired not to seriously injure the victim, the attacker may "pull the blow" (p. 122), attacking with less than his full ST.

Black Powder Weapons (Physical/Easy)   Defaults to DX-4

This is the ability to use any black-powder weapon, including musket, pistol and rifle. Add 1 to your skill for an IQ of 10 or 11, and 2 for an IQ of 12 or better. Modifiers are as per Guns, p. 51.

Blowpipe (Physical/Hard)   Defaults to DX-6

This is the ability to use a blowpipe to shoot small (usually poisoned) darts. Such a dart cannot pierce normal clothing except on a critical success, and never penetrates cloth or better armor. If a dart hits exposed flesh or light clothing, the poison can take effect. Modifiers: -2 and up for wind, if outdoors.

Bolas (Physical/Average)   No default

This is the ability to throw the bolas – a length of leather cord with two or more weights attached – to entangle a victim. It is primarily used to stop herd animals and to hunt small game and birds. It can also be used in combat; it can be dodged or blocked, but an attempt to parry makes it hit and entangle the parrying arm automatically. Exception: a successful parry with an edged weapon will cut the cords, ruining the bolas!

A bolas may be aimed at a body part, or the hit location table may be used for a randomly-cast one. If the bolas hits, it automatically wraps around its target, as well as doing its damage. If the arm, hand, or weapon is hit, roll a Quick Contest of Bolas skill vs. target's ST. If the target loses, he drops the weapon (does not affect shields strapped onto the forearm).

If the leg is hit, two legs are entangled. A running target must make a DX roll or fall – taking 1d-2 damage. Once entangled, a victim requires three successful DX rolls (and one free hand) to escape; during this time, no other actions can be taken. Animals roll to escape at DX-3 if they have paws, or DX-6 if they have hooves.

Combat/Weapon Skills

Bow (Physical/Hard) — *Defaults to DX-6*

This is the ability to use the longbow, shortbow and all similar bows. It also covers the compound bow, though a person who had never seen a compound bow would need to make an IQ roll to figure it out before he could use it properly.

Brawling (Physical/Easy) — *No default*

This is the skill of unscientific roaring-and-punching close combat. When you attack with bare hands or feet, roll vs. Brawling skill to hit. Add $^1/_{10}$ of your Brawling skill level (round down) to the damage you do. When you defend with bare hands, you may parry twice per turn (once with each hand) and your Parry is $^2/_3$ your Brawling skill. See p. 101 for rules on parrying bare-handed.

Broadsword (Physical/Average) — *Defaults to DX-5, Shortsword-2 or Force Sword-3*

Ability to use any 2- to 4-foot, balanced, one-handed weapon – including broadswords, one-handed bastard swords, baseball bats and anything similar.

Buckler (Physical/Easy) — *Defaults to DX-4 or Shield-2*

This is the ability to use a medieval-style buckler – a small shield held in the hand or strapped to the arm. This skill is used exactly like the *Shield* skill, p. 52, and can be used to calculate a Block defense if you have a buckler instead of a shield.

Crossbow (Physical/Easy) — *Defaults to DX-4*

Ability to use all crossbows, including a "prodd" or stonebow. If you have this skill, you understand the use of crossbow-type siege engines, but have no special skill in firing them.

Fast-Draw (Physical/Easy) — *No default*

This is a separate skill for each type of weapon. Fast-Draw is available for the following weapons: Knife, Blackjack, Sword (one-handed), Two-Handed Sword, Arrow (including crossbow bolts), Pistol, Rifle (including submachine guns, etc.), Magazine, Speedloader. The GM may add a new Fast-Draw skill for any weapon if it can reasonably be drawn quickly, but is significantly different from all the above weapons. This skill is used when you wish to ready a weapon from its holster, scabbard, etc. A successful roll means you ready the item instantly (this does not count as a maneuver). You may attack with the weapon (or load the bow) on the same turn. A failed roll means you ready the item normally, but may do nothing else that turn (if it's an arrow, you *drop* it). A critical miss means you drop the weapon – or, for arrows, the whole quiver!

Combat Reflexes advantage gives a +1 on Fast-Draw skill.

Fencing (Physical/Average) — *Defaults to DX-5*

This is the ability to use the fencer's weapons – rapier, smallsword and saber. The rapier is a long (2-hex reach), light, thrusting weapon. The smallsword is a shorter (1-hex reach), light thrusting weapon, somewhat like a modern fencing foil with a point. The saber is a light cut-and-thrust weapon.

If you have one of these weapons, no larger than a small shield, and no greater than light encumbrance, your parrying ability is $^2/_3$ your Fencing skill (round down). Furthermore, you can parry *twice* per turn, instead of just once. If you are on All-Out Defense, you may parry *any number* of attacks each turn. Many fencers carry a dagger as a second weapon. It may also parry (making three parries per turn!) – but only at the fencer's regular Knife Parry skill level.

The only disadvantage of the fencing Parry is that the fencer's weapons are very light and may break when used to parry – see pp. 99, 110.

GURPS Martial Arts treats fencing in much more detail.

Flail (Physical/Hard) — *Defaults to DX-6*

Ability to use unbalanced weapons with the head attached to the handle by chain or rope, such as the flail, morningstar or nunchuku. Flails are hard to use, but also hard to defend against. Any attempt to *block* a flail weapon is at -2. Any attempt to *parry* it is at -4. Knives and fencing weapons cannot parry flail weapons at all! Martial-arts defenses *can* parry flails, but at -4.

Force Shield (Physical/Easy) — *Defaults to DX-4*

Ability to use the force shield, an ultra-tech device which is worn on the wrist and projects a circle of force. It gives a Block defense, just like a regular shield. Also see *Shield*, p. 52.

Anyone who has the Shield skill may use a force shield after only 1 hour of practice (or use a force shield at -2 with no practice). But anyone skilled with a force shield will default at -2 to a regular shield, which is heavy, clumsy, and *opaque*. 50 hours of drill reduce this penalty to -1. Another 100 hours eliminate it entirely, giving Shield skill equal to Force Shield skill; thereafter, any increase in one skill increases the other. A character who starts with both skills at the same level is assumed to have gained this familiarity already, at no extra point cost.

Force Sword (Physical/Average) — *Defaults to DX-5, or any Sword skill-3*

Ability to use all force swords (TL11 and above). A typical force sword looks like a flashlight and weighs 2 lbs.; at TL11 it costs about $3,000. It takes one turn to activate it, one further turn for the blade to form and stabilize. It runs for 5 minutes on a $100 C power cell (p. 119). A force sword has a reach of 1, and does 8 dice cutting damage or 4 dice if used to impale.

Gunner/TL (Physical/Average) — *Defaults to DX-5 or (other Gunner skill)-4*

This is the ability to operate a heavy weapon, including a vehicle-mounted weapon. Make your Gunner roll each time you fire that weapon. Modifiers: See *Familiarity*, p. 43. -2 for an unfamiliar vehicle, aiming system, etc.; -2 for an unfamiliar weapon of a known type (e.g., .30-cal when you are used to .50s); -4 or more for a weapon in bad repair; -4 or more for a weapon of unfamiliar type (e.g., a laser when you are used to firing recoilless rifles). All normal modifiers for missile-weapon fire also apply. Add 1 to your skill for an IQ of 10 or 11, and 2 for an IQ of 12 or better.

A Gunner can also serve as a substitute Mechanic for his weapon. Roll at -4 to find each problem, and -8 to fix it. See *Mechanic*, p. 54.

If you want to learn Gunner skill for two or more types of weapons, start learning the second one at a reasonable default from the first – usually -4 (check this with the GM). A weapon of a different TL is considered a different "type." Some weapon types include:

Arbalest	Catapult
Machine gun	Recoilless rifle
Rocket launcher	Naval cannon
Laser	Tank cannon

Guns/TL (Physical/Easy)
Defaults to DX-4
or (other Gun skill)-4

This is the ability to use any type of 20th-century cartridge-type gunpowder weapon. Add 1 to your skill for an IQ of 10 or 11, and 2 for an IQ of 12 or better. Modifiers: See *Familiarity,* p. 43. -2 for an unfamiliar weapon of a known type (e.g., .22-cal when you are used to .38s); -4 or more for a weapon in bad repair; -4 or more for a weapon of unfamiliar type (e.g., a rifle when you are used to firing pistols). All normal modifiers for missile-weapon fire also apply.

Judo (Physical/Hard)
No default

This represents the general skill of unarmed throws and grapples, rather than any specific school of unarmed combat. You may not use judo if you have anything in your hands, or if your encumbrance is greater than Light. Using judo, you may parry with either hand as though it were a weapon, using 2/3 your Judo skill as your Parry defense. You are also less likely to be injured when you parry a weapon bare-handed – see p. 101.

If you successfully parry, you may try to throw that foe on your next turn if he is in an adjacent hex; this is an attack. Make your Judo skill roll. Your foe may use any active defense – he *can* parry your hand with a sword! – but PD of his armor doesn't count. If he fails to defend, he is thrown. An attack roll of 17 or 18 means *you* are the one who falls. Note that in an All-Out Attack, you cannot attempt two throws, but you can make one attempt at +4. You may also use your skill to throw a foe if you are Grappling him (*Close Combat,* p. 111); -5 if you are lying down!

When you throw a foe, he falls where you please: in any two hexes near you. One of these hexes must be *his* starting hex, *your* hex, or any hex adjacent to one of these hexes. He must roll against HT; a failed roll means he is stunned! If you throw him into someone else, *that person* must roll either ST+3 or DX+3 (whichever is better) to avoid being knocked down.

You may also use your Judo skill, instead of your DX, in any DX roll made in Close Combat *except* to draw a weapon or drop a shield.

Karate (Physical/Hard)
No default

This represents the general skill of trained punching and kicking, rather than any specific school of unarmed combat. There is no penalty for using the left hand. The hand(s) you use must be empty, and your encumbrance must be Light or less.

You may parry with either hand as though it were a weapon, using 2/3 your Karate skill as your parry defense.

Used offensively, Karate increases the amount of damage you do when you strike without weapons. Roll against your Karate skill to hit. (If you kick, roll against Karate-2. If you miss your kick, you must roll against DX to avoid falling.) 1/5 of your Karate skill, rounded down, is added to the basic damage you do with hands or feet. Bare-handed parries can still cause you injury if they fail – see p. 101.

Note: Although you can break bricks to show off, you cannot punch through armor unscathed. Any time you hit a target with a

---

DR of 3 or better, roll against your HT. A failed roll means you take 1d-2 damage to the hand or foot. Your foe's Toughness does *not* count as DR for this. Your *own* toughness (or boots, etc.) will protect *you,* though.

Knife (Physical/Easy)
Defaults to DX-4

The ability to use, but not to throw, any type of knife, dagger or stiletto.

Knife Throwing (Physical/Easy)
Defaults to DX-4

The ability to throw any sort of knife.

Lance (Physical/Average)
Defaults to Spear-3
for those who have Riding at 12+;
DX-6 for others
Prerequisite: Riding

The ability to use the lance – a spear-like weapon 12 or more feet long, used from horseback. The parry is not normally used in lance combat; a lance-wielder must Block or Dodge enemy attacks.

Lasso (Riata) (Physical/Average)
No default

This is the skill of throwing the lasso or lariat. It is used primarily to snare animals. A body part may be targeted, or the Parts of the Body table (p. 211) used for a random result. If an arm or the body are lassoed, make a Quick Contest of ST; if the lassoer wins the victim is immobilized, but if he loses, he loses the rope. If the head is lassoed, the target is at ST-5 for the Contest of ST. If the foot is lassoed, then the target must make a DX roll to remain standing (DX-4 if the target was running at the time lassoed); no Contest of ST is used. If the DX roll fails, the target takes 1d-4 falling damage; 1d-2 if target is running.

To keep the target immobilized requires the lasso to be taut at all times; this can be done by hand, but while doing so you cannot take any other actions. If a horse is trained to keep the lasso tight (p. 143), its ST is substituted for the thrower's in the Contest of ST.

A lasso thrown around the neck (-5 to hit on a human, -2 on most herd animals) will cut off the victim's breathing as long as it is kept taut. Treat this as suffocation (see p. 122).

One cannot escape from a taut lasso without cutting the rope. Escaping from a limp lasso is done as for a bolas, p. 49.

Net (Physical/Hard)
No default

The ability to fight with the net as a weapon. A thrown net can be dodged, but not blocked or parried. On a successful throw, the victim is enfolded and is unable to move or attack until the net is removed. Three successful rolls at DX-4, not necessarily consecutive, are required to remove a net, using both hands (DX-6 for animals or humans with only one hand available). If three consecutive rolls are failed, the victim has become so entangled that the net will have to be cut free. An animal net weighs 20 lbs., and can be thrown (ST/2) yards plus 1/5 Net skill (round down).

A small net may also be used as a melee weapon, with a reach of 1 or 2 hexes. Treat as a lasso (above), but the victim can attempt to free himself as from a bolas (p. 49). A melee net weighs 5 lbs.; it can be thrown (ST) yards plus 1/5 Net skill (round down). All rolls to escape from a melee net are at +3.

Polearm (Physical/Average)
Defaults to DX-5

Ability to use any very long, unbalanced pole weapon, including poleaxe, glaive, halberd, guisarme and the hundreds of variations on the type.

COMBAT/WEAPON SKILLS

Shield (Physical/Easy)   *Defaults to DX-4 or Buckler-2*

This is the ability to use a medieval-type shield or a police riot shield. This skill is necessary to *attack* with a shield. However, the *passive defense* from a shield (1-4 points) protects the carrier, even if he doesn't know how to use it. The *active defense* from a shield – your *Block* score – is ½ of your Shield skill. Thus, you can block much better if you have studied Shield than if you are using default skill. The average person's DX is 10, so his default Shield skill is 6, and his Block score is only 3!

See also *Force Shield*, p. 50.

Shortsword (Physical/Average)   *Defaults to DX-5, Broadsword-2, or Force Sword-3*

This is the ability to use any balanced weapon, 1-2 feet long – including the shortsword, gladius, baton or billy club.

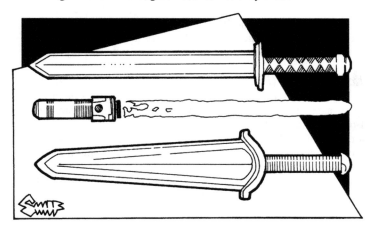

Sling (Physical/Hard)   *Defaults to DX-6*

This is the ability to use the sling or staff sling.

Spear (Physical/Average)   *Defaults to DX-5 or Staff-2*

Ability to use (but not throw) any sort of spear, javelin, trident, fixed bayonet, pike or similar long, light, pointed weapon.

Spear Thrower (Physical/Average)   *Defaults to DX-4 or Spear Throwing-4*

This device, and the skill to use it, are distinct from the Spear Throw*ing* skill, but each defaults to the other at -4. A spear thrower is a long, flat stick with a notch and loop on one end. It increases the force with which a javelin or similar weapon is thrown. It takes 1 turn to place a spear into the thrower after both are in hand and ready. Modifiers: -5 in tight quarters (needs at least a 6-foot clearance overhead for effective use).

Spear Throwing (Physical/Easy)   *Defaults to DX-4 or Spear Thrower -4*

Ability to throw any sort of spear, javelin, etc.

Speed-Load (Physical/Easy)   *No default*

This is the skill of quickly getting ammunition into a firearm. It is not the same as Fast-Draw. But you could, with the right skills, reload *very* quickly by Fast-Drawing a speedloader or magazine from your pocket or belt, and then Speed-Loading.

A different Speed-Load skill is needed for each firearm, and affects loading time as follows:

Black powder weapons: -10% (round down) from normal loading time.

Simultaneously-ejecting revolvers: Without a speedloader, -⅓ sec. per round (round down). With a speedloader, -3 sec.

Single-ejecting revolvers or *integral-magazine weapons:* -⅓ sec. per round (round down).

Removable-magazine, clip-loading, or *ultra-tech power-cell weapons:* -1 second.

Belt-fed weapons: -2 seconds.

A failure on a Speed-Load attempt adds to normal loading time the amount that would have been saved had the attempt succeeded. A critical failure drops or damages the ammunition; the whole loading procedure must be started over or the ammunition recovered (2d seconds or GM's decision).

Some weapons of peculiar design may have different Speed-Load effects, at the GM's discretion.

Staff (Physical/Hard)   *Defaults to DX-5 or Spear-2*

Ability to use a quarterstaff, or to use any improvised pole like a quarterstaff. This is a two-handed skill. Your Parry is ⅔ your skill.

Thrown Weapon (Physical/Easy)   *Defaults to DX-4*

The ability to throw any one type of "throwable" weapon. This skill is different for each type of weapon. Examples are Knife Throwing, Axe Throwing, Spear Throwing. See also *Throwing*, p. 49.

Two-Handed Axe/Mace (Physical/Average)   *Defaults to DX-5*

Ability to use any long, heavy, unbalanced weapon, such as the battleaxe or maul.

Two-Handed Sword (Physical/Average)   *Defaults to DX-5 or Force Sword-3*

Ability to use a long (4- to 5-foot) bladed weapon, in two hands. Note that a "bastard sword" is used with this skill when held in two hands, but with Broadsword skill when held in one.

Whip (Physical/Average)   *No default*

This is the skill of using a whip as a weapon. Whips come in different lengths; for game purposes, a "1-yard" whip has a reach of 1 yard. Such a whip would actually be about 4 feet long. Time to re-ready a whip depends on its length: 0 turns for a 1-yard whip, 1 turn for a 2-yard whip, 2 turns for a 3-yard or larger whip. Whips may be up to 7 yards long; a whip 2 yards long cannot strike at 1 yard or closer.

A whip is a very poor parrying weapon; your parrying skill with a whip is 1/3 your combat skill, rounded down.

A whip can be made to "crack" – the sound is caused by the tip breaking the sound barrier! If the user makes the whip crack just as it hits its target, it does +2 damage, but this is -4 to skill.

Whip blows are very painful. A character who takes more than 1 point of arm or hand damage from a whip must make a Will roll, at a penalty equal to the damage taken. A failed roll means anything in that hand is dropped.

A whip-user can also strike directly at a foe's weapon (at normal penalty for weapon size). If he hits, immediately roll a Contest of ST; at +1 for the whip-user due to leverage. If the whip-user wins, he yanks the weapon away. A critical success on the original strike produces the same result.

A whip may be used (at -4 to skill) in an attempt to entangle the target, exactly like a lasso. This does no damage, but (if successful) follows lasso rules.

CRAFT SKILLS

Any of these skills can be self-taught, with or without books. But many craft techniques, though simple, are not obvious! All craft skills except Carpentry and Leatherworking must be learned at only $^1/_4$ speed (that is, 4 times the point cost) if no teacher is available.

Armoury/TL (Mental/Average)
Defaults to IQ-5, (weapon skill)-6, or Blacksmith-3 (for weapons at TL4 or below)

This is the ability to build and repair weapons and armor at the appropriate tech level. A successful roll is required to find the problem with a weapon (unless it is obvious). A second roll lets you repair it. The GM should determine a reasonable time for each repair attempt. Modifiers: -4 if the weapon is unfamiliar; -4 to try to repair without proper tools (-5 at TL9+).

An armourer at TL5 or below *may* specialize (see p. 43) in one or two of the following fields:

Black powder hand weapons — Armor
Hand weapons (knives, swords, maces, etc.) — Siege engines — Bows and arrows
Guns (e.g., black powder cannon)

An armourer above TL5 *must* specialize (see p. 43) in one or more of the above fields, and/or any of the following fields that exist at his tech level:

Rifles and handguns — Body armor
Beam handguns — Needle handguns
Vehicular weaponry (tanks, autoduelling, etc.) — Airplane weaponry — Psi weaponry
Spaceship weaponry — Spaceship armor
Artillery (includes naval guns) — Any other specialty

Note that above TL5, there is no default between Armoury specializing in armor, and Armoury specializing in any weapon type. They are totally different. The exception would be a specialization in Armoury (Battlesuit), which would cover all systems of the battlesuit and its own armor.

Blacksmith/TL (Mental/Average)
Defaults to IQ-5 or Jeweler-4

This is the ability to work iron and other non-precious metals by hand. A forge is necessary for this work, but a smith can build one, given suitable materials, in about 30 days. Modifier: -1 for every point of ST below 13.

Carpentry (Mental/Easy)
Defaults to IQ-4 or DX-4

This is the ability to build things out of wood. A successful roll lets you do one hour's worth of competent carpentry. A failed roll means the work was bad. Modifiers: +5 if you are being supervised or assisted by someone with skill 15 or better; -5 if you do not have good tools.

Cooking (Mental/Easy)
Defaults to IQ-4

This is the ability to prepare a pleasing meal from raw materials (not just heat water and open boxes). In any "outdoor" society, it includes the ability to dress out game – that is, to prepare a fresh-killed animal for cooking.

Jeweler/TL (Mental/Hard)
Defaults to IQ-6 or Blacksmith-4

This is the ability to work with precious metals of all kinds, make jewelry, decorate weapons and so on. A forge is necessary (see *Blacksmith,* above) to work metal. A Jeweler can identify any precious metal, or determine the value of any precious bauble, by making his skill roll.

Leatherworking (Mental/Easy)
Defaults to IQ-4 or DX-5

This is the ability to work with leather to make belts, saddles, armor, et cetera. A leatherworker can make new goods and repair old goods. By making his skill roll, he can also determine the value of goods made of leather.

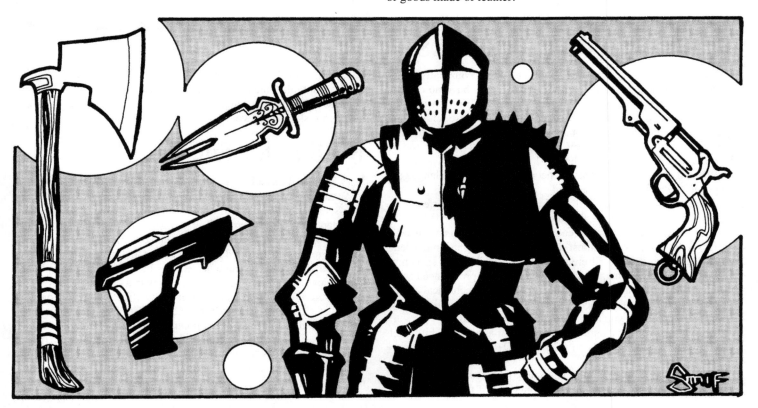

CRAFT SKILLS

Mechanic/TL (Mental/Average)   Defaults to IQ-5 or Engineer-4*

This is the ability to diagnose and fix ordinary mechanical problems – usually, but not always, on a vehicle engine. Specialization is required; types include:

Wagon	Steam engine
Clockwork and small gadgets	Small electric motor
Gasoline engine	Propellor plane engine
Jet plane engine	Hovercraft engine
Fuel cell/electric motor	Ocean-going vessel
Spaceship drive	Starship drive
Robotics	

A successful skill roll can find one problem; a second successful roll can repair it. Modifiers: -5 if proper equipment is not available; -2 for an unfamiliar vehicle, engine, etc. (e.g., a diesel when you are used to gasoline engines); -4 or more for a machine of unfamiliar type (e.g., a plane when you are used to fixing automobiles). All normal modifiers for tech-level differences also apply (see p. 185).

If you want to learn Mechanic skill for two or more types of machine, start learning the second one at a reasonable default from the first – usually -4 (check this with the GM).

* Special default: If you have the skill to operate a particular vehicle (car, cycle, battlesuit, etc.) or the Gunner skill for a particular large weapon, you can default to this skill for Mechanic rolls when you work on that particular machine. To *diagnose* a problem, default to your appropriate Driver or Gunner skill-4. To *fix* it, default to your appropriate Driver or Gunner skill-8.

Pottery (Mental/Average)   Defaults to IQ-5

This is the ability to work with various sorts of ceramics. A potter can make new pots and other items out of clay. By making his skill roll, he can identify proper building clay (for bricks, etc., as well as for tableware); determine the origin or value of pottery; etc.

Shipbuilding/TL (Mental/Hard)   Defaults to IQ-6

This is the ability to design and build ships, boats, etc. A successful roll on this skill will let you determine whether a ship is seaworthy and approximately what it is worth.

At TL8+, shipbuilding and *starship* building are two different skills, both easier because they're computer-assisted; see p. CI137.

Woodworking (Physical/Average)   Defaults to DX-5 or Carpentry-3

This is the ability to do "fine" work with wood; cabinet-making, decorative carving, etc. By making his skill roll, a woodworker can also determine the origin and fair value of a woodcarving, or identify a type of wood.

HOBBY SKILLS

Many fields of study have little to do with either adventuring or making a living – but they are studied nevertheless. No particular teacher is required. Some examples: comic books, model railroading, rock music, tropical fish, opera, cinema, science fiction, gaming . . . In general, these skills are Mental/Average, defaulting to IQ-5 or thereabouts. A few points in a hobby skill can make role-playing more fun – and possibly come in handy once in a while.

Since hobby skills are typically studied during "free time," the GM may allow them to be taken initially at *half price*. Don't do this with anything obviously useful. Fencing, for instance, might be a rich man's hobby – but for game purposes, he can't learn it at half price.

LANGUAGE SKILLS

Each individual language is a separate skill. Your native language defaults to IQ (see below). Other languages have no default unless they are closely related (for instance, English and an English-based "pidgin" trade language). In such a case, either language skill can default to the other, -4. A dialect of a language will default to the base language (or vice versa) at from -1 to -3. Dialects may default to each other at -1 to -4.

Without a teacher (or at least someone who speaks the language) language study is four times as hard.

A language is a Mental skill. Difficulty of languages varies:

Easy: Pidgin English, Esperanto, and the like.

Average: Most languages – French, Chinese, Elvish, Rumanian, etc.

Hard: Basque, Navajo, most alien languages, or any other language based on concepts different from "ordinary" human speech.

Very Hard: Alien languages which cannot be pronounced with the character's natural vocal equipment or simple mechanical aids.

Modifiers: Language Talent (see p. 20) and the Linguistics skill (p. 61) will both give you a bonus to learn any language.

To study your own language, start with an automatic skill level equal to your IQ. IQ+1 costs only 1 point, IQ+2 costs 2, IQ+3 costs 3, and so on.

If you live in another country and speak its language at all times, that is the automatic equivalent of 4 hours/day of training; there is no need to allocate specific study time unless you want to get more than this default. Thus, every 50 days would give you one character point to spend in that language. This "automatic training" ceases when your skill equals your IQ.

Rolling for Successful Communication

When two people try to communicate in a language, and one or both speak it badly, the GM may want to roll to see if a particular important idea comes across. Roll against the *poorer* language skill plus 1/5 of the better speaker's skill (round down). *Example:* Jacques speaks French at a 12; Fred has only an 8. On a roll of 10 or less, a particular idea can be communicated. For hurried speech, bad phone connections, complex directions, etc., roll with a -2 to -8 penalty!

To determine if you can *read* or *write* effectively in a foreign language (if you are literate), the GM will roll against your language skill *only*. He may allow bonuses for simple material (shopping lists, one-line instructions) and penalties for very difficult material. Thus, it is harder to read and write (where you have no feedback) than it is to talk face to face (where you can quickly correct many errors).

Levels of Language Skill

This table will give you an idea about what sort of success to expect at each level of language skill.

4 or under: Recognizes some important words.

5-6: Usually understands simple sentences, spoken slowly.

7-8: Adequate reading and speaking vocabulary. Non-native speakers will have a thick accent, very amusing to natives.

9-10: Command of the language equivalent to that of an average native speaker. Non natives will retain a distinct foreign accent.

11-12: Command of the language equivalent to that of an educated native. Non natives will retain a slight foreign accent.

13-14: Full mastery of the language, including idioms. No foreign accent. Can adopt regional accents if desired.

15 or better: Absolute fluency. If non native, can think in the language.

Literacy

This ability varies widely in availability and importance, depending upon your game world. Furthermore, it is normally acquired when you are very young – or not at all. Therefore, it is treated as an *advantage* (see pp. 17 and 21) in cultures where reading is not common. In cultures where most people can read, you are assumed to be literate unless you took the *disadvantage* of Illiteracy (see p. 33).

If you never have the chance (or never take the time) to learn basic literacy, you may become skilled with many languages without being able to read or write any of them. Therefore, you do not have a score for Literacy; you are either literate or illiterate. If you are literate, your degree of literacy in each language is measured by your skill in that language.

Gesture (Mental/Easy)   Defaults to IQ-4 or Sign Language

This is the ability to communicate through simple, improvised hand signals. Deaf and/or mute individuals have a +3 to use this skill. A successful Gesture roll will let you communicate one simple idea to another, or understand one simple idea communicated by another. For lengthy "conversations," use the communication

LANGUAGE SKILLS

rules under Language. Simple gesture is not suited for complex communication! Different cultures develop different gesture vocabularies; for Westerners dealing with Japanese, for instance, effective Gesture skills are at -4. For humans dealing with aliens of inhuman type, Gesture communication might be nearly impossible – but let the players try!

Sign Language (Mental/Average)   No default

This is any of the many true languages of gesture. One of the better-known is American Sign Language (Ameslan). Other examples might be the language of a speechless alien race, a sign code used by spies or revolutionaries, etc. A sign language is complex, stylized and can communicate almost any concept. Knowing one form of sign language does not let you understand others – but you can recognize that some form of language is being used by making an IQ roll. Deaf and/or mute individuals have a +3 on any Sign Language roll.

Telegraphy (Mental/Easy)   No default

This is the ability to send and receive Morse code, to do simple troubleshooting on a telegraph system, and to recognize other individual operators by their "fist" – that is, the characteristic way they send. This skill is normally found at Tech Levels 5 through 7; at TL8+, humans rarely send code themselves. They use a computer instead.

At TL5, a telegrapher can send or receive 2 words per minute (wpm) for each point of his skill. At TL6+, with a semi-automatic key, this becomes 3 wpm per point of skill. However, skill improves slowly even for the intelligent; your *effective* rate of sending or receiving, in wpm, may not exceed the number of *weeks* since you first acquired the skill.

An operator may attempt to send or receive messages at a speed greater than his skill would normally allow, at -2 to skill for each additional 2 wpm (TL5) or 3 wpm (TL6+) attempted. Maximum rate at TL5 is 25 wpm; at TL6+, maximum is 75.

Sending or receiving messages in code, rather than plain English (or another known language) is at -4 to skill. Sending or receiving in a non-native language is at -1 for every point by which the operator's skill in that language is less than 10, to a maximum penalty of -4.

MAGICAL SKILLS

Each magic spell is considered a separate "skill." Magic is best learned from a wizard, but can be self-taught (at half-speed) from a good grimoire. Magic is covered in Chapter 19.

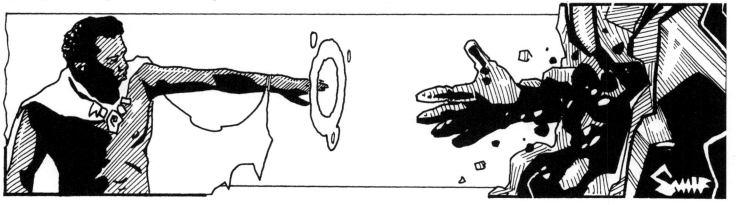

MEDICAL SKILLS

Medicine is a complex subject. The "Physician" skill represents general "doctoring" ability. A good M.D. would have skills of 16 or better in Physician, Diagnosis and First Aid, and at least 14 in Surgery; a skilled surgeon would have all the above and a 20 or better in Surgery. A nurse might be a character with a very high level of First Aid, or a moderate level of Physician, plus the Empathy advantage. An EMT might be a nurse with Electronics Operation (Medical Equipment) and Combat Reflexes. A midwife would be a Physician with an optional specialization in delivering infants.

Note that most of these skills are interrelated and default to each other. Note also that the Physician skill can be used, without a penalty, in place of any First Aid roll! For more information about use of medical abilities, see *Injuries*, p. 126.

Medical skills can be learned (aside from the obvious places) in any military force. First Aid can be learned at half-speed without a teacher. Other medical skills are learned at quarter-speed if no teacher is present, and both medical texts and actual subjects are required.

In campaigns with several very different races, all medical skills *require* specialization (see p. 43) for a chosen type of physiology (e.g., mammalian, avian, arthropod). Lack of familiarity with a specific race within the type will give a -2 penalty. *Exception:* First Aid requires only familiarity with the race, not specialization.

Diagnosis/TL (Mental/Hard)   Defaults to IQ-6, First Aid-8, Veterinary-5 or Physician-4

This is the ability to tell what is wrong with a sick or injured person, or what killed a dead person. A successful roll will give *some* information about the patient's problem – *limited to realistic knowledge for the character's tech level* (see pp. 181 and 185). It may not determine the *exact* problem (if the GM feels the cause is totally beyond the doctor's experience, for instance), but it *will* always give hints, rule out impossibilities, et cetera. Modifiers: -5 for internal injuries; -5 or more for a rare disease; +½TL if diagnostic equipment of that TL is available. Note that no Diagnosis roll should be required for obvious things, like open wounds and missing limbs.

First Aid/TL (Mental/Easy)   Defaults to Physician, IQ-5, Veterinary-5 or Physiology-5

This is the ability to patch up an injury in the field (see p. 127). A successful First Aid roll will halt bleeding, neutralize or partially neutralize poison, give artificial respiration for a drowning victim, etc. If a problem is unusual, it must first be identified through Diagnosis. Modifiers: +1 or more for a first-aid kit, crash kit or other facilities.

Hypnotism (Mental/Hard)   No default

This is the skill of affecting another mind through verbal and mechanical means. Once hypnotized, an individual will be extremely suggestible. Roll a contest of Hypnotism skill vs. the victim's Will-1 for each command that is given. Any command that threatens the victim's life or loved ones will be resisted at +4 to his Will. The effects of hypnotism last 1d hours unless terminated sooner by the person doing the hypnosis.

Post-hypnotic suggestions may also be given, instructing the victim to do something long afterward. Normally these are at +1 to the victim's Will for each full week of delay.

Hypnotism can be made more effective by use of telepathy (+2 to Hypnotism roll if Telepathy is successful – one attempt only). A successful Hypnotism roll will cause the subject's mind shields to be lowered automatically.

The first attempt at hypnotism takes 5 seconds. If this fails but the subject is cooperative, a second attempt may be made at -5, taking 5 minutes. If that one fails, the subject is resistant and may not be hypnotized that day. Of course, a subject who is not familiar with Hypnotism will not know exactly what has been attempted, but he may suspect witchcraft. Should the victim resist hypnotism deliberately, a Contest of Skills is made: Hypnotism skill vs. the patient's (Will+3).

A successful Hypnotism roll gives +2 to any use of Surgery skill, being a quick and safe anesthetic. Successful hypnotism also puts a subject to sleep, and can thus be used as an attack, though only against one person at a time. A successful Hypnotism roll can also help the subject remember something he had forgotten.

Physician/TL (Mental/Hard)   Defaults to Veterinary-5, First Aid-11 or IQ-7

This is the general professional ability to aid the sick, prescribe drugs and care, etc. This is the skill to use if a GM requires a single roll to test *general* medical competence or knowledge. A physician may take an optional specialization.

At Tech Level 4 and below, Physician includes the ability to find healing herbs in the wild. If you are in familiar territory, a successful roll will *always* turn up some sort of medicinal plants – the better the roll, the more useful they will be. Obviously, someone with this ability will also be able to find edible plants, and identify/avoid poisonous ones!

At and above Tech Level 5, knowledge of drugs becomes largely "book learning." A high-tech Physician will know a great deal about drugs, and will be able to identify most drugs fairly easily, but will not be able to go into the wild and find useful drugs. Exception: If the Physician has Naturalist ability of 20 or better, he can function as a "primitive" Physician as well! Modifiers: -5 to identify a drug without laboratory facilities; +3 if the Physician takes the risk of smelling/tasting the substance.

Surgery/TL (Mental/Very Hard)   Defaults to Veterinary-5, Physician-5, Physiology-8 or First Aid-12 Prerequisite: Physician

This skill is used when someone attempts to operate on a character to cure sickness, injury, or bodily malfunction. A surgeon may take an optional specialty in a certain part of the body.

A successful roll means the operation proceeded without undue complications. A failed roll means the patient took damage – 2 dice for simple amputations, etc., 3 dice for more complex attempts. Modifiers to skill: -2 if proper equipment – *minimum* of a doctor's black bag – is not available; -3 for head or chest surgery; -5 for undiagnosed problems; -3 or worse if the area or equipment cannot be properly cleaned and sterilized.

Most outdoor skills can be learned just as quickly by solo practice as they can with a teacher (if you survive, of course). The exceptions are Boating, Navigation, Seamanship and Tracking, which can be learned only at half-speed without a teacher. Country characters will easily find teachers and opportunities for these skills; urban folk may have difficulties.

Area Knowledge
See *Social Skills,* p. 62

Boating
See *Vehicle Skills,* p. 68

Climbing (Physical/Average) Defaults to DX-5 or ST-5
This is the ability to climb mountains, rock walls, trees, the sides of buildings, and anything else that may get in your way. Modifiers: +3 if you have the advantage of being double-jointed; *minus* your encumbrance level. Climbing is fully discussed on p. 89.

Fishing (Mental/Easy)
Defaults to IQ-4

This is the ability to catch fish – with net, hook and line, or whatever method is used in your own culture. If you have proper equipment and there are fish to be caught, a successful roll will catch them. If equipment is not available, you can improvise. Modifier: -2 or more, depending on the circumstances, for improper equipment (trying to catch sharks with a bent pin is *very* hard).

Hunting
See *Tracking,* below

Naturalist (Mental/Hard)
Defaults to IQ-6

This is a general knowledge of animals and plants, and of nature in its various forms. It is the sort of knowledge you would expect from a good 20th-century biology teacher. A successful roll will let you identify a plant and its uses or tell you something about an animal and its habits. Modifiers: +3 if you are in familiar territory; up to -5 if you are in a very unfamiliar environment.

Navigation/TL (Mental/Hard)
Defaults to Astronomy-5 or Seamanship-5

This is the ability to find your position (on earth, not in space) by the stars, ocean currents, etc. A successful roll will tell you where you are, at sea *or* on land. Note that if you do not have the skill and are trying a default roll, you cannot default to Seamanship

unless you are actually at sea! Special note: *if* you have this ability, you have no penalty at any lower tech level.

Modifiers: -3 if you are on land (you have no currents to guide you); -3 if you are in a totally new part of the ocean (the currents are new to you); -4 if you do not have the proper instruments for your TL, be they compass-and-sextant or naviscope-and-wrist-comp; -5 (and no use of Astronomy default) if the weather is bad and the stars are hidden; -5 on a brand-new world (the stars are different); +3 if you have Absolute Direction.

Seamanship/TL (Mental/Easy)
Defaults to IQ-4

This is the ability to man a large seagoing vessel. You will need it to crew a ship (or to captain it!). Modifiers: standard tech level penalties (see p. 185).

Survival (area type) (Mental/Average)
Defaults to IQ-5, Naturalist-3, or Survival (other area type)-3

This is the ability to "live off the land," find good food and water, avoid hazards, build shelter, etc. A different Survival skill is required for each type of terrain, including:

Desert	Woodlands
Plains	Jungle
Arctic	Island/Beach
Mountains	Swampland
Radioactive (no default use)	

One successful roll per day is required to live safely (if not comfortably) in a wilderness situation. One person with this ability can look after up to ten others. A failed roll means each member of the party takes 1 die of injury. Modifiers: -2 on an unfamiliar continent or planet; up to -5 for extreme weather conditions; -5 if you are wholly without equipment.

This skill also gives an "eye for country." It can be used to pick the best direction of travel to find flowing water, a mountain pass, or whatever other terrain feature is desired – assuming that it exists.

This is also the skill used to *trap* wild animals. (A city-bred thief could use his Traps ability, but he's used to different game . . . so the roll would be at a -5.) Make one roll for each trap set. It takes about 30 minutes to improvise a trap from ordinary materials, or 10 minutes to set and hide a commercial steel trap. Pit traps for large game, of course, take several hours to dig.

Tracking (Mental/Average)
Defaults to IQ-5 or Naturalist-5

This is the ability to follow a man or animal by its tracks. Make one Tracking roll to pick up the trail, and one further roll for every 5 minutes of travel. Modifiers: -5 if the trail is more than a day old, -10 if it is more than a week old; +5 if you are following a man, +10 if you are following a group of men. Terrain also matters – for instance, -3 in desert, -5 through parched rock, -10 along city streets! All Vision bonuses also count here.

This skill is also used if you want to *cover* your tracks. (Note that your travel time is doubled if you are doing this!) A successful roll means you have hidden your tracks well enough that they will not be seen except by someone else with this skill. If you are followed by another tracker, the GM will roll a "contest of skills" between your ability and his, modified as above. One roll will be made for every mile of travel. If at any time the follower loses the contest of skills, he loses the trail.

To stalk close to game once you have tracked it, use the Stealth skill (p. 67).

PROFESSIONAL SKILLS

This is a general term for those skills that are useful for making a living, but will (almost) never have any other use in the game. Such skills are not given individual listings here – but you can still learn them if you want to! For a character whose "adventuring" skills aren't worth much money, a professional skill is a great way to qualify for a job (see p. 192) and a steady income.

If a character is created specifically as a professional, the GM should require him to take the appropriate professional skill at a level of at least 12, unless the character is *supposed* to be incompetent!

Professional skills include barber, construction worker, game designer, journalist, law enforcement officer, mason, salesman, stockbroker, stock clerk, tailor, vintner, weaver, zookeeper . . .

Important professional skills for a specific game world will be listed in that gameworld book. Players can work out and use as many professional skills as they like, with the consent of the GM. As a rule, professional skills will be Mental/Average, and default to IQ-5 or thereabouts. A specific professional skill may also default to an already-listed skill (e.g., Journalist would reasonably default to Writing-3) or have a skill as a prerequisite (Animal Handling for Zookeeper, for instance). This, too, is up to the GM.

Most professional skills are only learned in school or "on the job." A few professional skills of value in game terms:

Accounting (Mental/Hard)
Defaults to IQ-10, Merchant-5 or Mathematics-5
Prerequisite: Literacy

This is the ability to keep books of account, to examine the condition of a business, etc. Mostly useful as a job skill. However, a successful Accounting roll (requiring about two hours of study) can tell you whether financial records are correct – which can sometimes be important! Modifiers: -5 if you only have a hurried glance at the figures; +5 if you have all day; +5 if you have the Mathematical Ability advantage.

Computer Operation/TL (Mental/Easy)
Defaults to IQ-4

This is the ability to operate a computer, call up data, run existing programs, play video games, et cetera. This is *not* the same as programming – that is a separate and harder skill. Modifiers: -3 or more for an unfamiliar computer or unfamiliar program. This skill is only available at TL7 and above. Characters from tech levels below 7 cannot even use it by default unless they have had time to gain some familiarity with computers!

Electronics Operation/TL (Mental/Average)
Defaults to IQ-5 or appropriate Electronics-3

This skill allows use of all electronics gear within a known specialty. For normal, everyday use of equipment, no skill roll is required. Rolls should be required in emergency situations, or for "abnormal" use of equipment, or for use of complex gear by the unskilled.

A successful roll will also let you perform repairs on known types of equipment. Time required for each attempt is up to the GM. Modifiers: -2 without plans or schematics; -5 without proper tools; -4 when working outside your specialty. *Note:* Electrical *motors* are covered by the Mechanic skill, not by Electronics.

Examples: Someone is jamming your radio transmission. Roll a Contest of Skills in Electronics Operation (Communications) – radio vs. jammer – to see whether or not you can get a clear signal out.

You're trying to pick up a speedy target on radar. Make your Electronics Operation (Sensors) roll. The GM might also assess (for instance) a penalty due to the target's ECM gear.

Characters with Electronics Operation skill may attempt to improvise new gadgets (like an engineer), at a -4 penalty in their specialty, or a -8 outside it.

A specialty must be chosen. Some samples include:

Communications. Long-range radios, FTL radio and satellite receivers. The Communications specialty also encompasses knowledge of any standard, current communications codes appropriate to the character's background. No skill roll is necessary for these, though attempting to understand or use unfamiliar codes does require a roll.

Computers. Aiming and fire control systems, calculators, robot brains, artificial intelligence.

Force Shields. Personal, portable, vehicular, base and starship force shields and deflectors.

Holographics. Holographic projectors.

Matter Transmitters. All matter transmitters, teleporters or transporters.

Medical. Cloning tanks, life support equipment and bionics.

Security Systems. This is the electronic version of the Lockpicking skill! Useful for designing (and circumventing) high-tech traps and alarms.

Sensors. Detection gear of all types, plus ECM and ECCM gear.

Weapons. High-tech personal weapons such as lasers. This is, for game purposes, very similar to Armoury skill specializing in these weapons.

Heraldry (Mental/Average)
Defaults to IQ-5 or Savoir-Faire-3

This is the skill of recognizing and designing coats of arms, colors and devices, plaid setts and other emblems. On a successful roll, a herald could recognize a knight or noble by the banner or shield being borne, and describe it in proper heraldic terms; create attractive and proper arms for a new noble (without conflicting with existing designs), and so on. Heraldry is also important in some science fiction backgrounds!

The herald's roll would be modified based upon whether the design is well-known (up to +5), rare (-1 or more), or from a land wholly foreign to the herald's own experience (at least -5).

Law (Mental/Hard)
Defaults to IQ-6

Modifiers: +4 if dealing with the law of your specific area. A successful roll lets you remember, deduce or figure out the answer to a question about the law. But remember that few legal questions have a clear-cut answer – even an expert will hedge his advice. Many lawyers specialize in one particular field (e.g., patent and trademark; contract; criminal defense).

A successful Law roll may also be required if you (or your client) wind up in court. This depends largely on the legal system of your particular game world. In some worlds, *being a lawyer* is a serious offense . . .

PSIONIC SKILLS

These are special mental abilities. In most cases, you must be born with the potential for a psychic ability (i.e., create your character with that ability), and then train in that ability, in order to use it. Like magical skills, they are Mental/Hard. Psi is covered in Chapter 20.

SCIENTIFIC SKILLS

In general, scientific skills are useful as sources of information. A character with a scientific skill is more likely to roll to *know* something than to *do* something. There are exceptions, of course – a chemist might roll to analyze or concoct something, a mathematician might roll to solve a complex problem. But as a rule, some problem will be presented and the scenario (or the GM) will say, "Make your roll on Archaeology to translate that strange inscription," or "Make your roll on Metallurgy, or Chemistry-5, to identify the greenish metal of the door." In many cases, the GM will roll for the characters and give them some item of information *only if the roll is successful*. If the roll fails, the GM will not even tell the players why he was rolling.

Where a listing below describes expertise – e.g., "A chemist would be able to identify elements and simple compounds" – it should be understood that a successful skill roll must be made to use this expertise! The time required is up to the GM.

Most scientific skills are differentiated by tech level (see p. 185). If you make a default roll on a skill you do not have, you default to that skill at the TL of your own home culture.

Some scientific skills require the learner to *specialize* (see p. 43). If specialization is not required, an optional specialty may still be chosen. You may have up to two optional specialties. If you choose to specialize, you will have a +5 on questions relating to your specialty, and a -1 on questions outside it (or -2 if you have two optional specialties). For instance, an archaeologist might specialize in ancient Egypt and Sumeria, or a zoologist might specialize in felines.

Agronomy/TL (Mental/Average)   Defaults to IQ-5
This is the science of growing things. An agronomist could answer questions or solve problems related to farming and agriculture. A skilled farmer *is* an agronomist, whether he knows the term or not!

Alchemy/TL (Mental/Very Hard)   No default
This is the science of magical transmutations. It is covered in detail in the *Magic* sourcebook.

Anthropology (Mental/Hard)   Defaults to IQ-6
This is the science of human evolution and culture. An anthropologist is knowledgeable in the ways of primitive (and not-so-primitive) groups of men (or the other intelligent creatures he studies). Anthropology rolls could be used to explain, or even predict, unusual rituals and folk customs a traveler might encounter.

Archaeology (Mental/Hard)   Defaults to IQ-6
This is the study of ancient civilizations. An archaeologist is at home with excavations, old potsherds, inscriptions, etc. On a successful roll, an archaeologist can answer questions about ancient history, identify artifacts and dead languages, et cetera. Sometimes an archaeologist will have information relating to the occult – e.g., Ancient Secrets and Things Man Was Not Meant To Know . . .

Architecture/TL (Mental/Average)   Defaults to IQ-5
The ability to design buildings and to deduce the design of buildings from their function, and vice versa. A successful Architecture roll will let you learn things about a strange building, find a secret room or door, etc. Modifiers: -2 if the building is of a strange type; -5 if it is alien.

Astrogation/TL (Mental/Average)   Defaults to Navigation-5, Astronomy-4 or Mathematics-4
This skill covers navigating through interstellar and interplanetary space. There is a different Astrogation skill for each type of faster-than-light drive. Astrogation skills may default to each other at up to -4, depending on how different the drives are. Modifiers and results of failures are up to the GM, since this skill can be defined very differently for different universes. (And, in some science-fiction backgrounds, the skill might not be Average.)

Astrogation rolls are also required to find the ship's position if it gets lost, or to determine likely routes for another ship that is being followed.

SCIENTIFIC SKILLS

Astronomy/TL (Mental/Hard)   *Defaults to IQ-6*

This is the study of the stars and other extraplanetary objects. An astronomer could answer questions about the Sun, the planets of the solar system, meteorites, and so on. At Tech Level 4 and below, this skill is Astrology, combining a knowledge of the stars and constellations with a great amount of mythology and fortune-telling.

Biochemistry/TL (Mental/Very Hard)   *Defaults to Chemistry-5*
Prerequisite: Chemistry

This is the study of the chemistry of living beings. A biochemist is an expert in the chemical reactions that sustain life.

Biology

This is such a wide field that there is NO "general" Biology skill; its specialties are skills in their own right. These include Biochemistry, Botany, Ecology, Genetics, Physiology and Zoology. A general "biologist" would have studied some or all of these areas.

Botany/TL (Mental/Hard)   *Defaults to IQ-6 or Agronomy-5*

This is the study of plants. A botanist would be able to identify plants, make a guess about the habitat and properties of an unfamiliar plant type, etc.

Chemistry/TL (Mental/Hard)   *Defaults to IQ-6*

This is the study of matter. A chemist would be able to identify elements and simple compounds (but not necessarily drugs, magical substances, etc.). Given proper equipment, he could conduct complex analyses and syntheses.

Computer Programming/TL (Mental/Hard) *No default*
Prerequisite: Computer Operation

This is the ability to write and debug computer software. A successful roll will (among other things) let you find a program "bug"; determine a program's purpose by reading a printout; answer a question about computers or computer programming; or, given sufficient time, write a new program. The time required varies widely! Modifiers: -5 if you are rushed (GM's decision); +5 if you have ample time; -5 or worse if the program is written in an unfamiliar language.

Criminology/TL (Mental/Average)   *Defaults to IQ-4*

This is the study of crime and the criminal mind. A criminologist would use his skill to find and interpret clues, guess how criminals might behave, et cetera. Though this skill does not actually default to Streetwise, the GM may allow a Streetwise roll instead in certain situations – especially to predict or outguess a criminal.

Ecology/TL (Mental/Hard)   *Defaults to IQ-6 or Naturalist-3*

This is the study of the natural relationships of living beings, or of whole environments. Below TL6, this science does not exist – use Naturalist instead. An ecologist would be able to tell (for instance) which creatures are vital to an environment and which are not; whether man could fit into a new environment; what effect a certain change might have on an environment; or what function a creature plays in its habitat.

Economics (Mental/Hard)   *Defaults to IQ-6 or Merchant-6*

This is the study of money, exchange and banking. An economist could answer questions about investment, economic policies, et cetera. He could also predict local effects of economic changes – the introduction of new materials or techniques, the destruction of a power plant or a merchant house, and similar situations.

Electronics/TL (Mental/Hard)   *Defaults to (other Electronics)-4*
Prerequisite: Mathematics

This is electronics *engineering* – the ability to design and build electronic apparatus. A successful roll will let you (for example): identify the purpose of a strange device; diagnose a glitch; perform a repair; design new systems; improvise a gadget to solve a problem.

Modifiers: +5 to build a gadget if you (the player) can give the GM a good description of what you want to do; -5 if you try to diagnose or repair without proper tools; -4 if you are working outside of your specialty. Tech level differences (p. 185) will be very important!

An electronics engineer *must* specialize in one of the types of electronics listed under *Electronics Operation* (p. 58).

Note that an electronics engineer is not necessarily a skilled operator of the things he designs and fixes; Electronics Operation defaults to Electronics at -3.

Engineer/TL (Mental/Hard)
Defaults to appropriate Mechanic specialty-6
Prerequisites vary with specialty chosen (see below)

This is the ability to design and build complex machinery. A successful roll will let you (for example): identify the purpose of strange machinery; diagnose a mechanical or electrical problem; perform a repair; design new machinery; improvise a gadget to solve a problem. Time required for each attempt is up to the GM. Modifiers: as for *Electronics,* above.

An engineer *must* specialize (see p. 43) in one particular field. Some specialties:

Primitive machines: catapults, etc. (prerequisite: Mechanic).
Mining (prerequisite: Geology).
Vehicles (prerequisite: Mechanic).
Bombs and traps (prerequisite: Traps).
Plumbing (no prerequisite).
Clockwork (prerequisite: Mechanic).
Electrical work (no prerequisite).
Combat engineering (fortifications, etc. – no prerequisite).
Guns (no prerequisite).

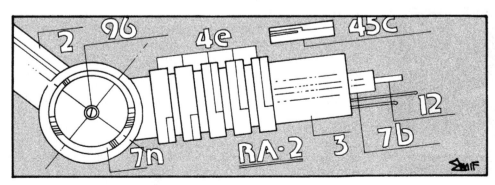

Forensics/TL (Mental/Hard)
Defaults to Criminology-4

This is the general science of "laboratory" criminology . . . computation of bullet paths, microscopic or chemical analysis of clues, etc. Depending on the situation, a GM may allow a default to Chemistry or another field of study appropriate to the particular investigation.

Genetics/TL (Mental/Very Hard)
Defaults to Biochemistry-5 or Physiology-5

This is the study of heredity. A geneticist could tell how to breed for desired traits; how to identify genetic diseases; and how to keep the fruit flies from overrunning your lab. At TL9+, the optional specialty of Genetic Engineering becomes available.

Geology/TL (Mental/Hard)
Defaults to IQ-6 or Prospecting-4

This is the science of earth study. A geologist knows about oil, rocks, metal ores and minerals; about earthquakes and volcanoes; and about fossils. In the field, he can try to find water by using an "eye for country" as under *Survival* (p. 57).

History (Mental/Hard)
Defaults to IQ-6 or Archaeology-6

This is the study of the recorded past (as opposed to archaeology, which also studies the prehistoric past). A historian would be able to answer questions about history, and might (at the GM's option) be allowed a roll to remember a useful parallel: "Ah, yes. Hannibal faced a situation like this once, and here's what he did . . ."

Linguistics (Mental/Very Hard)
No default

This is the study of the principles on which languages are based. A linguist could identify an obscure language from a snatch of speech or writing, if he made his skill roll. If you have this skill, add $^1/_{10}$ of your skill level (round down) to your skill with any language you learn.

Literature (Mental/Hard)
Defaults to IQ-6

This is the study of the great writings. A student of literature would be knowledgeable in the realms of old poetry, dusty tomes, philosophy, criticism, etc. This can be useful for finding clues to hidden treasure, sunken lands, Secrets Man Was Not Meant to Know, and the like. The work in question must be available in a language you speak. Modifiers: -5 if you're illiterate (oral tradition).

Mathematics (Mental/Hard)
Defaults to IQ-6

This represents general mathematical expertise. While there are dozens of mathematical specialties, the differences are not likely ever to affect the game. A mathematician, for game purposes, can roll to answer any sort of math-related question. If the problem is simply one of calculation or computation, the GM may allow a modifier for the computing facilities (or lack of same) available.

Metallurgy/TL (Mental/Hard)
Defaults to Blacksmith-8, Jeweler-8, Armoury-8 or Chemistry-5

This is the study of metals and their properties. A metallurgist could identify metals or alloys, or solve a problem concerning metals, their use, mining or refining.

Meteorology/TL (Mental/Average)
Defaults to IQ-5

This is the study of the weather and the ability to predict it. The GM always makes Meteorology rolls for the player; a good roll means he tells the truth, while a bad roll means he answers randomly or lies.

At low tech levels, this skill may be called Weather Sense. Anyone of TL4 or below gets a +2 for Weather Sense in his home area.

At high tech levels, this skill includes the ability to read instruments, interpret satellite maps, etc. But a high-tech meteorologist can still function without his instruments; if he can't, he's not a meteorologist, but a meter-reader. Instrumentation becomes useful at TL5 (the barometer). If instruments are available, add (TL-4) to effective skill. This works only for a trained meteorologist – not on a default roll.

A basic skill roll will predict the weather for tomorrow. 2 days: -1. 3 days: -2. 4 days: -4. 5 days: -6. Another -2 for each further day. Note that a separate roll is required for each day; a 3-day forecast requires 3 rolls, rolling first for tomorrow and again for each following day. If one day's roll fails, subsequent ones can't succeed.

A Meteorologist will also know, on a successful roll, what sort of *general* climate to expect from any area he has heard of or visits.

Naturalist
See *Outdoor Skills*, p. 57

Nuclear Physics/TL (Mental/Very Hard)
No default
Prerequisites: Physics-15+ and Mathematics-15+

This is the study of nuclear processes. A nuclear physicist would be able to answer questions about the interior of the sun, nuclear weapons or nuclear power plants.

Occultism (Mental/Average)
Defaults to IQ-6

This is the study of the mysterious and/or supernatural. An occultist has a special knowledge of mysticism, primitive magical beliefs, ancient rituals, hauntings, etc. Note that an occultist does not have to *believe* in the material he studies. In worlds where magic is common, "occultism" is replaced by magicians' professional knowledge!

Physics/TL (Mental/Hard)
Defaults to IQ-6

This is the science of force and motion. A physicist could answer questions about the basics of the universe, the behavior of moving bodies, and matter and energy.

Physiology/TL (Mental/Very Hard)
*Defaults to IQ-7, or to any medical skill-5**

This is the study of the human body and its function. A physiologist knows how the muscles, bones and organs work, and where they are located.

*Note that this skill cannot default from Hypnotism.

SCIENTIFIC SKILLS

Prospecting/TL (Mental/Average)
Defaults to IQ-5 or Geology-4

This is applied geology: the skill of finding valuable minerals by on-site examination. Prospecting from a distance, by instrument or map readings and extrapolation, requires Geology skill. A prospector will be at -1 in a new area of familiar type, -2 or more in an unfamiliar type of area, until he has been there long enough (a month of work) to gain familiarity.

A successful Prospecting roll will also tell good ore or minerals from a small sample, and judge their commercial value.

In the field, a prospector can try to find water by using an "eye for country" as under *Survival* (p. 57).

Psychology (Mental/Hard)
Defaults to IQ-6

This is the study of behavior. A psychologist deals with the human mind (and perhaps other types as well). A successful Psychology roll can predict, in general, the behavior of an individual or small group in a defined situation, especially a situation of stress. Modifiers: +3 if the psychologist knows the subject well; +3 if the psychologist has the Empathy advantage and meets the subject; +3 if the subject is of a known deviant personality type – i.e., suffers from a phobia or other mental problem.

Research (Mental/Average)
Defaults to IQ-5 or Writing-3

Also defaults to *any* scientific skill-2 if you are researching material connected with that skill. Research is the general ability to do library and file research. A successful Research roll in an appropriate place of research will let you find some useful piece of data, *if* that information is to be found.

Research skill requires either Literacy or Computer Operations (in a high-tech campaign world).

Theology (Mental/Hard)
Defaults to IQ-6

This is the study of religion. A theologist knows about ancient and modern religious beliefs, history of religion, etc. If your character is a priest or holy man, you should consider taking this skill, *specializing* in your own particular religion.

Zoology/TL (Mental/Hard)
Defaults to IQ-6 or any Animal skill-6

This is the study of animals. A zoologist can identify animals; make a good guess about their natural diet, habits and habitat; and predict their behavior.

SOCIAL SKILLS

Acting (Mental/Average)
Defaults to IQ-5, Bard-5 or Performance-2

This is the ability to counterfeit moods, emotions and voices, and to lie convincingly over a period of time. It is *not* the same as Disguise or Performance. A successful Acting roll will let you pretend to think or feel something that you do not feel. The GM may require an Acting roll whenever you try to fool someone, lie to them, etc. Modifiers: +1 for every point of IQ you have over the person you are trying to fool (or the smartest one in the group), and -1 for every point of IQ if your victim is smarter than you.

Impersonation of a particular person is a special type of acting. To mimic a particular person, you must first successfully disguise yourself (see *Disguise*, p. 65) – unless, of course, your victims cannot see you! Modifiers for any mimicry: -5 if you are not well-acquainted with your subject; -5 if the people you want to fool are acquaintances of the original; and -10 if they are well-acquainted.

Administration (Mental/Average)
Defaults to IQ-6 or Merchant-3

This is the skill of running a large organization. Primarily useful for earning money or qualifying for high rank. A trained Administrator (skill 15+) would also get a +2 reaction bonus when dealing with a bureaucrat, and (on a successful roll) could predict the best way to go about dealing with a bureaucracy.

Area Knowledge (Mental/Easy)
Defaults to IQ-4*

*A default roll is allowed only for an Area Knowledge roll based on a place where you live or once lived. See the last paragraph.

This is the skill of familiarity with the people, politics and geography of a given area. Normally, a character will have Area Knowledge only for the area he considers his own "home base," whether that's a single farm or a solar system. If information about

other areas is available, the GM may allow characters to study Area Knowledge for other places. Spies, for instance, will try to acquire detailed Area Knowledge of their target areas before going there.

The GM should not require an Area Knowledge roll for ordinary situations – finding the blacksmith, tavern or your own home. But he could require a roll to locate a smith to shoe your horse at 3 a.m., or to find the best ambush location along a stretch of road. "Secret" or very obscure information will carry a penalty, or may not be available through Area Knowledge at all. For instance, Area Knowledge of Washington will give you the location of the Russian Embassy, but not the KGB's current safe-house.

The things that can be known with Area Knowledge overlap Streetwise, Navigation, Naturalist, Politics and more. The difference is that Area Knowledge works for a single area; you know the habits of *this* tiger or gang boss, but this does not give you general insight into the species.

Area Knowledge can be bought for any sort of area. The larger the territory, the less "personal" and more general your knowledge becomes. Almost every character will have Area Knowledge of some type. Some examples (the GM may add more for his particular campaign):

Few Hundred Acres: Knowledge of farmers or tribesmen, trails, streams, hiding places, ambush sites, flora and fauna.

Hamlet, Village, or Small Town: All important citizens and businesses and most unimportant ones; all public buildings and most houses.

City: All important businesses, streets, citizens, leaders, etc.

Barony, County, Duchy, or Small Nation: General nature of its settlements and towns, political allegiances, leaders, and most citizens of Status 5 and up.

Large Nation: Location of its major cities and important sites; awareness of its major customs, races, and languages (but not necessarily expertise); names of folk of Status 6+, and a general understanding of the economic and political situation.

Planet: As for a large nation, but more general; knowledge of people of Status 7+ only.

Interplanetary State: Location of major planets; awareness of major races (though not necessarily expertise); knowledge of people of Status 7+; general understanding of economic and political situation.

When knowledge is needed about a place distant from the "home base" area, the GM should assess a penalty. For instance, if the home base is a small town, facts about the neighboring farms might be rolled at -1. The next town (a mile away) would be at -2; the big city 50 miles away would be at -5. The capital of a neighboring state or nation would be at -7, and a faraway country would be at -10. The long-distance modifiers in the sidebar on p. 151 can be used if specific rules are needed.

Bard (Mental/Average)   See *Artistic Skills*, p. 47

Carousing (Physical/Average)   Defaults to HT-4

Buy this skill based on your HT, not DX. This is the skill of socializing, partying, etc. A successful Carousing roll, made under the right circumstances, will give you a +2 bonus on a request for aid or information, or just on a general reaction. A failed roll means you made a fool of yourself in some way; you get a -2 penalty on any reaction roll made by those you caroused with. If you do your carousing in the wrong places, a failed roll can have other dangers! Modifiers: GM's discretion, but up to a +3 for buying drinks or other entertainment for your fellow carousers.

Diplomacy (Mental/Hard)   Defaults to IQ-6

This is the skill of negotiating, compromising and getting along with others. A Diplomacy roll may be substituted for any reaction roll in a non-combat situation (see *Influence Rolls*, p. 93). A successful roll will also allow you to predict the possible outcome of a course of action when you are negotiating, or to choose the best approach to take. If you have the Diplomacy skill at an expert level (20 or better), you get a +2 bonus on all reaction rolls! Modifier: +2 if you have the Voice advantage.

Unlike other influence skills, Diplomacy will never give you a worse result than if you had tried an ordinary reaction roll. A failure of Fast-Talk or Sex Appeal will alienate the subject, but Diplomacy is always safe.

Fast-Talk (Mental/Average)   Defaults to IQ-5 or Acting-5

This is the skill of talking others into doing things against their better judgment. It is not taught (intentionally, that is) in school; you study it by working as a salesman, confidence man, lawyer, etc. If you have Fast-Talk at an expert level (20 or better), you get a +2 on all reaction rolls where you're allowed to talk! The GM may require the player to give details of the story he is using, rather than just letting him say "I'm using Fast-Talk."

Fast-Talk is not the same as Acting. In general, Fast-Talk is used to get someone to make a snap decision in your favor. Acting is used for long-term dissimulation. But there are many situations in which the GM could allow a roll on either skill.

In any situation where a reaction roll is called for, you may *substitute* a Fast-Talk roll instead; all normal reaction modifiers apply to the Fast-Talk roll. A successful roll gives you a "Good" reaction. A failed roll gives you a "Bad" reaction.

Gambling (Mental/Average)   Defaults to IQ-5 or Mathematics-5

This is skill at playing games of chance. A successful Gambling roll can (among other things) tell you if a game is rigged; identify a fellow gambler in a group of strangers; or "estimate the odds" in *any* tricky situation. When you gamble against the house, just make your own roll (with a modifier if the GM says the odds are poor). When you gamble against someone else, you both make your Gambling rolls (see *Contests of Skill*, p. 87) until one of you wins. Modifiers: +1 to +5 for familiarity with the game being played; -1 to -5 if the game is rigged against the players. The Sleight of Hand skill (p. 67) can be helpful if *you* want to cheat!

To spot a cheater, roll a Contest of Skills; your Gambling roll (or just your Vision roll) vs. the opponent's Sleight of Hand for card or dice tricks, or IQ for other kinds of cheating.

Leadership (Mental/Average)   Defaults to ST-5

This is the ability to coordinate a group in a dangerous or stressful situation. Some level of Leadership is required to hold rank in a military or paramilitary group. A successful Leadership roll is required to lead NPCs into a dangerous situation (player characters can decide for themselves if they will follow you!). Modifiers: Charisma (if you have it); -5 if the NPCs have never been in action with you; -5 if you are sending them into danger but not going yourself; +5 if their loyalty to you is "Good"; +10 if their loyalty is "Very Good." If their loyalty is "Excellent," no roll is necessary! (Defaults to ST because in a random group, if nobody has leadership training, the strongest usually leads.)

Social Skills

Merchant (Mental/Average) — Defaults to IQ-5

This is the ability to act as a "trader," buying and selling merchandise. It involves salesmanship, understanding of trade practices, and psychology. On a successful skill roll, a Merchant can (among other things): judge the value, *in his own culture,* of any piece of common goods; find out where any commodity is bought and sold; find the local fair market value of any commodity; etc. Modifiers: If the commodity is illegal, the Merchant is at a -3 penalty *unless* he has Streetwise at 12+ or specializes in those goods.

A merchant in an unfamiliar area will have a penalty (-2 to -6, GM's decision) until he has had time to become familiar with the customs and prices there.

A merchant can choose to *specialize* (see p. 43) in some single class of goods. In this case, he has a +5 when dealing with this class of goods, but a -1 with other goods.

When two merchants are haggling, the GM may settle it quickly by a Contest of Skills between the two. The winner adds or subtracts 10% of fair value, depending on whether he was trying to sell or buy.

A character who has this ability at *any* level gets a +1 on reaction rolls when buying or selling. A character who has this skill at *expert* level – 20 or better – gets a +2.

Performance (Mental/Average) — Defaults to IQ-5, Acting-2 or Bard-2

This is the ability to act on the stage or screen. It is different from Acting in that you are trying to impress and entertain people, but not necessarily to fool them. If this skill is studied, it also includes the professional knowledge of the type of acting appropriate for the period (stage directions, actor/agent/producer relations, types of cameras, etc.).

Politics (Mental/Average) — Defaults to IQ-5 or Diplomacy-5

This is the ability to get into office, and to get along with other politicians. It has nothing to do with administration! This skill can only be learned in office or by working for someone in office. A successful Politics roll will give you +2 on any reaction from a fellow politician. When running for office, roll a Contest of Politics Skills. Modifier: +2 if you have the Voice advantage. In some jurisdictions, money is another important reaction modifier . . .

Public Speaking — See Bard, p. 47

Savoir-Faire (Mental/Easy) — Defaults to IQ-4

This is the skill of "good manners" – whatever they may be in this particular culture. A successful Savoir-Faire roll is required to get along in "high society" without embarrassing yourself – roll once for each party or meeting. A successful roll can also detect someone who is *pretending* to high rank or good breeding.

In any "high society" situation where a reaction roll is called for, you may *substitute* a Savoir-Faire roll instead; all normal reaction modifiers apply to the Savoir-Faire roll. A successful roll gives you a "Good" reaction. A failed roll gives you a "Bad" reaction. Modifiers: +2 if you have higher rank or "class" than the NPC you are trying to impress; -2 if your social status is lower; +2 if you seem to have important friends!; -2 or more if the culture is very different from your own (-6 would be appropriate for an *alien* culture).

It can also be difficult to pass yourself off as a wildly different social class than yours. The prince would have a hard a time portraying a pauper and vice versa. In general, a Savoir-Faire roll is required to impersonate anybody more than 3 social levels away from your own. If your "native" social level is negative and you are trying to pass yourself off as someone from level 1 or better, or vice versa, a Savoir-Faire roll is required at -2.

Sex Appeal (Mental/Average) — Defaults to HT-3

Based on HT, not IQ. This is the ability to impress the opposite sex. It can only be studied in your "free time" – say, a maximum of three hours a day – unless you are a member of a harem or the equivalent. The Sex Appeal ability has as much to do with your attitude as it does with your looks. If you are not willing to "vamp" someone to get what you want, you won't have this talent or *want* it. Modifier: +2 if you have the Voice advantage. *Double* all normal disadvantages for appearance!

In any encounter with the opposite sex, if reaction roll is called for, you may *substitute* a Sex Appeal roll instead; all normal reaction modifiers apply to the Sex Appeal roll. See *Influence Rolls,* p. 93. A succcessful roll gives you a "Very Good" reaction. A failed roll gives you a "Bad" or worse reaction. Usually, only one attempt is allowed per "victim," though the GM might allow you another attempt after a few weeks.

Strategy (Mental/Hard) — Defaults to IQ-6, Tactics-6 or other Strategy type-4

This is the ability to plan military actions and to predict the actions of the enemy. It is usually taught only by the military. A successful Strategy roll will let you deduce, in advance, enemy military plans *unless* they are led by another person with this skill. In that case, the GM rolls a Contest of Skills between the two strategists; if the player-character loses, he guesses wrong (i.e., is given false information) about the enemy plans. The amount of information the strategist gets depends on how good his roll was, but *not* how good the foe's plans are. A howling mob uses strategy – they just don't know it themselves, and they are easy to out-think.

A strategist must specialize (p. 43) in a type of strategy: important types are land, naval and space. The specific units being commanded are less important; at worst, a strategist might have a -1 or -2 when planning for units of another nation or TL, as long as he has accurate information about their capabilities.

Tactics (Mental/Hard) — Defaults to IQ-6 or Strategy-6

This is the ability to outguess the enemy when the fight is man-to-man or in small groups. It is usually taught only by the military. A successful Tactics roll during a battle will *sometimes* (GM's discretion) allow you information about immediate enemy plans. If you have studied this skill at all, you get a +1 bonus on initiative rolls. If you have Tactics at an expert level (20 or above), you get a +2 bonus on initiative rolls.

Teaching (Mental/Average) — Defaults to IQ-5

This is the ability to instruct others. In order to teach someone, you must know the skill being taught at a higher level than your student knows it. Anyone with a Teaching skill of 12 or better should be allowed to act as a teacher for most game purposes. A roll should only be required if it is vital to the "plot" of the adventure that some difficult point be taught to someone. If a language barrier exists, the GM should *also* roll to see if the teacher and student are communicating properly!

Many skills in this category are taught only by military, espionage or ninja-type groups, or the underworld. Exceptions include Streetwise (learned in the streets); Detect Lies (learned anywhere); Escape and Ventriloquism (learned in the theater).

Acting   See *Social Skills*, p. 62

Climbing   See *Outdoor Skills*, p. 57

Camouflage (Mental/Easy)   *Defaults to IQ-4 or Survival-2*

The ability to use natural material and/or paints to disguise yourself, your position, your equipment, and so on. A Contest of Skills (Vision vs. Camouflage) is made to determine whether camouflage is successful. Depending on the circumstances, successful camouflage may hide its subject entirely, or blur its outlines to make it harder to hit (-1 to attacker's skill). Camouflage will not improve your Stealth roll, but if you are well-camouflaged, the enemy may overlook you even after you *fail* a Stealth roll. Base skill is to hide yourself: The larger the item being camouflaged, the greater the penalty to skill. Use the reverse of the Size modifiers on the *Size and Speed/Range Table*, p. 201.

Demolition/TL (Mental/Average)   *Defaults to IQ-5, Underwater Demolition-2, or Engineer-3*

This is the ability to blow things up. A Demolition roll is necessary whenever you use explosives; it takes 15 minutes to an hour to properly plant and fuse explosives. A successful roll means everything went all right. A failed roll indicates you made a mistake; the worse the roll, the worse the failure. A badly-failed roll in close quarters can blow *you* up. Modifiers: -3 or more for unfamiliar equipment; -2 if you are rushed; +2 if you have all the time in the world to prepare.

When setting an explosive trap, use this skill rather than the Traps skill. Setting a "trap" fuse like a land mine, instead of a timed fuse, is at -2 to skill. If you are an engineer of a type concerned with explosives (e.g., mining, ordnance, etc.), you may use your Engineer skill instead of Demolition, at no penalty. Underwater demolition (p. 68) is a separate skill.

Detect Lies (Mental/Hard)   *Defaults to IQ-6 or Psychology-4*

This is the ability to tell when someone is lying to you. It is not the same as Interrogation; the Detect Lies skill works in a casual or social situation. When you ask to use this skill, the GM rolls a Quick Contest of Skill between your Detect Lies skill and your subject's IQ (or Fast-Talk or Acting skill). If you win, the GM will tell you whether you are being lied to. If you lose, the GM may lie to you about whether you were lied to . . . or just say "You can't tell."

Modifiers: +4 if you have the Empathy advantage. If the liar is of a different species, the GM may assess a penalty (usually -2) unless the questioner is very familiar with that species!

Disguise (Mental/Average)   *Defaults to IQ-5*

This is the ability to make yourself look like someone else, using clothes, makeup, etc. It takes 30 minutes to an hour to put on a good disguise. Roll a Quick Contest of Skills (Disguise vs. IQ, usually) for each person (or group) that your disguise must fool. People with professional skills in law enforcement or espionage may substitute those skills for IQ when rolling to penetrate a disguise. Modifiers: +2 if you had powders and paints available (does not help on a default roll); -1 through -5 (GM's discretion) to disguise yourself as someone or something very different from you. If your own appearance is distinctive, this also reduces your effective skill by 1 to 5, at the GM's option. Large groups may require multiple rolls, again at the GM's option.

Note that a quick disguise (grabbing a lab coat when you enter a laboratory, for instance) requires no skill roll, but will fool only inattentive enemies!

When you are combining Acting (p. 62) with Disguise (that is, when you must change your face *and* your personality), you only need to make one roll for each person or group – but it must be the *harder* of the two rolls.

Escape (Physical/Hard)   *Defaults to DX-6*

This is the ability to free oneself from ropes, handcuffs and similar bonds. The first attempt to escape takes one minute; each subsequent attempt takes 10 minutes. Modifiers: The more thoroughly you are tied up, the greater a penalty the GM will apply to the roll: modern police handcuffs, for instance, would be a -5 to escape from. If you have the advantage of being Double-Jointed (p. 20), you get a +3 on this skill.

Fast-Talk   See *Social Skills*, p. 63

Forgery/TL (Mental/Hard)   *Defaults to IQ-6, DX-8 or Artist-5*

This is the ability to make up a fake passport, banknote or similar document. It is not taught except by intelligence agencies and by the underworld, though you can always study it alone. When you use a forged document, a successful Forgery roll is needed *each time* the document is inspected – unless you roll a critical success on your first attempt.

Actual production of a document can take days, if not weeks. Modifiers: -5 if you did not have access to good inks and equipment; -5 if you did not have a sample to copy; +3 if you are merely altering a genuine document rather than making up a new one. The GM may also assign modifiers based on the severity of the inspection the document must pass; a routine border check, for instance, would give a +5 bonus. Note also that coordination and eyesight are required. You must be able to see; your skill is -1 for every point of DX below 10.

THIEF/SPY SKILLS

Holdout (Mental/Average)
Defaults to IQ-5 or Sleight of Hand-3

This is the skill of concealing items on your person or the persons of others (usually with their cooperation). It is also the skill of finding such hidden items.

Detection

Spotting a concealed item is a Quick Contest of Skill; the detector's Vision roll (or Holdout skill +/- Vision modifiers) against the concealer's Holdout skill. GMs should modify this for circumstances. For instance, the "searcher" is at -5 if he is not specifically looking for a concealed item, and -2 if he is looking at a lot of people quickly as they walk by. Contests should be rolled secretly; it defeats the purpose to say, "You don't notice the gun under his jacket.'"

Roll separately for each concealed item. Searchers who find one item are likely to suspect more.

Every part of the human body can be used to conceal weapons (including the inside; that's the reason for a body-cavity search at the jail). A fairly thorough "pat-down" hands-on search of an unresisting person takes one minute. It gives a +1 bonus to find each concealed item. A thorough "skin search" of a person's hair and clothing takes three minutes and gives a +3. A complete search, including body cavities, takes five minutes and is +5 to skill. An X-ray or similar device gives an extra +5 to spot any object containing metal. If more than one person is making the search, there must be a separate contest of skills for each searcher.

The GM is free to skip unnecessary rolls; no human can get a sawed-off pump shotgun through a body search. Likewise, a knife or jewel simply *cannot* be found on a normally-dressed person without (at least) an X-ray or skin search. In general, if net bonus to the roll is +3 or better, a skin search is *required*. If *size* penalty is -2 or worse, a skin search will *automatically* find the hidden item.

Concealment

The size and shape of the item governs its concealability. Some examples:

+6: A pea-sized jewel; a postage stamp
+5: One lockpick; a large jewel; a dime; a TL8+ computer disk; a letter
+4: A set of lockpicks; a dagger; a silver dollar
+3: A 20th-century floppy disk or CD, without case
+2: The smallest ordinary handguns (e.g., a Baby Browning); a small knife
+1: A large knife; a slingshot
0: An average handgun (e.g., a Luger)
-1: A large handgun (e.g., a Colt Government Model)
-2: The largest handguns; a shortsword
-3: A hand grenade
-4: A broadsword
-5: A Thompson submachine gun; a bastard sword

Clothing also affects effective skill. A Carmelite nun in full habit (+5 to skill) could conceal a bazooka or a battle-axe from an eyeball search. A Las Vegas showgirl in costume (-5 to skill) would have trouble hiding even a dagger. Of course, the showgirl might escape search entirely (unless the guards were just bored) because "she obviously couldn't hide anything in *that* outfit . . ." Full nudity is -7 to skill. Clothing designed specifically to hide things can give a bonus of up to +4.

A properly designed holster helps to conceal a weapon. A custom holster costs about $200 and gives +2 to Holdout for the weapon it contains. A good concealment holster from a commercial maker will cost about $100; it is +1 to Holdout. A reasonably good concealment holster costs about $50 and gives no Holdout bonus. No holster, or a non-concealment or cheap holster, is -1 to Holdout on gun-type weapons.

Things that move or make noise are at least -1 to Holdout skill.

Intelligence Analysis/TL (Mental/Hard)
Defaults to IQ-6

The ability to analyze and interpret intelligence data (usually military), to determine enemy plans and capabilities.

Interrogation (Mental/Average)
Defaults to IQ-5 or Intimidation-3

This is the ability to question a prisoner. It is not taught except by intelligence agencies, police, prisons, military units and the underworld.

To interrogate a prisoner, you must win a Contest of Skills: your Interrogation ability vs. the prisoner's IQ. The GM will roleplay the prisoner (or, if *you* are the prisoner, the GM will roleplay the interrogator) and make all die rolls in secret. Each question roll costs 5 minutes of time; a successful roll gets a truthful answer to one question. On a failed roll, the victim remains silent or lies. A bad failure (by 5 points or worse) means a *good, believable* lie is told! Modifiers: +2 for lengthy interrogation (more than two hours); -5 if the prisoner's loyalty to his leader or cause is "Very Good" or "Excellent"; +3 if severe threats are used; +6 if torture is used.

Note that "torture" does not necessarily mean thumbscrews and the rack. Exposing a prisoner to the object of his phobia (see *Phobias,* p. 35) is a very effective torture if the prisoner fails his Will roll to endure the fear. A believable threat against a loved one is also torture. *Note also* that torturing a prisoner is usually considered vile behavior and will likely bring retribution.

Lip Reading (Mental/Average)
Defaults to your Vision roll-10

This is the ability to *see* what others are saying. You must be within 20 feet, or use magic or binoculars to bring your point of view this close. Each successful roll will let you make out one sentence of a discussion – assuming, of course, that you know the language. If your subjects suspect you can read lips, they can hide their mouths or subvocalize to make lip reading impossible. A critical failure on a lip reading roll – if you are where your victims could see you – means that you stared so much you were noticed! Modifiers: All Vision modifiers (see p. 92).

Lockpicking/TL (Mental/Average)   Defaults to IQ-5

This is the ability to open locks without the key or combination. Each attempt to open a lock requires one minute; if you make the roll and open the lock, each point by which you succeeded shaves five seconds off the required time. (A vault, safe or other challenging lock can take more time, at the GM's discretion.) Note that if the lock has a trap or alarm attached, a separate Traps roll will be needed to circumvent it. Modifiers: -3 if you have only improvised equipment rather than real lockpicks; -5 in darkness (working by touch); up to +5 for very good equipment at high TLs. Inside information gives a bonus at GM's discretion.

Pickpocket (Physical/Hard)   Defaults to DX-6 or Sleight of Hand-4

This is the ability to steal a purse, knife, etc., from someone's person – or to "plant" something on him. Modifiers: +5 if the victim is distracted; +10 if he is asleep or drunk; up to -5 for goods in an inner pocket; and up to -10 for a ring or similar jewelry.

If your victim is aware someone may try to pick his pocket, or if he is generally wary, the GM should roll a Quick Contest of Skills – his IQ (modified by Alertness) against your Pickpocket skill (modified by difficulty of the job). If your victim has Streetwise, he uses that skill instead of his IQ! A similar roll may be required for you to outwit a third party who is watching you and the victim.

Poisons (Mental/Hard)   Defaults to IQ-6, Chemistry-5 or Physician-3

Also defaults to Cooking-3 or Savoir-Faire-3 in the appropriate culture. This is the general practical knowledge of poisons. A successful skill roll will let you (among other things) recognize a poison-bearing plant in the wild; distill the poison into useful form; recognize a poison by its taste in food or drink; identify a poison by observing its effects (+3 if *you* are the one poisoned); know a proper antidote; recognize or distill the antidote from its sources. Note that each of these feats requires a separate roll. Modifiers: Acute Taste and Smell will help to recognize a poison.

Scrounging (Mental/Easy)   Defaults to IQ-4

This is the ability to find, salvage or improvise useful items that others can't locate. Each attempt takes an hour. The scrounger does not necessarily steal his booty; he just locates it – somehow – and then acquires it by any means necessary. Note that if the scrounger finds something that is "nailed down," he must decide how to try to get it, and a roll on another skill may be necessary. Modifiers: As the GM sees fit, for the rarity of the item sought.

Shadowing (Mental/Average)   Defaults to IQ-6 or Stealth-4 (on foot only)

This is the ability to follow another person through a crowd without being noticed. (In the country, use Tracking and Stealth.) Roll one Contest of Skill every 10 minutes: your Shadowing vs. the subject's Vision roll. If you lose, you lost the subject; if you lose by more than 5, you were seen. Modifiers: -2 or more (GM's decision) if your looks are distinctive; -3 if the subject knows you.

Once the subject is aware he is being shadowed, make a Contest of Skills every 5 minutes: your Shadowing skill vs. his Shadowing or Stealth skill. If he wins, he eludes you. If he loses by more than 5, he *thinks* he eluded you. If you fail critically, you lose him and follow the wrong person.

To follow someone in a car or similar vehicle, use the same rules, but the shadower is at a -2; it's harder than shadowing on foot.

Sleight of Hand (Physical/Hard)   No default

This is the ability to "palm" small objects, do coin and card tricks, etc. Each successful roll will let you perform one piece of simple "stage magic"; a failed roll means you blew the trick. Modifiers: -3 if the person you want to fool has Acute Vision or knows the Sleight of Hand skill himself; +3 if the light is dim; +3 if you have a confederate to distract attention; +5 if you have prepared in advance (cards up your sleeve, etc.).

This skill can also be used to cheat while gambling. A successful Sleight of Hand roll will give you a +5 on your Gambling roll in a Contest of Skills. A failed roll will cause you to be denounced as a cheater!

Stealth (Physical/Average)   Defaults to IQ-5 or DX-5

This is the ability to hide and to move silently. A successful roll will let you conceal yourself anywhere except a totally bare room, or move so quietly that nobody will hear you, or follow someone without being noticed. (To follow someone through a crowd, use Shadowing skill, above.) Modifiers: minus your encumbrance level; -5 to hide in an area without "natural" hiding places; +3 or more if there are many hiding places; -5 to move silently if you are running instead of walking (walking speed with Stealth is 1 yard/second); -5 to fool dogs instead of people.

If you are moving silently, and someone is *specifically* listening for intruders, the GM will roll a Contest of Skills between your Stealth and their Hearing roll (see p. 92).

This skill is also used to stalk game, once you have spotted it. A successful roll (and about 30 minutes) will get you to within 30 yards of most animals. Another roll, at -5, will get you to within 15 yards. After that, you will have to make a weapon skill roll to hit it.

THIEF/SPY SKILLS

Streetwise (Mental/Average)　　　　Defaults to IQ-5

This is the skill of getting along in rough company. A successful Streetwise roll can (among other things) let you find out where any sort of illegal "action" is; which local cops or bureaucrats can be bought, and for how much; how to contact the local underworld; etc. Note that if you belong to an organization with good connections (Assassin's Guild, Brotherhood, police, Illuminati, etc.), you may be able to get this information by asking a contact. "Streetwise" is a measure of your ability to make your *own* contacts at need.

In any underworld or "bad neighborhood" situation where a reaction roll is called for, you may substitute a Streetwise roll instead; all normal reaction modifiers apply to the Streetwise roll. A successful roll gives you a "Good" reaction. A failed roll gives you a "Bad" reaction. Modifiers to this Influence roll only: +3 if you have a tough reputation (either "good" or "bad") in the area; -3 if you are obviously a stranger in the area.

Tracking　　　　See Outdoor Skills, p. 57

Traps/TL (Mental/Average)　　　Defaults to IQ-5, DX-5 or Lockpicking-3

This is the skill of building traps and detection devices, and of nullifying them. A successful Traps roll will (among other things) detect a trap if you are looking for it; disarm a trap once you have found it; reset it after you pass; or (given proper materials) build a new trap. Note that a "trap" can be anything from a pit trap with stakes to an elaborate security system! Time: As for Lockpicking (p. 67). Modifiers: Infinitely variable. The more sophisticated the trap, the harder it will be to see and to disarm/reset. Note that a trap may be (for instance) easy to find, but hard to disarm! This is all up to the GM or the designer of the adventure. Vision modifiers help you to find traps, but not to disarm or reset them. Note also that, if you don't possess this skill, a DX default should apply only to disarming or resetting a trap – NOT to detecting or building one!

Note that at TL7 and above, the Traps skill is essentially the same as Electronics (Security Systems).

Underwater Demolition/TL (Mental/Average)　　　Defaults to Demolition-2
Prerequisites: Scuba, and either Demolition OR appropriate Engineer

Ability to prepare and set an explosive charge underwater. Otherwise, similar to Demolition (above). If a demolitions engineer is using this skill by default, he rolls against his Demolition-2 to prepare the charge. But his demolitions training teaches him nothing about scuba; if scuba work is required to set the charge, he must roll against default Scuba skill or find someone else to place the explosives.

Ventriloquism (Mental/Hard)　　　　No default

This is the ability to disguise and "throw" your voice for a short distance. A successful roll will let you throw your voice well enough to fool your audience. Modifiers: +5 if you have a dummy or confederate to distract your audience (it's easier to "see" a face talk than it is to believe the voice comes from an immobile object); -3 if the audience has reason to be suspicious.

VEHICLE SKILLS

Most vehicle skills are learned in practice, though they can be taught in school. Learning without a teacher is only possible if you have the appropriate sort of vehicle for practice, and even then learning proceeds at half speed.

When a vehicle skill is used *by default,* a roll is necessary when you start the vehicle; failure may mean anything from the engine's failing to start immediately . . . to an immediate accident! The GM may require a further roll any time a hazardous or challenging situation occurs; landing a flying craft always requires a roll. If the pilot/driver has expert skill (15 or over), any critical failure requires an immediate second roll. Only if this second roll is a failure does a mishap really occur. Otherwise, it was a "near thing" averted by experience.

Battlesuit　　　　See Combat Skills, p. 49

Bicycling (Physical/Easy)　　　Defaults to DX-4 or Motorcycle

This is the ability to ride a bicycle without falling off. You can also roll at -5 to repair a damaged bicycle, assuming tools or parts are available.

Boating (Physical/Average)　　　Defaults to IQ-5, DX-5 or Powerboat-3

This is the ability to handle canoes, rowboats, small sailboats, etc. At default, one roll is required when the boat is entered (to keep from falling in the water) and one to get the boat moving. The GM may require other rolls whenever a hazard is encountered. Modifiers: -5 if the boat is an unfamiliar type (a day's experience, *if* you already have the Boating skill, will let you become familiar with a new type); foul weather will give a -3 or greater penalty.

Driving/TL (vehicle type) (Physical/Average)　　　Defaults to IQ-5 or DX-5

This is the ability to drive a specific type of vehicle – a specialization (p. 43) is required. Modifiers: -2 for an unfamiliar vehicle of a known type (for instance, from automatic to stick-shift); -2 or more for a vehicle in bad repair; -2 or more for bad driving conditions; -4 or more for a vehicle of unfamiliar type (e.g., a Model T when you are used to TL7 vehicles or a racecar when you are used to stock cars). Note that the ability to drive a team of animals is not Driving; it is the Teamster skill (p. 47).

If you want to learn Driving skill for two or more types of vehicles, start learning the second one at a reasonable default from the first – usually -4 (check this with the GM). Some vehicle types include:

Automobile	Hovercraft
Construction Equipment	Locomotive
Halftrack	Mecha
Heavy Wheeled	Tracked

A vehicle of a different tech level is considered a different "type."

Gunner/TL   See *Combat Skills*, p. 50

Mechanic/TL   See *Craft Skills*, p. 54

Motorcycle/TL (Physical/Easy) Defaults to DX-5, IQ-5 or Bicycling-5

This is the ability to ride a motorcycle. You must specialize in either motor-scooters/light cycles, or medium and heavy cycles.

Modifiers: -2 for an unfamiliar cycle of a known type (e.g., a Harley when your own cycle is a Shogun); -4 or more for a cycle in bad repair; -2 or more for bad road conditions; -4 or more for a cycle of unfamiliar type (e.g., a cycle of a different tech level); +3 if the cycle has a sidecar.

Piloting/TL (aircraft type) (Physical/Average) Defaults to IQ-6

This is the ability to pilot a specific type of aircraft or spacecraft. A specialization (p. 43) is required. The default is to IQ, because intelligence would be required to figure out the controls in an emergency. But when the skill is learned normally, it is based on DX like other physical skills.

A Piloting roll is required on takeoff or landing, and another roll is required in any hazardous situation. A failure by 1 indicates a rough job; failure by more indicates damage to the craft; a critical failure is a crash. If the pilot/driver has expert skill (15 or over), any critical failure requires an immediate second roll. Only if this second roll is a failure does a mishap really occur. Otherwise, it was a "near thing" averted by experience.

Piloting rolls can also be used when resolving air combat.

Modifiers: -2 for an unfamiliar aircraft of a known type (e.g., a Piper when your own plane is a Beech); -4 or more for a plane in bad repair; -2 or more for bad flying conditions; -4 or more for a plane of unfamiliar type (e.g., a twin-engine plane when you are used to single-engine craft). Craft with very complex controls (e.g.,

space shuttle) or primitive craft (e.g., Wright brothers) should always have penalties, even for experienced pilots. Tech-level differences *definitely* count (see p. 185).

If you want to learn Piloting skill for two or more types of craft, start learning the second one at a reasonable default from the first – usually -4 (check this with the GM). Types include:

Aerospace	High-Performance Spacecraft
Autogyro	Light Airplane
Contragravity	Lightsail
Flight Pack	Lighter-Than-Air
Glider	Low-Performance Spacecraft
Heavy Airplane	Starship
Helicopter	Ultralight
High-Performance Airplane	Vertol

In most science fiction campaigns, Free Fall and Vacc Suit skills should be prerequisites for spaceship or starship piloting.

Powerboat/TL (Physical/Average) Defaults to IQ-5, DX-5 or Boating-3

This is the ability to handle small powered watercraft of all kinds. (For non-powered watercraft, see Boating, above, and Seamanship, p. 57.) Default skill users must make a Powerboat, Boating or DX roll when the boat is entered (to keep from falling in the water). Another roll is required in any potentially hazardous situation. Modifiers: -4 if the boat is an unfamiliar type; foul weather will give a -3 or greater penalty.

Teamster   See *Animal Skills*, p. 47

Vacc Suit/TL (Mental/Average) Defaults to IQ-6

Available at TL7+ only. This is the ability to use a "space-suit" in environments where there is no air (or no breathable air). A separate Free Fall roll is required for zero-G work. See *GURPS Space* for more detail about vacc suits.

EXAMPLE OF SKILL SELECTION

Let's go back to Dai Blackthorn, the character we started to create on p. 14. We've already determined his basic attributes, his advantages and his disadvantages. All that is left is to select skills suitable for a quick, bright, overconfident little thief.

Dai's beginning attributes are ST 8, DX 15, IQ 12 and HT 12. Obviously, he will do best in things where dexterity and intelligence are important. If he chooses skills that default to DX and IQ, he will be able to do much better than if he defaults to ST. Fortunately, most physical skills *do* default to DX, and nearly all mental skills default to IQ.

We haven't defined Dai's age, so we'll make him the standard starting age: 18. The only reason to make him older would be to let him put more points into education. At age 18, he is limited to 36 character points for skills, but that's no problem; Dai has only 25 points left anyway.

25 points will let you learn quite a lot, especially if you start out as smart as Dai. So . . . what shall we say Dai has learned in his life so far?

Every thief ought to be able to pick locks. Lockpicking (see skill description, p. 67) is a Mental/Average skill; it defaults to IQ-5. That makes Dai's default skill 12-5, or 7. Not too good. We want Dai to have at least a 12 in this skill, so he'll have a better than 50-50 chance to open the average lock. A skill of 12 would be equal to Dai's IQ; referring to the Average column of the Mental Skill table, we see that this skill would cost him only 2 points at this level! 4 points would buy a skill of 13; 6 would buy a skill of 14! We'll go for a Lockpicking skill of 13.

Area Knowledge is equally important for a street kid. It's a Mental/Easy skill. 2 points will buy it to a level of IQ+1, or 13.

A good thief is also a pickpocket. The Pickpocket skill (p. 67) defaults to DX-6, giving Dai a default level of 9. It's a Physical/Hard skill – hard to learn. And Dai wants to be *good* at it, since it's dangerous to fail at pocket-picking! To get to a skill equal to his DX of 15, he needs to spend 4 points. A skill of 15 should be good enough.

A good thief should also be able to hide. The Stealth skill (p. 67) defaults to either IQ-5 or DX-5. Dai's DX is better than his IQ, so he would default to DX, giving him a default level of 10. Still not good enough for safety – so let's study it. Stealth is a Physical/Average skill, so a skill equal to Dai's DX of 15 costs only 2 points.

Climbing (p. 57) is another useful skill in Dai's line of work. It defaults to DX-5 or ST-5. Dai's DX is better than his ST. His default Climbing skill is 10. Because he is *double-jointed* (remember, we took that as one of his advantages), his Climbing skill is increased by 3, to 13. That's pretty good, as long as he's not faced with any sheer walls. So for now, he'll spend no points, and rely on his default Climbing skill of 13.

Not absolutely necessary – but very useful for a character like Dai – is the Fast-Talk skill (p. 63). His default in this (IQ-5) would give him only a 7. This is a Mental/Average skill. For two points, Dai can get it at a level equal to his IQ, or 12.

And, to survive in the underworld, Dai needs a good helping of Streetwise (p. 68). His default (IQ-5) would be only 7. This is also a Mental/Average skill. For 2 points, he can get it at a level equal to his IQ, or 12.

At this point, Dai has spent 16 points on skills, leaving him a total of 9 yet to spend. And Dai probably needs some sort of weapon skill if he's to survive. With 9 character points left for training, he could choose to be pretty good with one weapon, or competent with two or three. He chooses to study two weapons: Knife (p. 51) and Shortsword (p. 52). Knife is Physical/Easy, defaulting to DX-4; Shortsword is Physical/Average, defaulting to DX-5. His default abilities would be Knife-11 and Shortsword-10 . . . not too bad, but not good enough to keep him alive in a serious fight.

So – Dai puts 4 character points into Knife. 4 points in a Physical/Easy skill gets him to DX+2 level, or 17. He also puts 4 points into Shortsword. This gets him to DX+1 level; his Shortsword skill is now 16. He's no professional soldier, but his opponents won't be professionals, either. He can hold his own in a back-alley brawl.

Dai has only one point left – not enough to increase either Knife or Shortsword by another level. But let's get tricky and add a skill that defaults to another skill. Since Dai's Lockpicking skill is 13, and since Traps (p. 68) – a Mental/Average skill – defaults to Lockpicking-3, Dai's default Traps skill is already 10. Not bad, but not great. A better Traps skill could be useful for Dai. Can we raise it?

To find out, we'll go back to the table. Dai's IQ is 12, so his current Traps skill is equal to IQ-2. To go from IQ-2 to IQ-1 on the Mental/Average column is a difference of only 1/2 point! So we can raise his Traps skill from 10 to 11. We can't get it up to 12; that would require another full point, which we don't have.

So: 1/2 character point left. We'll put it in a Physical/Easy skill where 1/2 point can actually make a difference. Dai takes Knife Throwing skill, at DX-1 – which is still a skill of 14!

SKILLS	Pt. Cost	Level
AREA KNOWLEDGE	2	13
CLIMBING	-	13
FAST-TALK	2	12
KNIFE	4	17
KNIFE THROWING	1/2	14
LOCKPICKING	4	13
PICKPOCKET	4	15
SHORTSWORD	4	16
STEALTH	2	15
STREETWISE	2	12
TRAPS (from lockpicking)	1/2	11

That uses up all his character points, and completes the character of Dai Blackthorn . . . and quite a rogue he is. His "positive" totals (advantages plus skills) plus his "negative" totals (disadvantages and quirks) add up to exactly 100. In the next section, we'll buy Dai some equipment, double-check his stats and write his character story . . . and he'll be ready to go.

8 EQUIPMENT AND ENCUMBRANCE

Now you need to decide what equipment and possessions you have . . . and find out whether they weigh you down enough to make a difference! This section will also give you enough information about weapons and armor to let you choose your combat gear intelligently.

MONEY

The first question, of course, is how much money you have. Money and wealth are different for each game world and adventure (see p. 189). Prices are always listed in $, for convenience – but $ can stand for dollar, credit, silver piece, or whatever is appropriate. Remember that if you take relative wealth or poverty as an advantage or disadvantage (see p. 16), the amount of money you start with is different from the average for your game world.

Money and economics are explained in more detail in Chapter 22.

BUYING EQUIPMENT

In some adventures, some (or all) of your starting equipment is specified already. Other adventures will let you buy whatever you want, within your starting budget. Remember to leave a little for spending money.

Each game world or adventure will have one or more *equipment lists*, giving cost, weight and other information about important items. You *can* buy items not on the list if the GM decrees them "reasonable." Price, cost and weight are set by the GM. Game Masters: Just be logical here, and use your own judgment. Especially in a modern scenario, there are hundreds of items not likely to be listed – but you could go into the department store and pick them up. If somebody really wants a vegetable dicer or a talking baby doll, let them buy one.

The *Charts and Tables* section includes lists of weapons, armor and general equipment for medieval/fantasy, modern and futuristic campaigns. You are welcome to make copies for your own use.

All equipment you buy should be listed on the Character Sheet. If you accumulate a lot of gear, you may want to keep it on a separate sheet. To keep proper track of encumbrance (see p. 76), the items you are actually carrying should be listed separately from possessions you leave at home.

Clothing and Armor

These will be dealt with as one subject, because armor is only specialized clothing. And, in an emergency, your clothing is better than no armor at all. Armor is vital in combat situations. If your foes can hit you, and you do not have some sort of armor protection, you will soon be dead.

Heavy armor gives the best protection. But it adds encumbrance! Another limitation is your wealth; the best armor is *very* expensive, and few starting characters will be able to afford it. Armor is more important in some periods than in others. In low-tech combat, it's a lifesaver, especially for fighters with a low HT and no Toughness. *Armor can be more important than weapon skill in determining who wins a fight with low-tech weapons!*

When guns come into play, armor becomes less important because heavy guns can defeat it (though cops will still want their woven body armor). In some science-fiction backgrounds, armor may be worthwhile; in others, lasers can cut through anything, and ducking is the best defense.

Armor protects you in two ways. Its *passive defense*, or PD, (1 to 6) adds to your defense roll when you wear it. Its *damage resistance*, or DR, protects you when you *do* get hit.

Do You Need Armor?

The short answer is *yes!* Unless you are in a high-tech campaign where hand weapons defeat any armor, or a modern-day campaign where wits are more important than weapons, armor is literally a lifesaver.

Armor protects you in two ways. First, good armor makes you harder to hit, by causing blows to glance off. This is its *passive defense*.

Second, when you *are* hit, your armor will stop some of the blow. This *damage resistance* varies with the type of armor. Cloth armor has a damage resistance, or DR, of 1. It stops 1 hit of damage from each attack. Plate armor made of steel has a DR of 7. Some exotic materials have a very high DR indeed.

The types of clothing and armor available will differ in each game world; therefore each game world book will have a *Clothing and Armor* section. Gear from one country, time or game world *will* work in others. Exception: A GM may declare that highly magical items will not work in a technological (low-mana) world, or vice versa. And *availability* of otherworldly items will always be limited. A 20th-century flak jacket will not be found in a medieval world, and a bronze breastplate will be very hard to find in modern-day America.

Contrary to popular belief, good armor does *not* make you clumsier (i.e., decrease your DX) when you are used to it. It's quite possible to do acrobatics in plate armor! The real disadvantage of armor is that it's *heavy*. It slows your movement, and is terribly uncomfortable in hot weather.

Furthermore, a full-head helmet limits your vision somewhat, and makes hearing almost impossible. When you wear such a helm, reduce all Vision or Hearing rolls by 3, and reduce all effective weapon skills by 1. In the Basic Combat System, when you buy a complete suit of armor, full-head helmets are considered part of "half-plate" and plate armor. Above TL7, helmets are designed to avoid this problem.

Note also that gloves or gauntlets reduce your effective DX by 8 (!!) if you are trying to do delicate work like lockpicking. This is true even at high tech levels.

Listing Armor on Your Character Sheet

Your armor, along with its cost and weight, should be listed in your "Possessions" box (center column).

The *passive defense* of your armor goes on the "Armor" line of the "Passive Defense" box (left column, center).

The *damage resistance* of your armor goes on the "Armor" line of the "Damage Resistance" box (left column, low down).

Layering Armor

Normally, you can only wear one suit of armor at a time! But there are exceptions.

If you wear chainmail, you *should* wear cloth armor underneath. The cost of this padding is included in the price of a full "suit" of chain. If you wear chainmail without the cloth padding, it has PD3 and DR3 (but PD0 and DR1 against an impaling weapon).

If you wear plate, half-plate, heavy leather, a flak jacket, etc., you can wear cloth armor or a leather jacket underneath. This adds weight, and does *not* add passive defense – but it does give you one more point of damage resistance. Chainmail under plate will give 2 more points of DR, but the added weight will be prohibitive to all but the strongest!

In a high-tech campaign, you may wear "reflec" armor to protect against laser attacks. Reflec is worn over all other clothing and armor. Any attack must pierce the reflec before affecting the armor beneath.

In general, the inner layer of any layered armor adds damage resistance, but not passive defense. The GM's common sense is the final guide to armor layering.

Armor Types

For each type of clothing and armor, the following information is listed:

General Description. The item's name and how it is used.

Passive Defense (PD). Armor that is smooth and hard (metal, plastic or hardened leather) is likely to "turn" a blow. It may even reflect an arrow, lightning bolt or laser beam! This adds to your *passive* defense; your defense roll is better, because some blows will bounce off. PD of armor normally ranges from 1 to 6.

Damage Resistance (DR). This is the amount of protection the item gives, in terms of hits subtracted from a blow which strikes the wearer. For instance, if you are hit in the chest while wearing a DR6 breastplate, and the attacker rolls 8 points of damage, only 2 will affect you. Some types of armor have two different DRs, depending on the type of weapon that hits them. Some typical damage resistances are shown below.

Weight. This is given in pounds; it adds to your total encumbrance.

Cost. Translate "$" to your world's currency. Like other costs, this assumes a typical sale, made by an ordinary merchant in an area where the item is usually found, when it is neither more scarce nor more common than usual.

Suits of Armor

In the Basic Combat System, you just buy a full "suit" of one type of armor. (The Advanced Combat System gives you the option to put your armor together from its component parts, using the *Armor Table* in the *Charts and Tables* section.)

common types of armor

Type	TL	PD	DR	Cost	Weight
Summer clothing	any	0	0	$20	2
Winter clothing	any	0	1	$60	5
Padded cloth armor	1-4	1	1	$180	14
Light leather armor	1-4	1	1	$210	10
Heavy leather armor	1-4	2	2	$350	20
Chainmail	3-4	3[1]	4[2]	$550	45
Scale armor	2-4	3	4	$750	50
Half plate[3]	2-4	4	5	$2,000	70
Light plate[3]	3-4	4	6	$4,000	90
Heavy plate[3]	3-4	4	7	$6,000	110
Flak jacket[4]	6	2	3	$220	17
Kevlar (light)[4]	7	2[1]	4[2]	$220	5
Kevlar (heavy)[4]	7	2[1]	12[2]	$420	9
Light body armor	7+	4	15	$270	22
Reflec[5]	8-9	6	2	$320	4
Medium body armor	8+	6	25	$1,520	32
Heavy combat armor	9+	6	50	$2,520	52

[1] PD 1 vs. impaling.
[2] DR 2 vs. impaling.
[3] all combat skills at -1 due to helm; Vision and Hearing at -3.
[4] protects torso only.
[5] against lasers only; PD3, DR0 against sonics; no protection vs. other weapons.

Each suit of "real" armor includes a set of light, common clothing to wear underneath it; you do not have to buy clothing separately and add in the weight! A suit of chainmail includes heavy cloth padding under the chain.

Choosing Your Weapons

The weapons you carry should be determined first by your skills, and then by your strength and budget. If you can't use it, don't buy it. Note, too, that most places have laws or customs that govern the sort of weapons and armor you may wear on the street without attracting attention. A suit of plate armor in the average medieval village would be every bit as conspicuous – and threatening – as a machine gun in the corner grocery store!

High-tech weapons (like guns) will work for anyone who knows how to use them. Low-tech weapons, like clubs and swords, do more damage when wielded by a strong person, and you will usually want to carry the heaviest weapon that your strength and skill will allow.

The combat rules are in Chapters 13 and 14. This section will present just enough information to let you equip yourself intelligently. If your character is a total non-fighter type, you can skim through this section.

Basic Weapon Damage

"Basic damage" is the *impact* damage a weapon does, *before* its point or cutting edge is considered. The table on p. 74 is used to figure how much damage each weapon does, based on two factors: the *attack type* and the *strength of the user*. Some weapons do more or less damage (in particular, large weapons do extra damage), so check the *Weapon Table* listing for your particular weapon.

Damage is shown as "dice plus adds." For example, "2d" means you roll two dice to calculate the damage done. "2d+1" means that you roll two dice and add 1 to the result. Thus, a roll of 7 would mean 8 hits of damage. "2d-1" means that you roll two dice and *subtract* 1 from the result – and so on.

If you hit with a cutting or impaling attack, or a bullet, you always get at least one hit of basic damage if the basic damage roll was capable of wounding. Thus, if you strike with a dagger for "1d-4" damage, and roll a 2, you do not do -2 hits, or even zero hits. Any time your damage works out to zero or a negative number, count it as 1 hit. (Remember, this is *before* the effects of armor. It is quite possible to do zero damage once armor is accounted for.)

However, if you hit the foe with a crushing attack, you can do zero damage. If your *fist* does "1d-4" damage and you roll a 2, you did no damage.

Types of Attack

There are two main types of weapon attack: *thrusting* and *swinging*. A *swinging* attack does more damage, because the weapon acts as a lever to multiply your ST. The following table shows how much basic damage each type of weapon does, according to the user's Strength.

The columns show the number of dice rolled to determine damage. *Example:* If your ST is 10, you will do 1d-2 basic damage with any thrusting type attack, or 1 die of basic damage when you *swing* a weapon. So: if you attack with a sword and roll a 6, you will do 6 points of basic damage if you swing the sword, or only 4 if you thrust.

Weapon Effects

Different weapons do different types and amounts of damage, because they are used in different ways.

Each weapon is described by two terms: *damage type* (cutting, crushing or impaling), and *damage amount* (defined by the way the weapon is used), which tells how hard it hits.

Thrusting Attacks

These blows strike with only the force of your muscle behind them. (Some weapons, like crossbows, add a "lever" effect, and they get damage bonuses.)

A *thrusting/crushing* weapon (fist, blunt arrow, end of a staff) is the least deadly type!

A *thrusting/impaling* weapon (spear, arrow, knife) is far deadlier. It always does at least one hit of basic damage. And whatever damage the target's armor does not stop will be doubled!

Note that, at the same strength, an arrow does the same impaling damage as a sword or spear. This is intentional! An arrow makes a smaller but deeper wound. Overall damage is roughly equivalent.

Swinging Attacks

Swung weapons, like polearms and swords, are *levers* to increase your force when you strike. Thus, your basic damage is greater when you swing a weapon than when you thrust with that same weapon. Of course, a *heavy* swung weapon does even more damage, and will get a damage bonus (see *Weapon Tables*).

A *swinging/crushing* weapon, like a club or maul, can do a great deal of basic damage if it is heavy. It can also knock your foe backwards (see p. 106) if you hit him hard enough. But it does no bonus damage.

A *swinging/cutting* weapon, like a sword, will get a 50% damage bonus if it gets through your foe's armor.

A *swinging/impaling* weapon, like a pick, halberd or warhammer, can be the deadliest of all. It will have a high basic damage, which lets it get through armor – and the damage that penetrates armor is doubled, as for any impaling weapon. The drawback of such weapons is that they can get *stuck* when you hit your foe (see p. 96).

Alternative Attacks

Some types of weapons can be used in different ways. For instance, some swords can be swung for a cutting attack, or thrust for an impaling attack. This is shown on the *Weapon Tables*. Before you strike with such a weapon, specify how you are attacking.

Weapon Tables

A "Weapon Table" is a list of weapons, showing damage, weight, cost and other information. The *Weapon Tables* are in the *Charts & Tables* section.

Each game world released for **GURPS** will include the appropriate *Weapon Tables*, armor lists, etc., for that world.

Weapon Quality

The Weapon Table prices assume weapons of "good" quality. Fine quality weapons may be made for Good quality prices at TL7+ due to improvements in metallurgy. The qualities and relative prices are:

Swords. Swords are very costly. This is because, especially at low tech levels, it is no mean feat to temper a piece of steel to make it thin, light, yet strong and capable of holding an edge! Thus, there is a wide range of quality among knives and swords.

A *cheap* sword (bronze or poor steel) has a 2/3 chance of breaking when it parries a very heavy weapon, and is more likely to break on a critical miss. But it costs only 40% of the price shown in the table.

A *good* sword is as listed in the table. It has a 1/3 chance of breaking when it parries a very heavy weapon (see pp. 99 and 111). All weapons mentioned will be of this quality unless specified otherwise.

A *fine* sword has only a 1/6 chance of breaking when it parries a very heavy weapon. It holds a better edge, so it does +1 basic damage. It costs 4 times the listed price.

A *very fine* sword will not break on a parry. It does +2 damage. It costs at least 20 times the listed price – and very fine swords are not available in most places!

Axes, polearms, and other cutting and impaling weapons of fine quality are unusual (because the armorer must, in effect, use sword steel). Therefore, they cost 10 times the listed price. They also do +1 basic damage. Very fine and cheap weapons of this type are rarely made.

Maces and other crushing weapons may be of fine quality; they cost three times the listed amount and resist breakage, as above, but do no extra damage.

Bows and crossbows of fine quality will shoot 20% farther than normal weapons. They cost four times the listed amount.

Guns, beam weapons, etc. of fine quality will be more beautiful, or more accurate, or both, but usually have no extra range or damage. Cheap guns are often available; cost depends on the game world (generically, 60% of listed price). They are less accurate (a minus to Acc of 1 to 10) and more likely to malfunction in upsetting ways.

Magical weapons are covered in Chapter 19, *Magic.* They are more likely to vary in Power than in physical quality.

basic weapon damage

attack of attacker	Swinging attack (fist, spear, etc.)	Strength Thrusting (sword, club, etc.)
1	1d-9	1d-9
2	1d-8	1d-8
3	1d-7	1d-7
4	1d-6	1d-6
5	1d-5	1d-5
6	1d-4	1d-4
7	1d-3	1d-3
8	1d-3	1d-2
9	1d-2	1d-1
10	1d-2	1d
11	1d-1	1d+1
12	1d-1	1d+2
13	1d	2d-1
14	1d	2d
15	1d+1	2d+1
16	1d+1	2d+2
17	1d+2	3d-1
18	1d+2	3d
19	2d-1	3d+1
20	2d-1	3d+2

See p. 248 for a chart covering higher levels of ST.

Listing Basic Damage On Your Character Sheet

On the table above, find your Strength. Read across to the two types of basic damage: thrusting and swinging. Copy these two numbers onto your Character Sheet. The "Basic Damage" box is just below the "ST/Fatigue" box, since basic damage is based on ST.

You will refer to this whenever you need to figure how much damage you do with a primitive weapon. The specific weapon you use will affect this number – a greataxe does more damage than a shortsword. See p. 75.

Damage Types and Damage Bonus

Weapons do three basic *types* of damage: impaling, cutting and crushing. Impaling weapons are those that strike with a sharp point. Cutting weapons strike with an edge. Crushing weapons strike with a blunt surface. So, for instance, a fist or club is a crushing weapon. A spear or arrow is an impaling weapon, a sword or axe is a cutting weapon.

Cutting and impaling weapons are more effective on flesh than on armor. Therefore, they do *bonus damage* – but only if they penetrate the armor.

When you hit with a *cutting* weapon, all damage that gets through the target's armor (and other Damage Resistance) is increased by 50%, rounded down. Suppose you strike with a sword and do 8 points of damage, 5 of which get through the armor. Half of 5 is $2\frac{1}{2}$. So the victim takes an extra 2 points of damage, for a total of 7.

When you hit with an *impaling* weapon, the damage that gets through the armor is *doubled.* If you hit your foe with a spear, and 5 points of damage get through the armor, he takes 10 "hits" of injury!

Thus, impaling weapons are deadly against unarmored targets. For a well-armored target, a heavy, swung weapon (an axe or maul) may be best, because it can overcome the DR of the armor and get through to the wearer!

Bullets are a special case; different types of bullets have different damage multipliers. Dum-dums, for instance, are treated as impaling because they do terrible damage to flesh. Armor-piercing bullets have a high basic damage, to punch through armor, but the damage that gets through the armor is *halved* because the bullet cuts right through the target without mushrooming.

Listing Weapons On Your Character Sheet

Carry as many weapons as you need – but not so many that you will be weighed down. Even a non-fighter may want a knife or sidearm! List each weapon in the "Weapons & Possessions" box on your Character Sheet, as follows:

Cost and *Weight* are copied directly from the *Weapon Table*.

Damage is also copied from the *Weapon Table*. For weapons that do two types of damage (like shortswords – either cutting or impaling), use two lines.

Total Damage is the damage *you* do with that weapon. Refer to the Basic Damage box you just filled in (below the ST/Fatigue space). Take your basic damage for that *type* of attack, and add the damage shown on the table for your weapon. *Example:* If your ST is 10, your basic swinging damage is 1 die. And a broadsword does "swing+1." So *your* damage with a broadsword is your basic swinging damage, plus 1 . . . for a total of 1d+1. Record this on your Character Sheet. When you hit with a broadsword, you will roll 1 die and add 1 to the result. *Exception:* Some weapons have a "MD" (maximum damage) listed. No matter how strong *you* are, the weapon cannot do more basic damage than this. So use your own calculated damage *or* the weapon's MD, whichever is less.

Skill is your skill level with the weapon . . . the number you must roll against in order to hit with it. If you have spent points to learn the weapon, get your skill from the "Skills" box. If you have not studied the weapon, put down your "default" or untrained skill – see p. 44.

Listing Ranged Weapons On Your Character Sheet

If you have a "ranged" weapon (anything that can be thrown or fired), you should fill in the "Weapon Ranges" box. List each ranged weapon. Then fill in the four "range stats" for that weapon, from the *Ranged Weapon Table*. Note that for some weapons the ranges depend on your ST. For instance, if your ST is 12 and a range is given as STx10, you would write 120 (yards).

Ranged weapons are explained on p. 100 and explained in more detail on p. 114.

Choosing Your Shield

Shields are very valuable in low-tech combat, but almost worthless in high-tech environments. A bullet or beam will go right through a medieval shield, slowed only slightly if at all. Plastic riot shields and science-fiction "force shields" can stop some high-tech attacks. The following discussion assumes shields are being used against weapons of their own tech level, giving them a reasonable chance to work!

Shields protect the user both actively and passively. A shield will stop many blows automatically, with no particular effort on the part of the user. The bigger the shield, the better it does this. This is the shield's *passive* defense.

You may also deliberately try to block a blow (see *Blocking*, p. 98). This is an "active" defense. If you have the Shield skill, you can make yourself very hard to hit!

A shield has no "damage resistance." It does not reduce the damage from any blow that hits you. It makes you hard to hit, by active and passive defense – but that's all! (Certain high-tech weapons may lose a bit of their force as they penetrate shields, of course.) An advanced rule allows shields to take damage, for those who want more complexity. See p. 120.

Improvised Shields. In an emergency, you may snatch up just about anything with which to block a blow! You may do this even if you do not have the Shield skill; your default skill is DX-4. The GM will rule on the effectiveness of any improvised shield.

Improvised Weapons

Occasionally you will want to hit someone with something besides a "real" weapon. In that case, the GM should determine what weapon it is most similar to, and treat it that way.

Most improvised weapons will be equivalent to clubs or quarterstaves. A length of chain would be a clumsy but dangerous morningstar. And so on.

If an improvised weapon is particularly clumsy (e.g., a crossbow being used as a club), reduce the user's effective Club skill. If it would do less damage than a "real" weapon of the same type, subtract from its damage roll.

Minimum Strength

Most low-tech weapons, and some high-tech devices, have a "Minimum ST" listed. This is the minimum ST required to use the weapon properly.

You may still fight with a weapon if you are too weak for it. But for every point of ST by which you are too weak, you will be at -1 to your weapon skill, and you will suffer 1 extra point of fatigue at the end of each fight.

Drawbacks of Shields

While you are using a shield, you may not use any two-handed weapons.

A large shield will interfere with your weapon use – and sometimes your *foes* will use it for shelter! Therefore, while you are using a large shield, subtract 2 from your effective weapon skill and 1 from your Parry defense.

Any shield will interfere with your dexterity and weapon use if you enter close combat (see p. 111). The bigger the shield, the more it gets in the way. Subtract the shield's passive defense from all attacks and DX rolls you make in close combat after your first full turn of close combat.

Listing Your Shield on Your Character Sheet

Write your shield on the last line in the "Weapons and Possessions" box. Copy its cost and weight from the table at left. If you are using the optional rules for attacking with a shield (see p. 123), you can fill in the lines for damage and skill. Otherwise, they don't matter.

You should also fill in the "Shield" line of the "Passive Defense" box. The bigger the shield, the more passive defense it provides.

Don't Let the Encumbrance Rules Weigh You Down

GURPS provides *very* detailed rules for weight and encumbrance, for the benefit of those who like a great deal of realism in their games. If you like, you can calculate the *precise* weight your character is carrying, down to the coins in his pocket!

But most roleplaying campaigns don't require that much realism – indeed, extra detail can slow a game down. For most campaigns, it would be ridiculous to count the weight of individual coins. Indeed, you may choose to ignore the weight of *any* item that weighs less than, say, five pounds. Now, when you pick up a battleaxe, or a 50-pound chest of copper coins, go ahead and add *that* weight in . . .

Detailed encumbrance rules are most important in combat situations, boardgame tournaments, etc. But remember: The encumbrance rules are here to provide detail *if you want it*. Don't saddle yourself with more complexity than you enjoy!

The easiest way to simplify encumbrance is to use the "generic armor" rules (p. 72) instead of calculating individual cost and weight of each piece. Note that all four of the sample characters (pp. 214-217) were made up using the "generic" armor rules. If you want to use the more complex rules, you can adjust their armor to match the pictures; this will vary their weight slightly.

Shields may be divided into six general types, as shown below:

Type	Passive Defense	Cost	Weight	Hits
Improvised	1 or 2	–	varies	varies
Buckler	1	$25	2 lbs.	5/20
Small	2	$40	8 lbs.	5/30
Medium	3	$60	15 lbs.	7/40
Large	4	$90	25 lbs.	9/60
Force (TL11+)	4	$1,500	½ lb.	–

(worn on left wrist, leaving hand free)

Type. The kind of shield. "Improvised" represents anything you happen to grab to defend yourself in an emergency. The GM will rule on its effectiveness.

Passive Defense. This amount contributes to your defense roll – even if you have no idea how to use a shield.

Weight. Weight in pounds, for a wooden shield with metal banding. A 20th-century plastic riot shield weighs half this much.

Cost. For a medieval world; double this, in $, for a modern riot shield.

Hits. This column is used only for the optional *Shield Damage* rule (p. 120). It shows the amount of damage a shield can take before it is destroyed.

ENCUMBRANCE

Your *encumbrance* is the total weight you are carrying, *relative to your strength*. Items you do not carry on your person don't count as encumbrance.

Encumbrance reduces your movement rate in combat, and the distance you can walk in a day. It also makes swimming and climbing much more difficult.

A strong person can carry more than a weak one. Therefore, the ratio of weight to strength determines encumbrance, as follows:

Weight up to *twice* ST: no encumbrance. You have no penalty.

Weight up to *four times* ST: light encumbrance. Movement penalty of 1.

Weight up to *six times* ST: medium encumbrance. Movement penalty of 2.

Weight up to *12 times* ST: heavy encumbrance. Movement penalty of 3.

Weight up to *20 times* ST: extra-heavy encumbrance. Movement penalty of 4. You cannot carry a weight more than 20 times your ST for more than a few feet at a time. 30 times ST is the absolute *most* you can carry.

ST	None (0)	Light (1)	Medium (2)	Heavy (3)	Extra-Heavy (4)
6	12 lbs.	24 lbs.	36 lbs.	72 lbs.	120 lbs.
7	14 lbs.	28 lbs.	42 lbs.	84 lbs.	140 lbs.
8	16 lbs.	32 lbs.	48 lbs.	96 lbs.	160 lbs.
9	18 lbs.	36 lbs.	54 lbs.	108 lbs.	180 lbs.
10	20 lbs.	40 lbs.	60 lbs.	120 lbs.	200 lbs.
11	22 lbs.	44 lbs.	66 lbs.	132 lbs.	220 lbs.
12	24 lbs.	48 lbs.	72 lbs.	144 lbs.	240 lbs.
13	26 lbs.	52 lbs.	78 lbs.	156 lbs.	260 lbs.
14	28 lbs.	56 lbs.	84 lbs.	168 lbs.	280 lbs.
15	30 lbs.	60 lbs.	90 lbs.	180 lbs.	300 lbs.
16	32 lbs.	64 lbs.	96 lbs.	192 lbs.	320 lbs.
17	34 lbs.	68 lbs.	102 lbs.	204 lbs.	340 lbs.
18	36 lbs.	72 lbs.	108 lbs.	216 lbs.	360 lbs.
19	38 lbs.	76 lbs.	114 lbs.	228 lbs.	380 lbs.
20	40 lbs.	80 lbs.	120 lbs.	240 lbs.	400 lbs.

Recording Encumbrance on Your Character Sheet

Copy the encumbrance levels for your Strength into the blanks in the "Encumbrance" box (left center). For instance, if your ST is 15, you would list "30" in the "no encumbrance" space. That means that, at or below 30 lbs., you are effectively not encumbered at all.

Whenever it becomes necessary to check encumbrance, you can refer to this box and find out just how much you can carry. (If you have a cart or wagon, you can carry more. See p. 89.)

YOUR MOVE SCORE

Your "Move" is the distance (in yards) you can actually run in one second. To find your Move, add up the total weight in your "Weapons and Possessions" box. Compare this with the encumbrance levels you have marked down. This will tell you what your actual encumbrance is.

If you have the Running skill, add 1/8 of your skill level to your Speed *for this calculation only*. Running doesn't affect your Speed score (it doesn't make your reflexes faster), but it will help your Move.

Now subtract your encumbrance *penalty* from your Speed score, and *round down*. The result is your Move score – always a whole number, not a fraction. If you have no encumbrance, your Move is the same as your Basic Speed, rounded down. If you have light encumbrance, your Move is 1 less than your Basic Speed – and so on.

Mvmt	**BASIC SPEED**	**MOVE**
	6.75	6
	(HT+DX)/4	Basic – Enc.

ENCUMBRANCE

		PASSIVE DEFENSE
None (0) = 2×ST	16	Armor: _1_
Light (1) = 4×ST	32	Shield: ____
Med (2) = 6×ST	48	
Hvy (3) = 12×ST	96	TOTAL
X-hvy (4) = 20×ST	160	1

ACTIVE DEFENSES

DODGE	**PARRY**	**BLOCK**
6	7	5
= Move	KNIFE Weapon/2	Shield/2

DAMAGE RESISTANCE

Armor _JACKET : 1_ TO 1

Your Move controls:
(1) how fast you can move.
(2) *when* you move, if you use the "realistic" combat sequencing option (p. 95).
(3) your Dodge defense. This "active defense" is equal to your Move. The less weighted-down you are, the quicker you can dodge!

List your Move on your Character Sheet, beside your Basic Speed. If your encumbrance level changes, you should change your Move to match. This can happen if you pick up a heavy object – or if you drop your shield to run away! The levels shown in the "Encumbrance" box will make it easy to tell when you cross over to a slower or faster Move.

Your Move can never be reduced to *zero* unless you are unconscious, unable to use your legs, or lifting over 30 times your ST – see *Lifting and Moving Things*, p. 89.

Dai Blackthorn has the disadvantage of Poverty, so instead of the normal $1,000 to spend, he has only $200. He can spend it on anything from the low-tech equipment lists. He settles on the following:

Clothes – lower-class – 1 lb. – $10
Shoes – 1 pair, leather – 2 lbs. – $40
Leather jacket – 4 lbs. – $50
Small knife (at belt) – 1/2 lb. – $30
Set of lockpicking tools – weight negligible – $20
Dagger (strapped to leg) – 1/4 lb. – $20

This accounts for $170. The other $30 represents Dai's current life savings. $20 of it is in a gold ring, which he wears; $10 he carries in cash on his person – the safest place for it!

All Dai's equipment and money is recorded on his Character Sheet. The protective values (Passive Defense and Damage Resistance) for his armor are copied directly from the book to the Character Sheet.

WEAPONS AND POSSESSIONS

Item	Damage Type Amt.	Skill Level	$	Wt.
SMALL KNIFE	cut 1d-5	17	30	½
	imp 1d-4			
DAGGER	imp 1d-4	17	20	¼
LOCKPICKS			30	–
CLOTHES (low-class)			10	1
SHOES			40	2
LEATHER JACKET			50	4
RING			20	–
SILVER $			10	–

Totals: $ 200   Lbs. 7¾

When Dai gets some more money, he's likely to buy a shortsword – since he knows how to use it, and since it's a far more effective weapon than a knife. But even a *poor-quality* shortsword costs $160, and a good one would be $400. He would also benefit greatly from some sort of light armor, if he expects to get into any combats more serious than the occasional tavern brawl. But for skulking and thievery, his leather jacket is about right.

The total weight of Dai's gear is 7¾ lbs. Even with his low ST, he can carry anything less than 16 pounds at "no encumbrance" – so he's fine. He can still pick up some loot without slowing down!

Your *GURPS* character is almost finished. At this point, you should have filled in most of your Character Sheet, and checked your math to be sure that everything balances. The Character Sheet for Dai Blackthorn is on p. 214. If you go back and check it against the description of Dai's character as we developed it (pp. 14, 15, 18, 25, 40, 41, 70 and 77), you'll see that everything matches. Dai Blackthorn is a balanced 100-point character.

Starting at the top of the character sheet and working down:

Name. You ought to know this by now.

Player. That's the *real* you.

Appearance. List race (if not human), age (your decision), height and weight (set by you, or left to the dice – see p. 15), and anything else interesting about the way you look.

Character Story. A two-line version of your background and history.

Date Created. This is in the calendar of your *game world.* Your character's birthday, time use sheets, etc., all refer back to this "birth date."

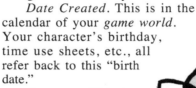

Sequence. This is explained in the sidebar, p. 95. Skip it for now.

Unspent Points. This will be used to record character points earned in play. When you spend them, erase them here and increase *Point Total.*

Point Total. Dai is a 100-point character.

ST. Your strength. The space to the side lets you mark off fatigue. If you are playing a magic-user, fatigue will come and go often, and you should keep track of it on a separate piece of paper.

DX. Your dexterity. The space is big enough to let you show an "effective" DX, if something happens to change your dexterity temporarily.

IQ. Your intelligence.

HT. Your health. The space to the side lets you mark off hits taken. However, if you are playing a game with a lot of combat, keep track of hits on a separate piece of paper.

Basic Damage. This is based on your ST; it's the amount of damage you do with a "generic" weapon – see p. 74. With ST 8, Dai does a puny 1d-3 thrusting, or 1d-2 swinging.

Movement. Compute *Basic Speed* as follows: add your HT and DX, and divide the total by 4. Your *Move* score is the speed at which you actually travel; figure your encumbrance (below and p. 76) to get your *Move.* Dai's Speed is (12+15), divided by 4 . . . 2⁷/₄, or 6.75.

Encumbrance. This is the weight you are carrying, compared to ST (see p. 76). Dai has a ST of 8, so he can carry 16 pounds of gear and will have "no encumbrance." Dai's meager possessions have a total weight of only 7 ³/₄ lbs. – so he is certainly unencumbered. With no encumbrance, his Move score is the same as his Basic Speed, rounded down – a 6.

Passive Defense. The first blank is for armor. All Dai has is his leather jacket – torso armor with a passive defense of 1. He has no shield, and no magical or special protection. So his total passive defense is a 1, filled in the last blank. Not good, but a lot better than nothing.

Active Defenses. These are explained on p. 98. For "Dodge," Dai has the same as his *Move* score – a 6.

The "Parry" box is usually filled in with half your *best* weapon score, rounded down. Dai is most skillful with his knife (skill of 17), so his "parry" is 8. However, knives are short weapons and parry at a -1 penalty, so his parry is 7. If Dai gets a short-sword, his skill of 16 will give him a shortsword parry of 8.

The "Block" box is filled in with half your Shield skill. This is not too important for Dai – he has no shield, so he cannot block. And he has not studied the Shield skill. His default skill is DX-4, or 11. Half of this, rounded down, is 5, so he has a Block of 5. Should he snatch up a shield, he can try to use it.

Damage Resistance. Your resistance to injury. Dai's leather jacket "armor" gives him a DR of 1. He has no Toughness, magic or other special protections, so that is also his total Damage Resistance. He'd better avoid being hit!

Advantages, Disadvantages and Quirks. Here we fill in Dai's four advantages and three disadvantages. Extra lines are provided, to allow for explanations. Finally, we list the five "quirks" we chose to flesh out Dai's personality.

Reaction +/-. This is in the second column, under your picture. It is based on the values from appearance, as well as any advantages or disadvantages which affect others' reactions to you. The value for Dai is zero; there is nothing about him that makes him especially likeable, or especially obnoxious either. A character with good Charisma (for instance) would have a positive number here; someone with an Odious Personal Habit, bad Physical Appearance or some other problem would have a minus. If you have both positive and negative modifiers to reaction, fill in the net total. Two lines are given in case a note is needed.

Weapons and Possessions. Each line represents one item that you carry with you, with the following information:

(a) *for a weapon only*, the total *damage* you do with it, based on your ST – see p. 74 to compute this. Dai's knife has both "cutting" and "impaling" damage – it does (1d-5) basic damage when it cuts, and (1d-4) when it impales.

(b) *for a weapon only,* your skill level with that weapon.

(c) and (d) the item's *cost* and its *weight*.

Money. Use the bottom line of the "Possessions" box for the money you have on your person, and the back of the sheet for any "bank account" or hidden wealth you might possess. To avoid frequent writing and erasing, you may want to use a sheet of scratch paper to keep track of money earned and spent during an adventure, and fill in this blank only at an adventure's end.

Weapon Ranges. This area is used for thrown- and missile-weapon ranges. Fill it in as described on p. 75. Dai's knife and dagger can both be thrown. Their ranged-weapon stats are copied from the *Weapon Table* (p. 207). They do the same damage when thrown as they do normally.

Skills. Here you fill in all your skills, points spent on each and their final levels. Languages and spells also go here. If you run out of space (and you may), continue the list on an added sheet of paper.

Summary. This box is used to record the point totals from the various sections, for an easy double-check. You'll want to update the summary any time the point totals change.

That completes Dai Blackthorn's character sheet. When you play Dai – and you can, with the adventure in this set – you will be able to find anything you need to know about him, just by referring to this sheet.

Dai Blackthorn's Story

Dai knows nothing about his birth or early childhood. His first memories are of the streets; he was a slum kid in the metropolis of Kotat (where he still lives). He remembers no parents; like the other street kids, he lived on what he could beg or steal.

When he was about seven, he was taken in by an old man named Sekelshen Mat. Old Sekky was a fagin; he taught children to steal, and lived off the loot they brought home. Dai was lucky, in that Old Sekky was a kind master and an honest thief, well-thought-of in the neighborhood. Dai became fairly good at picking locks and pockets, and an accomplished "second-story man." He loved to climb buildings – on the job or just for fun. Because he was bright, agile and inconspicuous, Sekky used Dai mostly as a messenger and spy. By the time he was 15, Dai knew the city like the back of his hand . . . its roofs as well as its alleyways.

That saved his life. One night, Dai awoke to find the house in flames. When he and his "family" tried to escape, crossbow bolts flew from the darkness. Someone *meant* for them to burn! As the flames rose higher, Dai took refuge on the building's roof – then, with a terrified leap, he made it to an adjoining building, and vanished from sight. He was the only survivor. The old thief who had been father and mother to him, as well as all his "brothers," died in the flames.

Dai soon learned who was responsible. An ambitious young ruffian had taken over the lazy Thieves' Guild of Kotat, and given the "independents" like Sekelshen Mat just two choices: join or die. Old Sekky, crotchety to the last, hadn't taken the threat seriously. It was his last mistake.

Dai swore revenge on the killers – and, over the next couple of years, managed to become a minor thorn in the Guild's side. But only a very minor thorn. To his great pride, there is now a price on his head. To his chagrin, it is only 50 copper farthings . . .

Continued on next page . . .

Dai had a close call last year, when three bravoes from the Guild caught him in an alleyway and beat him up. They finished by binding his arms behind him, tying his feet to an anvil, and dropping him off the dock. The limber Dai managed to work free and escape before he drowned – but the experience left him uncomfortable around any body of water bigger than a horse-trough.

Dai is now 18 years old. He is small and not strong – and sensitive about both these things. But he is quick, wiry and fairly good with weapons. He loves to boast of his exploits, and tends to embroider the truth a little.

He lives by himself in a third-story garret in the worst part of town, rented for a few pieces of silver from a drunken old couple who sell carpets down below. He makes his living by stealing (and occasionally does an almost-honest day's work, acting as messenger or go-between). He takes chances, but he has so far managed to stay alive – and that's all. Though he refuses to touch drugs or alcohol (he has seen too many people kill themselves that way), he manages to waste his money almost as soon as he steals it. He wants to be rich, famous and feared – and he wants revenge on the Thieves' Guild – but he also wants to have a good time, and that often takes priority over any grandiose plans he might have.

THE CHARACTER ILLUSTRATION

In the center of the sheet on p. 214, we have illustrated Dai, as we see him. If you're not an artist, you can trace the outline one of the character illustrations and customize it to suit yourself.

The illustration is by no means necessary. If you don't care for it, just use this area for extra notes.

THINGS NOT SHOWN ON THE CHARACTER SHEET

There are several things that you *may* want to keep track of on a separate sheet, for one reason or another. These include:

Time Spent in Studies. This will be shown on your weekly Time Use Sheets (if your campaign uses them). But you may want to make up a separate tally sheet so you know exactly how much time you have spent studying.

Possessions in Other Places. The "Possessions and Equipment" box shows those items you have on your person. For a wanderer, that may be everything he owns. But if you are (for example) a medieval duke, or a rich 20th-century super, you will have a home, stored wealth and many other possessions that you cannot carry with you. These should be recorded separately.

Character Story. You may want to keep notes of the things that happen to you, to develop your character – see below.

You may also want to keep a separate piece of scratch paper for money, wounds and expendable possessions, since these can change rapidly. That way, you won't wear a hole in your record sheet by constant writing and erasing.

CHARACTER STORIES

A "character story" is the life history of a game character, as written by the person who plays that character. The story is a great aid to roleplaying. You may even want to write the story first (or at least write some of it), and *then* work out your character's actual statistics.

A story can really help bring your character to life. You don't *have* to do it – but it's recommended.

If you write the story down, you should show it to the GM, but not necessarily to the other players. After all, your character probably has *some* secrets, even from his friends.

As your character adventures and gains experience, his "story" will get longer and more detailed. Not only will you have the adventures themselves to remember . . . the more you play a character, the more you will work out about his background, past history, etc.

In time, the combined stories of all your characters will make quite a tale – a fantasy epic, war story, spy novel, Western or some other sort of home-grown masterpiece – depending on your game world.

JOBS

Characters can, and probably should, get jobs. This lets them earn money and practice their skills; it also keeps them busy between adventures.

The jobs open to your character will be limited by his game world, his basic attributes and his skills. In certain cases, your job will be determined by your patron. Everything else being equal, more accomplished characters will be able to get better jobs and earn more money.

Jobs also provide a convenient starting point for adventures. Newspaper reporters, mercenaries, detectives, wizards' apprentices and freelance writers are especially adventure-prone.

This subject is covered in more detail on p. 192, and in the *Jobs* section of each game world book.

10 CHARACTER DEVELOPMENT

The longer (and the more skillfully) you play your character, the better that character will become. This can happen in two ways: through study, and through "character points" that you earn during play.

IMPROVEMENT THROUGH ADVENTURE

After a successful play session, the GM will award you "bonus" character points (see p. 184). These are the same kind of points that you used when you first created your character. Note them in the top right corner of your Character Sheet until you spend them. They are spent the same way, with a few differences:

Basic Attributes

To improve one of your basic attributes (ST, DX, IQ or HT), you must spend character points equal to *twice* the beginning point-cost difference between the old score and the new one. *Example:* To go from ST 10 (beginning cost 0) to ST 11 (beginning cost 10) would cost 20 points. To go from ST 11 to ST 12 (beginning cost 20) would cost another 20 points. And so on.

If you improve an attribute, all skills based on that attribute also go up one level. For instance, if you raise your DX, all your DX-based skills go up one!

Changes in ST do not affect height and weight once a character has been created (except for a child!). Height and weight are based on *original* strength.

Physical Appearance

To improve your physical appearance, you must (a) earn and spend the character points for the upgrade and (b) find a reasonable way – in the game world – to improve your appearance. *Example:* Maureen O'Shea, a 20th-century adventuress, is attractive – but she wants to be very beautiful. The difference, in terms of beginning point cost, is 20 points. Maureen must spend the 20 points – and pay the 20th-century "cost" for such an improvement. In this case, the player does a little research and presents it to the GM. The GM then rules that Maureen must spend $40,000 for extensive plastic surgery, two months recuperating and another two months improving her figure in a spa. At the end of four months, game-time, she can re-enter play – as a *knockout*.

Adding Advantages

Most of the advantages listed are inborn, and cannot be "bought" later with experience. Common exceptions are Literacy and Combat Reflexes (which can be learned); Acute Hearing, Taste/Smell and Vision (which, in certain game worlds, can be bought at a high cash price); and Patrons (which can always be acquired). To add an advantage, you must pay the appropriate amount of character points, plus the appropriate game world cost (determined by the GM) if a physical ability is being added.

Although advantages should not be freely added, the GM can make an exception whenever it seems reasonable. The GM should provide a good rationale in his game world or challenge the player to come up with a good explanation why he should be allowed (for instance) to suddenly have better hearing.

If your campaign includes psi abilities (Chapter 20), these may be improved like skills and new ones may sometimes be acquired during play.

Unspent Points

You may keep your earned character points for as long as you like before "spending" them. Ignore these unspent points when evaluating your character. Suppose your character began at 100 points and earned 30 points, but hasn't spent the extra yet. He's still a 100-point character – it is fair for him to go on adventures designed for 100-pointers.

Now, suppose this character spends all 30 of his points on improving his attributes. This buys him only 15 points' worth of improvements (because attributes count double if bought later). So he's now a 115-point character, and should be shown that way on his Character Sheet.

But if he spends those points on skills, he gets a full 30 points' worth of skills. So he is now a 130-point character.

Disadvantages Gained During Play

It is possible to gain a new disadvantage during play. A crippling injury, for instance, might cost you a limb; this disadvantage must be recorded on your Character Sheet.

However, you do *not* get any extra points for a disadvantage gained during play. That's just the breaks of the game! Instead, the disadvantage reduces the total "value" of your character.

One exception to the no-new-disabilities rule: If you acquire a new Patron, you can have a Duty to him or it – and the point value of the Duty can be used to reduce the point cost of the Patron.

As the GM, you may also allow a character to "buy off" a disadvantage acquired during play. If he can come up with enough character points to buy it off, and you are feeling merciful, you may arrange events to eliminate the disadvantage. It's your option.

Improvement Through Study

You may also gain skills, and improve those you already have, by spending time studying them. Anyone can gain or improve skills this way, as long as an opportunity for study is available.

This improvement does *not* depend on the actual play of the character. It would be possible to design a character, keep track of his age, and let him work, study and learn for 40 game-years *without ever bringing him into play.* (It might not be much fun, but it *would* be possible.) Of course, things that happen during play can offer great opportunities for study. If you befriend a master wizard, his gratitude may take the form of some training in magic. And if you're shipwrecked with a Frenchman for six months, you might as well learn some French – it could come in handy someday.

To improve skills by study, a player must fill out a weekly Time Use Sheet (see the *Instant Characters* booklet). With or without a teacher, you must allot time for study. Mark this time on your character's Time Use Sheet. When you have spent enough time to increase your skill, tell your GM and change your character sheet. This is too much bookkeeping for some campaigns. If you don't enjoy this, *don't do it.* Instead, the GM may slightly increase the number of "earned character points" he gives on each adventure, and let those points be used to "buy" skill increases, as described above. Then it will not be necessary to keep track of study time.

Normally, 200 hours of study are worth one character point for that skill. Under certain conditions (military basic training, slave-training, high-tech hypno-study, etc.), GMs may permit faster learning, but make it rare and either painful or expensive!

Finding a Teacher

In order to study a new skill, you must (usually) find a teacher. For some skills, finding a teacher will be automatic; for others, it will be difficult. GMs should follow the guidelines on the *Skill List*, modifying freely to suit their own concept of what is "reasonable." If the players want to study something really outlandish (magic in a non-magical world, ninja murder methods, mating habits of the Great Blue Whale, etc.), the GM should make an adventure out of the search for a teacher!

Education may also cost money. This is left up to the GM. In general, make a reaction roll to see how the teacher feels about the student. Then, if the teacher wants to be paid, use the *Job Table* (see p. 194) to determine what the teacher's time is worth, and go from there. Barter may be possible . . . or the teacher may demand a service (in advance) in exchange for his aid. There are endless adventure possibilities here.

Continued on next page . . .

Buying Off Disadvantages

No character may get extra points by adding disadvantages after he or she is created. Any disadvantage that occurs during play (accidental maiming, for instance) is worth no points – it's just part of the game.

However, characters may *get rid* of most beginning disadvantages by "buying them off" with character points equal to the bonus originally earned when the disadvantage was taken. For most disadvantages, no other payment is necessary. Some specific cases and exceptions:

Poverty and *Social Stigma* cannot be "bought off" with points alone. To cure poverty, you must earn money! To cure social stigma, you must either change your position in society or change your society. The GM will tell you when you have succeeded – at that time, you must pay enough points to buy off the original disadvantage.

Enemies may be bought off by paying the appropriate point cost. The GM should require you to deal with them in the game world, as well: kill them, jail them, bribe them, flee from them, make friends with them . . . whatever works. Note that enemies can *never* be permanently disposed of unless the point cost is bought off . . . they will return or new enemies will appear in their place.

Dependents can be bought off at their original point value. The player (or GM) should provide a game world explanation of where they went: died, grew up, moved away, fell in love with someone else . . .

Odious Personal Habits and *mental problems* may be bought off at their original bonus value. It is simply assumed that you got over your problem.

Physical disadvantages may, in general, be bought off – but the degree of game world difficulty varies. A 20th-century character could buy a hearing aid that would solve his problem while it was worn. In the 21st century, he could have an operation to fix the problem permanently. In the 19th century, the best he could do would be an ear trumpet. Earlier, he would need magic!

It is up to the GM to determine whether curing a specific physical disadvantage is possible in any given game world . . . and, if so, what the cost and time will be. For guidance, refer to the *Medical Skills* listing, and the *Medical* section, in the description of your game world. If a buy-off is possible, the point cost will be equal to the bonus originally gained from the disadvantage.

Youth cannot be bought off until you age naturally; then it *must* be bought off. *Age* cannot be bought off unless the character uses magic or medical technology to halt or reverse aging. Note that a character who started at age 50 or younger, and aged naturally to 70, can set his age back without paying *any* character points. This is because he did not take the years past 50 as disadvantages; he lived through them naturally. However, if you start as an "old" character (over 50) and reverse your age past the age at which you started, you must "buy off" the points you got for those extra years, to keep everything fair.

Adding and Improving Skills

Earned character points can be used to increase your skills or add new ones. Each character point is the equivalent of 200 hours of education.

This is not to say that your character found time to hit the books for a semester in the midst of his adventures. Rather, it assumes that the genuine experience of an adventure can be equivalent to a much longer period of study.

Therefore, earned character points can *only* be spent to improve those skills that, in the GM's opinion, were *significantly* used in the adventure in which those character points were earned. If the only thing you do on the adventure is trek through forests and slay monsters, the only skills you can improve are Forest Survival and your combat abilities. If you used *any* spells, the GM may allow you to put your points into *new* spells if he feels they are reasonably related; the same holds for psi abilities.

When you improve a skill, the cost is the *difference* between your current skill level and the cost of the new skill level. Example: You have a DX of 10 and a Shortsword skill of 13. This is DX+3 level, which, from the table on p. 43, costs 16 points for a Physical/Average skill. The next level of skill, DX+4, costs 24 points. The difference between 16 and 24 is 8, so it will cost you 8 points to raise your Shortsword skill to a level of 14.

Money

You may also trade your earned character points for money. Each point is worth one month's income at your current rate, whatever that is (see *Jobs*, p. 192). The GM should provide a reasonable explanation for your windfall: tax refund, buried treasure, inheritance, gambling winnings or whatever seems appropriate. Be creative. If a character is a spy, and his cover is "professional tennis player," you could tell him that he earned the money by making a commercial for cornflakes.

AGE AND AGING

Heroes, just like other people, eventually grow old . . . though they are less likely to die in bed.

A character is assumed to be 18 years old when created, unless the player specified otherwise. Youth is a slight "disadvantage" – see p. 29. Age is not a "disadvantage" unless the character is over 50 when created – see p. 27. A character who is older than 18 when he is created can put more character points into skills, because he has had longer to learn. (He does not get any *bonus* points unless he is over 50 – he is just allowed to spend more on education. See *Choosing Your Beginning Skills*, p. 43.)

Decline Due to Age

Beginning on his or her 50th birthday, each character must roll yearly to see if old age is taking its toll. If you do not wish to keep track of a character's exact birthday, just assume it as January 1, and roll every game-year as needed. Starting at age 70, roll every 6 months. Starting at age 90, roll every 3 months!

Roll 3 dice vs. Health for each of the four basic attributes; add your world's medical tech level (see p. 186), *minus 3*, to your HT for the purpose of this roll. Thus, in a medieval (TL4) world, a person with HT 10 needs an 11 or less to succeed. A failed roll means that the attribute in question is reduced by one point – and a roll of 17 or 18 *automatically* fails and causes the loss of *two* points. Roll in the following order: ST, DX, IQ, HT.

Obviously, if the last roll is failed, HT itself goes down by one . . . and the next "old age" roll is more likely to fail. Thus, the decline accelerates. When an attribute is reduced by age (or by anything else, for that matter), all skills involving that attribute are also reduced. Thus, if aging reduces your IQ by 1, all your mental skills are lowered by 1. If any attribute reaches 0 from aging, the character dies a natural death. In a "real life" situation, a person would be carried away by a "minor" disease or accident long before HT reached zero, and this would still be considered as natural death.

Certain magical and technological processes can halt aging, or even "set the clock back" to make a character younger. These devices, potions, etc., are extremely valuable, and will be described in specific game world books. If lost IQ (for instance) is restored, lost skill levels in mental skills are also restored.

The timetable above is for humans. Aging for other races is described in the appropriate game world books.

Improvement Through Study (Continued)

Self-Teaching

Most skills can be self-taught under the proper circumstances. If a skill can*not* be self-taught, this will be indicated in the skill description. In any case, double the training time for a self-taught skill. A good teacher – one who can guide your studies and answer your questions – is tremendously valuable in any field of learning.

Jobs

If you have a job, that counts as "study" of the skill (if any) used in the job. However, since most of the time on the job is spent doing what you *already* know, rather than learning new things, time on the job counts only ¼ for learning. If you put in a 40-hour week, you can count it as 10 hours of training in the work you're doing. That works out to 500 hours of training in a year. If a job requires more than one skill, you can split the training time between them as you like.

School

On the other hand, if you go to school, you might spend three to six hours a week in each class, plus another three to six in homework – say an average of nine hours per week. A semester is 21 weeks – so a semester of classroom study equals around 200 hours per subject.

Adventuring Time

Adventuring time can also count as "study" of the appropriate things; GMs should be *generous* in allowing this. For example, a trek through the Amazon would count for every waking moment – say 16 hours a day – as study of Jungle Survival.

You may study any number of skills at one time, but each hour of time only counts toward study of one subject unless the GM allows an exception. Language study is a good example of an exception: If you already speak French well, going to school in Paris would count both for improving your command of the language and for study of the classroom subject. As a rule, time spent in a foreign country, speaking the native language, counts as four hours per day of language study no matter what else you are doing, until your skill with the language is equal to your IQ level.

Skin, Hair and Eyes

You may give your character any coloring you like, as long as it is appropriate to his or her background. If a random character is being rolled up, the following table may be useful. Roll 3 dice three times – one roll for skin, one for hair and one for eyes. Discard any result (or combination of results) inappropriate to the adventure being played. A light-haired Oriental, for instance, would be quite possible in San Francisco in 1930, but most unlikely in Peking in 1870. If you are playing in a far-future game world, you may wish to add some even more exotic possibilities to the table.

Die Roll	Skin Color
3	Blue-black
4-6	Black
7	White with freckles
8	White, tanned
9-10	White
11-12	Brown
13-15	Light golden (Oriental)
16	Golden
17-18	Red-bronze

Die Roll	Hair Color
3	Blue-black
4-5	Black
6	Blond
7	Bald (males only)
8	Red-brown
9	Light brown
10-11	Brown
12-13	Dark brown
14	Gray
15	Strawberry blond
16	Bright red/orange
17	Golden blond
18	Pure white

Die Roll	Eye Color
3	Purple
4	Black
5	Ice-blue
6	Gray
7-8	Blue
9-11	Brown
12	Hazel
13	Green
14	Dark blue
15-16	Dark green
17	Golden
18	Different colors! Roll again for each.

This system lets you create a character just by rolling dice. It can be used when the GM needs a non-player character in a hurry, or when you want to play without taking time to create detailed characters. The *average* character will be about 100 points – but there will be lots of variation! This can be fun, especially if you like to "take what the dice give you" and then roleplay that character faithfully. It is likely to give you at least one attribute far lower than anything you would choose on your own!

Basic Attributes

Roll 3 dice for each of the four basic attributes – ST, DX, IQ and HT. If you wish, you may discard any *one* of the four rolls and try again – but you must keep the new roll, whatever it is!

Completing Your Character

After rolling up basic attributes, you have two choices. If you want a completely random character, skip down to *Physical Appearance*. Determine advantages, disadvantages and skills randomly, as described.

Alternatively, you can keep your randomly-rolled attributes and take an additional 50 points (assuming your campaign uses 100-point characters) to finish him any way you want, choosing advantages, disadvantages and skills for yourself. Do *not* take 50 points *and* roll random skills, etc. – you'll get a superman.

Physical Appearance

All characters have average appearance unless they roll good or bad looks as an advantage or disadvantage (below). Height and weight are determined as per p. 15. Skin, hair and eye color are determined by the table in the sidebar.

advantages and disadvantages

Roll three dice and consult the table below to find your advantage (usually one per character). Then roll again for a disadvantage.

Die Roll	Advantage(s)	Disadvantage(s)
3	Roll twice more	Roll twice more
4	Voice	Poor
5	Charisma (+6)	Cowardly
6	Alertness (+4)	Odious Personal
7	Common Sense	Habit: -2 reaction
8	Magical Aptitude (+2)	Bad Temper
9	Acute Vision (+5)	Unlucky
10	Alertness (+2)	Greedy
11	Charisma (+3)	Overconfident
12	Acute Taste/Smell (+5)	Honest
13	Danger Sense	Hard of Hearing
14	Attractive Appearance	Unattractive Appearance
15	Acute Hearing (+5)	Bad Sight
16	Handsome/Beautiful	Hideous Appearance
17	Roll twice more	Roll twice more
18	Roll twice more	Roll twice more

Ignore any roll, and roll again, if:
(a) you roll the same advantage or disadvantage twice;
(b) you roll two kinds of personal Appearance (only the first one counts);
(c) you roll a disadvantage that conflicts with an advantage you already have (e.g., Bad Sight after you have Acute Vision);
(d) you roll an advantage or disadvantage that is meaningless in your game world (e.g., Magical Aptitude in a game world without magic).

Not all the advantages and disadvantages are found on this table – just the more common ones. If you want a more exotic advantage or disadvantage, ask the GM for permission to choose it – or create your character without the random die rolls.

Skills

To determine the *number* of skills a character has studied, roll 2 dice. Give the character that many logically-chosen skills. If you want to chance some illogical skills, use the table below (roll 3 dice and pick one skill from the indicated row):

randomly chosen skills

(roll three dice and pick one skill from the indicated row)

3	Calligraphy	Armoury	Biochemistry
4	Botany	Merchant	Sleight of Hand
5	Diplomacy	Physician	Sports (any)
6	Singing	Language (any)	Veterinary
7	Animal Handling	Bard	Acting
8	Stealth	Scrounging	First Aid
9	Hand Weapon (any)	Fast-Draw (any)	Climbing
10	Hand Weapon (any)	Traps	Shield
11	Running*	Brawling	Driving or Riding (any)
12	Missile Weapon (any)	Pilot or Gunner (any)	Swimming
13	Carousing	Law	Savoir-Faire
14	Gambling	Streetwise	Politics
15	Musical Instrument (any)	Survival (any)	Lockpicking
16	Forgery	Disguise	Mechanic
17	either Judo *or* Karate	Naturalist	Sex Appeal
18	History	Navigation	Poisons

If you roll a ridiculous result, or one inappropriate to your game world, discard it and roll again. If you roll a result that says (any), pick any appropriate skill from that category.

* If you roll this skill, you have it at just high enough a level to raise your Move score by 1.

Skill Levels

Now that you know *what* skills you have, you need to determine the *level* of skill you have in each one. Roll 1d-3 for each skill, and add the result to your controlling attribute for that skill (IQ for mental skills, DX for most physical ones). That's your skill level. *Example:* You get a weapon skill. Weapons are DX-based. Your DX is 12, and you roll a 5. (5-3) is 2, so add a 2 to your DX of 12, and your final skill level is 14.

Note that this 1d-3 roll for added skill levels can never be below zero. If you roll a 3 or less, you simply add nothing – your skill level is the same as your IQ or DX.

Instant NPCs

Sometimes the GM will need a character *immediately*. Rather than stop to roll one up randomly, it may be better to determine only the things that are actually needed for play.

Let's suppose that Dai Blackthorn is finishing a midnight visit to the Duke's palace (without the Duke's knowledge). He climbs the garden wall to leave . . . and he absolutely *blows* his Climbing roll! You, as the GM, decide that he fell and made a lot of noise – so a guard will come to investigate.

Unfortunately, you don't have any guards made up and ready. (Careless of you . . .) No matter. All you really *need* to know are the guard's four basic attributes and his Shortsword skill. You can roll them up – or you can just assign him reasonable numbers (say, ST and DX 12, HT 11 and IQ 9, with a Shortsword skill of 17). Decide what armor the guard is wearing, and go!

Likewise, armor and equipment are simply "issued" to the NPC according to the GM's logic and his rationale for having the character there in the first place. If a question arises, after the fact, as to whether some NPC possessed a specific item, the GM can handle this two ways:

(a) A random roll. The GM decides what the odds are, rolls the dice and goes from there.

(b) Fiat. If, from the GM's viewpoint, there is only one "right" answer to make the game run smoothly, then that's the answer. "Of course the guard had a knife. Take it and run!"

When you are the GM, you can generate an NPC *any way you want*. Some people prefer to leave everything to chance; others prefer "logic." It's up to you.

Critical Success and Failure

A *critical success* is an especially good result on a skill roll. You score a critical success as follows:

A roll of 3 or 4 is always a critical success.

A roll of 5 is a critical success if your effective skill is 15+.

A roll of 6 is a critical success if your effective skill is 16+.

In general, when you roll a critical success, the GM determines what happens to you. It is always something good; the better the roll, the better "bonus" he gives you. Even if you do not score a critical success, the GM may give you some extra bonus if you roll well under the required number.

A *critical hit* is a critical success scored on an attack. The GM does not determine the result. Instead, use the *Critical Hit Table* (p. 202).

A *critical failure* is an especially *bad* result on a skill roll. You score a critical failure as follows:

A roll of 18 is always a critical failure.

A roll of 17 is an ordinary failure if your effective skill is 16 or better, and a critical failure if your effective skill is under 16.

Any roll of 10 greater than your effective skill is a critical failure. That is, 16 on a skill of 6, 15 on a skill of 5, and so on.

In general, when you roll a critical failure, the GM determines what happens to you. It is always something bad; the worse the roll, the worse the result. Even if you do not roll a critical failure, the GM may penalize you if you roll well over the required number. Note also that for some things (e.g., defusing a bomb), it can be just as deadly to fail by 1 as to fail by 10!

A *critical miss* is a critical failure scored on an attack. The GM does not determine the result. Instead, use the *Critical Miss Table* (p. 202).

These rules may vary slightly for specific situations. For instance, on an IQ roll to avoid the effect of a phobia or other mental disadvantage, a roll of 14 or over is an automatic failure – see p. 30.

When your character attempts to use a skill, perform an action, attack a foe, etc., 3 dice are rolled to determine whether you succeed. This is a *success roll*. Sometimes you roll; sometimes the GM rolls for you (see sidebar, p. 87).

For your character to succeed in his attempt, the total rolled on the dice must be *less than or equal to* the skill or attribute you are using. For instance, if you are attempting to pick a lock, and your Lockpicking skill is 9, you must roll a 9 or less on 3 dice.

In many cases, special rules will provide modifiers for the type of action being attempted. For instance, the description of the Lockpicking skill states that a character working in the dark has a "-5" to succeed. This means that 5 must be *subtracted from his skill* for that attempt. 9 minus 5 is 4; thus, in the dark, a character with a Lockpicking skill of 9 must roll a 4 or less to succeed . . . not impossible on 3 dice, but very difficult.

Furthermore, a specific scenario may provide modifiers to allow for the relative ease or difficulty of a specific situation. For instance, let us assume that a certain lock is primitive and clumsy. The scenario states (or the GM has previously determined) that this lock is +10 to open because it is so primitive. 9 plus 10 is 19; thus, your character with the Lockpicking skill of 9 would need to roll 19 or less on 3 dice. Since the highest roll possible on 3 dice is 18, it would seem that success is assured. This is almost true, but not quite – see *Critical Failure* in the sidebar.

All modifications are cumulative. Suppose that you are attempting to open that primitive lock . . . in the dark. Both modifiers apply, 9 minus 5 is 4 – plus 10 is 14 – so you need a 14 or less to succeed.

Your *basic* skill is your actual level in that skill. Your *effective* skill is your basic skill plus or minus any appropriate modifiers. In the example above, your effective skill is 14. You may not attempt to roll if your effective skill is less than 3, unless you are attempting a *defense roll* (p. 98).

Default Rolls

Some actions *cannot* be attempted except by a character with the necessary skill. Ventriloquism, nuclear physics and magic are examples.

However, other things can be attempted even by someone who is totally untrained. Only a warrior can use a broadsword skillfully – but *anyone* can pick it up and swing it. Swimming, interrogation and gesture communication are examples of actions that can be attempted, with a reasonable chance of success, by an untrained individual.

An action that can be attempted by someone without that special skill is said to "default" to another skill, or to one of the character's basic attributes. For example, default Lockpicking skill is based on intelligence. The smarter you are, the better your chances of opening a lock, even without training. Similarly, default Riding skill is based on DX. If you have no training in riding, your instincts will help you stay astride – and the better coordinated you are, the likelier you are to suceed. The description of each skill shows what other skill(s) or attribute(s) it defaults to.

But it is always better to have training! When a skill defaults to another skill or attribute, there will be a minus number shown. For example, Lockpicking defaults to "IQ-5." That means that your IQ, minus 5, is your "default" Lockpicking skill. If you have an IQ of 10, you can open an ordinary lock on a roll of 5 or less on 3 dice, *without training*.

In many cases, a skill will default to two (or more) different skills or attributes. You can pick whichever one you want to default to (and you should choose the best). For instance, Climbing defaults to "ST-5" *and* "DX-5." In other words, if you're not a trained climber, either ST or DX can help you. You should default to the better of the two. If you have ST 16 and DX 8, use your strength to climb; 16-5 is 11, which gives you a reasonable chance on 3 dice.

A "default" roll is made just like an ordinary success roll. Refer to the *Skill List* for possible default skills or attributes. Pick the best one for your character, add or subtract any modifiers for the situation and roll 3 dice. Good luck.

But remember . . . some skills have no defaults listed. If you don't have training in that specific skill, you can't attempt it at all. No matter how clever or dextrous you are, you can't throw your voice, build an A-bomb or speak Ancient Egyptian without training.

Note also that if you have a superhuman basic attribute, it is treated as 20 for default purposes. *Example:* Super-Fist has a DX of 25. His default Swimming skill (DX-4) is 16, not 21.

Automatic Success

Some things are totally trivial. No roll is required when common sense says that both failure and critical success are impossible. However, if there is any chance of failure, a roll is required. Finding your corner store requires no roll. Hitting a target at point-blank range, even for an experienced warrior, does, since his weapon might break or he might slip on an unexpected banana peel.

CONTESTS OF SKILLS

Sometimes a situation will come up in which two characters will need to compare their relative skills to settle a battle or competition. The one with the highest skill does not always win . . . but that's the way to bet. As the GM, you will often find that a Contest of Skill is a quick way to resolve a competitive situation without playing it out in detail. Set the rules of the specific contest as you see fit – and let the characters roll!

When a Contest of Skill is called for, both characters make their success rolls in the appropriate skill. Any appropriate modifiers are used.

There are two types of contest. A *quick contest* is usually over in one turn. *Examples:* two people grabbing for the same weapon; two knifethrowers seeing who gets closer to the bullseye. Each character makes his skill roll. If one succeeds and the other fails, the winner is obvious. If both succeed (or fail) the winner is the one who succeeded by the most, or failed by the least. A tie means nobody won (both fighters grabbed the weapon at once; the knives hit the same distance from the bullseye).

A *regular contest* may last several turns. *Examples:* arm wrestling, foot racing. Each character tries his skill roll. If one succeeds and the other fails, the winner is obvious. If both succeed or both fail, the characters' relative positions are unchanged and they may try again.

The length of *game-time* each attempt takes will depend on the activity, and is up to the GM to determine. In a combat situation, each attempt takes one second. In a library-research contest, with the fate of the world hanging on who finds a certain obscure reference first, each attempt could represent days of time.

If both characters have a very high skill, the contest could go on indefinitely. Therefore, shorten it as follows: If both skills are over 14, reduce the higher one to 14, and subtract the same amount from the lower one. *Example:* For a 19 vs. 16 contest, subtract 5 from each to make it 14 vs. 11.

Eventually, one character will make his roll and the other one will miss. At this point, the one who made his roll is the winner of the contest.

When the GM Rolls

When a character tries to do something, most success rolls will be made by the player himself. But there are two important cases in which the GM makes the roll. He does *not* let the player see what he rolls.

First is any situation in which the character shouldn't be able to tell whether he has succeeded – especially when he is trying to get information. Examples would be skills such as Detect Lies, Meteorology, Interrogation, the various scientific skills and the advantage of Empathy.

When the player says that he wants to use such a skill, the GM rolls in secret. If the roll succeeds, the GM gives the player true information. If the roll fails, the GM lies or gives no information at all – whatever seems more appropriate. The worse the failure, the worse the GM lies.

Second is any situation in which the player simply shouldn't know what's going on. This includes most Sense, Danger Sense and similar rolls. Suppose the party is walking along a jungle trail. A jaguar is on a limb ahead. The GM should *not* say, "There's a jaguar ahead of you. Roll to see if you notice it." Neither should he say, "Everybody make a Vision roll. Does anybody have Danger Sense?" Either of these approaches gives too much away.

Instead, the GM should refer to his GM Control Sheet, check the necessary information for each character and roll. If anyone makes their roll, the GM can say, "Harry! You notice a jaguar on a branch 20 yards ahead!" If nobody makes their roll . . . they're in for a surprise.

Contest of Skill Examples

Close combat (p. 111) includes a number of situations which call for contests of strength and/or dexterity. A Contest of Skill is appropriate any time two characters (especially two PCs) are striving directly against each other. The two characters will usually (but not always) roll against the same skill. Some examples:

Logrolling: DX, with a +3 bonus to the stronger contestant.

Arm-wrestling: ST.

Private argument or debate: IQ vs. IQ or Fast-Talk, Diplomacy, etc.

Shooting craps: Gambling.

Interrogation: Questioner's Interrogation skill vs. prisoner's Will.

Mental battles: Telepathy.

Public debate: Bard, modified by all normal reaction bonuses (from the audience, not the opponent).

Drinking: Carousing; -2 penalty if you are not accustomed to the type of liquor being imbibed.

Winning an election: Politics, modified by all normal reaction bonuses.

Haggling: Merchant.

Seduction: Sex Appeal vs. Will.

Marathon dance contests: ST vs. ST.

Jumping During Combat

The jumping distance formulas assume you take at least a couple of seconds to crouch and prepare for the jump. Halve the distances if you jump with no preparation.

If you jump over a small obstruction during a fight (one hex across, less than a couple of feet tall), you must use a *Move* maneuver; the jump costs one extra movement point. This is the same cost as to step *into* an obstructed hex; it takes just as long to step around a body as to jump over it. But some obstructions (a man-trap, for instance, or a pool of lava) should *not* be stepped into . . .

If you jump over a larger obstruction (a pile of bodies, a chair, etc.) or jump *onto* something during a fight (a table, for instance), it is a *Move* maneuver; you can do nothing else that turn. Unless something really extreme is being attempted, assume that any fighter can make any jump, and get on with the battle. Don't calculate ST and distance every time somebody jumps onto a chair!

However, a DX roll *is* required when you make a vertical jump or a long horizontal one (GM's discretion). If you fail the roll, you fall and you will have to take the next two turns to stand up. If you roll a 17 or 18, you fall *off* the thing you jumped onto, or land badly if you were jumping down. Take 1d-2 damage for each yard you fell.

If you don't want to risk a DX roll, but you do want to get onto that table, you can take two turns of *Move* instead of one, and "scramble" to the top. No DX roll is required.

For a long or hard jump (down into a pit, for instance), the GM should subtract from 1 to 5 from the jumper's DX and roll as above.

Jumping With Encumbrance

An optional rule, for realism: Subtract your encumbrance level from your ST when you jump. If your encumbrance level is heavy (3) and you have a ST of 13, calculate any jump as though your ST were 10.

PHYSICAL FEATS
Running

In combat, running is just a series of *Move* maneuvers. Your running speed is equal to your *Basic Speed* score, plus Running skill bonus, plus one yard per second "sprint bonus" if you are running in a straight line (see sidebar, p. 108).

But sometimes characters will have to run a *long* distance – to catch a plane, avoid a bomb blast, escape the savage pygmies or whatever. The GM need not play out every single step – he just needs to know *how long* the sprint will take. If the distance to be run is over 500 yards, your average speed will be less.

For distances of 10-500 yards, each point of Speed is good for 1 yard per second, and you can add one more yard for the "sprint bonus" if the ground is good. So, with a Speed of 7, you can run 8 yards/second. (That works out to a time of 12.5 for the 100-yard dash. The world record is about 9.0, which would indicate someone with a Speed of 10, sprinting 11 yards per second!) Do not round down your Speed when figuring long-distance speed. A Basic Speed of 5.5, if you are unencumbered, would let you run 65 yards in 10 seconds.

For distances of 500 yards and up, you will run just half as fast as indicated above. So, with a Speed of 7, you can run 4 yards/second over a long distance if the ground is good. That works out to 7 minutes 20 seconds for a full mile.

These figures assume the runners have *no encumbrance!* Divide the speeds by two for light encumbrance, by three for medium encumbrance, by four for heavy encumbrance, by five for extra-heavy encumbrance. The moral is this: If you have to run very far, drop your load first!

Exhaustion from Running: After every 100 yards of top-speed running or 200 yards of long-distance (half-speed) running, you must roll against HT. A failed roll means you take 1 point of fatigue. Keep in mind that when your ST is reduced to 3, your Speed is halved . . . and when ST reaches 1, you can no longer run!

Jumping

In most cases, when you want to jump over something, the GM should say "Okay, you jumped over it," and get on with play. In combat, jumping over an "ordinary" obstacle costs one extra movement point – that is, jumping over one hex counts as two hexes of movement. But it is automatically successful. Only if the obstacle seems really significant, or if the GM put it there as a deliberate hazard, should you resort to math to see if the character could actually make the jump! But, when you need them, the rules are as follows.

The distance you can jump is determined by your ST score (but see below). For an "ordinary" jump – no die roll required – the maximum distances are:

High jump: 3 times your ST, minus 10 inches – e.g., ST of 11 lets you jump 23" straight up. Add 2 feet to the above if you have 4 yards for a running start.

Standing broad jump: Your ST minus 3 feet – e.g., ST of 11 lets you jump 8 feet from a standing start. Remember that 1 hex equals 3 feet, or 1 yard.

Running broad jump: As above, but add 1 foot for every yard of "takeoff" distance, up to double your standing broad jump distance.

Extra effort: If the "automatic" distances above are not enough, you can always try a little bit harder. Any time you put in extra effort – whether you succeed or fail – you lose 1 point of fatigue. For a high jump, subtract the extra distance (in inches) from your ST or DX (whichever is better) and roll. For a broad jump, divide the extra distance (in inches) by 4, round up and subtract from ST or DX. For a running broad jump, divide the extra distance (in inches) by 6 and proceed as above. A successful roll means you make the jump.

Jumping skill: If you have this skill, you may *substitute* your skill level for either ST or DX in any of the height or distance formulas above. With a high level of skill, this will let you make Olympic leaps.

Climbing

To climb anything more difficult than a ladder, a Climbing roll is required. Climbing skill defaults to DX-5 or ST-5. One roll is required to start the climb, with a further roll every five minutes; a failed roll means you fall. If you are secured by a rope, you will fall only to the end of the rope unless you roll a critical failure. Modifiers to the roll depend on the difficulty of the climb – see the table below. Your encumbrance level is also subtracted from your Climbing skill; climbing while heavily laden is a dangerous matter.

Regardless of encumbrance, a normal human character can manage about three ladder-rungs per second going up, or two per second going down. Any climbing during combat movement will only last a little while, and will be inspired by rage or terror, so it will go quickly. For a *long* climb, use the speeds in the second column. Climbing during combat requires the *Move* maneuver.

climbing speed and modifiers

Type of Climb	Modifier	Short Climb	Long Climb
Ladder going up	no roll	3 rungs/sec.	1 rung/sec.
Ladder going down	no roll	2 rungs/sec.	1 rung/sec.
Ordinary tree	+5	1 ft./sec.	1 ft./3 secs.
Ordinary mountain	0	1 ft./2 secs.	10 ft./min.
Vertical stone wall	-3	1 ft./5 secs.	4 ft./min.
Modern building	-3	1 ft./10 secs.	2 ft./min.
Rope-up	-2	1 ft./sec.	20 ft./min.
Rope-down			
(w/o equipment)	-1	2 ft./sec.	30 ft./min.
(w/ equipment)	-1	12 ft./sec.	12 ft./sec.

Lifting and Moving Things

In general, the GM may let characters lift whatever they need to, without die rolls. But when very heavy weights are involved, a check against ST may be needed. The weight you can lift is governed by ST. GMs may let characters combine their STs whenever it seems reasonable – e.g., to pull a wagon.

One-Handed Lift: Maximum weight is equal to 6 times your ST, in pounds.

Two-Handed Lift: Maximum weight is equal to 25 times your ST, in pounds.

Carry on Back: Maximum weight is equal to 30 times your ST, in pounds. Thus, you can carry more than you can lift by yourself. Note that every *turn* that your encumbrance is over 20×ST (that is, "extra-heavy" encumbrance), you lose 1 *Fatigue* point – see *Fatigue,* p. 134.

Shove and Knock Over (see sidebar for details): 25 times ST, or 50 times ST with a running start.

Shift Slightly: Depending on the way the character is braced and the ground surface, 100 times ST, or more, could be shifted or rocked slightly.

Drag: On a rough surface, you can drag only about as much as you can carry. If you are dragging something on a smooth, level surface, halve its effective weight (that is, at a given encumbrance, you can drag twice as much as you can carry). Halve it again if you are dragging a sledge on snow. Remember to include the sledge's weight. Movement rate is governed by effective encumbrance.

Pull on Wheels: As for dragging, but divide effective weight by 10 for a two-wheeled cart, or by 20 for a good four-wheeled wagon. Halve effective weight again if it is being pulled on a good road.

Extra Effort: If you are not quite strong enough to lift or move something, you may make an *extra effort*. This increases the weight you can handle. Roll against ST, subtracting 1 for an extra 10% of weight, 2 for an extra 20%, and so on. For a continuing effort (e.g., pushing a stalled car), roll once per minute. Remember that a 17 or 18 always misses.

A successful roll moves the item. A failed roll means the item did not move and you strained yourself! Lose 1 ST to fatigue. A critical failure also costs you 1 HT of actual injury which cannot be cured by First Aid, but only by rest.

Shoving Things and Knocking Them Over

There will be times – especially in combat – when you will want to knock something down. For instance, you might want to block the way, inconvenience a foe, etc. In maneuver terms, this is an attack. To knock a table over, for instance, you "attack" the table.

The weight you can knock over this way – whether by kicking, body-blocking, shoving or whatever – is equal to a maximum of 25 times your ST. Players and referees should assume any reasonable attempt to be *automatic*, rather than calculating every time. For heavy objects, go ahead and calculate if there is a disagreement.

If you take a running start – that is, if you take your full movement for one turn and *then* run into something – you can knock over twice as much weight. The GM can also make allowances for precariously balanced objects, to make them easier to tilt. Use common sense. Make it fun.

When something is knocked over, place a counter (homemade, if necessary) to indicate its new location. This is especially important for a feature that was drawn on the map! Characters must then jump over it, move it again or otherwise deal with it.

Extra Effort. If you are not quite strong enough to shove something, you may make an *extra effort* as for lifting (see main text).

Note that these rules apply to *inanimate* objects. To knock over a person or creature, see *Slam Attacks,* p. 112.

Throwing Distance Table

Round the object's weight *down*, and multiply the distance given in the table by *your ST*. (If you have the Throwing skill, add ⅙ of your skill level to ST first). This gives the distance, in yards, that you can throw that object.

Weight	Distance
1 lb. or less	3.5
1.5 lbs.	3.0
2 lbs.	2.5
3 lbs.	1.9
4 lbs.	1.5
5 lbs.	1.2
7.5 lbs.	1.0
10 lbs.	.8
15 lbs.	.7
20 lbs.	.6
25 lbs.	.5
30 lbs.	.4
40 lbs.	.3
50 lbs.	.25
60 lbs.	.2
80 lbs.	.15
100 lbs.	.1
200 lbs.	.05

Very light objects, and things so oddly shaped that they are hard to throw, don't go as far as "normal" objects; the GM can allow for this if he wishes.

If something weighs more than 25 times your ST, forget the formula. You can barely carry it. You can't throw it, or even pick it up by yourself.

This table assumes that gravity is normal. In (for instance) half gravity, things weigh half as much; modify weight accordingly and use the table normally. For more detail on different gravity, see *GURPS Space*.

If you're trying to hit a specific target, there are penalties for its speed and distance. See p. 201.

Examples of Throwing Things

Suppose your ST is 12. You have a 2-pound grenade. The distance for 2 lbs. is 2.5 yards – times your ST of 12 is 30 yards. You can throw the grenade 30 yards.

Suppose your ST is 16. You have a 50-pound sack of flour. The distance for 50 lbs. is .25 yard; 16 times .25 is 4, so you can throw that sack four yards.

Suppose your ST is 14. You are holding the unconscious body of a 120-lb. companion, which you must get across a six-foot crevasse. 120 rounds down to 100, which has a distance of .1 yard. 14 times .1 is 1.4 yards – less than six feet. If you throw your friend across, he will fall in – so you had better not try! (Of course, you will not be allowed to work this out in advance. Try to guess right!)

Picking Things Up In Combat: In combat, a light item is picked up with the *Ready* maneuver, which takes one second. It takes two full seconds to pick up a heavy item (weight in pounds greater than your ST).

Throwing Things

Anything you can lift – that is, anything with a weight of 25 times your ST or less – can be thrown. To hit a target, roll against DX-3 or your Throwing skill (see p. 49). To lob something into a general area, roll against Throwing or DX. The GM should allow any reasonable attempt to throw something. Only if a precise answer is needed should he take time for formulas. But in that case . . .

The distance you can throw an object depends on its weight and your ST. Round the weight *down,* refer to the table in the sidebar and multiply the distance given by your ST. This gives the distance, in yards, that you can throw it.

If you have the Throwing skill, divide it by 6 (round down) and add the result to your ST to determine how far you can throw something. This applies only to the general Throwing skill, not to "thrown weapon" skills.

Throwing Things in Combat

Throwing an object during combat (whether as an attack or not) requires the *Step and Attack* maneuver. You must pick up the item first, as described above.

damage from thrown objects

If you are hit by a (blunt) thrown object, the damage it does depends on its *weight* and the *strength* with which it was thrown. This table does *not* take sharp edges into account; don't use it for weapons.

ST	½ to 10 lbs.	10+ to 50 lbs.	50+ to 100 lbs.	over 100 lbs.
5-6	1d-5	1d-4	1d-5	–
7-8	1d-4	1d-3	1d-3	–
9-10	1d-3	1d-2	1d-2	1d-3
11-12	1d-2	1d-1	1d-1	1d-2
13-14	1d-1	1d	1d	1d
15-16	1d	1d+1	1d+2	1d+2
17-18	1d+1	1d+2	2d-2	2d-1
19-20	1d+2	2d-2	2d-1	2d

Note that, especially at lower strength, a heavier missile does *not* necessarily do more damage, because it can't be thrown with any force.

A fragile object (or a thrown character) will *take* the same amount of damage that it *does*. Roll damage separately for the thrown object and the target.

Damage done by *falling* objects (for instance, the boulder that you rolled onto the foe) is covered under *Combat,* p. 131.

Digging

Digging rate is determined by the digger's ST, quality of his equipment, and the type of soil. In ordinary soil, with an iron-bladed shovel, a man can dig .075×ST cubic yards (cy) per hour. One man with an iron pick can break up .3×ST cy per hour, making it into loose soil, which is easier to remove. The most efficient way to dig is with one man with a pick, and two shovelers clearing behind him.

In loose soil (sand, etc.), shovel rate is .15×ST cy/hr.

Hard soil, clay, etc., *must* be broken up first by a pick, working at half speed, and then shoveled at .15×ST cy/hr. A lone man with both pick and shovel can remove .05× ST cy/hr (he loses time switching between tools).

Hard rock must be broken by a pick at 1/4 speed (or less, for very hard rock!), and removed by shovels at half-speed.

Wooden tools (common at TL5 and below) work at half-speed. Improvised shovels (bare hands, mess kits and so forth) work at 1/4 speed at best.

Digging is hard work. One hour of digging in loose dirt costs 1 Fatigue point; 2 Fatigue for ordinary soil; 3 for hard dirt; 4 for rock.

Swimming

The Swimming skill (p. 49) defaults to ST-5 or DX-4.

One Swimming roll is required when you first enter water over your head with a further roll every five minutes. If you fail a roll, you inhale water! Lose 1 point of Fatigue and try another roll in five seconds – and so on, until you (a) drown, (b) are rescued or (c) make a successful roll and get your head above water. If you successfully recover, roll again in one minute; if you succeed on this roll as well, go back to making rolls five minutes apart.

If you fall into the water, you may try to get rid of armor, etc., after making your first *successful* Swimming roll. Roll vs. DX for each item you try to remove. Shields, helmets and body armor are at -4 DX. A failed roll means you inhale water, with penalties as above. Yes, you can shout for help!

If your ST reaches 0 from drowning, you fall unconscious. You will die in four minutes (very cold water will prolong this period significantly) unless you are removed from the water *and* a successful First Aid roll is made. See the sidebar for rules on holding your breath and recovering from lack of air.

Modifiers for the Swimming roll: +3 if you entered the water intentionally; *minus* twice encumbrance level. Thus, a warrior in plate armor who makes his encumbrance Heavy has a -6 to Swimming skill. Characters with the Fat disadvantage get +5 to all Swimming rolls, and their fat encumbrance does not count agains them.

Swimming speed: If you manage to swim successfully, your Move when swimming short distances is equal to $^1/_{10}$ your Swimming skill (round down). This means that only the fastest swimmers, wholly unencumbered, will manage to swim two yards per second. Most people will have a Move of 1 when swimming. (If you can stay afloat, you can always swim at least one yard per second.)

To swim long distances, use a 10-second time scale. The number of yards you can swim in 10 seconds is equal to your Swimming skill, minus *twice* your encumbrance.

Swimming long distances costs fatigue as per Running. After every 100 yards of top-speed swimming, roll vs. HT. A failed roll costs 1 point of Fatigue. When ST is reduced to 3, your swimming speed is halved. If you are swimming *slowly,* or just staying afloat, make a HT roll every 30 minutes.

Combat in and under water: This is very tiring. Make a Swimming roll every five *seconds*. A failed roll costs 1 Fatigue. If fighting completely *underwater*, roll every *two* seconds.

Weapon use and damage are reduced by water drag. The penalty to weapon skill underwater is determined by its maximum reach. Any Close weapon (including fists) is -2 to wield. A 1-hex weapon is at -4; subtract an additional -4 for each hex of reach. Also, take a skill penalty equal to your encumbrance level.

Damage (even automatic maximum damage) is halved underwater.

If you are fighting in, but not *under,* the water, halve the above penalties to hit, and reduce damage by only 1/3 (rounding the result down).

Lifesaving

Swimming skill can be used to rescue a drowning person. Make a Swimming roll at -5, plus or minus the difference in ST between you and the person you are rescuing. A failed roll means *you* inhale water: -1 ST. A critical failure means the victim nearly drowned you: -6 ST, and you must break off the rescue attempt. This roll will be easier if the players think of good lifesaving techniques.

Digging: Some Comparative Holes

All times assume a single ST 10 man shoveling in ordinary soil, and ignore resting periods.

1.5 cy: A one-man foxhole. 3'×3'× 4$^1/_4$' deep, with the loose dirt piled in a foot-high berm in front. 2 hours.

4 cy: A grave. 6'× 3'× 6' deep. 5 hours, 20 minutes.

8 cy: A pit trap for a wild boar. 6'× 6'× 6' deep. 10 hours, 40 minutes.

55 cy: A pit trap for a tiger. 12'× 12'× 10' deep. 73 hours, 20 minutes, plus whatever time is required to camouflage it, set stakes if desired, and so on.

Holding Your Breath

These rules don't apply just to swimming. Characters in vacuum, faced with poison gas, or being strangled will also need to hold their breath. See the Breath Control skill, p. 48, for more information.

When not exerting yourself, you may hold your breath for HT×10 seconds. During mild exertion (swimming slowly or walking, for example), you may hold your breath for HT×4 seconds. During heavy exertion such as combat, you may hold your breath for HT seconds. Double these times if you hyperventilate first. Quadruple them if you hyperventilate with pure oxygen. Halve these times if you are caught totally by surprise and don't have a chance to take a deep breath.

Once out of breath, a character loses one Fatigue per turn. When ST reaches 0, he falls unconscious. He will die in four minutes unless he gets air. If the victim was actually drowning (i.e., has water in his lungs), a rescuer will also need to make a successful First Aid roll to save him. Otherwise, just getting clean air will bring the victim around. The victim recovers 1 ST immediately, but must recover the rest of his lost fatigue normally.

There is a chance of brain damage (permanent -1 to IQ) if the victim is saved after more than two minutes without air; roll vs. HT to avoid this.

Repeated Attempts on Success Rolls

Sometimes you will only get one chance to do something (defuse a bomb, jump over a crevasse, remove an inflamed appendix, please the King with a song). Other times you can try over and over again until you succeed (pick a lock, catch a fish, analyze a poison). Still other times you will not know whether you succeeded or failed until it's too late to try again (translate an old treasure map, order in a French restaurant, build a ship). Finally, there will be times when you are injured by failure but can afford to fail a few times (climb a wall, impress a savage tribesman).

The GM will have to use his common sense to distinguish between these, according to the exact situation in which the players find themselves. As a rule:

(a) If the first failure kills them (or destroys the object of the attempt), that's that.

(b) If a failure causes damage of some kind, assess the damage and let them try again after a "reasonable" time passes. Time-per-attempt is listed for those skills in which it is very important.

(c) If a failure causes no damage, let them try again after a reasonable time, but *at a penalty* for each attempt. For instance, you could try all night to pick a lock . . . but if you don't get it pretty soon, that particular lock is probably beyond your skill. So the GM should subtract 1 on the second attempt, 2 on the third, and so on, until the lockpicker succeeds or gives up.

SENSE ROLLS

Sense rolls include Vision rolls to see, Hearing rolls to hear, and Taste/Smell rolls. All Sense rolls are made against the character's IQ. The Alertness advantage is a bonus to all Sense rolls. Acute senses help the appropriate Sense rolls; some disadvantages interfere with Sense rolls.

Vision

To see something small or hidden, make a Vision roll. The GM may make this roll easier or harder, for things that are more or less well-hidden. Blind characters, or those in total darkness, can of course see nothing! In total darkness, action requiring sight is either at -10 (e.g., combat) or totally impossible (e.g., reading a map).

Positive modifiers include your bonuses for Alertness (which improves all senses) and for Acute Vision.

Negative modifiers include partial darkness (-1 to -9) and Bad Sight. A nearsighted character (without vision correction) will have a -6 to Vision rolls for items farther away than three feet. A farsighted character will have a -6 on Vision rolls for things within three feet.

A character with Peripheral Vision should get a roll to see *anything* in the area, unless it is absolutely, positively, directly behind him. A character with Night Vision suffers no penalties for darkness unless the darkness is total.

If the item in question is dangerous, anyone with the Danger Sense advantage should get a *second* roll against IQ to sense the danger.

Hearing

To hear a faint sound, roll your IQ. The GM may make this roll easier or harder, depending on the loudness of the sound, surrounding noises, etc. Once a sound is heard, a regular IQ roll may be required to *understand* its significance – e.g., realizing that the "owl hoot" is actually an Indian warrior. Deaf characters can of course hear nothing!

Positive modifiers on a Hearing roll include your bonuses for Alertness and for Acute Hearing.

Negative modifiers are the Hard of Hearing disadvantage (-4), and any the GM wishes to apply for the particular situation (e.g., for noisy surroundings).

If the sound in question represents a danger, anyone with the Danger Sense advantage should get a *second* roll against IQ to sense the danger.

Smelling and Tasting

These are two manifestations of the same sense. To notice an odor or a taste, roll your IQ. In some cases, the GM may require a separate IQ roll to *understand* the significance of a smell or taste that everyone notices – e.g., realizing that faint scent belongs to the flower of a man-eating plant, or recognizing the taste of a drug! Sometimes the GM could require an appropriate *skill* roll (Chemistry, Cooking or Poisons, depending on the circumstances).

Positive modifiers include Alertness and Acute Taste/Smell. And, of course, a strong taste or odor would be easier to notice than a faint one.

There are no specific negative modifiers except those the GM applies to the particular situation – e.g., a faint or disguised taste or odor might carry a penalty. Characters with the disadvantage of No Sense of Smell/Taste can taste and smell *nothing*.

If the taste or odor in question represents a danger, anyone with the Danger Sense advantage should get a *second* roll against IQ to sense the danger.

WILL ROLLS

When a character is faced with a frightening situation, or needs to overcome a mental disadvantage, the GM should require a Will roll. Normally, Will is equal to IQ, so this is just an IQ roll. However, if the character has the advantage of Strong Will (p. 23) or the disadvantage of Weak Will (p. 37), the appropriate number of levels add to or subtract from IQ. For instance, a person with IQ of 14, and 2 levels of Weak Will, has a Will of 12.

On a successful Will roll, the character overcomes his fear, bad impulse, or whatever. On a failed roll, the character is frightened or gives in to the "lower impulse," whatever that is. Any Will roll of 14 or over is an automatic failure.

Many mental disadvantages allow the character a chance to overcome them temporarily with a Will roll. But if a *player* constantly tries to avoid his mental disadvantage, rather than roleplaying it, the GM should penalize him.

Furthermore, if a character has an IQ of more than 14, treat his IQ as only 14 before subtracting Weak Will. If you have an IQ of 14 *or higher* and 3 levels of Weak Will, your Will is only 11.

FRIGHT CHECKS

A Fright Check is a special type of Will roll, made when something occurs that should *terrify* the characters. The advantage of Combat Reflexes gives a +2 on any Fright Check. The GM should require a Fright Check whenever a character meets the object of his *phobia* (p. 35). If the Phobia is severe, roll at a -4 penalty to Will!

Other Fright Checks can be required, at the GM's pleasure, for other horrifying events. In a Horror campaign, where ordinary people meet shockingly gruesome Things, Fright Checks can be very common. In other campaigns, they can be rare. Fright Checks are not required for "ordinary" frightening things, but for events so unusual and terrifying that they might mentally stun their victims, or even permanently scar them.

In an "ordinary people" campaign, Fright Checks should be required for face-to-face encounters with monsters, discovery of dead bodies, and supernatural happenings. But in a fantasy campaign, all these things may be quite normal . . . threatening, but normal. A fantasy character, on the other hand, might have to make a Fright Check if transported to the 20th century and given a ride down the Interstate . . .

Likewise, a Fright Check might be required of an ordinary person, or even a rookie cop, if someone tries to kill him (or *does* kill someone nearby). For a veteran cop or soldier, this is unfortunately routine.

Bonuses and penalties. If an event is especially violent, gruesome or terrifying, or involves a friend, the GM may require a penalty on the Fright Check, of anywhere from -1 (discovery that the victim's ears are missing) to -6 (discovery that one of the victims was your Dependent).

Likewise, an occasional Fright Check may be easier. For instance, seeing a monster at a great distance would allow a check at +1 to Will; seeing a body after being warned would be at +3.

Heat of battle. In combat, you are usually too excited to be scared. Any Fright Check made in the heat of battle is at +5. This applies only if you are already in combat when the terrifying thing happens or is first noticed. If Officer Jordan suddenly realizes that the suspect he's grappling with *has no head,* he rolls at +5. His partner, covering him from several feet away, rolls without the bonus.

Influence Rolls

An Influence roll is a Contest of Skill vs. Will, made when one character wants to influence another. The PCs may try to influence NPCs . . . but equally often, NPCs will try to influence *them.* Influence rolls include Contests of Skill between the Will of the "victim" and any of the following skills: Diplomacy, Fast-Talk, Savoir-Faire, Sex Appeal. Any reaction modifiers that the *influencing* character has, good or bad, apply to an Influence roll.

PCs with an appropriate "influence" skill can always elect to substitute an Influence roll for a regular reaction roll in an appropriate circumstance. However, GMs should assess a slightly *worse* reaction for a failed Influence roll, *except* Diplomacy, than for a regular failed reaction roll. Diplomacy is relatively safe . . .

Long Tasks

The GM may define very large jobs or projects as "tasks." Each task requires a number of hours, set by the GM, to perform. Several different skills may be required, with an appropriate number of man-hours assigned to each. For instance, a rope bridge must be built over a chasm. The GM decides this will take 40 man-hours of ordinary labor (using DX as a skill); 24 man-hours of Carpentry work; and eight man-hours of Engineering at TL2+.

Normally, a person can do eight man-hours of work per 24-hour day. At the end of each day, each character rolls vs. the skill used that day, with the GM rolling for NPCs. Each successful roll accomplishes eight man-hours toward the task. A failed roll does only half as much. A critical success counts 50% extra. A critical failure does no work, and *ruins* 2d hours of work already done!

PCs may work longer shifts, and may (on good reaction rolls) convince NPC hirelings to do the same. A HT roll must be made each day that extra work is done; this roll is at -1 for each hour worked over ten. If the HT roll succeeds, roll normally vs. skill, and (except on a critical failure) more work will be done. But if the HT roll fails, the skill roll is made at a penalty equal to the amount by which the roll was failed (minimum -2) and the worker takes Fatigue equal to the same amount. On a critical HT failure, the character is exhausted and can do no work the next day!

Special abilities, stimulants (which may be harmful in the long run) and other special items may make it easier to work long hours safely.

The GM may modify skill rolls or time required as he sees fit. Special equipment, clever player ideas for shortcuts, and special abilities might all justify bonuses. Encourage players to use their imaginations!

When a character fails a Fright Check, roll 3 dice. *Add the amount by which the Fright Check was missed,* and consult the following table.

Many of these results will give the character a new Quirk, Phobia, Delusion, or other mental disadvantage. The GM assigns the disadvantage. It must be related to the frightening event. If possible, it should also be related to an existing Quirk, Delusion or Phobia!

Disadvantages acquired this way *do* reduce the point value of the character.

4, 5 – Stunned for one turn, then recovers automatically.

6, 7 – Stunned for one turn. Every turn after that, roll vs. unmodified IQ to snap out of it.

8, 9 – Stunned for one turn. Every turn after that, roll vs. Will, plus whatever bonuses or penalties you had on your original roll, to snap out of it.

10 – Stunned for 1d turns. Every turn after that, roll vs. modified Will, as above, to snap out of it.

11 – Stunned for 2d turns. Every turn after that, roll vs. modified Will, as above, to snap out of it.

12 – Lose your lunch. Treat this as being stunned for 15 turns, then roll vs. HT each turn to recover. Depending on the circumstances, this may be merely inconvenient, or humiliating.

13 – Acquire a new *Quirk* (p. 41). This is the only way a character can acquire more than five Quirks.

14, 15 – Take 1d of fatigue, and 1d turns of stunning, as per #10 above.

16 – Stunned for 1d turns, as per #10, and acquire a new Quirk, as per #13.

17 – Faint for 1d minutes, then roll vs. HT each minute to recover.

18 – Faint as above, and roll vs. HT immediately. On a failed roll, take 1 hit of damage as you collapse.

19 – Severe faint, lasting for 2d minutes; then roll vs. HT each minute to recover. Take 1 hit of injury.

20 – Faint bordering on shock, lasting for 4d minutes. Also, take 1d fatigue.

21 – Panic. Victim runs around screaming, sits down and cries, or does something else equally pointless for 1d minutes. At end of that time, roll vs. unmodified IQ once per minute to snap out of it.

22 – Acquire a *Major Delusion* (p. 32).

23 – Acquire a *Mild Phobia* (p. 35) or other 10-point mental disadvantage.

24 – Major physical effect, set by GM: hair turns white, you age five years overnight, you go partially deaf. In game terms, acquire 15 points worth of physical disadvantages (for this purpose, each year of age counts as 3 points).

25 – If you already have a Mild Phobia that can logically be related to the frightening incident, it becomes Severe. If not, add a new Mild Phobia or 10-point mental disadvantage.

26 – Faint for 1d minutes, as per #18, and acquire a new 10-point Delusion, as per #22.

27 – Faint for 1d minutes, as per #18, and acquire a new 10-point mental disadvantage, as per #23.

28 – Light Coma. You fall unconscious, rolling vs. HT every 30 minutes to recover. For 6 hours after you come to, all skill rolls and attribute checks are at -2.

29 – Coma. As above, but unconscious for 1d hours. Then roll vs. HT; if the roll fails, remain in a coma for another 1d hours, and so on.

30 – Catatonia. Stare into space for 1d days; then roll vs. HT. On a failed roll, remain catatonic for another 1d days, and so on. If you have no medical care, lose 1 HT the first day, 2 the second, and so on. If you survive and awaken, all skill rolls and attribute checks are at -2 for as many days as the coma lasted.

31 – Seizure. You lose control of your body, and fall to the ground in a fit lasting 1d minutes and costing 2d Fatigue. Also, roll vs. HT. On a failed roll, take 1d damage. On a critical failure, you lose 1 HT *permanently*.

32 – Stricken. You fall to the ground, taking 2d damage in the form of a mild heart attack or stroke.

33 – Total panic. You are no longer in control; you may do *anything* (the GM rolls 3 dice; the higher the roll, the more useless your reaction). For instance, you might jump off a cliff to avoid the monster. If you survive your first reaction, roll vs. IQ to come out of the panic. If you fail, the GM rolls for another panicky reaction, and so on!

34 – Acquire a *Severe Delusion* (see p. 32).

35 – Acquire a *Severe Phobia* (see p. 35) or other mental disadvantages worth 15 points.

36 – Severe physical effect, as per #24, but equivalent to 20 points of physical disadvantages.

37 – Severe physical effect, as per #24, but equivalent to 30 points of physical disadvantages.

38 – Coma, as per #29, and a Severe Delusion, as per #34.

39 – Coma, as per #29, and a Severe Phobia or other 30-point mental disadvantage, as per #35.

40+ – As #39, above, but victim also loses 1 point of IQ *permanently*. This automatically reduces all IQ-based skills, including magic and psi skills, by 1.

13 BASIC COMBAT

The *GURPS* combat system is designed to allow a realistic simulation of all kinds of combat action. This involves a great deal of detail. Therefore, combat is presented in two versions: Basic, for the beginner and for the group more interested in roleplaying than combat . . . and Advanced (p. 102) for those wanting playable detail and realism.

COMBAT TURN SEQUENCE

Characters act one at a time, until they have all taken a turn; then they start over. The *sequence* in which they act can be determined in either of two ways (see sidebar). Your turn *starts* when you choose a maneuver, and *ends* when you choose your *next* maneuver – that is, after all other characters have acted once. Each turn represents *one second* of real time.

MANEUVERS

Start each turn by choosing any *one* of the following maneuvers. The maneuver you choose will also affect your *defenses* if you are attacked before your next turn. You do not select a defense until you are actually attacked – but the maneuver you choose will govern the defenses you can use. Defenses are explained on p. 98.

Move

Move, and do *nothing* else (except for the "free" actions listed on p. 97). You may use any legal active defense.

Movement and special actions are wholly abstract; no gameboard is required. If a decision about movement becomes important ("How long will it take me to run across the room and grab the jewel?"), the GM provides it. A character's Move is equal to the number of yards he can run per second – a Move of 5 lets you run 5 yards per second, and so on. If you prefer more detailed and accurate movement rules, use the Advanced System.

Change Position

Go from standing to prone, kneeling to standing, or any other position change. (It takes *two* turns to go from prone to standing: first you kneel, then you stand.) *Exception:* You can go from kneeling to standing, or vice versa, *and attack* on the same turn (below).

You can use any defense on the turn you change position.

Ready

Ready any weapon or other item (see sidebar, p. 104). Any weapon is "unready" if it is in its scabbard or holster. An axe, mace or other heavy weapon becomes "unready" when you swing it; it must be readied again before each use! Some weapons must be "readied" for more than one second after each use.

You can parry with a weapon, or block with a shield, as soon as you have readied it – that is, on the same turn! You can also use any other legal active defense on the turn when you ready an item. *Exception:* If you are "readying" a missile weapon by reloading it, your only defense is to Dodge – and if you Dodge, you lose the benefit of that turn of reloading.

Note that, even if you are ambidextrous, you cannot ready one weapon on the same turn you attack with another.

Turn Sequence

There are two ways to determine who goes first: the easy way, and the realistic way.

The Easy Way

Each player rolls a die. The winner goes first. After that, players take their turns in order, moving clockwise around the table. If a player controls several characters, they may act in any order – and it does not always have to be the *same* order.

This system has the advantage of simplicity. However, there is a slight advantage in going first in each rotation. Realistically, this advantage would go to the fastest characters. If you would prefer to play this way, use . . . .

The Realistic Way

Before combat begins, compare the Move scores of all characters. The highest Move goes first; put a "1" in the "Sequence" box at the top right of his character sheet, as a reminder. (Use pencil!) The second-highest Move score goes next, and gets a "2." And so on. In case of ties, the highest *basic Speed* goes first; here is where a 5.5 is better than a 5.25, for instance. (If anyone is *still* tied, roll dice to see who goes first.)

Which is Better?

Over a few turns of combat, the advantages and disadvantages of sequencing tend to average out. Use the method you are most comfortable with. If there are more than a dozen fighters in the game, though, the easy way is *much* faster.

Flails

A weapon with a length of chain between the handle and the head is a *flail*. The one-handed flail is a "morningstar."

Because of the chain, a flail can "wrap around" a foe's weapon when he tries to parry it. Therefore, any parry against a flail weapon is at a -4. And fencing weapons, with their light blades, cannot parry a flail at all! Even a shield is less useful against a flail; blocks are at -2.

Reloading Time

Sling: 2 seconds to reload – can be fired every 3 seconds.

Bow: 2 seconds to reload – can be fired every 3 seconds.

Crossbow (your ST or less): 4 seconds to cock and reload – can be fired every 5 seconds. If ST is up to 2 greater than yours: 8 seconds to cock and reload – can be fired every 9 seconds.

Guns: Repeating guns are divided into three kinds: replaceable magazine, integral magazine and revolvers.

Integral magazines take 3 seconds of preparation, plus one second *per round.*

Changing magazines for a replaceable magazine gun (or stripping a clip into a Mauser-type action) takes 3 seconds (one to prepare, one to acquire, one to insert).

Revolvers: *Single-ejecting* revolvers take one second to prepare for unloading and one second *per round* to unload the empties. Reloading takes one second to prepare and two seconds *per round* to load, plus one second to ready for firing or carrying. *Simultaneously-ejecting* revolvers take three seconds of preparation plus one second *per round* of loading time.

See also the Speed-Load skill (p. 52).

"My Weapon's Stuck!" – The Problem with Picks

Weapons that are swung for *impaling* damage – picks and the like – do a *great deal* of damage. The drawback is this: they may get stuck in your foe!

Any time such a weapon penetrates the foe's armor, it may stick. On your next turn, roll against your ST. A successful roll means your weapon is not stuck, and you may re-ready it on the following turn.

A failed roll means it *is* stuck. You cannot use it or ready it. You may roll again at the beginning of each turn to try to unstick it, but you can do nothing until you succeed. A critical miss on this roll (a 17 or 18) means the weapon is permanently stuck, and you might as well drop it; you can recover it after combat, if you survive.

When the pick comes unstuck, it does half as much damage as it did originally. For example, if the final damage done by the original wound was 4 or 5 hits, it does another 2 hits when it is pulled free.

If you cannot pull your pick free during combat, your attempts do your foe no extra damage (for game purposes). After combat, you will be able to recover the pick if your foe is lying on the battlefield.

If your weapon is stuck in a foe, and he tries to move away, roll a Quick Contest of Strength. If your foe wins, he pulls the weapon out of your hands. If you win, your foe can't move. If you tie, the weapon comes loose and does damage as above.

Weapons with this drawback include picks, warhammers and (when *swung to impale)* halberds.

Reloading

Use the "Ready" maneuver to reload a missile weapon. This will require several turns. With a sling, for instance, you need one second to "ready" the rock, and one second to put the rock in the sling. If you don't aim, you can fire on the third second. Crossbows take much longer. First you must *cock* the bow – this takes 2 seconds for a bow of your ST, or more for a heavier bow. Then you must ready the arrow (1 turn) and load the bow (1 turn).

Reloading time for missile weapons is shown in the sidebar. Note that the Fast-Draw skill (p. 50) can speed reloading for an archer (to draw arrows) or a gunman (to grab a magazine or speedloader).

Aim

Aim a ready *ranged* weapon at a specific target. You must name your target. Your attack is at -4 if you use a ranged weapon without aiming *unless* your effective skill is at least equal to the weapon's Snap Shot number (p. 115). If you aim for one turn, your attack is at your normal skill level plus the weapon's Accuracy modifier (p. 115). You may aim for up to three more turns, getting a further +1 bonus for each turn you aim.

You can use any defense while you are aiming . . . but to do so will spoil your aim and you lose all the accumulated benefits. If you are injured while aiming, you must make your Will roll or lose your aim.

Attack

Attack any foe with your ready weapon. The GM always has the option of ruling (for any reason having to do with the situation) that some characters may not attack certain enemies. For instance, ten characters could not hit the same human-sized foe at once. (Even three or four attackers at once would be unlikely unless their victim had no allies!) Note also that if the battle is in close quarters, bows and similar missile weapons should only be allowed one shot each – then the fight will go to hand weapons.

You may parry (with a ready weapon), block (with a ready shield) or dodge on the same turn you attack.

All-Out Attack

Attack any foe with hands, feet or a ready *hand* weapon. You have four choices:

(a) Make two attacks against the same foe, *if* you have two ready weapons, or one weapon that does not have to be readied after use;
(b) Make one *feint* (see below), and then one attack;
(c) Make a single attack, at a +4 bonus to your skill!
(d) Make a single attack, at normal skill, doing +2 damage if you hit.

However, if you choose this maneuver, you may make *no active defenses at all* until your next turn.

Feint

"Fake" an attack with a hand weapon. You cannot feint at someone unless you *could* have hit him with an attack or all-out attack.

When you feint, roll a Quick Contest of Skills (see p. 87): your weapon skill against your foe's shield or weapon skill. (If he has no shield or hand weapon, or if his DX is better than his shield or hand weapon skill, he rolls against his DX instead.) A feint does *not* make any weapon unready.

If you fail your roll, your feint is unsuccessful. Likewise, if you succeed, but your foe succeeds by *as much or more* than you do, your feint fails.

If you *make* your roll, and your foe *fails,* the amount by which you made your roll is subtracted from the foe's active defense if you attack him on your very next turn. For instance, if your skill is 15 and you roll a 12, your feint is a success and your foe defends against you at -3 next turn. (Your allies cannot take advantage of *your* feint; the defense penalty applies only to *your* attack.)

If you and your foe *both* succeed, but you succeed by more, the *difference* between the amounts is subtracted from the foe's defense. *Example:* Your skill is 15, and you roll a 10. You succeeded by 5. Your foe's skill is 14, and he rolled a 12. He succeeded by 2. The difference is 3, so he will defend at -3 next turn.

This maneuver can be a lifesaver – or a total waste of time. Use it wisely.

Wait

Do nothing *unless* a foe comes within your striking range before your next turn. If that happens, you may attack (a regular attack, not all-out). Because movement is entirely abstract in the Basic System, you will rarely need this maneuver. You may use any defense on a turn you Wait.

All-Out Defense

Defend yourself; do nothing else this turn. If you fail your defense roll against any attack, you may try *another* (different) defense – in other words, you get two defense rolls, using two different active defenses against the same attack. You are limited to *two* blocks and *two* parries per turn when you choose All-Out Defense, and you can't parry twice with a weapon that becomes unready after a parry.

Concentrate

Cast a spell, or do anything else requiring mental concentration. If the character is hurt, knocked down, forced to use an active defense, or otherwise distracted, he must make a Will-3 roll to maintain his concentration.

Long Action

This is not a specific maneuver; it is a "generic" choice that allows you to do one second's worth of *any* multi-second action. The GM decides how many turns each "long action" will take; see p. 107 for a table of some common actions. As a rule, no defense except dodging is possible during a long action, but the GM can vary this as he sees fit. Any sort of defense may also interfere with whatever you are trying to do.

Free Actions

These are things you can do during *any* maneuver. These include talking, dropping weapons or other objects, *maintaining* magical spells (if you are using magic), etc. See p. 107 for more detail.

MAKING AN ATTACK

Each attack is resolved by three die rolls. First is your *attack roll*. If your roll is successful, your attack was a good one. Now your *foe* must make a *defense roll* to see if he can defend against your blow. If he makes this roll, he is not hit. If he misses his defense roll, your blow struck home and you *roll for damage*.

If you choose the *Attack, All-Out Attack* or *Wait* maneuvers, you may try to hit a foe. In the Basic Combat System, you don't need to worry about the enemy's precise location. You may attack any foe, unless the GM rules that attack is impossible for some reason.

You cannot attack unless your weapon is *ready*. A sword or knife is ready every turn. An unbalanced weapon, like an axe, becomes unready when you swing it, so it can only be used every other turn. See p. 104.

Rolling to Attack

Your "attack roll" is a regular success roll. Figure your *effective skill* (your basic skill plus or minus any appropriate modifiers) with the weapon you are using.

Example of Combat

Louis LeBlanc is the attacker. His weapon is a machete, which is considered a shortsword. His Shortsword skill is 15, and there are no adverse conditions to subtract from his roll. Therefore, he needs a 15 or less to hit his foe. He swings and rolls a 13, so he hits.

His opponent, Filthy Pierre, has a Move of 4 (giving him a Dodge of 4). He has a Shield skill of 14 (giving him a shield-block defense of 7) and a Shortsword skill of 13 (giving him a parrying defense of 6). His Block is his best defense, so he will use it whenever he can.

Pierre's small shield is also good for a *passive* defense of 2 (see *Types of Shields*, p. 76).

Pierre is wearing cloth armor, which gives a passive defense of 1 (see *Suits of Armor*, p. 72).

So Pierre's defenses are 7 + 2 + 1, or a total of 10. If he Blocks and rolls a 10 or less, he can defend against the accurate blow that Louis just threw. But 10 misses half the time on 3 dice. He rolls – and gets an 11. Too bad! He's hit.

Although the combat calculations may seem complex at first, they are *simple* in play! The attacker rolls against his skill, as shown on his record sheet. The defender adds up his defenses, as shown on *his* record sheet, and rolls against the total. That's it!

To continue the example: Louis is attacking Pierre. His blow was good, and Pierre failed to defend. So the blow got through.

Now Louis rolls for damage. Louis' player has already figured how much damage he does with a shortsword, and written it on his record sheet . . . . his strength is 11, so his swing does "1d+1" damage. He rolls one die and gets a 4. Adding one point yields a 5. So Pierre is hit for 5 points of basic damage.

However, Pierre is wearing cloth armor (Damage Resistance of 1.) This gives him 1 point of protection. So only 4 points of damage get through the armor.

But a sword is a cutting weapon! The damage that got through the armor is increased by 50%, to 6! So Pierre takes 6 hits of damage. That blow could knock a lesser man down. Sad but true . . . . one good sword blow can settle a fight.

Pierre's player subtracts 6 points from Pierre's HT. Luckily, this is not *more* than half of Pierre's original HT of 12. So Pierre is not stunned, and does not have to roll to see if he is knocked down. However, if he attacks on his next turn, he must subtract 6 from his skill! And the fight continues.

Many things can make it harder to hit your foe. Each one has a "hit penalty" which is subtracted from your skill before you roll.

Bad light: -1 to -9
Total darkness: -10
Bad footing: -2 (more, at GM's option). *Exception:* If you are firing a missile weapon, taking time to aim will also eliminate this penalty!
Attacker is standing in water (kneedeep or more): see p. 91
Attacker is swimming: -6, or Underwater penalty (p. 91).
Attacker is in a strange position: -2 or more (GM's decision – see p. 123)
Blind: -6. Blinded suddenly: -10
One eye: -1 for hand weapon attacks, -3 for ranged attacks
Clothes are on fire: -2
Crawling: -4
Crouching: -2
Sitting: -2
Off-hand attack: -4 (no penalty if Ambidextrous)
Shield: -2 to attacks if using a *large* shield
ST under minimum ST for that weapon: -1 for each point of difference
Wounds: Penalty equal to hits you took on preceding turn. If you are using a mounted weapon with an electronic sighting mechanism, this penalty is halved. High Pain Threshold advantage eliminates this penalty.
GMs may add or change modifiers as they see fit!

Critical Hits

A "critical hit" is an especially good blow. It automatically hits home – your foe does *not* get a defense roll. On an attack roll of 3, you do not roll for damage – your blow automatically does the *most* damage it could do. For instance, maximum damage for a 1d+2 blow would be 6+2, or 8 hits.

A roll of 4 is also a critical hit, but it does normal damage.

A roll of 5 or 6 *may* be a critical hit, depending on your skill. If your effective skill is 15, then a roll of 5 or less is a critical hit. If your effective skill is 16 or more, than a roll of 6 or less is a critical hit. This means that a bonus to hit (e.g., when you make an all-out attack) *will* increase your chance of getting a critical hit. However, a natural 3 is still the only roll that automatically does maximum damage.

The maximum-damage rule is a *substitute* for the more complex Critical Hit Tables. Do *not* use both!

(See p. 86 for success rolls, and p. 201 for combat modifiers.) Then roll 3 dice. If your roll is *less than or equal to* your "effective" skill, you have rolled well enough to hit the foe, and he must roll to defend. Otherwise, you missed!

No matter what your skill, a roll of 3 or 4 always hits, and is a "critical hit" – see sidebar. A roll of 17 or 18 always misses.

DEFENSE

If you make your attack roll, you have not (yet) actually struck your foe (unless you rolled a critical hit). You have thrown a blow that is *good enough* to hit him – *unless* he defends.

Your foe's defense is equal to the total of his *passive* defenses (armor, shield and/or magic) and his *active* defenses (dodge, block or parry). Passive defenses always protect, but active defenses must be specifically chosen from those that are "legal" at the moment. This depends on the maneuver he chose on his last turn – see above.

The defender rolls 3 dice. If his roll is *less than or equal to* his total defense, he blocked the blow (or dodged it, or whatever). Otherwise, his defense was ineffective and your blow struck home. If your blow hits your foe, you can roll for damage.

A defense roll of 3 or 4 is *always* successful – even if your total defense was only 1 or 2! A roll of 17 or 18 is always a failed defense.

Your foe does not get to attempt a defense roll if you rolled a critical hit against him.

Active Defense

There are three *active defenses* that can protect you against an attack. Each of these defenses is calculated in advance. When you are attacked, you may choose one active defense as part of your total defense roll. (If you took *All-Out Defense,* you may make *two* separate defense rolls, using different defenses.)

Your active defense will depend on your situation – *especially* the maneuver you chose last turn. Some maneuvers limit the active defenses you can make. A stunned character's active defense is at -4.

Sometimes you will have *no* active defense. A stab in the back from a "friend," a sniper's shot or a totally unexpected booby trap would be attacks against which no active defense is possible.

The Combat Reflexes advantage gives a +1 to each of your active defenses.

Dodging

Your Dodge defense is the same as your Move score. Dodging is often the best defense when you are not skilled with your weapon and you have no shield.

You may dodge *any* attack, except one that you did not know about! There is no limit to the number of times you may dodge in one turn.

If you have the Acrobatics skill, you may try an "Acrobatic Dodge" (p. 48).

An animal's Dodge score is half its Move or half its DX, whichever is better – up to a maximum of 10.

Blocking

You must have a *ready* shield, which you use to "block" the attack. Your Block defense is ½ your Shield (or Buckler) skill, rounded down. In general, you can block any blade weapon, club, axe, spear, polearm, etc., whether swung or thrown. You may also block arrows, quarrels, slung stones and similar low-tech missiles. You *cannot* block bullets or beam weapons . . . these come too fast to be stopped with a shield. (However, the shield's *passive* defense helps against *all* missile weapons – see p. 99.)

You may only block one attack per turn, unless you chose the *All-Out Defense* maneuver. In that case, you may block two attacks per turn.

Parrying

Hand weapons (blades, clubs, axes, spears, polearms) can be used for defense as well as offense. When you parry with a weapon, *half* your skill with that weapon (round down) counts as active defense. Thus, if you have a Sword skill of 20, you would have a Parry defense of 10 when you use a sword.

You cannot parry unless your weapon is *ready*. Parrying with an unbalanced weapon will make it "unready." For instance, you can't parry with an axe on the same turn you attacked with it; you have to re-ready it first. See p. 104.

A weapon parry won't stop anything except hand weapon attacks. A further exception: A weapon has a $\frac{1}{3}$ chance of breaking if it parries anything of three or more times its own weight! (If it breaks, that parry counts.) In general, only rapiers and knives are likely to break this way. See *Striking at Weapons*, p. 110.

You can also parry with a non-weapon of the proper size and shape, using the closest weapon skill. A pole or rifle could parry like a spear, a bow like a light club. However, parrying just once with a bow will ruin it *as* a bow, though it may survive for a few seconds longer as a club.

You may only parry one attack per turn, unless you have two weapons (in which case you may parry twice) or you chose the All-Out Defense maneuver. In that case, you may parry twice (with each weapon). Fencers also have an improved parrying ability – see below.

If you successfully parry a bare-handed attack with a weapon, you may injure your attacker. Immediately roll against your own weapon skill. If you hit, your parry struck the attacker's limb squarely; roll normal damage. (If your attacker used Judo or Karate, you are at a -4 to this "to hit" roll.)

Special Parrying Rules

Thrown weapons may be parried, but at a -1. Thrown knives and similar weapons are parried at -2.

Knives and equally small weapons are at -1 to parry *with*.

Flails are at -4 to parry *against*.

Quarterstaves parry at $\frac{2}{3}$ of skill rather than $\frac{1}{2}$.

Fencing weapons use a unique fighting form. A fencer uses a light weapon and a very light shield (or none at all). The fencer's "ready" position keeps his weapon pointed toward the foe. Thus, he can parry better than other fighters.

If you have the Fencing skill and appropriate gear (a smallsword, rapier or saber, no larger than a small shield and no greater than "light" encumbrance), your Parry is $\frac{2}{3}$ your Fencing skill (round down). Furthermore, you may parry *twice* per turn, rather than just once. (An all-out defense will let you parry *any number* of times!)

Many fencers carry a dagger as a secondary weapon. The dagger can also parry – at $\frac{1}{2}$ the fencer's Knife skill. (-4 to skill for an off-handed weapon; -1 to Parry ability for using a knife; total, $\frac{1}{2}$ Knife skill, -3). See also the Main-Gauche skill (p. CI134).

The only disadvantage of the fencer's parry is this: Fencing weapons *are* light, and likely to break if they parry a heavy weapon – see above.

Passive Defense

When you are attacked, you *may* also have a "passive" defense factor operating in your favor, thanks to your armor, shield, etc. Passive defense *always* protects you, even if you are unconscious or unaware of the attack. If you have *any* passive defense at all, a defense roll of 3 or 4 will succeed for you!

Armor: The passive defense from your armor depends on its type – see p. 72 – varying from 1 to 6.

Shield: The passive defense of your shield depends on its size: 1 for a buckler, up to 4 for a large shield. It does not protect against a "sneak attack" – i.e., one where the GM rules you are struck from behind. See *Shields*, p. 75.

Etc.: Magic spells and other things (whatever the GM dreams up!) may also add to your passive defense.

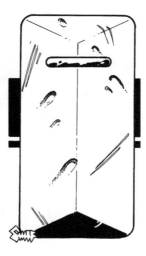

Basic Weapon Effects

There are two types of attack (*thrusting* and *swinging*) and three types of basic weapon damage (*crushing, cutting* and *impaling*). They are explained in the sidebar on p. 73.

Effects of Injury

In the Basic Combat System, *all* injuries are assumed to be to the torso. Subtract the hits you take from your HT score.

If you take a wound, your attack roll will be reduced (on your next turn only) by the number of hits you took. Thus, a scratch will have little effect . . . . but if you take a major wound, you'd better go on the defensive for a moment. Wounds taken during the same turn are cumulative.

Knockdown and Stunning

If you take a single wound that does damage of *more than half* of your *basic* HT score, you must roll against your basic HT. If you fail the roll, you are *knocked down!* You cannot attack until you stand up again. (If you insist on using your weapon while lying on the ground, the GM may allow it, assessing a huge penalty. If you want to stay down and play dead, that's legal. Good luck.)

Whether or not you fall down, you are *stunned*. All active defense rolls are at -4 until your next turn. At that time, you must roll against your basic HT. A successful roll means you recover, and can act normally that turn and thereafter. A failed roll means you are still stunned, and continue to stand there (or lie there) without making any maneuvers – and at a continuing -4 on each active defense roll!

Severe Wounds

If you are reduced to 3 hit points (or less), your Move score and your Dodge are both cut in half (round down). Your wounds are slowing you!

Unconsciousness

If you take enough wounds to reduce your HT to *zero or less,* you are hanging on to consciousness by sheer willpower. At the beginning of each turn that your HT is zero or less, make a roll against *basic* HT. A successful roll means you can take your turn normally – the last-gasp effort of the true warrior. A failed roll means you fall unconscious! Roll each turn, until you fail a roll and fall unconscious.

Death

If your HT goes fully negative (for example, -10 if your basic HT is 10), you risk death.

For more about injuries – and how to recover from them! – see *Injuries*, p. 126.

DAMAGE AND INJURY

Rolling for Damage

If an enemy fails his defense roll, you have hit him, and you may make a "damage roll." This roll tells how much damage you did to your target. The number of dice you roll for damage is determined by your weapon (and, for low-tech weapons, by your own strength). It is shown in the "Weapons and Equipment" box of your character sheet, in the "Damage Amount" blank for the weapon you are using.

If the enemy is wearing armor, the armor's Damage Resistance is subtracted from the damage you roll. For more details, see *Armor Types*, p. 72. Magic spells and inborn "toughness" (see p. 23) may also provide Damage Resistance which works just like armor.

If you are lucky, you will roll enough damage to exceed your foe's protection, and injure him!

Injury

If the total damage you roll *exceeds* the Damage Resistance of the armor/skin/etc. protecting your foe, the excess hits are taken as damage. *Example:* Your "basic damage" when swinging your sword is 2d. You roll 2 dice, and an 8 is the result. The target has 3 points of Damage Resistance, so 5 points of damage got through. Add the 50% damage bonus for a cutting weapon (2 points, because you always round down). The total is 7. So the target took 7 hits of damage.

Effects of injuries are explained in the sidebar – and covered in greater detail in the section on *Injury, Illness and Fatigue* (p. 126).

RANGED WEAPONS

Thrown Weapons

In the Basic Combat System, anyone can (usually) hit anyone else with a hand weapon. But there may still be times when you want to throw a weapon. If you want to do it, it's legal. Do *not* roll against your weapon skill when you throw a weapon; roll against a "throwing" skill instead. A Snap Shot (one made without aiming) is at a -4. See *Aim*, p. 95. (Note that the Advanced Combat System adds more detail to the question of snap shots and accuracy!)

If a weapon can be thrown, throwing it is a *separate* skill. All weapon-throwing skills are "easy" to learn, defaulting to DX-4.

There is also the "generic" skill called Throwing. This is a "hard" skill. But if you have this skill, you can use it to throw *anything* – a knife, a baseball, a brick, a spear. (If you don't have this skill, you throw rocks, etc., at your basic DX.) Your target can Dodge, Block or Parry a thrown weapon.

If you hit, you do normal damage. Whether you hit or miss, your weapon falls on the floor. In a big fight, the GM probably shouldn't let you recover the weapon at all; in a small battle, he may roll one die to see how many turns it takes you to get your weapon back!

Special Ranged Attacks

Advance Shots: If the battle is in an open area or large room, the missile-weapon users will get at least one free shot before the charging foe can reach them. The average armored foe will move about 3 yards per second. Unarmored attackers will move about 5 yards per second. (*Remember:* the Move score is equal to the movement rate, in yards per second).

Missing: In the Basic System, if you miss with a thrown or missile weapon, you won't accidentally hit someone else – you just missed. Rules for hitting the wrong person are added in the Advanced System.

Missile Weapons

Missile weapons are treated like other weapons; make your attack roll, let your foe make his defense roll, and then roll for damage. In the Basic Combat System, assume all attacks are at a fairly close range unless the GM rules otherwise (see p. 116 for missile-weapon range rules). To hit with a missile weapon, roll against your weapon skill. Attack at -4 for a Snap Shot (no aim); see *Aim,* p. 95. The target of a missile weapon may Dodge, but may not Parry. Arrows and quarrels may be Blocked with a shield; higher-tech missiles cannot be Blocked.

Bows and slings do not fire every turn. A bow, for instance, normally takes two seconds to re-ready, so it can only fire every third second.

UNARMED COMBAT

Sometimes you will have to fight without weapons, or with improvised weapons. This is *unarmed combat.* Anyone can engage in unarmed combat, but there are certain skills – Judo, Karate and Brawling – that will make you a more effective unarmed fighter.

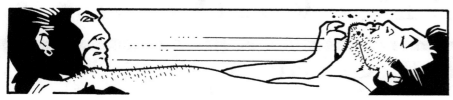

Punching

A punch is an attack with a Reach (see p. 102) of C or 1. Your "skill" for a punch is your basic DX, unless you have Brawling or Karate skill. Damage is determined by your ST: it is Thrust-2 crushing damage, determined from the Basic Weapon Damage Table. *Example:* With ST 12, your Thrust damage is 1d-1, so your punch does 1d-3 damage.

Brass knuckles or plate-mail gauntlets add +2 to your punching damage.

Improvised Weapons

If you have no weapons, you can sometimes improvise. A rock, roll of coins, etc., can be held in your fist. A small, heavy object will add +1 to the damage you do with a punch. A larger object (such as a beer mug) will add +2. Anything larger must be treated as a weapon – usually a club.

Kicking

A kick is treated exactly like a punch, except skill is DX-2, Brawling-2 or Karate-2, and you do straight Thrust/Crush damage – or Thrust+1 if you are wearing heavy boots or something similar. If you kick at a foe and miss, you must make your DX or skill roll to avoid falling down! A kick has a Reach (see p. 102) of 1 without Karate training.

Parrying Bare-Handed

If you are fighting bare-handed, you may parry a *kick* or *punch* with your hands, using half your basic DX as your Parry. Unarmed combat skills give you a better bare-handed parry: ²/₃ your Brawling, Judo or Karate skill (round down).

If you parry a weapon bare-handed, your defense is at -3 unless you parry a *thrust,* or you are using Judo or Karate (in either case, use your normal parry). A failed parry means the weapon hits; the attacker may choose to hit where he was aiming, or to hit your arm! If your arm takes damage of more than half your HT, that arm is automatically *crippled* (see p. 127).

Unarmed Combat Skills

These three skills (see pp. 50 and 51) let you fight more effectively with your bare hands. Brawling is easy to learn; Judo and Karate are hard.

This completes the Basic Combat System. Get out there and fight!
When you are comfortable with these rules, you can proceed to the next chapter if you want more realism and detail.

Carrying Weapons (and Other Things)

You cannot use a weapon or shield unless it is "ready." At any time, you may have (at most) two one-handed weapons ready – *or* a weapon and a shield – *or* a two-handed weapon.

But you may *carry* more weapons than this. A weapon can be carried in a variety of ways.

First, it can be *in hand* (whether or not it is ready). This is the *only* way to carry a bow or most weapons with a reach of more than 1 hex; balanced in one hand or slung over a shoulder. They don't make holsters for halberds! The number of items you can have in hand is limited by your number of hands – usually two.

Second, it can be carried in a scabbard, or a leather loop hanging from your belt. It takes one *Step and Ready* to draw a weapon carried like this, and two seconds of *Step and Ready* to *return* a weapon to a scabbard or belt-loop. Rifles, SMGs, greatswords and bastard swords are the only "long" weapons that can be carried this way; a greatsword scabbard hangs at your back, and the weapon is drawn over your shoulder.

Theoretically, you could have a dozen weapons hanging at your belt or scabbarded about your person. In practice, anybody who carries more than one or two extra weapons (plus a dagger) is usually being unrealistic, or just silly. The GM is the final arbiter.

Third, a weapon can be carried inside a pack, pocket, etc. It will take time to find a weapon that is packed away like that: roll 1 die for your pocket, or 2 dice for a pack, and take that many seconds to find the item. You must take a pack off before you can search it; roll 1 die to see how long *that* takes. Your encumbrance is the only limit on the number of weapons you can carry this way.

Animals in Combat

Combat against animals is played out like combat against humans. The only stat that has a different meaning is HT. Very large or very small animals have a split HT score, with the first number being "health" (to roll against when checking for stun, etc.) and the second number being "hits" (damage taken). These numbers are the same for a human, but not for a large or small animal. *Example:* An elephant might have HT 17/50 – Health of 17, able to take 50 hits.

Animals are described in more detail in Chapter 18, starting on p. 140.

ADVANCED COMBAT

The Advanced Combat System is intended for gamers who want more "realism" in their roleplaying. It can also be played as a *stand-alone boardgame* of man-to-man combat.

The Advanced System has five sections: *Movement* (which turns the game from an abstract system to a realistic combat simulation), *Hit Location, Close Combat, Ranged Weapons* and *Special Situations*.

MOVEMENT

THE COMBAT MAP

This system uses *combat maps* marked off in hexes. There are two in the *Instant Characters* section. When combat starts, pick an appropriate *map,* or just draw one, and choose a miniature figure to represent each character. Each hex represents one yard. Since the hexes are an inch across, this is a 50mm scale. For ease of handling, though, we suggest using 25mm figures.

Each figure must occupy one hex. A fractional hex is considered a full hex (unless the GM rules otherwise), and can be occupied without penalty. Ordinarily, only one figure can occupy each hex. Exceptions include close combat (see p. 111) and any situation in which people are crowded close together but are not trying to *do* anything. You could crowd up to four ordinary-sized people into a single hex, if they were friendly. You may also move through a friendly character's hex, though the movement cost is higher.

The basic unit of movement is one hex, or one yard. The number of hexes you can move depends on your Move score and the *maneuver* you choose each turn – see p. 103.

FACING

Each figure on the combat map must occupy one hex, and "face" toward one of the six adjacent hexes. Your facing defines your *front, right, left* and *back* hexes (see illustration). Your front hexes are the hexes you can *see* into, and easily *move* into. You can move into any adjacent hex, but sideways and backwards movement are slower (see *Maneuvers,* p. 103).

Normally, you can only attack forward. The *distance* you can attack depends on your weapon's *reach* (see sidebar).

For a right-handed fighter, the right side is the weapon side, and the left side is the shield side. For a left-handed fighter, these are reversed.

Facing Changes During Movement

Most maneuvers let you move only one hex. If you move one hex (or stand still) you may turn to face *any* direction at the end of your movement.

On an All-Out Attack, you may stand still and change facing. If you move, you must go *forward*. You may keep the same facing as you move forward, or turn to face each hex as you enter it (see diagram on the next page). You *cannot* change facing at the end of your move. Thus, you cannot start in front of someone and strike them from behind or the side, except with a wild swing (p. 105).

On a *Move* maneuver, you must change facing appropriately for *each hex you enter,* as follows: When going forward, either turn to face the hex you enter (movement cost 1) or sidestep into it (cost 2). When you move to the side or backwards (cost 2), you keep the same facing. See diagram on opposite page.

"Reach" of a Weapon

If you have a *hand* weapon, the hexes you can hit with it are defined by its *reach,* as follows:

"Close" reach: you can strike only at targets in your own hex. See *Close Combat,* p. 111.

1-yard reach: you can strike into any of your front hexes, as shown below.

2-yard reach: you can strike into any of your "2" hexes.

3-yard reach: you can strike into any of your "3" hexes.

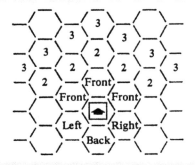

Most weapons have a 1-yard reach, and can hit only your three front hexes.

Some weapons have two reaches. For instance, a billy club can strike at "close" and "1-yard" range. With a spear, you can have a reach of either 1 or 2 yards, depending on how you hold the weapon! An impaling-type pole weapon can have a reach of 1, 2 or 3 yards.

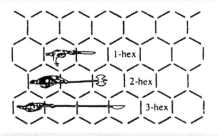

Most "long" weapons (those with two or more reaches) must be readied for a turn to "change grips" and go from one reach to another. For example, if you are holding a halberd with a grip that allows you to strike 3 hexes away, you will have to re-ready it for a turn before you can use it to strike someone 1 or 2 hexes away. The *Weapon Table* shows which weapons require a grip change, and which (e.g., greatsword and quarterstaff) do not.

The reach for each weapon is given in the *Weapon Table.* The reach of a bare-handed fighter is close and 1 yard.

At the end of your move, if you have used half (or less) of your possible movement, you may turn to face in any direction, unless you used an all-out attack. If you have moved more than half of your Move score, you may change your facing by *one hexside* (see diagram).

You may also change facing *before* you start a Move maneuver, or *during* the move – but this costs movement points. A facing change costs 1 for each hex-side of change – thus, turning 180° costs 3.

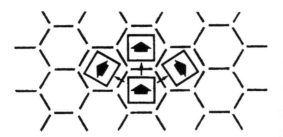

MANEUVERS

The ten maneuvers introduced in the Basic Combat System are still used. However, each maneuver now has a *movement* component added. Some of the names have been changed to reflect this.

When your turn comes to act, you may perform any *one* maneuver from the list below. If a maneuver has two or more parts (i.e., movement and attack), you may do them *in any order* unless the maneuver specifies otherwise.

Where movement is part of a maneuver, you may always choose to move *less* than the distance called for, but never *more*. You may also stand still and/or change facing. When a maneuver requires "forward" movement, each move may take you only into one of your three front hexes.

Change Position

This maneuver is used to get from any position to any other position, including standing, sitting, kneeling, lying face down (prone) or lying face up.

You may not move on the turn you use this maneuver. Note, though, that if your position change is from kneeling to standing, or vice versa, you may do this as part of any "Step and . . ." maneuver, below.

If you are lying down, you occupy *two* hexes. You cannot stand directly up from a lying position; you must kneel first (in either hex) and then stand up. This takes *two* turns.

You can move while in almost any position, but only while standing can you run at full speed. Movement restrictions for other positions are listed below.

Crouching does *not* require a "change position" maneuver. If you are in a standing position, you can elect to crouch at the beginning of any turn without a separate maneuver. If you don't move, you may crouch at the end of movement. However, you may not move and then crouch at the *end* of movement to avoid attacks – not in one second! If you are crouching, you *may* stand up at any time without using a maneuver.

You may use any defense on the turn you change position, though some positions give you a penalty for defense. Each position has advantages or disadvantages for attack, defense and movement, as summarized in the *Positions* table (p. 203).

Aim

This is the maneuver used to aim a thrown or missile weapon. Your weapon must be ready to fire. You must choose a specific target to aim at. You may change facing before you aim, but you may move only 2 yards or half your move, whichever is less.

Your attack is at -4 if you use a ranged weapon without aiming, *unless* your effective skill is at least equal to the weapon's Snap Shot number. If you aim for one turn, your attack is at your normal skill level *plus* the weapon's Accuracy modifier (p. 115), though you cannot get an Acc modifier higher than your skill.

You may aim for up to 3 more turns, getting a further +1 bonus for each turn you aim, for a maximum +3 bonus. See p. 115 for more about aiming.

You can use any defense while you are aiming, but to do so will spoil your aim and you lose all the accumulated benefits. If you are injured while aiming, you must make your Will roll or lose your aim.

This rule governs facing when you move forward. It is only important on a *Move, Wait* or *All-Out Attack* maneuver. Other maneuvers do not restrict your facing when you move!

A forward move is a move into one of your three front hexes. You must *turn to face the hex* as you enter it (see illustration). If you go *straight* ahead, your facing will not change; otherwise it will change by one hex-side (see illustration).

This means that you *can* change direction while moving "forward." In three "forward" moves, you can run in a half-circle and end up facing the opposite direction (see below).

If you don't want to move forward, you can step backward (A) or sideways (B), keeping the *same* facing (see below). Backward or sideways movement is not allowed in an all-out attack. As part of a *Move* maneuver, each hex costs double – that is, 2 movement points on good ground.

You can also "sidestep" into a *front* hex (C) while keeping your same facing. This *is* allowed on an all-out attack, as well as a regular *Move* maneuver. It also counts double.

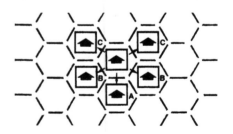

If you want to be more realistic, you can let your Encumbrance level affect the time it takes for a Change Position maneuver. At an encumbrance level of 0 or 1, it still takes 1 second for each Change Position. At an encumbrance level of 2 (medium), it takes *two* seconds to change position – and so on. While you are part-way through a position change, you are considered to be in the *old* position. This rule definitely slows play, but it means that falling down while wearing heavy armor can be fatal.

When Is a Weapon Ready?

A weapon is "ready" if it is in your hand and ready to attack. One turn is required to ready a weapon from its scabbard (but see *Fast-Draw* skill, p. 105).

Swords and knives do not become "unready" after use, because they are balanced and easy to maneuver.

Unbalanced hand weapons (like axes) *do* become "unready" after each attack or parry. Their momentum carries them away; it takes a turn to ready them again.

3-hex hand weapons (e.g., polearms like the halberd) require *two* turns to ready after a *swinging* attack, or one turn to re-ready after *thrusting*. A polearm swing carries it downward, so it takes longer to ready. But a polearm does not become unready after a parry, because you parry with the shaft.

Changing Grips: It takes one extra turn of readying to go from a 1-yard to a 2-yard reach, or a 2- to a 3-yard reach, or vice versa, with most weapons. An unready weapon may be re-readied to either reach, regardless of how you used it before.

Falling: If you fall down, lose your balance or are stunned, and your weapon is one that requires readying after each use, it becomes unready!

Scabbarding: It takes *two* turns to return a weapon to a scabbard or belt-loop.

Quick Readying with High ST

If a weapon becomes unready after use, the reason is its unbalanced *weight*. Therefore, high ST lets you ready it faster.

If your ST is 5 over the *minimum* ST required for an "unbalanced" weapon, it takes you one less turn to ready it after each attack. Thus, you could attack every turn with an axe, or every other turn with a polearm. And you could parry with an axe, and attack with it, on the same turn.

This also applies to crossbows: with ST 5 over the crossbow's ST, you can cock it in 1 second instead of 2.

If your ST is 10 over the minimum required for an unbalanced hand weapon, you can attack with it every turn. This does *not* apply to crossbows.

Parrying and Readiness

You may only parry with a *ready* weapon. Parrying does not make most weapons unready. You may attack with a sword, parry your foe's counterattack, and then attack again on your next turn. However, parrying does make a weapon unready if attacking would make it unready. *Exception:* polearms.

Example: John Falcon is fighting Fiendish Fredrick. John is faster; he swings with a sword. Fredrick's axe is ready, and he parries. Fredrick now cannot throw a blow – his axe is now unready. On his turn, he readies the axe.

Continued on next page . . . .

If you are prone, sitting down, beside or behind a wall, or in some other position appropriate for "bracing" a missile weapon, you get an extra +1 bonus to hit *if* you aim. You do not get this bonus for a snap shot or while moving.

Step and Ready

This is the maneuver used to pick up or draw *any* item and prepare it for use. You may move one hex before or after you draw the weapon. To pull a sword from its sheath or a gun from its holster, choose this maneuver.

You can also "ready" an item if you *stand still* and take it from a table or wall rack, etc. It must be in your own or an adjacent hex.

You can *stand still* and accept an item someone else holds out to you. The person must be in your own hex or any adjacent hex. You may use the same maneuver to hold out an item for someone else to take. Two objects may not be exchanged simultaneously (remember that these turns are one second long).

You may dodge normally after choosing this maneuver. You may block normally *if* your shield is already ready when you are attacked. You may parry normally *if* your weapon is fully ready when you are attacked. If your weapon requires more than one turn to ready, you cannot parry with it until it is fully ready. See below.

Readying a Weapon: You cannot use a weapon that is not "ready" – that is, in your hand and ready to use. Some weapons must be "readied" again after each attack. An axe, for instance, must be readied after each swing, because its momentum carries it away. A polearm must be readied for *two* seconds after each swing, or when you pick it up from the floor (because it is both long and heavy). The *Weapon Tables* show which weapons require readying after use.

Reloading a weapon requires repeated "ready" maneuvers. For instance, to fire a longbow (assuming the bow itself is ready in your hand), you must (1) ready the arrow by taking it from your quiver; (2) ready the bow by placing the arrow to the string. That took two turns. On the third turn, you can aim or fire. A crossbow would require the same two *Ready* maneuvers, plus at least two more to *cock* it! See sidebar, p. 96.

When a weapon requires more than one *Ready* maneuver to prepare, you should keep track by saying (for instance); "Cocking the bow, one second . . . cocking the bow, two seconds . . . readying the arrow . . . readying the bow." That took four turns, so you could fire on the fifth. Reloading times for different weapons are shown on the *Weapon Tables*. See also the sidebar on p. 96.

You may use any legal defense while readying a hand weapon; you may dodge, block or parry with another weapon. You may not block or parry while you are reloading a missile weapon. You *may* dodge, but you do not get the benefit of that turn of reloading. If you are cocking a crossbow or doing something else complex, you will have to start over if you dodge!

Readying a Shield: If a shield is on the ground, or slung on your back, the number of turns it takes to ready it is equal to its passive defense. It takes the same time to sling a shield on your back again. It takes one turn just to get a shield *off* your arm.

Picking Something Up from the Ground: This requires two turns. On the first turn, you Change Positions to *kneel*. On the second turn, you pick up the weapon and Change Positions again to *stand*. A sword, knife, etc., is automatically ready when you do so. An unbalanced weapon must be readied. It takes *two* turns to ready a polearm after you pick it up!

Step and Attack

This maneuver is used to attack with *any* ready weapon. Step one hex in any direction (or stand still), and use your weapon! The maneuver is the same, whether you strike with a hand weapon, fire a gun or throw a weapon. You may attack first and *then* move, if you choose. If you had been aiming a ranged weapon, moving before your attack will limit the bonus you can get from aiming (see p. 103).

The rules for attacking a foe are explained in the Basic Combat System (see p. 97). The foe you attack must be within your weapon's *reach* (see p. 102). He must be *in front* of you unless you are swinging wildly (see sidebar this page).

You *may* defend normally on the turn you attack. You may dodge, block or (if your weapon is still ready) parry. If you are using an axe or similar weapon, it becomes unready as soon as you swing it. So you can't use it to parry until after you take a turn – or more, if necessary – to ready it.

Attacking through an occupied hex: It is possible to attack "through" someone else if you have a hand weapon with a 2- or 3-yard reach. You may attack through friendly characters at no penalty (this is a basic part of your training with any long weapon). If you attack through an enemy's hex, the penalty is -4.

If your attack passes along a line between two hexes, there is no penalty at all unless both hexes are occupied. If they are, treat it as a single occupied hex – friendly, unless both hexes are occupied by foes.

All-Out Attack

This is the berserker's maneuver – the complete attack, with no thought to defense. You don't *have* to be crazy, but it helps.

You may use any hand weapon (not a missile or thrown weapon). You must move first and then attack – not vice versa. You may turn in place, or move up to two hexes (or half your movement, whichever is more) *forward*. You may ignore bodies on the ground and bad footing! You may not change facing at the end of your move. You have four choices for your attack:

(a) Make two attacks against the same foe, *if* you have two ready weapons, or one weapon that does not have to be readied after use;

(b) Make one *feint* (see below), and then one attack;

(c) Make a single attack, at a +4 bonus to your skill!

(d) Make a single attack, at normal skill, doing +2 damage if you hit.

However, if you choose this maneuver, you may make *no active defenses at all* until your next turn. You must depend on your passive defense to protect you – which is probably a forlorn hope.

This is a good maneuver if (a) your enemies are all otherwise occupied; (b) you have a long weapon and nobody can reach you, or (c) you're desperate.

Step and Feint

Move one hex in any direction and "fake" a hand weapon attack. You cannot feint unless you *could* have attacked that foe with a regular or all-out attack.

When you feint, roll a Contest of Skills (see p. 87): your weapon skill against your foe's shield or hand weapon skill. (If he has no shield or hand weapon, or if his DX is better than his shield or hand weapon skill, he rolls against his DX instead.) A feint does *not* make any weapon unready.

If you fail your roll, your feint is unsuccessful. Likewise, if you succeed, but your foe succeeds by *more* than you do, your feint fails.

If you *make* your roll, and your foe *fails*, the amount by which you made your roll is *subtracted* from the foe's active defense if you attack him on your next turn. (Your allies cannot take advantage of *your* feint; the defense penalty applies only to *your* next attack).

If you and your foe *both* succeed, but you succeed by more, the *difference* between the amounts is subtracted from the foe's defense. *Example:* Your skill is 15, and you roll a 10. You succeeded by 5. Your foe's skill is 14, and he rolled a 12. He succeeded by 2. The difference is 3, so he will defend at -3 next turn.

A feint is no good if your foe cannot see you. You cannot feint in the dark, from behind, etc. If your foe turns his back on you, or loses sight of you in some way, you will *not* lose your bonus if you attack on your next turn. However, if *you* lose sight of the foe, the bonus is lost.

A feint is good for *one* turn! But if you feint and then make an all-out attack, swinging twice, the feint applies to both attacks.

When Is A Weapon Ready? (Continued)

On John's second turn, he swings his sword again. Fredrick could parry – but he would rather be able to attack! So he has to dodge or block instead. On Fredrick's second turn, he swings with his axe. It is now unready. John parries the blow.

On John's third turn, he swings again. Fredrick's axe is unready, so he cannot parry – he must dodge or block again. On his own third turn, he can ready his axe – which will let him either parry or attack on his fourth turn. And so on . . .

The Fast-Draw Skill

This is an "easy" skill. It cannot be used by default; you must actually have learned the skill to attempt a fast-draw.

Fast-Draw is the ability to ready a weapon from its holster, scabbard or hiding place in (effectively) zero time. Roll against your Fast-Draw skill. A successful roll means the weapon is *instantly* ready and can be used to attack on that same turn. A failed roll means you perform an ordinary *Ready Weapon* maneuver. A critical miss means you drop the weapon.

You may also try Fast-Draw at the *end* of your turn, after doing something else. If you succeed, your weapon is ready. If you fail, you *must* take the "Ready Weapon" maneuver on your next turn – you've already started it.

Fast-Draw can be learned for pistols, longarms (rifles/SMGs), knives, arrows, regular swords, two-handed swords, speed-loaders and detachable-weapon magazines. Each of these is a *different* skill.

Wild Swings

A "wild swing" is a blow thrown at a foe to your *side* or *rear*. It's not likely to hit, but sometimes it's better than nothing.

A wild swing is at a -5 hit penalty, or a maximum attack roll of 9, or the current Darkness penalty, whichever is worst. You cannot aim at any particular part of the foe's body. If you are using hit-location rules, roll randomly. The foe you attack *must* be within your weapon's reach. You may not make a "wild" impaling attack at more than a 1-hex distance.

You may swing wildly on an all-out attack – but it's not usually a good idea. An all-out attack can*not* get a +4 skill bonus if you are swinging wildly.

Defense is normal against a wild swing. It does normal damage if it hits.

If you have Peripheral Vision, your right and left hexes count as "front." Therefore, an attack into your right hex is not a wild swing. An attack into your left hex *is* a wild swing (unless you have a two-handed weapon) – you can see, but the angle of attack is clumsy!

Knockback

When you hit someone very hard with a weapon, you may knock him backward. For every *full* 8 hits of *bullet, crushing* or *cutting damage* you roll, move the foe one hex directly away from you. Calculate knockback damage *before* the damage resistance of the foe's armor is subtracted. It may protect him from injury, but it won't keep him from feeling the blow!

Anyone knocked backward must make a DX roll to avoid falling down. A successful roll means he lands on his feet. If you knock your foe into something large, he will stop when he hits it. The results (including possible damage to whatever is hit) will be as if you had thrown him into it. See *Throwing Things*, p. 90.

Knockback from Slam Attacks

When one fighter knocks another down in a slam attack, there is a chance the fallen fighter will be knocked backward as well as down. This happens only when one fighter keeps his feet and the other falls.

Roll a Quick Contest of Strength. If the fallen fighter wins or ties, he is not knocked backward. If he loses, he is knocked back one hex for every 2 points by which he lost – round down, but always at least 1 hex. Any wall, fighter or other obstruction will stop him. If he hits another fighter, he stops in the hex *with* that fighter, who must make a roll (ST+3 or DX+3, whichever is better) to avoid falling down himself!

The fighter who *initiated* the slam attack cannot "bounce" back more than 2 hexes.

You may use any legal defense on any turn you feint. However, if you feint and then parry with an unbalanced weapon, rendering it unready, you cannot attack on the next turn and your feint becomes pointless.

Shield Feints: After you have attacked your foe once by striking with your shield (see p. 123), you may also feint with your shield, rolling vs. your Shield skill.

Step and Concentrate

This maneuver allows you to step one hex in any direction (usually) and then *concentrate* on one mental task. This may be the casting of a magical spell, use of a psi power, attempt to disbelieve an illusion, or any similar action.

If you are hurt, knocked down, forced to used an active defense, or otherwise distracted, you must make a Will-3 roll to maintain your concentration.

Step and Wait

This maneuver lets you move one hex in any direction, change facing or stand still, and *wait* for a foe to approach. At any time before your next turn, if a foe is close enough, you may attack. If you stood still on your turn, you may step one hex *forward* and *then* attack. If the foe is moving to attack *you,* the longer weapon strikes first. If they are the same length, roll a Contest of Weapon Skills. With high skill, this allows a "stop thrust" strategy.

You do not *have* to attack the first foe that comes within reach; you may ignore one enemy and wait for another. You do not have to attack at all.

If more than one fighter is Waiting, and one announces an attack, then that attack (and the target's reaction, if it was the target's move) are both played out before another Waiting fighter can attack.

If no enemy comes within step-and-attack range, or if you choose not to attack, your turn is simply lost; you stood there waiting, and did nothing.

You may choose any legal defense on the turn you Wait.

This maneuver is also used for *opportunity fire* with a ranged weapon (see sidebar, p. 118).

All-Out Defense

This is the maneuver to choose when you're beset by foes – especially foes who like all-out attacks. You may move one hex *in any direction.* You may do nothing else – except defend!

If you fail your defense roll against any attack, you may try *another* (different) defense – in other words, you get two defense rolls, using two different active defenses, for each attack made during the turn. You are limited to a total of *two* blocks and *two* parries per turn when you choose All-Out Defense (if you have two weapons, each can parry twice). If you run out of blocks and parries, you may only dodge each attack once – you can't dodge the same attack twice!

Long Action

Many actions will take more than a second to complete. In a combat situation, use the generic "Long Action" maneuver each second until you are finished. The GM will tell you how long it will take. In some cases, dice will be rolled to determine how long you will take to finish.

Some things (like piling up rocks to stand on) can be interrupted in the middle if necessary, to take any necessary maneuver or other action. Other things (like dialing a telephone number) cannot be interrupted; if you stop in the middle, you will have to start over entirely.

examples of long actions

Pick up a heavy object (weight greater than your ST) .... 2 sec.
Open an unlocked box, book, chest, briefcase, etc. .... 1 sec.
Find a loose item in a box, briefcase, etc. (if it's not hidden) .... 2d seconds
Find some item in your own pocket .... 1d seconds
Write a brief note .... 5 sec. per sentence
Read a brief note .... 2 sec. per sentence
Swallow a pill or potion .... 2 sec.
Light a match, cigarette, fuse, candle, torch, etc. .... 2 sec.
Replace a weapon in its scabbard, drop a small item into your pocket .... 2 sec.
Search an unresisting person fairly thoroughly .... 1 min.
Change clothes .... 1 min.
Put on a suit of light armor .... 5 min.
Put on full plate or ultra-tech combat armor .... 10 min.

While carrying out a long action, you should count the seconds each time you announce the maneuver. For instance, to replace a weapon, you would say "Replacing my weapon – one second" on the first turn, and "Replacing my weapon – two seconds and finished" on the second turn. That way, the GM and the other players can keep up with what you are doing.

The GM determines your legal defenses while you are taking a long action. As a rule, Dodging is the only legal defense, and a Dodge will usually force you to start your action over. But the GM may vary this whenever it seems realistic.

Move

This is the maneuver to choose when *all* you need to do is move. You can *Move* in almost any position, but only if you are standing can you travel at full speed. Other positions will slow you, as shown in the sidebar.

For example, if you want to move *backward* for some reason (such as to keep your eyes on a foe), each hex counts double. Thus, someone with a Move of 6 could go only three hexes backward in a turn, without turning around. If you move in a *crouching* position, you will be slower but harder to hit.

You may use any legal active defense on a turn you pick the Move maneuver.

You may use a hand weapon during a Move – before, during or after your movement – but it is a Wild Swing (p. 105).

You may aim or fire a ranged weapon while moving, but there will be a substantial penalty to your accuracy. See p. 117.

Free Actions

Some actions may be taken during any maneuver. Some examples:

Talk. You can *always* talk. (If the GM wants to be realistic, he should only allow one sentence's worth of communication per second. It is usually more fun when you ignore this limitation.)

Maintain spells (when magic is used). As long as a spell-caster is not injured or knocked unconscious, he can maintain a spell no matter what else he does.

Dropping an item. Any "ready" item can be dropped at any time during any maneuver. It may be dropped in any hex you move through, or any adjacent hex.

Crouching. You may crouch (to avoid missile weapons) at the beginning of any turn – but movement costs are increased by 50%. You *cannot* crouch and sprint. You may stand up again at any time.

Costs for Movement

Use the following costs only when you choose the *Move* maneuver. For other maneuvers, "cost" does not matter.

If you have (for instance) a Move of 6, you have 6 "movement points" per turn. A hex of forward movement costs 1; sideways and backwards movement costs 2.

Penalties for obstructions, etc., add to this. If you step sideways (cost 2) into an obstructed hex (cost+1), the total cost to enter that hex is 3. However, you can always move 1 hex per turn. Peripheral vision does *not* affect the cost to move sideways or backwards!

Direction of Travel
Forward: 1
Sidestep or Backward: 2

Positions
Crouching: $+\frac{1}{2}$
Kneeling: +2
Crawling: +2
Lying down: move only 1 hex per turn (belly-crawl or rolling)
Sitting: cannot move!

Facing Changes
If you want to change facing *before* or *during* a move, each hex-side of change costs 1. At the *end* of your move, you may change facing freely if you used half (or less) of your movement points. If you used more than half of your Move score, you may change facing by *one hex-side* at the end of your move.

Obstructions
Minor obstruction (e.g., a body, or another character, in the hex): +1 per body or person. You cannot go through an *enemy's* hex unless you *evade* (p. 113).
Severe obstruction (several bodies): hex must be bypassed or actually climbed.

Bad Footing
On treacherous ground, the cost to enter each hex is increased by 1, 2, or more. It depends on the GM's "realistic" view of the situation (mud, loose gravel, waxed floors, or whatever!). Movement on stairs (up or down) costs double.

Movement in foot-deep water costs double. Deeper water reduces all movement to 1 hex per turn. If such a stream is swift-moving, roll vs. DX (minus encumbrance) each turn. A failed roll means you fall, and must make a Swimming roll to regain your feet. Every failed Swimming roll sweeps you 3 yards downstream and has its normal choking effects (see p. 91).

Anyone in an obstructed or bad-footing hex also suffers a -2 on any attack they make. Defense is unaffected. Exception: If you are firing a missile weapon, taking time to aim will also eliminate this penalty!

Continued on next page . . .

Costs for Movement
(Continued)

Sprinting

If you run *forward* for two or more turns in a row, your second (and later) moves get a "sprint bonus" of 1 extra yard per turn. You may not take the sprint bonus unless the ground is good and you are running (more or less) straight toward some goal. Any deviation from "forward" movement will require you to run at normal speed for one turn before you can get the sprint bonus again.

Example: Your Move is 4. You can run 4 yards forward. But on your second and later turns of running, you get the sprint bonus, and you can run *five* yards forward.

Quicker Combats

If your combats are taking too long, here is an alternate rule you can use. Note that this rule will make it *much easier* for a high-skill fighter to slaughter a low-skill one. But with fighters of equivalent skills, it will not affect balance much.

Treat each attack/defense as a *Quick Contest of Skills* (p. 87). If the attacker hits, the defender must make his defense roll by *as much, or more*. This makes successful defense rolls harder, and speeds combat!

Passive Defenses in the Advanced Combat System

Your passive defenses – your armor and shield – add to your defense roll when the foe has attacked you, just as in the Basic Combat System. Armor and Toughness work just the same (though armor can have different PDs at different parts of your body – see the *Armor Table*).

However, your shield's PD only protects against attacks from *in front* of you and your *shield* side. It protects against all attacks while you are lying down, unless you state, for some insane reason, that you are *on top of* the shield.

If you have your shield slung on your back, it will offer a *little* passive defense. Subtract 1 from the regular PD of the shield, and apply this to attacks from the back (only), but *not* to other attacks. You could carry an extra shield strapped to your back – but it would add weight!

"Runaround" Attacks

A very fast character can sometimes start in front of a foe and run behind him to strike from his rear hex. Against a true attack from the rear, no active defense is possible because the victim did not know the attack was coming. If the attacker starts in front and runs behind (outmaneuvering his victim through sheer speed), the victim *does* know he's being attacked. Treat it as a side attack – -2 to active defense.

ATTACKS

In general, attacks are carried out just as in the Basic Combat System. Two special kinds of attack are covered in detail in later sections: *close combat* in the same hex with your foe (see p. 111), and *ranged attacks* with thrown and missile weapons (see p. 114).

DEFENSE

The rules for defense are essentially the same as in the Basic Combat System – but more detailed, to allow for your position relative to the enemy.

Active Defenses

There are three *active defenses* that can be used to protect you against an attack. Each of these defenses is calculated in advance. When you are attacked, you may choose one active defense as part of your total defense roll. (If you took *All-Out Defense*, you may make *two* separate defense rolls against each attack.)

The active defense you choose will depend on your situation – *especially* the maneuver you chose on your last turn. Some maneuvers restrict the active defenses you can make. For instance, if you make an All-Out Attack, you have *no* active defense.

If you are stunned, any active defense is at -4. Sometimes you will have *no* active defense. A stab in the back from a "friend," a sniper's shot, or a totally unexpected booby trap would be attacks against which no active defense is possible. Likewise, an unconscious person has no active defense. But you always have your *passive defense* – see sidebar.

The advantage of Combat Reflexes gives +1 to any active defense.

Dodging

Your Dodge defense is equal to your Move score. An animal's Dodge score is half its Move or half its DX, whichever is better – up to a maximum of 10. Dodging is the best defense when you are not skilled with your weapon.

You may not dodge an attack from your *back* hex – that is, directly behind you. Subtract 2 from your Dodge when you dodge an attack from a *side* hex. *Example:* If your Dodge is 5, your Dodge against a side attack would be 3. You may not dodge a ranged-weapon attack from a foe outside your field of vision.

There is no limit to the number of times you may dodge in one turn.

Acrobatic Dodge: If you have the Acrobatics skill, you can try a "fancy" Dodge maneuver once per turn. You may define this as jumping over a sword-blow, cartwheeling away, or whatever else you like. Attempt your Acrobatics roll (no defaults!). If you succeed, you get a +1 to your Dodge roll; if you fail, you get a -2. This may be combined with a Retreat (see p. 109).

Blocking

Your "block" defense is half your Shield skill, rounded down. You must have a *ready* shield, which you use to "block" the attack. Blocking follows the Basic Combat rules (p. 98) with the following additions:

You may block only attacks made from your front hexes *or* your shield-side hex (left, unless you are left-handed). A block against a shield-side attack is at a -2. You may block thrown weapons coming from a side hex, but not missiles.

You may only block one attack per turn, unless you chose the *All-Out Defense* maneuver. In that case, you may block *two* attacks per turn.

Parrying

Your Parry defense is half your hand-weapon skill, or 2/3 your Fencing or Quarterstaff skill (round down). Parrying follows the rules given in the Basic Combat System (p. 99) with the following additions:

You may only parry attacks made from your front hexes or your *weapon*-side hex (the right, unless you are left-handed). A two-handed weapon can parry attacks from either side hex. You Parry at -2 against an attack from the side.

You may normally parry only one attack per turn, unless you are a fencer (see p. 99). If you take *All-Out Defense,* you may parry *two* attacks per turn. You may parry a bare-handed attack with a weapon – see p. 99.

Retreating

This is not a separate defense; it is an option you may add to any active defense, by moving one hex in any direction away from your attacker. Retreating adds 3 to any attempt to Dodge, Block or Parry.

You may not retreat into an occupied hex. You may change facing by *one* hex-side, if you wish. (A retreat cannot be used to defend against a *ranged* attack.) Your "retreat" move takes place immediately.

If a retreat takes you out of the reach of a hand weapon, *the foe still gets his attack.* And if your foe was making an all-out attack, retreating does *not* put you beyond the reach of his second attack.

You cannot retreat in a sitting or kneeling position, or while stunned. You *can* retreat (by rolling) if you are lying down.

You can retreat only once per turn. In other words, once you retreat, you may not retreat again until after your own next turn.

HIT LOCATION

When you strike at an enemy, you may choose *what part of his body* you will attack. Each part of the body is different – easier or harder to hit in a fight, and having different reactions to major damage. The table on p. 203 shows this. You can also refer to this table when you want to choose a random body part to be hit (for instance, by falling rocks or an arrow fired from far off). Roll 3 dice to see what was hit. Some parts will never be hit randomly.

Hit Penalties for Different Body Parts

If a blow is aimed at any part of the body except the torso, the difficulty of the target will add a hit penalty. Subtract this penalty from the attacker's skill. The torso is easy to hit (no penalty). Arms and legs are harder (-2); hands and feet harder yet (-4). The head is still harder to hit (-5), and the *brain* area – the vital part of the head, as opposed to the face and jaw – is -7, because it is both small and *hard*. See the table on p. 203.

If the target of the blow is armored with some substance that "turns" blows – metal or hard plastic – it will have a *passive defense* that will add to the target's defense roll. For instance, heavy leather gives a passive defense of 2. See the *Armor Tables,* pp. 210 and 211. Armor protection for specific body parts should be marked by the character's picture on his Record Sheet.

CRITICAL HITS

A "critical hit" is an especially damaging blow. Any time you roll a natural 3 or 4 when attacking, you hit automatically – the defender gets no defense roll – *and* you may roll on the *Critical Hit* tables on p. 202.

If you are very skillful, you get critical hits more often. With an *effective* skill of 15, a roll of 5 is a critical hit. With an effective skill of 16 *or better,* a roll of 6 is a critical hit. Hit bonuses (e.g., for an all-out attack) *do* make critical hits more likely. Hit penalties (e.g., for a hard target) make critical hits less likely.

Deciding Where to Attack

Where you should hit your foe depends on many things – your skill, your foe's armor, and whether you want to kill him!

Brain – Lets you stun with minimal damage, and kill easily with a good shot. But this is a hard target, especially if a helmet is worn.

Body – Easy to hit, and no damage is "wasted" except from very powerful attacks – it all goes into killing the foe. The best target for strong, clumsy types or long-range attacks. The best target for an impaling weapon.

Limbs – Lets you eliminate a foe from combat with less total damage, leaving him alive for questioning or prisoner exchange. If you do *not* want to kill, this is the best target. Attacking the limbs is often a good move if you have high skill but low strength.

Hands or feet – Hard targets, but give you a chance to cripple the foe with little real damage. Don't try this if your real objective is to kill.

Weapon – The place to strike if you need to take the foe unharmed, if you have to disarm a friend, or if you just want to show off. See *Striking at Weapons,* p. 110.

Random Hit Location

You do not *have* to choose a target; you can always swing randomly. Roll 3 dice and check the table to see where your blow falls. Then proceed normally with the attack. Random hit location is also used when a booby trap goes off, when a missile weapon is fired from a long way off, etc. In that case, though, you should *first* determine whether the missile hits (with no penalty for part-of-body) and *then* determine where it hits.

If a random attack comes from above (e.g., a halberd stroke, or falling rocks), subtract 3 from the roll before referring to the table. This makes the head and arms the most likely targets.

Massive Damage: "Blow-Through"

The amount of damage the limbs can take is limited; damage over HT/3 on the hands and feet, or HT/2 on the arms or legs, cripples the limb instead of dealing additional hits of damage.

For a single blow to the torso, *Impaling or bullet* damage of more than HT is lost . . . it just goes "through" the victim and is wasted. For the head or vitals, damage over HT×3 is lost.

Beam, fireball or lightning attacks do double the above maximum damage to torso, head or vitals.

However, there is no maximum damage for injuries to the brain. There is also no maximum damage cutoff for weapons doing more than 15 dice basic damage; such huge weapons do so much damage going through that any "wastage" is moot.

Advanced Injury Rules

Different types of weapon affect different parts of the body in different ways. An arrow through the head, for instance, is bad news – but the same arrow through the foot may be little more than a nuisance.

Bullets and Impaling Weapons

When you choose a specific part of the body as your target, bullets and impaling weapons can do special damage.

If you hit the foe's *vital organs* with an impaling weapon, the damage that gets through the armor is *tripled!* Vital organs cannot be targets except with an impaling attack. (Exception: A punch or kick to the solar plexus or groin may be played as a crushing attack to the vitals.)

If you hit the foe's *arms, legs, hands or feet* with a bullet or impaling weapon, there is *no* damage bonus; the damage is not multiplied at all. An arrow wound to a limb is fairly trivial; an arrow in the head can kill.

Crippling Injuries

If the target is hit on a limb, and enough damage is done, the limb is crippled . . . crushed, slashed, or badly burned, as the case may be.

A fighter immediately loses the use of a crippled limb. This can cause him to fall, drop a weapon, etc. See the chapter on *Injuries, Illness and Fatigue,* p. 126, for more detail. A crippling injury automatically *stuns* the victim (see p. 127).

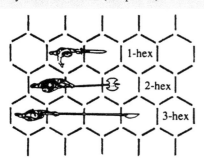

Striking at Weapons

You may strike at a weapon because you want to take its user alive . . . or because (in the case of a polearm) the weapon is the only thing you can reach.

A "close" weapon is in the user's hex. A 1-hex weapon is in the user's hex and directly in front (see diagram), and a 2-hex weapon is in the two hexes directly in front of the user. However, you can always strike at a 2- or 3-hex weapon on the turn after it struck or feinted at *you.*

There is a -5 penalty for striking at a knife, pistol or other small weapon, -3 for a polearm, spear, rifle, or greatsword and -4 for any other weapon. A hit on a weapon may *chop through* the wood shaft of an axe or polearm, and knock down or break a metal weapon.

Continued on next page . . .

Example: Louis LeBlanc needs to roll a 15 or less to hit Filthy Pierre. He rolls a 5. That's a critical hit for him! (A 3 or 4 would be a critical hit for *anyone!*) Because this is a critical hit, Pierre gets *no defense roll*. The blow automatically hits!

A critical hit is the *only* way that an unskilled character can injure a superior opponent in a fair fight. It's also the only way you can get through heavy armor with a light weapon. Once in a while, everybody gets a lucky shot. But note that the most likely result on the table is "no extra damage." Even if you get lucky and hit a superior foe, your blow may not be especially hard . . .

Stunning

Critical hits, and several other things, can stun the victim. This is discussed in detail on p. 127. A stunned character defends at -4 and can do nothing!

This rule is realistic but *deadly*. If you want to ignore it, go right ahead.

CRITICAL MISSES

The opposite of a "critical hit" is a "critical miss." You suffer a critical miss when you roll *very badly* on your attack roll. A roll of 18 is always a critical miss. A roll of 17 is a critical miss unless your effective skill is 16 or better; in that case, it is an ordinary miss. A roll that exceeds your needed roll by 10 or more is also a critical miss. *Example:* You need a 6 or less to hit. A roll of 16 or more is a critical miss! You may break your weapon, throw it away, or even hit yourself.

When you roll a critical miss, you should immediately refer to the appropriate *Critical Miss Table* (p. 202) and roll 3 dice. Apply the results immediately. Some results call for a second roll to "confirm" an especially unlikely fumble.

Obviously, if your effective skill is 7 or more, you will not get a critical miss unless you roll a 17 or 18. Therefore, skilled fighters won't fumble very often . . . unless they try a difficult blow, or attack under adverse conditions.

CRITICAL HITS AND MISSES ON DEFENSE ROLLS

Defenses can also fail disastrously on a critical miss. If you tried to *dodge*, you lose your footing and fall. if you tried to *block*, you lose your grip on your shield and must take a turn to re-ready it before you can block again (its passive defense still counts). If you tried to *parry*, you go to the *Critical Miss Table.*

However, if you get a critical success on any defense roll, then your *foe* goes immediately to the *Critical Miss Table*. You "faked him out," or knocked the weapon from his hand, or otherwise defended *very* well. Exception: against a *ranged* attack, a critical success has no special effect.

CHOOSING YOUR ARMOR – ADVANCED RULES

When you use the Advanced Combat System, you may purchase armor for six different parts of the body: head, torso, hands, feet, arms and legs. See the diagram on p. 211. Cost and weight for hands, feet, arms and legs always assume that a pair is being purchased, since it is rare for anyone to want one sort of gear on one limb and one on the other. However, it is perfectly legal to do this if you want to!

The *Armor Tables* (pp. 210-211) give cost, weight, passive defense and DR for many different pieces of armor, from cloth to futuristic plastics, and show what coverage each item gives.

If this is too complex to be enjoyable, you may simply go back to the Basic System and assume that the passive defense and damage resistance of a suit of armor apply equally to all its parts.

Cost and weight in the two systems are equivalent. However, the Basic armor rules *are* more advantageous to characters using hit location rules, because (for instance) a figure in plate gauntlets has DR 4 on his hands, while a figure in "generic" heavy plate, if hit on the hand, has a "generic" damage resistance of 7!

CLOSE COMBAT

Using the *Move, Step and Attack* or *All-Out Attack* maneuvers, you may move into an enemy-occupied hex if you can reach it. When you move into an enemy's hex, you may attack him in any of several ways. Attacking a foe in the same hex is *close combat*.

You may also try to *evade* and slip past the enemy without contact. If you use the *Move* maneuver to enter an enemy-occupied hex, you *must* either try to evade, or to *slam* the opponent!

When you enter an enemy-occupied hex, you occupy *half* the hex (see diagram). You have the half of the hex from which you entered; he has the other half. To enter any of your front hexes on the enemy's side, you will have to *evade* him and "move through" him.

MANEUVERS IN CLOSE COMBAT

Step and Attack Maneuver

You can step into the foe's hex and attack him. If you are already in his hex, you can step out and attack with a 1-hex weapon – or stay in the hex, make a close attack, and step out – *unless* he has grappled you. If he is holding you, you may still choose a maneuver every turn, but you cannot leave the hex until you break free – you're trapped. Possible attacks are:

Grapple. You grab the foe. To do so, you must win a Quick Contest of Dexterity (see p. 87); you are at +3! You must have at least one empty hand to grab with. Grappling does no damage, but the foe is at -4 DX and may not leave until he breaks free, or you let go. (Note that if you grapple with a foe of more than twice your ST, you do *not* prevent him from leaving. At the most, you're a nuisance. A man can grab a bear, but he can't keep the bear from walking away.)

You may grapple with both hands, or only with one. If you are holding your foe with both hands, the only further attack you can make is to try for a strangle, takedown or pin.

If your foe is kneeling, lying down, etc., you are at +6 on your DX roll. But you must kneel or lie down yourself in order to grab him! You may do this as part of your "grapple" attack – just dive right in there!

Grab the foe's weapon. You must have an empty hand and win a Quick Contest of Dexterity. On later turns, you may then try to wrest it from the foe; each attempt takes a full second and requires you to *win* a Contest of Strength. If you *lose* the contest, you lose your grip on his weapon.

Grab the foe's weapon arm. As above, but for a weapon you *cannot* grab (like a dagger). If you win the Contest of Dexterity, you grab the weapon arm or hand. This counts as a Grapple. You cannot take the weapon away, but you can force the foe to drop it by winning a Contest of Strength; you could then try to pick up the weapon yourself.

Attack with a weapon. If you have a legal close combat weapon in hand (see sidebar, p. 112) you can use it. Weapon attacks in close combat are at a -2 to hit.

Attack bare-handed. This may be an ordinary punch (Thrust-2 crushing damage); an attempt to bite (1d-4 crushing damage for human teeth, more for some creatures); a punch using the Karate or Brawling ability (see p. 51, 50); or a Karate kick doing -1 damage.

Attempt a takedown. You may only do this if your foe is standing and you

Striking at Weapons
(Continued)

Cutting Through a Weapon

To chop through a wooden shaft (destroying the weapon) you must hit it with a cutting weapon. Only *basic* damage counts – there is no 50% bonus when you cut an inanimate object. Typically, a spear or axe would have a wooden shaft 2" in diameter, which would have a DR of 3 and 8 hit points. A well-made *polearm* would have a 2" shaft protected by metal facings; it would have a DR of 4 and 12 hit points. Keep track of the damage your weapon takes! For more information on the amount of damage that weapons (and other items) can take, see p. 125.

Breaking a Sword

To break a foe's sword, rapier, knife or other blade weapon, you must strike it with a cutting or crushing blow. It takes 4 hits of damage *in a single blow* to break a dagger, smallsword or rapier, 6 to break a knife, short-sword or saber, 8 to break a broadsword, 10 to break a larger sword. If your weapon is of better quality (see p. 74), it takes only half as much damage to break the enemy's weapon. If his weapon is of better quality than yours it takes *twice* as much damage to break it.

Any weapon can be broken by parrying a heavier weapon. If you parry a weapon of at least 3 times the weight of your own weapon, there is a ¹/₃ chance that your weapon will break!! This becomes a ¹/₆ chance if you have a *fine* weapon, or a ²/₃ chance for a *cheap* weapon.

To determine this, roll one die. A ¹/₆ chance comes up on a roll of 1, a ¹/₃ chance on a 1 or 2, and so on.

Defense Against Weapon Attacks

You may dodge an attack on your weapon. You may parry, if your weapon is ready – in effect, you are turning your weapon so the foe's blow misses or slides off harmlessly. You may *not* block an attack on your weapon. Your passive defense does *not* count into this defense!

Knocking a Weapon Away

To knock a weapon from a foe's hand, use an Attack maneuver, but state that you are attacking to disarm. Instead of regular attack and defense rolls, roll a Quick Contest of Weapons Skills. If you are striking at a hand-held missile weapon, your foe uses his DX instead of skill. You attack at a penalty appropriate to the weapon's size (see above). Weapons *other* than fencing weapons are at a further -2 for a disarm attempt. The defender rolls at +1 if his weapon is heavier than yours, +2 if it is twice as heavy, and so on.

If you win, your foe drops his weapon in that hex; if you roll a critical failure, *you* are disarmed. Otherwise, there is no effect.

Weapons for Close Combat

Most weapons cannot be used in close combat. The exceptions are knives and daggers; pistols (slug-throwers or beam weapons); certain magic items; brass knuckles and similar devices; and anything else small and easily managed. All weapon attacks (except for fists) are at -2 in close combat.

Pistols can be used in close combat, but not aimed. Ignore speed/range modifiers!

Brass knuckles will add +2 to the damage you do with your fists. A set of brass knucks (one for each hand) costs $30 and weighs one pound. It takes two seconds to put each brass knuck on. They cannot be grabbed by the enemy or dropped accidentally, but give you a -2 to use any other weapon in that hand.

A *blackjack*, or "sap," can only be used in close combat or when you are adjacent to an unsuspecting foe. A blackjack does Thrust/Crush damage.

If you are assembling armor piece by piece, here's how to show it on your Character Sheet.

HEAD
POT-HELM
PD 3; DR 4

TORSO/ARMS
SCALE
PD 3; DR 4

HANDS
BARE
PD Ø; DR Ø

LEGS
BARE
PD Ø; DR Ø

FEET
LEATHER
PD 2; DR 2

have already grappled him. Roll a Quick Contest of Skills: your ST, DX *or* Judo skill (whichever is better) against your foe's ST. (If *you* are already on the ground, you have a -5 penalty.) If you win, your foe falls down in the same hex *and* any adjacent hex (your choice – remember, a prone man occupies two hexes). If he was holding you, he loses his grip. If you lose, *you* suffer the same effects! If nobody wins, nothing happens.

Attempt a pin. You may only do this if your foe is already on the ground. Roll a Contest of Strength. The *heavier* fighter gets +1 to his roll for every 10 pounds he has over his foe. If you win, your foe is *pinned* and helpless; you must stay there to hold him down, but you can free one of your hands for other actions. If you lose or tie, nothing happens.

Choke or strangle. You must already have grappled the foe by the neck, with both hands. You cannot do anything else with your hands until next turn!

Roll a Quick Contest – your ST vs. your foe's HT. If you win, your foe takes as many hits of damage as you win by, and you also inflict suffocation damage as per the sidebar on p. 122. Otherwise, nothing happens.

Break free. For maneuver purposes, this is an "attack," even though it does no damage. If you are being grappled, you cannot move away until you break free by *winning* a Quick Contest of Strength. Your foe is +5 if he has you pinned but is only using one hand, or if you are not pinned but he is holding onto you with both hands. Your foe is at +10 if he has you pinned; in that case you may make only one Break Free attempt per 10 seconds.

If you successfully break free, you may immediately move one hex in any direction. Note: If your foe falls unconscious, you are automatically free!

Slam. This attack is described below under the *Move* maneuver.

Step and Ready Maneuver

Draw a weapon. This should be a weapon you can use in close combat (see sidebar). Use the *Step and Ready* maneuver (even if you can't step) to draw a weapon from its sheath or holster, or to pick it up off the ground in your hex or an adjoining one. Make a DX roll to get it successfully. A critical failure (17 or 18) means you *dropped* the weapon while trying to draw it!

If you have the Fast-Draw skill, you may use it in close combat – but you must make *two* rolls, one (vs. DX) to get the weapon, and one (vs. your skill) to get it *fast*. If you miss the second roll, you readied the weapon normally.

Change Position Maneuver

You may change positions freely during close combat. *Exception:* If you are on the ground and pinned, you cannot change positions unless your can break free, as described above.

Move Maneuver

Slam. You may try to slam your foe when you *first* enter his hex. You are trying to run into him and knock him down. A shield helps. You cannot make a slam attack if you start in the same hex with your foe!

To hit your foe, roll a Quick Contest of DX. He is at a -2 if you entered from the side or if he's not standing; you win automatically if you entered from behind. If you win (or tie), you slam into him; if you lose, he avoided you, and you must move at least two more hexes, if you have that much movement left.

If you slam into your foe, roll a Quick Contest of ST, with the following modifiers, to see if you fall down:

+2 if you moved more than one hex toward the foe, or if you were running last turn and moved one hex this turn.

-2 if the *foe* moved more than one hex toward *you*, or was running last turn and moved one hex this turn.

+2 if you have a medium or large shield; -2 if the *foe* has one of those shields.

+2 if you slam the foe from behind.

The loser falls down, and may also be knocked *backward* – see sidebar. p. 106. The *winner* falls down, too, if he fails to roll at least his (adjusted) ST! Note that a shield helps knock your foe down, and that your foe is more likely to keep his feet if he was also running toward you!

A slam attack does no damage to either fighter unless he rolls a 17 or 18 on his ST roll. In that case, he is unhurt but stunned.

If you slam your foe, knock him down, and win the Contest of ST by more than 5 points, you can keep right on moving! This is an "overrun," and is most often seen when a large creature slams into a man.

Flying Tackle. This is a special type of slam. The tackler gets one extra hex of movement. The target may attempt to Dodge unless being tackled from behind; if he dodges, the tackler falls to the ground. If the tackle is not dodged, roll the Contest of ST as for a Slam. The tackler is at +2, but he automatically falls down. The target is at -2 if he tried to Dodge and failed. If the tackler wins the contest by more than 4, he automatically grapples his foe.

Trample. This tactic is only effective if used by a large foe – see *Trampling,* p. 142. A large creature can take a turn to trample its foe – or do half the regular "trampling" damage just by moving through. The attacker rolls against DX to hit; the defender gets a Dodge bonus. A man-sized fighter cannot "trample" without stopping unless he is running through a swarm of small creatures (see p. 143).

Escape. If you start in the foe's hex and he is not grappling you, you can move out of the hex through any of the three hexes on "your side" of the combat hex. You cannot leave through the hexes on the foe's side unless you can *evade* him – see below.

Evading

"Evading" is moving "through" the foe, to leave the hex on *his* side. You can attempt this as part of any maneuver that allows movement.

You *cannot* evade if a foe is holding you. You must also have enough movement to get out of the enemy hex! If your movement ends in the enemy hex, you *cannot* evade or escape on that turn.

First, ask if your foe is trying to stop you. If he chooses to let you go, you have *automatically* "evaded." No roll is needed.

If your foe wants to stop you, roll a Quick Contest of DX, with *your* DX modified as follows:

-5 if the foe is standing up.
-2 if the foe is kneeling.
+2 if you entered the hex that turn, from his right or left.
+5 if you entered the hex that turn, from *behind* him.
+5 if the foe is lying down.

If you win, you have evaded him and you are free to move out. If you lose or tie, he got in your way and stopped you.

Free Actions
(combine with any maneuver in close combat)

Release your grip. Let go of the foe, if you are grappling him.

Throw away your weapon. This automatically succeeds and takes no time. You may do this to get a useless weapon out of your way, or to deprive the foe of a chance to grab a useful weapon (e.g., a blackjack) from you.

Other Maneuvers

All-Out Attack, All-Out Defense, Feint, Aim, Concentrate and *Wait* maneuvers are not possible in close combat. Any close combat is – by definition – almost "all-out" anyway, and the other maneuvers require a degree of planning and coordination that is impossible when you are nose-to-nose with your opponent. If you want to try some other action during close combat, the GM will be the judge of its feasibility.

Dropped Weapons

When a weapon is dropped for any reason, place a counter in that hex to indicate the dropped weapon. Any character in that hex, or next to it, can pick up the dropped weapon. It takes one turn to kneel in the weapon hex or an adjacent hex, and a second turn to grab the weapon and stand up.

Once you have readied the weapon in hand, it must be *readied* if it is a weapon that requires readying after each use. Thus, a sword is automatically ready, but it takes two turns of readying for a polearm. It takes a number of turns equal to a shield's passive defense (1 for a buckler, up to 4 for a large shield) to ready it on your arm after you pick it up.

Broken Weapons

Knives, bows, crossbows, slings and similar weapons are always useless after breaking. For other weapons, roll one die. There is a 50% chance that it is still *partially* usable – refer to the appropriate paragraph below.

Swords: A broken sword does half its normal cutting damage, but is almost useless as an impaling weapon: Thrust damage, crushing only (because the tip is gone). A broken 2-hex sword has only a 1-hex range.

Smallswords and Rapiers: A broken smallsword is treated as a dagger, and a broken rapier is treated as a smallsword. The broken tip does not make the weapon less deadly – just shorter!

Spears: There is a 50% chance the head will break off where it joins the shaft – in which case, you now have a quarterstaff. Otherwise, you have a club, and there is a 1-yard spear, doing normal damage, lying on the ground in front of you.

Battleaxes: There is a 50% chance you now have a club, and a 50% chance the shaft breaks near your hand – in which case, there is a clumsy (-4 to hit) 1-yard axe lying in front of you.

Polearms: It all depends on where it breaks. There is a 33% chance you are left with an 8-foot pole (parries normally, attacks as a blunt pike); a 33% chance you are left with a quarterstaff, and there is a very clumsy (-4 to hit) axe on the ground; and a 33% chance you are left with a short club and there is a clumsy (-2 to hit) 2-hex battleaxe on the ground. Figure skill and damage according to the *new* weapon type!

Axes and Maces: The head is broken off, leaving you holding a short club.

Other Weapons: Use the closest type of weapon listed above, or let the GM make a logical decision about the possibilities (and roll, if there is more than one way for the weapon to break).

Striking Into a Close Combat

If you are not, yourself, involved in a close combat, but your allies are, you may want to help them. You can do this by standing outside the close-combat hex(es) and striking at a foe who **is** in close combat.

Your attack is at a -2, plus any modifier for the foe's position (lying down, for instance). If you hit, your foe's only legal defense is to dodge.

If you **miss**, or if your foe successfully dodges, you may hit someone else in the hex. Roll randomly to see who you "attack" first, if there is more than one other fighter in the hex. No attack roll you make, whether it is against a friend or foe, can be at better than a 9. If you hit, the victim may dodge. Keep rolling until you run out of targets or you actually hit someone.

Shields in Close Combat

In close combat, a shield becomes a potentially deadly nuisance. It still provides its passive defense. However, it hampers **you** while you wear it. **Any** attack you make in close combat (except for the **initial** slam or step-and-attack, when you move into the foe's hex) has a penalty equal to the passive defense of your shield!

Any DX roll you attempt in close combat, **after** your first turn of close combat, has the same penalty.

It takes one turn, with a successful DX roll, to get rid of your shield during a close combat.

Karate Kicks in Close Combat

The Karate skill allows you to kick in close combat – something normally forbidden. All normal Karate rules (falling down, etc.) apply.

Modifying Dice + Adds: An Optional Rule

Sometimes, accumulated modifiers will give large plusses – e.g., an attack of 2d+5. In this case, the GM may rule that any +7 be turned into two dice, or any +4 be turned into one die. Thus, an attack of 2d+5 would be equivalent to a 3d+1. This gives more realistic results, but requires an extra step when character sheets, etc., are filled out – so it's up to the GM.

DEFENSE IN CLOSE COMBAT

The only active defense that works in close combat is **Dodge. Exception:** if you have the Brawling, Judo or Karate skill, allowing you to parry bare-handed, you can use the Parry defense.

You **may** choose to "dodge and retreat" in close combat, **if** the enemy is not holding you. Add 3 to **your** defense and back out of the hex – that is, leave on your side, moving one hex! If the foe is grappling you, you cannot do this.

MULTIPLE CLOSE COMBAT

Any number of people may be involved in a close combat. This can be difficult to show with miniatures – especially if some figures are standing and other figures are lying down. A good compromise is to allow a fighter to declare himself in "close combat" with an opponent while still in the next hex.

Up to two figures may combine in an attempt to take a single foe down; up to three may combine in an attempt to pin a single foe. In either case, use the ST (or DX) of the attacker with the best score, and add 1/5 (round down) of the ST or DX of each of his helpers.

RANGED WEAPONS

A "ranged weapon" is any weapon that is used at a distance. This includes thrown weapons, missile weapons, beam weapons and (in a magical world) many types of hostile magic. There are several different types of ranged weapons, each with its own characteristics.

Thrown Hand Weapons

If a hand weapon is designed to be thrown, anyone may throw it by rolling against the appropriate thrown-weapon skill. Thrown-weapon skills are different from regular weapon skills. For instance, the Knife-Throwing skill is **not** the same as the Knife skill, even if the knife is the same. The general Throwing skill gives you a bonus for throwing **any** weapon (or anything else you have handy).

The **Weapon Table** indicates which weapons can be thrown.

Thrown Objects

Throwing a brick, rock, flask or similar object is considered an attack. Use your Throwing skill (p. 49), or DX-3. See p. 201 for penalties for hitting a specific target.

A rock, grenade or similar item weighing a pound or less can be thrown 3.5 yards **times** your basic ST. For characters of normal ST (7 and above), a rock does 1 hit **less** than your basic Thrust damage. For detailed rules on throwing things of all weights, see p. 90.

Missile Weapons

Missile weapons include bows, crossbows, slings, guns and beam weapons. A low-tech missile weapon's range and damage are governed by its user's ST.

Bows and Crossbows are an exception; range and damage are governed by the ST of the bow. You may use a weaker bow or crossbow than your ST. If the ST of the bow exceeds that of the archer, Bow skill is at -1 per point of excess, and a contest of ST is required for each turn spent aiming the bow. A crossbow that exceeds your ST will do more damage – but it takes longer to cock. A crossbow of your ST or less takes 2 seconds. A crossbow with ST 1 or 2 greater than yours takes 6 seconds. A crossbow with ST 3 or 4 greater than yours requires a "goat's foot" device to recock each time – this device weighs 2 lbs., costs $50, and cocks the bow in 20 seconds. (Remember that in addition to cocking time, it takes one turn to ready an arrow – unless you have Fast-Draw for arrows – and one turn to place the arrows on the bow.)

You cannot cock a crossbow, except by slow mechanical devices, if its ST exceeds yours by more than 4. You can still fire it!

Ranged Weapon Stats

For each ranged weapon, four numbers are listed, describing that particular weapon's special characteristics:

Snap Shot Number (SS): If your adjusted "to hit" roll is greater than or equal to this number, you may fire *without aiming,* yet incur no -4 snap-shot penalty, as long as the target was in view at the beginning of your turn. Snap-shooting is relatively easy with some weapons, very hard with others. Larger, closer, and slower targets are easier to hit with snap shots . . . and a skilled shooter can succeed with a snap shot where an unskilled one would have little chance.

Accuracy Modifier (Acc): This is the bonus a user gets with this weapon *if he takes at least one turn to aim.* For instance, if your Pistol skill is 15, and your .45 has an Accuracy modifier of +2, you have an effective skill of 17 after you aim for a turn. *Scopes* add to a weapon's Accuracy modifier in aimed fire. Add half a scope's power of magnification to its Acc – e.g., a 4× scope adds +2. Scopes give -1 to effective skill of unaimed shots; they are clumsy.

Some weapons have a very high Acc, but you can never get an Acc bonus of more than your skill. For example, if your Beam Weapons skill is only 8, and you use a Laser Rifle (Acc 15), you only get a +8 with it.

Half Damage ($^1/_2$D): The range (in yards) at which the power of the weapon has fallen off so much that it only does half its normal damage (roll normally, and then divide the result in half, rounding down). Realistically, most weapons lose striking power gradually as air resistance slows them down, but a detailed calculation would be unplayable. When firing at a target beyond the $^1/_2$D range, ignore the weapon's accuracy modifier; random variations have canceled whatever inherent accuracy the weapon had.

Maximum Range (Max): No attack is possible beyond this range, because the weapon won't reach that far – or, for a thrown weapon, because it won't be traveling point first!

sample ranged-weapon stats

Weapon	SS	Acc	$^1/_2$D	Max
Small Knife	11	0	ST-5	ST
Baseball or rock	12	0	ST×2	ST×3.5
Spear	11	+2	ST	ST×1.5
Longbow	15	+3	ST×15	ST×20
Crossbow	12	+4	ST×20	ST×25
.45 pistol	10	+2	175	1,700
Laser rifle	15	+13	900	1,200

There will be specific notes for some weapons. For example, a .50-caliber sniper rifle will have an extra -3 penalty for snap shots. Its recoil is so strong that if you fire it with less than minimum ST, it takes two turns to recover.

Arc of Vision

If you have a ranged weapon, you can attack into any of the *white* hexes to your front, as shown below. This is your "arc of vision." A character with Peripheral Vision can fire into any hex in *his* arc of vision, as shown by the *gray and white* hexes.

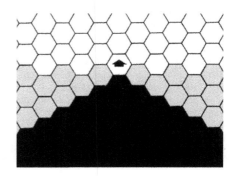

Fast-Draw for Archers

If you learn Fast-Draw for *arrows* (or crossbow bolts – same skill), a successful Fast-Draw roll will let you ready an arrow in "zero time." This will shave one second off your overall readying time with your bow.

However, the penalty for missing a Fast-Draw is greater for an archer. If you miss your roll, you *drop* the arrow. But on a critical miss, you spill your whole *quiver!* Picking up each arrow is a separate "ready" action from then on, and you can't fast-draw an arrow that's lying on the ground.

Shooting Blind

If you have a ranged weapon, you may attack someone outside your arc of vision by "shooting blind." Your attack is at a penalty of -10, or a maximum "to hit" roll of 9, whichever is worse. (As Murphy's Law predicts, you are often *less* likely to hit your target than anyone else in the vicinity.) Needless to say, you cannot get a bonus by aiming. See *Hitting the Wrong Target,* p. 117.

Ranged Attacks on Human Targets

When using a ranged weapon against a human target, you may almost always simplify the calculation by using only the *Range* modifier. Size of an adult human gives a zero modifier. Speed should be neglected (unless the target is flying or something similiar), because the target will get an active defense.

Pop-Up Attacks

A pop-up attack is a special Attack maneuver in which you emerge from cover, move one hex or less, throw a weapon, and *return* to your cover – in the space of one turn. This is also possible with most missile weapons, but not with any bow except a crossbow. Pop-up attacks include ducking around a corner, around a tree, out of a trench, and the like.

A pop-up attack cannot be aimed and always has a -4 Snap Shot penalty. There is an extra -2 penalty for the pop-up maneuver because you can't see your target at the beginning of your turn.

While you are out of cover to throw your weapon, you *may* be attacked by anyone targeting that hex with opportunity fire. Your only legal defense is a Dodge.

Aiming

The *Aim* maneuver is used to target a single foe when you have a thrown or missile weapon, or to target a single hex when you are planning to take opportunity fire. Aiming slows down your rate of fire, but makes you more accurate. Aiming for a turn eliminates the Snap Shot penalty and gives you the weapon's Accuracy bonus (though you cannot get an Accuracy bonus higher than your base skill with the weapon). You may hold your aim as long as you like. Each turn of aiming, after the first, gives you +1 to hit, up to a maximum +3.

Standing still to aim also eliminates the -2 penalty for firing from an obstructed hex, or one with bad footing.

If you are in a suitable position for "bracing" your missile weapon, taking even one turn to aim gets you an *extra* +1 to hit.

If your target moves while you are aiming, your aim is unaffected. However, if you lose sight of the foe, all Aim bonus is lost! If you are injured while aiming, you must make your Will roll or lose your aim.

Aiming on the Move

A firer can aim while walking if the pace is no more than two yards per second (or half his Move, whichever is less). The maximum aiming bonus while walking is +1. Archers, except for crossbowmen, cannot aim while walking.

Thrown Weapons

Throwable weapons include knives, axes and spears. Each of these is a different "thrown weapon" skill.

Thrown weapon skills are actually easy, as "combat" skills go. They improve quickly with practice. They are only considered difficult, in today's world, because few people practice!

ATTACKING WITH A RANGED WEAPON

When using a ranged weapon, your to-hit number is figured by:

(1) Taking your base skill with the weapon.

(2) Modifying for *size of target,* as shown on the table on p. 201.

(3) Modifying for target's *range and speed* (done as a single modifier), also from the table on p. 201.

(4) Modifying for the specific weapon's *accuracy,* if you have taken at least a turn to aim. Your bonus for accuracy cannot exceed your base skill level.

(5) Modifying for conditions (snap shot or extra aim, bracing, darkness, and so on) including any special conditions determined by the GM.

The result is your *effective skill*. A roll of this number, or less, is a hit.

Size of Target

The larger the target, the easier it is to hit. The table shows a range of sizes; round up to the next larger size, and read the modifier in the *second* column of the table. Objects larger than man-sized give a bonus to hit; smaller objects give a penalty.

Target's Speed and Range

The target's speed and range give a single modifier. The *sum* of range (in yards) and speed (in yards per second) gives a number from the table. This means that if the target is very fast, its distance becomes less important . . . or if it is very far away, its speed becomes less important.

For very large or distant targets, the table gives a subsidiary column using *miles* and *miles per second*. If you use miles for the range, always use mps for the speed.

Tracking systems in high-tech campaigns will add to the firer's effective skill – see Chapter 16.

Examples: A target at 50 yards, with a speed of 30 yds/sec (60 mph) has a speed/range of 80 yards: modifier -10. A target at 5 yards, moving 1,000 yds/sec, has a speed/range of 1,005 yards: modifier -17. A target at 60 yards, moving 2 yds/sec, has a speed/range of 62 yards: modifier -9.

This system uses the same geometric progression for both size (generally a positive modifier) and the combination of speed and range (generally a negative modifier), and gives reasonable results whether the target is a fly or a planet, at 1 yard or 100,000 miles, stationary or traveling at half the speed of light

Speed and range are combined so that when one is relatively small and the other relatively large, only the relatively large factor has much effect on the outcome. Small speed (or range) becomes negligible when firing at a target at extreme range (or speed).

If a rocket is going 1,000 yards per second, it doesn't matter much whether it's 50 or 100 yards away. If an elephant is 1,000 yards away, it hardly matters at all if it is walking at 1 hex/second or 2 hexes/second.

If a target gets twice as big, twice as far away, and twice as fast, the difficulty of hitting it stays the same. (Twice as far away cancels twice as big; twice as far away also cancels twice as fast, since angular speed hasn't changed.)

Examples of Range Calculation

Example: The target is a car, 5 yards long (+3 to hit). It is 40 yards away, and moving 30 mph. 30 mph is 15 yards per second. 40 + 15 = 55; on the table on p. 201, 55 rounds up to 70, giving a speed/range modifier of -9. The cumulative modifier is -6 to hit, before the particular weapon is taken into account.

Example: You are throwing an axe at a cask a foot across. Your Axe Throwing skill is 16. The size of the cask gives you a -5 to hit. The cask is 5 yards away, and is rolling slowly (1 yard per second). These combine for a speed/range modifier of 6 yards per

second. On the table, this rounds up to 7, for a -3 penalty. Your total penalty is -8, giving you an effective skill of 8. If you throw without taking a turn to aim, your effective skill is less than the axe's Snap Shot number of 10, so you'll take an added -4 penalty for the snap shot. If you aim for a turn, you will not have the -4 penalty. Instead, you'll get the axe's Acc bonus of +2.

Example: You have a ST of 12 and a longbow. Your skill is 15. The target is a man, so there is no modifier for size. He is 200 yards away and not moving (-12). The total penalty is -12, so your effective skill is 3. Better aim for a long time, and cross your fingers!

Note also that the "Half Damage" range for a longbow is ST×15. Two-hundred yards is greater than your ST×15, so you will only do half damage if you hit.

Firing Upward and Downward

Firing downward increases the distance you can fire a ranged projectile weapon; firing upward decreases range. This is not likely to matter at short distances, but can be important at long range. Ignore it entirely for beam weapons like lasers.

Firing downward: For every two yards of elevation you have over your target, subtract 1 yard from the effective distance. *Example:* You are 40 yards away from your target, and 10 yards higher. Subtract 5 yards from effective range. You fire as though you were only 35 yards away. Note: Whenever this formula would reduce the effective range to less than half the *real* ground distance, use half the real ground distance instead.

Firing upward: For every yard of elevation from you to your target, add 1 yard to the effective distance. *Example:* You are 40 yards away from your target, and 10 yards lower. Add 10 yards to effective range. You fire as though you were 50 yards away.

Firing on the Move

Any ranged weapon can be fired while the firer is walking or running, but it cannot be braced. Normal penalties (in addition to the snap shot penalty) are -1 for walking, -2 for running, and anything else the GM assesses if the firer is otherwise handicapped or distracted. *Triple* these penalties for crossbows; multiply by 6 (!!) for bows.

Firing Through an Occupied Hex

You can target an enemy if you can draw a straight line between *any* part of your hex and *any* part of his without passing through a solid obstacle. A straightedge is a useful tool for determining this. However, if your chosen straight line passes through an occupied hex, the figure(s) in that hex are in the way. You may hit them if you miss your intended target – see below.

Any character in the way (friend or foe) gives you a -4 penalty (-8 for ultra-tech *sonic* weapons, which have a wide beam). If your attack passes through several occupied hexes, add the total penalty for *each* character in the way!

If your attack passes along a line *between* two hexes, there is *no* penalty unless *both* hexes are occupied. If they are, treat it as a *single* hex penalty.

Someone lying down is never "in the way" unless you, too, are on the ground. Someone kneeling or sitting is not in the way unless *either* you *or* your target is also kneeling or sitting.

Hitting the Wrong Target

If you attack with a ranged weapon, and *miss*, you may hit someone else. You *must* check for this if you fail your attack roll.

Any character (friend or foe) may be hit if he was in your line of fire. To determine this, check the line along which you attacked. Any hex this line passed through is "in the way."

The GM may add to-hit modifiers up to -4 for unpredictable movement of the target. A target which doesn't deviate from a straight line by at least its own size per second is not unpredictable!

Sample modifiers:

-1 for a vehicle swerving or a man side-stepping and dodging as he runs (halving Move).

-2 for a man evading rapidly (making little forward progress, Move 2).

-3 for a rat running across the floor.

-4 for a hummingbird or equally unpredictable target.

Opportunity Fire

A character with a thrown or missile weapon may stand still, watching a specified area, and fire as soon as a target presents itself. This is *opportunity fire*.

To take opportunity fire, you must choose the *Step and Wait* maneuver. Your character is now staying still, facing the direction you choose and watching for a target *in a specified area*. If a target appears, you *must* fire (or throw) your weapon (but see below). This takes place *immediately*. You may do *nothing* else that turn. If no target appears, you simply wasted that turn.

All of the area to be "covered" must be within your arc of vision (see p. 115). The larger the area you have to watch, the greater the penalty when you fire:

One hex being watched: -2
Two hexes being watched: -4
Three or four hexes being watched: -5
Five or six hexes being watched: -6
Seven to ten hexes being watched: -7
More than ten hexes being watched: -8

You may also specify a single straight line, and say that you will fire at the first target that crosses that line. The penalty for this kind of opportunity fire is -5. All normal modifiers apply to opportunity fire.

If you want to keep your foes from knowing where you are planning to fire, just tell the GM secretly.

If two or more people are taking opportunity fire at the same target, they all fire at effectively the same time.

When you announce that you will take opportunity fire, you *must* fire at the first enemy that appears in the designated area! The GM should make sure that players carefully specify the area they are watching for opportunity fire.

Opportunity shots are automatically snap shots, regardless of your effective skill; the -4 penalty is built into the above numbers. Exception: if you are watching a *single hex,* you can Aim while you wait for a target. This will give you the normal aiming bonus when you finally fire. Each turn you wait for a target counts as a turn of aiming. However, if you are watching more than one hex, you cannot get an aiming bonus at all.

If you want to specify that you are *not* firing automatically, you may do so. When a target appears, the GM makes your Vision roll for you and tells you whether you *think* it's friend or foe. You are at a -2 to your shot because of the time you will spend deciding.

Characters who are kneeling or lying down are not in the way unless you, too, are at their level.

Because hitting the wrong target is a matter of pure chance, your attack roll against each character is the same: a flat 9 – or the number you would have had to roll to hit them on purpose, whichever is *worse*.

Roll first for the target closest to you. If you miss (or if the target dodges) roll for the next target, and so on. Keep rolling until you hit, or your attack is blocked or parried, or you run out of targets. If your attack went along a line between two occupied hexes, roll randomly to see which one you check first.

Anyone (friend or foe) gets the same defense against this attack that he would have had if it had been directed against him intentionally.

Head only: -5 to hit.

Head and shoulders exposed: -4 to hit.

Body half exposed: -3 to hit.

Behind light cover: -2 to hit.

Behind someone else: -4 to hit, see above.

Lying prone without cover: -4 to hit.

Lying prone, minimum cover, head up: -5 to hit.

Lying prone, minimum cover, head down: -7 to hit.

Crouching or kneeling, no cover: -2 to hit

Cover and Concealment

If you hide behind something, you will be a harder target for ranged weapons. The better the cover, the harder you will be to hit; anyone shooting at you must target an exposed part of your body. Some examples:

Head only: -5 to hit

Head and shoulders exposed (e.g., firing a weapon from a trench): -4 to hit.

Body half exposed (e.g., firing from behind a tree, or standing behind a small embankment): -3 to hit.

Behind light cover (e.g., a screen of bushes): -2 to hit.

Behind someone else: -4 for each human-sized figure in the way. See *Firing Through an Occupied Hex,* p. 117.

You can also make yourself a harder target, even without cover, by crouching or lying down:

Lying prone without cover: -4 to hit.

Prone behind minimum cover (e.g., a body), head up to observe: -5 to hit.

Prone behind minimum cover, keeping head down: -7 to hit.

Crouching or kneeling without cover: -2 to hit.

Based on these examples, GMs can interpolate a reasonable penalty for any exotic method of concealment the players may devise.

If you are using the "hit location" rules, you may target specific parts of the body (e.g., the head), at specific "to hit" penalties. Do *not* add these penalties to the ones listed above unless some extra difficulty is really being added. Example: If only the target's head is showing, the penalty to hit it is the same -5, whether you consider it "aiming at the head because you want to," or "aiming at the head because that's all that's exposed."

Overshooting

If you *make* your attack roll, but your foe blocks or parries successfully, your weapon or missile has been knocked to the floor. There is no chance that you hit anyone.

If your foe *dodges,* the weapon/missile went *past* him and may hit someone else. Proceed as above, but start with the closest character on the *other side* of your foe. (You already know you didn't hit anybody *between* you and your foe, or he would not have had to defend.)

Scatter

When you *throw* a grenade or similar object, you may say that you are "lobbing" it with a high trajectory rather than throwing it in a straight line. You still pick one hex to aim at, and make your attack roll in the usual way. But you need not worry about anybody who might be in your way. And if you miss, your grenade will hit fairly close rather than shooting past!

If you miss your attack roll, you missed your target by a number of yards equal to the amount by which you missed your roll – or half the distance to the target, whichever is less. Round up.

To determine the *direction* of your miss, roll one die. Take the direction *you* are facing as #1, the next direction clockwise as #2, and so on. Your grenade misses in that direction, by the number of yards determined above.

GUNS

This section will give general rules for all type of high-tech hand weapons, from black-powder weapons through 20th-century guns and on to science-fiction weapons such as blasters. Stats for a variety of guns are given on the *Weapon Tables,* pp. 208-209.

Single-Shot Weapons

The earliest guns (TL4 and early TL5) must be loaded with loose powder and bullets. Each barrel or chamber must be loaded separately. Loading time for matchlocks and wheellocks is 60+ seconds. Loading time for smoothbore flintlocks and caplocks is 20+ seconds; for rifled versions, 30+ seconds. Rate of Fire (RoF) given for such weapons is the time necessary to load; e.g., the RoF of a matchlock is 1/60+. A roll on Black Powder Weapons skill is required to successfully *load* such a weapon. A matchlock pistol is a "fire and forget" weapon. Fire it once, then forget about it until the next fight!

Many TL5 through TL7 guns, as shown by the RoF of 1 on the Weapon Table, may be fired once a turn; they take time to reload, charge or cycle.

However, many "single-shot" weapons may be fired up to three times a turn with repeated trigger pulls. This is shown by a RoF of "3~." For recoilless weapons, such as lasers, there is no added penalty for the second and third shots. Weapons which recoil have a hit penalty for each added shot; this is the Rcl number on the Weapon Table. This penalty is applied to each successive shot until there is a minimum 1-second pause between shots. If your ST is below the minimum listed for the weapons, the penalty is doubled for each point of difference, and a 2-second pause is required to re-establish shooting position.

Automatic Weapons

By definition, a fully-automatic weapon continues to fire as long as the trigger is held. The shots fired by one trigger pull are a *burst.* Many automatic weapons (and all made at TL8+) have *selective-fire* capability – they can be set to fire single shots. It takes one turn to change from single-shot to automatic mode, or vice versa.

The *Wait* maneuver can be used for *any* "reflex action" you want to plan in advance – e.g., "If Dora sees any Orcs, she will pull this rope immediately – otherwise, she does nothing." No action can be taken as a "reflex" unless it can be done in a *single motion.* The GM's decision is final.

Note: This is the rule to use in a "knife at the throat" situation!

Counting Shots (an optional rule)

Sometimes it is critical to control exactly how many rounds are being fired from an automatic weapon: "Make every shot count, men, we're down to the last few rounds!"

In such situations, the firer announces how many rounds he wishes to fire, and rolls against his weapon skill. A successful roll allows the desired number of rounds if RoF is less than 12. For RoF over 12, a success allows the desired number of rounds, plus or minus two GM's choice (but never less than one round!). Failure means that the full RoF is fired (if there are enough rounds).

Stunners

Stunners are non-lethal sonic weapons. They will *not* work in vacuum. Anyone hit by a hand stunner must roll HT-3 (HT at 12 yds or more) to avoid its effects. Every 5 points of DR gives a +1 to this roll; this is the only protection armor offers. If a limb is hit, it is incapacitated for 20-HT minutes; on a head or body hit, the victim is unconscious for the same period of time. A critical failure on the HT roll triples the duration. Victims cannot be revived before this.

For stun rifles, the roll is HT-6 (HT-3 at 300 yards or more).

Shotguns

Shotguns may fire either *shot* or *slugs.* Shot does the listed amount of damage for the weapon, and gives +1 to hit at all times. Each die of damage is rolled individually and applied separately vs. armor.

A slug does double basic damage with no damage modifiers, but at -2 to the firer's skill. Slugs triple the 1/2D and Max ranges.

Power Supplies

Some ultra-tech (futuristic) weapons use *power cells.* This is noted on the *Shots* column of the *Weapons Chart* by a slash followed by a letter indicating the type of cell. For instance, a stunner (40/C) gets 40 shots from a C power cell. See p. 247 for details.

A B cell costs $30; 20 weigh 1 pound. A C cell costs $100 and weighs 1/2 pound.

Damage to Shields: An Optional Rule

This rule allows shields to take combat damage, eventually becoming worthless. Do *not* use this rule unless you are willing to tolerate some bookkeeping in order to achieve more realistic combat!

Whenever you make a defense roll by only the number of points of your shield's passive defense, the blow hit your shield. For instance, if you have a large shield (4 points protection), and your total defense roll is 12, then any roll of 9 through 12 missed you but hit your shield. Any blow that hits your shield can damage it.

Any wooden shield has an inherent damage resistance of 3 – equivalent to an inch of wood, or thinner wood with a $^1/_8$" metal facing. Subtract 3 from any blow your shield takes before you assess damage to the shield.

Shield Damage Table

Shield type	PD	Damage
Improvised	1 or 2	varies
Buckler	1	5/20
Small	2	5/30
Medium	3	7/40
Large	4	9/60

PD: The passive defense of the shield.

Damage: This is given as two numbers separated by a slash. The first number shows the amount of damage, in one blow, that will penetrate the shield. For instance, five hits in a single blow will penetrate a buckler or small shield. If a shield is penetrated by a *crushing* or *cutting* weapon, you are not hurt, but the shield is rendered useless. If it is penetrated by an *impaling* weapon, the weapon comes through and hits you, with its force weakened by as many points of damage as the shield took, plus 3 for its DR. Except for that damage, the shield remains intact.

The second number shows the *total* damage your shield can take. Most medieval shields were wood, or wood with a thin layer of metal. After one good battle, a shield was worthless. Keep track of the total number of hits your shield takes for you. When this total is exceeded, your shield is destroyed!

At Tech Levels 2-4, metal shields (usually bronze) are available, but uncommon. For a bronze shield 1/2" thick, quadruple the cost, triple the weight, and double the damage it can take before destruction. It has DR6 – it will turn most arrows and some bullets! Passive defense remains unchanged – which is why such shields were rare.

TL7 riot shields (Lexan, etc.) have the same damage numbers as wood shields but weigh half as much. Shields made of more advanced materials are certainly possible.

Force shields may exist at TL11; see p. 76. They do not take damage when hit.

Rate of Fire

The Rate of Fire (RoF) for an automatic weapon is the number of rounds it fires *each turn*. If the gun starts firing at the beginning of the turn, and the trigger is held for the whole turn, the gun fires the RoF number of rounds.

If the gunner takes any other action (such as moving, changing facing or dodging) before firing, some of the time that could have been used in firing is expended. Any action that takes less than $^1/_2$ of Move allows full RoF; an action that takes 1/2 Move or more allows $^1/_2$ RoF. The GM rules in any disputed case.

Number of Hits in a Burst

It is very unusual for all the rounds of a burst to hit the target. To game this, the burst is divided into *groups* of no more than four shots. A separate roll to hit must be made for each group fired. The firer rolls against Guns skill, modified by Recoil of the weapon.

The table below shows the number of shots that hit, depending on the success of the roll. Note that if three or four shots were fired, a roll that *misses* by 1 is still a hit with one shot. A miss by 2 or more is a miss with all.

A critical hit with a group of shots is a hit with all the rounds. *One* shot does damage according to the Critical Hit Table. Likewise, a critical miss with a group means *one* roll on the Critical Miss Table.

hits in a burst

Rounds in Group	Roll Made by						
	-1	0	1	2	3	4	5+
1	0	1	1	1	1	1	1
2	0	1	1	1	1	1	2
3	1	1	1	1	2	2	3
4	1	2	2	3	3	3	4

Damage from a Burst

Every round in a burst has a chance to damage the target separately. Damage is separate for each round, not cumulative. This affects armor penetration. The PD and DR of the target must be applied separately to each round that hits.

Exception: For *lasers* with automatic fire, *total* the damage from all rounds striking the target in each one-second burst. If eight 2d rounds are fired, and five of them hit, apply them to the target's armor as a single 10d attack.

Recoil from Burst Fire

Burst firing is harder to control than single-shot. Each round of the burst has the same recoil impulse as would a round fired by itself, so a long burst is harder to control than a short burst. Among the things that determine recoil are weight-to-recoil ratio, stock design, compensators and rate of fire.

When a weapon is fired on automatic, the Rcl number is a penalty to the effective skill level on the firing roll for the first *group*. This penalty is added again for each four-round group, or partial four-round group, after the first. (-1 becomes -2 and then -3; -2 becomes -4 and then -6; and so on.) This penalty continues to add as long as that burst continues, even in subsequent turns!

At TL7 and below, all automatic weapons have significant recoil; the best Rcl number is -1. At TL8 and 9, some automatic weapons have a Rcl of 0 – they are effectively recoilless. At TL10+, almost all weapons are recoilless.

The Rcl number is doubled for a base Skill level below 12. Rcl is also doubled for each point of ST below that required for the weapon. These doublings are cumulative – that is, ST below list *and* Skill below 12 *quadruples* the Rcl number.

Removing or folding the stock of a weapon multiplies Rcl by 1.5 (round up). Firing any weapon with one hand *doubles* the Rcl penalty. These apply to non-automatic weapons as well. Note that folding the stock also lowers SS by 2 and Acc by 3.

Hitting the Wrong Target

Any bullet that does not hit the intended target might hit the wrong one (see p. 117). It is only necessary to track the fate of every stray projectile if something significant is likely to be hit.

Aiming Successive Groups

An automatic-weapon firer can use his weapon like a hose, aiming even as he fires, as long as he can see where his rounds are going (GM's decision, or make a Vision roll). After one four-shot group, this adds the weapon's Accuracy bonus. Each successive group fired this way *also* gives +1 for aiming, up to the normal maximum +3 for aiming.

Automatic weapons can use the "garden-hose" effect even when firing on the move, *if* the firer watches his target while running. However, on any but the flattest ground, this requires a roll vs. DX or Vision (whichever is worse) every turn, to avoid a fall. GMs may apply penalties for especially bad terrain; aliens with lots of eyes may not need to roll at all . . .

Area Effect

Automatic weapons can be fired against several targets in one burst. All these targets must be within a 30° angle. When playing on a hex-grid, let this be any angle described by two spots which are 5 hexes apart and 10 hexes from the firer (see below).

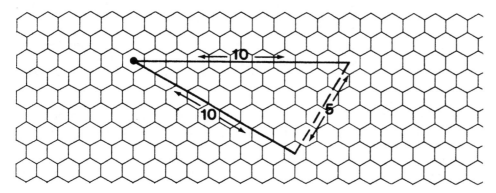

The targets must be engaged in succession, and the firer must announce, before rolling to hit, how many rounds he will use on each one. Calculate the attack separately for each target. If the targets are more than one yard apart, traversing between targets wastes some rounds. For RoF of 16 or below, one round is lost for each yard between targets. For RoF over 16, two rounds are lost for each yard.

EXPLOSIONS

Explosions do two kinds of damage: concussion and fragmentation. In combat, most explosions will be from grenades, mortars and so on.

Concussion Damage

Concussion damage for grenade-sized explosions falls off rapidly with distance. Base damage for the weapon applies only to targets in the hex of impact and adjacent hexes. It is $1/4$ that in the next two hexes; $1/4$ *that* in the next two, and so on. Roll total damage separately for each target, and then divide by the appropriate number (4, 16, and so on). Damage less than 1 is ignored.

Concussion does crushing damage. Armor protects normally.

Fragmentation Damage

Explosions may also do fragmentation damage, if there is anything that can be shattered and thrown about at the explosion site. Significant fragment damage is done

Molotov Cocktails and Oil Flasks

In a game at TL4 or above, a "Molotov cocktail" – a bottle filled with gasoline – can be used as a firebomb. A rag is tied to the outside. Light the rag and throw the bottle; when it hits, it will break, spilling flaming gas.

However, before the 18th century (that is, before TL4 on Earth), no flammable, hot-burning liquid was available. (Alcohol is flammable but burns with a cool flame. Pitch is sticky but will *not* flare up instantly.) Still, in a *fantasy* low-tech game, you may use the "oil flask" weapon. Just assume that the ancient secret of "Greek fire" was not lost, and fill an earthenware flask with the concoction. It should be very expensive!

It takes one second to ready a flask hanging at your belt; one second to light its "fuse" if you have a torch or lighter; one or more seconds (optional) to aim; and one second (an Attack maneuver) to throw it.

A bottle will always break if it hits the floor. There is a five in six chance that the fuse will stay lit and catch the contents on fire. It will produce a 1-hex pool of fire, with tiny spatters all around. Place a marker to indicate that the hex is on fire.

If your target is a person, he may dodge or block (but not parry). A dodge means the bottle hits his hex (but not him). A block means it breaks on his shield – see below.

If a Molotov cocktail or oil flask hits a *living being*, it will always break if its target is wearing plate or other rigid armor. Otherwise, there is a 50% chance it will bounce into an adjacent hex (choose randomly) and break on the floor. If it breaks on a shield or living being, there is a four in six chance that it will ignite.

The flame will burn for one minute – longer than most combats will last.

Being on fire (or in a flaming hex) does 1d-1 damage per turn. Toughness *does* protect you; so does armor – up to a point. See *Flame*, p. 129, for details.

If your *shield* is on fire, you may use it normally (the fire is on the outside). But the shield must be discarded after the battle. If you are using the Shield Damage rules (p. 120), the shield takes one hit per turn for one minute or until the fire is put out.

Disadvantages: Because a bottle is so fragile, there is a four in six chance of breakage for each one on your belt if you fall down. Also, a foe may strike at a bottle or flask on your belt (-5 to hit); it automatically breaks if hit. In either event, you will be soaked in flammable liquid from the waist down. If you enter a fire hex, you will catch fire yourself.

Suffocation

It is possible to render a victim unconscious or even dead without inflicting significant HT damage, by *suffocating* him. This may be done either by preventing him from breathing, or by restricting the flow of blood (and thus oxygen) to his brain.

While struggling, a character can "hold his breath" – that is, survive without damage while no fresh oxygen is reaching his brain – for a number of turns equal to his HT. If the victim does not resist in any way – a feat which requires a Will roll – he may lie passively in the grip of his assailant, holding his breath for HT×4 turns. If the victim can win a Contest of Skills (Acting vs. IQ), the attacker may be fooled into thinking he's unconscious.

Once the victim is "out of breath," he loses one Fatigue point per turn. When he runs out of Fatigue, he falls unconscious. If his assailant continues to restrict the flow of oxygen to his brain, he will die in four minutes, regardless of his current or starting HT. If his assailant releases him, he will regain consciousness fairly quickly.

A victim may be suffocated to unconsciousness or even death in a variety of ways. You may hold his nose and mouth shut by hand, cover his face with a pillow or other suitable object, or constrict either of his carotid arteries (which may be found on either side of the throat, just below the hinge of the jaw). None of these methods inflicts any HT damage on the victim – they simply induce brain death. All these ways would require either that the victim be tied or otherwise helpless already, or that the attacker win a Contest of ST *every turn* until the victim falls unconscious.

If you attempt to choke a foe to death by squeezing his trachea, you *do* inflict HT damage, as described under *Choke or Strangle* on p. 112. At the same time, you are also suffocating him, as described here – so he may pass out from lack of oxygen before you actually crush his windpipe. The difference is that by simply suffocating him, you will not harm him in any lasting way; by choking him, you are inflicting potentially fatal damage.

over a radius of 5 yards times the dice of the concussion damage. So, for example, a grenade doing 4 dice of concussion damage would throw fragments over a 20-yard radius.

The farther a target is from the burst, the less likely he is to be hit by fragments. Start by assuming a hit, then roll passive defense (no active defense is possible). PD is +1 for each yard from the explosion. For ground bursts, kneeling gives +1 PD and prone position gives +2. The maximum possible PD vs. fragments is 15. Position does not protect against airbursts.

Damage done by fragments depends on the ground at the site of the explosion, from 1d-4 for ordinary earth, up to 1d for an explosion on loose scrap. Fragmentation shells (grenades, etc.) produce *deadly* fragments: 2d damage if hit, regardless of the ground at the site.

SPECIAL SITUATIONS

SUBDUING A FOE

At times, you will want to subdue an enemy without killing him. Knockout gas, magic and similar tricks are the best way to take prisoners – most weapons are entirely *too* final! But if you need to defeat someone without harming him, and you have only ordinary weapons, you still have several options:

Disarm him. You can do this by striking at his weapon (see p. 110) to knock it out of his hand or break it. Of course, he may not surrender even then.

Pull your punches. You do not have to strike with your full strength. You can always choose to use less strength – as much or as little as you like – when striking with your hands or with a weapon. *Example:* If your normal damage with your sword is 2d+1, you can say, "I'm using less strength; I only want to do 1 die of damage." You can specify any amount of damage you want, but you still have to roll the dice to see how much you actually did.

Turn your blade. You can strike with the flat of a sword or axe. The weapon then does the same basic damage but gets no damage bonus. You can also turn a spear around and poke with the blunt end. Again, it does the same basic damage but no extra damage for impaling.

Pin him. If you can engage the foe in close combat, you can "pin" him and then tie him up. This takes about a minute, and requires ropes.

Suffocate him. See the sidebar.

SURPRISE ATTACKS AND INITIATIVE

When the PCs surprise a group of adversaries, or vice versa, the party that is surprised may not be able to react immediately. In this case, the attackers should get one or more "free turns." The GM is responsible for determining when the attackers have achieved surprise.

Note that a character with Combat Reflexes is rarely surprised. He will never "freeze." His side gets a +1 on initiative (+2 if he is the leader, but not cumulative for more than one character). He also gets a +6 (!) on his IQ roll to recover from surprise. Most wild animals automatically have Combat Reflexes.

Total Surprise

When the defenders are totally taken by surprise, they will "freeze." The GM rolls 1 die. This is the number of seconds that passes before the defenders can react at all, unless they have Combat Reflexes. Adventurers, guards and the like will rarely be taken totally by surprise unless they are actually asleep. But total surprise would be appropriate if a group of werewolves came charging through the door of the local library. (In fact, such an extreme case might justify a Fright Check, at least for the librarian.)

After the initial "freeze" ends, each defender must roll against his basic IQ at the beginning of each turn until he recovers. A successful roll means that character can move and act normally *for the rest of the combat*. A failed roll means that character is still mentally "stunned." A really stupid character, taken totally by surprise, could miss the whole combat!

Partial Surprise

This may occur when the defenders were expecting trouble – or when each party surprised the other! The GM should require each side to roll for *initiative*.

To determine who gets the initiative, the leader of each side rolls 1 die. A leader with Combat Reflexes gets +2, or +1 if another party member has Combat Reflexes (not cumulative). The *smarter* leader gets +1. Tactics skill gives a +1 on initiative rolls; a skill over 20 gives a +2. The GM can add other bonuses or penalties as he sees fit – for instance, if he thinks that one side was more alert than the other. The side whose leader has the highest roll will get the initiative.

If one side is totally leaderless, the GM rolls for them. They get an automatic -2 to initiative. (This does not apply to animals.)

The side that gets the initiative can move and act normally. Each character on the other side is mentally stunned and must roll vs. IQ each turn, as described above, to snap out of it. However, with partial surprise, each character gets a +1 bonus to IQ on the second turn, +2 on the third turn, and so on – so even the stupid characters will catch on after a few seconds.

If the initiative roll is a tie, nobody was taken by surprise.

ATTACKING WITH A SHIELD

A shield is an excellent defense against low-tech weapons, but it can also be used offensively. To attack with a shield, roll against Shield skill.

Shield Bashing

A shield "bash" is an attack. It can only be made against a foe in your front or left hexes. Roll against your Shield skill to hit. The foe may dodge or block normally, or parry at -2. Weapons of 2 lbs. and under cannot parry at all! A shield-bash does thrust/crushing damage.

Some shields are spiked, and do +1 damage in a bash attack. However, this is not treated as impaling damage, because the spikes are typically blunt and short. As a rule, "chivalric" shields are not spiked, but a barbarian or Viking shield might be. A spike adds 5 pounds to shield weight and $20 to cost.

Shield Rushes

A "shield rush" is an attempt to knock your foe down by slamming into him with a heavy shield. You must have a medium or large shield. A successful shield-rush will knock the foe down. See p. 112 for details.

COMBAT AT DIFFERENT LEVELS

Suppose you want to jump onto a table and strike down at the foe? Or fight your way up a staircase? If you and your foe are at different levels, the vertical distance affects combat. This rule is for *hand* weapons. For *ranged* weapons, see *Firing Upward and Downward*, p. 117.

A long weapon (reach over 1 yard) brings the foe closer! If a fighter has a weapon with a 2-yard reach, he attacks as though his foe were 3 feet closer, but a foe with a one-yard weapon would get no corresponding advantage when striking back. *Example:* An attacker with a greatsword, standing 6 feet below his foe, attacks as though his foe were only 3 feet higher.

One foot of vertical difference, or less: Ignore it.

Up to two feet of vertical difference: Ignore it unless you are using hit locations. In that case, the higher fighter has a -2 hit penalty to attack feet and legs, and a +1 hit

Mass Combat

A very large battle – one involving over 20 fighters – can last a long time. If this is not your cup of tea, you may want to limit yourself to the Basic Combat System in large fights, just to save time.

In particular, *sequencing* (remembering who goes in what order) can make a mass combat play very slowly. This is a good time to use the "clockwise around the table" rule. Note: If the combat starts with the opponents right next to each other, the first side to attack will have an advantage . . . so be realistic, and let the fighters start out at some distance from each other.

As an alternative, you can use the abstract mass combat system from *GURPS Compendium II* (to be released in fall, 1996) for resolving very large battles and determining their effect on the PCs.

Dirty Tricks

Creative players will constantly be inventing new combat tricks – for instance, throwing sand in an enemy's face to blind him. This presents a problem for the GM. On the one hand, creativity should be encouraged; it makes the game more interesting. On the other hand, tricks only work when they're new and original. If sand in the face worked every time, barbarian warriors would leave their swords at home and carry bags of sand instead!

The best solution is to let "tricks" work once – maybe twice – and then assume that word has gotten around. If you, as the GM, think that the players' clever idea is a good one, you should give it a fair chance to work. But remember that elaborate tricks can fail elaborately . . . . and word gets around. The first Trojan Horse was a great success. It hasn't worked since then.

IQ and Dirty Tricks

Often, a GM will find it appropriate to require an IQ roll when a clever trick is attempted. Depending on the circumstance, the GM may:

(a) make the *trickster* roll vs. his IQ to pull the trick properly;

(b) make the *victim* roll vs. his IQ to see through the trick;

(c) require a Contest of IQ to see which one outsmarts the other.

No hard-and-fast rule can be given. Just remember: nobody who takes an IQ 8 fighter should be allowed to play him as a genius!

bonus against the head. The lower fighter has a +2 bonus to hit feet and legs, and a -2 hit penalty against the head.

Up to three feet of vertical difference: As above, but the lower fighter also *subtracts 1* from his defense roll, and the upper fighter adds 1 to his defense.

Up to four feet of vertical difference: As above, but subtract 2 from the lower fighter's defense; add 2 to the upper fighter's defense. The upper fighter *cannot* strike at the lower fighter's legs or feet.

Up to five feet of vertical difference: The lower fighter *cannot* strike at the upper fighter's head, and the upper fighter *cannot* strike at the lower fighter's feet or legs. Subtract 3 from the lower fighter's defense; add 3 to the upper fighter's defense.

Up to six feet of vertical difference: The upper fighter may only strike at the lower fighter's head; no special bonuses or penalties. The lower fighter may *only* strike at the upper fighter's feet and legs; no special bonuses or penalties. Subtract 3 from the lower fighter's defense; add 3 to the upper fighter's defense.

Over six feet of vertical difference: Combat is impossible unless the fighters adopt some strange position (e.g., the upper fighter lies down and reaches over the edge). In that particular case, he would effectively bring himself three feet closer, and his foe could strike at his head and arm. The GM may offer appropriate bonuses and penalties for any odd tactics that the players employ.

Distances are set by common sense and mutual agreement (beforehand, if possible). Some examples: Ordinary stairs rise 8 inches per step (for simplicity, you may want to call them 1 foot). The seat of a chair is less than two feet tall. An ordinary dining table is less than 3 feet tall. The counter in a shop is about four feet tall. The hood of a car, or the bed of a wagon, is about three feet tall. The roof of a car, or the seat of a wagon, is over four feet tall.

Torches and Flashlights

A torch or flashlight reduces the hit penalty for darkness. In caves, dungeons, etc., any such light within line of sight turns the hit penalty from -10 (total darkness) to -3.

A torch can be used as a weapon – treat it like a baton (a light club) – plus one point of damage for the flame. And, of course, a torch can be used to set other things on fire – given enough time. Most oil you're likely to encounter in a medieval world will catch fire three seconds after contact with an open flame; ordinary clothing will catch in four seconds; kindling will take ten seconds to set ablaze. Other types of objects will vary – GM's judgement.

It is possible to carry a light in your "off" hand, leaving your weapon hand free for combat. It's even possible to parry with it – taking appropriate minuses if it is carried in the off hand. Bear in mind that a torch or ordinary flashlight will smash on the first blow if used to parry a weapon of significant heft!

At TL7, "police flashlights" (see *Modern Equipment* list, p. 213) are available. Such a flashlight performs for all purposes like a light club.

ATTACK FROM ABOVE

Ambush from above is a good surprise tactic; roll a Contest of Skills (Stealth vs. Vision) to see if the surprise works. When walking along a trail, alley, etc., anyone will be at -2 to notice someone lurking *above,* unless they specifically state they are looking in the trees/high windows, etc.; then they get a +2. Peripheral Vision does not help you spot a foe *above* you.

An attack from above may paralyze its victims with surprise (p. 122) if the GM so rules. If the victim knew he was being attacked (unlikely in an ambush) his active defense is at -2. If he did not know he was being attacked, he has no active defense. An attack *against* a foe above suffers penalties as above. A "stop-thrust" may be attempted if you are aware that a foe is dropping on you (see p. 106).

Some ambushers (animals, in particular) may ambush you by actually dropping onto you. As a rule, this produces identical damage for both attacker and victim (see p. 131). Remember that a victim is a *soft* thing to land on. Thus: 1d-5 damage per yard for a 1- or 2-yard jump, 1d-4 per yard for a 3- or 4-yard jump, and so on. Animals that are natural ambushers-from-above (e.g., jaguars) are built for jumping, and so take a further -2 damage per yard jumped – thus, only a very unlucky cat, or one jumping a long ways, will get hurt.

GMs, use common sense for special cases. An attacker in heavy boots would do +1 damage per yard, an armored man is not a soft target – and so on.

ATTACKING INANIMATE OBJECTS

There are many situations in which you will want to attack *something* rather than *someone*. Go right ahead. It can't hit back. Any inanimate object will have a DR (damage resistance) representing its innate "toughness," and a HT (hit point) score, representing the amount of damage it can take before it is cut, broken, or smashed. Almost any attack on an inanimate object can be generalized as (a) cutting through a rope or bar; (b) breaking through a flat surface; (c) smashing a solid object to rubble. Use the listing nearest to the object you're attacking; modify as appropriate. To attack an object:

(1) *Figure hit modifiers* for size, speed, distance, etc. – see p. 201. If you are using a hand weapon, and have a second to "aim" your blow at a motionless object, take a +4 to hit.

(2) *Roll to hit,* as with a normal attack. Inanimate objects get no defense roll, unless they are actually combatants (e.g., robots, military vehicles).

(3) *Roll damage* normally for your weapon, if you hit.

(4) *Subtract the object's damage resistance.*

(5) *Apply the remaining damage to the object.* Edged and impaling weapons do not get a "damage bonus" – that only applies to living targets. When the object's "hit points" are reduced to zero, the object has been cut, broken, or otherwise destroyed.

HT of a bar or rope is the damage required to cut it. HT of a wall or slab is the damage required to force a 2-foot-diameter hole. *Impaling* damage of the listed amount will make a *small* hole in a slab.

A complex object will have two HT listings. The first *breaks* it and makes it nonfunctional; the second *destroys* it. For example, a weapons locker might have a DR of 4 (thin steel), and HT of 20/50. If you use it to block the door, it will take 50 hits to reduce it to rubble. But 20 hits will ruin it as a locker!

"Weapon to use" is intended as a guideline for the players and GM, rather than a hard and fast rule. In general, just make sure that the weapon being used is one that could reasonably affect its target! Use common sense. A hard-driven spear could easily penetrate a door, but that would not break the door down. A club is unlikely to damage a basketball unless the basketball has nowhere to bounce. A sword may eventually cut down a door, but the sword will be dulled before the job is over. And so on.

---

damage resistance and hit points for some typical objects

Object	DR	Hit Points	Weapon to use	Object	DR	Hit Points	Weapon to use
Light rope (³/₈" diameter)	1	2	Any	Wallboard (¹/₂" thick)	1	5	Not impaling
Heavy rope (³/₄" diameter)	3	6	Edged	Plywood (¹/₂" thick)	3	15	Not impaling
Hawser (1¹/₂" diameter)	4	10	Edged	Wooden slab (1" thick)	2	10	Any
Steel cable (¹/₄" diameter)	2	8	Not impaling	Wooden slab (2" thick)	4	20	Not impaling
Steel cable (¹/₂" diameter)	4	16	Edged	Wooden slab (3" thick)	6	30	Axe, hammer, club
Steel cable (1" diameter)	6	30	Axe				
Wooden pole (1" diameter)	1	3	Any	Thin iron/bronze (¹/₈")	3	6	Not impaling
Wooden pole (2" diameter)	3	8	Not impaling	Thin iron/bronze (¹/₄")	4	12	Axe, hammer, club
Wooden pole (3" diameter)	4	12	Edged	Iron slab (¹/₂" thick)	6	25	Axe, hammer, club
Wooden pole (4" diameter)	6	20	Axe	Iron wall (1" thick)	8	50	Axe, hammer, club
Wooden pole (6" diameter)	6	30	Axe				
Wooden pole (8" diameter)	6	50	Axe	Thin steel (¹/₈")	4	10	Not impaling
				Thin steel (¹/₂")	6	20	Axe, hammer, club
Bronze/iron bar (¹/₂" diameter)	1	4	Not impaling	Steel slab (¹/₄" thick)	7	40	Axe or hammer
Bronze/iron bar (1" diameter)	3	20	Axe or hammer	Steel wall (1" thick)	8	80	Axe
Bronze/iron bar (2" diameter)	3	60	Axe				
				Brick wall (3" thick)	6	40	Axe, hammer, club
Steel bar (¹/₂" diameter)	2	6	Axe or hammer	Concrete wall (6" thick)	4	60	Axe or hammer
Steel bar (1" diameter)	6	25	Axe	Stone wall (6" thick)	8	90	Axe or hammer
Steel bar (2" diameter)	8	80	Axe	Stone wall (12" thick)	8	180	Axe or hammer

Example of Injury

Fiendish Friedrick has a basic HT score of 14. He has the ill fortune to be trapped in a dead-end corridor by a huge band of orcs. He fights valiantly, but the orcs keep coming, and Friedrick takes more and more wounds.

When his HT is reduced to 3, his movements slow and falter. Soon he takes another blow which reduces his HT to *exactly* zero. At the beginning of his next turn, he tries his HT roll – and succeeds! Grimly, he hangs on to consciousness, slaying another orc. For the next two turns, he continues to make HT rolls. Each time, he succeeds (with a HT of 14, it's hard to miss) and stays conscious.

Then he fails a HT roll. Instantly, he falls unconscious.

The orcs keep hacking at him. When his HT reaches -14, he must roll 14 or less on 3 dice – or die. He makes the roll. The orcs keep hacking (they're too stupid to cut his throat). At -19 HT, and again at -24 HT, further rolls are required. Each time, he rolls 14 or less, and clings to life. But the orcs keep hacking. Eventually, Friedrick will reach -70 or miss a roll; then he is automatically dead. Only strong magic can help him now! And if the orcs keep on hacking until his hits go to -140 (which might take a while), there will not even be a body to revive – just a Friedrickburger.

Instant Death

Regardless of HT, anyone can be killed by a cut throat, decapitation, etc. If a helpless or unconscious person is attacked in an obviously lethal way – he's dead. Don't bother to roll for damage, calculate remaining hit points, etc.

This does not apply to a merely *unaware* victim. If you sneak up behind a sentry, you can't automatically kill him. But you can play it out realistically. Aim for a vital organ and attack; if the sentry is just standing there, he can be attacked as an "inanimate object" (p. 125) and you get a +4 to your roll. Your attack roll will almost certainly succeed. Your victim will get no active defense at all. You will probably do enough damage to incapacitate or kill him. But it's not *automatic*.

The life of an adventurer is not all song and glory. You get tired. You get your clothes dirty. You may actually get *hurt,* or even worse, *dead.*

Fortunately, all these problems can be cured. Even death. Read on . . .

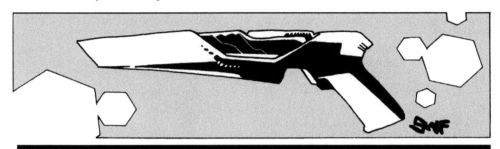

INJURIES

Wounds and other injuries cause bodily damage, or "hits." Your HT (health) score tells how many hits you can take. A character who goes down to 0 hit points will soon fall unconscious. It *is* possible to survive with a negative hit point total.

The average character has 10 to 12 hit points. It should be obvious from the *Basic Weapon Damage* table (p. 74) that this much damage can often be done by just one or two blows! This is realistic. Remember that most weapons are *levers* (to vastly increase your strength), or impaling devices to reach your foe's vital organs. In reality, an average man can kill another average man with *one* good head blow from a club . . . let alone a sword, spear or gun. Armor helps . . . but fights are *deadly.* Avoid them!

General Damage (Lost Hit Points)

Someone who is wounded repeatedly will eventually weaken and collapse, even if no single injury is very great. Record hits on your Character Sheet. Characters who lose most of their hit points are affected as follows:

3, 2, 1 hit points left: Your Move is cut in half; you are reeling from the wounds.

0 or less hit points left: You are in immediate danger of collapse. At the beginning of each turn, roll against your basic HT, plus or minus Strong/Weak Will. A success means you may take your turn normally. A failed roll means you fall unconscious.

-HT hit points: You must make your HT roll (use *basic* HT) or die. If you don't die, you are still able to talk, fight, etc. (assuming you are still conscious!). Another roll is required after each further loss of 5 hit points. If you take 6 or more hits at once, you cross two levels and must make *two* HT rolls. (*Example:* If your HT is 8, then -8 is "-HT." When you reach -8 hit points, you must make your HT roll or die. If you survive, you must roll again at -13 hit points – and so on.)

-5×HT: Automatic death. This means you have lost a total of 6×HT hit points; nobody can survive that much injury.

If your character is killed, you may wish to keep track of further damage anyway. In some magical or high-tech game worlds, a dead character can be brought back to life if some or all of his body is recovered.

But there is a limit even to that. If a character's hit point total goes to -10 times his original HT, his body may have been *totally* destroyed. Whether any portions remain intact will depend on the means of destruction. 200 points' worth of arrow wounds will leave a messy, but recognizable, corpse. 200 points' worth of fire damage will leave nothing but a lump of charcoal.

Shock

Whenever you are injured, your IQ and DX are reduced by that amount, *on your next turn only. Example:* If you take 3 hits of injury, your IQ and DX, and skills, will be -3 on your next turn. Active defenses are not DX-based skills.

This subtraction will most often affect weapon attacks or attempts to cast magical spells – but *any* use of IQ, DX or skill you initiate is affected. Defensive reactions (resisting psionic powers, Fright Checks, etc.) are not penalized. Therefore, on the turn after you are badly hurt, it may be a good idea to try flight, all-out defense, etc., rather than counterattacking instantly.

This is only a temporary effect from shock. On your following turn, your skills are back to normal.

Knockout

Any blow to the head or brain, or any crushing blow to the vitals, may knock the victim out, even if it does *exactly 0* damage (in other words, one more hit would have caused actual injury). The victim must make a HT roll. On a failed roll, the victim falls unconscious.

A blow to the "brain" area which does more than HT/2 hits is an *automatic* knockout.

Knockdown

Anyone who is hit for *more* than half his HT in one blow must immediately roll against his basic HT. If he fails the roll, he *falls* and is *stunned* (see below). If he makes his HT roll, he keeps his footing, but he is still stunned.

Note that this is not the same as *knockback* (see p. 106), in which a blow may knock you backwards, but not necessarily make you fall down.

Stunning

A character may be "stunned" by taking damage of *more* than half his HT in one blow – or by a critical hit – or by a brain blow that does more than HT/3 damage. A crippling or blinding injury also causes stunning.

If you are stunned, all your active defenses are at -4 until your next turn. At that time, roll against basic HT to see whether you recover. A successful roll means you can act normally *on that turn*. A failed roll means you are still stunned and stand there mindlessly . . . The "stunned" state continues until you can make your HT roll and snap out of it. You may act again on the turn you roll successfully and shake off the daze.

A surprised or shocked character may also be *mentally* "stunned" – this is what happens when the foe gets the initiative on you (see p. 122). The effects of this sort of stunning are just the same, but you must make your IQ roll, rather than your HT roll, to snap out of it. You're not *hurt* – you're *confused*.

Crippling Injuries

In the Advanced Combat System, you do not take "generic" damage; each wound hits a specific part of the body. Enough damage to a hand, foot or limb *in one blow* will cripple it. A hand or foot is crippled by being hit for more than 1/3 your HT. An arm or leg is crippled by being hit for more than 1/2 your HT. Damage *over* the crippling amount, either in that blow or a later one, does not affect you at all; ignore it.

A crippling injury may (or may not) take the hand, foot or limb right off; it depends on the type and amount of damage – GM's ruling. For simplicity, any part that has been rendered useless will be referred to as "crippled." Effects of crippling injuries are described in the sidebar. See p. 129 for recovery.

First Aid

Most of the HT loss from an injury is due to shock rather than actual physical damage. Therefore, prompt treatment after a fight can restore some of the lost hit points. A medical kit (see the appropriate *Equipment List*) will help!

Simple bandaging, etc., *even done by a totally unskilled person,* will restore one lost hit point per fight – but no more, no matter how badly you were hurt. This takes 30 minutes per victim.

Starvation and Dehydration

When the party buys equipment, they shouldn't forget food! The traveler's rations listed in the equipment table are the minimum necessary to keep you healthy on the road; missing even one meal will weaken you.

For each meal that you miss, lose 1 point of ST. Treat this as fatigue, except that "starvation" fatigue can be recovered only by a day of rest – no fighting or travel, and three full meals. Each day of rest will make up for three skipped meals.

When your ST reaches 3 due to "starvation" fatigue, you start losing HT instead, at the same rate. This HT loss is regained in the normal fashion.

Water: In temperate areas, where water is easy to come by, just assume that supplies are renewed as needed. But if water is in short supply, watch out! A person (human, elf, dwarf, etc.) needs 2 quarts of water a day – 3 in hot climates, 5 in the heat of the desert! If you get less than you need, you lose a fatigue point *and* a HT point each day. If you drink less than a quart a day, you lose 2 fatigue and HT points a day. If ST or HT goes to 0 from lack of water (even if that is not the only cause) you become delirious and – if in the desert – die within a day if no help arrives. Fatigue lost due to lack of water is regained after a day of rest with ample water supplies. Lost HT is regained in the normal fashion.

Foraging: In hospitable terrain, you can supplement your supplies by foraging for food. On any day, each character can "forage" as the party travels. A successful Survival or Naturalist roll will collect enough edible plants and berries for one meal. (A roll of 17 means you poisoned yourself; make your HT roll. Lose 1 hit if you make the roll, 1d hits otherwise. A roll of 18 means you shared with your friends and the whole party suffers likewise.)

In the right terrain, a successful skill roll with a missile weapon (at -4) will bag a rabbit, providing enough meat for two meals. Each character gets one Survivalist/Naturalist roll and one missile roll each day.

Alternatively, the party can take some time off from travel and do some *serious* foraging. Each character can make five Survivalist/Naturalist rolls and five missile-weapon skill rolls per day. Meat can be smoked over a fire and added to the regular store of rations.

Game Masters: If keeping up with the party's meals doesn't sound like fun, feel free to ignore this whole section. Travel is much more hazardous if you have to keep track of food and water!

Technological level	Time per victim	Hits restored
0 (Stone Age): No First Aid skill exists. Use bandaging only.		
1 (Bronze Age)	30 minutes	1d-4
2, 3 (Roman/medieval)	30 minutes	1d-3
4 (up to U.S. Civil War)	30 minutes	1d-2
5 (Civil War – WWI)	20 minutes	1d-2
6, 7 (WWII/modern)	20 minutes	1d-1
8 (near future)	10 minutes	1d
9 and up: As for TL8, with the addition of various special healing drugs and devices. See science-fiction game-world books.		

First aid (a successful First Aid skill or default roll) will restore a variable number of hit points, depending on the tech level of the First Aid skill and the degree of success. A *minimum* of one 1 point is always restored. This is *not* cumulative with simple bandaging – i.e., sometimes the first aid is no more effective than plain bandaging.

Great Success or Failure: On a critical success, the victim regains the maximum possible HT. On a critical failure, the victim *loses* 2 hit points, and bandaging will not help.

Natural Recovery

Gradual recovery will cure any number of hits, unless the victim gets sick (see *Illness*). At the end of each day of rest and decent food, the victim may roll against his basic HT. A successful roll results in the recovery of one hit point. The GM may modify the roll downward if conditions are bad, or upward if conditions are very good.

Medical Care

If the victim is under the care of a competent Physician (skill level 12 or better) the victim gets a +1 on all healing rolls. The *healer* may also roll against his Physician skill to cure the patient. Frequency of this roll depends on the tech level of his skill (see below). Medieval-level Physicians, for instance, roll once per week. A successful roll lets the patient recover 1 extra hit point; a critical success gives 2. A badly-failed roll *costs* the patient 1 hit point.

Exotic methods of healing are available in some game worlds.

Medical TL	Frequency of roll	Patients per doctor	Medical TL	Frequency of roll	Patients per doctor
0	There are no physicians. Get well by yourself.				
1-3	Weekly	10			
4	Every 3 days	10	10	3×daily	50
5	Every 2 days	15	11	4×daily	100
6	Daily	20	12	5×daily	100
7	Daily	25	13	6×daily	100
8	Daily	50	14	8×daily	200
9	Twice daily	50	15+	10×daily	200

Physicians at high tech levels depend heavily on equipment, but are still given good basic training in med school. Therefore, a physician above TL6 performs as though he were TL6 if he has to make do without the gadgetry to which he is accustomed, as long as the surroundings are clean.

Only one physician per patient may roll (no, 20 doctors can't cure you in a day). However, one doctor can be responsible for up to 200 patients at a time, depending on the tech level of his skill and whether he has assistance.

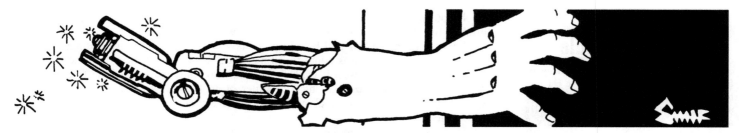

Psionic healing (p. 175) and magical healing (p. 162) are both much faster than normal healing.

High tech levels bring advanced medical techniques, to accelerate the body's processes to the point where almost any injury can heal quickly. Lost parts can be replaced by "bionic" prosthetics that are as good as new (or better), or by cloned transplants. See *GURPS Space.*

Recovering From Unconsciousness

This depends on the severity of your injuries, rather than the medical care you get or don't get. If your HT is 0 or higher, you will awaken in an hour; if you have lost no more than 2 HT, you will awaken in 15 minutes.

If your Ht is below 0, but not fully negative, make a HT roll to regain consciousness after a number of hours equal to the amount by which your HT is negative (maximum 12 hours); roll hourly after that. Example: Your HT is -8 after the battle. You may roll to wake up (still with -8 HT) after 8 hours, and every hour after that. When you awaken, you can call for help or even try to drag yourself to shelter. Details are up to the GM, who should be merciful. However, you regain no hit points unless you can get food and shelter; you will remain weak for a long time.

If your HT has gone "fully negative" – e.g., HT of -10 or worse for someone with a basic HT of 10 – you are in bad shape. If you can make a roll on basic HT, you will awaken (as above)- after 12 hours, and can try to help yourself. If you fail the roll, you stay in a coma and die unless you are helped within (HT) hours.

Recovering from Crippling Injuries

At the end of any fight in which a character is crippled, that character makes a roll vs. Health for each crippling injury. A *successful* roll means that the injury is *temporary.* If and when the character gets back up to full health – i.e., regains all his hit points – the crippling injury is fully healed. Until that time, the character is lame, one-armed, or one-handed, as the case may be.

If the HT roll is failed by *3 points or less,* the injury is lasting. A bone was broken, or muscles were badly torn. Roll 1 die. This is the number of months it will take for the injury to heal fully. (Subtract 3 from the roll for a medical tech level of 7 or better, 2 for a TL of 6, and 1 for a TL of 5 – but the period of healing is never less than a month.)

If the HT roll is failed by *more* than 3 points, the injury is *permanent.* It is up to the player and the GM to determine whether the limb was actually lost, or just permanently damaged. It would be logical to assume (for instance) that an axe-wound would cause a clean amputation, while a mace would just pulverize the bone and muscle. In general, effects on play will be the same.

Assorted Hazards

Besides the ordinary combat risks of knives, swords, guns and spells, there are a number of other hazards commonly faced by the adventurer.

Flame

These rules assume the adventurers are dealing with flames of "ordinary" heat – at most, a bonfire. The extreme heat produced by a blowtorch, pyrokinetic attack, volcano, etc., cannot be resisted by anything except magic or armor specifically made to stop heat.

A torch, wielded as a weapon, does ordinary "club" damage plus one point for the flame (see p. 124). However, if the enemy has armor or skin of DR2 or better, he will not feel the flame and will take no extra damage. Certain magical weapons create flame, which does more damage than ordinary fire.

Sometimes you will have to walk *through* fire. The most common sources of fire are flaming oil (see sidebar, p. 121), burning rubble (as a side-effect of combat), and magic. For game purposes, a hex is either "on fire" or not.

Accumulated Wounds: An Optional Rule

Normally, a character is crippled only if he takes enough damage (over $\frac{1}{2}$ HT for a limb, over $\frac{1}{3}$ HT for a hand or foot) in a single blow. For more realism, you may keep track of where hits are taken, and let a limb be crippled when its total damage reaches the appropriate level. However, this makes record-keeping more complicated. You may want to use tally marks by the character's picture, or make notes in the "Hits Taken" box.

Excess damage is still lost. For instance, if your HT is 11, then damage of 6 or more hits would cripple the arm. Once you have taken 6 hits to the arm and crippled it, further wounds are ignored. Even if the crippling blow theoretically did 20 hits of damage, only the first 6 would count. That way, you cannot be killed by (for instance) repeated blows to the arm.

Last Wounds: An Optional Rule

In a game, it can happen that a sorely wounded character is knocked out, or even killed, by a 1-point blow to the foot. There are those who find this unrealistic.

If you wish, use the following optional rule: Once a character's HT is reduced to 3 or less, no wound to the arm, leg, hand or foot affects him at all unless (a) it is a critical hit; (b) it is enough to cripple that limb; or (c) it does 3 or more points of damage at once.

Dying Actions

When a PC or important NPC is killed in any but the most sudden and thorough fashion, the GM should allow a "dying action." If this is a final blow at the enemy, it should take no more than a turn. If it is a deathbed speech, the GM can stretch time a little bit for dramatic purposes!

This has nothing to do with realism, but it's fun.

Bleeding: An Optional Rule

The victim of a cutting, impaling or bullet wound may continue to lose HT due to bleeding. At the end of every minute after being wounded, the victim rolls against HT, at a -1 penalty for every 5 points of damage he has taken. If he fails this HT roll, he bleeds for a loss of 1 HT. On a critical failure, he bleeds for *3* points of damage. On a critical success, the bleeding stops completely. On an ordinary success, he does not bleed this minute, but must continue to roll every minute. If he does not bleed for three consecutive minutes, the bleeding stops for good.

If someone makes a First Aid roll to help his wounded comrade, or if a wounded but conscious character makes a First Aid roll on himself, the bleeding stops immediately. One First Aid roll may be attempted per patient per minute; this roll comes *before* the bleeding roll. Once first aid has been successfully administered, no more bleeding rolls are made. If a successful First Aid roll is made within the first minute after the wound was delivered, there will be no HT loss due to bleeding.

Note that it takes only one minute to apply pressure or a tourniquet in order to stop bleeding. Once bleeding has been halted, the character administering first aid may spend 30 minutes to treat the victim for shock. To do this, he must keep the victim warm, comfortable, calm and still; at the end of 30 minutes, he makes another First Aid roll. If he succeeds, he has alleviated the victim's shock and restored a single HT point of damage, as per p. 127.

This rule is realistic, but remains optional for two reasons. First, it adds to bookkeeping. Second, it markedly increases the deadliness of combat!

The GM decides what wounds may bleed. Most crushing wounds won't bleed significantly, but there are always exceptions. Burns and similar wounds do not bleed significantly because the damage sears the wounded flesh, cauterizing the wound and preventing blood loss automatically. Examples of this type of wound include fire and electrical damage, laser fire, and chemical burns.

If you spend *part* of a turn in a fire, you will take 1d-3 damage. If you spend *all* of a turn in a fire (or on fire) you will take 1d-1 damage.

Low-tech armor (TL7 and below) protects you *completely* against ordinary heat or flame for a number of turns equal to 3 times its DR. After that, it still protects against *flame*, but the wearer must roll vs. HT every turn to resist the *heat* of the fire. A failed roll costs 1 *Fatigue. Example:* heavy leather protects against all damage for 6 turns. After that, the wearer starts making HT rolls. Note that if you are using the advanced armor rules, you take fire damage according to the *lightest* armor you have on.

Higher-tech armor may be airtight; in that case, armor of DR4 or better will protect indefinitely against ordinary flame. Reflec armor protects against flame for one minute; after that, the wearer must roll vs. HT, as above, once every 10 seconds, as heat builds up. Airtight armor of DR3 or less protects like low-tech armor, but may (GM's decision) be ruined by the fire!

A shield offers no protection if you are walking *through* flame. It can block a *jet* of flame (dragon breath, for instance) as it would block any other attack. If you have to go *near* a source of intense heat, but not actually *in* it, the shield's PD will count as damage resistance (it reflects the heat). Increase the PD by 50% (round down) if it is highly polished.

Heat

In weather of 80° or above, make a HT (or Desert Survival) roll every 30 minutes. If the weather is very humid, the GM may increase the effective temperature! A failed roll costs 1 point of Fatigue. When ST reaches 3, start losing HT instead. This assumes you are wearing appropriate clothing (light-colored and loose). If you are wearing heavy clothing or armor, subtract its DR or your encumbrance level, whichever is less, from effective HT.

Reduce your effective HT by 1 for every five degrees over 90° Fahrenheit.

Any extra exertion in hot weather will cost extra fatigue, too. See sidebar, p. 134. And remember that extra water will be needed in hot weather (see p. 128).

Armor offers no protection at all against heat. *Exception:* "Reflec" armor raises the wearer's effective temperature by 10° – it retains body heat. Certain types of airtight high-tech armor, including all battlesuits and all TL9+ combat armor, will have integral cooling systems.

A related problem, and a very real danger in some places, is sunburn. After a day of full sun on unprotected skin, an albino will be near death, and a light-skinned Caucasian will be very uncomfortable (1d-3 damage). Darker characters may itch, but aren't in as much danger. Details must be left to the GM. Ingenious PCs will quickly find ways to protect themselves!

Freezing

Cold can be deadly, but only magic or super-science can produce cold quickly enough to affect a combat. Medieval-style armor offers its normal protection against such "instant" cold, but is no protection at all against cold *weather*. High-tech airtight battlesuits, etc., protect completely against cold if they have DR5 or better. Airtight suits of DR4 or less give +1 on the wearer's HT roll to resist cold, unless they are specifically designed to keep the wearer warm. Reflec armor also retains heat, giving a +1.

Against "normal" freezing weather, make a HT (or Arctic Survival) roll every 30 minutes. A failed roll costs you 1 point of Fatigue. When ST reaches 3, start losing HT instead. This assumes you are wearing normal winter clothing. Subtract 5 from effective HT if you are wearing light clothing or if your clothes are wet; add 5 if you are dressed for really cold weather.

Reduce your effective HT by 1 for every 10 degrees below zero Fahrenheit. Strong wind (the "wind chill factor") can reduce the effective temperature dramatically; this is up to the GM.

Drowning

See the rules for *Swimming,* p. 91.

Falling

When you fall, roll for damage as follows:

1 or 2 yards: (1d-4) damage per yard
3 or 4 yards: (1d-3) per yard
5 or more yards: (1d-2) per yard

A successful Acrobatics roll will reduce the effective distance of your fall by 5 yards.

Terminal velocity – the maximum speed a falling object can achieve – varies for humans, but is normally reached after 3 or 4 seconds of falling. Therefore, treat any fall of more than 50 yards as only 50 yards.

If you land on something soft, subtract 1 point per yard fallen. If you land in deep water, make a Swimming roll immediately. A successful roll means the water counts as "soft" – you entered well. Otherwise, treat it as "hard"!

Example: If you fall 5 yards, you would take (5d-10) damage – that is, roll 5 dice and subtract 10 from the total rolled. If you fall 5 yards but land on something soft, roll 5 dice and subtract 15 from the result.

Cloth, leather or flexible plastic armor will protect against a fall with its normal DR (maximum 3). Medieval-style metal armor has half its normal DR (round down) against a fall. TL8+ combat armor is very well padded inside, and protects with 1/3 its normal DR (which is very high). Shields don't help.

Falling Objects

If you are hit by a *hard* falling object, calculate the damage done as follows: Round its weight off to the nearest 10 pounds, and the distance it fell to the nearest 10 yards. Multiply the number of 10-pound and 10-yard increments . . . and take that many dice of damage.

Example: A 20-lb. rock, falling 30 yards, does (2×3):6 dice of damage. A 43-pound suit of armor, falling 39 yards, does (4×4) or 16 dice of damage.

"Terminal velocity" is reached after something falls far enough that air resistance stops further acceleration. Exact terminal velocity depends on the object – the more air resistance, the less its maximum speed. For simplicity, when dealing with falling *inanimate* objects, treat any fall of more than 200 yards as 200 yards. Falling *beings* reach terminal velocity at 50 yards, as described under *Falling,* above. Mattresses and the like reach terminal velocity sooner, but dealing with this is left to the GM – if he cares about that much detail!

A very *light* object, or one that falls a short distance, does less damage. Any weight or distance of 2 or less should be treated as 10 – but halve the final damage. Example: a 2-lb. weight falling 29 yards does *half* of (1×3) damage. Rather than trying to roll 1½ dice, you can roll 3 dice and halve the result, rounding down.

Thus, an object of 2 lbs. (or less) which falls 2 yards (or less) does only ¼ die of damage – so unless you roll 4 or more, the damage is zero! That is not to say that it won't hurt – but it would not do any real injury.

Soft objects (living things, for instance) do half damage, or less, for their weight.

If a large item is tipped over onto you, rather than falling freely, it does much less damage. Divide its weight by 100, round down, and roll that many dice.

Any *bulky* object – over 50 lbs. and/or 6 cubic feet – will impede the movement of anyone it falls against. The victim may only move one yard on his next turn. Furthermore, his active defense is reduced by 3 (distraction!). This is a good time to use the *All-Out Defense* maneuver.

If you drop a rock on someone, treat it as a thrown-weapon attack and make your DX (or Throwing) roll normally. Your target cannot avoid the rock unless he knows it's coming. If he's aware of it, let him make his Dodge roll, or roll against his basic DX (whichever is better) to avoid it. But note that passive defenses like armor might deflect a falling rock, but *not* a boulder or piano!

Hit Location from a Fall

If you are using the Hit Location rules, you may roll on the following table to see what *type* of injury you sustain from a fall.

Roll 2 dice:

2: Hit head. Knocked out. Roll vs. HT every 30 minutes to see if you come to.
3: Both arms crippled.
4: Both legs crippled.
5: Right leg crippled.
6: Left leg crippled.
7: Right arm crippled.
8: Left leg crippled.
9, 10: General bruises, but no special injury.
11, 12: Hit head. Stunned.

If you took less than 5 hits of damage, any "crippling" result is temporary, and you will be able to use the limb again in 10 minutes. (The HT is *not* recovered, though.) If you take 5 or more hits, your injury is a break or bad sprain, and you must roll against HT to see if you can recover (see p. 129). But such injuries are usually "clean," so you get a +5 bonus to your effective HT for this roll.

Poisoned Weapons

Poisoned weapons are unchivalrous, unsporting, expensive and usually less effective than their users would like. But they have their advantages . . .

A blood agent may be applied to any cutting or impaling weapon. It takes effect only if the weapon actually does damage. Most weapon poisons will only take effect the first time the weapon strikes someone; after that, most of the poison will have worn off. Three *unsuccessful* strikes with a poisoned weapon (blocked or parried) will also make the poison wear off.

A contact agent may be applied to any weapon at all. It takes effect if the weapon breaks the skin or touches bare skin. It wears off as above.

Some examples of poisons include:

Caustic tar. A preparation of powerful alkali and sticky pitch, especially for weapons. Blood agent (causes pain but no other effect on skin contact). $30 per dose. In a wound, it causes *intense* pain but no real damage; the victim loses no HT, but has -1 to DX, for the next hour, for *each* time he is hit with the poisoned weapon. This effect is immediate. A successful HT roll prevents all effects. Caustic tar adheres well to a weapon; roll 1 die each time it strikes. The tar wears off only on a 1 or 2, and not at all on blocks and parries.

Wolfsbane. A vegetable poison, often used by savages. Both a blood and digestive agent. Common wolfsbane might cost $40 per dose. Does 2 dice damage and causes numbness and spasms; reduce victim's DX by 4 for two hours. A successful HT roll will prevent any effect. Effects take 1 hour to show.

Cobra venom. Very costly ($100 per dose). Blood agent. Must be relatively fresh. One adult cobra gives 4 doses. Does 3 dice of damage, or 1 die if the victim makes his HT roll. Multiple doses each take full effect! Effects take 1 hour to show.

Examples of Poison Gas

Tear gas chokes you if you breathe it, doing 1 point of damage per turn. Roll vs. HT to resist. Damage ceases when you fall unconscious. Tear gas is also a contact agent (eyes only). Roll vs. HT to resist if it gets in your eyes. A failed roll means you are partially blinded – -5 on DX. Recovery takes about 10 minutes.

Mustard gas chokes you if you breathe it, doing 2 points of damage per turn. Roll vs. HT to resist. Damage continues until you die. It is also a contact agent. Treat it like tear gas if it gets in your eyes. It also does 1d-3 damage each turn to unprotected *skin* – roll vs. HT each turn to resist. Damage continues until you die. (Realistically, mustard gas does not kill that cleanly; you can linger for hours or days. But the fatal damage occurs very quickly.)

Poisons

Specific poisons will be discussed in the appropriate game-world books. As a rule, the higher the medical tech level, the deadlier and more subtle will be the poisons available. But even primitive hunters can envenom their arrows . . .

Types of poison include *contact* agents (which only have to touch the skin); *blood* agents which must enter the body through a wound or injection; *digestive* agents which must be swallowed; and *respiratory* agents which must be inhaled (see *Poison Gas*).

Poison is commonly met on weapons (see below); on darts, needles, or spikes in traps; in food or drink offered by a treacherous foe; and anywhere else you did not expect it. Human foes are not the only ones that can poison you. Snakes, insects and certain other creatures have natural poison (usually blood agents); eating the wrong plant or animal may treat you to a dose of digestive poison. These are treated just like other poisons.

A very common poison effect is to temporarily reduce ST, DX or IQ. If this happens, *all skills* relating to the reduced attribute are also reduced until the poison's effects are gone.

As a rule, anyone who is poisoned will get a HT roll to avoid the poison's effects. Depending on the poison, some rolls will be harder than others! And some especially virulent poisons cannot be resisted, or have a reduced effect even on those who resist.

The description of a poison will include the following information:

Name, general description, and source.

Type: contact, blood, respiratory or digestive (or some combination).

Cost per dose (a dose is enough to poison one person or envenom one weapon).

Effects of the poison if it is not resisted. Most poisons are *slow;* time will be specified. Unless specified otherwise, multiple doses will have no extra effect.

HT roll (if any) allowed to resist the poison.

Effects of the poison (if any) on someone who successfully resists it.

Poison Gas and Smoke

Poison gas uses the poison rules, with certain additions. *Smoke* can be considered a weak "poison gas." Breathing it does 1 HT damage per turn; a HT+3 roll will avoid its effects. For smoke, as for any poison gas, roll *each turn* to resist the effect.

All poison gases are *respiratory* agents – affecting anyone who breathes them. Some are also *contact* agents. A gas mask, or even a towel over the face, will protect against respiratory effects, but not against contact effects. Your DR from Toughness helps against contact agents, but not against respiratory agents. Your skin may be tough, but your lungs aren't.

A single "dose" of gas is enough to affect one person if projected right in his face (from a spray can or a trap, for instance). Ten doses will make a gas grenade that will affect a whole room, or small outdoor area (say 4 yards×4 yards, with no wind).

Internal effects (from breathing gas): Some types of gas kill; others just incapacitate. As a general rule, deadly gases do damage every turn (unless resisted). Incapacitating gases have the same effect whether you get one lungful or a dozen – again, unless you resist. You *can* hold your breath to keep from breathing gas, if you know it's coming – see p. 91. If you are knocked out or stunned, you inhale automatically!

External effects (from contact with gas): Not all gases affect the skin, but the worst ones do. They can simply blister the skin, like mustard gas – or they can be absorbed through the skin and attack internally, like modern nerve gas. Clothing protects covered areas completely for two turns – then the gas has full effect. Any sort of non-airtight armor will protect completely for five turns – then the gas takes effect.

Airtight armor protects completely. Toughness protects you against physical blistering, but not from absorbing nerve gases and the like.

Insects and Loathsome Crawlers

Each game world will have its own "nuisance creatures." Stinging insects, slimy vermin and similar horrors are treated like skin-affecting gas (above). Airtight armor will protect against almost all varieties. Clothing will keep them off for two turns, armor for five. After that, they attack you, doing whatever damage they can do. The result of an insect attack can range from harmless misery to quick death. See p. 143.

Most insects attack by injecting poison, so Toughness is no help. Some creepy-crawlers attack by *eating* you, and Toughness is a *big* help there!

ILLNESS

Maladies and strange diseases may affect the adventurer in far lands. The search for a cure – whether for a princess' wasting disease, or for a plague ravaging a kingdom – is an excellent plot device. Invention of diseases is an excellent opportunity for the GM to exercise a morbid sort of creativity.

You may be wholly or partially protected from disease by magical or technological items, the Immunity to Disease advantage, or just a high HT. Risks are greatest in warm, moist areas. If you catch something, you won't know until the symptoms start to show . . . the GM makes your roll to avoid it!

Disease

A disease is usually a "plague" caused by microorganisms and spread by infected humans or animals – but sometime diseases have other causes! News about disease-ridden areas travels fast. And a roll against IQ, Physician or Diagnosis tells when many people around you have the same illness.

However, characters may enter (for instance) a jungle area where animals are suffering from a disease that humans can catch. Then they would need to examine a specimen and make a successful Vet roll, or a roll on IQ-5 or a medical skill -5, to realize the danger.

Symptoms

Disease symptoms usually appear at least 24 hours after the disease is caught. Most diseases aren't contagious until after symptoms appear. Typical symptoms include daily HT loss (which may endanger the victim) for several days; loss of ST, DX or IQ; increased fatigue; sneezing, coughing, spots, sores or rash. Severe symptoms could include delirium, unconsciousness, blindness, etc.

Diagnosis

When symptoms of a disease are apparent, the GM should roll each character's Diagnosis skill, or IQ-6. (Use Vet skill to identify an animal illness.) Success means the character identifies the disease. Totally new illnesses can't be identified, but a very good roll might give enough information to do some good.

Recovery

Typically, a disease sufferer must make a daily HT roll. This roll, and the effects of failure, vary with each illness. For a "generic" disease, a failed roll might mean you lose 1 HT; a success lets you regain 1 HT.

When you have recovered all HT lost to an illness, you are cured. If your illness allows HT rolls to attempt to recover, a roll of a natural 3 or 4 means the disease has vanished (lost HT must be recovered in the normal fashion).

For some diseases, recovery will be aided by use of appropriate drugs. For most diseases, a physician's care (as for injuries) will aid attempts to recover.

Contagion

Anyone in a plague-ridden area, or encountering a plague carrier, is in danger. Roll against HT once per day; a failed roll means you catch the plague. From the table below, choose the *least* advantageous roll each day:

Avoided all contact with possible victims: HT+4

Entered dwelling or shop of victim: HT+3

Spoke with victim at close quarters: HT+2

Touched victim briefly: HT+1

Used victim's clothes, blankets, etc.: HT

Ate victim's cooked flesh (animal, we hope!): HT

Ate victim's raw flesh (ditto!!): HT-1

Prolonged contact with living victim(s): HT-2

Kissing or other intimate contact with victim: HT-3

These chances are not cumulative; roll anew each day. The GM may require a harder roll for a virulent plague, or an easier one for a less contagious one. Proper precautions (masks, antiseptic washes, etc.) will also decrease the chances of catching plague, but only if the *characters* know and understand them – no modern techniques are allowed in a low-tech world!

Immunity and Susceptibility

Some illnesses may not affect members of certain races or groups. For instance, the GM may decide that Dwarves never get the Purple Shakes at all, and that Elves have a +2 on all HT rolls against it . . . but that mortality rate among male Giants is 100% unless they are treated within two days. Such cases of differential susceptibility may be known to someone with Physician or Diagnostic skill.

Some *individuals* are immune to a specific disease. If the GM rolls a 3 or 4 for your first attempt to resist a disease, you are immune! He should note this fact and not tell you – under normal circumstances, you have no real way of knowing about your immunity.

At TL5 and above, *vaccination* is available for many plagues (though not diseases or infections). At TL6 and above, vaccines are widespread and can be stored for long periods of time like other medicines. A vaccination will not cure illness, but will provide almost certain immunity. At TL9 and above, "panimmunity" treatments (see *GURPS Space*) can increase your effective HT against any form of disease.

Finally, anyone who survives a given plague or disease may be immune in the future. This depends on the illness. You only catch measles once, for instance – but mumps can come back over and over.

Fatigue Costs

Fighting a Battle

Any battle that lasts more than 10 seconds will cost Fatigue points as follows, at the *end* of the battle:

No encumbrance: 1 point
Light encumbrance: 2 points
Medium encumbrance: 3 points
Heavy encumbrance: 4 points
Extra-heavy encumbrance: 5 points

This is a cost per battle, and not a cost per 10 seconds of battle! The GM (or adventure writer) may assess extra Fatigue for a very long battle – but a fight should run at least 2 or 3 minutes (120 to 180 turns) before extra Fatigue costs would be realistic.

If the day is hot, add 1 extra point to the above, or 2 extra points for anyone in plate armor or an overcoat. Full-coverage armor at TL8 and above includes cooling systems!

Marching

Exactly as above, for each hour of road travel. An hour of marching while lightly encumbered would cost 2 Fatigue points (3 in hot weather), and so on. If the party enters combat while on the road, assume (unless the scenario specifies otherwise) that they have been walking for an hour, and assess fatigue penalties accordingly.

Running or Swimming

After each 100 yards of running or speedy swimming, roll vs. HT. A failed roll means you lose 1 point of Fatigue. This is not affected by encumbrance, though heavy encumbrance will make you run more slowly (see p. 76).

Overexertion

Carrying more than extra-heavy encumbrance, or pushing/pulling a very heavy load, costs 1 Fatigue per *turn* (see p. 89). Extra effort when lifting, jumping, etc. (see p. 88) also costs 1 Fatigue per attempt.

Losing Sleep

A night without sleep costs 5 Fatigue. Losing a half-night of sleep costs 2 Fatigue.

Spells and Psychic Powers

Use of most magic spells (see Chapter 19) and many psychic abilities (see Chapter 20) will cost Fatigue points.

Infection

An "infection" is caused by a microorganism which attacks open wounds. Infections are possible anywhere, but some locales (especially jungles) may harbor especially severe forms of infection.

The GM may require a roll for infection if (a) the circumstances of a battle insure that a wound will be dirty, or (b) some special sort of infection is present in the area. A single roll against HT is made; details are at the GM's discretion.

Otherwise, infection is healed just like disease. Some sample rolls:

To avoid ordinary infection from dirt in the wound .... HT+3
As above, in an area with a special infection .... HT
To avoid infection from a spike envenomed with dung .... HT+1
As above, in an area with a special infection HT-2

If the infected wound is in the head or body, all HT loss is "generic." If the wound is on a hand, foot or limb, and it progresses to the point where it has cost the victim more than half his HT, the affected member must be amputated to save the victim's life. The infection is then considered cured.

FATIGUE

Fatigue represents lost *strength,* just as injury represents lost health. If your ST is 10, you can lose 10 "Fatigue points" before falling unconscious from exhaustion. When you suffer Fatigue, keep separate track on your Character Sheet, in the box beside your ST. Fatigue does not affect HT at all.

You can suffer from fatigue due to overexertion, running long distances, lack of air, use of psi powers, casting magic spells, etc. You will also suffer fatigue at the end of each battle that lasts more than ten seconds (you expend energy fast when you fight for your life!). The fatigue you suffer at the end of a fight is equal to your encumbrance level plus 1. That is, an unencumbered fighter suffers 1 point of Fatigue. A fighter with extra-heavy encumbrance suffers 5 Fatigue! Spell-casters who do not actually "cross swords" with the foe will not suffer this fatigue drain, but their magic *will* cost them Fatigue.

While your ST is reduced due to fatigue, any "test of skill," attempt to lift or throw an object, or other use of strength will be made at the reduced ST score. Likewise, your score in any ST-based skill will be reduced by the amount of your fatigue. For instance, if you have ST 10 and have suffered 4 points of Fatigue, you perform as though your ST was 6!

However, the basic damage you do with weapons will remain unchanged. This is for playability, to avoid constant recalculation of weapon effects.

Likewise, your Move score is not affected by fatigue *until your ST reaches 3.* At that point, cut your Move in half (rounded down).

If fatigue reduces your ST to 1, you collapse and can do nothing physical until you have rested (see below) for long enough to recover at least 1 point of Strength. You *can* continue to talk, cast spells, use psychic abilities, etc. If you are drowning, you can keep struggling!

If fatigue reduces your ST to 0, you fall unconscious and automatically rest until your ST reaches 1 and you awaken. You cannot have "negative" Fatigue.

Recovering From Fatigue

Anyone suffering from fatigue may regain the lost ST points by resting quietly. Talking and thinking *are* all right; walking around, or anything more strenuous, is *not* all right. Each ten minutes of rest will cure 1 point of Fatigue. The GM may allow 1 extra point of Fatigue to be regained if the characters eat a decent meal *while resting.*

Fatigue caused by *lost sleep* is automatically regained after one *full* night of sleep, but is not regained *until* you get that night of sleep.

Certain drugs will remove Fatigue. In a magical world, there are also spells and potions to remove Fatigue, cure injury and illness, etc.

Resolving mounted or vehicular combat falls into three basic steps, whether the fighters are astride horses or grav-buggies: (1) Get into weapon range. (2) Attack the enemy and resolve the combat. (3) If anyone was hit, resolve the results of damage to the fighters or their mounts . . . and see whether the fighters are still *in control* of their mounts or vehicles. If not, resolve the fall or crash.

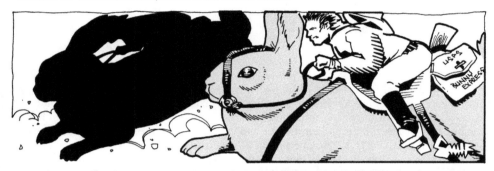

MOUNTED COMBAT

With the exception of occasional camels and elephants, historical cavalry forces have been horse-mounted. Fantasy and science-fiction worlds will certainly have other potential mounts, and the same rules would be used for fighters "mounted" in the back of a pickup. But, in general, this section will assume we are talking about horses.

Horse types and training are described on p. 144. War-trained riding animals are worth more than other mounts. At TL2-3, they are taught to enter battle and fight savagely, even if their rider is unhorsed. And a trained warhorse is likely to attack anyone who approaches it, except its owner. Past TL4, they are not taught to fight, but to be reliable transportation, *not* afraid of gunfire or screams. In any period, a year of war training (after "basic" training) is required before the mount is fully fit to ride into battle; this doubles its value. Up to 3 more years of training are possible, giving +1 per year on all Riding and Animal Handling rolls in combat, and increasing base value by 50% per year.

Horses without war training will "spook" at danger, and especially at the sounds of gunfire and hurt horses! *All* combat Riding rolls are at -3 for a well-broken horse without war training, -6 or worse for one that is not fully broken.

Movement

A rider is in the center of a 3-hex horse, or the front of a 2-hex mount like a mule. An elephant or similar mount would have a flat back, and a rider could stand up and move around; elephants carried the driver, or *mahout,* on the neck, and a *howdah,* a platform with several fighters, on the back.

Mounting a horse or similar creature takes 3 turns; you can leap astride in 1 turn if you make your Riding roll at -3. For simplicity, the horse moves on its rider's turn.

An average cavalry horse, unencumbered, has a Move of 16. With an average rider and gear, the horse will be carrying 200+ lbs., which is Light encumbrance for a strong horse with a light rider, but Medium encumbrance for most. Thus, Western-style cavalry will move at 12 to 14. Indians and Mongols are more lightly equipped, but their ponies are bred for endurance rather than speed, and will probably move at 10.

Unencumbered, a horse may accelerate from a standing start to its full Move in a single turn. Even lightly encumbered, however, a horse may change speed by only ⅓ of its Move in any given turn. For example, a mounted horse with Move 12, beginning from a standing start, may move up to 4 hexes on the first turn, up to 8 hexes on the second turn, and full speed on the third turn. If it is running at full speed and begins to slow, it must still run 8 yards on its next turn – some caution should be exercised when riding in close areas!

Losing Control of Your Mount and Other Equestrian Disasters

Roll 2 dice on this table whenever you lose control of a spooked mount. Refer to the appropriate result, without rolling, whenever a rider is thrown, a horse falls, and so on. Any time a rider falls from his mount, add +1 injury for each five hexes of speed over 10.

2 – You are thrown from your mount. Take 2d-8 damage (assuming normal, soft ground). If you remain conscious, make one Animal Handling-3 roll immediately to try to call your horse back. If you fail, further attempts may be made every 5 minutes.

3 – You aren't thrown, but you lose your grip and fall. Take 1d-4 damage and try to recover your horse as above.

4 – You drop whatever you were holding. Now roll again.

5 – The horse charges directly toward the foe.

6, 7 – The horse is exhausted and will not fight or move at faster than a slow walk (Move 2) until it gets several hours of rest.

8, 9 – The horse seems to settle down, but it is now fractious. -1 to all Riding rolls during this engagement. This may be cumulative.

10 – The horse charges directly away from the foe.

11 – The saddle comes loose. All Riding rolls, and all attack rolls made while riding, are at -3 until you can dismount and spend 4d seconds tightening the straps.

12 – The horse falls! If it fails to roll DX+1 or better, its leg is broken and it may be considered lost. In any case, the rider must roll vs. Riding-2. If he fails, he is unseated, and takes damage as above. If he succeeds on that roll, the rider makes *another* Riding roll (at a penalty equal to his Encumbrance) to leap clear of the falling horse. If he leaps clear, he takes damage as for a 2-yard fall (usually 2d-8). If he fails, the mount falls on him, doing 1d-1 crushing damage (if the horse's speed was 10 hexes or more, the rider takes 1d+1), *plus* the damage for a 2-yard fall.

Lance Combat: Thrusting Damage for ST 21-50

ST	Thrust	ST	Thrust
21, 22	........2d	37, 38	.......4d
23, 24	........2d+1	39, 40	......4d+1
25, 26	........2d+2	41, 42	......4d+2
27, 28	........3d-1	43, 44	......5d-1
29, 30	........3d	45, 46	.......5d
31, 32	........3d+1	47, 48	......5d+1
33, 34	........3d+2	49, 50	......5d+2
35, 36	........4d-1		

A lance does thrust+3 damage, based on the *horse's* ST. For example, Sir Actys' warhorse, Axehoof, has ST 45. At 5 or fewer hexes per turn, Actys and Axehoof do thrust+3 with a lance, based on a ST of 11 (one quarter of Axehoof's ST), or 1d+2. From 6 to 10 hexes per turn, they do thrust+3, based on ST 22 (half Axehoof's ST, rounded down), or 2d+3. At any speed of 11 or higher, they do thrust+3, based on Axehoof's full ST 45, or 5d+3!

A mount may decelerate by twice the normal amount if it makes a DX+2 roll *and* the rider makes a Riding-2 roll. If the horse makes its roll and the rider fails, the mount slows but the rider is unseated (see sidebar). If the mount fails its roll, it falls (see sidebar).

Turning

A horse moving slower than 4 hexes per turn must move at least one hex in a straight line after every one-hexside change of direction. A horse moving 4 or more hexes per turn must move at least two hexes in a straight line after each one-hexside change of direction – and so on. See *Turning Radius,* p. 139.

Maneuvers

The available maneuvers for a mount are Move, Step and Attack, and All-Out Attack. Riders may take any maneuver, but may not Move except to leave the horse.

Spooking

The usual result of a failed Riding roll in combat is a "spooked" horse. When a horse is spooked, it shies and bucks; the rider must make a Riding roll every second. A critical success calms the horse immediately; three ordinary successes in a row will have the same result. Three failures in a row, or a single critical failure, means a total loss of control (see the sidebar). A long alternation of successes and failures means you spend your time fighting your horse and not the enemy! (Fortunately, a bucking horse, or its rider, are at -2 to be hit due to unpredictable movement.)

Weapon Fire from a Moving Vehicle or Howdah

Use these modifiers whenever weapons are used from a moving platform, whether it's tommy guns from a getaway car or javelins from one of Hannibal's elephants. All normal size and range/speed modifiers also apply. In vehicular combat, it becomes important to consider the *apparent* relative speed of the vehicles. If two cars are rushing toward each other on I-35, the speed of one, relative to the other, may be over 120 mph, but the *apparent* relative speed is almost zero.

Hand weapon attack by the driver: -4
Hand weapon attack by a passenger: -2

Roughness of the ride, from:
A car on a good road, or a WWII fighter: 0
A WWI fighter plane: -1
A motorcycle on the road, or an elephant: -2
A car on a bad road: -3
Car, tank or pickup, off the road: -4
Horseback: Depends on Riding skill. See p. 137.
Firing through smoke, paint, etc.: up to -10

Ordinarily, a trained warhorse can be directed by voice and foot pressure, leaving both hands free for weapon use. However, all Riding rolls are at -3 for "no hands," or -1 if only one hand is on the reins. Riders who need both hands to control the horse may drop what they are holding. It requires a DX-3 roll to put a weapon back in its scabbard while a horse is bucking, at 1d+1 seconds per attempt; a critical failure drops it!

Cavalry Weapons

A rider uses hand weapons at his weapon skill or his Riding skill, whichever is less. Thus, a trained rider has no penalties using hand weapons on horseback.

Lance skill is described on p. 51. Impacting with the force of a charging warhorse, a lance can easily pierce the heaviest contemporary armor. A lance requires a minimum ST of 12; it takes one turn to ready a lance after a miss, 2 turns to ready it after a hit. A lance longer than 12 feet may be used, to give an advantage in reach, but for every additional foot of lance, the lancer takes a -1 to his skill. The reach of the lance goes up by one hex for every three full feet of length above 12. A lance weighs an extra 2 lbs. for every foot of length over 12.

The lance does thrust+3 impaling damage, based on the *horse's* ST and velocity (see sidebar). If the horse is moving 5 or fewer hexes per turn, the lance does thrust+3 damage based on $^1/_4$ of the horse's ST, rounded down. If it is moving 6-10 hexes per turn, the lance damage is based on $^1/_2$ of the horse's ST. If it is moving 11 hexes or faster, lance damage is based on the horse's full ST. To use a lance or similar weapon, a rider *must* have a saddle and stirrups.

Tournament jousting is done with blunted wooden lances, specially designed to break if they strike very hard. These do thrust+3 *crushing* damage. If more than 15 points of damage is rolled, the lance snaps, doing 15 points of damage.

Swords, axes, spears, etc. may be *swung* by a rider. If the mount's speed is at least 6 relative to the foe, assess -2 to hit but +2 to damage. A cavalryman is effectively three feet above infantry (see p. 123).

Using Ranged Weapons From Horseback

Firing from a moving animal is a test of both marksmanship and riding. Roll against your Riding or weapon skill, whichever is worse, adjusted as per the sidebar. If your weapon is noisy, make a Riding roll after each shot. A failure means the horse is spooked; see above. On a critical failure, you lose control (see sidebar, p. 135).

Aiming: You may Aim a ranged weapon from horseback, but only to get the Acc bonus; aiming for additional turns gives no extra bonus. Your Accuracy bonus may not exceed *either* your skill with the weapon *or* your Rider skill.

Tricks: To turn in the saddle and fire at the foe behind you: -4 to weapon skill, -1 to any Riding roll made that turn.

To hang on the far side of the horse and shoot over it or underneath it: -6 to weapon skill, -3 to any Riding roll made that turn. Your foe is at a -8 to hit you, and his only targets are your heel, head and one hand. But if he shoots at you and misses by 4 or less, he hit your horse.

Horse Attacks

A trained medieval warhorse will attack footmen and other horses, by biting (2 points of crushing damage) or kicking (1d for small horses, 1d+2 for large ones, +1 for iron shoes). It will also trample, doing the same damage as a kick. The rider's attack will be at an extra -2 on any turn the mount attacks.

An 18th- or 19th-century cavalry horse will not attack; in fact, a Riding+2 roll is required to get any horse *except* a medieval warhorse to charge into or over any obstacle or bad footing. Horses are very cautious about bad footing!

Defense

A mount's only defense is Dodge. A horse has a Dodge of DX/2 or Move/2, whichever is better. In medieval campaigns, warhorses can have *barding,* or armor, which gives a PD of up to 4 for full plate.

A rider rolls his own defense; he may Dodge, Block or Parry. For a rider of skill 12+, all these skills are at normal levels. For a rider of less skill, all active defenses are reduced by the difference between 12 and the rider's skill (so, for instance, a rider with a skill of 9 has a -3 to his defenses).

Combat Results

When a rider is hit in combat, he must make a Riding roll to keep his seat. This roll takes a -1 penalty for every full 4 points of basic damage delivered by the blow (*before* subtracting armor). If the rider fails this roll, he falls from his saddle (see *Losing Control* sidebar, p. 135). If the rider was stunned by the blow, the Riding roll is made at -4.

A character who Blocks a blow may still be unhorsed by the impact. If the Block roll is less than or equal to the blocker's PD, then the blow glances off the shield or armor. If the Block roll was *greater* than the PD – which is to say that he actively Blocked the blow – then the blow was caught squarely upon the shield. In such a case, the character takes no damage from the attack, but still must make the Riding roll described above, or be unhorsed.

If any attack aimed at a rider *misses by 1,* roll the exact same attack against the horse. Of course, the horse itself may be attacked intentionally.

If the *mount* is hit, the rider must roll vs. Riding, *minus the damage taken,* to keep it from spooking (see p. 136). A horse that takes more than 1/4 its hit points in one blow must roll vs. DX to avoid falling. A horse that takes more than half its hit points in one blow is affected like a human.

Vehicle Weapon Mountings

The purpose of a vehicle weapon mounting is to stabilize the weapon. A good weapon mounting will give a Gunner or Guns skill bonus. However, this bonus only offsets any penalties for a rough ride; if your vehicle moves so smoothly it's like standing still, the mounting doesn't matter.

The simplest vehicle mount is a fixed mounting, with no elevation or traverse. You aim the gun by aiming the vehicle. This gives a +2 bonus to help offset a rough ride. Gunner skill with such a weapon cannot exceed your vehicle-control skill-3.

Any heavy man-portable weapon can be set up on an improvised mounting, like a tripod in the back of a Jeep. Such a mounting would give no bonus – but of course it's far easier to track a target with this than with a fixed mounting.

At TL6, an ordinary military gun mount is a pintle; machine-guns, light auto-cannon, rocket-launchers and recoilless rifles are often mounted this way. This gives a +1 bonus. Mass-produced military mounts are 20% of the cost of the weapon involved. Custom jobs require individual negotiation; any machinist can make a good one in two days. One could be built for (for instance) a tommy gun on a civilian vehicle.

Slightly better is an unstabilized turret, which permanently braces the weapon. This gives a +2 bonus.

Stabilized turrets use gyroscopes to keep the weapon aimed at the target regardless of the motion of the vehicle. They are available on some tanks, aircraft and ships at the very end (after 1943) of TL6. (Only the U.S. managed to put a tank with a stabilized turret into action in WWII, and that was only stabilized in elevation.) A fully stabilized turret gives a +5 bonus. A turret stabilized only in elevation gives a +3 bonus.

Stabilized turrets at TL6 are rare, expensive and unreliable. They are not available at all until after 1930. A custom-built stabilized turret takes precision parts and at least two man-months of very skilled labor. The work will almost certainly attract the attention of the government's spy-catchers. Cost for a simple MG turret is $10,000. At TL7 and later, turrets are fairly easy to build, though they will be very unusual accessories for civilian vehicles in most game worlds

The Human Target

In World War I, it was considered unsporting for one fighter pilot to shoot at another. The gentlemanly aviator tried to cripple the opposing plane, leaving his opponent unharmed. Not that all the pilots wore chutes . . .

In general, though, taking out the enemy pilot (or driver, or *mahout*) is the quickest way to cripple an enemy unit. But that's not always an easy target. Assess speed/range modifiers. Then assess the penalty (see p. 118) for the enemy's coverage. If you are shooting at the driver of an automobile, this depends on the weapon you are using. With a .22, you must shoot through the window, and only his head is exposed. With an assault rifle, you can shoot right through the side of the car, and the driver essentially has no cover.

Shots Penetrating An Automobile

Roll 2 dice for each shot that penetrates a TL6 or 7 car. Remember that some of the shot's damage has been used up in coming through the car body. This table assumes that the *car* was the target, and that shots were not aimed specifically at (for instance) the driver.

2 – Hits driver. If driver survives, he must make a Driving roll at -4 to keep control. If stunned, he automatically loses control.

3, 4 – Hits passenger – roll randomly to see which one.

5 – Windshield shattered; -3 to Driving rolls until it is fixed.

6-8 – Bullets exit harmlessly.

9 – Tire hit; reduce speed by 10 mph.

10, 11 – Cargo damaged (GM provides details).

12 – Engine crippled. Car coasts to a stop.

When a critical hit is scored against an automobile, roll one die; on a 1-3, it hit the driver, and on a 4-6, it took out the engine. See also *GURPS Vehicles*.

VEHICULAR COMBAT

There are two main types of combat from vehicles. The first is with personal weapons (e.g., firing from a getaway car). This will happen from time to time in many campaigns; these rules cover it adequately.

Other combats use weapons actually mounted on the vehicle (tanks, planes, auto-duelling, etc.). The drivers either use their own Gunner skill, or carry gunners as passengers. This is more complex, and different for every type of vehicle. It is covered in detail in *GURPS Vehicles*.

Maneuvers and Movement

You can represent vehicles by multi-hex counters drawn at 3 feet to the inch. Scale speed is based on reality. A speed of 60 mph, for instance, is equivalent to a Move of 30. For airplanes and automobiles, use the turning-radius rules given on p. 139. In general, vehicles move in Move order (fastest first). In case of ties, the highest control skill goes first.

Someone in a vehicle takes no maneuvers as such. If he is controlling the vehicle, he makes the appropriate "control" rolls (Driving, Powerboat, Piloting, etc.) as needed. If he is using a weapon, he attacks by making the appropriate weapon rolls (usually Guns or Gunner). Detailed rules for vehicle movement can be found in *GURPS Vehicles*.

A control roll is required any time the vehicle is damaged or attempts a risky maneuver. A failed roll erases any accumulated aiming bonuses; any attack on the next turn is at a penalty equal to the amount by which the roll was failed. The vehicle may also skid or stall, and a very unstable vehicle, like a motorcycle, can crash. A critical failure always indicates a loss of control. Results depend on the vehicle; a biplane will crash, while a tank will just roar ahead.

Attacks

If the driver of a vehicle tries to use a *personal* weapon (forcing him to divide his attention between driving and shooting) he is at an extra -4 to hit. This penalty does not apply for using weapons built into his vehicle!

Heavier weapons will use Gunner skill. Vehicle weapons are usually formidable; the *lightest* would be a .30-caliber machine-gun, with SS 20, Acc 12, $\frac{1}{2}$D 1,000, Max 4,700, a RoF of 8 to 20 and doing 7d+1 damage *per round!* A TL7 tank would fire shells doing at least 6d×25 per round.

Aiming: With single-shot weapons, aiming is the same as from horseback. With a vehicle-mounted or automatic weapon, you can Aim while firing, up to the maximum of +3 bonus!

Targeting Systems: At TL7 and above, many vehicles have targeting systems (radar, computers, etc.). A targeting system adds to the effective skill of the user.

Defense

This varies widely. Some vehicles (e.g., a fighter plane) would be allowed a Dodge roll against enemy fire. A tank would get no Dodge roll, but its heavy sloped armor would give it a high passive defense.

When a shot hits, treat as for any other combat, comparing the weapon damage to the armor of the target vehicle. Again, this varies. An early fighter plane has no armor at all. A TL6 or 7 automobile has a sheet-steel skin with PD3, DR5. The armored sides of a TL7 main battle tank have a DR of 100 or more, and its front has at least DR600. (Even so, its survival depends mainly on *not being hit*.)

Shots that penetrate a vehicle may affect the crew. For an automobile, roll on the table in the sidebar. GMs playing other types of combat can construct equivalent tables, or see *GURPS Vehicles*.

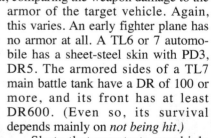

This section covers special rules for aerial movement and combat. PCs themselves could fly using psi powers; powerful magic, not covered in the *Basic Set,* will also let wizards fly. And *Space* campaigns can include personal grav belts and flying alien races . . . For much more detail, though, see *GURPS Vehicles.*

Movement

If the ceiling is high enough, fliers can go over other figures. Humans normally fly in a horizontal position (so they can watch the ground and see where they're going), making them 2-hex figures.

Changing height: Vertical movement costs the same as horizontal. A yard of diagonal movement at 45° would cost the same as 1.5 horizontal yards.

Turning Radius

The faster *anything* moves, in the air or on the ground, the more space it needs in which to turn. A tight turn on the ground can make a vehicle (or creature) lose traction and fall/spin out of control.

The safety of a turn depends on *speed* and *turning radius.* In game terms, turning radius equals the number of hexes a figure travels between one 60° (one-hexside) facing change and the next. See illustration.

If, for instance, turning radius is 1, you move 1 hex between facing changes (describing a circle whose radius is 1). If your turning radius is 2, you move 2 hexes between turns, and so on.

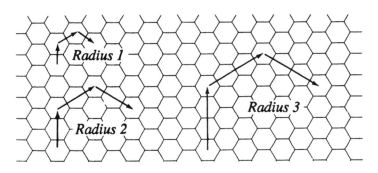

To find the turning radius, *square* the figure's current speed and divide by (10 times G), where G is the G-force of the turn. Round down for movement on land or water; round up for air movement. For most cases, use G=1. More than that is unlikely for men, animals, unpowered fliers and most automobiles. To make a one-hex-sharper turn, roll vs. your control skill (DX, Piloting or Flight skill, levitation, etc.) minus 4! A failed roll means you fall, lose control of the vehicle, or lose control in the air, as the case may be. (For simplicity, you may ignore this for running humans unless they are moving at super-speeds.)

Example: A gryphon's flight speed is 15; with light encumbrance (see below) that becomes 11. 11 squared is 121; 121/10 (rounded up) is 13. At full speed, this creature can change facing by 60° (one hexside) every 13 hexes. If it makes a DX-4 roll, it can change facing after moving only 12 hexes. A failed roll would make it tumble in the air; in this case, the GM should make the rider roll vs. Riding to stay on!

Because turning at high speeds requires making a wide circle, it is often faster to slow down, turn, and speed up again.

Encumbrance

Use the following encumbrance rules for flying animals:

No encumbrance (up to 2×ST): Move is unaffected.

Light encumbrance (up to 6×ST): reduce Move by 4.

Medium encumbrance (up to 10×ST): reduce Move by 8.

Heavy encumbrance (up to 15×ST): reduce Move by 12. Most creatures cannot fly with Heavy encumbrance, and some cannot fly even with Medium.

Flight Ceiling

On Earth, an unprotected human will have trouble breathing past 10,000 feet. Double Fatigue costs for any exertion between 10,000 and 15,000 feet. Past 15,000 feet, an oxygen mask (or magical assistance) is needed. Some nonhumans will be able to fly much higher. On worlds with a greater air pressure, higher flight will be possible. On worlds with little atmosphere, the reverse will be true.

Combat Maneuvers

Combat maneuvers are the same for flyers as for other characters. with the following exceptions:

Change Position is a free action in flight.

Aim is treated as for a man on horseback (p. 137).

Step and . . . maneuvers allow a 3-yard "step" in flight.

Concentrate can be performed during a full move, if the flyer is going in a straight line.

All-Out Attack: A flyer can go up to half his Move and make an all-out attack.

Attacks and Defenses

Weapon use is difficult in flight. The penalty for use of a weapon in flight is (15-Skill); if your skill is 15 or better, you have no penalty. The penalty for use of a *ranged* weapon in flight is (17-Skill). Note also that a flyer's own speed counts into his speed/range total for a ranged weapon attack!

When flyers use hand weapons against foes on the ground, use the modifications for relative height (p. 123). Weapon reach becomes very important! But don't worry about relative height of two battling flyers.

Flying humans have a +2 to Dodge. They have a -2 to Parry and Block unless the skill (or spell) used for flying is at 15 or better.

18  ANIMALS

Biting Damage

When a carnivore bites, this is treated as a *cutting* attack, unless specified otherwise. Fangs and claws are much more effective on flesh than they are on armor. The bite of a herbivorous creature like a horse is *crushing* damage and usually does damage appropriate to about half its actual ST.

An animal bite – even from a carnivore – *can* do zero damage. A small dog, for instance, doesn't necessarily do significant harm every time it bites.

In general, an animal's biting damage depends on its ST. But there are always exceptions. For instance, a sabertooth tiger would do extra damage!

ST	Biting Damage
1-2	1d-5
3-5	1d-4
6-8	1d-3
9-11	1d-2
12-15	1d-1
16-20	1d
21-25	1d+1
26-30	1d+2
31-35	2d-1
36-40	2d
41-45	2d+1
46-50	2d+2
51-55	3d-1
	and so on . . .

Each *GURPS* worldbook includes a listing of animals, monsters, etc., peculiar to that setting. Also available is the *GURPS Bestiary,* with complete descriptions of more than 200 creatures. A few very common beasts will be described here.

All animals and monsters are controlled by the GM or Adversary. Since these creatures are not PCs, they are not built on a point system, but described in simple terms. For each animal, the following data will be given:

General description, including size, weight and habits.

Value for a domestic animal. No values are given for wild animals, though a specific campaign or adventure may assign them specific values.

Attributes. If two numbers are given for HT, the second is hit points. Note that GMs may vary animal attributes – see p. 145.

Basic speed. Except in the case of loaded riding and draft animals, this will also be the creature's Move. Note that Dodge (an animal's only active defense) is half DX or half Move, whichever is better, up to a maximum of 10.

PD and DR, if any, from the creature's hide or armor.

Attacks, if the creature is likely to be involved in combat.

Special abilities and other information relevant to gaming the creature.

Abilities and Skills

Most creatures that live in the wild have keen senses. The "generic" roll for an animal to sense something (sight, hearing, smell, etc.) is 14, regardless of its IQ. This varies, as noted, for specific creatures.

Some animals also have the equivalent of human skills. For instance, a bloodhound is considered to have the Tracking skill at a level of 18.

Size

Small creatures take up less than a hex; several can fit in the same hex. See *Swarm Attacks,* p. 143.

If it is necessary to calculate (for instance) a dose of poison for a nonhuman, compare its weight to the 150-lb. human average. For instance, it would take twice as much poison to affect a 300-lb. beast as it would to affect a man.

Combat

In general, use the same combat rules for an animal that you would for a human. A few special cases – e.g., trampling by a heavy creature – are noted in the chapters on combat, earlier in this book. Some special notes:

Attacks: To hit, an animal rolls against its DX; use the same modifiers as if a human were attacking.

Reach: Most animals attack by "close combat" – a grapple or slam, followed by an attempt to crush the foe or tear him to pieces. Assume that any creature's "reach" is "C" – close – unless the description states otherwise.

Defense: Animals do not block or parry, but may defend by *dodging*. A creature's Dodge score is equal to half its Move, or half its DX, whichever is better, up to a maximum of 10. (Some small creatures can't run as fast as man, but dodge much better.)

Armor: Many creatures have PD and/or DR from hides, shells, etc.

HT: Health and Hit Points

For a roughly man-sized creature, HT represents both "health" – the creature's overall state of wellness – and "hits" – the amount of injury it can take. For very large or small creatures, this is not true. For instance, an elephant can take many more wounds than a man, but its chance of recovering from a stun is no different than a healthy man's.

Therefore, some creatures will have *two* numbers for HT. The first number, from 3 to 18 (usually) is the "health" that you roll against. The second number is the "hits" that the creature can take. Thus, an elephant might have HT 17/50, and a rat might have HT 17/2. Both are hardy creatures, but the elephant takes a lot more wounds before dying!

Realism

If you want to play animals realistically, remember that:

Most animals fear man and will flee rather than attack. Exceptions include a mother defending young; an insect swarm defending its nest; an old or wounded "man-eater" predator; a creature so stupid it doesn't realize men are dangerous; a creature so powerful men *aren't* dangerous; or a large herbivore (bison, rhino, Triceratops) which may charge anything, just out of orneriness.

In a balanced ecology, predators will be comparatively rare, prey species common.

Multi-Hex Creatures

Some animals, monsters, etc., occupy more than one hex. This is important primarily if you are using the Advanced Combat System and playing with a combat map. It may be helpful to use miniature figures and cut cardboard bases of the appropriate size.

Movement

Movement of a multi-hex figure is controlled by its head. Determine the distance moved, and "forward" movement (see p. 103), as though the creature's head were a normal one-hex figure. The rest of the body follows. This may mean, for instance, that a dragon's head moves 3 hexes while its tail sweeps through 10. That's all right – and it's a good way for the dragon to knock people over.

A multi-hex figure cannot fit through a map space narrower than its widest point. However, GMs should be lenient in allowing large figures to overlap walls, etc., where a partial hex is adjacent to a wall. Remember that when a hex is cut by a straight wall, etc., a partial hex counts as a full hex.

Arc of Vision

The arc of vision of a multi-hex creature is controlled by its head. Note that most animals have eyes set to the sides of their heads, so they have a wider field of vision than humans.

Ape

Apes and monkeys are intelligent – too intelligent to be really predictable. Any Animal Handling roll is at -1 with such creatures. Apes are very strong, but attack in close combat only, by grappling and biting, rather than punching or kicking.

All apes and monkeys are 1-hex creatures or smaller.

Chimpanzee: ST 14-18, DX 14, IQ 6, HT 12-14. Speed 7. PD0, DR0. Weight 100-180 lbs. (males are larger than females). Bites for 1d-1 cutting damage.

Gorilla: A peaceful plant-eater; will not normally fight unless it or its young are threatened. ST 20-24, DX 13, IQ 6, HT 14/16-20. Speed 7. Hide has PD1, DR1. Weight 200-600 lbs. (males are larger than females). Bites for 1 die cutting damage.

Bear

Most bears are omnivorous, eating both plants and animals. Make a reaction roll for a bear to determine whether it's hungry/aggressive or just gets out of your way. Grizzly bears and polar bears are mostly carnivorous and react at -3. Mother bears with cubs are almost always aggressive!

A bear walking or running on four legs is a two-hex creature; when it stands on its hind legs to fight, it is a 1-hex creature.

Black or brown bear: ST 14-17, DX 13, IQ 5, HT 14/14-18. Hide has PD1, DR1. Weight 200-400 lbs. Bites for 1 die of cutting damage; strikes with its claws (close combat only) for 1 die of crushing damage.

Grizzly bear: ST 22-28, DX 13, IQ 5, HT 14/18-22. Speed 8. Hide has PD1, DR2. Weight 400-1,000 lbs. Bites for 1d+1 cutting damage; strikes with its claws (reach 1 hex) for 1d+2 crushing damage. May grapple (bear hug) in close combat and bite while grappling.

Polar bear: ST 27-33, DX 13, IQ 5. HT 15/18-24. Speed 7, or 3 if swimming. Hide has PD1, DR2. Weight 600-1,400 lbs. Bites for 1d+2 cutting damage; strikes with its claws (reach 1 hex) for 1d+2 crushing damage. May bear-hug like a grizzly.

Cave bear: A prehistoric creature. ST 27-33, DX 12, IQ 5, HT 14/30. Speed 7. Hide has PD1, DR2. Weight 1,200-1,600 lbs. Bites for 2d-2 cutting damage; strikes with claws (reach 1 hex) for 2d-2 crushing damage. May bear-hug like a grizzly.

Camel

A dry-plains creature domesticated for draft use. See *Riding and Draft Animal* table for stats.

As for a horse, except that it can go for four days without drinking at all. Any use of Animal Handling skill is at -4 because a camel is *very* nasty and stubborn.

Continued on next page . . .

Animal Descriptions (Continued)

Cat

A domestic animal, kept as a pet. Cost ranges from free to outrageous.

ST 3, DX 14, IQ 5, HT 13/3. Speed 10.

Skin is not thick enough for armor. Weight 5-15 lbs.; size <1 hex.

Cats, if provoked, attack by biting and scratching, doing 1d-4 damage (treated as cutting damage because claws are short).

Deer

Hunted for food. ST 5-14, DX 15, IQ 4, HT 13/6-8. Speed 9, depending on age and species. PD0, DR0. Weight 70-200 lbs. Occasionally attacks by kicking or trampling (1d crushing damage) or by butting with antlers (1d impaling damage).

Dog

A domestic animal, used for hunting or as a pet. Because there are so many different breeds, the descriptions here will not be precise. Weight ranges from 5 lbs. to 150 or more; size is 1 hex. Cost ranges from negligible to $10,000 or more, though a fully-trained healthy dog, even if it has no breeding, is always worth at least $200.

ST 1-12 (depending on breed), DX 11-12, IQ 5. HT 12-15 (but a very small dog may have only 3 or 4 hit points).

Basic speed ranges from 4 (small lap dog) to 20 (greyhound or saluki). Average is about 10. Large dogs can be used as draft animals. A thick-coated breed will have PD1 and DR1. Most dogs' hide is not thick enough to serve as armor.

Dogs attack in close combat, doing normal biting damage for their ST. Some breeds (e.g., bloodhounds,) have keen noses, and Smell and Tracking rolls of 18.

Elephant

Often domesticated. Intelligent, loyal and hard-working. Stats as given in *Riding and Draft Animal* table. Size: 10 hexes. An elephant will not carry more than Medium encumbrance (10 × ST) on its back.

Attacks by trampling (3d damage per turn!) or with trunk. The trunk has a reach of 2. DX roll to strike (1 die damage) or to grapple (no damage, but victim can then be thrown, pulled to be trampled, etc.).

The elephant is so large that it effectively has no Dodge roll. Its trunk has a ST of 12 for lifting, carrying, etc.

Falcon

A bird of prey used for sport hunting. A large falcon would have ST 3, DX 15, IQ 4, HT 12/3-5. Speed 20 in level flight (when diving on prey, the falcon's scale speed would be 70 or 80!). Weight 2-8 lbs.

A very well-trained falcon, or one disturbed by a stranger, might attack a human with beak and claw, doing 1d-2 damage. Though the falcon's claws are sharp, they are much too short to impale, so treat this as cutting damage.

Continued on next page . . .

Front, Side and Rear Hexes

Each multi-hex creature has front, right, left and rear hexes, corresponding to those of a human. See below.

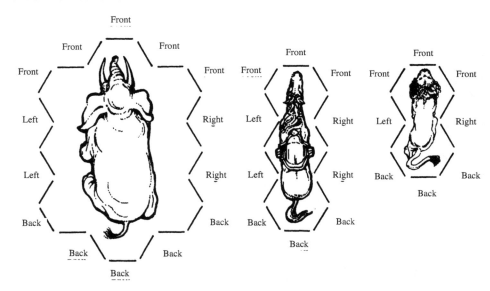

Knockdown and Overrun

When a figure of 2 or more hexes moves through a smaller one, treat it as a "slam" attack (see p. 112). This gives the small figure a chance to get out of the way. If it fails to do so, it will probably lose the ensuing Contest of ST and be knocked down!

Unless the larger figure is itself knocked down, it can keep right on moving. In either case, it is a Quick Contest of DX.

A figure knocked down by one that is at least twice its size or weight may be trampled.

Trampling

When a very large animal runs over, or stamps, an enemy, it does *trampling* damage. This damage depends upon weight, and on whether the creature has hooves. If a non-hoofed creature tries a "trample," treat it as though its weight were only 1/4 its true weight. Claws are not ordinarily effective in a trample – that's not what they were designed for. If a tiger tramples you, it may take your breath away, but that's all.

The figures below assume that the victim is on yielding ground. For special cases (i.e., an elephant trampling a foe on a concrete floor) double damage, at least, would be appropriate!

If an animal takes the "trample" maneuver in close combat, staying in the foe's hex and stamping him, it does damage as listed below. If the animal "slams" the foe, does not fall, and keeps running, it does half the damage listed below. In either case, the attacker must roll against DX to hit, and the victim gets a Dodge defense.

A human may also "trample" small creatures (see *Swarm Attacks,* p. 143). No DX roll is required; if you trample into a swarm, you'll get *something*.

trampling damage table

Attacker	Trampling Damage
Under 150 lbs.	no effect
150-300 lbs.	1d-2
300-599 lbs.	1d-1
600-999 lbs.	1d
1,000-1,999 lbs.	1d+1
1-1.99 tons	1d+2
2-2.99 tons	2d
3-4.99 tons	2d+1
5 tons and up	3d

Weight of

Swarm Attacks

A group of small creatures is treated as a unit when it attacks. Such a group (filling one hex on the combat map) is called a "swarm." A swarm attacks the victim(s) in its own hex (if you are not using a combat map, it attacks one person each second). It will not change victims without a good reason.

A swarm attack automatically hits; there is no attack or defense roll. Each attack made by a swarm does the same damage, until the swarm has taken enough "hits" to disperse it by killing or confusing its members.

Special clothing (a wet-suit or beekeeper's suit, or high-tech airtight armor) may protect against some types of swarm. Against tiny creatures like insects, clothing is complete protection for two turns and low-tech armor for five; then the bugs get in and the armor ceases to protect! Against larger creatures like rats, armor would protect indefinitely with its normal DR.

Depending on the type of swarm, special tactics may work. For instance, bees could be destroyed by insecticide or baffled by leaping into a pond. This is up to the players' cleverness and the GM's common sense.

Attacking a Swarm

Any attack against a swarm will automatically hit; the swarm gets no defense roll. (A swarm of hard-to-hit creatures simply requires more "hits" to disperse it.) Against a swarm attack, fists and most weapons (regardless of the user's ST) do only 1 hit of damage per turn. Exceptions:

Torches and flaming weapons do 2 hits.

Shields can crush flying creatures; a shield does 2 hits and can be used at the same time a weapon is used.

Stamping attacks do 1 hit per turn against non-flying vermin; this can be done at the same time that weapons are used. You can't stamp on fliers.

Swarm Attack Examples

Bees. A "swarm" is about 1,000 common bees, with a Move of 6. Does stinging damage of 1 hit per turn unless foe is *completely* covered. Dispersed by 12 hits; will give up the attack if foe is chased 50 yards from hive. Note that bothering a hive may get *several* such swarms after you!

Rats. A "swarm" is about a dozen rats, with a Move of 4. Does 1d of cutting damage per turn; armor protects with its normal DR. Dispersed by 6 hits.

Bats. A "swarm" is about a dozen carnivorous bats, with a Move of 8. Does 1d of biting damage/turn; armor protects with its normal DR. Dispersed by 8 hits.

Pets and Trained Animals

Characters may purchase trained animals. These are not considered "advantages," but just property. A trained animal, like any other creature, is controlled by the GM. But the better an animal is trained, the more likely it is to do what its owner wishes.

Animal Training

The level of training an animal can absorb depends strictly on its IQ. See the *Animal Handling* skill, p. 46.

IQ 3: Average reptile. Can learn to recognize master and come when called for food, and not to attack master (usually).

IQ 4: Average horse or hawk. Can learn commands suitable for its work – hunting commands for a hawk, riding or pulling commands for a riding or draft animal, and general tolerance for all humans or for specific masters (trainer's choice). Will learn its name and come when called (if it feels like it).

IQ 5: Average dog. As above, plus "fetch," "attack," "find," "sit," etc., as appropriate for the particular type of animal. Will try to warn its owner of dangers it perceives. Will fight and even die for its master.

Animal Descriptions (Continued)

Horse and Mule

Domestic animals, kept for riding and draft purposes. See the *Riding and Draft Animal* table for stats. A riding horse is considered a 3-hex figure, with the rider in the middle. Donkeys and small mules are 2-hex figures.

Skin is not thick enough for armor.

Horses fight by kicking into any front or back hex. A horse under 1,000 lbs. does 1 die of crushing damage; a larger one does 1d+2. A horse may bite in close combat, doing 2 hits of crushing damage.

Lion

A big, lazy cat, found in both plains and jungle, which hunts in small groups.

ST 24-30, DX 13, IQ 4, HT 15/16-20. Speed 10, in short bursts. Hide has PD1, DR1. Weight 400-600 lbs.; size 2 hexes. Attacks by biting and clawing (close combat) for 2d-2 cutting damage.

Snake

Python: A large constricting snake (up to 30 feet in length). ST 12-24, DX 13, IQ 3, HT 15/15-30. Speed 4. Non-poisonous; attacks by crushing. Once the snake gets a successful "grapple," it starts to squeeze, continuing until it dies or is forced off. This does 1d-4 to 1 die of crushing damage, depending on size of the snake. Only plate armor protects against this attack, but it protects with its full DR.

Rattlesnake: A common poisonous snake. ST 2-10, DX 13, IQ 3, HT 15/4-20. Speed 3 or 4. Even the little ones are dangerous; a big diamondback (up to 8 feet long) is *very* dangerous. The bite of a small snake can penetrate DR1; a big rattler can bite through DR2 leather (but not metal).

Anyone bitten must make a HT roll, at -4, each day for 3 days. A failed roll means the venom does damage; a critical failure means *death*. Venom damage ranges from 1d-1 for a small rattler to 2 dice for a big one. Modifiers to the HT roll: +1 if venom is immediately sucked out; +2 if antivenin (TL 6 or better) is used for treatment.

Coral Snake: A tiny (1 or 2 feet long), brightly-colored, poisonous snake. ST 2, DX 11, IQ 3, HT 15/2. Speed 2. Its bite will not penetrate *any* protection – affects bare skin only. Roll as for rattlesnake poisoning, except that venom does 1 die damage and victims are -6 to resist. Any victim will be at -2 DX for 3 days, or -4 DX if he takes HT damage from the venom.

Continued on next page . . .

Animal Descriptions (Continued)

Tiger

A solitary hunting cat, usually found in jungle.

ST 35-40, DX 14, IQ 4, HT 15/20-25. Speed 10, in short bursts. Hide has PD1, DR1. Weight 500-700 lbs.; size 2 hexes. Attacks by biting and clawing (close combat) for 2d-1 cutting damage.

Wolf

A wild carnivore, hunting in packs. Can be (more or less) domesticated, but never like a dog.

A typical wolf would have ST 8-10, DX 14, IQ 5, HT 11-13. Speed 9. Hide has PD1, DR1. Weight 70-170 lbs.; size 1 hex. Attacks by biting (close combat) for 1d-2 cutting damage.

Wild Boar

Wild hogs are hunted for food – but they're dangerous game. Boars are smart, evil-tempered, and likely to attack even when encountered by accident. Sows are less aggressive and smaller (give them weight and ST at the low end of the scale).

Large boar: ST 20-24, DX 14, IQ 6, HT 15/20-25. Speed 8. Hide PD1, DR2. Weight 400+ lbs.; size 2 hexes. Attacks by slashing with tusks (1d+1 cutting damage) or trampling (1d-1 crushing damage). Will try to knock men down with a slam attack (which includes a tusk-slash) and gore them while they are helpless.

Small boar (javelina or peccary): ST 8, DX 14, IQ 6, HT 12. Speed 7. Attacks as above: tusk-slash does 1d-2 cutting damage; trample does no real harm. Weight 40-50 lbs.; size 1 hex.

IQ 6: Average monkey. As above, with more complexity. GMs may allow anything they ever saw a trained animal do in the movies . . .

Training time depends on IQ and the level of training. A trainer can work with a given creature for as much as 4 hours a day in two 2-hour sessions (though this is a generalization):

animal training

IQ Level of animal	IQ Level of Training			
	3	4	5	6
3	60 days	Impossible	Impossible	Impossible
4	30 days	360 days	Impossible	Impossible
5	7 days	180 days	360 days	Impossible
6	2 days	90 days	180 days	720 days

This is the time needed to train the animal to the general level given above. To teach some specific new trick, if the GM agrees the animal can learn it, allow 14 days for an IQ 6 creature, 30 days for one of IQ 5, 90 days for an IQ 4 animal.

Value of Trained Animals

Training can affect the value of domestic animals, as follows:

IQ 3 creatures can learn so little that training doesn't enhance their value.

IQ 4 creatures are of little use unless trained. *Decrease* the value of an IQ 4 domestic animal by 1/3 if it is "unbroken" – i.e., untrained. Any young specimen is automatically unbroken and therefore cheaper.

IQ 5 creatures are assumed to be trained to IQ 4 level when bought – otherwise, decrease price by 1/3, as above. When an IQ 5 creature is fully trained to IQ 5 level, increase its base value by 50%.

IQ 6 creatures follow the IQ 5 rule; in addition, when an IQ 6 creature is fully trained to IQ 6 level, double its base value.

If a domestic animal has a higher intelligence than normal for its species, it will be worth *much* more when fully trained. As a general rule, multiply the creature's worth by 4 if it is 1 point smarter than normal, by 10 if it is 2 points smarter. Thus, an IQ 6 horse would be worth 10× base value.

If a "wild" animal is captured and trained, its value will go up markedly – especially if the creature is intelligent and/or ferocious. Details are up to the scenario and the GM.

Riding and Draft Animals

These creatures are trained as described above. For mounted combat rules, see p. 135.

riding and draft animals table

Type	ST	DX	IQ	HT	Move	Cost	Wt. (lbs.)	Notes
Donkey	25	10	4	13	8	$1,000	500	2 hexes; too
Small mule	30	10	4	14	8	$1,000	800	small to ride.
Large mule	40	10	4	14	9	$2,000	1,400	
Pony	30	10	4	13	13	$1,500	800	
Racehorse	32	9	4	13	18	$4,000+	1,100	Some are faster!
Saddle horse	35	9	4	14	12	$1,200	1,200	Ordinary riding horse.
Cavalry horse	40	9	4	15	16	$4,000	1,400	A light warhorse.
Heavy warhorse	50	9	4	16	15	$5,000	1,900	Usually vicious.
Draft horse	60	9	4	16	12	$2,000	2,000	
Ox	80	8	4	17	8	$1,500	2,500+	
Camel	40	9	4	15	10	$1,500	1,400	Vicious; drinks little.
Elephant	300	12	6	17/50	8	$10,000	12,000+	10 hexes. PD1, DR2.

Encumbrance and Movement

Encumbrance for beasts works as it does for men (see p. 76). The level of encumbrance reduces the beast's Move score. However, the encumbrance table for four-footed creatures is different:

No encumbrance (up to 2×ST): Move is unaffected.

Light encumbrance (up to 6×ST): Move is reduced by 2.

Medium encumbrance (up to 10×ST): Move is reduced by 4. Few animals will carry greater than 10× ST on their backs!

Heavy encumbrance (up to 15×ST): Move is reduced by 6.

Extra-heavy encumbrance (up to 20×ST): Move is reduced by 8, but never to less than 2.

Maximum encumbrance (up to 30×ST): Move is reduced to 1. Only a very willing beast will attempt to move a load this heavy.

Distance traveled in a day for horses and most other large beasts is the same as for humans (see p. 187).

Effective weight is reduced if it is carried on a sledge or wagon, and reduced further on a good surface – see the rules on p. 89. If a team of animals is used, just add their Strengths. A team of four oxen, for instance, has ST 320.

Rules for pulling a load assume proper harness and collars. Without these, using for instance an improvised harness of ropes, the pulling power of any draft animal is halved. Drawing a load with a lasso is even less efficient, since the angle of pull is bad. A horse can draw at most medium encumbrance with a lasso firmly anchored to the pommel.

Grain-fed horses have an advantage in strength, speed and endurance over grass-fed horses. In any straight Contest of Skills between horses, the grain-fed horse has +2 to the appropriate skill.

Value of Riding and Draft Animals

Base values are given in the table above. Increased IQ will raise the worth of an already valuable animal as described under *Training*.

Increased ST, if anyone cares enough to do the math, will raise the value of the beast by the same percentage that ST increases. A 10% increase in ST raises value by 10%. *Very* strong specimens will be worth more than this formula would indicate, of course.

Increased Speed will raise a riding animal's value drastically. Double value for +1 Speed. Quadruple value for +2 Speed.

Other value-changes are up to the GM, or the PC's haggling ability.

Individualizing Animals

GMs are not totally bound by the written descriptions of animals. These describe typical creatures – individuals may vary.

ST: May vary by several points, especially on large creatures. ST is valuable for draft animals, and a very strong horse, etc., is worth more.

DX: Should not vary from the suggested value by more than a point, except for a very unusual creature.

IQ: Realistically, should not vary up or down by more than a point – and even a 1-point increase in IQ makes a beast a genius of its kind. For game purposes, allowing an occasional animal of any species to be IQ 6 will allow for some interesting pets. This also increases their value – see above.

HT: True health can vary by a couple of points in either direction. Hit points, especially on a large creature, may vary by up to 20% in either direction.

PD and DR of skin won't vary much.

Speed and Move can vary a little bit. Horses and similar creatures can go up drastically in value if they are faster than average.

Cost: Any increase in an animal's stats can be reflected by an increase in its market value, but unless specific formulas are given, the details are up to the GM. Likewise, decreased stats would decrease the creature's value.

These three creatures have been selected because (if the GM changes the name and files off the serial numbers), they work in an SF background, too!

Cockatrice, or Basilisk

This creature resembles a small snake with a hideous face and a crested head.

ST 3, DX 12, IQ 3, HT 12/4. Speed 4, Dodge 6. Skin PD1, DR0. Weight 1-2 lbs.; size 1 hex. Its attack is special; the Middle Ages called it a "gaze of death." Treat as a telekinetic attack (p. 172) with a Power and Skill of 16. It may attack anyone who it sees or touches, if it concentrates for one turn first. If its victim sees *it,* or makes any psi contact, the cockatrice can attack instantly! It rolls against its Telekinetic skill, at -1 for every yard to the target. If it succeeds, the victim takes 2d+2 damage *per second* until the cockatrice's concentration is broken or the victim leaves its sight. Then the beast must roll again, at the new range, to continue its attack. DR and Toughness do not protect; no defense roll is allowed.

Gryphon

This beautiful creature has the head, wings and forefeet of an eagle and the hindquarters of a lion.

ST 30-35, DX 14, IQ 5, HT 15/20-25. Speed 6 on the ground, 15 in the air; Dodge 7. Skin PD1, DR1. Weight 500-600 lbs.; size 2 hexes. Attacks by clawing and pecking in close combat for 2d-1 damage.

Gryphons can be tamed if captured young, but their handlers are at a -3 to all animal-control skills. Since the gryphon is neither bird nor mammal, neither type of animal-control spell affects it! An untamed gryphon in good health might sell for $5,000; a tame one is priceless, and will not cooperate with anyone except its trainer. In flight, the gryphon's maximum encumbrance is Light, so only a small rider can be carried.

Strix

A strix (plural striges) is a blood-sucking, birdlike creature about the size of a crow, with a long beak and large eyes. Striges are nocturnal. ST 2-5, DX 17, IQ 4, HT 12/3-5. Speed 12 in the air, 1 grounded; Dodge 7. PD2, DR0. Weight 10-25 lbs.; size <1 hex.

A strix attacks with its long, barbed beak, doing 1d-3 impaling damage. If it hits, it inserts the beak and begins to suck the victim's blood, doing 1 hit of damage every 10th second. A successful Physician or Surgery roll must be made to pull it out; otherwise it does an extra die of damage.

It attacks its victim's most lightly armored spot, and will go for the eyeslits (at -10) of a person in metal armor. Only two striges can strike thus per turn – but a successful strike will blind the eye!

19  MAGIC

Magic is a powerful and fickle force, controlled through procedures called *spells*. Magic draws upon an energy called *mana* – but even the most powerful wizards do not fully understand magic. Or, if they do, they haven't told *us* about it.

Certain people have an inborn ability to learn and use magic. This advantage is called Magical Aptitude (see p. 21). Anyone with any degree of Magical Aptitude is called a *mage*. In many game worlds, only mages can use magic. In all worlds, they are *better* with magic than are non-mages.

LEARNING MAGIC

Most spells can be learned by anyone (but in some worlds they can only be *used* by mages). Some spells can only be learned by mages – this is a *prerequisite* for the spell.

Each magic spell is considered a *skill*, and is learned the same way that any other skill is learned. Spells have no default level; you *must* be trained in a spell to use it. Spells are Mental/Hard skills (except for a few, specified in the Spell List, which are Mental/Very Hard). However, your level of Magical Aptitude *adds to your IQ* for the purpose of learning spells. Thus, if you have an IQ of 12 and 3 levels of Magical Aptitude, you learn spells as though you had IQ 15. No one may have a Magical Aptitude of more than 3.

To learn a spell, you must put a *minimum* of one point in it – even if you are brilliant and blessed with Magical Aptitude. Eidetic Memory is not too useful for spells; it gives you rote memory, but not true understanding. First-level Eidetic Memory gives a +1 to IQ for learning spells; second-level gives a +2. It gives no other bonuses.

When you play a character who knows a number of spells, you may wish to make a "grimoire" for that character. A grimoire is a book of spells. Your character's grimoire is a list of the spells he knows, his skill with each, the energy each costs to cast, and other important details about them. This will save a lot of reference time in play – not even the most dedicated player will know the details for every spell!

Prerequisites

All spells except the most basic have *prerequisites* – requirements that must be met before the spell can be learned. If the prerequisite is another spell, it must be known at skill level 12 or better before the higher spell may be studied. Thus, a magic-user must learn simple spells first, and proceed to advanced ones as his knowledge increases. "Magery" is a prerequisite for most of the stronger spells. This means that no one but a mage – a person with Magical Aptitude – can learn them. "Magery 2" means that *two* levels of Magical Aptitude are required to learn the spell, and so on. Some spells also require a minimum *basic* DX or IQ.

CASTING SPELLS

In order to cast a spell, you must *know* that spell, or possess an item that lets you use the spell (see p. 153). Then you must spend one or more turns in *concentration*. At the beginning of the turn *after* your last turn of concentration, you must make your skill roll for that spell. You may then do something else on that turn (use a weapon, start concentrating again, etc.).

Casting a spell works just like any other use of a skill. The caster rolls three dice and compares the result with his "skill level" in that spell. If his roll is less than or equal to his skill level, the spell works. If his roll is greater than his skill, the spell fails. Various modifiers will add to or subtract from the caster's basic skill with the spell. The modifiers depend on the *class* of spell – see p. 149.

A successful roll means the spell was cast, and the spell's energy cost (see below) is marked off of your ST (as fatigue) or your HT (as injury).

A *critical success* means the spell worked especially well. Magic is fickle; the *nature* of this great success is left entirely up to the GM, who should be both generous and creative. There is *never* an energy cost if you get a critical success when you cast a spell.

A failed roll means the spell was not cast. If a successful use of the spell would have cost energy, the caster loses 1 energy point. If the spell would not have required energy, the caster loses nothing.

In a world in which magic is common, it will probably be taught just like any other trade. You may apprentice yourself to a wizard to learn his whole craft . . . or hire a magic instructor to teach you a few spells. Of course, there is always the possibility that magic will be a closely-guarded secret in your world. This can lead to interesting complications!

In a world in which magic is rare (or in which few believe in it), finding an instructor will be much harder. Most wizards will shroud themselves in secrecy – or belong to mysterious, far-off cults – or prove to be fakes!

Like any other intellectual skill, magic can be learned without a teacher. You must be Literate and have access to good textbooks. Even with the *best* textbooks, an unsupervised student learns at half speed (each spell costs twice as many character points). And most spell-books – *especially* those found in non-magical worlds – are complex and deliberately obscure!

Hiring a Wizard

PCs may want to hire a wizard for a teacher. Or a group of adventurers may need a mercenary magician! Use the same procedure and pay rules as for any other hireling (see p. 194). The more common magic is, the easier it will be to find any sort of wizard and the less you will have to pay him. See sidebar, p. 152, for some basic cost and pay figures for "common" magic campaigns.

However, it will be harder to find a wizard hireling if you want to specify his spells, especially if you specify complex ones. To find a wizard with Create Fire, for instance, you would need to roll at only a -1, since this is a common spell. But to find a wizard who knew both Create Fire Elemental and Major Healing (two complex, unrelated spells) you might have to roll at a -8!

Setting these penalties is up to the GM. Any mage gets a +1 when searching for another mage as a hireling; connections with the local wizardly guilds or power structure could be good for a further +1 to +3 bonus.

A *critical miss* means the energy cost of the spell was spent, but the spell failed *badly*. A table of "backfire" results is provided. However, the GM may improvise *any* "backfire" that he finds amusing, as long as he does not actually *kill* the caster.

If this seems arbitrary or unfair . . . it is! Again, *magic is fickle*. Any time you cast a spell, you are using powers you do not fully understand, and exposing yourself to the whim of the fates – as represented by the GM.

Critical Spell Failure Table

Roll 3 dice. The GM does not have to use this table; he is free to improvise (though improvisations should be appropriate to the spell and the situation). If a result on this table is inappropriate, or if it is the result that the caster actually *intended,* roll again.

3 – Spell fails entirely; caster takes 1d of damage.
4 – Spell is cast on spellcaster.
5 – Spell is cast on one of the caster's companions (roll randomly).
6 – Spell is cast on a nearby foe – roll randomly.
7 – Spell produces only a whining noise and an awful odor of brimstone.
8 – Spell affects someone or something other than its target – friend, foe, or random object – roll randomly, or GM makes an interesting choice.
9 – Spell fails entirely; caster takes 1 hit of damage.
10 – Spell fails entirely; caster is stunned (IQ roll to recover).
11 – Spell produces nothing but a loud noise and a flash of colored light.
12 – Spell produces a weak and useless shadow of its intended effect.
13 – Spell produces the reverse of the intended effect.
14 – Spell has the reverse of the intended effect, on wrong target (roll randomly).
15 – Nothing happens except caster temporarily forgets the spell – make an IQ roll after a week, and again each following week, until he remembers.
16 – Spell seems to work, but it is only a useless illusion.
17 – Spell fails entirely; caster's right arm is crippled – 1 week to recover.
18 – Spell fails entirely. A demon (see p. 154) appears and attacks the caster, unless, *in the GM's opinion,* caster and spell were both lily-white, pure good in intent.

Caster and Subject

The "caster" of a spell is the person who is attempting to cast it.

The "subject" of a spell is the person, place, or thing upon which the spell is cast. If you are casting a spell on yourself, you are both caster and subject. The subject can also be another person; another being; an inanimate object; or even an area on the game map. If the subject is a place, the caster can "touch" it by extending a hand over it or touching the ground, as appropriate for the spell.

Time Required to Cast Spells

Most spells take one turn to cast. The caster uses the "Concentrate" maneuver for one second. At the *beginning* of his next turn, he attempts his skill roll. If the roll succeeds, the spell takes effect instantly. The caster is then free to make another maneuver, or to concentrate again.

Example: Wat wants to cast Create Fire (a one-second spell). On Turn 1, Wat says "I'm concentrating." He must tell the GM what he is casting. He can do nothing else that turn. At the *beginning* of his second turn, he rolls. He makes his roll; fire is created. Now Wat may take any maneuver, or announce another spell and Concentrate again.

Some complex spells take more than one turn to cast. All this time must be spent in the "Concentrate" maneuver.

Example: If a spell takes 3 seconds to cast, the wizard must spend three turns doing nothing but concentrating. The spell is cast at the beginning of the caster's fourth turn. The caster may "abort" the unfinished spell before then, at no penalty, but must start over if he wishes to try again.

Magic Rituals

The higher your skill with a spell, the easier it is to cast. This applies both to the energy cost and to the "ritual" required to cast it. If you cannot perform the ritual, you cannot cast the spell! For instance, if the ritual requires you to speak, you can't cast the spell if you are gagged or under a spell of silence. These skill levels are not "effective" skill, but the level at which the skill is *known,* at a -5 penalty if in a low-mana area (see sidebar). If you don't know a spell, you can't cast it without an appropriate magical item.

Skill 11 or below: The wizard must have both hands and both feet free for elaborate ritual movements. He must speak certain words of power in a firm voice. The spell takes *double* the listed time to cast – it is not yet fully known.

Mana

Mana is the energy behind magic. Magic will work only if the mana of the game world (or the specific area) allows it. Mana is rated as follows:

Very high mana: Anyone can cast spells, if he knows them. Energy spent by a mage is renewed every turn. However, any slip is likely to be disastrous. Even an ordinary failure is treated as a "critical failure" – and critical failures produce spectacular disasters. Very high mana is extremely rare.

High mana: Anyone can cast spells, if he knows them. This condition is rare in most worlds, but some game worlds have high mana throughout them.

Normal mana: Only mages can cast spells. These spells work normally, according to all rules given in this section. This is the "default" condition for fantasy game worlds; mages use magic, others don't.

Low mana: Only mages can cast spells, and all spells perform at an effective -5 to skill level, for all purposes. Power of magical items is also at -5 – so items with Power below 20 *will not work at all*. However, critical spell failures (see main text) have very mild effects or no effect at all. Our Earth is a low-mana world.

No mana: No one can use magic at all. Magic items do not function (but regain their powers when taken to an area with mana). No-mana conditions occur in isolated spots in magical worlds. Some entire game worlds may have no mana, making magic use impossible.

The Ethics of Magic

Some religions teach that magic is inherently evil, and that any magic-user is endangering his immortal soul. Certainly, badly-cast spells seem to attract the attention of *something* powerful and malicious – and occasionally a clumsy spellcaster is devoured by a genuine demon!

But it is also true that many good men know and use magic – and the saintliest of these seem to be immune to the worst magical "fumbles."

No one really knows. The consensus is that magic, of itself, is neither good nor evil. It is the intent behind it that determines whether magic is "white" or "black." But there is no doubt that certain forms of magic – that powered by human sacrifices, for example – are inherently evil and are despised by all honest mages.

Magical Terms

abort: To stop the casting of a spell before its completion.

backfire: A critical miss when a spell is cast. Same as "fumble."

base skill: A level of spell skill given by spending 1 character point (the minimum) for an ordinary (Mental/Hard) spell, or 2 points for a M/VH spell.

basic spell: A spell with no other spells as prerequisites.

cancel: To end your own spell before it would normally be over.

caster: The person casting a spell.

effective skill: Your true skill, plus or minus any bonuses or penalties (usually penalties) for range, circumstances, etc. A caster rolls against *effective* skill.

energy: The "cost" to cast a spell. Energy cost may be paid in either ST points (fatigue) or HT points (hits). Lost energy of either kind is recovered as usual: resting for fatigue, healing for hits.

grimoire: A book of spells. Specifically, the list of spells available to a particular character, and their cost.

mage: Anyone with the advantage of Magical Aptitude.

magery or *Magical Aptitude:* Two words for the same thing. Magery is the advantage of being "in tune" with the powers of magic; see p. 21.

maintain: To continue a spell after it would normally end. Costs more energy, unless the caster has high skill.

mana: The energy of magic. Different areas (or worlds) have different levels of mana. See sidebar, p. 147.

mastered spell: A spell known at a high enough skill to eliminate the need to concentrate to cast it.

missile spell: A spell which is first cast, and then "thrown" at the subject. Requires two rolls: a skill roll to cast, a Throwing or Spell Throwing roll to hit.

prerequisite: A requirement for learning a spell.

resisted: Any spell that has to overcome the "power" of its subject before it works.

subject: The person, place or thing on which a spell is cast.

wizard: Any user of magic, whether he is a mage or not.

Skill 12-14: The wizard must speak a few quiet words and make a gesture to activate the spell. At this level (and above) spells take the listed time to complete.

Skill 15-17: The wizard must speak a word or two and gesture – a couple of fingers are enough. He is allowed to move one hex per turn while taking the Concentrate maneuver. *At level 15, the spell's energy cost is reduced by 1.*

Skill 18-20: The wizard must speak a word or two *or* make a small gesture, but not necessarily both. *At level 20, the spell's energy cost is reduced by 2.*

Skill 21-24: No ritual is needed. The wizard simply seems to stare into space as he concentrates. Casting time is halved (round up). A spell that would normally take one second can now be cast without a turn of concentration, even while taking another maneuver – fighting, talking, etc. You may never cast two spells at once!

Skill 25 or over: As above, but casting time is now ¼ normal, rounded up. *At level 25, the spell's energy cost is reduced by 3.* Each further 5 levels of skill will halve casting time again and reduce cost by 1 more.

Some spells always require a certain ritual or item; this is noted in the spell lists, and overrides the general rules. Note that time to cast *missile* spells is not reduced by skill.

Distraction and Injury

If the caster is hurt, knocked down, forced to use an active defense, or otherwise distracted while concentrating, he must make a (Will-3) roll to maintain his casting. A failed roll means he must start over. If he is *injured* while concentrating, his effective skill for that spell is lowered by the number of hits he suffered.

Energy Cost for Casting Spells

Each spell has an energy cost. When you cast a spell, it costs you energy – either HT or ST. The better you know a spell, the less energy is required to cast it. If you know it well enough, you can cast it at *no* cost. The mana level of the area (see sidebar, p. 147) affects a wizard's effective skill with spells. Low mana also prevents use of the Recover Strength spell (p. 162), reducing the frequency with which *any* spells can be cast.

If your *basic skill* with a spell (modified by mana level) is 15+, the cost to cast that spell is reduced by 1. If your skill is 20+, the cost to cast it is reduced by 2 – and so on. *The energy is still going into the spell – but your skill lets you draw it from the surrounding mana rather than supplying it yourself!* Thus (for instance) at skill 20, in a normal-mana area, you can cast a 2-die fireball (requiring 2 energy points) at *no* energy cost. To make it a 3-die fireball, you would need to add 1 point of your own energy.

The entire cost for a spell is calculated before any subtraction for high skill. A mage who can create small fires repeatedly, at no cost, might still be exhausted by creating a single multi-hex fire. High skill also lowers the cost to *maintain* a spell – see below.

Normally, the energy cost from a spell is considered "fatigue" – see p. 134. Lost fatigue can be recovered by rest. A *mage* who knows the Recover Strength spell (see p. 162) can regain lost ST faster than normal. A caster *may* take energy from his body's vital force instead of just his Strength. He marks off some or all of the spell's cost against HT rather than ST. In other words, the spell is doing actual harm to the caster! This is dangerous, but may be necessary if the caster is badly fatigued and *has* to throw another spell. HT lost this way is treated just like any other injury.

A wizard's skill is at -1 for every point of HT he used to cast that spell.

A wizard may "burn" HT until he falls unconscious. Should a failed HT roll indicate he has died, the HT for that particular casting wasn't actually spent, and he falls unconscious instead of dying, thus ending the HT drain.

Duration of Spells and Maintaining Spells

Some spells take effect instantly and cannot be maintained. Other spells last for a given time (see the Spell List) and then wear off – unless they are *maintained*.

If a spell can be maintained, it will continue for a time equal to its original duration. A spell may be maintained as often as the caster wants, if he keeps paying the energy cost. He cannot maintain a spell while he sleeps! But only the caster can maintain a spell. *No new skill roll is required.*

However, further energy must be spent. If a spell can be maintained, the cost is in the Spell List. *Example:* The Light spell has a 1-minute duration, and a maintenance cost of 1 per minute. So the spell ends after a minute – *unless,* at the end of that minute, the caster spends one more energy point to maintain it. If a caster is conscious, he will know when one of his spells needs to be renewed. *Distance is not a factor* in maintaining a spell.

Concentration. Most spells can be maintained without "concentration" on the part of the caster. But any spell that requires constant manipulation and change – e.g., control of a living being – naturally requires constant concentration by the caster. This requires the caster to take only the "Concentrate" maneuver. If he is distracted, a Will-3 roll is required each turn. A failed roll will not end the spell, but the spell's subject will do nothing until the caster can once again concentrate on it. A critical failure *will* break the spell. Casting another spell will *not* break concentration – but the caster suffers a skill penalty for doing two things at once. See below.

Reduced Cost. If you know a spell so well that its energy cost is reduced (see above), then its cost to maintain is reduced by the same amount. If you cast a spell at a skill of 15 or better, it costs 1 less point of energy to *maintain* it. This can be very important! For instance, if a spell's "cost to maintain" is only 1, and you cast that spell at level 15, you can maintain it indefinitely at *no energy cost!*

Canceling Spells. A caster may wish to have a spell end *sooner* than it normally would. For instance, he might want a created fire (normally good for one minute) to end after only 30 seconds. If he specifies this at the time the spell is cast, it will last exactly the time desired. But if he suddenly decides to "cancel" a spell before its time is up, there is an energy cost of 1, regardless of the spell.

Casting Spells While Maintaining Other Spells

A character may only cast one new spell at a time. However, a caster *may* cast a new spell before older ones end. This is relatively easy if the existing spells do not require *concentration* – that is, active control. If existing spells require control, it becomes much harder to cast a new spell! These modifiers apply to spellcasting in all conditions.

-3 for each other spell you are *concentrating* on at the moment. The Spell List specifies which spells require concentration.

-1 for each other spell you have "on" at the moment. A spell which lasts permanently (e.g., Beast-Soother, Purify Water, Enchant) *does not carry a penalty.*

DIFFERENT KINDS OF MAGIC

There are many different types of magic. Spells are divided into "colleges" according to subject matter, and "classes" according to the way they work.

Colleges of Magic

Spells related by subject matter belong to the same college. Twelve colleges of magic are represented in the Spell List here; there are others. Basic spells of a college are "prerequisites" for the harder spells. Most mages specialize in only a few colleges (thus making it possible to learn some advanced magic), but it is possible to learn spells from every college. Some spells fit in more than one college. For instance, *Earth to Air* is both an Earth and an Air spell. This is only important when counting prerequisites.

Spell Classes

Each spell falls into one or more classes: Regular, Area, Missile, Information, Resisted, Enchantment and Special.

Regular Spells

Most spells fall into this category. A regular spell only affects one subject at a time. For a subject larger than 1 hex (e.g., a 3-hex chunk of earth, or an elephant) multiply energy cost by the subject's size in hexes. If the caster cannot *touch* the subject, apply a skill penalty equal to the distance in hexes from caster to subject. If the spell takes time to cast, figure distance at the moment the spell is finished and cast.

If the caster can't touch *or see* the subject, there is a further -5 penalty. He does not have to see through his own eyes; any spell that lets him see by magical means will do.

There are two ways to direct such a spell.

"The hex on the other side of this door." You'll get whoever is in that hex. If there is nobody there, you wasted the spell.

"The closest person in the next room." Or, "George, who I know is around here somewhere." The GM figures the actual range to the subject. (This is risky. The caster is inviting failure, or even critical failure. If the subject is farther away than he thinks, or not there at all, he may get a backfire!)

Aside from this, no physical barrier affects a regular spell. Unless the spell backfires, a regular spell never hits the wrong target.

Area Spells

These spells can be cast over an area of several hexes. If the spell affects living beings, all those within the area are affected. Otherwise, these are just like regular spells.

The size of the area governs the energy cost, but not the difficulty of the roll. The cost for these spells is given as *Base Cost*. This is the cost to affect *just one hex*. To affect a circle with a 2-hex radius (e.g., a hex, and all adjacent hexes), double the base cost – and so on.

The Mage's Touch

Touching a subject negates any distance penalty; a wand or staff may be used. Some spells *require* that the caster touch the subject. This is "the mage's touch." First the mage casts the spell. As his next action (assuming the spell roll was successful), the mage tries to strike his foe with his hand, wand or staff.

In combat, roll as for any other attack. If a touch is scored (the mage hits, and the foe's defense fails), the spell succeeds. If the mage misses or the foe defends, the spell is lost. PD from armor and shield will not normally help against the "mage's touch," and a parry with an arm won't save the subject. A bare-handed or staff attack does its normal physical damage (if the mage wishes), in addition to whatever damage the spell does. A wand touch does no damage. Note that a wand is very light, and has a 1/3 chance of breaking if parried by anything heavier than a hand or knife!

A wizard who enters close combat and attempts a touch on the same turn must roll it as a normal attack; the foe may use any active defense.

A wizard who is already in close combat at the beginning of the turn may "touch" already, unless both his hands are immobilized. But since it is impossible to concentrate while in close combat, only *mastered* spells may be used this way.

Wand and Staff

Wands and staffs are magic items, made by the Staff spell (p. 161). Many wands are enchanted so that only their owner may use them; some contain other powerful spells as well. Only once-living materials (wood, bone, ivory, coral, etc.) can be used to make a wand.

Touching an item with a wand is as good as touching it with a finger, for casting purposes. Thus, the basic use of a wand or staff is to increase the mage's "touching" reach. Pointing with the staff reduces the range to the subject by 1 hex. A wand or staff can't extend range on a missile spell unless it is specifically enchanted to contain that spell.

Magic in the Basic Combat System

These rules give precise descriptions of range and area-of-effect, on the theory that most campaigns will use some or all of the advanced combat rules. But if you are playing without a map, use these guidelines for "range modifiers" to skill:

Missile spells are always cast at the caster's basic skill. Other combat-type spells are cast at basic skill *if* the GM rules the subject is in "striking range" of the caster. Otherwise, subtract 3 from the caster's effective skill.

For other spells: On the rare occasion when a "mapless" GM needs a precise range or distance, use those given. Otherwise, just make it fun!

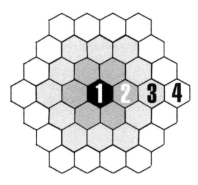

The Area of Effect

The area of effect of an *area* spell is a circle. Its size depends on the energy put into the spell. (1) above is a single "ring" of hexes (i.e., 1 hex). Cost to cast the spell in this area is equal to base cost. (2) is an area equal to two rings of hexes – the center, and the ring around it. Cost to cast here is double base cost. (3) is three rings of hexes – triple base cost. (4) is four rings – four times base cost. And so on . . .

Some area spells have a minimum cost to cast – e.g., Sense Foes has a base cost of 1 but a minimum cost to cast of 2 points. This means it will cost 2 to cast, even if you choose to restrict it to one hex.

Hints for Spellcasting

Several small spells can often be better than one big one. If you know the Fog spell well, you could cast several individual hexes of fog at little or no cost – but a large area would cost you several energy points. Furthermore, if you cast several spells in succession, you can enter each hex and cast the spell around you, avoiding any penalty for distance. And, of course, a small spell wastes less energy if it fails. Large, quick spells are best saved for emergencies.

Ranged Attack Modifiers

Missile spell attacks are treated as "ranged weapons" (pp. 100, 114-119) for all purposes. Ranges for these spells are:

Stone Missile: SS 13, Acc +2, $\frac{1}{2}$D 40, Max 80.

Lightning: SS 13, Acc +3, $\frac{1}{2}$D 50, Max 100.

Fireball: SS 13, Acc +1, $\frac{1}{2}$D 25, Max 50.

Ice Sphere: SS 13, Acc +2, $\frac{1}{2}$D 40, Max 80.

Limits on Protection

Several spells (Blur, for instance) offer variable levels of protection. In all such cases, the *most* protection anyone can get from these spells, whether from one caster or several, is 5 points' worth.

If the same protective spell is thrown more than once on the same subject, only the strongest one takes effect; they do not add together. The same is true for attack spells that reduce the subject's attributes.

Some spells have a very low base cost – e.g., $\frac{1}{10}$ of a point for Rain. You must spend a minimum of 1 point on these spells. You may choose to affect only a part of the area, rather than the whole circle, but the cost is still the same.

If the caster cannot touch some part of the affected area, the skill penalty is equal to the distance, in hexes, from the caster to the *nearest hex* of the area.

Assume that area spells reach 4 yards up from the ground, except for weather spells.

Missile Spells

Certain long-distance attacks (Fireball, Lightning, etc.) are "missile spells." These spells require *two* skill rolls. The first is the regular skill roll to determine whether the spell succeeds; this is made when you start the spell, with no modifier for distance. The second is a roll on the caster's Throwing or Spell Throwing skill (p. 244), made when the spell is *thrown,* to see whether it hits its target! Figure this like any other ranged attack, taking into account the target's size, speed and range.

A missile spell flies in a straight line. If it hits a physical barrier and breaks that barrier, its remaining power continues through. An accurately-thrown missile spell may be blocked or dodged – but not parried. If the defender fails his defense roll, the spell takes effect. Armor *does* protect against damage from missile spells.

The *strength* of a missile spell depends on the energy put into it. For instance, a fireball does 1 die of damage for each point of energy used in creating it.

Time to prepare a missile spell depends on the energy put into it; each turn gives it 1 point of energy. The caster concentrates for a turn, and then tries his spell roll at the beginning of his new turn. If he succeeds, the missile has 1 point of energy and can be thrown on that turn. Or he can hold it and *enlarge* it! Another second of concentration gives it another point of energy. A third second of concentration makes it a 3-point missile – as big as most missiles can get.

Thus, a wizard could create and throw a 1-point missile every turn – or a 2-point missile every second turn – and so on. He may not aim while he is creating the missile; if he is going to aim, he must take another turn to do so *after* the missile is created.

A wizard may keep a missile spell "in hand" after it is ready to throw. He may move while holding it, or use the Aim maneuver. He does not have to throw the spell until he wants to. This is the *only* sort of spell that can be "held until ready." A wizard cannot cast another spell while holding a missile spell.

If a wizard is injured while he has a missile "in hand," he must roll vs. Will. If he fails, he loses control of the missile. A solid missile will simply fall to the floor, but other missiles (fireballs, etc.) will immediately affect the caster!

Information Spells

An "information" spell is cast to gain knowledge. Some information spells require that the subject be touched by the caster. Modifiers for each information spell are given in the Spell List. When an information spell is cast, *the player doesn't make the roll.* The GM rolls, *in secret.* If the spell succeeds, the GM gives the caster the desired information – the better the roll, the more information. If the spell fails, the caster is told, "You sense nothing." On a critical failure, the GM *lies* to the player.

Therefore, the caster always pays the full energy cost for each information spell – he does not know whether it succeeded or not. Most information spells can only be tried once per day by each caster (or group)! "Seek" spells are an exception to this.

Most information spells are less likely to succeed if the subject is a long distance away; see sidebar, p. 151, for long-distance modifiers.

Resisted Spells

Certain spells may be *resisted.* These are noted on the Spell List. When such a spell is cast, it works automatically only on a critical success. If it "merely" succeeds, use a "quick contest" procedure to see whether the spell overcomes the subject's resistance. *(The subject is always aware that something is happening, and has a chance to resist. But he does not have to resist if he doesn't want to, even if he has Magic Resistance!)*

In a "resisted" situation, the caster first tries his skill roll. If he fails, he fails, and the subject notices nothing. If he succeeds, note *how much* he succeeded by. For example, a roll of 6, when a 13 was needed, succeeds by 7 points. If the subject is a living creature, the caster rolls against a 16 or the subject's actual resistance, whichever is higher, if his effective skill is over 16 and the subject is a living creature; thus, "automatic victory over resistance" is impossible. If the subject is a *spell,* there is no limit on the caster's effective skill! Note that if the subject has Magic Resistance (p. 21), it always affects this roll, even if the subject is willing.

The subject may then try a *resistance roll.* A living subject may resist a combat spell with IQ, ST, DX or HT, depending on the attacking spell. Strong Will always adds to resistance; Weak Will always subtracts. The subject's Magic Resistance, if any, adds to his resistance. It counts *double* against *area spells only.* For instance, Magic Resistance 1 adds 1 to resistance of Sleep, or 2 to Mass Sleep.

If the subject makes the resistance roll by *as much or more* than the amount by which the caster's skill roll succeeded, the spell has no effect – but the energy *is* spent! If the subject is conscious, he feels a slight mental or physical wrench (depending on which attribute he resisted with) but no other effect. The caster knows his spell was resisted.

Resistance against Area Spells: If an area spell can be resisted by subjects in the area, roll normally to see if the new spell is cast. If it is, each subject in the area rolls separately to see whether he (or it) succumbs to the spell.

Enchantment Spells

Spells of the College of Enchantment are used to make or unmake magical items.

Special Spells

These are spells that don't fit into any of the other categories; follow the rules given in the spell description.

CEREMONIAL AND GROUP MAGIC

Ordinary magic is cast by a single wizard, and is relatively quick. Ceremonial magic is much slower (since it involves complex ritual), but it allows others to help the caster. Thus, more powerful spells can be cast, and they can be maintained longer. Spells like Power are almost never cast except by ceremonial methods.

Time required: When ceremonial magic is used, casting time is ten times as long as shown on the Spell List.

Energy cost: Same as normal. All the energy required is spent at the *end* of the casting, when the caster rolls to see if the spell succeeded. Whether it succeeds or fails, all the energy is spent at this time.

There are two ways to cooperate in ceremonial magic:

Circle. Any number of mages can "link" to cast a spell, if they *all* know it at level 15 or better. They must be physically joined in some way – e.g., holding hands, touching a common center, etc. Any one of them can act as the caster and make all die rolls.

The energy cost may be shared among the linked mages in any way they agree on. If there is a backfire, the GM may assess one huge result, or roll separately for each person in the Circle. A backfire involving a dozen mages can be a chaotic event indeed!

If the physical link is broken during the casting of the spell, the caster must start over. If any of the linked mages is wounded, the effect is as if the caster himself had been wounded (see p. 148). If any linked mage is knocked out or killed, all mages in the Circle are stunned, and must roll vs. IQ to recover!

Mages who do not know the spell at level 15, or non-mages who *do* know it at level 15, can aid in a lesser way. They may join the Circle, as above, and suffer the same ill effects if the Circle is broken. But each may contribute only 3 energy points to each spell.

Spectators. Unskilled observers can aid a ceremonial casting; they usually chant, hold candles, etc. Each spectator contributes 1 and only 1 energy point to each spell cast, up to a maximum of 100 "spectator" energy points per spell. Sincere belief and desire to help is required; you cannot hire people off the street!

If anyone present is *opposed* to the spell, each *subtracts* 5 from the energy (maximum 100) contributed by the mass of spectators! If this means that there is insufficient energy to cast the spell, then the caster (and/or the Circle) will have to contribute more energy – possibly from their HT – or abort the spell, losing all the energy put into it. This is one reason that covens and temples don't hold their ceremonies in public.

Tradeoff: *Energy for Skill*

If a great deal of energy is available for ceremonial magic, the caster gets a bonus on his skill roll. This can ensure the success of an ordinary spell (except for automatic failures). It can also make a defensive spell able to resist almost any attack. Extra energy gives a skill bonus as follows: +1 for 20% of extra energy, +2 for 40%, +3 for 60%, +4 for 100%, and an additional +1 for each additional 100% of the required energy. This method can also be used to make magical items of increased Power.

Notes on Ceremonial Magic

A group aids concentration. If a caster of ceremonial magic is distracted but not injured, he rolls at Will, not Will-3, to continue. A ceremonial casting is also harder to "coordinate" than a regular spell. It fails automatically on a roll of 16. 17 and 18 are always backfires, even if the caster's effective skill is 16+. If a magical ceremony fails, *all the energy is still spent.*

A Circle may be maintained for a long time, with wizards entering and leaving. They may not do this during an actual casting, but if the Circle is merely maintaining its spells, its composition may change. Thus, a Circle can maintain a spell indefinitely.

Long-Distance Modifiers

Use these skill modifiers for "Seek" spells, and for other specified spells which work over a long distance.

Less than 100 yards: 0
Up to a half-mile: -1
Up to a mile: -2
Up to 3 miles: -3
Up to 10 miles: -4
Up to 50 miles: -5
Up to 100 miles: -6
Up to 300 miles: -7
Up to 1,000 miles: -8
Another -1 for each additional 1,000 miles.

Also, subtract 1 from effective skill for each "known" item you choose to ignore in your search. For instance, you would need to ignore the water in your canteen when you cast Seek Water in the desert!

Alternate Systems of Magic

The system presented here is the "official" *GURPS* magic system. However, magic is not amenable to reality checks. Every fantasy author treats magic a little differently. This system is designed to encompass, in a playable manner, the most common literary concepts of magic. This system treats magic in a *somewhat* mechanistic fashion. A given spell usually produces a given effect, and these effects are carefully defined in game terms, for playability. However, the effects of many spells are complex and individualized – and spell failure can produce unpredictable, and disastrous, results.

Mages can learn large numbers of spells, and can be more expert with some spells than with others. Almost anyone can learn a little bit of magic, but some are born to it and gain power quickly and easily. Inborn talent, intelligence and long study are the most important requirements for a magic-user; strength and dexterity are useful but not vital. Spells fall into logical groupings, but mages are not limited to a single grouping in their studies.

This system will work as is, or with very minor changes, for campaigns in most fantasy game worlds. If you want to base a campaign on the works of an author whose view of magic diverges *widely* from that presented here, you will simply have to modify the system.

To do so, start by just changing or reversing some of the features listed above! Then you can add entirely new features – Divine Favor, influence of the moon, or whatever you like. Enjoy. You may also want to refer to *GURPS Magic,* which offers a number of special and optional rules that can be used to create your own magic system.

Cost to Make Magic Items

The economics of magic can be as basic or as detailed as you like. The GM is perfectly welcome to ignore everything that follows, and set magic prices to suit himself. For those who enjoy economic realism, though, here are some "hard" numbers. The *value* of an item is what it will bring, as discussed on the next page. But the actual cost to *make* an item can be calculated. The calculations below assume that:

(1) Enchanter mages normally spend an average of 10 energy (ST only) on each "Quick and Dirty" casting.

(2) When Powerstones are used, the return to the stone's owner is 36% per year, so the cost of 1 point of energy from a stone is $1/1,000$ of the stone's cost.

(3) Most enchanter mages make around $25 per day. Very few enchanters have a skill over 20, so the largest circle will be 6.

(4) Most items are made at Power 15.

As a consequence of (1) and (3), energy from mages' own ST costs about $1.00 per point used. As a consequence of (2), energy from Powerstones smaller than 5 points is cheaper than using a mage. But if a Powerstone is larger than 35 points, its energy costs more than $25 per point, which makes Slow and Sure enchantment cheaper than using such a stone.

This means that: An item whose total energy cost is 100 or less, made in a single casting, will cost an average of only $1.00 per point to produce, because small, cheap Powerstones can provide all the needed energy. For items requiring more energy, prices rise quickly, as larger, less economical stones must be used.

Energy Cost	Cost to Make
105	$180
110	$205
120	$235
130	$320
140	$435
150	$505
160	$685
170	$915
180	$1,055
190	$1,385
200	$1,790
210	$2,065
220	$2,615
230	$3,275
240	$3,650
250	$4,510
260	$5,520
270	$6,090

Any item with an energy cost over 270 should be made by the "slow and sure" method. This will cost a flat $25 per energy point, plus costs for any materials required and the actual item to be enchanted.

For intermediate values, use a weighted average of the values above and below.

Since ceremonial spell rituals cannot be hurried, neither the caster's skill, nor anyone else's, reduces the time or cost. The Luck advantage can *not* be used to improve a caster's chances with ceremonial magic.

MAGIC ITEMS

Objects may be given magic powers by use of the Enchantment spells. Use of an appropriate magical item is the *only* way to cast a spell you don't know. Most such items can be used by anyone. Some can be used only by mages. If an item has *any* mage-only spells in it, the *entire* item can be used *only* by a mage.

Magic items last indefinitely. Enchantments may be removed by the Remove Enchantment spell (see p. 160). Enchantment is also removed if an item is broken, worn out, etc. Repair of a broken formerly-magical item does *not* renew the spell.

An item may carry any number of spells; each one requires a separate enchantment. The presence of a spell on an item does not affect further enchantments. But if such an item breaks, *all* its spells are lost!

ENCHANTING: CREATING A MAGIC ITEM

Magic items *must* be created by ceremonial magic – usually, but not always, in a group. An enchantment can be "quick and dirty" or "slow and sure" – see below. Some items require a particular item or material to start with – e.g., a gem. Others require a certain cash expenditure for "generic" magic supplies. Still others require no special ingredients – just time and energy. To create a magical item, the caster (and any assistants) must know the Enchant spell *and* the spell to be put into the item – both at level 15 or better (20 in a low-mana area). For instance, to create a Stone Missile staff, the Enchant spell and the Stone Missile spell must both be known.

Power of a Magic Item

Each magic item has a "power," set when it is created. Normally, an item's Power equals the caster's skill with (a) the Enchant spell or (b) the spell contained in the item – whichever is lower. This should be recorded for each magic item found or created (skill of found items will be known only to the GM until Analyze Magic is used on the item). An item may have several spells on it . . . each the result of a separate enchantment. In this case, each spell's Power is recorded separately.

If attacked with a magic item, you roll against its Power when you try to resist. Obviously, an item created by a highly skilled mage is better than one created by a caster of lesser ability. An item's Power must be 15 or above, or it will not work. The Power of any item in a low-mana area is temporarily reduced by 5, so items with a Power below 20 *will not work at all* in a low-mana area. In a no-mana area, *no* magical items work.

Success Rolls When Creating Magic Items

The GM makes the success roll when PCs try to create a magic item. A *success* means the spell works and the item becomes enchanted. Results of a *failed* roll depend on the method being used to enchant the item – see below.

On a *critical success* the enchantment succeeds greatly. The Power of the item created is higher; roll 2 dice for the amount of increase. A roll of 3 may also enhance the object in some further way – GM's discretion. The caster will know that his spell went well, but he will have to use Analyze Magic to know *how* well.

A *critical failure* will destroy the item and all materials used.

Quick and Dirty Enchantment

This method is used when a magic item is needed *now*. It takes one hour for each 100 points of energy required (round up). At the end of that time, all the energy is spent, and the roll is made. Thus, a lone caster is limited to the energy provided by his own HT and ST, and *one* Powerstone (see p. 161).

The caster may have assistants. Each of these may also use a single Powerstone – so assistants can dramatically multiply the available energy. The drawback is this: his effective skill is at -1 for each assistant! The number of permissible assistants is limited to the number that will reduce the caster's effective skill to 15. With more assistants, the enchantment won't work. If anyone but the caster and assistants is present (within 10 yards, or able to see the caster), the spell is at a further -1. Thus, keeping guards to protect against a possible backfire adds to the danger of a backfire.

A *failed* roll means the enchantment is perverted in some way, or is a wholly different spell – GM's choice. The caster won't know his spell went wrong unless he uses Analyze Magic or tries the item!

Slow and Sure Enchantment

This method is used when the "quick and dirty" method can't generate enough power, or when a mage wants to be sure it's done *right*. The process takes one mage-day for each point of energy required. Thus, if an item has an energy cost of 100, it may be created by one mage in 100 days, two in 50 days, three in 34 days, and so on. Again, full eight-hour days of work are required. As for other types of ceremonial magic, all the caster's assistants must be present every day. Spectators may not help.

Example: Four mages are making a Stone Missile staff (see p. 156). This requires 400 points of energy. So the casting takes 400/4, or 100, days.

Each mage in the Circle must be present for each day of work. If a day's work is skipped or interrupted, two days will be required to make up for each day skipped. Loss of a mage simply ends the project! The final skill roll is made on the last day. No energy expenditure is required; the energy has been put in gradually as the spell progressed.

A *failed* roll means the enchantment simply didn't work. The time and energy are lost, as are the materials used in the spell. (Exception: If the item was already magical, it is unharmed, though *extra* materials are lost.) Note that, as with other ceremonial magic, a roll of 16 fails automatically.

This method can be combined with "energy for skill," p. 151, to let a mage take a *very* long time and make an item of very high Power.

USING A MAGIC ITEM

Magical items follow the rules given for the spell(s) they contain – see the Spell List. Most items *give the user the power to cast that spell*. Some let him cast the spell only on himself; others let him cast it on any subject. If a spell can be put into a magic item, this will be detailed at the end of the spell description. Unless specified otherwise:

Casting time is as described for the spell; high Power does not affect this.

No ritual is required unless specified for a particular item. In general, the user just wills it to work.

Energy cost is the same as for a normal casting of the spell, and is *not* affected by the item's Power (though an item may be "self-powered" to reduce the energy required to use it – see p. 160).

Success is determined normally, using the item's Power as the caster's *basic* skill and applying normal modifiers. Power is at -5 in low-mana areas.

The item can be used indefinitely – the magic does not "wear out."

All other effects are as described for normal use of the spell.

Only one person at a time can control a magic item. If two people are touching a magic item (struggling for control of a staff, for instance), only the first to touch it can use it. If one *can't* use it (e.g., because it is only for mages) his touching it doesn't count.

Resistance and Power: If a spell can be resisted when cast normally, it can be resisted when cast from a magic item. Roll a contest: the item's Power (see p. 152) vs. the subject's resistance for that spell. Therefore, items of high Power are harder to resist. And magic items are easier to resist in low-mana areas – their Power is reduced by 5.

"Always On" Items

Certain magical items are described as "always on." They must be worn or carried in order to work. These items don't let the wearer cast the spell; they automatically cast it *on the wearer* at no energy cost. If the spell is one which could be resisted if cast normally, a resistance roll may be made.

Picking an item up momentarily, to examine it, is not "wearing" it. But carrying it in your hand, or putting it on, is. As a rule, a beneficial item must be worn or touched in order to work, but a harmful one will affect you even if carried in your pocket.

If an arrow or dart is enchanted with hostile magic, it may be carried without harm. It only affects the person it sticks in! That person is "wearing" it until it is removed by a successful Physician or First Aid roll (requires one minute) or by brute force (does the same damage the missile initially did)!

The new owner of a magic item may not immediately learn its powers. Some effects (e.g., increased ST or DX) will be obvious immediately. Others (e.g., water-breathing) will

Powerstone Costs

Powerstones (see p. 161) are a special case, because a Powerstone is built up by a number of small castings, each requiring 20 energy. The size of a gem, in carats, gives the maximum strength it can have as a Powerstone – a 20-carat gem can become a ST 20 Powerstone, but no more.

We make the following assumptions:

Cost for each casting of the spell Powerstone: $20. Cost for a gem that is suitable for making a strength P Powerstone: $10 \times P^2 + $40 \times P$. Daily pay for an average enchanter mage: $25. Expected rate of return for money invested in Powerstones: 0.1% per day (36% per year).

The average cost of Powerstones, especially large ones, is increased by a cumulative factor which represents the chance that one of the castings will result in a critical failure, destroying the stone. For a Powerstone of ST 60, the chances are over 2 in 3 that the stone will be destroyed before it reaches the desired size! Thus, the *expected* cost to make a ST 60 Powerstone is more than three times that which would be given simply by adding the cost of the gem to the cost of casting the spell 60 times.

There is always a demand for good Powerstones without peculiar quirks (see p. 161), so retail magic-sellers always mark the price up. Typical retail prices are shown in the second column.

Size	Cost to make	Typical retail
1	80	150
2	175	300
3	300	500
4	450	900
5	620	1,200
6	850	1,600
7	1,050	2,000
8	1,350	2,500
9	1,650	3,100
10	2,000	4,000
12	2,750	5,500
15	4,250	8,200
20	7,700	15,000
25	12,500	24,000
30	19,000	40,000
35	28,000	58,000
40	39,000	80,000
45	54,000	110,000
50	72,000	150,000
60	120,000	250,000
70	195,000	500,000
80	305,000	850,000
90	460,000	1,200,000
100	680,000	2,000,000

Making Magic Items in a Campaign

Players will often want magic items which aren't available in the marketplace. One way to get these is to have them made by PC mages. "Quick and dirty" enchantments will be possible for less powerful items. But for most important items, the "slow and sure" method will be needed. This requires eight-hour days of work from all participating mages. But that does not take the character out of play. He may do other things while he's not working . . . or foes may interrupt him while he works.

The following rules apply to any mage involved in making a magic item by the "slow and sure" method:

(1) If interrupted while at work, he will be somewhat fatigued; roll 1 die to determine the amount of lost fatigue.

(2) If interrupted while at work, he must keep concentrating on his enchantment. Therefore, any other spell use will be at -3. Or he may stop concentrating – but then he loses the day's work.

(3) Time spent in making a magical item counts 50% as study of the Enchantment spell, and 50% as study of the spell being placed on the item.

(4) A wizard who is molested while *not* actively working on his enchantment is under *no* disadvantage, unless he has just quit work and is fatigued (the GM may decide this).

(5) A mage may work on only one enchantment at a time. He may not "work two shifts," either on the same or different items.

GMs do not have to permit the creation of PC wizards who do nothing but make magic items. Players who want such a wizard in their service must hire one!

Controlling PC Enchantment

GMs will probably want to limit the number of magic items in the campaign. Restricting magic items may cause players to decide to make their own. If the GM feels that any item is too easy to make, here are some ways to make it more difficult:

Rare materials: The item could require rare ingredients in addition to the energy and time. Attempting to get the needed materials could become an adventure in itself . . .

Side effects: After making the item, the PCs might discover that strange things happen when they try to use it. The GM could rule that additional obscure precautions or rituals are needed to make the item safe.

Additional expenses: The GM can rule that additional common but expensive materials (such as gems or rare metals) are needed to make the item, raising the cost to whatever level is necessary.

not be noticed until a situation occurs where they can take effect. In such a case, the GM should try not to drop inadvertent clues to the item's true nature!

For all "always on" items, unless specified otherwise: *Casting time* is irrelevant. The item does not let the wearer cast the spell; it puts the spell on *him.* "Hostile" magic items are sometimes designed to take effect over a period of about five minutes, so it is not immediately obvious that they are dangerous. Beneficial items work instantly.

Energy cost is zero.

The subject gets a resistance roll, if the spell is hostile and can normally be resisted.

The item can be used indefinitely; the effect lasts as long as the item is worn.

All other effects are as usual for that spell.

MAGICAL ENTITIES

There are many different kinds of spirits and magical entities; see *GURPS Fantasy Bestiary* and *GURPS Magic* for thorough listings. Two important sorts of entities are:

Demons

Demons are malign magical creatures, summoned from another plane by spells. They often appear because of magical backfires. When "summoned" thus, a demon attacks the caster and anyone else in sight, until it is killed. But a demon cannot injure a truly good or innocent person (GM's decision), though it can destroy his property.

The GM generates stats for the demon as he wishes. A simple formula for a demon that attacks with its claws only: ST = 3d; DX = 3d; IQ = 2d; HT = 4d; Move = 2d. Some demons may have magic spells or attack with weapons!

Elementals

Elemental spirits, or "elementals," are the embodiments of the elements: Earth, Air, Fire and Water. Spells to summon, control and create them are listed on p. 156.

Elementals will have DX and IQ no greater than 12, but ST and HT are unlimited.

Earth elementals have a +2 on any roll to resist control, and a -1 on reactions to most people (+1 to farmers, etc.). Move 3; DR2. Affected by all spells and weapons, but take only half damage from Fire and Water combat spells, and none from Air (except Lightning). Fight with their hands, doing Thrust/Crush damage for their ST.

Air elementals have +1 on any roll to resist control. Move 12. They are unaffected by material weapons, and attack by using Shape Air (p. 157) for knockback and nuisance.

Fire elementals, or "salamanders," have a -2 reaction to people in general, +2 to any proposal to *burn.* Move 6; no DR. Attack with hands; do Thrust-2 fire damage for their ST. The hex each occupies is a "fire hex." They take double damage from Water combat spells; *regain* 1 point of ST from a 1-die Fireball, and so on.

Water elementals react at -4 to proposals to set fires. Move: 4 out of water, 10 in water. No DR. Attack as a bare-handed human. Immune to Water spells; take double damage from Fire spells. Can merge with any large body of water, becoming invisible and regaining 1 HT per minute. Freezing them solid will immobilize them but not hurt them.

SPELL LIST

On the following pages are 97 magic spells. These are by no means all the possible spells; for much longer lists, see *GURPS Magic* and *GURPS Grimoire.* We have selected spells that are suitable for a beginning campaign. Each spell description includes:

Name of Spell and *Class(es)* it belongs to. A (VH) indicates a Very Hard spell; otherwise, it's Hard.

Description of Effect, and special rules. If any particular items are required, assume the spell uses them up unless the description states otherwise.

Duration: the time the spell's effect lasts. If maintained, it lasts for a time equal to the original duration. Some spells have an instantaneous effect, so no duration is given.

Cost: the energy (ST or HT) spent when the spell is cast. If given as *Base Cost,* it is the cost for each one-hex radius of an "area" spell – see p. 150. Some spells also have a cost to maintain. Those with an instantaneous effect can't be maintained.

Time to Cast: If no time is given, the spell requires *one second* of concentration and takes place at the beginning of the caster's next turn.

Prerequisites: Magery and/or IQ requirements, and other spells that must be known at a skill level of 12 or better before this spell may be studied.

Item: Type of permanent magical item that can be made with the spell, and special rules (if any). Energy costs to create it, and costs for required materials (if any). See p. 152 for rules on creating magical items, and p. 160 for the spells used. If there is no "Item" listing, no magic item can be made with the spell, at least as far as the PCs know.

ANIMAL SPELLS

These are the spells related to animal control and communication. None of these spells give their subjects any special powers; animals controlled will not be able to do anything they would normally be unable to do, but they will follow the caster's mental commands to the best of their abilities. Likewise, the ability to talk to an animal only lets you learn what the animal knows and understands.

These spells will not work on creatures of races which normally have IQ 8 or greater. All magical items of this college must depict the appropriate type of animal, or contain an inset tooth from that creature.

Beast-Soother   *Regular*

Lets the caster calm a single animal. The beast's reaction roll to the caster is improved by twice the energy put into the spell.
Duration: Permanent, until something disturbs animal.
Cost: 1 to 3.
Prerequisite: Persuasion or the Animal Empathy advantage.
Item: Staff, wand or jewelry. Energy cost to create: 600.

Beast Summoning   *Regular*

Lets caster call one creature of a named type (anything under IQ 8). Range does not matter for this spell. If the spell is successfully cast, the caster will know the location of the closest creature of the type, and how long it will take for that creature to come to him. It will move toward the caster as fast as it can, until the spell ends or the animal can see the caster. It will stay nearby, without attacking, until the spell ends. The summoned animal will then have a +1 on its reaction to the caster (only). Note that if the creature is attacked by the caster or someone near the caster, the spell will be broken.
Duration: 1 minute.
Cost: 3 to cast; 2 to maintain. To call *many* animals, double the cost of the spell. All creatures within a certain area (usually about a 10-mile radius; more for a very successful spell) will be drawn. The time they take to arrive depends on the speed at which they can travel. If the spell ends before they arrive, they will turn and go about their business.
Prerequisite: Beast-Soother.

Item: Staff, wand or jewelry. Energy cost to create: 400 for an item that summons one particular species, or 800 for an item that can summon any beast.

Reptile Control   *Regular; Resisted by IQ*

Lets the caster control the actions of one large reptile (any size) or a group of small ones, up to about 100 lbs. total. Concentration is required. This spell will not work on an intelligent being (IQ 8 or more).
Duration: 1 minute.
Cost: 4 to cast; 2 to maintain.
Prerequisite: Beast-Soother.
Item: Staff, wand or jewelry. Energy cost to create: 400 for an item that controls one particular species, or 800 for an item that can control any type of reptile.

Bird Control   *Regular; Resisted by IQ*

Lets the caster control the actions of one large bird (any size) or a flock of small ones, up to about 100 lbs. total. Concentration is required. This spell will not work on an intelligent being (IQ 8 or more).
Duration: 1 minute.
Cost: 4 to cast; 2 to maintain.
Prerequisite: Beast-Soother.
Item: Staff, wand or jewelry. Energy cost to create: 400 for an item that controls one particular species, or 800 for an item that can control any type of bird.

Mammal Control   *Regular; Resisted by IQ*

Lets the caster control the actions of one large mammal (any size) or a group of small ones, up to about 100 lbs. total. Concentration is required. This spell will not work on an intelligent being (IQ 7 or more).
Duration: 1 minute.
Cost: 5 to cast; 3 to maintain.
Prerequisite: Beast-Soother or Charm.
Item: Staff, wand or jewelry. Energy cost to create: 600 for an item that controls one particular species, or 1,200 for an item that can control any type of mammal.

COMMUNICATION AND EMPATHY SPELLS

Sense Life   *Information; Area*

Tells the caster if there is any life in the subject area, and gives a general impression (on a good roll) of what kind. Caster can also specify he is looking for a specific sort of life; plants, elves, redheaded girls, or a named person whom the caster knows.
Base Cost: 1/2 (minimum 1).
Item: Staff, wand or jewelry. Energy cost to create: 80.

Sense Foes   *Information; Area*

Tells the caster if the subject has hostile intent, and what the degree of hostility is. Can be cast on one person, or a whole area. If cast over an area, it will only detect that *someone* is hostile, but not *who*.
Base Cost: 1 (minimum 2).
Item: Staff, wand or jewelry. Energy cost to create: 200.

Sense Emotion   *Regular*

Lets the caster know what emotions the subject is feeling at the moment. Works on any living being, but not much use except on intelligent creatures! Will also tell how loyal the subject is to the caster (see *Loyalty*, p. 195).
Cost: 2.
Prerequisite: Sense Foes.
Item: Staff, wand or jewelry. Energy cost to create: 300.

Truthsayer   *Information; Resisted by IQ*

Tells whether the subject is lying or not. May be cast in two ways: (a) to tell whether the subject has told *any* lies in the last five minutes; (b) to tell whether the *last* thing the subject said was a lie. May also give an indication of how great the lie is. If caster is not touching subject, calculate range as for a regular spell.
Cost: 2.
Prerequisite: Sense Emotion.
Item: Crown, helmet or other headgear. Energy cost to create: 500.

Mind-Reading   *Regular; Resisted by IQ*

Lets the caster read the subject's mind. Works on any living thing, but most useful on intelligent creatures. Detects only *surface thoughts* (what the subject is thinking at that moment). The subject is not aware his mind is being read, except in case of a critical failure. Modifiers: if caster does not know the subject's *native* language, -2 to skill; if subject is of a different race, -2 ; if subject is totally alien, -4 or more!
Duration: 1 minute.
Cost: 4 to cast; 2 to maintain.
Time to cast: 10 seconds.
Prerequisite: Truthsayer.
Item: Crown, helmet or other headgear. Usable only by a mage. Energy cost 1,000.

Persuasion   *Regular; Resisted by IQ*

Used when a reaction roll is required, this spell makes the subject (one intelligent creature – IQ 8 or better) likelier to react favorably.
Duration: 1 minute.
Cost: Twice the bonus to be added to the roll.
Prerequisite: Sense Emotion.
Item: Cap, crown, helmet or other headgear. Energy cost to create: 1,000. Must include a purple jewel (garnet or amethyst) worth at least $200. Usable only by a mage.

ELEMENTAL SPELLS

There are four different colleges of Elemental magic: Earth, Air, Fire and Water.

EARTH SPELLS

These spells concern themselves with the element Earth. Typically, they are very powerful, but also very fatiguing; Earth is the hardest and most obstinate of elements. In all these spells, one "hex" of earth, where it matters, is assumed to be six feet deep. None of these spells will affect stone or metal unless the description specifically says so.

Seek Earth   Information

This is the basic Earth spell. It tells the caster the *direction and approximate distance* of the nearest significant amount of any one type of earth, metal or stone. Use the long-distance modifiers (p. 151). Any known sources of that material may be excluded if the caster specifically mentions them before beginning.

Cost: 3.

Time to cast: 10 seconds.

Item: A forked stick with an ounce of the desired earth/stone/metal set in the tip; each stick will find only that earth. Energy cost to create: 50 energy, and cash to buy an ounce of the material sought.

Shape Earth   Regular

Lets the caster move earth about and shape it into any form. If the form is stable (e.g., a hill), it will remain permanently after shaping. An unstable form (e.g., a column or wall) will last only while the spell continues – no special concentration is required – and then collapse.

Earth *moved* with this spell travels at only 2 hexes per turn. It can harm no one except by flowing over an immobile person and burying him. If earth is moved into a person's hex – or *out of* his hex, to create a hole – that person may move normally on the next turn, to escape. Only if he fails to do so will he be buried.

Anyone buried by this spell may try to claw his way out of the loose earth. One roll, at ST-4, is allowed every turn. GMs may make this roll harder if a character is buried under more than a hex-worth of earth! See *Holding Your Breath*, p. 91.

Duration: 1 minute.

Cost: 2 per hex of earth shaped; 1 per hex to maintain.

Prerequisite: Seek Earth.

Item: Staff, wand, jewelry or digging tool. Energy cost to create: 200.

Earth to Stone   Regular

Turns an item of earth or clay into hard stone (but not gemstone).

Duration: Permanent.

Cost: 3 for an item up to 20 lbs.; 5 for a larger item up to 1 hex, plus 5 more for each additional hex.

Prerequisites: Magery, Shape Earth.

Item: Staff, wand or jewelry. Energy cost to create: 300.

Stone to Earth   Regular

Turns any kind of stone (including gemstone) into simple earth. Must be cast on a whole stone or block, rather than a part of it.

Duration: Permanent.

Cost: Double that of Earth to Stone.

Prerequisite: Earth to Stone *or* any four Earth spells.

Item: Staff, wand or jewelry. Energy cost to create: 400.

Create Earth   Regular

Lets the caster create good, solid earth where none existed before. This earth must be created in contact with the Earth itself – not hanging in the air or floating in the sea!

Duration: Permanent.

Cost: 4 per hex to create earth from nothingness (to fill a pit, for instance), or 2 per hex to solidify mud into good earth.

Prerequisite: Earth to Stone.

Item: Staff or wand. Energy cost to create: 500.

Stone Missile   Missile

Lets caster create a ball of stone and fire it from his hand. When it hits, it does crushing damage and vanishes. This spell has SS 13, Acc +2, 1/2D 40, Max 80.

Cost: From 1 to 3; the missile does 1d + 1 damage for each energy point.

Time to cast: 1 for each point of energy used.

Prerequisite: Create Earth.

Item: Staff or wand – missile is fired from end of item. Usable only by a mage. Energy cost to create: 400.

Earth to Air   Regular

This spell turns earth or stone into air; it can therefore be very valuable to one trapped underground. It is also considered an Air spell.

Duration: Permanent.

Cost: 1 to transform a cubic foot of earth/stone to air, giving enough air for one person to breathe for 1 minute – this is about 1 1/3 six-foot-deep hexes of earth or stone per hour. To transform large quantities of earth or stone at once, the cost is 8 per hex.

Time to cast: 2 seconds.

Prerequisites: Create Air (p. 157), Shape Earth.

Item: Staff, wand or jewelry. Usable only by mages. Stone to be transformed must be touched by item. Energy cost to create: 750 energy; item must include $1,000 in jewels.

Earth Vision   Regular

This spell lets the subject see through the earth – to find caves, bodies of ore, buried treasure, entombed victims, etc. Earth and uncut stone (up to 50 yards deep) are transparent to the subject, wherever he looks. Metal is *not* transparent; cut stone, bricks, etc.,are also not transparent. Thus, this spell won't let you look through castle walls.

Duration: 30 seconds.

Cost: 2 per 10 yards of depth to cast; the same to maintain.

Prerequisite: Shape Earth.

Item: Any. Energy cost to create: 400.

Elemental Spirit Spells

The following descriptions of Earth Elemental spells also hold true for the corresponding Air, Fire and Water spells. For descriptions of the nature and abilities of the four types of elementals, see p. 154.

Summon (Earth) Elemental   Special

This is a different spell for each of the four elements. It allows the caster to call a nearby elemental – *if one exists.* Air and Water elementals may travel several miles within their element to answer a summoning, but Earth elementals will come only a mile, and Fire elementals will travel only a hundred yards from a fiery place. In general, the GM should assume that an elemental is available if the location is appropriate, *unless* the scenario or situation requires that elementals are opportunely absent. The GM determines the elemental's attributes – by rolling 2 dice for each, if the plot of the adventure does not require some specific sort of elemental. A very successful summoning may call several elementals – on a critical success, roll 1d+1 for number called, and roll 3 dice for ST and HT.

The summoned elemental is *not* under the caster's control, but must remain for one hour unless it is dismissed – or destroys the caster. Note that a dismissal does not *guarantee* the elemental will leave; if it is hostile, or simply curious, it may choose to stay!

The caster may question the summoned elemental, request a service, etc. A *reaction roll* is immediately made to see how the elemental(s) feel toward the wizard. Fire elementals always react at -2. On a good reaction, an elemental will cooperate for an hour – no longer – and then vanish. (When summoning elementals, remember that they can be bargained with – if you are wise enough to know what an elemental might desire.)

If the summoning spell is repeated, roll 1 die. On a 1-3, a new elemental appears. On a 4 or 5, the same elemental appears. On a 6, there are now no elementals available. If the same elemental is summoned again within a week, it will react at a -4.

Duration: One hour. May not be maintained.

Cost: 4.

Time to cast: 30 seconds. The elemental appears in 2d minutes.

Prerequisites: Magery; at least 8 other spells of the appropriate element, *or* 4 spells of the element and another Summon Elemental spell.

Item: Staff, wand or jewelry decorated with appropriate elemental images – a different enchantment is required for each of the four types. Energy cost to create: 800 energy, $1,300 gold and platinum.

Control (Earth) Elemental   Regular; Resisted by higher of ST or IQ

Lets the caster control all actions of a single elemental while the spell continues. For direct control, the elemental must remain within the caster's view. If the elemental is simply told to leave, it will do so. If it is to be sent to do a task, rather than controlled directly, its IQ must be sufficient (GM's decision) to comprehend its instructions!

This spell can also be used as an information spell, to judge the four attributes of that type of elemental (within 15 feet). A successful roll is required, but there is no energy cost.

Duration: One minute.

Cost: ⅛ the total of the elemental's four attributes (round up) to start; half that amount (round up) per minute thereafter.

Time to cast: 2 seconds.

Prerequisite: Summon Elemental for the appropriate element.

Item: Staff, wand or jewelry decorated with appropriate elemental images – a different enchantment is required for each of the four types. Does not let user cast spell; gives a +2 on any attempt to use the spell. Noncumulative. Energy cost to create: 1,000 energy; item must include $1,300 in gold and platinum.

Create (Earth) Elemental   Special

Lets the caster create a spirit of the appropriate element. Its maximum IQ and DX are 12 each; there is no limit to ST and HT. There is no minimum to any of the four attributes, though a very stupid elemental will not understand complex commands. A newly created elemental will serve the caster obediently for one hour. At the end of that time, roll a contest between the caster's skill with the spell, and the elemental's combined IQ and ST. If the caster wins, the elemental will serve for a further hour – and then another contest will be required, and so on. When the caster loses, the elemental escapes control and flees (or attacks, on a very bad reaction).

Cost: 1/4 the total of the elemental's 4 attributes. *Double* this cost if cast in a place inappropriate to the element being invoked – e.g., creating a water elemental near a volcano.

Time to cast: Seconds equal to the total attributes of spirit created.

Prerequisite: Magery 2, appropriate Control Elemental.

AIR SPELLS

These are the spells dealing with the Air element. A "hex" of air may be assumed to be a volume of air 1 hex by 6 feet, composed of normal breathing air at 1 atmosphere of pressure.

Purify Air   Area

This is the basic Air spell. It removes all impurities from the air in the subject hex. It is often used to neutralize the effects of poisonous gas or vapors. Note that a room full of smoke may safely be purified one section at a time – but truly deadly vapors must all be removed at once, or some may escape. This spell will also turn old "stale" air into fresh breathable air. One hex of air, if not renewed from the outside, will last 45 minutes for one person at rest. This time will be less for multiple persons or someone violently exercising (GM's discretion).

Duration: Works instantly. Purification is permanent.

Base Cost: 1. Cannot be maintained; must be recast.

Item: Staff, wand or jewelry. Energy cost to create: 50.

Create Air   Area

This spell manufactures air where none exists. Cast where there is already air, it will produce an outward breeze lasting for about five seconds. Cast in a vacuum, it will instantly create breathable air. Cast within earth, stone or other material, it will fill any empty spaces with air, but will not burst the stone. Cast underwater, it makes bubbles!

Duration: 5 seconds. Air created is permanent.

Base Cost: 1 (for 1 hex of air at normal air pressure).

Prerequisite: Purify Air.

Item: Staff, wand or jewelry. Energy cost to create: 200.

Shape Air   Regular

Lets caster create movements of air over a small area. The wind starts at the "subject" hex; it blows in a stream 1 hex wide, for a distance in hexes equal to 5 times the energy put into it, and then dissipates. This may cause "knockback" (p. 106) on someone it hits; roll 1 die for every full 2 points of energy in the spell, each turn the wind hits them. 8 points of "knockback" will push someone back 1 hex.

Duration: 1 minute.

Cost: 1 to 10. 1 produces a gentle breeze; 4 a wind; 6 a heavy wind; 8 or more a violent blast. Cost to maintain is the same as to cast.

Prerequisite: Create Air.

Item: Staff, wand or jewelry. Energy cost to create: 200.

Predict Weather   Information

Lets the caster forecast the weather accurately for a given location over a given time. This forecast does *not* take magical meddling into account, or predict the actions of other spellcasters!

Cost: 2 times the length of the forecast, in days. Double the cost for a location outside the general area (say, over the horizon). Quadruple the cost for a place on another continent. Weather on other planets or planes cannot be predicted with this spell.

Time to cast: 5 seconds per day forecast.

Prerequisites: At least 4 Air spells.

Walk on Air   Regular

Air behaves as though solid under the subject's feet; thus, he can walk (or run) across chasms, or walk up and down imaginary "stairs." If the subject falls for any reason (e.g., injury), the spell will be broken! If the spell is recast immediately, he will fall for only 1 second (about 5 yards) and will then "land" on the air (taking 1 die damage) – unless he hits ground before then. If you're 10 feet over a lava pit, too bad!

Duration: 1 minute.

Cost: 3 to cast; 2 to maintain.

Prerequisite: Shape Air.

Item: Staff, wand, jewelry, or shoes. Works for wearer only. Energy cost to create: 500 energy. $1,000 in materials.

Breathe Water   Regular

Lets the subject breathe water as though it were air. Subject does *not* lose the ability to breathe ordinary air!

Duration: 1 minute.

Cost: 4 to cast; 2 to maintain.

Prerequisites: Create Air, Destroy Water (p. 159).

Item: Clothing or jewelry. Energy cost to create: 400.

Clouds   Area

Creates or dispels outdoor cloud cover, as the caster chooses.

Duration: 10 minutes, after which normal clouds leave/return unless spell is maintained.

Base Cost: ¹/20. Same cost to maintain.

Time to cast: 10 seconds.

Prerequisite: At least 4 Water spells and 4 Air spells.

Item: Staff, wand or jewelry. Energy cost to create: 300.

Rain   Area

Creates (or prevents) 1 inch of rain, in a normal outdoor setting.

Duration: 1 hour.

Base Cost: ¹/10. Cost to maintain is the same per hour. Cost to make rain doubles in a desert or other area (GM's determination) where rain is unnatural. Cost to prevent rain doubles in a naturally rainy or swampy area.

Time to cast: 1 minute.
Prerequisite: Clouds.
   Item: Staff or wand. Energy cost to create: 600. Can be used only by a mage. Must be kept in water when not in use; loses powers if it stays dry for more than an hour.

Earth to Air   *Regular*
   As listed under Earth, p. 156.

Lightning   *Missile*
   Lets spellcaster shoot a bolt of lightning from his fingertip. Not as destructive as Fireball, but accurate at longer ranges. It has SS 13, Acc +3, ½D 50, Max 100. Tends to short out electronic equipment when used in a high-tech environment. However, a lightning bolt *cannot* be fired through a metal grid, between bars, from within a car, etc. – it will jump to the metal and be lost. Metal armor will not protect well against this spell – treat any metal armor as PD0, DR1.

   Lightning can have unpredictable effects. The GM may, for instance, allow a wizard to shoot a lightning bolt into a metal floor. This would not electrocute those on it, but could shock them all, injuring concentration and doing slight (perhaps 1 hit?) damage. GMs may encourage creative use of lightning until it becomes a nuisance . . .
   Cost: Any amount from 1 to 3; the bolt does 1d-1 damage for each energy point spent in casting it.
   Time to cast: 1 to 3 seconds (the caster's fingers will be seen to sparkle as the spell builds up).
   Prerequisites: At least 6 other Air spells.
   Item: Staff or wand – bolt is fired from end of item. Energy cost to create: 800; item must inlcued $1,200 for platinum decorations. Usable only by a mage.

Summon Air Elemental, Control Air Elemental, Create Air Elemental – see pp. 156-157

FIRE SPELLS

   These are spells for use and control of the element Fire. Any time a "hex" of fire is mentioned, it is assumed that the whole hex is filled with fire (see *Flame*, p. 129.). If the volume of an area of flame is important, assume a hex of flame shoots 6 feet high.
   Burning Clothes: Clothes being worn are hard to burn. In general, 4 hits of fire injury at once, or Ignite Fire at its third level of effect, will set fire to part of the victim's clothing. This is very distracting (-2 to DX) and does 1d-4 damage each turn. Anyone may put out the fire by beating it with their hands (takes 1 turn if a DX roll is made).
   Ten hits of fire damage at once will ignite *all* the victim's clothes, producing a human torch and doing 1d-1 damage per turn. This can only be put out if the victim rolls on the ground for 3 seconds or jumps in the water. The victim can do nothing else until the fire is out, unless he is protected (e.g., by Resist Fire). If a wooden shield takes 10 or more fire hits in one turn, the bearer is at -2 DX and 1d-5 damage per turn until he gets rid of it.
   These guidelines assume ordinary clothing. Armor is good protection against fire attacks; clothes under armor are almost impossible to ignite and will not stay lit! Clothing worn over armor (e.g., a surcoat) could be ignited, but the armor would protect from the burning effects as per pp. 129-130. On the other hand, fancy dresses or lace cuffs would ignite very easily.

   Magic Items: All magical items involving Fire spells must include a ruby; the size of the ruby depends on the spell. If an item has several spells on it, it needs only one jewel, of a size sufficient for the most powerful spell.

Ignite Fire   *Regular*
   This is the basic Fire spell. It produces a single spot of heat, and is used to set fire to a *readily* flammable object. It works best on paper and cloth, and will not affect any item that would not burn in an ordinary fire. In particular, it will *not* set fire to a living being! Once ignited, the fire burns normally.
   Duration: One second.
   Cost: Depends on the amount of heat desired. Cost to maintain is the same as the original cost.
   1 – for an effect as though a match had been held to the subject: will light a candle, pipe or tinder in one second.
   2 – for an effect as though a torch had been held to the subject: will ignite paper or loose cloth in one second, ordinary clothes being worn in four seconds.
   3 – for an effect as though a blowtorch had been held to the subject: will ignite dry firewood or clothes being worn in one second, leather in two seconds, heavy wood in six.
   4 – for an effect as though burning magnesium or phosphorus had been held to the subject: will ignite coal in one second, heavy wood in two seconds.
   Item: Staff, wand or jewelry. Energy cost to create: 100; item must include a small ruby worth $50.

Create Fire   *Area*
   As for Ignite Fire, but requires no fuel. Produces up to a hex of flame (or, in midair, a sphere of flame which falls). This is real fire, which will eventually ignite any flammable objects it touches. Cannot be cast within rock, foes, etc.
   Duration: 1 minute.
   Base Cost: 2. Cost to maintain: Half the cost to create. No maintenance required if there is fuel for the fire to ignite.
   Prerequisite: Ignite Fire.
   Item: Staff, wand or jewelry. Energy cost to create: 300; item must include a ruby worth $200.

Shape Fire   *Area*
   Lets caster control the shape of any flame. A natural fire will not move to a place that it can't burn, but flame made with the Create Fire spell needs no fuel and can move. A flame keeps its same volume. Each shape-change requires a second of concentration by the caster, and *moving* a flame requires constant concentration – but once shaped, the flame will keep that shape until the spell expires, without concentration. Maximum speed is 5 yards per second, moving on the caster's turn. However, if the fire in one hex is "shaped" to spread out across two hexes, it will only do half damage to those who enter the hex. One hex spread into three hexes does ⅓ damage, and so on.
   Duration: 1 minute.
   Base Cost: 2. Cost to maintain: Half the cost to cast.
   Prerequisite: Ignite Fire.
   Item: Staff, wand or jewelry. Energy cost to create: 400; item must include a ruby worth $300.

Extinguish Fire   *Regular*
   Puts out a hex of fire – or a smaller area, if necessary. A larger area can be affected at an increased cost in fatigue. Affects ordinary and magical fires, but not molten steel, lava, etc.
   Duration: Once out, a fire stays out.
   Cost: 3 per hex extinguished.
   Prerequisite: Ignite Fire.
   Item: Staff, wand or jewelry. Energy cost to create: 400; item must include a ruby worth $300 *and* a black onyx worth $100.

Heat   *Regular*
   This spell increases the heat of an object by up to that which could be achieved by a smith's forge. It does not necessarily produce fire, though most things will burn if heated enough. Useful for cooking, etc. Heat will be radiated away normally. (GMs, use this as a guideline for playable effects – don't try to turn the spell into a physics exercise.)
   Any wizard planning to make extensive use of this spell should arm himself with a list of the melting points of various materials. The spell can have drawbacks. If you were in jail, you might melt your way through the bars . . . but radiated heat would probably broil you first.
   Duration: 1 minute.

Cost: 1 for an object up to the size of a fist, 2 for up to a cubic foot, 3 for a one-hex object, 3 more for each additional hex. Continuing the spell costs the same as the original casting, per minute.

Time to cast: 1 minute. Each minute raises the target's temperature by 20°. Time can be halved by doubling the energy spent, and so on, but one cannot use *less* energy per minute for a *slower* heating.

Prerequisites: Create Fire, Shape Fire.

Item: Staff, wand or jewelry. Energy cost to create: 400; item must include a ruby worth $300.

Cold   *Regular*

The reverse of the above spell. Reduces the temperature of any object to absolute zero (if maintained long enough).

Duration, cost and time to cast: As for Heat. Each minute lowers the target's temperature by 20°.

Prerequisite: Heat.

Item: Staff, wand or jewelry. Energy cost to create: 400; items must include a $300 ruby *and* a $300 sapphire.

Resist Fire   *Regular*

The subject (person, creature or object), and anything he carries, become immune to the effects of heat and fire (but not electricity).

Duration: 1 minute.

Cost: 2 per person or 1-hex area; 1 per minute to maintain. Cost doubles if subject must resist a blast furnace or volcano; cost triples if subject must resist the heat of a star, nuclear bomb, etc. Only the first level of protection is necessary against combat-type Fire spells.

Prerequisites: Extinguish Fire, Cold.

Item: Staff, wand or jewelry. Affects wearer only. Energy cost to create: 800; must include a ruby worth $500 and a black onyx worth $200.

Fireball   *Missile*

Lets caster throw a ball of fire from his hand. When it strikes something, it vanishes in a puff of flame which may ignite flammable objects. It has SS 13, Acc +1, 1/2D 25, Max 50.

Cost: Any amount from 1 to 3; the fireball does 1 die damage for each energy point spent in casting it.

Time to cast: 1 to 3 seconds.

Prerequisite: Magery, Create Fire, Shape Fire.

Item: Staff or wand – ball is fired from end of item. Energy cost to create: 800; must include a ruby worth $400. Usable only by a mage.

Summon Fire Elemental, Control Fire Elemental, Create Fire Elemental – *see pp. 156-157*

WATER SPELLS

These are the spells for use and control of the element Water. Note that, although the human body is almost entirely water, these spells will *not* affect the water in a human body (or any other living creature) unless specifically noted. One hex of water, one foot deep, is about 60 gallons, and can put out one hex of fire.

Seek Water   *Information*

This is the basic Water spell. It lets the caster determine the direction, distance, and general nature of the nearest significant source of water. Use long-distance modifiers – p. 151. Any known sources of water may be excluded if the caster specifically mentions them before beginning. Requires a forked stick; -3 to skill if this is not available.

Cost: 2.

Item: A forked stick (may also be carved of bone or ivory). Energy cost to create: 40 energy, must include $300 of spell materials.

Purify Water   *Special*

Lets the caster remove all impurities from water, by pouring it through any hoop or ring (or, in a pinch, his own fingers) into a container. Only one skill roll is required as long as the flow continues.

Duration: Purified water stays pure unless re-contaminated.

Cost: 1 per gallon purified.

Time to cast: Usually 5 to 10 seconds per gallon, unless a large container and ring are being used.

Prerequisite: Seek Water.

Item: A hoop of bone or ivory. Energy cost to create: 50.

Create Water   *Regular*

Lets the caster create pure water out of nothing. This water may appear in any of several forms. It may appear within a container, or as a globe in midair (it falls immediately). Or it may appear as a dense mist of droplets; in this form, one gallon of water will extinguish one hex of fire. Water cannot be created (for instance) inside a foe to drown him!

Duration: The created water is permanent.

Cost: 2 per gallon created.

Prerequisite: Purify Water.

Item: Staff, wand or jewelry. Energy cost to create: 200.

Destroy Water   *Area*

Causes water (in any form) to vanish, leaving a vacuum and/or specks of dry impurities. Good for drying things out, saving a drowning victim, etc. (If more water is all around, it will of course rush in to fill the hole.) *Cannot* be used as a "dehydrating" attack on a foe.

Duration: Permanent.

Base Cost: 3. In deep water, a hex is only 2 yards deep.

Prerequisite: Create Water.

Item: Wand, staff or jewelry. Energy cost to create: 300.

Shape Water   *Regular*

Lets the caster sculpt water (or ice or steam) into any form, and even move it about. Once given a shape, the water will hold it without further concentration, until the spell ends. Water moved with this spell will travel at 3 hexes per turn.

A useful shape is a Wall of Water to stop fiery attacks. Twenty gallons will create a six-foot-high wall across 1 hex. This will stop fireballs and ordinary fire; it will do 2 dice of damage to any fire elemental that penetrates it. Twenty gallons of water is about 2.5 cubic feet, or 160 lbs.

Duration: 1 minute.

Cost: 1 per 20 gal. shaped; 1 (for the whole shaping) to maintain.

Time to cast: 2 seconds.

Prerequisite: Create Water.

Item: Staff, wand or jewelry. Energy cost to create: 400.

Breathe Water   *Regular*

As listed under Air Spells, p. 157.

Walk on Water   *Regular*

Lets the subject walk on water as though it were land. If the water is moving, the GM may assess a DX penalty for anything attempted while on the water. If the water is choppy or wildly moving, a DX roll (perhaps with a substantial penalty) is required each turn, or the subject will fall. Only a critical failure will break the spell.

Duration: 1 minute.

Cost: 3 to cast; 2 to maintain.

Time to cast: 4 seconds.

Prerequisite: Shape Water.

Item: Staff, wand, jewelry or clothing. Works only for wearer. Energy cost to create: 500.

Fog   *Area*

Creates an area of dense fog. Even 1 hex of fog will block vision. Flaming weapons and missiles lose their extra power in fog. Entering *each* hex of fog does 1 point of damage to Fire elementals, and subtracts 1 point from the damage a Fireball will do when it hits. However, no amount of fog will extinguish a fire.

Duration: 1 minute.

Base Cost: 2; half this to maintain.

Prerequisite: Shape Water.

Item: Staff, wand or jewelry. Energy cost to create: 300.

Ice Sphere — Missile

Lets caster throw a ball of ice from his hand. When it strikes, it does crushing damage and vanishes in a gout of water. A 1-die Ice Sphere will also extinguish 1 hex of fire, if accurately aimed. It has SS 13, Acc +2, 1/2D 40, Max 80.

Cost: Any amount from 1 to 3; does 1 die damage for each energy point spent in casting it, or *double* damage to creatures of fire.

Time to cast: 1 to 3 seconds.

Prerequisite: Shape Water.

Item: Staff or wand – ball is fired from end. Energy cost to create: 400; must be tipped by a $500 sapphire. Usable only by a mage.

Rain — Area

As listed under *Air*, p. 157.

Summon Water Elemental, Control Water Elemental, Create Water Elemental – see pp. 156-157

ENCHANTMENT SPELLS

These are the spells used to make and unmake permanently magical items. They can ony be cast by ceremonial magic (see p. 151).

Enchant (VH) — Enchantment

This is the basic Enchantment spell. If any spell is to be placed on an item, the caster must *also* know the Enchant spell. This is also a *prerequisite* for all spells of the College of Enchantment except Scroll.

When an item is enchanted, the caster's spell roll is determined by the *lower* of his skills with this spell and the specific spell being placed on the item. If the caster has assistants, their skills with both spells must be 15 or greater, but the roll is based on the *caster's* skill.

Duration: All magic items are permanent until destroyed or the enchantment is removed – see below.

Cost and Time: See pp. 152-153.

Prerequisites: Magery 2, and at least one spell from each of 10 other colleges.

Scroll — Enchantment

Lets the caster write a magical scroll embodying any spell of the other Colleges. Read aloud by a mage who understands its language, this scroll will cast the spell *once.* Its power is then lost and the writing vanishes. Reading a scroll requires *twice* the normal casting time for the spell; the mage reading the scroll pays the normal energy cost. No skill roll is required when the spell is read, *unless* the spell is resisted. In that case, roll using the skill level of the mage who wrote the scroll.

A scroll can be read *silently,* to see what it says. Any mage who understands the language will know what spell it is supposed to be. This does not cast the spell!

Spells may be written on any material; parchment is usual. Damage to a scroll does not affect it as long as the scroll is legible.

Time to cast: The number of days needed to write a scroll is equal to the energy cost required to cast the spell originally (base cost for area spells), not counting any bonuses for skill. Multiply this by $25 to get the normal market value of the scroll. *Example:* The Rear Vision spell normally costs 3 energy to cast. A Rear Vision scroll would take 3 full days to write, and would normally cost $75. At the end of the writing time, the GM rolls against the writer's skill with Scroll or the spell being written – whichever is lower. A successful roll means the spell is good. A failure means the scroll will not work. A critical failure means it will cast a flawed spell!

Duration: As long as the spell would normally last. The mage who read the scroll can maintain the spell, if it could normally be maintained.

Prerequisite: Magery, Literacy. A mage may not write a scroll for a spell he does not know.

Remove Enchantment — Enchantment

Takes one enchantment spell off the subject item. Does not affect other enchantments on that same item. Exception: A failed attempt to remove a "limiting" enchantment will remove all enchantments from the item.

Skill modifiers: -3 if the caster does not know how to cast the enchantment he is trying to remove. -3 if he does not know exactly what that spell is. -3 for each other spell on the item. These are cumulative.

Duration: Removal is permanent.

Cost: 100, or 1/10 the cost to place the enchantment originally, whichever is more.

Time to cast: as per Enchantment (pp. 140).

Prerequisite: Enchant.

Power — Enchantment

Makes a magic item "self-powered," partially or completely. That is, it decreases the energy required to use that item. The extra energy is drawn directly from the surrounding mana. Self-powered items are in great demand, because they do not fatigue their users.

If an item has 1 point of self-power, that item's wearer spends 1 less point of energy to *cast* or to *maintain* the spell. Example: A ring of Flight has 1 point of self-power. It normally costs 5 to cast this spell and 3 per minute to maintain it. But with the self-power, it costs only 4 to cast and 2 per minute to maintain!

This assumes the area has normal mana. In a low-mana area, only half as much power is produced (round down). In a high-mana or very-high-mana area, double the amount of power provided. A self-powered item can never provide "extra" power, though.

If an item has enough self-power that the cost to maintain is 0, it may be treated as "always on" after the cost to cast is paid – but the wearer must still stay awake, etc., to maintain the spell normally. But if an item has enough self-power that the cost to *cast* is zero, the item is "always on" for all purposes, and requires no conscious maintenance of any kind! The owner may still turn it off if he wishes.

Energy cost to create: 500 each for the 1st and 2nd points of self-power, 1,000 for the 3rd, and double for each additional point. May be re-cast at a higher level, as per Accuracy (below).

Prerequisites: Enchant, Recover Strength.

Weapon Enchantments

Unless specified otherwise, the subject of any of these spells must be a weapon. The last one to pick the item up is its "owner." All are permanent and do not require the weapon-user to spend energy.

Accuracy — Enchantment

Makes the subject weapon more likely to hit, by adding to user's effective skill. The Accuracy spell can add from +1 to +3 to skill.

Energy cost to cast: Depends on the bonus. +1: 250. +2: 1,000. +3: 5,000. *Divide* cost by 10 if subject is a missile – e.g., an arrow +3 to hit would require only 500 energy.

If a weapon already has this spell at a low level, a caster may recast the spell at a higher level (making the weapon more accurate). The energy cost for the new spell is the difference between the levels.

Prerequisites: Enchant, and at least 5 Air spells.

Puissance — Enchantment

Makes the subject weapon do extra damage when it hits. The spell increases *basic* damage; enchanted weapons are more likely to penetrate armor.

Energy cost to cast: Depends on the bonus. +1: 250. +2: 1,000. +3: 5,000. *Double* cost if subject is a missile weapon. *Divide* cost by 10 if subject is a missile (e.g., an arrow). Note that this spell may be recast at a higher level as per Accuracy (above).

Prerequisites: Enchant, and at least 5 Earth spells.

Armor Enchantments

These spells work only on clothing, armor and shields. They are "always on," and are excellent protection. The drawback is that when the item is damaged badly enough, the spell also vanishes. Keep track of the number of times the item is *penetrated* by enemy blows. When it has been penetrated (DR× 5) times, using *natural* DR, it is damaged enough that the enchantment leaves. If a piece of clothing has no natural DR – e.g., a cotton shirt enchanted into armor – it loses its power after the fifth penetration.

Ordinary repairs may fix the item but will *not* count against the number of penetrations for purposes of deciding when the enchantment wears off. However, the Repair spell *will* accomplish this.

If the advanced armor rules are used, armor may be enchanted and bought by the piece. Costs for pieces: 40% of full for the torso (30% for front only!); 10% per pair for arms, legs, hands or feet; and 20% for the head.

Fortify   Enchantment
Adds to the damage resistance of the item upon which it is cast. DR may be increased by up to 5 with this spell. If you are building armor part by part, each item's enchantment protects only itself, and several Fortified items may be worn. If you use "generic" armor, use Fortify on the torso armor; it adds DR wherever the user is hit.
Energy cost to cast: 50 for DR +1, 200 for DR +2, 800 for DR +3, 3,000 for DR +4, 8,000 for DR +5. The spell can be recast to strengthen it, as per Accuracy (p. 160).

Prerequisite: Enchant.
Item: Clothing or armor (but not a shield).

Deflect   Enchantment
Adds to the passive defense of the item upon which it is cast. PD may be increased by up to 5 with this spell. If you are building armor part by part, each item's enchantment protects only itself, and several items with Deflect may be worn. If you are using "generic" armor, use Deflect on the torso armor; it adds to PD wherever the wearer is hit.
Energy cost to cast: 100 for PD +1, 500 for PD +2, 2,000 for PD +3, 8,000 for PD +4, 20,000 for PD +5, as per Accuracy (p. 160). This spell can be recast to strengthen it, as per Accuracy (p. 160).
Prerequisite: Enchant.
Item: Clothing, armor, or shield.

Lighten   Enchantment
Makes armor or shield lighter and easier to carry. The subject becomes lighter only when it is actually being worn. Armor in a backpack would still have its full weight.
Energy cost to cast: 100 to cut the item's weight by 25%; 500 to cut its weight in half.
Prerequisite: Enchant.

Wizardly Tools

Items enchanted with these spells can be used only by mages. All these spells are always on.

Staff   Enchantment
Anything touched by a mage's staff is considered to be touched by the mage. (This also means a mage can set a Powerstone in his staff and use it normally.) See p. 149.

Though many magic items must be in the form of a wand or staff, they do *not* necessarily have to have this spell on them. The Staff spell is used only when the mage needs an item to extend his own touch.
Energy cost to cast: 30.
Prerequisite: Enchant.
Item: Any rod-shaped piece of organic material (wood, bone, ivory, etc.) up to 6 feet long. May be decorated with other materials, like gems and precious metals. A small staff is often called a "rod," and a very short and slender one, a "wand."

Powerstone   Enchantment
A Powerstone is used to *store* mana until it is used by a mage. Any mage touching a Powerstone can take any or all of the energy it contains, using it instead of his body's own energy to cast a spell, like a magic battery.

Each Powerstone is said to have a "strength." This is the maximum amount of energy it can hold. Since a mage can only use one Powerstone per turn, a large Powerstone is more useful than a handful of small ones. A large Powerstone can be used to cast a large spell; a group of small ones can be used one at a time to help *maintain* a spell, but cannot be used all at once.

A Powerstone "recharges" itself after use, by absorbing mana from the surrounding area. The rate varies with the area's mana level:

No mana: No recharge   High mana: 1 point/12 hrs.
Low mana: 1 point/week.   Very high mana: 1 point/6 hrs.
Normal mana: 1 point/day.

A Powerstone will not recharge within six feet of a larger Powerstone. Stones of the same size split the available mana and recharge more slowly. This means the owner of several Powerstones must let some of them out of his sight to get them recharged!

Special rules for creating Powerstones: A jewel (see below) is required. The first casting of the spell turns it into an uncharged Powerstone with strength 1. Each new casting increases its ST by 1. Thus, 15 castings would create a Powerstone with a Strength of 15. But note that with this many castings, there would be a cumulative chance of nearly 1 in 4 that a critical failure would be rolled at some point, destroying the stone. For 60 successive castings, the cumulative chance of critical failure is 2 in 3!

And each *ordinary* failure while casting will put some sort of magical "warp" on the stone. Thus, it is possible to work for many months and end up with a ST 20 Powerstone that smells like tuna fish and can only be used on Wednesdays . . . This makes big stones without serious flaws more valuable than others of the same strength. Warps and quirks of a Powerstone are set by the GM, and can be used as a tool for campaign balance. Most of them will be peculiar, arbitrary limitations on how the stone can recharge (e.g., only while bathed in iguana blood) or how it can be used (e.g., only on Fire spells; only by a green-eyed virgin; not by anyone wearing a hat). A severe quirk will affect the user of the stone (e.g., render him mute for an hour).

The caster will know if his spell has failed, but not what quirk his Powerstone now has. The Analyze Magic spell can determine what quirks a Powerstone has. Two failures in a row indicate that no further growth is possible for that stone.

A Powerstone must be made from a jewel (usually opal). Its maximum strength is equal to its weight in carats. Since there are some 140 carats in an ounce, this is not a significant weight limitation, but it means that a strong Powerstone will be noticeable if it is worn where it can be seen. A gem of over 10 carats is unusual; over 20 is very unusual. And since large jewels cost proportionately more than small ones, this will raise the cost of big Powerstones even more. See p. 153.

A Powerstone is uncharged when created (though if it already contained energy, that energy is unaffected by a casting to increase its ST). The energy from a Powerstone can*not* be used to power enchantments on *that* stone – a Powerstone cannot be used to help enchant itself!
Energy cost for each casting: 20.
Prerequisite: Enchant.

"Dedicated" Powerstones
If a Powerstone is attached to an item *before* that item is enchanted, the Powerstone becomes a part of the magical item. It is then a "dedicated" Powerstone. Its energy may be tapped by the item's user – but *only* to power the spells cast by or through that item.

If a dedicated Powerstone is removed from a magical item, the magical item is automatically broken and loses its enchantment, but the Powerstone is intact, and becomes a "normal" Powerstone again. (Of course, if the Powerstone is built into the item in some way – e.g., set in a magic ring – a successful Jeweler skill roll is required to remove it without breaking the stone, too.)

The advantage of a dedicated Powerstone is that its energy, being specifically channeled, is used twice as efficiently. A 1-point dedicated Powerstone gives 2 points of energy (but still recharges in one day in a normal-mana area).

"Exclusive" Powerstones

An item can also be made with a built-in Powerstone, in such a way that it can *only* be powered by its integral Powerstone(s). This is done exactly as for dedicated Powerstones, but the energy of an exclusive Powerstone is *three* times as efficient – i.e., a 1-point exclusive Powerstone delivers 3 points of energy, but then the item is useless until the stone recharges.

HEALING SPELLS

These spells are the whitest of white magic. Yet the healing spells are precursors of the dark spells of necromancy . . . Some healers even refuse to learn Resurrection (listed in *GURPS Magic*), because of the "unclean" necromantic knowledge required to make the spell function.

Anyone who tries to heal *himself* will have a skill penalty equal to the amount of injury he has. For example, if a wizard takes 4 hits and tries to heal himself, he will be at a -4 to cast any healing spell on himself.

A *critical* failure with a Healing spell will always have some appropriate bad effect on the patient – aggravating the injury, creating a new wound, or the like.

Lend Strength   Regular

Restores the subject's lost fatigue, at an energy cost to the caster. Cannot increase ST above its original level.

Cost: Any amount; the energy spent by the caster goes to the subject as restored ST. *Example:* The caster spends 5 ST; the subject regains 5 lost Fatigue points. Casting cost is not reduced by high skill.

Prerequisite: Magery, *or* the advantage of Empathy.

Item: Wand, staff, or jewelry. Energy cost to create: 100.

Lend Health   Regular

As above, but restores the subject's lost HT rather than fatigue. However, this is a *temporary* "healing." HT gained from this spell lasts only an hour, and then vanishes. HT cannot be raised above its original level.

This spell cannot be maintained; it must be recast. Therefore, it is only a stopgap measure. Casting cost is not reduced by high skill.

Duration: 1 hour.

Cost: 1 per point of HT loaned.

Prerequisite: Lend Strength.

Item: Wand, staff, or jewelry. Energy cost to create: 250.

Recover Strength   Special

Works on the caster himself; cannot restore ST to others. Allows the caster to rest and recover Fatigue more quickly than "normal." A normal person recovers 1 point of Fatigue every 10 minutes. A mage who knows this spell at level 15 recovers twice as fast – 1 point every 5 minutes. A mage who knows this spell at a skill of 20 can recover a point of fatigue every 2 minutes. No further improvement is possible.

The mage must rest quietly, but no ritual or die roll is required. He just "rests faster" by drawing strength from the mana around him. While resting, he can maintain ordinary spells, but not those that require concentration.

This spell does not function in low- or no-mana areas.

Cost: none.

Prerequisites: Magery; Lend Strength.

Item: Jewelry. Permits wearer to recover as though he had this spell at a level equal to item's Power; always on. A very rare item! Energy cost to create: 1,000; must be made of alloyed gold and platinum (minimum value of a small ring is $500).

Awaken   Area

Renders subject(s) awake and alert; instantly counters the effects of stunning or the Suspended Animation spell. If a subject is very fatigued (ST 3 or less), this spell renders him alert for only an hour and *costs* him 1 Fatigue point. It won't work on anyone with ST 0 or less. Subjects must make a HT roll to awaken, with a bonus equal to the amount by which the spell roll succeeded. A subject rolls at -3 if he was unconscious because of injury; -6 if he was drugged.

Base Cost: 1.

Prerequisite: Lend Health.

Item: Staff. Must touch subject. Energy cost to create: 300.

Minor Healing   Regular

Restores up to 3 HT to the subject. Does not eliminate disease, but will cure harm already done by disease.

This spell is risky if used more than once per day by the same caster on the same subject. If you try, your skill will be at -3 for the first repetition, -6 for the second, and so on.

If you have the Physician skill at level 15 or better, a "critical failure" roll with this spell counts only as an ordinary failure – unless you are trying the spell more than once per day on the same subject.

Cost: 1 to 3; the same amount is restored to the subject.

Prerequisite: Lend Health.

Item: Wand or staff, decorated in a snake pattern. Subject must be touched by item. Usable only by mages, or by non-mages with Physician skill 15+. Energy cost to create: 600.

Major Healing (VH)   Regular

Restores up to 8 HT to the subject. Does not eliminate disease, but will cure harm already done by disease.

This spell is risky if used more than once per day by the same caster on the same subject. If you try, your skill will be at -3 for the first repetition, -6 for the second, and so on.

If you have the Physician skill at level 15 or better, a "critical failure" roll with this spell counts only as an ordinary failure – unless you are trying the spell more than once per day on the same subject. However, a caster can use both Major and Minor Healing on the same subject in the same day, without penalty.

Cost: 1 to 4. Twice the amount spent is restored to the subject.

Prerequisites: Magery, Minor Healing.

Item: Wand or staff, decorated in a snake pattern. Subject must be touched by item. Usable only by mages, or by non-mages with Physician skill 20+. Energy cost to create: 1,500.

KNOWLEDGE SPELLS

These spells provide information. Duration is "instantaneous" unless noted otherwise – that is, the caster gets one flash of knowledge, but not a continuing picture.

Detect Magic   Regular

Lets the caster determine whether any one object is magical. If the spell is successful, a second casting will tell whether the spell is temporary or permanent. A critical success on either roll will fully identify the spell, as for Analyze Magic.

Cost: 2.

Time to cast: 5 seconds.

Prerequisite: Magery.

Items: (a) Staff, wand, or jewelry. Usable only by mages. Energy cost to create: 100. (b) Ring or necklace. Usable by anyone; always on. Vibrates, alerting wearer, when any magical item is within 5 yards.

Energy cost to create: 300.

Aura — *Information*

Shows the caster a glowing halo, or "aura," around the subject. This aura gives the caster a general insight into the subject's personality – the better the skill roll, the better the insight. In particular, the aura also shows whether the subject is a mage (and about how powerful); whether the subject is possessed or controlled in any way; and whether the subject is in the grip of any violent emotion. All living beings have auras; inanimate things do not. A zombie is detectable by his faint, death-haunted aura. A vampire retains the aura he had in life.

Illusions and created beings have no auras, so a successful casting of this spell will also distinguish them from real persons. A critical success will detect secret magical traits like lycanthropy, vampirism, unnatural longevity and the like.

Cost: 3 (for any size subject).
Prerequisite: Detect Magic.
Item: Staff, wand, or jewelry. Usable only by mages. Energy cost to create: 100.

Seeker — *Information*

Attunes caster to one individual, or one manmade object, he is looking for. Useful for finding lost items. A successful roll gives the caster a vision of the item's whereabouts, or leads him to it if it is within a mile. Skill modifiers: Standard long-distance modifiers (see p. 151). Something associated with the item sought (e.g., part of a lost person's clothing) should be available at the time of casting; roll at -5 if it is not. +1 if the caster has held the item sought or is already familiar with it.

Cost: 3. One try per week.
Prerequisites: Magery, IQ 12+, and at least two "Seek" spells (e.g., Seek Earth, Seek Water.)
Item: A forked stick (wood, bone, or ivory) or compass-needle (carved out of ivory) which always points to a certain subject, chosen when the item is created. Something pertaining to the subject must be incorporated into the item. Energy cost to create: 500.

Trace — *Regular*

May be cast on any person, animal or object. As long as the spell is maintained, the caster will know where the subject is if he concentrates for a second. Either the subject must be with the caster when the spell is first cast, or Seeker must first be successfully cast. Standard long-distance modifiers if subject is not in caster's presence.

Duration: 1 hour. One try per day.
Cost: 3 to cast; 1 to maintain.
Time to cast: 1 minute.
Prerequisite: Seeker.

Identify Spell — *Information*

Lets the caster know what spell or spells have just been cast (within the last five seconds), or are being cast at the moment, *on* or *by* the subject. Does not identify the spells on a permanently-enchanted item. One casting will identify *all* spells cast on or by the subject. However, if any of these spells are totally unknown to the caster – not just spells he doesn't know, but spells he has never *heard of* – the GM should provide only a general, vague description – e.g., "Some kind of physical protection." As a general rule, wizards will have heard of every spell in this list, unless the GM rules that some are secret. But wizards will *not* have heard of new spells created by the GM or players.

Cost: 2.
Prerequisite: Detect Magic.
Item: Staff, wand, or jewelry. Energy cost to create: 1,100.

Analyze Magic — *Information; Resisted by spells to conceal magic*

Tells the caster exactly what spell(s) are on the subject. If the subject has more than one spell on it, Analyze Magic will identify the one that took the least energy, and tell the caster "there are more spells." It can then be cast again to determine the next spell, and so on.

Like Identify Spell, above, it will give limited results when faced with a spell the caster has never heard of.

Cost: 8.
Time to cast: 1 hour.
Prerequisite: Identify Spell.
Item: Staff, wand, or jewelry. Energy cost to create: 1,200.

LIGHT AND DARKNESS SPELLS

Light — *Regular*

Produces a small light like a candle-flame. It stays still unless the caster concentrates on moving it; then it can move at a speed of 5.

Duration: 1 minute.
Cost: 1 to cast; 1 to maintain.
Item: Wand, staff, or jewelry. Energy cost to create: 100.

Continual Light — *Regular*

Cast on a small object (up to fist-sized or 1 pound) or a small part of a larger object, makes that object glow with white light.

Duration: Variable. Roll 2 dice for number of days.
Cost: 2 for a dim glow, 4 for the brightness of a fire, 6 for a glare so bright as to be painful at close range.
Prerequisite: Light.
Item: Any item can be made to glow permanently, for 100 times the above energy cost (e.g., 200 for a dim glow, etc.).

Flash — *Regular*

Creates a brilliant flash of light. This will totally blind some who see it, and reduce the DX of others by 3 (which reduces all DX-based skills). It may affect anyone who is facing the flash and has his eyes open (GM's decision, if miniatures are not being used). The caster himself is not affected if he closes his eyes as he casts the spell. Each other creature in range must make a HT roll to avoid the worst effects:

Distance	If HT roll is made	If HT roll is not made
Within 10 hexes	1 minute at -3 DX	3 sec. blind, 1 min. at -3 DX
11 to 25 hexes	10 sec. at -3 DX	1 minute at -3 DX
26 or more hexes	no effect	3 seconds at -3 DX.

Cost: 4.
Time to cast: 2 seconds.
Prerequisite: Continual Light.

Darkness — *Area*

Covers one or more hexes in pitch darkness. A person in a dark hex can see out of the hex normally, but can see nothing else in his own hex or other dark ones. Those outside a dark hex can see nothing inside it but darkness. Thus, attacks out of darkness suffer no penalty, but attacks into darkness are at a penalty: -4 to skill if the defender is in a lone darkness hex, -6 if there are several such hexes and the defender's location isn't known for sure. The Dark Vision spell (listed in *GURPS Magic*) allows one to see through dark hexes. Infravision does not.

Duration: 1 minute.
Base Cost: 2 to cast; 1 to maintain.
Prerequisite: Continual Light.
Item: Floor, ground, or a rug can be enchanted so that the area above (about 6 feet) is in permanent darkness. Energy cost to create: 120 per hex.

Blur — *Regular*

Makes the subject harder to see, and therefore harder to hit with any physical attack or ranged spell. Each point of energy subtracts 1 from the effective skill of any attack on the subject – maximum 5.

Duration: 1 minute.
Cost: 1 to 5 to cast; the same amount to maintain.
Time to cast: 2 seconds.
Prerequisite: Darkness.
Item: Staff, wand, or jewelry; affects wearer/holder only. Energy cost to create: 100 per point of subtraction.

Making and Breaking Spells

Find Weakness — Information

Lets the caster sense the weakest part of the subject, if any. Can be cast on any part of a large object; you would not have to cast it on a whole city wall, for instance, but could check one hex of wall at a time.

Cost: 1 per hex (minimum 1). Double this if subject is alive.

Time to cast: 2 seconds.

Prerequisites: One spell for each of the four elements.

Item: Jewelry. Works for wearer only. Energy cost to create: 100.

Weaken — Regular

Does 1 die of damage to the weakest part of the subject (works only on inanimate items). See p. 125 for strengths of various items. No caster may use this spell on the same subject more than once per hour. Subjects's DR does not protect it.

Duration: Permanent.

Cost: 2.

Time to cast: 5 seconds.

Prerequisite: Find Weakness.

Item: Wand, staff, or glove. Works for wearer only; must be used to strike subject. Energy cost to create: 200.

Shatter (VH) — Regular

Similar to Weaken, but quicker – can be cast in a single turn, and may be cast repeatedly. Can do up to 3 dice damage. But if the spell does not do enough damage to actually *break* the subject, the subject takes *no* harm. Inanimate objects only.

Cost: 1 to 3; does 1 die damage for each energy point put into it.

Prerequisites: Magery, Weaken.

Item: Wand, staff, or glove. Works for wearer only; must be used to strike subject. Energy cost to create: 500.

Restore — Regular

Temporarily makes a broken inanimate object *look* as good as new. Other senses will not be fooled, nor will Mage Sight.

Duration: 10 minutes.

Cost: 2 per hex of the subject to cast; half that to maintain. Very small subjects still cost 2.

Time to cast: 3 seconds.

Prerequisite: Either Weaken *or* Simple Illusion.

Rejoin — Regular

Temporarily fixes a broken inanimate object. If some small parts are missing, skill is at -3, but if the spell succeeds the object will hold together without the missing parts.

Duration: 10 minutes.

Cost: 1 per 10 pounds of subject's weight (minimum 2) to cast; half that cost (rounded up) to maintain.

Time to cast: 4 seconds per 10 lbs. of subject's weight.

Prerequisites: Weaken and Restore.

Repair — Regular

Permanently repairs a broken inanimate object. If some small parts are missing, skill is at -5, and appropriate material to *make* the missing parts must be provided – e.g., a lump of gold to make gold filigree-work. If the spell succeeds, the missing parts will reappear. Broken once-magical items will not regain their magic when repaired, but this spell will restore a weakened magic item to full durability.

Duration: Permanent.

Cost: 3 per 10 pounds of subject's weight (minimum 6) to cast.

Time to cast: 1 second per lb. (minimum 10).

Prerequisites: Magery 2, Rejoin.

Mind Control Spells

Fear — Area; Resisted by IQ

The subject(s) feel fright. A subject who fails to resist must make a reaction check at -3 OR +3; the GM decides whether that particular subject will have a "better" or "worse" reaction because he is frightened. A foe might surrender, or attack madly; a merchant might be intimidated, or order you away. Thus, this spell is chancy! A subject who *does* resist will be angered. PCs subjected to this spell may be required to make a Fright Check, at -3, instead of a reaction roll.

Duration: 10 minutes unless countered by Bravery.

Base Cost: 1. Cannot be maintained.

Prerequisite: Sense Emotion.

Items: (a) Any item. Always on; causes wearer to feel fear. Energy cost to create: 200. (b) Staff or wand. Usable by mage only; must touch subject. Energy cost to create: 300.

Bravery — Area; Resisted by IQ-1

Makes the subject(s) fearless. Anyone under this spell must make an IQ roll to *avoid* being brave, should caution be called for.

Duration: 1 hour unless countered by Fear.

Base Cost: 2. Cannot be maintained.

Prerequisite: Fear.

Items: (a) Any item. Always on; keeps Bravery spell on wearer. Energy cost to create: 500. (b) Staff or wand. Usable by mage only; must touch subject. Energy cost to create: 500.

Foolishness — Regular; Resisted by IQ

Reduces subject's IQ temporarily. Ability with all IQ-based skills, and all spells, is also reduced. The GM may also require an IQ roll to remember other complex things while under the influence of this spell.

Duration: 1 minute.

Cost: 1 for every point of IQ reduction (maximum 5); half that amount (round up) to maintain.

Prerequisite: IQ 12+.

Items: (a) Any item. Always on; reduces wearer's IQ. Energy cost to create: 100 for each point of IQ reduction. (b) Staff or wand. Usable by mage only; must touch subject. Energy cost to create: 800.

Daze — Regular; Resisted by HT

Subject looks and acts normal, but will not notice what is going on around him, or remember it later. A dazed guard will stand quietly while a thief walks past! Any injury, or successful resistance to a spell, causes the subject to snap out of the daze and return to full, alert status.

Duration: 1 minute.

Cost: 3 to cast; 2 to maintain.

Time to cast: 2 seconds.

Prerequisite: Foolishness.

Items: (a) Any item. Always on; causes effects of Daze spell. Energy cost to create: 400. (b) Staff or wand. Usable by mage only; must touch subject. Energy cost to create: 1,000.

Mass Daze — Area; Resisted by HT

As above, over a large area.

Base Cost: 2 to cast; 1 to maintain. Minimum radius 2 hexes.

Time to cast: 1 second for each energy point spent.

Prerequisite: Daze, IQ 13+.

Sleep — Regular; Resisted by HT

Subject falls asleep. If standing, he falls; this does *not* wake him. He can be awakened by a blow, loud noise, etc., but will be mentally "stunned" (see p. 127). The Awaken spell will arouse him instantly.

Cost: 4.

Time to cast: 3 seconds.

Prerequisites: Daze.

Items: (a) Any item. Always on; wearer sleeps until it is removed. When the item is created, the caster can specify whether its effects are gradual or immediate. Energy cost to create: 600. (b) Staff or wand. Usable by mage only; must touch subject. Energy cost to create: 1,200.

Mass Sleep — Area; Resisted by HT

As above, but can be cast over an area.

Base Cost: 3. Minimum radius 2 hexes (costs 6).

Time to cast: 1 second for each energy point spent.

Prerequisites: Sleep, IQ 13+.

20 PSIONICS

Psionics, or "psi" abilities, are powers of the mind. Psi abilities are learned just like other skills, except that, for each skill, there is an underlying psi *power* – an inborn advantage – which is a prerequisite. If you don't have the appropriate power, you can never learn these psi skills.

If you have a psi power, you may learn any or all of the psi skills within that power. You may also be able to use some skills by *default* – that is, without spending any points to "learn" them. Eidetic Memory gives *no* bonus to learn psi skills.

A character who starts with a psi power can increase it later, at the same cost per level, by spending earned character points. But totally new powers can't be acquired; you have to start with at least one level in a power if you are ever to have the power. (GMs may make exceptions to this if they like – see *Latent Powers,* p. 166.)

POWER AND SKILL

Each of your psi abilities is described by two factors: *power* and *skill*.

Power is the raw "strength" of your psi. It controls range, damage done, weight affected, etc., depending on the power.

Power is bought in levels. Your Power is the same for all skills within each power. If your Telepathy Power is 10, *all* your Telepathy skills have a Power of 10. Telepathy (TP), Psychokinesis (PK) and Teleport cost 5 points per level; Extra-Sensory Perception, Healing and Antipsi cost 3 points per level.

Skill is bought as for normal skills; psi skills are Mental/Hard. Skill determines how well you control your ability. A die roll is required only when there is a significant question of skill. For instance, no skill roll is needed to shove something with TK, just as you don't roll vs. DX to pick up a book. A roll is required to move something to a precise spot, especially if you want to move it *fast*.

Example: A character buys a Telepathy Power of 10 (50 points); his Power is 10 for all of his telepathic skills. He buys Telesend at 9 and Telereceive at 18; these are Skill numbers, based on IQ. His power of 10 would give him good range for these skills. He can receive complex thoughts under stressful situations, but sending his own thoughts can be hard.

Example: A Telekinetic of Power 18 and skill 5 could lift large weights by mental power, but his control would be poor. He could shove an elephant across the street, but trying to perch it on a parked car would be difficult.

On the other hand, a TK of Power 5 and skill 18 could maneuver a dime into a coin slot while carrying on a conversation, but couldn't lift a suitcase.

One-Skill Powers

If you have only *one skill* under a power, and can never learn any more, that power can be bought more cheaply. A star (★) by the name of a skill shows the cost per point of Power if that skill is the only one the psi can learn for that power. If there is no star, the skill is not available as an "only" skill.

USING PSI ABILITIES

Fatigue Cost

Most uses of psi require no expenditure of energy, just as ordinary walking and talking require no significant effort.

Other uses are more strenuous. When use of a psionic power costs energy, it is always taken as *fatigue* – 1 point of Fatigue per attempt, unless specified otherwise.

This whole chapter, like that on magic, is *optional*. The GM does not have to allow psi powers. Adding these powers to a campaign can be very interesting. But it can create new problems, which the GM should consider before the players surprise him!

The first has to do with allowable power in the campaign. In a supers campaign, for instance, world-cracking levels of PK may be perfectly all right. In a "psychic investigator" campaign, such a character is out of place. The GM should decide in advance what the allowable maximum Power will be for beginning PCs. This can be very low . . . you can get a fascinating campaign with a Power limit of 5 or so. The peepers will have to get very close to their victims, and the psychokinetics will use their skills for lockpicking rather than car-throwing.

Requiring all psis to take certain Limitations (see pp. 175-176) can also help keep them from turning into superbeings. Untrainable, Fickle and Roll to Activate are all suitable for this.

Or the GM can simply limit the number of character points that may be put into psi powers.

The second problem is related to the power level; the higher the power level, the worse it is. Several psi powers, *especially* Telepathy, can make a mockery of most adventure plots. When an investigator can finger the criminal on first meeting (or, for that matter, touch the murder weapon and name the killer), the mystery doesn't last long.

One solution, of course, is to reduce power levels. Another is to make sure that all the criminals, and a lot of important non-criminals, have psychic powers of their own, or at least very good mind shields. The most interesting solution of all is to contrive a situation where the PCs are hindered from using their powers; perhaps psi is against the law in your game world, or telepathy is a violation of the subject's privacy and civil rights! The investigators can still use their powers, but they must avoid leaving any evidence that they've done so!

Latent Powers

Psi powers, like most other advantages, are inborn. As a rule, if you don't start as a psi, you can't gain psionic powers later in your career.

Therefore, if you want a character with a wide variety of psi abilities, you should consider starting with two or more powers, but only buying one at a useful level. The other powers, bought at Power 1 only, are "latent." The character has little Power and no Skill; he won't be able to use them effectively. But later in his career, he will be able to train his latent powers and develop other types of skill.

Adding New Powers

Alternatively, GMs may choose to let PCs gain powers they didn't start with, as long as the appropriate character points are paid. Here are some good excuses for gaining a psi power:

Severe blows to the head.

Encounters with powerful psi-users (human or monstrous).

Lightning strikes, radiation accidents, alien diseases.

Mysterious artifacts.

Deliberate experiments in creating psi powers. But there *must* be some reason why the experiment's success was partial, unknown, accidental, or unrepeatable, or we'd all be psionic!

Critical Success and Failure with Psi

A critical success on a psi skill roll has no automatic special effect *except* that no Fatigue is spent, even if it ordinarily would have been. Of course, especially where ESP is involved, the GM may provide some extra information or other bonus.

On a critical failure, roll 1 die and lose that many points of Fatigue, in addition to any Fatigue that the effort would normally have cost. Also, after a critical failure, a psi may not attempt the same feat again until all lost Fatigue is recovered. Some skills may have other critical failure effects.

Extra Effort

A psi can put "extra effort" into an attempt and get an effective increase in Power. For every 3 Fatigue points spent on an attempt, increase effective Power by 1, but *decrease* effective Skill by 2. If the psi use continues for more than a minute, each extra minute costs another 3 Fatigue.

A psi can*not* spend his own HT as energy for psi use; this is one of the differences between magic and psionics.

Psi use costs fatigue under the following circumstances:

(a) For an "extra effort" use of psi – that is, an attempt beyond your ordinary Power. See below.

(b) For each *repeated* attempt to use a skill, when the first attempt has failed. See below.

(c) For any use requiring a Contest of Skills, *unless* you win the contest by 5 or more. In that case, the effort was so easy it cost no fatigue.

(d) For any skill specifically requiring energy expenditure.

(e) For any critical failure.

Concentration and Time Required

Use of a psi ability requires the *Concentrate* maneuver. Unless specified otherwise, each use of an "active" psi skill requires one turn of concentration – that is, you stand for a second, doing nothing. At the beginning of the next turn, make your skill roll to see if you succeeded.

If the effect you were trying to achieve is instantaneous (e.g., setting someone's hair on fire) it takes place as soon as you make your roll, and you may take some other action that turn (or start concentrating again).

If something – especially an injury – disturbs you while you concentrate, a Will roll is required to maintain your concentration. Use the same rules as for magic (p. 148).

For an effect that takes longer (e.g., reading someone's mind), further time must be spent in concentration after the initial contact is made. If you want to do something else while you continue the psi use, you can try – but a skill roll is required every minute, at a penalty.

Some examples:

Carry on light conversation: -2

Carry on intelligent conversation: -4

Do repetitive manual labor: -2

Combat at a distance (e.g., fire a gun): -6

Repeated Attempts

When a psi tries to use a power and fails (misses his roll), he may wait five minutes and try again without a penalty. If he tries again sooner, this is considered a *repeated effort,* and costs a point of Fatigue. Furthermore, this second effort is at a -1 on skill. Should this effort fail, he can spend another point of Fatigue and try again at -2, and so on until Fatigue reaches 0 and he falls unconscious, or effective skill drops to 2, at which point no success is possible.

Once a psi starts spending fatigue in repeated attempts to perform a feat, *every* attempt at that feat is considered a repeated effort, until he rests long enough to recover *all* lost fatigue, at one point per 10 minutes of rest.

Psi use is only considered a repeated attempt if the psi is trying the same feat – that is, the identical skill on the same (or identical) subject. Two people are not identical subjects. Two bullets (to be lifted with PK) would be. If *distance* is the only thing that changes, it is still a repeated attempt, though the new distance may modify the die roll for some powers. In case of doubt, the GM rules.

Default Use

Most psi skills cannot be used without training, even if you possess high Power. There are a few exceptions which have a *default* skill, usually of IQ-4. These are noted in the individual skill descriptions.

TELEPATHY

Telepathy is the power of mental communication and control. For these skills, the *subject* is the person you are trying to detect, control, or communicate with. Telepathy is unaffected by physical barriers. Your Telepathy Power controls the *range* at which you can use telepathic skills, as follows:

telepathy range table

Power	Range		
1	Touch only, and required time is multiplied by 10.		
2	Touch only	12	400 yards
3	1 yard	13	½ mile
4	2 yard	14	1 mile
5	4 yards	15	2 miles
6	8 yards	16	4 miles
7	15 yards	17	8 miles
8	30 yards	18	15 miles
9	60 yards	19	30 miles
10	100 yards	20	60 miles
11	200 yards	21	125 miles

Further increases in power continue to double range. These ranges are for contact with a single target. For powers involving a "global" use of psi (e.g., a Shout directed at everyone around you), divide range by 100!

Any *skill roll* for one of these abilities will have the following modifiers:
Subject has Mind Shield skill: minus Telepathy power.
User is touching subject: +1. Exception: If your Power is 1 or 2, you *must* touch the subject, and you do not get a skill bonus.
User knows subject slightly (GM's decision): +1.
User knows subject intimately (GM's decision): +2.

Psi Sense ★1

This is the ability to detect use of psi ability. The possessor of the power (sometimes called a Sniffer) gets a *passive* Skill roll to detect any *active* use of psi within his range. He may also use the skill actively, by concentrating.

A Sniffer has the following bonuses and penalties:
Sniffer is concentrating exclusively on detection: +5
Subject is using a Telepathic ability: +2

The success of the skill roll determines the amount of information the Sniffer gets, as follows:
Failed roll: No psi use detected.
Roll succeeds: Sniffer knows psi was used within his range.
Succeeds by 1: Sniffer knows approximate direction.
Succeeds by 3: Sniffer also knows approximate distance.
Succeeds by 5: Sniffer also knows what psi power was used.
Succeeds by 7: Sniffer also knows what psi skill was used.
Succeeds by 9: Sniffer also knows what the skill was being used on or for.
Succeeds by 11: Sniffer also gets image of user's personality (or recognizes user, if he knows him already).
This skill detects only a psi *user*. A short-range Sniffer, in the same room with another person, would not know that person's mind was being read unless the spying telepath was also within the Sniffer's range. This sense uses full range, not range divided by 100.

Emotion Sense ★2

This is the ability to tell, not what someone is thinking, but what he is *feeling*. When a subject is in range of your power and you hear him speak, you can tell whether he is lying – not what the truth really is, but whether he's being truthful. This is a "passive" roll, made automatically.

Active and Passive Skills

An "active" psi skill is one which you use deliberately. Telesend and Pyrokinesis are examples of active skills. An active skill always requires a skill roll. Clairvoyance skill rolls are made by the GM, so the player won't know how well his skill is working. Other skill rolls are made by the player himself.

A "passive" skill is one which works automatically when circumstances call for it. Some passive skills (for instance, the low-level precognition called Danger Sense) still require a skill roll – but the roll is made by the GM. Others (e.g., Mind Shield) always work, without the need for a roll. For instance, Mind Shield always subtracts from the skill of a telepathic attack against you, even if you don't know you are being attacked.

Extra effort cannot be put into a passive use of skill, since it is by definition automatic.

Multiple Feats

A psi can *initiate* only one skill use at a time. But he may do several things simultaneously, as long as they are started one at a time. For each simultaneous "feat" there is a -1 to skill.

Example: A multi-powered psi is using Telekinesis to juggle three balls with his hands behind his back. This requires a skill roll at -3 to start, and another roll every minute to continue. If he now attempts to use Telereceive to read the mind of someone in the audience, his mind-reading roll *and* his Telekinesis roll will both be at -4.

You can also get a general "feeling" for someone's personality; the better your Skill roll, the more detailed a feeling you get. This is also a "passive" process; the GM rolls for you and provides the information.

Finally, you can also sense other emotions. If someone is sad but pretending to be happy, for instance, a successful Skill roll will reveal it. This is not a passive process, but requires an active attempt.

Default use: At a Power of 3 or better, the passive aspects of this skill can be used without training. You can sense lies, but not other emotions, by rolling vs. your IQ. You get only one "personality" roll for each person you meet (if you are separated for more than a month, you get another roll). This works exactly like the Empathy advantage (p. 20) – because they're the same thing! If you have Empathy, you *are* a psi. The 15 points you spent for Empathy make you a Telepath with Power 3 and no training, rolling at your IQ level by default.

Telesend ★3

This is the skill of *sending* thought. The user sends his thoughts to the subject at about the speed of talking, though simple pictures may also be sent (by visualizing them) at the speed it would take to draw them on paper.

A successful Skill Roll is necessary. If the roll fails, the psi may spend Fatigue and try again (see *Repeated Attempts*).

If the psi has no language in common with the subject, the skill roll is at -4. If the roll is then failed by 4 or less, the subject feels a mental contact, but understands nothing!

The Shout: Telesend ability can also be used for a telepathic *Shout* which can stun those who receive it. If the Shout is broadcast, no skill roll is required. It will affect everyone within the psi's range (a lesser range can be specified, if the psi Shouts less loudly). Everyone within range of the Shout must roll vs. Health. A failed roll results in a mental Stun (see *Total Surprise*, p. 122). (So high HT helps you avoid a Stun, and high IQ helps you recover quickly.)

The Shout may also be aimed at one area (seen through the psi's own eyes or another's), or at one single person (seen through the psi's eyes or those of another with whom the psi has made contact through Telereceive).

Telereceive ★3

This is the skill of *receiving* thought – often called "mind-reading" or "peeping." Received thought comes at the speed of speech, except between two very skilled telepaths (see sidebar, p. 169).

To receive thoughts from a *willing* subject within range, a skill roll is necessary. Remember the bonus for familiarity with your subject!

To receive thoughts from an *unwilling* subject, two rolls will be necessary. The first roll tests your subtlety. Roll a Contest of Skills: your Telereceive vs. the subject's Mind Shield skill (see below), or IQ if he has no shield up. If you win the contest, your mind-reading attempt is not noticed. If you lose or tie, the subject notices you (whether he realizes what was happening will depend on his experience with telepathy!).

The second roll is the actual attempt to enter the subject's mind. Roll your Telereceive skill, modified downward by the subject's Shield *Power*, to see if you made contact with his mind. Subtract the subject's Strong Will from your Skill as well (or add his Weak Will!).

Glossary

ESP – Extra-Sensory Perception. The power to see, hear, or know things that cannot be detected with the ordinary five senses.

Blinker – A person with the power of teleportation.

Esper – A person with ESP.

Peeper – Any telepath, but specifically someone with the Telereceive skill.

PK – Psychokinesis. The mental power to affect matter.

Precog – A person with precognitive powers, or a precognitive vision.

Psi – Short for "psionics" – the generic term for unusual mental powers. Also, any person who possesses a psionic power may be called a "psi."

Screamer – A person with antipsi powers.

Sniffer – Someone with Psi Sense skill.

Subject – The person or object against which a psi skill is being directed.

Teleport – A person with the power of teleportation, or the act of teleportation.

TP – Telepathy. The power to read, affect, control, or shield minds.

User – The person using a psi skill.

Victim – The subject of hostile psi use.

Thus, it is possible for an intruder to bounce off a powerful shield without being noticed, or penetrate a skillful shield yet be observed.

If the subject is talking, or even *subvocalizing* (talking under his breath), you get a +2 to all skill rolls.

A new skill roll is required each minute that you stay in the subject's mind, but this does *not* cost Fatigue. If a roll fails, contact is broken.

If you get into your subject's mind, the level of thought you get depends upon the amount by which you make your skill roll:

0-2: Surface thoughts only. If the subject is talking or subvocalizing, you pick up only what he is saying.

3-4: All surface thoughts, plus occasional mental associations and background. You can also pick one of the subject's senses (sight, hearing, telepathy, etc.) to "tap into" and perceive.

5-6: As above, but with all significant mental associations and background (but still only if the subject thinks about it!). You can also pick up all of the subject's sense impressions.

7-8: The subject's subconscious mind is also exposed.

9-10: The subject's memories of the last day are also exposed.

11-12: The subject's memories of the last week are also exposed.

13+: All the subject's memories are exposed, though a separate skill roll is necessary to "locate" any particular memory over a year old. A failure means the memory cannot be located; try again another day.

Mental Blow — Prerequisite: Telesend at 12+

This is a direct mental attack. It always costs the user 1 Fatigue. If successful, it Stuns the subject (as per Shout) and does *fatigue* damage as well. Once the victim's ST reaches zero and he falls unconscious, no further damage can be done. *Exception:* A critical success with a Mental Blow does *physical* harm to the victim instead! A critical failure backfires, doing physical harm to the attacker in addition to the normal fatigue loss from a critical failure.

Damage is based on the attacker's Power. Roll one die for every *full* 10 points of power, and add 1 point if the remainder is 5 or more – thus, Power of 16 does 1d+1 damage. The victim, if he is still conscious, gets an automatic roll against his own Telereceive, Mind Shield or Psi Sense skill. A successful roll gives information about the attacker, as per Psi Sense. Ignore critical failures.

Mind Shield ★2

This is the ability to hold a mental "shield" that warns you of telepathic attacks, and helps defend as well. This involves a Contest of Skills and a Telereceive roll by the invading psi, as described under Telereceive.

You may turn your shield on or off at will; this may be done at any time, *even when it is not your turn during combat phasing.* When you go to sleep or become unconscious, your shield remains as it was set. If there is some need for your shield to come up or go down while you are asleep or unconscious, you get a *single* Mind Shield skill roll (at -2 if you are unconscious rather than merely asleep). If the roll fails, your shield stays as it was until you awaken.

Power of Shield: Your Telepathy Power is the shield's strength. Subtract this number from the skill of any psi use affected by the shield (see below). *Example:* A Telepath with skill 18 is trying to read your mind. Your Telepathy Power is 5. The TP rolls at an effective skill of 13.

Repeated Attacks: If a telepathic attack meets a Mind Shield and fails, each repeated attempt is at a -2 (not the normal -1) to skill, and costs 1 Fatigue point.

Effects of Skill: The user's *skill* with Mind Shield determines the *type* of protection it gives:

Two-Way Communication

A two-way contact between Telepaths can be initiated with Telesend power. Once the other Telepath is aware of you, he makes his own Telesend roll, at +4 because the contact has already been made. After each minute of conversation, each Telepath must make another Skill roll, but *all* rolls to maintain a two-way contact are at +4.

For true two-way conversation, each TP must be within his own Telesend range of the other. But a very powerful TP could hold a two-way talk with someone wholly untalented, talking with Telesend and picking up subvocalized answers with Telereceive.

If two Telepaths are "talking," and each has *both* Telesend and Telereceive skills at 10 or better, they may choose to enter "full communion." Each is aware of *everything* the other thinks and perceives, and communication is 10 times faster than speech!

Three-Way Interaction

If two Telepaths are reading the same subject's mind, they *will* notice each other unless one is deliberately hiding. In that case, a Contest of Skills is rolled (the GM may make this roll for one or both characters, to keep secrecy). If one character is *looking* for mental intruders, he is at a +2 to his skill to notice.

If *both* characters are trying to hide, and neither is aware of the other, the GM should roll *two* Contests – one to see if A notices B, and one to see if B notices A.

Even if two or more Telepaths are "in" the same mind, they cannot communicate directly through the third mind. They can use it as a "relay station" only if that third mind is another Telepath, actually listening and repeating the message from one mind to another.

8 or less: Interferes with all uses of Telepathy, friendly or hostile, against *or by* the subject. In other words, when the user's shield is up, it interferes with his own telepathic abilities!

9 to 11: Interferes with all use of Telepathy, friendly or hostile, when Mind Shield user is the subject – but not with the user's own Telepathy.

12 to 14: Interferes with all uses of Telepathy when Mind Shield user is the subject, unless user consciously designates a use as "friendly." That use then suffers only half the normal interference (round up).

15 to 17: The shield automatically discriminates between friendly and hostile contacts. Friendly contacts are detected, but can work through the shield without opposition. The user can decide, at any given time, whether "neutral" contacts will be treated as friendly or hostile.

18 to 20: As above – and if a "friendly" contact turns hostile, the attacker must make a new skill roll, against the shield.

Over 20: As above, but any psi contacting the shield must win a Contest of Skills (Telereceive vs. Shield) even to perceive that the user is psionic. Otherwise, he will merely perceive surface thoughts appropriate to a non-psi. This is called "cloaking." (A successful Telecontrol or Mindwipe roll will penetrate the cloak – possibly to the surprise of the invading psi!)

"Get Out Of My Mind!"

It can happen that a hostile psi penetrates your shields with Telereceive, and that you *later* become aware of his presence – for instance, because he failed a Telecontrol or Mindwipe roll. Or he might have entered your mind while your shields were down. In either case, you may attempt to close him out of your mind. Roll a contest: your Telepathy Power + Mind Shield skill, vs. his Telepathy Power + Telereceive skill. If you win, you push the intruder out of your mind, and he will be at a -2 (repeated attempt) if he tries to return.

But if you lose, the enemy psi is in your mind for as long as he likes. And you must make an IQ+4 roll to control your own thoughts, or you will immediately think of whatever it is you fear he is trying to learn – which can give your secrets away even to an unskilled attacker.

Sleep   *Prerequisite: Telesend at 12+*

After making a normal contact as for Telereceive, the user rolls a Contest of Skills: his Sleep skill vs. the subject's Will. If the user wins, the subject falls into a normal sleep lasting for 1d hours unless awakened. On a failure, the subject gets an IQ roll to realize he is under attack. (*Exceptions:* Any Telepath rolls against his best Telepathy skill. And in a world where neither magic nor psi is commonly known, most victims will have no experience of Sleep attacks and will just think they're sick.)

Psionics and Magic

Magic and psionics are two different things. Many of the same effects can be achieved by both disciplines. For instance, a fire-mage and a pyrokinetic can both set your clothes afire.

However, the techniques *are* different. An anti-magic spell will not affect psi attacks in the least.

Likewise, a wizard's mind-reading spell will have no more (or less) success if his subject is a telepathic psi.

However, the purely physical effects of the two disciplines can interact, or even cancel. If a pyrokinetic creates a fire, it is like any other fire, and water magic can extinguish it normally.

On the rare occasions when magic and psi interact physically, roll a Contest of Skills between the magic skill and the psi skill.

So Which Is Better?

Neither magic nor psi is better than the other – but, again, the disciplines are very different.

Magic is more diverse. There are many more spells than there are psi skills. Furthermore, the average mage knows many more spells than the average psi knows skills.

However, magic (except for a very skilled mage) requires a lot of energy. Many psi powers require no effort at all – they are as simple as thought.

Magic can give unpredictable results, or even backfire. Psi doesn't always work, but won't blow up in your face or summon a demon unexpectedly.

Both mages and psis can be deadly. But neither is immune to bullets . . .

Mindwipe Prerequisite: Telesend and Telereceive at 12+

This is the ability to edit or remove a subject's memories. To use this skill, you must first make contact with the subject, using Telereceive, and get past his shields, if any. Then try your Mindwipe skill (once per hour for long processes). A failed Mindwipe roll will alert the subject that his mind is being tampered with. If you make several rolls but then fail one, the subject will lose memory, but it will return in 3d days.

The time required to do (or undo) a memory change, or to find traces of a change in the subject's mind, varies with the complexity of the change. The more subtle the change, the harder it is to make, repair, or find:

Delete all the subject's memories (leaving a babbling idiot): 2 hours.

Delete all subject's memories *permanently*: 1 hour.

Delete a lot of memory (e.g., several weeks of time): 3 hours.

Replace a lot of memory with a false memory: 5 hours.

Remove one memory: 1 hour (10 minutes for a memory within the past day).

Change one memory: 2 hours (20 minutes for a memory within the past day).

Plant a *compulsion* (a single order the subject will have to follow at an appropriate time): 4 hours.

Detecting Mindwipe

Total memory deletion is obvious. You may detect lesser tamperings when you are in mental contact with the victim. Roll vs. Mindwipe, or Telereceive-5 if you don't have Mindwipe. You only get one such "passive" roll – the first time you contact the person after the tampering takes place. You are at -2 to notice a compulsion, and -4 to notice a single memory has been changed. You are at a further -1 for every week since the tampering took place, up to 6 weeks.

If you are deliberately looking for mental tampering, having failed the passive roll to notice it, you must make mental contact using Telereceive, and then make the above skill roll. This effort takes an hour, and any further check within a day is a "repeated effort."

Undoing Mindwipe

Any memory alteration except a deliberate, permanent mindwipe can be undone. This requires as many *weeks* as the original process took *hours*. The psi trying to reconstruct the memories must make his own Mindwipe skill daily; failed rolls mean the day doesn't count, and critical failure means the process must start over. A critical success counts as a full week of success. A psi is always at +4 to undo his own work.

Telecontrol Prerequisite: Telesend and Telereceive at 15+

This is the ability to actually take over the victim's mind, and operate him from a distance like a puppet. This requires great concentration: a psi using Telecontrol is at an extra -4 to skill if he is doing *anything* else. It is possible to control more than one victim, at a -4 to Telecontrol rolls for each extra person, and the puppets will have slurred speech and DX-4.

To use this skill, you must first make contact with the subject, using Telereceive, and get past his shields, if any. Then try your Telecontrol roll. A successful roll puts the victim under your control; you can use all his physical and psychic skills, but you do not have access to his memories. A failed roll alerts the victim to your attempt; he feels you in his mind.

Once established, Telecontrol may be continued as long as you concentrate. When it ends, the victim will remember nothing. After a victim has been controlled once, you have a +2 to any further attempt on the same victim.

Using Psi With Other Skills

Psi skills can be used in a number of creative ways. In general, the GM should let a successful psi roll give a *bonus* on an appropriate skill roll. What is "appropriate" is left up to the players' creativity; as always, the GM has the final word.

In general, the psi roll must first be attempted. If it is successful, the real task is made easier. A failure does not affect the task, but a critical failure gives a penalty equal to the bonus that would have been gained. Some examples:

A successful Telekinesis roll gives a +4 to Lockpicking skill with any tumbler or combination-type lock.

A successful Clairvoyance roll also gives a +4 to skill – this time, to *see* the tumblers. If the lockpicker made both rolls, he would get both bonuses. A psi thief could be formidable . . .

Reading a foe's mind would be good for a +2, or better, on a Strategy roll – the trickier the foe's plans, the better the bonus.

Levitation could give a +2 on any Acrobatics roll (if you want to conceal your power) or +6 (if you don't care who knows you're a psi).

And so on . . .

PSYCHOKINESIS

This power covers moving things at a distance, making them colder or hotter, etc. A PK must visualize the subject. Normally, this means he must see or touch it. A familiar subject (a person well known to the psi, or an object he has handled repeatedly) may be affected at a distance even if it is unseen: -1 to skill for 1 yard distance, and an extra -1 each time the distance doubles. Any *skill roll* for PK will have a +1 bonus if the user is touching the subject.

Telekinesis ★4

This is the ability to move objects by mental power. Your PK Power controls the *mass* you can move mentally, as follows:

telekinesis table

Power	Mass	Power	Mass
1	1/4 oz.	12	30 lbs.
2	1/2 oz.	13	60 lbs.
3	1 oz.	14	125 lbs.
4	2 oz.	15	250 lbs.
5	4 oz.	16	500 lbs.
6	8 oz.	17	750 lbs.
7	1 lb.	18	1,000 lbs.
8	2 lbs.	19	1,250 lbs.
9	4 lbs.	20	1,500 lbs.
10	8 lbs.	21	1,750 lbs.
11	15 lbs.	22	2,000 lbs. (1 ton)

Further increases in power continue to add 250 lbs. per level.

Telekinetic Contests

If two psis are both trying to move the same subject, a Contest of Skills is made. The psi that wins the contest gets control of the subject *for a second,* but the other psi "keeps a grip" on it. However, if one psi wins by 5 or more, he has broken the other psi's mental grip and is in full control of that subject until he releases it voluntarily.

Obviously, each psi needs to have enough power to move the subject. The psi with the stronger Power is also at +1 to effective skill for every *two* points by which his Power exceeds his opponent's. Brute strength is less important than control in a contest of this type.

Getting Tricky

Any time telekinesis is used for anything beyond simple straight-line movement, a skill roll is required to *aim* it. A failed roll means that the subject misses its target (or otherwise performs badly – GMs can be creative here). The GM sets the skill penalty, with the following guidelines:

Precise aim, slow movement (guiding a coin into a slot): -2.
Precise aim, fast movement (*throwing* a ball through a hoop): -4.
Precise aim, bullet-fast movement: -6.
Precise orientation (keeping an arrow going point-first): -3. This adds to the above penalties for aim.
Complex movement (writing your name with a crayon): -2 or more.
Target is moving when you try to control it: -1 for every yard per second that it is moving, up to a maximum of -10 (thrown weapons and arrows fall into this category). You cannot catch a bullet, because you can't see it coming.

You may try to *deflect* a missile if you can see it coming. The roll to deflect something is 4 easier than the roll to control it (6 easier for long objects like spears and arrows). Thus, the net roll to deflect a fast-moving arrow is -4. A successful roll moves the subject off course – it automatically misses its target.

Telekinetic Attacks

Telekinesis can be used to attack a victim's *body* – squeezing blood vessels, etc. The damage this does is taken from the Swinging damage chart (p. 74, based on the psi's PK power). So, for instance, a PK power of 6 would do 1d-4 damage per second, and a power of 10 would do 1 die per second.

To initiate this attack, the psi must see (or touch) the victim, and visualize the interior of the body. This requires a successful IQ roll, or Surgery+3 if he has that skill. It takes a second of concentration (and only one try is allowed).

If this roll is successful, the psi may start his telekinetic attack. A skill roll is required, with the following modifiers:

-1 for every yard of distance.
-3 to do *Fatigue* damage rather than real injury.

If this roll is successful, the victim takes damage every second, as described above. No further skill rolls are required unless the victim gets out of the attacker's sight. In that case, a new roll is required (at the new range) to keep contact.

Levitation ★3

This skill works to lift only the psi's own body (and whatever he is carrying). It is the psionic form of flight. Weight and speed are figured as for Telekinesis (above), except that the psi can move *only* his own body plus whatever he is carrying (no more than his own weight).

Power is effectively increased by 10, for this skill only. This means that a levitator with a power as low as 5 (4, for a child) can "fly" at a yard per second. And a high-powered levitator can go *fast*. Maximum practical speed, without special protection, is about 100 mph.

A psi who has Telekinesis, but not Levitation, can still lift himself if he has enough power. Use the Telekinesis weight chart, above.

Pyrokinesis ★3

This is the ability to increase the temperature of an object. The target must be visible to the psi (though a telepath could look through another's eyes to use the power, at -3 to Power). Once started, a pyrokinetically-set fire burns normally. The psi cannot use this power to put it out (but see *Cryokinesis*, below).

A skill roll is *always* required when this power is first activated. A miss by 1 to 5 means nearby objects are also affected. A worse miss means the target isn't burned, but other things are. A critical failure affects everything within sight; the GM works out the details, maliciously. If the psi misses, he can continue (accepting the inaccuracy) or try again (paying Fatigue for a repeated attempt).

Each level of Power lets the pyrokinetic raise the temperature of ten cubic inches of material (which does not have to be in cubical form) by 50°. Larger items can be heated more slowly, but smaller items do not heat any quicker. Continued concentration will continue to raise the temperature by 50° per second for each level of power. Thus, at Power 10, you could heat up a 10-cubic-inch item at 500° per second! So in a single second, you could set a book ablaze.

Items must be heated as a unit; you cannot, for instance, focus on a victim's finger and burn it off while ignoring the rest of his body. Hair or clothes *can* be ignited separately. The GM must use common sense, tempered by dramatic license, to decide what constitutes a "unit" here.

Pyrokinetic heat is *trapped within the subject*; very little escapes to the outside world until the psi stops concentrating. Thus, a sufficiently powerful Pyrokinetic can burn a victim to ashes while his clothing is almost unaffected. Or a weaker psi could set your *clothes* on fire; you would notice nothing until they burst into flames, but then the flames *would* hurt you!

Some important temperatures (all in degrees Fahrenheit): Room temperature: 75-80°. Person becomes unconscious: 120°. Water boils: 212°. Paper bursts into flame: 451°. Wood bursts into flame: 550°. Meat broils: 550°. Lead melts: 621°. Copper melts: 1,980°. Iron melts: 2,786°.

For a living being, treat each pound of body weight as 20 cubic inches (this allows for an innate resistance by living flesh; a steak would cook faster). Thus, a 150-pound man would be 3,000 cubic inches. A Power of 20 would increase the temperature of a unit volume (10 cubic inches) by 1,000° per second. So he could increase the man's temperature by 1/300 of that, or 3.3° per second.

Cryokinesis ★2

Works exactly like Pyrokinesis, in reverse – *cools subject down* by 50° per 10 cubic inches per second. Less spectacular, but occasionally useful. Ice forms at 32°. Absolute zero is reached at -460°.

Very cold metals, glass, etc., become more brittle; this has to be left as a GM judgment call, but in general, halve the HT of any metal item below -50°.

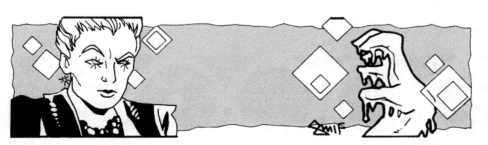

Telekinetic Throwing

In general, PK Power of 15 or better is needed to move an object fast enough to do harm. A lesser Power can still cause a distraction, even if the objects thrown aren't heavy or fast-moving enough to cause injury.

The weights given for Telekinesis assume that the subject moves one yard per second. For barely visible motion (the subject shifts a tiny bit and stops), effective Power is at +1, doubling weight that can be affected.

For greater speeds, consider the object's weight. Take the difference between the PK's actual Power and the minimum Power required (from the table on p. 172) to move it continuously.

Now look up this "excess power" on the chart below, to see the speed at which that object can be moved. For every 2 points of difference, speed doubles. If the excess power is an odd number, multiply the next lower speed by 1.4.

Excess Power	Speed
-1	0 (tiny shift in position)
0	Move 1 (1 yard/sec)
1	Move 1.4 (5 feet/sec)
2	Move 2 (2 yards/sec)
3	Move 3 (3 yards/sec)
4	Move 4 (4 yards/sec)
5	Move 6 (6 yards/sec)
6	Move 8 (8 yards/sec)
7	Move 12 (24 mph)
8	Move 15 (30 mph)
10	Move 30 (60 mph; thrown rock)
12	Move 60 (120 mph; arrow speed)
14	Move 120 (240 mph)
16	Move 250 (500 mph; bullet)
18	Move 500 (Mach 1.5)

If something is thrown at Move 30, treat it as though it had been thrown by a ST 12 man; use the *Throwing* table on p. 90.

With a Power of 16 or better, you can throw small stones, etc., as though they were bullets; use range and damage as for guns (see p. 208), as follows:

Power 16: .22 pistol (Ruger STD)
Power 17: .32 pistol (Walther PPK)
Power 18: .38 pistol (FN HP35)
Power 19: .357 magnum (Colt Python)
Power 20: .44 magnum (S&W M29)

For each level of power over 20, add 25 yards to half-damage range, 50 yards to maximum range, and 1 point of damage. Note that you have no weapon, so you have no Accuracy bonus available, and *any* attack is a Snap Shot unless you take time to aim.

Pside Effects

Psi skills can have "side effects" that are unique to a particular character. That is, *your* Telesend (for instance) has a special side effect that occurs when you use it.

Side effects are optional, and are determined when a character is created. There are two general categories:

Special Effects

A *special effect* is a side effect which is essentially unimportant, though it may occasionally inconvenience the user. For example, if your Telekinesis skill makes a low humming noise, those nearby will notice something (and those who know you will know you're using your TK). A special effect is worth 1 point as a trivial disadvantage, or 2 if the GM feels it might be a bit more inconvenient. You may take up to 5 points' worth of special effects for all your psi skills combined.

Drawbacks

Drawbacks are side effects that cause real trouble to the user or those around him. For instance, if your use of Telesend causes mild headaches in everyone within 20 feet, that's a problem!

A drawback is worth points as a disadvantage – but only if it makes *real* trouble for the character. 15 points is the maximum allowed for *all* damaging special effects. As an example, the effect described above might be worth 5 points – mostly because it keeps the psi from using his power up close without being noticed.

A really obnoxious special effect will give its possessor a reaction-roll penalty. This is worth 5 points per -1 of reaction if it is always in effect (which would be rare), 5 points per -2 reaction if it is noticeable only some of the time, and 5 points per -3 reaction if it is relatively rare.

Character Points

Points for special effects do *not* count against the normal (suggested) disadvantage limit. Thus, a psi character can have up to 20 points' worth of extra disadvantages – 5 for side effects and 15 for drawbacks.

Illegal Side Effects

No character may take a side effect which is obviously useful as a controllable weapon or advantage. If a player finds a clever way to make a seemingly worthless side effect *very occasionally* useful, that's all right.

PK Shield ★2

To get this skill, the PK must also have at least 1 point of ESP power, in order to sense the air next to his body. PK Shield lets the psi "lock on" to that air and hold it in place as a shield. This gives +1 PD, and DR equal to his $\frac{1}{2}$ his PK power, against solid objects only (no effect against beams, sonic attacks, etc.).

A new skill roll is required each second to keep the shield active, though critical failures after the first roll are treated as ordinary failures. Activating this skill costs 1 Fatigue, plus 1 more for each full minute the shield is held.

ESP

The power of "extra-sensory perception" covers the various "sixth sense" skills – to see things hidden to ordinary people. When an ESP skill is used, a skill roll – made by the GM – is always required. The better the roll, the more accurate and useful will be the information he gives. On a failed roll, he says "You learn nothing." But if a Psychometry or Precognition roll is failed by more than 5, he *lies*. Repeated attempts cost *two* Fatigue apiece, at -2 skill for each repeated attempt.

Clairvoyance ★2

This is the ability to see through walls and other solid objects. Its range is sharply limited by Power, but not by what is in the way. You will not accidentally see "through" what you are looking for. Each time the psi looks at a different thing or in a different direction, a new roll is required.

The range of Clairvoyance is equal to your Power *squared,* expressed in *inches*. Thus, even a Power of 1 will let you see inside an envelope in your hand. Power of 20 will let you see 400 inches – almost exactly 11 yards.

Clairaudience ★2

As above, except that it lets the user *hear* what is being said behind walls, etc., and listen indefinitely to any conversation of interest.

Psychometry ★1

This talent lets the psi learn something about the history of a place or inanimate object: general impressions, use, user's personality, etc. The length of history sensed is equal to Power squared, expressed in *years*.

Normally, a deliberate effort is required. But very strong "vibes" may be noticed passively; the GM rolls in secret. Psychometry will not detect magic. But (for instance) a holy object would have "good vibes" because it had been handled by holy men, and an evil altar would have a pall about it because of the sacrifices made on it. Psychometry would also detect an unnatural air about an artifact from another dimension.

Precognition ★2

This is the ability to see the future. It is the chanciest and least-understood of all known psi skills. A "precog" vision may be sight, sound, or just a flash of knowledge. And remember that nothing about the future is *certain*; even if the GM has made his mind up, he could reconsider . . .

An *active* attempt to Precog requires 10 minutes, and costs 2 Fatigue points. It is made at a -10 (!!) to skill.

A *passive* Precog roll may be made at the GM's whim. Precognition is usually associated with a person or thing. For instance, if you meet a person who has some very important event in his future, the GM will give you a roll (which *he* makes) to detect the possibility of that event. Or seeing a picture of a place could set off a vision having to do with that place.

Precognitive range is based on Power. Physical distance is figured as for Telepathy (p. 167). Time is equal to Power squared, expressed in *days*. But if you are dealing with a person's future, the fact that he may later travel out of your physical range does not affect your skill.

Default use: Without training, this skill gives you a roll vs. IQ any time you are in immediate danger; a successful roll means you are aware of danger, and a very good roll gives you some details. This works the same as the Danger Sense advantage (p. 20) – because it *is* the same. If you have Danger Sense, you *are* a psi: an Esper, with Power 5 and no training.

Special Limitations: If your precognition is limited to one particular type of event, skill levels may be added at half cost. Some examples of legal limitations:

Only events involving you personally; Only disasters (fire, explosions, etc.); Only events related to death.

TELEPORTATION

This is the power of moving things from place to place *without traversing the distance between*. A teleported object simply "blinks" from one place to another, in *no time*.

Autoteleport ★4

This is the basic Teleport ability – the ability to move yourself (and up to 5 lbs. of clothing and carried items) from point to point without crossing the space between. You cannot go somewhere unless you have been there or can see it at the moment you teleport there. You *can* try to teleport to a place you are seeing on live TV (at -5) or through someone else's mind (at -3).

To carry more weight, learn the Exoteleport skill (below). Distance is regulated by Power, as per Telepathy range. Accuracy is regulated by skill. Failures will send you someplace unplanned, usually somewhere similar to your intended destination, and cost 2 Fatigue. Critical failures send you somewhere *unpleasant,* and stun your Teleport power, rendering it unusable, for 1d hours.

Special limitations: (1) Some Teleports can carry nothing, and always arrive nude. If you take this limitation, cut your Power cost in half. You cannot learn Exoteleport.

(2) Your teleported objects retain any orientation and speed vector they had. If you are falling, and transport yourself to the surface of the earth, you will hit hard! This limitation also halves Power cost.

Exoteleport ★4

This is the ability to transport objects from point to point. Power regulates distance, as above, *and* weight; weight is equal to 10% of that shown on the weight table for TK (p. 172). Skill modifiers: +3 if you carry the item by Autoteleporting (roll separately, at no extra penalty for the arrival of yourself and your cargo); +1 if you are touching the object when you send it; -3 if you can neither see nor touch it.

You may try to *bring* an object to you rather than sending it. This is at -5 to skill, or -8 if you cannot see it. The object must be a very familiar one, and you must know exactly where it is. A failure on the roll will lose the item forever, embed it in a wall, etc. A critical failure could bring it to a spot over or *in* the teleporter.

HEALING

The power of psychic healing seems to combine aspects of psychokinesis and telepathy, but it is effectively a separate power. Only one skill, also called Healing, is known.

Limitations

One Skill: variable

You can learn only *one* of the skills associated with the power. See p. 165.

Untrainable: -40%

You can't learn to control your power well. You learn all skills under the affected power as though your IQ were only 8 (or at -1 IQ, if already IQ 8 or below). You can never learn any skill at higher than level 10.

Emergencies Only: -20%/-30%

The power is triggered by your fear or excitement, and cannot be used under "routine" conditions. The GM is the final arbiter of the emotional state of your character. The GM may rule that multiple successive failures of your power make you angry enough that it begins to work, but this is entirely up to him.

A less severe form of this limitation is Full Power in Emergencies Only (-20%). You can work at half Power, rounded down, under normal conditions, but at full Power only under stress.

Uncontrollable: -30%

This limitation is only available for the Antipsi, Psychokinetic and Teleport powers. Your power tends to manifest by itself – even against your will – when you are angry or excited. This can be especially interesting if your skill is destructive and you have a high power.

Whenever you are under stress (GM's decision, but a phobia situation is *always* stressful) you must make a Will roll to control your power. If you fail the roll, the GM takes over your power, playing it as though it were a separate entity of hostile or prankish nature. Usually only one roll is required per stressful situation, but a 14+ always fails.

GMs may wish to base the actions of an uncontrollable skill on the character's "suppressed desires" as reflected in his Quirks and mental disadvantages. Your power will go after obvious foes first, and will never turn on *you,* but nobody else is safe. After each uncontrolled act (or *before* an attack on a dependent or other loved one), you get another Will roll to control your power. This continues until you master the power or destroy everything around you!

Continued on next page . . .

Fickle: variable

Your ability has the disturbing tendency to stop working suddenly. A Fickle power always works right if you have not used it for a 24-hour period. After that use, and after every successive use, you must make the Fickleness roll: roll the Fickleness number, or less, to get the power to work. A failed roll means that power is unavailable for the next 5d turns. When this time is up, the power will work normally on the next use – but you must make another roll *after* that use!

For an Fickleness number of 5, this limitation is worth -70%; for 8, -30%; for 11, -20%; and for 14, -10%.

Accessibility

This is a catch-all term that can be used to cover all limitations not specifically defined. Accessibility limitations fall into two groups: usable only against certain things or usable only in certain situations.

Examples:
Useless Under Stress: -60%
Usable Only vs. Psis (or Non-Psis): -50%
Usable Only vs. Opposite Sex (or Own Sex): -20%
Usable Only in Hypnotic Trance (or under Incapacitating Drugs): -30%
Usable Only by One Side of Split Personality: -40%

If the power is only weakened (half power) instead of becoming useless, halve the power of the limitation.

Unreliable: variable

Sometimes your Power works and sometimes it doesn't! It just comes and goes; you've never identified why. This is completely separate from the skill roll to hit a target. You can have skill 15 and still have problems making it work!

Every time you want to use the Power, you must roll the activation number or less (see below) on 3d. Once you succeed, the Power will work for that particular use. When you stop using the Power, another activation roll will be required to start it again.

If it fails to activate, you may continue to try on subsequent turns, at no penalty. Each successive attempt costs 1 point of fatigue. If your ST drops below 3, you must rest until all fatigue is regained before you can attempt to use the power again.

A failed attempt to activate *can* be noted by someone with the Psi Sense skill, just like a normal use of a psi skill.

For an activation number of 5 or less, this limitation is worth -70%; for 8 or less, it is worth -30%; for 11 or less, -20%; and for 14 or less, -10%.

The user must be in physical contact with the subject. On a successful Healing roll, he can restore lost HT up to his own Power. Failure costs 1d fatigue; critical failure also costs the subject 1d *hits!* Successful healing costs 1 fatigue for every 2 hits healed. The cost to cure disease is always at least 6 fatigue.

Healing skill is at -2 when the victim is unconscious, and -2 or worse to cure disease. It can't restore a lost limb, and is at -6 to restore a crippled but whole limb (each Healer only gets one try at any one limb). It can't bring back the dead.

Special limitations: (1) In addition to the Fatigue cost, the psi takes actual damage equal to half the hits healed (round up). $1/2$ Power cost.

(2) The psi can only use the power on others. $1/2$ Power cost.

(3) The psi can only use the power on himself. $2/3$ Power cost.

ANTIPSI

This is the psionic power of *interfering* with psi use. *Special limitation:* $1/2$ Power cost if it only affects one other Psi power.

Psionic Resistance see p. 22

Psionic Resistance is considered an advantage, not a psionic skill. See p. 22 for a complete description.

Psi Static ★2

Those with this ability are sometimes called "Screamers." A few Screamers are in full control of their skill, but most are untrained . . . because of this, few psis want anything to do with a Screamer.

A Screamer can activate his power "globally," to interfere with *all* psi use within an area defined by his Power (range as for global use of Telepathy – p. 167). This requires no skill roll. While the Psi Static power is on, any use of psi that normally requires a skill roll requires a Quick Contest of Skills – the Screamer's Psi Static skill vs. the skill of the psi being attempted. This also costs the other user (but not the Screamer) 1 Fatigue point per attempt, in addition to any other cost. If the Screamer wins the roll, the psi use is a failure. If the other psi wins the contest, he can attempt psi use normally.

By making a successful Psi Static skill roll, a Screamer can also *specifically* interfere with psi use by any individual that he can see (through his own eyes or another's). This roll is at +2 if the Screamer is touching his victim.

Default Use: Without training, this skill may be used at IQ-4.

LIMITATIONS

You can take a *limitation* on any psi power, which makes it cheaper but less reliable. A limitation cuts the cost to buy that power. It affects all skills under that power. Cost to *learn* individual skills is not affected.

You may take more than one limitation on the same ability. However, the total cost modifier may never never exceed -75%.

The cost modifier is applied to your *total* Power cost, and *then* rounded up. *Example:* You have a cost modifier of $1/2$. You are buying Telepathy (5 points per level). Your first level costs 3 (half of 5, rounded up). Your second level costs 2 more, for a total of 5 (exactly half of 10). Your third level costs 3 more, your fourth level 2 more, and so on.

21 GAME MASTERING

The Game Master is the referee of a roleplaying game. But that's putting it too simply. He is like a mystery writer . . . a storyteller . . . an umpire . . . a cosmic bookkeeper . . . the "house" at a gambling casino . . . and (to the characters) a minor deity.

The GM is the final authority. Rules are guidelines . . . the designer's opinion about how things *ought* to go. But (as long as he is fair and consistent) the GM can change *any* number, *any* cost, *any* rules. His word is law!

And many things *are* left up to the GM to decide. A roleplaying game gets realism from its completeness. The GM adds all the little details that make a game world come alive. With a good Game Master, even a *bad* set of rules can be a lot of fun. With a *good* set, the sky's the limit. We semi-modestly believe that *GURPS* is a very good set of rules indeed – but without the GM, the rules are nothing. Read on . . .

STARTING A GAME SESSION

There are a few things the GM should do before play actually starts, to make things easier for himself *and* the players:

Introduce the characters. If you are in the middle of a continuing campaign, you can skip this step! But if you are just starting out, each player should have the opportunity to describe "himself" or "herself." If there is an artist in the group, he can help by drawing the characters as they are described.

Check for skills, etc., improved since the last play session. In a continuing campaign, players will earn character points which they can spend to improve their abilities. In some campaigns, the PCs can work at their jobs, study, etc., *between* play sessions by using the weekly Time Use Sheet (in the *Instant Characters* section).Therefore, some characters may have better skills or abilities than they did in the last game session. This is the time for them to tell the GM about it.

Fill out the GM Control Sheet. While the players are getting to know each other (or each other's characters), the GM should check over the character sheets, make sure everything balances, and copy necessary information onto his own *GM Control Sheet*. This is a reference sheet which gives ST, DX, IQ and HT, along with certain other basic information, for each player character. When the GM needs to determine (for instance) who saw something, who *understood* something that everyone saw, who was affected by a certain spell, or who that bad-tempered dwarf took a dislike to, this sheet will be valuable. A master for this sheet is in the *Instant Characters* book.

Brief the players. Tell them what's going on, and give them some idea what the adventure will be about. There are many ways to do this. You can always just *tell* them. But it's much more fun to start play, and *then* "set the scene." Let the characters immediately find a map or old book . . . meet someone who tells them an interesting rumor . . . befriend someone in need of help . . . witness a wrong that needs righting . . . or whatever.

Let the game begin!

Maps

Most prepackaged scenarios will include maps. The GM can prepare his own maps (in different scales) in advance, to help him plan and to keep track of events. He may also give maps to the players as clues. And the players themselves may want to map their progress, whether it be through jungles, dungeons, or downtown New York City, to make sure they can find their way back . . .

Maps in *GURPS* use hexagons, or "hexes" (see p. 178) to regulate movement and combat. Each hex is adjacent to six other hexes.

Advance Preparation

There are several things for the GM to do well in advance, before the players arrive on the scene:

Prepare the adventure. If you are playing a prepared adventure, all you need to do is read through it, and possibly make up some character sheets. But if you are designing your own adventure, you may spend weeks of work – a labor of love – before it is ready for the players. In any event, be sure you're fully familiar with the adventure *before* the players show up!

Brief the players about the adventure. If your players are already familiar with the system, you should tell them in advance (*before* they arrive to start the game) what sort of characters will be legal – how much money, equipment, etc., they are allowed, and maybe a hint about useful skills. If everyone has his character made up in advance, you'll be able to get right to the action when the players arrive.

Set up the play area. You will need pencils, paper and dice; maps and miniatures if you are using them (and a table to play them on); and a supply of snacks!

Campaign Style

Before you Game Master for the first time with a new group of players, you should also discuss the *style* of campaign you will run. There are many alternatives:

A "by-the-book" campaign, vs. one where the GM uses many of his own rule interpretations.

A campaign in which death is common and permanent, vs. one where PCs rarely die, or the dead are easily raised.

A "puzzle and mystery" campaign, vs. a "combat and adventure" campaign.

A humorous campaign where everything is played for laughs, vs. one which is very serious about "realistic" situations and "dramatic" roleplaying.

A "realistic" campaign, vs. a "cinematic" one (see p. 183).

All these are legitimate approaches to roleplaying. But if the players and the GM have different ideas about how the game should be run, everyone can be disappointed. The game should be a story that develops as it is played – not a battle between players and GM. But to achieve this, a little mutual understanding is necessary. A few minutes of pre-game discussion can increase everyone's enjoyment.

Player-Made Maps

Whenever the players enter an area for which they have no map – be it an underground dungeon, a laboratory complex or a network of jungle trails – they will want to map it themselves. (That is, they will if they are smart!)

However, mapping is not as easy as all that. Unless the party carries a tape measure and spends a lot of time using it, they should *not* be told "You go 12 yards down the stairs and turn north. The tunnel is seven feet wide and nine feet high. It goes north for 120 yards and then turns northeast. In another 20 yards it opens out into a room 10 yards by 6 yards." This is the sort of information a team of surveyors might get – but not a group just walking through the tunnel!

Instead, the GM might give them information like this: "You walk down the stairs – they go down a little farther than an ordinary flight of stairs. At the bottom, there's a tunnel going right. It's wide enough for two to walk side by side, and so high you can barely touch the ceiling with your swords. It goes on for a ways in a fairly straight line . . ."

"How far?" asks a player.

"Is somebody pacing it off? Okay. Around 128 paces. It then turns to the right a bit . . ."

"How much?"

"Did you bring a protractor? Surveying tools? Anybody got Absolute Direction? No? All right. Standing at the intersection, with the old tunnel behind you at six o'clock, the new tunnel looks like it turns away at between one o'clock and two o'clock. Got that? Now, it goes along for another 19 or 20 paces, and then opens out into a big room. The door's in the middle of the long wall. The room is roughly rectangular. From where you stand, it might be ten yards long, 6 or 7 yards wide."

Very different, yes? But also much more realistic. The players are given only the information they actually get with their senses. In the example above, the GM fudged all the distances a little bit, assuming that whoever was pacing would have a standard pace a bit less than a yard.

If you do this, the players may come up with ingenious ways to measure time and distance. Let them!

Note that, if mapping is difficult in ordinary circumstances, it becomes next to impossible if the party is in a hurry! Suppose the group were being chased through the area described above. The GM would say:

"Okay. You're running? Stop mapping. Here's where you go. Down the stairs! Turn right! Run for several seconds! The tunnel bends to the right! Run a little farther! You're in a room!"

And so on. When the party stops running, they can sit down and try to remember where they went. (Eidetic Memory, of course, is a big help here!)

Travel Maps

These maps may be drawn to any convenient scale. Examples include continents, highway maps, city maps, etc. These maps are used purely for information; they are not "playing boards." In a modern adventure, the players will have access to travel maps. In a far-past or far-future campaign, the travel map may be the GM's secret. (*Finding* a map can be a great adventure objective.)

Area Maps

These are usually drawn to a scale of 1" = 18', or 6 hexes to the inch. Each hex is still one yard across – it is just drawn to a smaller scale. A sample sheet of small hex-grid is supplied in the *Instant Characters* section. This scale can be used by the GM to map an entire building, dungeon, arena, etc. Use a different sheet for each floor or level, indicating shafts and stairways. Mark each room (or other point of interest) with a letter or number for use with a map key.

This map should be kept secret from the players – though they will usually try to make their own map. The GM may place a marker on his area map to show where the party is at any given moment.

Room Maps

These maps can be drawn to any convenient scale. One good one is 1" = 6' – half the size of the combat maps. They are used by the GM when he needs to sketch a room in some detail, but does not want to draw up a combat map for the room.

The map key will have a description for each room, with:

(a) Its size (though this may be clear from the area map).

(b) A general description of the room.

(c) A description of the people or creatures in the room. This may be very simple: "Two ordinary wolves." Or it may be complex: "This room is empty except between midnight and 9 a.m., when two guards are there. There is a 50% chance that each one is asleep. They are ordinary guards from the Character List elsewhere in this adventure, but one of them also has a gold ring worth $200. They will surrender if outnumbered more than 2 to 1, but will not cooperate, even if threatened with death."

(d) If necessary, any special notes about the room, and descriptions of anything that might be found if the room were *carefully* examined.

(e) If necessary, a larger-scale map of the room to show precise location of furniture, characters, etc.

Combat Maps

Combat maps are not required in the Basic Combat System (though they can still be handy to help the players visualize the action). They should be used in the Advanced Combat System.

Combat maps are drawn to a scale of 1" = 3'. Thus, each hex is 3 feet, or 1 yard, across. When the characters enter a room, tunnel, or other area where combat might occur, lay out a map and have them place their figures on it to show exactly where they are. If combat occurs, the fight will be played out on the combat map.

Any partial hex is treated as equal to a full hex. This allows a realistic representation of either a hex-walled room or an irregular cavern.

Players and GMs may photocopy the blank combat grid (*Instant Characters* booklet) in order to make their own combat maps. Several sheets can be taped together to make a large-sized map.

RUNNING THE GAME

The GM's task during the game is simple. All he has to do is listen to the players describe what *they're* doing, and then use the rules of the game to tell them what happens, so the players can describe what they want to do next . . . and so on. Well, perhaps it's not *quite* that simple!

The sections below will help you, as GM, determine "what happens next" in a variety of situations. But the most important things are not "rules" at all, but guidelines for good GMing.

Use your common sense. When *any* rule gives a silly result, follow common sense, instead. No matter how much we playtest, *no* rules are perfect – including these. Don't let the players turn into "rules lawyers." *Your* decision is final. See the sidebar.

Be fair. Give all the players an even chance, and try to keep all of them involved in the action. And when you change a rule or make a special exception, apply it equally to everybody.

Keep the action moving. A roleplaying game is like a story. As the GM, you're the author. Your main characters have free will, and often the story goes where *they* want it to! But when things lag, it's your job to liven them up. Improvise an encounter . . . introduce a clue . . . do *something* to get things back on track, or to help the players get some ideas!

Don't lean on formulas of any type. This *definitely* includes the various formulas in the rules! Use them when you need them – but don't let them become crutches. And don't let adherence to a formula spoil the game. If Dai really *needs* to lift that rock to keep the action going – let him lift it.

Thou shalt not kill. Not much, anyway. In some RPGs, life is cheap. A GM doesn't think he's doing a good job unless he slaughters half the party within the first hour of play. But this isn't much fun if you just finished creating your character! *GURPS* allows complete, detailed character creation. It's a shame to turn those detailed characters into cannon fodder. Remember – good adventure stories don't kill off their heroes without a reason. This is discussed in greater detail below – see *Keeping The Characters Alive* (p. 181).

If you and your players *really* like hack-and-slash games, go right ahead. But you may want to roll up your characters randomly, rather than taking time to design them in detail. That way, you can get right to the blood and gore.

Playing the NPCs

An NPC, or "non-player character," is any character played by the GM. The Game Master gets to play dozens of characters throughout an adventure – from chance-met travelers to powerful patrons and villains.

As the GM, you may create your NPCs in any way you like. The important NPCs should usually be designed just like player characters, but "cannon fodder" and other unimportant characters can be rolled up randomly, or even created on the spur of the moment and given "logical" abilities, without regard to point value. See p. 84.

Once you create an NPC – major or minor – *play the role!* As your NPCs interact with the characters, they will try to earn money, look important and admirable, protect their skins, and achieve their various goals – just like anybody else! The more skilled you become at roleplaying, the better a GM you will be and the more fun you (and your players) will have.

Some of your NPCs will automatically be friendly to the players, and some will be "natural enemies." These reactions will be pre-set when you work out the scenario. But many NPCs have no "automatic" response to the characters. Instead, you will use the *Reaction Table* (p. 204) to see how they respond.

Mapping Overland Journeys

If the players are traveling through unexplored territory, they will no doubt wish to keep a large-scale map. The GM may make it automatic if they are following rivers, canyons and the like. But if they are trekking through trackless wastes, or trying to map a specific tiny inlet of a great river, an IQ roll should be required to map properly. Absolute Direction would be good for a large bonus; Navigation or the appropriate Survival skill could be substituted for IQ if someone in the group has these abilities.

This also makes a good adventure; the party is sent to explore and map the (trackless waste, virgin planet, mysterious dungeon, steaming jungle, dead city).

Settling Rules Questions

In any question of rules, the GM's word is *law*. The GM decides which optional rules will be used, and settles any specific questions that come up. A good GM will always discuss important questions with the players before deciding – but a good player accepts the GM's decision once it is made.

The GM should know the rules thoroughly. When a situation is not covered by the rules – or when a decision about the "real world" is needed – there are several techniques that can be used:

Success rolls. A "success roll" (p. 86) is a roll that tests a character's strength, dexterity, skill, etc. Use a success roll when a question arises about someone's ability to do some particular thing.

Random rolls. For a question like "Are the keys in the car?" or "Does one of the soldiers have a horse the same color as mine?" a random roll is often best. The GM decides what the chances are, and rolls the dice. Some things will have a 50-50 chance; others will be very unlikely. The GM decides what the odds should be, and leaves the rest to fate.

Arbitrary fiat. You don't have to use the dice at all. If there is only one "right" answer to fit the plot of the adventure – then that's the answer. "Luckily for you, the grenade bounced down the stairwell. Nobody was hurt. But the guards are alerted now!"

Predetermined Reactions

Certain NPCs may have reaction modifiers (mostly bad) worked out in advance. For instance, a street gang might have a -5 reaction to *anybody*. A mountain man could be a reclusive type, with a -3 reaction to any outsider – and no matter what, his reaction will never be better than "neutral." In this case, any reaction better than neutral is simply treated as neutral; do not roll again.

Second Reaction Rolls

If the players get a reaction roll they don't like – unless the first roll started a fight – they may change their approach and try again. Some ways to change their approach are: (1) offer a bribe of some kind; (2) offer a better deal; (3) have someone else ask; (4) present new information; (5) use a particular skill (see below). If the NPC, as played by the GM, feels that the characters are becoming a nuisance, subtract 2 from the second roll, 4 from the third, and so on! This penalty can be avoided by a reasonable wait between requests. "Reasonable" is entirely up to the GM!

Special Skills

Certain skills can be used *instead* of regular reaction rolls in appropriate situations. These skills are Fast-Talk, Savoir-Faire, Sex Appeal and Streetwise. If you have one of these skills, you may choose to use it instead of depending on a regular reaction. The GM still applies the appropriate modifiers, as though you were making a reaction roll, but they are treated as modifiers to the skill you are using. See the descriptions of these four skills for details.

Playing the Adversary

When the GM plays an NPC who is an enemy of the player characters, he should try to limit his knowledge to those things that the NPC would really be aware of. The GM knows all about the party's strengths and weaknesses – but the enemies don't. One good way to solve this problem is to have another person play the adversary characters.

The GM should tell the Adversary as much as possible about the characters he is to play. But the Adversary should know no more than is "realistic" about the overall situation. In particular, he should know very little about the PCs and their abilities – especially at the beginning of an adventure! For total realism, you might even want *two* Adversary players – one for knowledgeable enemies who are familiar with the party, and one for stupid cannon fodder.

The Adversary is like an "assistant GM." His job is to roleplay the foes as well as possible. He should *not* play them as mindless killing machines (unless they really are). If the "appropriate" thing for those particular enemies to do is to attack, they should attack. But they might also throw rocks from ambush, shout insults, or even run away immediately!

In any disagreement between the Adversary and the GM, the GM's word is law. But a good GM will give the Adversary as much leeway as possible, and will take any disagreement into another room to avoid distracting the players.

Playing the Adversary is a good way to build up experience if you would like to be a Game Master someday.

Reaction Rolls

When the players meet an NPC whose reaction to them is not predetermined, the GM makes a "reaction roll" on 3 dice. The higher the roll, the better the reaction. The GM then plays the NPC according to the guidelines on the *Reaction Table* (p. 204).

This roll should be kept secret from the players. They don't know, for instance, whether that friendly-looking old farmer is giving them straight advice or sending them into a trap.

Many factors can influence a reaction roll. A reaction *bonus* is a factor which will make the NPCs *more* friendly, and a reaction *penalty* is something that will bias the NPCs *against* the characters. Some common reaction modifiers:

Personal appearance and behavior of the player characters – especially the one who does the talking! A good personal appearance will improve the roll. So will Charisma. In most situations, so will a high apparent social status.

Appropriate skills for the situation – e.g., Streetwise in an underworld situation, Bureaucracy when dealing with an official. If the character has the skill at an "expert" level – 20 or better – it is more likely to help. Expert Diplomacy, for instance, is worth +2 on *any* reaction roll.

Racial or national biases between the NPCs and the character(s) in the party. These are usually minuses. Elves don't like dwarves; Frenchmen don't care for Germans, and so on. Common modifications will be found in the books for the appropriate game worlds. For uncommon ones (what do Germans think about elves?) the GM is on his own.

Appropriate behavior by the players! Here's another chance to reward good roleplaying. A good approach should be worth a +1 modifier – maybe more! A wholly inappropriate approach which antagonizes the NPCs should cost the party a -1 or -2 penalty on the reaction roll. Don't tell the players, "You blew it!" – just roleplay the offended character, and let them figure it out.

Don't forget: Random reaction rolls are great when they add a note of unpredictability to the game – and this is more fun for the GM, too! However, random die-rolling should never be substituted for reason and logic.

Knowledge

One challenge of roleplaying is to limit your character's knowledge to the things he "should" know. And part of the GM's job is to keep *players* from making use of information that their *characters* could not know.

Player Characters' Knowledge

Anachronistic technology. Players can't use high-tech knowledge that their *characters* could not have. If a medieval character wants to invent gunpowder – or build a compound bow – or use moldy bread for penicillin – you don't have to let them. Of course, time travelers can take knowledge into the past.

Similarly, modern characters should not be allowed free use of ancient techniques. Gunpowder is an example *here,* too . . . how many 20th-century people know *exactly* what to combine to make gunpowder, or how to mix, grind, sieve, and use it without blowing themselves up? However, modern characters can always *try* to "remember" ancient techniques, by making appropriate (and difficult) rolls in History or in the particular specialty involved.

Knowledge of history. If your game is set in the "real" past of Earth, the players will have advance knowledge of how things "really" came out. Don't let them use it – unless, of course, they are time travelers from the future. And remember that, in a game, history *can* be changed – so some of the things the players know *may not be true*.

Literacy. This is important – and lots of fun. If any of your characters are illiterate, *don't let them read anything!* It is amazing how many people will take the disadvantage of Illiteracy, and assume they can still read maps, street signs and shop-windows!

NPCs and Adversary Characters

Likewise, the GM (or the Adversary) should not use knowledge that *their* characters could not logically possess. This is the main reason for having an Adversary in the first place . . . so the GM's total knowledge of the player characters won't work against them. All the above warnings apply to the GM's characters as well. Specific things to watch out for:

Objectives of the party. This can cut both ways. The GM knows the players' true objectives; the Adversary *may* know. But when they play "ignorant" characters, they must roleplay their ignorance. This may mean that a NPC will act hostile when he "should" be friendly, or vice versa. It also means that when the party sneaks into the castle, the guards can't *all* rush to protect the treasure room. They don't know for sure where the PCs are going!

Abilities of the party. All NPCs – *especially* adversary characters – should react according to the *apparent* strength of the party. A simple example: If the players are exploring a dungeon populated by roving bands of orcs, each new band should find out *the hard way* that the mage has a Fireball wand – until some orc escapes to spread the word.

Special weaknesses of the party. If (for instance) two members of the party are deathly afraid of snakes, the adversary characters shouldn't know this unless there is a way they could have found out. In fact, the GM should *not* tell the Adversary things like this in the first place. Let him find out for himself! But even after he finds out, he can't use this sort of fact unless he is playing a character that *should* know.

Keeping the Characters Alive

There is a basic contradiction in RPGs. The players are all looking for adventure – and adventures are dangerous. On the other hand, nobody wants to get killed! The GM must walk a fine line between a "giveaway" adventure – where nobody is in real danger – and wholesale massacre.

The *GURPS* rules are designed for two main things: *good roleplaying* and *realism*. In that order. "Realism" means that, in any serious combat, someone is likely to get

Often, in spite of the GM's most careful preparation, something surprising will happen. It could be *anything*. No matter how much you plan ahead, or how well-tested a packaged adventure is, your players will come up with something you didn't expect.

That's all right. If they *didn't* come up with anything surprising, your duties as GM would be much less fun.

But you still have to cope with the problem. Let's say, for instance, that your players have just discovered the Shrine of the Mother-Goddess. Suddenly, they realize that they have been followed! A dozen huge, ape-like creatures stalk through the door and approach menacingly There are no other exits.

There are several things the players might do, and you're prepared. If they want to fight, you know the combat stats for the ape-things. If they try to make friends, you've already decided that they'll be dragged away to the ape-cave and fattened up for dinner. If they try to flee, or use magic to make a barricade, you know there is a secret door behind the altar – if they can find it in time. If they try to call on the Mother-Goddess, you've decided it won't work – they don't know the spells or rituals.

But one of the younger characters *panics* when he sees the ape-things. Running to the giant statue of the Mother-Goddess, he clasps her around the knees and bawls for help. He doesn't pray . . . he just *pleads*, like a terrified child. And you weren't *ready* for something like that!

Of course, you can just say, "Nothing happens. It doesn't work," whenever your players try something original. But that's no fun.

Or you can always say "I wasn't ready for that. Do something else." But that's no fun either.

The good GM will match the players' creativity with his own. In a really dramatic situation, like the one described above, just go with the flow! There's a very good chance that the Mother-Goddess will take pity on that poor sincere fool. Maybe she swats the ape-things out the door. Maybe she just picks up that one character and holds him safe, leaving the others to fight the apes. Who knows? You're the GM. In an unusual situation, *anything* is right if it's fair to the players and makes the story better.

Whatever you do, it's a good idea *not* to tell the players you were improvising. Let them think you had it all planned in advance. If you want to admit, *after* play, that you were just "winging it," that's up to you. But during play, don't interrupt the flow of the game. Roll the dice, shout, "You did it!" (or "You blew it!"), and keep going.

Dealing with the Players

Arguments

As the GM, you should *always* listen to reasonable suggestions from the players – and if you make a mistake on a rule, you should be willing to reverse yourself. But *you* are the final authority, and the court of last resort. If you make a decision that you think is fair, and someone insists on arguing . . . let them play with somebody else. Games are fun. Arguments aren't.

"I changed my mind!"

Certain players – if you let them get away with it – will "take back" actions when they see the bad consequences. Don't let them do it unless they could *realistically* have changed their minds in time to avoid the trouble. *Example:* If George says, "I'm dropping the nitroglycerine," and you roll the dice and tell him "It just blew up. Take 3 dice damage," George can't take it back. But if George says "I'm setting fire to the building," and then changes his mind – let him. "All right. You lit the match and found some newspaper, but then you changed your mind. Stomp out the newspaper." Buildings don't burn that quickly, so George had time to reconsider. (If George had a flame-thrower, of course, it would be different!)

In general, if a player announces that he is performing an *irrevocable* act . . . he really did it, and that's that.

Following the Leader

If the players select a leader, the leader should talk for the party, telling the GM what is being done – except in emergencies. Then, it's every man for himself. The leader can give orders, but he *cannot* enforce them unless his *character* can enforce them in the game world. If the leader appeals to you for help, tell him, "You're the leader. *You* keep discipline."

Table Talk

If your players are too noisy, tell them that "If you say it, your character says it." This means that the *characters* cannot be stealthy unless the *players* are quiet, and the *characters* cannot make a speedy decision unless the *players* decide quickly. Enforcing this rule can save the GM's sanity.

killed or badly hurt. And, since in real life nobody *wants* to get killed, "good roleplaying" means that most people will try not to fight until they *have* to! That goes for your NPCs as well as the player characters.

In the final analysis, good roleplaying (and having a good adventure) is the *most* important thing. When good roleplaying conflicts with realism, roleplaying should win out. As the GM, you should try not to let such a conflict occur. But if it does happen, tip the scales toward *fun*.

In particular, try not to kill too many of the PCs! In a hack-and-slash game, where the characters are no more than sets of numbers, a death is no loss. In a true roleplaying game, with fully-realized characters (who took a long time to develop), losing a character can *hurt*. That is not to say that PCs can't die. They can. But in the best games, they don't die too often.

Keep in mind that RPGs are meant to be *fun*. They simulate, not the reality of day-to-day life, but the reality of heroic fantasy. An RPG is a story that the GM and the players write together. And in the best stories, the heroes (most of them, anyway) survive and triumph. This is more important than "logic." Logically, Luke Skywalker would have been shot down . . . Frodo and Sam would have starved in Mordor . . . Tarzan would have been lion-bait before he was six years old. A classic defies logic, and *still* you believe it – because you want to. A good game is like that, too.

There are several techniques you can use to keep from killing off your "main characters." Some of these are totally contradictory. As GM, you're the boss. Use whichever one you like.

Intelligent scenario design. Don't fill an evening with traps, foes, and monsters to slaughter your players. That's good for ten-year-olds . . . maybe. Design a scenario to make the players *think* and *roleplay,* and to give them a fair chance. Perhaps – since they *are* the heroes – give them a better-than-fair chance.

Realistic NPC behavior. If your non-player characters are realistic, most of them won't risk their own lives unnecessarily. Not every encounter will turn hostile; not every hostile encounter will turn violent; not every violent encounter will involve weapons. Of course, some game worlds are more violent than others. But "life is cheap" usually makes for a very poor game.

Even in a violent game world, enemy characters will often have a reason to take the players prisoner, rather than killing them outright: slavery; interrogation; ransom; imprisonment; sacrifice, or what-have-you. Capture and escape are staples of adventure fiction, which is what the game is all about!

And if the PCs are *winning* a fight, your NPCs should try to save their skins. In real life, most guards, beasts, or bandits will flee – regardless of duty or greed – if a fight goes against them. Play them that way.

Realistic NPC abilities. In most game worlds, players start off as 100-point characters. But they are *unusual* people. The *average* person is about a 25-point character! Most people in your game world will be no match, physically or intellectually, for your characters. There will be exceptions . . . interesting, dangerous exceptions. But the "man on the street" will have poorer attributes and fewer abilities than the players. For the most part, the players should be facing inferior foes. This not only keeps the game in balance – it preserves the "reality" of adventure fiction.

That is not to say that an "average" person cannot be dangerous. A 20-point character can be a nasty fighter, if he takes a couple of disadvantages and specializes in ST, DX and combat training. He will be more than a match for a 100-point character who is not a fighter. But a 100-point fighter will chop him to bits.

Deus ex machina. This is the miraculous outside intervention that saves the day. The cavalry comes over the hill . . . the starship beams you up . . . the Governor issues a pardon. When the players did their best and things just went totally wrong, arrange a miraculous escape, against all odds. If it was good enough for Edgar Rice Burroughs, it's good enough for you. Needless to say, the beneficiaries of a *deus ex machina* should not gain wealth or bonus character points from the situation, since they did not escape on their own.

Cheat! When all else fails, roll the dice where the players can't see – and then lie about your roll. "It worked! You finally got the door open. You rush through, and slam it behind you. The orcs cannot follow." When an "honest" roll will end the game in a bloody massacre, a GM can be forgiven for cheating in the players' favor.

One last note: There *will* come a time when the players *insist* on getting themselves killed – through gross carelessness, total stupidity, or even (we can hope) good roleplaying, right down to the bitter end. You can't rescue them *every* time . . . that's no fun, either! If they really ask for trouble, *let them have it*. So it goes.

Game Time

Game time is the time that passes in the game world. The GM is the judge of how much time has passed.

Time During Adventures

Combat is played out in "slow" time. One combat turn equals one second. It may take a minute or so for each combat turn, especially if players are inexperienced or the battle is a large one. But combat is usually a life-or-death situation, and you need to give players time to think.

Conversations, attempts to pick locks, attempts to escape from traps, and similar situations are played in "real" time. If the players spend ten minutes discussing how to best approach an NPC merchant . . . their *characters* spent ten minutes talking outside the shop.

Routine travel, etc., is handled in "fast" time. When the party is walking along a trail, for instance, the GM can simply skip the time between encounters: "You walk for another two hours, and then, coming toward you, you see two young women with long poles . . ." Tell the players when they meet someone, when they come into a town, or when night falls. Just compress the rest of the time. Under some circumstances – a long ocean or space voyage, for instance – the GM could compress *months* of non-eventful time into "Nothing happens until July unless you make it happen yourself." This is a good time for the characters to dream up some interesting deviltry, or fill out a few Time Use Sheets for study and self-improvement.

Between Adventures

If you are running a continuing campaign (see p. 199), you also need to keep track of time *between* adventures, so characters can study, travel and age. This can always be the same amount of time, or the GM and the players can simply agree on a "logical" time to pass between the end of one adventure and the beginning of the next. It is often a good idea to let a month or two go by, to allow time for healing, earning money at "ordinary" jobs, and study of new skills – see *Time Use Sheets*, p. 184.

Or you can let X days of real time equal one day of game time, all the time. Thus, if X is 7, one day equals one week. If it has been seven days since your last adventure, seven weeks have automatically gone by in the game world.

Of course, no game time at all has to pass between *sessions,* if you can't finish an adventure in one session. If, when you quit play, the party has just confronted a rampaging Tyrannosaurus, that Tyrannosaurus will get no closer in the real-world week before you can play again.

ENDING A PLAY SESSION

At the end of each play session, the GM should do the following:

Discuss the adventure with the players. What went right, and what went wrong, and why? If the session was part of a continuing campaign, the GM should be careful not to give away any secrets.

The Cinematic Campaign

For the most part, these rules stress realism. Characters can get disappointed, injured, sick, or even dead. So it goes. The GM is expected to stretch reality in an emergency (defined as "whenever reality would ruin the game"). But the rest of the time, reality rules.

But (in the words of the sage): What is reality? Many people prefer to game out the "reality" of the cinema, where the heroes battle dozens of foes and emerge unscathed. *Don't* try that at home . . .

In a cinematic campaign, PCs should start at 200 points, rather than just 100. To maintain some touch with reality, PCs may not spend more than 150 points on their basic attributes; the rest must go into skills and advantages. Toughness, Luck and Combat Reflexes are especially appropriate cinematic advantages!

And for GMs who prefer this version of reality, here are two "official" alternate rules to use. Be sure to tell the players in advance if you're adopting Cinematic Reality!

Flesh Wounds

Any time when combat is not actually going on, any PC can be healed back to full HT by spending a character point (PCs should keep a few unspent points for this purpose.) "Zounds! It was only a flesh wound!"

Against All Odds

"Ten of us to a hundred of them, eh? Well, one British soldier is worth twenty of those beggars . . . so the odds are two to one in our favor. Hardly sporting!"

In a cinematic campaign, characters get twice the "standard" number of Parries and Blocks each turn; thus, for instance, a sword can parry twice per turn and a fencing weapon four times. Only one defense is allowed *per attack* unless All-Out Defense is chosen. Weapons which require re-readying after a parry may still parry only once! This rule will normally work in the PCs' favor, since they will be attacked by dozens of unskilled foes who, in a coldly realistic world, would swamp them with sheer numbers.

Time Use Sheets

The Time Use Sheet (*Instant Characters* section) is to be used by players to plan their characters' time *between* play sessions.

The amount of time covered by each sheet is set by the GM. An even number of weeks works best. At the end of each play session, the GM should tell the players how much game time will pass before the next session. When they show up for the new adventure, they can bring the records of how they spent the intervening time.

When an adventure "stops in the middle" – when one play session ends at night in the inn, and the next one starts the next morning – obviously no time use sheet is necessary. Use one when there is a hiatus in an adventure (for instance, when the players must wait two weeks to catch their ship). And use one *between* adventures, to give the characters a chance to rest, earn money, and improve their skills.

GMs: If this seems like too much bookkeeping, don't use it! Feel free to think of a substitute, or forget all this entirely, if it does not add to **your** *players' enjoyment.*

There are three major reasons to keep track of time outside of play:

Success Rolls

Characters may have important missions *between* play sessions. These might be tedious to game out, but vital – which is why you can do them "between times" and cover them with a few die rolls. For instance, in a treasure-hunting adventure, the group's scholar may need to spend a few weeks in the library making Research rolls to find useful maps. Meanwhile the thief is tavern-hopping, making Streetwise rolls to pick up useful rumors. The GM checks their sheets, sees how much time they spent at it, and rolls (one or more times) to see what they found.

Skill Study

Characters may wish to put time into actual study of their skills – or of new ones – to improve their scores or gain new skills. (If some characters are students, this is unavoidable!) The GM keeps a running total of the time they spend studying. When it's enough to buy a skill increase, the character's skill goes up immediately. See p. 82 for details.

Jobs

Time spent at work should also be recorded. It counts as study of the skill involved (though at only $\frac{1}{4}$ rate – that is, an eight-hour day of work counts as two hours of study). And it pays enough to live on – and maybe a little extra. (And in most societies, anyone who does *not* show up full-time for work will soon be fired, and hurting for money!) And a job can be a great springboard to adventure in the hands of a creative GM. See p. 192.

Award character points for good play – see below.

File away the play material. NPC records, GM Control Sheet, etc., will all be useful later – be sure to keep track of them! NPCs, in particular, can often be "recycled" in a later adventure.

Plan the next session with the players. This is especially important in a continuing campaign. Decide where the game will take up next week, how much game time will have passed, and anything else that the players need to know before the next session starts.

AWARDING CHARACTER POINTS

At the end of each play session, the GM awards bonus character points for good play. "Good play" is anything that advances the characters' mission, or shows good roleplaying – preferably both. Roleplaying is more important than mission success! If a player did something totally outside his character's personality (for instance, if a total coward performed a brave act), this would not be worth any points, even if it saved the day for the rest of the group!

Bonus points should be awarded separately (and probably secretly) to each character. Players should record their points on the character record sheets if they intend to play that character again; the GM may also want to keep his own record of bonus points granted.

Bonus points will be used by the players to develop and improve their characters – see *Character Development*, p. 81.

Some guidelines for point awards, per session of play:

For good roleplaying, within the original concept of the character: 1 to 3 points per play session.

For excellent roleplaying, even if it imperiled the mission: 4 or 5 points per session.

For poor roleplaying, ignoring or violating the stated personality or objectives of the character: -1 to -5 points.

For successful completion of the mission, or progress toward its completion in a multi-session adventure: 2 to 4 points.

For partial failure, or significant setbacks in a multi-session adventure: -1 or -2 points.

For disastrous failure of the mission: -4 or -5 points.

For a clever action or solution to a specific problem, as long as it is in character: 1 point per character per action.

It is strongly suggested that no PC *ever* get more than 5 points for any one play session. Two or 3 should be the usual ceiling. A character gets no points for a session in which his dependent NPC is killed, seriously wounded, or kidnapped and not recovered.

A character's net point total for an adventure can be zero, but it *cannot* be negative. The worst you can do, at the end of an adventure, is 0 points. A character *can* end a *play session* with a negative total, if that play session is part of a continuing adventure. The negative total is not subtracted from character points he has already earned, but it will count against anything he may earn during the *remainder* of that adventure.

Avoiding Character Inflation

As GM, you should try to balance the number of points you give out, so that characters improve fast enough to keep things interesting, but not so fast that they outrun their foes and unbalance your campaign. Also, if the original characters are now 400-point demigods, new players, and their characters, may tend to feel useless unless they are specifically brought into the action.

Some of this depends on the background; superheroic types are *expected* to improve fast (and their enemies improve, too), while ordinary cops or soldiers gain skills or promotions at a slower pace. In the final analysis, it's up to the GM to determine what is right for his own campaign and his own players.

22 GAME WORLDS

This chapter will cover some of the more important things the GM should consider about the campaign's game world. (For more about creating your own game worlds, see the next chapter!) Not coincidentally, these are also the things that a PC needs to know for successful travel and adventuring. Good luck . . .

TECH LEVELS

A *tech level* is a general description of a culture's highest achievement in technology (or a certain type of technology). If a WWII soldier (TL6) gets dropped back into the days of King Arthur (TL3) . . . things get interesting. Of course, time travel isn't necessary – even today, you can drop back three or four tech levels if you visit the right part of the world.

It is also quite possible for a locale, nation or world to have widely varying TLs in different subjects. For instance, weaponry and medicine might be well-advanced, but transportation and communication could lag behind by a level or so.

Tech levels run from 0 up. High tech levels are likely to seem like magic to anyone of a sufficiently low tech level!

Note that a party will always attract attention if it displays work of a tech level above that with which the local citizens are familiar. This attention may be mere curiosity – or it may be awe, worship or hatred. The greater the disparity between the local tech level and the party's, the greater the excitement.

Of course, locals may be familiar with technology they do not themselves possess. A highland village with Iron Age (TL2) technology might be quite familiar with the TL3 steel weapons carried by travelers, and the richer villagers would have a few, though the local smiths cannot duplicate or repair them. This would be expressed in parentheses – the village would be TL2(3).

Tech Levels and Skills

Many skills are different at each tech level. These skills are indicated by a /TL on the Skill List. When you take this skill, replace the TL by the tech level at which you learn the skill. An engineer in a medieval world, for instance, would learn the skill of Engineer/TL3.

If you plan to keep your characters in one game world, and to encounter nothing of different tech levels, none of this will matter. For instance, a purely medieval campaign would have no need of tech levels except (in the beginning) to define available equipment; tech levels of *skills* would not be needed at all! But a science-fiction or time-travelling campaign will need skill tech levels. Every time the characters change "worlds," they will enter a different tech level, and their relative abilities will change accordingly.

You are always most effective when dealing with the equipment and techniques of your own tech level. Higher tech levels will present unfamiliar developments; lower tech levels will challenge you to work with "obsolete" equipment. The farther away from your "home" tech level you get, the greater is the penalty when you try to use your skill. Modifications are as follows:

Tech level 4 (or more) higher than yours: Impossible

Tech level 3 higher than yours: -15	Tech level 1 lower than yours: -1
Tech level 2 higher than yours: -10	Tech level 2 lower than yours: -3
Tech level 1 higher than yours: -5	Tech level 3 lower than yours: -5
Your own tech level: No penalty	Tech level 4 lower than yours: -7
	and so on . . .

Note that this penalty only applies when you try to work with the unfamiliar technology. Your Tech Level 7 walkie-talkie will work just as well in 1800 (TL5) as it does today. But if it quits, the local technicians will be at a -10 to repair it (and will probably break it permanently if they fool with it). And *you* will be at a -3 to repair it if

Tech Levels – General Historical Comparison

0. Stone Age: fire, lever, language
1. Bronze Age (Athens): wheel, writing, agriculture
2. Iron Age (Rome): keystone arch
3. Medieval (pre-1450): steel weapons, mathematics with zero
4. Renaissance/Colonial (1450-1700): gunpowder, printing
5. Industrial Revolution (1701-1900): mass production, steam power, telegraph
6. World War I/World War II (1901-1950): cars, airplanes, radio
7. Modern (1951-2000): nuclear energy, computer, laser, rockets
8. Spacefaring (2001-2050?): slower-than-light space travel, fusion power, implants
9. Starfaring: faster-than-light star travel, sentient computers, longevity, deteronic frombotzer
10. Antimatter: antimatter power, artificial gravity, slow FTL radio
11. Force: force screens, tractor beams, fast FTL radio
12. Gravitic: contragravity, grav compensators, personal force screens
13. Worldbuilding: full terraforming of planets
14. Dysonian: construction of worlds, ringworlds and so on
15. MT: matter transmission, cosmic power
16+. As you wish . . .

Transportation

0. Feet; canoes; sledges
1. Horseback; horse-drawn carts; sailing rafts and small galleys
2. Horseback with a saddle; ocean-going galleys
3. Horseback with a saddle and stirrups; sailing ships
4. Fully-rigged ships; hot-air balloons
5. Steamships; railroads; zeppelins
6. Automobiles; aircraft; ocean liners; submarines
7. Jet aircraft; space shuttles; mag-lev monorails; hovercraft
8. Spaceships; orbital towers; ballistic airliners
9-11. Faster-than-light star travel; space yachts
12. Contragravity vessels and personal flying belts
15. Matter transmission
16+. POOF. You're there.

Weapons and Armor

0. Fists and stone weapons.
1. Metal-tipped spears and arrows; bronze swords; leather armor
2. Iron swords; shields; scale armor
3. Steel weapons; lances, flails, crossbows; plate and chainmail; castles
4. Black-powder muskets; cannon; sailing warships
5. Ironclad warships; dynamite; repeating handguns
6. Battleships; tanks; machine-guns; fighter aircraft; fission bombs; flak jackets
7. Nuclear missiles; atomic submarines; jet fighters; Kevlar
8. Cybertanks; orbital lasers; bioweapons; BPC combat armor and battlesuit; reflec; Gauss needlers
9. Starships; genius bombs; flamers; particle-beam blasters; stunners
10. Nerve pistols; superheavy combat armor; disruption beams
11. Force screens; personal force shields; tractor beams; antimatter missiles
12. Grav tanks; personal force screens
13. Planetary missiles
14+. POOF. You're dead.

Power

0. Slaves
1. Horses and mules; water wheels
2. Windmills
3. Horses with horse-collars
4. (No significant improvement)
5. Steam engines; direct current
6. Hydroelectric power; alternating current
7. Fission and hot fusion; solar
8. Fission/electric; orbital-collected solar power
9. Cold fusion/electric
10-12. Antimatter
13. "Pocket" antimatter
14. Total conversion
15. Cosmic power

Medicine

0. None
1. Supportive treatment; herbs
2. Bleeding the sick; chemical remedies
3. Amputations and crude prosthetics
4. Experiments that killed the patients
5. Germ theory of disease; anesthetics; vaccines
6. Major surgery; antibiotics
7. Organ transplants
8. Cloning; simple implants; bionics; plastiskin
9. Longevity; panimmunity; braintapes; complex implants; suspended animation; automedic
10. Genericillin; Torpine
11. Sensa-skin
12. Full panimmunity; regeneration
16+. POOF. You're healed.

you have to depend on 1800s testing equipment, etc. (A little GM creativity will help here. In this particular case, even if you *do* figure out the problem, it will take you weeks or months to come up with a substitute part, since you can't just go down to the radio store and buy it!)

Building Up Local Technology

There may be times when you need to improve the local tech level. A group of castaways might have high-tech knowledge, but little or no equipment to work with. In that case, they would need to "build the tools to build the tools" to use their technological knowledge. In extreme cases, your castaways may have to go all the way back to primitive mining to get the ore to refine to metal to build the tools to build the tools . . . ! Or a single traveler may want to impart his high-tech knowledge to the people he is visiting. (We assume that he has the cooperation of his hosts, or he doesn't have a chance.)

Any such situation is largely at the GM's discretion. But it *can* be done. Some of the best adventure stories of all time have revolved around one of these premises: *Swiss Family Robinson, Lord Kalvan of Otherwhen,* the *Riverworld* series, *A Connecticut Yankee in King Arthur's Court,* et multiple cetera.

General guideline: A "science" is one of the categories of knowledge listed in the sidebars on pp. 185-186. It takes *two* years of work to move each science from one tech level to the next, assuming that (a) you have an ample supply of labor; (b) you have an ample supply of raw materials; (c) you are fully familiar with the lower tech level (all relevant skills at 12 or better), and (d) you know where you're going, and are fully familiar with the higher tech level (all relevant skills at 12 or better).

IMPORTANT: This rule does *not* cover inventions. This is only to be used by high-tech-level characters when re-inventing, or introducing, technology to a low-tech society or situation.

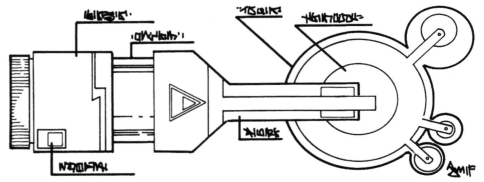

New Inventions

Although they are rare in the real world, fiction holds many gadgeteers who sit down over coffee and invent marvelous world-shaking devices to solve the day's problems. The following rule is intended to simulate this sort of incredible inventiveness. It is most useful in modern or science-fiction game worlds, and GMs are free to ignore it entirely if they so choose! This rule leaves a lot to the GM's discretion . . .

To invent a new gadget, the *player* must have a clear idea of what he wants to invent and how it will work. This must be described to the GM. A very clear description, or clever idea for a particular approach, should be worth a die-roll bonus. A cloudy idea will lead to a die-roll penalty. The new gadget should be, at most, one tech level in advance of the inventor's skill.

Inventing a new gadget requires skill in the appropriate sort of Engineering. It may also require skill in another subject; for instance, inventing a new and improved telescope would require skill in Astronomy, to understand the problem. Extra skill requirements are up to the GM.

Two successful skill rolls are required to develop an invention. Each is made on Engineering, or on the "problem area" skill if it is lower than your Engineering skill. Each is made by the GM, so the engineer never knows for sure if he's on the right track!

The first roll is a "conception" roll. Make it at Skill-15. No equipment is required, except perhaps a tablecloth to draw on and several gallons of coffee. One roll is permitted per inventor per day. A successful "conception" roll gives a theory which can be tested in the labs – proceed to the next paragraph. A critical failure gives a "flawed theory" which looks good but will never work – see next page.

The second roll represents laboratory work – this is the "working model" roll. Appropriate facilities are required – this is entirely up to the GM, but should include the most advanced possible shop and computer equipment for that tech level! Anything less will give a penalty (again, GM's discretion) on the "working model" roll.

This second roll is also made at Skill-15. One roll is permitted per week. Unless the shop is *tremendous,* only one gadgeteer (presumably the one with the highest skill) may roll. Add 1 to his effective skill for every "assistant" with a Skill level of 20 or more in either Engineering or the particular skill required for the invention – maximum of 4 assistants.

A successful roll will prove the theory and give a working model. For things like a stardrive, of course, the working model may not be big enough to do much good; this is entirely up to the GM! A critical failure will produce an explosion or other accident, doing a *minimum* of 2 dice damage to the gadgeteer and each assistant – more if they were playing with something very dangerous!

If the inventor was working with a flawed theory, a critical success in the lab will let the gadgeteer know his theory was bad. Otherwise, no matter how many times he tries, he will never succeed – so the GM must keep the rolls secret.

For campaigns in which gadgeteering becomes an important part of the action, more detailed rules can be found in *GURPS Supers,* pp. 66-72.

TRAVEL

Travel is, almost by definition, necessary to an adventure. Very little happens to most of us at home. The GM is free to pass over travel with a bit of narration, in order to get the party to the scene of action. But it's much more interesting to make travel, with its hazards, part of the game. The farther you have to go, and the wilder your game world (regardless of tech level), the more likely it is that travel itself will be an adventure.

A party going through unfamiliar territory should carry provisions, water and (if necessary) camping gear. The GM should be sure to arrange problems for any party that jaunts off into the wilderness with nothing more than weapons, armor and greed. See *Starvation and Dehydration* on p. 128, for starters.

Distance traveled in a day, either on foot or horseback, is a direct function of your encumbrance (see p. 76). Under ideal travel conditions, a party in good shape may plan on traveling the following distances in one day's march:

No encumbrance	50 miles
Light encumbrance	40 miles
Medium encumbrance	30 miles
Heavy encumbrance	20 miles
Extra heavy encumbrance	10 miles

A party's speed is equal to the speed of its slowest member. Whatever your daily mileage, you will spend about the same amount of time traveling. But the heavier your load and the worse the traveling conditions, the more slowly you will walk, and the more frequently you will stop to rest. See *Fatigue,* p. 134.

Parties with mechanical transport will move at that transport's best speed, depending on the terrain. Remember that driving or piloting for over 8 hours a day, or about 4 hours at a single shift, can be dangerously tiring or boring and may require a roll against the appropriate Vehicle skill to avoid a mishap.

Terrain and Travel

Terrain and weather affect travel both for good and ill. The GM has the final word on the effect of any condition on the speed and difficulty of movement. Some guidelines:

Off-Road

Adventurers frequently have to travel on whatever nature has provided. This can vary greatly in a very short time. A traveler in the North American west, for instance, can spend most of a day struggling a few miles through heavily forested mountains. Then he clears the mountains and can make five times his morning distance, in the same time, as he crosses the plains.

Improving Skill in Alternate Tech Levels

This rule is needed only for characters who travel between different tech levels. Treat each tech level as a different skill, defaulting to your "home" skill at the penalty listed on p. 185 for working at that level. For instance, Engineer/TL5 defaults to Engineer/TL7 at a -3.

However, by treating Engineer/TL5 as a *different skill,* you may study it in order to perform better at that tech level. This is handled as described under *Skill Defaults,* p. 44.

Example: Your IQ is 12, and your Engineer/TL7 skill is 17. Your default skill at Engineer/TL5 is 14 (17 minus 3). If you want to study Engineer/TL5, you start with your skill at level 14. This is (IQ+2) level for you. So your next level of skill is (IQ+3), which for this Mental/Hard skill will cost another 2 points. So, for 2 character points, you can raise your Engineer/TL5 skill to 15. This will not affect your Engineer/TL7 skill at all.

Thus, a high skill in another tech level will help you learn. (If your skill is not high enough to let you start from a favorable default, ignore the above system and learn the skill normally.) This will let you build up a character who is equally at home with transistors, vacuum tubes, crystal sets, and 25th-century deteronics. It just takes a little time . . .

Weather

Game weather is up to the GM. Weather should at least be consistent within climatological patterns. Surprises can happen; snow does fall in Miami in July, but not very often! Adventurers with Area Knowledge should have at least a chance to predict the weather.

Rain

Rain has only negative effects on transportation. This is usually a curse to adventurers, but sometimes can deter pursuit or invasion. In general, rain will halve travel speed in *any* terrain except on average or good roads. Even there, rain can cut motor vehicle travel speeds by 10% or so *if* the drivers are prudent. Drivers who push on at full speed are at -2 (or worse) to any Driving roll in case of emergency. The same is true of air travel.

A very light rain speeds sailing ships (wet sails catch more wind), but anything heavier will slow all marine traffic to some degree.

Rain can also spoil food supplies, wet powder, soak bowstrings (making them worthless until they dry) and destroy maps and papers. Most animals are bad-tempered in the rain (-2 to controllability).

Continued on next page . . .

Weather
(Continued)

Wind

Winds from gale to hurricane force can make even land travel impossible. At sea, the only solution is to run for open water, take in all sail, throw out a sea anchor, and hope she stays right side up until it's over. In the air, get as high as possible and hope the fuel outlasts the storm.

Even less-than-destructive winds can be hard on wind-driven transportation. It is possible to get somewhere at sea in any wind at all, as long as it isn't *no* wind. A ship can wind up sailing back and forth outside the destination port, waiting for a favorable wind to get in.

Winds are to some extent predictable. In the Indian Ocean, the summer monsoon blows from Africa toward India; and the winter monsoon blows from India toward Africa. In the North Atlantic, the wind blows mostly toward Europe; in the South Atlantic, the wind blows mostly toward America (until you hit latitude 40° South and the wind shifts back). On a smaller scale, the morning wind usually blows toward shore, and the evening wind toward the sea. Earth and water change temperature at a different rate, and the wind shifts to fit.

Heat

Too much heat can be deadly (see p. 130). But, though it makes travelers miserable, almost all terrain is unaffected, or actually improved for travel, by hot weather.

Cold

Exposure to cold can of itself be enough to kill (see p. 130). And cold greatly affects transportation. Wheeled vehicles are immobilized by snow and ice. Sleds can move faster on the snow than wheels can on solid ground. Frozen rivers are closed to boats, but become highways for skids and skates.

Ice can support weight as follows:

Under 1 inch: Small animals, possibly children, maybe elves

1-3": Children, fast-moving skaters, deer, wolves

3-4": Infantry in single file, adult explorers, lightly-loaded dogsleds

4-6": Cavalry, light horse-drawn artillery, snowmobiles, motorcycles, pack-mules, heavily-loaded dogsleds

6-8": Medium horse-drawn artillery, loaded wagons, herds of cattle, Stegosaurs, jeeps

8-12": Heavy horse-drawn artillery, trucks, light helicopters, Zulu dance performances

Over 12": Tanks, artillery while firing, Tyrannosaurs, C-130s, temporary towns (until the thaw)

Terrain changes with weather. Deep snow turns a plain into very bad terrain. The same cold changes a river from an obstacle into a solid highway.

Very Bad terrain: Jungle, dense second-growth forest, swamp, mountains, soft sand or deep snow. Daily rates of movement are only 20% of normal (10 miles a day for an unencumbered man). Such terrain is usually impassable for wheeled vehicles or animal teams.

Bad terrain: Steep hills, forest, or terrain "broken" by gullies, arroyos, or frequent steep-banked streams. Movement rates are halved for foot or mounted travel. Daily movement rates for teams and wheeled vehicles are 25% of normal.

Average terrain: Rolling hills, light forest or solid ice. Movement is normal.

Good terrain: Hard-packed desert or level plain. Daily movement rates are increased by 25%. Wheeled vehicles move as on an average road (see below).

Roads

In civilized country, honest travelers will usually keep to the roads; indeed, leaving the roads will be seen as a sign of bad intentions.

Very bad road: Little more than a guide to the way around the worst obstacles. It has no weather-proofing, and is not completely cleared. Rivers are crossed at unmarked fords, or by swimming. Daily rates of movement are the same as for the surrounding terrain, except in very bad terrain. Here, daily rates of movement are $1/3$ normal, and teams and wheeled vehicles usually can move. Weather affects movement just as it does on the surrounding terrain.

Bad road: Cleared but not *metalled*, that is, nothing is put on the surface to make it waterproof. Rivers are crossed at bridges, ferries or (at worst) marked fords. All travel is at standard rates, weather permitting. Weather affects movement on the road just as it does on the surrounding terrain, *except* for mud. Since the road is chewed up by traffic, the effect of mud is to turn the road into Very Bad terrain, forcing wheeled traffic to travel beside the road or stop moving.

Average road: Cleared and metalled. Daily travel rates are normal, and are not affected by rain (except for motor vehicles – see sidebar, p. 187). Rivers are crossed by all-weather bridges or ferries. Effective weights for animal-drawn loads on wheels are halved. Wheeled motor vehicles can travel at speeds up to 50 mph without difficulty and without damaging the road. Tracked vehicle traffic will degrade the road surface. Most roads below TL6 are average at best. Examples are Roman roads and the English coaching roads of the 19th century.

Good road: Permanent hard-surface road, effectively weatherproof and not damaged by wheeled or tracked vehicles at any speed. Only the worst weather (e.g., floods, car-toppling winds, sheet ice or blizzards) really affects travel conditions, though rain (see sidebar, p. 187) will slow prudent motor-vehicle drivers. The *autobahnen* and Interstates of TL6 and 7 rank as good roads.

LAWS AND CUSTOMS

Each game world will have its own laws and customs. Furthermore, *within* each world, laws and customs will vary greatly from place to place. In some worlds it is possible to research these things in advance (the Law skill helps here). In other worlds, you must learn them the hard way. (Law helps here, too, if you specifically investigate; Streetwise can find out "informally.")

As a rule, the use of *force* or the *threat of force* will be illegal or improper wherever you go. The stronger the local government, the more true this will be; government usually considers the use of force to be its own right and monopoly. Self-defense is sometimes an exception – but not always!

Note that the public display of non-customary weapons is a "threat of force," and will lead to bad reactions even if it's technically legal. If you walk down a village street in heavy armor, axes and polearms at the ready, the villagers will be *very* suspicious of your motives.

Violating a law will usually lead to some sort of trial and possible punishment. Violating someone's *rights* may lead to a "civil" trial and a fine – or just an informal beating. Violating a custom will simply give you a reaction penalty – possibly a big one – whenever you try to deal with a local. And the offended locals may not even tell you what you are doing wrong!

Law Enforcement and Jail

If you break the law, it will be the duty of *some* local to do *something* about it. This may be anything from a polite request that you clean up your act, to arrest and jail pending a trial. In some places, the police are also the judge, jury and executioner, empowered to make an instant decision and act on it.

Likewise, jails range from "honor system" to dungeons with chains. Many game worlds have widely varying types of jail, depending on the crime, the accuser, the social status of the prisoner and any timely bribes.

Trials

A trial may be totally fair and honest – or a show trial, with the outcome predetermined. It may be rigorously formal, or noisy and informal.

A simple game mechanism for a trial: The GM plays the judge and jury. In a criminal proceeding, he makes a reaction roll, with appropriate modifiers, and decides guilt or innocence based on his general reaction toward the characters. If the reaction roll is bad and the characters are guilty, the severity of the punishment is determined by how low the roll is.

In a lawsuit for damages, the judge makes a reaction roll toward each party to the suit. The party that gets the best reaction is the winner. The bigger the difference in the rolls, the more money (or other satisfaction) the winner gets.

Trial by Ordeal

This is a trial in which Fate is supposed to make the decision. *Example:* Anyone accused of witchcraft is thrown into a pond. Anyone who floats is a witch, and is taken out and burned. If they sink, they must have been innocent.

For a trial by ordeal, the GM should determine the skill rolls needed to survive. (The above example would be hard to survive!) Some other examples: Walk a beam across a canyon (roll DX-4 for each 10 feet of beam); hold a hot piece of iron (roll both ST-3 and Will-3); find your way out of a maze (roll IQ).

Trial by Combat

A trial by combat is like a trial by ordeal, in that Fate is supposed to determine guilt or innocence. As a rule, though, trial by combat provides the punishment as well. The guilty party dies.

A trial by combat may be fair (evenly matched champions); loaded (uneven champions) or totally unfair (throw the prisoner into a pit with a monster).

ECONOMICS

The economic situation of each game world is different. But money, in some form or another, is important in almost all campaigns.

Money is *anything* that can be exchanged for what you want. It varies from one game world to the next. In a high-tech world, everything may be done by credit card. In a low-tech world, gold and silver may be king.

All prices in **GURPS** (whatever the game world) are indicated by a dollar sign – $ – just to make it easy on the writers and typesetters. GMs are welcome to translate this to credits, copper farthings, Martian foomphra or whatever they feel is appropriate to the adventure.

In a low-tech world, rings and jewelry are also money. They may not have a set value imprinted on them – but they are small and portable, and are easily traded for coins or bartered directly for needed goods. In fact, many societies exist largely by barter – which can be a test of the players' ingenuity.

Gold and Silver

A traditional assumption of fantasy games (and many fantasy novels) is that gold and silver are heavy and inconvenient to carry around for purchases. If you are the GM, this is true only if you want it to be true.

Historically, gold and silver were *very* valuable – and many goods were cheap. For an authentic medieval English (14th-century) economy, treat the $ as a "farthing," a copper coin about the size of a quarter. A silver penny is worth $4 and is smaller than a dime; 250 such coins ($1,000) weigh one pound. If silver and gold trade at 20 to 1 (a reasonable ratio for much of history) then a pound of gold is worth $20,000! So a man could carry a king's ransom in his backpack.

On the other hand, a GM who wants wealth to be less portable may assume that the $ is a one-ounce silver coin, like a silver dollar. A one-ounce gold piece would then be worth $20 (interestingly, this was the denomination of the U.S. 1-ounce gold piece in the 1800s). At that rate, 12 coins (troy weight) would weigh a pound; a pound of gold would be worth only $240. In such a world, precious gems are the only way to carry a large amount of wealth in a small package, and caravans loaded with gold might actually exist!

Controlling Inflation

The GM should be careful not to let the players get too rich, too soon. Rather than drive up the prices of everyday goods, you can arrange an occasional catastrophe to keep the PCs broke – or encourage them to buy things (ships, noble titles, bridges, etc.) that cost a *lot* of money. Either that, or arrange adventures where no amount of money can replace brains.

In a high-tech world, there is no limit to the advantages you can buy with money. In a low-tech environment, once you have one good suit of armor, one fine weapon and a couple of fine horses, there's not much else you can do to buy personal prowess. Except hire an army . . .

Also, be realistic about the value of loot. Armor, combat vehicles and similar military materials are likely to be damaged after a fight – the PCs will be lucky to get ⅓ of their "retail value" if they drag them into town. (A *very* realistic GM will assess the PCs maintenance costs for repairing their *own* vehicles/weapons/ships/armor, too.)

Bankrolls and Possessions

The money a character has on his person should be listed on the front of his Character Sheet, just like his other possessions. If a lot of transactions are taking place, this can be recorded on a separate sheet of paper to avoid erasing a hole in the Character Sheet!

Money "in the bank" – that is, money a character does not carry with him – should be listed separately. The location of this "bankroll" should also be listed. GMs may arrange floods, bank robberies, tax increases and other entertainments to deprive the PCs of their savings – or at least make them work to get them back. The same is true of all other possessions they do not carry with them.

Buying and Selling

Players can buy and sell among themselves at whatever prices they can agree on.

For outside transactions, the GM (or Adversary) should roleplay a merchant dealing in the needed goods or services. For routine situations, no reaction roll is needed. But if the situation is in some way unusual, or if the players are new in town and have been swaggering around in armor and acting strangely, make a reaction roll to see if the merchants will have anything to do with them!

In general, the GM should set prices reasonably, following the laws of supply and demand. Camels will be valuable near the desert, worthless in the jungle. After a great battle, used armor may be on sale at scrap-metal prices. And so on.

The Merchant skill (p. 64) will help PCs get good deals.

Equipment and Supplies

Each game-world book will have a list of equipment and supplies, and their "normal" costs. Copies of this list can be given to the players when they plan for an adventure. Lists of equipment for Fantasy/Medieval campaigns, and for Modern (also usable for futuristic) campaigns, are included with this set.

The players will want to buy things that aren't on the list. The GM should allow any reasonable purchase – as *he* defines "reasonable" – setting prices by comparison with things on the list. A mail-order catalog is a useful resource.

Loot, and Disposing of It

Many adventures are overt quests for treasure. Many aren't. Nevertheless, it is customary to let the players find something of value if they complete an adventure successfully. If nothing else, this will let them pay for their supplies for the next adventure . . .

The classic fantasy adventure sends successful adventurers home with chests of gold and jewels. Very convenient! If you are writing a more realistic adventure, you will invent more interesting forms of treasure.

Let's say the party was hired as caravan guards. They drove off the bandits that attacked the caravan, tracked them to their lair, wiped them out and took their loot. Now, assuming that enough pack animals are available, it will be a simple matter to take the goods into town. Locate a merchant (using Streetwise if necessary). Make the best sales approach possible. The GM makes a reaction roll for the merchant. If he's interested in the goods, he makes an offer, which the players can accept or reject. Simple.

But it doesn't have to be that simple. Identifying treasure, and turning it into cash, can be a major part of the challenge! Some possibilities:

(a) The treasure is not portable. How will they get it home?

(b) The treasure is not recognizable as such without a skill roll. Or it looks like treasure to the unskilled observer but is really junk.

(c) The treasure is valuable only to certain collectors or specialists; getting it to a buyer may be an adventure in itself.

(d) The treasure is itself illegal or immoral and must be hidden.

(e) The treasure is perishable or dangerous and requires special handling.

(f) Somebody else is hunting the treasure.

(g) The treasure is not goods, but *information* – a clue to the *real* loot.

In spite of your best planning, the players will occasionally find "loot" you had not anticipated. For instance, the slavers had them trapped in iron cages – and when they escape, they take the cages with them to sell for scrap. This is when you improvise. If you have no clear idea what the goods are worth, just make the story interesting. If you want the party to have money, then there's a demand for scrap iron in the next village. If not – nobody is interested. Simple.

Social Level and Cost of Living

All characters are considered "middle class" unless specified otherwise, either by a specific game world or adventure, or because they have a specific advantage or disadvantage that changes their social level. In most game worlds, social level is directly related to wealth. In some societies, it is possible to be noble but dead broke, or wealthy but scorned. Therefore, Wealth and Status are separate though related advantages; see p. 16.

Anyone above the level of "slave" will have a *cost of living* related to their social class. This cost of living is subtracted from a character's job income to determine the amount that he has for his own use. Characters *must* spend the cost associated with their social class. Failure to do so should bring appropriate penalties from the GM. You may always spend *more* than the required amount; sometimes (GM's option) this may get you general reaction benefits or even help you into the next social level.

Social levels will be defined in each worldbook. A generic social level chart for fantasy/medieval and modern Western cultures is given below. Note that status is considerably "fuzzier" for modern-day cultures . . .

status and cost of living

Level	Fantasy/Medieval Example; Monthly Cost of Living	Modern Western Example; Monthly Cost of Living
8	Divine ruler: $50,000+	No equivalent
7	King, pope: $20,000+	President: $20,000+
6	Prince, duke, archbishop: $10,000	Governor, senator: $10,000
5	Baron, count, bishop: $5,000	Corporate head: $8,000
4	Landed lord: $2,500	Who's Who: $6,000
3	Lesser lord: $1,500	Large-city mayor: $4,000
2	Knight, mayor, great merchant: $800	Mayor: $2,400
1	Squire, captain, merchant: $400	Doctor, councilman: $1,200
0	Freeman: $200	Ordinary citizen: $600
-1	Bondsman or servant: $100	Poor: $300
-2	Outsider, underworld: $50	Street beggar
-3	Street beggar: $50	No equivalent
-4	Serf or slave: $50	No equivalent

In a campaign that does not use jobs, you can (a) subtract the cost of living from the characters' adventuring income, or (b) ignore this rule entirely!

In general, a high social level is more expensive to maintain, but gets you reaction bonuses and other benefits. Depending on the game world and the GM, your social class may bring various special benefits.

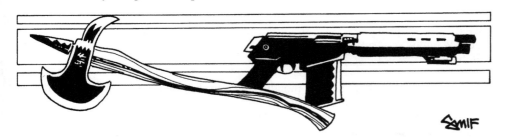

When characters move between game worlds (see p. 200) they will naturally want to take some cash with them. But what is "legal tender" in one world may be worthless in another. There are two principles for the GM to remember here:

First: Money in a new world isn't "legal tender." It is a commodity. If you take medieval gold coins to the 20th century, they will sell as curios – or as gold, for perhaps $400 a troy ounce. If you take American paper money to the 10th century, it will be worthless. So, rather than money, better take along a few plastic hard-hats and maybe a cassette tape recorder. ("What am I bid for this miraculous orchestra in a box?")

Second: A cross-world trading operation can get very rich very quickly. If a GM allows cross-world travel, it is up to *him* to preserve balance by limiting the quantity and/or type of goods that can be moved between worlds. A suggested limit: only what the travelers can carry on their persons – and trips should *not* be frequent.

Making Your Own Goods

Characters with the appropriate skills will probably want to save money by making their own equipment. This is legal, as long as the GM is willing to go along with it.

In general, this works better in low-tech worlds. Any Indian hunter ought to be able to make his own bow; a medieval smith or leatherworker could build his own armor. But a Tech Level 6 gunsmith, though he certainly *could* make his own flintlock, would be quite a while at the job – and a TL8 gunsmith would certainly find it easier to buy a .45 automatic than to go into the shop and build one. The availability of mass-produced items makes a lot of difference.

Things to consider:

(a) What raw materials are needed, and how much will they cost?

(b) How long will it take to do the work?

(c) Is there a chance that the work might be useless when finished? *Example:* forging of a high-quality sword blade is a tricky job, and would require repeated Blacksmith skill rolls.

Listings of all possible items, raw materials, skills and building times would take up several books – so this *must* be left up to the GM.

Defining New Jobs

Players are certain to come up with ideas for new jobs suited to their characters' talents. In general, the GM should allow any job that seems reasonable and realistic.

Required skills and monthly income can be set by common sense for modern worlds, and by the GM's fiat for fictional worlds. For a historical campaign, research may be required . . . the GM should invite the players to find and submit reliable information about the jobs they want! Whatever the campaign period, monthly income should be kept in line with existing jobs, to avoid unbalancing the campaign.

The success roll and critical failure results are *always* set by the GM, by analogy with jobs already listed on the Job Table in use by the campaign.

Remember that unless the economy is under some sort of stress or outside control, jobs will never be high-paying unless they are *difficult* (hard success roll), *dangerous* (severe consequences of a failed success roll), *highly trained* (difficult skill prerequisites), or *privileged* (difficult Status or Wealth prerequisites). If someone wants to be a wealthy movie star, he must buy appropriate Status and Wealth with character points, as well as the needed skills!

Jobs

The jobs available in each game world, and the pay for those jobs, will be defined in the Job Table of that game world book. This is important both when players need to find a hireling (see p. 194) and when they want to find jobs of their own. A *very simple* Job Table is given on p. 194 as an example.

Some jobs have skill or experience prerequisites. Default values don't count here; you must have at least a half-point invested in the skill.

Finding a Job

If a job is one requiring an employer, a PC may roll once per week to see if he found work. His base roll is equal to his IQ. Modifiers are as follows:

City size. The more people in the city, the better your chance to find the particular type of job that you are looking for:

Under 99: .... -5	10,000 – 49,999: .... +1
100 – 999: .... -4	50,000 – 99,999: .... +2
1,000 – 4,999: .... -2	100,000 or more: .... +3
5,000 – 9,999: 0	

Scarcity. Higher-paying jobs are harder to find. If the job (see p. 194) would be "lower-class," you are at +1 to find such a job. If "middle-class," no modifier. -1 for each "class" above middle-class.

Advertising. You can advertise that you are *looking* for work. +1 if you spend $30 to advertise, +2 for $300, +3 for $3,000, and so on. In a low-tech setting, "advertising" means posting handbills, hiring criers, etc.

Overqualification. If your skill for the job in question is higher than the minimum prerequisite, you are likelier to find the job. If your skill is 1 higher than required, add 1 to your chance. If it is 2 or 3 higher, add 2. GMs may improve a character's roll as they see fit if he has extra skills that would logically help him do a job (or impress a potential employer).

Multiple jobs. If you are qualified for more than one job, you can look for two jobs at once, at a -1 to each roll; 3 at once, for a -2 to each roll, and so on. Unless time and the GM allow, you can't actually *hold* two jobs at once – find one and keep it.

Income from Jobs

A character earns income from his job for every week spent on the job. Time spent adventuring is usually not "on the job." The GM can make exceptions for vacations, work done while traveling, etc., as he wishes.

The difference between a job's *pay* and the *cost of living* for a character's social level is his to save or spend as he wishes. In a fantasy world, an adventurer will save up to buy gear, training, etc. In other game worlds, he may have other things to do with his earnings.

job income

Character's Wealth Level	Job's Wealth Level				
	Poor	Struggling	Average	Comfortable	Wealthy
Poor	1	$^2/5$	$^1/5$	$^1/10$	NA
Struggling	1	1	$^1/2$	$^1/4$	$^1/10$
Average	1	1	1	$^1/2$	$^1/5$
Comfortable	1	1	1	1	$^2/5$
Wealthy	1	1	1	2	1
Very Wealthy	1	1	1	4	2
Filthy Rich	1	1	1	10	10

A character earns the standard monthly wage for his job if his *wealth level* is the same as that of the job. For example, someone with Comfortable wealth and a Comfortable job earns the wage listed for that job.

However, a Struggling character, at the same Comfortable job, earns only ¼ as much, while a Wealthy person would earn twice the listed amount. Use the table above to determine what multiple of the listed wage each PC earns. Note that low-level jobs never pay very much – you can't be a wealthy tenant farmer. And high-level jobs are not available to those in low brackets – no top administrator makes merely average money.

Skill Increases through Jobs

If the GM is using Time Use Sheets to keep track of the characters' doings between adventures, every eight hours spent on the job counts as two hours of training in that job skill. See p. 82 for complete rules.

Job Success Rolls

At the end of every month in which a character works, refer to the *Success Roll* column of the Job Table, and roll against the skill, attribute, or other number given there. *PR* stands for *prerequisite*; roll against the prerequisite given for that job. When there are two or more prerequisites, roll against your best unless *worst* PR is specified. Ignore advantages (e.g., Status, Charisma) unless they are specifically mentioned. One advantage that will be specified as helping some job rolls is *Reaction*: the total of all positive and negative general reaction modifiers.

Thus, a servant always needs to roll his IQ or less, a merchant rolls against his Merchant skill-2, and a knight rolls against Strategy, Savoir-Faire, or his best weapon skill, whichever is best.

Most jobs are with an established business or master. If you roll anything but a critical success or critical failure, just collect that month's pay and go on. On a critical success, you get a 10% permanent raise in income (but no more than one raise every six months). Results of a critical failure vary; check the table.

Some occupations are freelance (or at least variable) in nature. These are marked with an asterisk on the table. For these jobs, the base income is earned when the skill roll is made *exactly*. For other successful rolls, increase that month's income by 10% for every point the roll was made by. If the roll is failed, reduce income by 10% for every point the roll was missed by. A critical success *triples* the month's income. If a critical failure is rolled, earn nothing – and check the table for other penalties.

If a PC's time spent adventuring is part of his job (e.g., for our sample character, Dai), his success should depend mainly on regular play, not success rolls.

Critical Failures on Job Rolls

The last column on the table shows the consequence of a Critical Failure. "LJ" stands for Lost Job – you were fired, demoted or lost the client. The "d" means dice of damage – you were in an accident, fight, etc. The "i" indicates a lost month's income ("2i" means losing 2 months income) – you were fined, forced to pay for damages, had to replace equipment, etc. "C" is a crippling injury – a random limb is crippled in addition to the listed damage. Roll vs. HT as usual to determine whether it will be permanent. If there are two entries separated by a "/", use the second result only when a natural 18 is rolled.

Note that for some dangerous jobs, the result of a critical failure can be serious injury. The GM may choose to play out these episodes to give the PC a fighting chance.

Sample Job Table (Fantasy/Medieval)

The table on the next page is a very simplified guideline, suitable for campaigns without a heavy economic component. GMs requiring more detail (or a different background) can check the appropriate *GURPS* worldbook, or develop their own table; see the sidebar on p. 192.

Slavery

In some places, as determined by the GM, slavery will be legal. PCs may buy slaves either for workers or as an investment. On the other hand, the PCs may be enslaved themselves! Anywhere slavery is legal, slaves will make up a large part of the job market. Thus, there is a 50% chance that any hireling found will actually be a slave. Slaves can sometimes be rented but must usually be bought.

The price of a slave is generally equal to the amount he could earn in five years, if free and working at the standard rate for his highest skill. The GM may adjust this selling price for any number of reasons: extra skills, good/bad attitude toward slavery, physical appearance, health, etc. Slavemasters rarely give a real bargain!

Loyalty of Slaves

Determine a slave's loyalty per p. 195. However, slaves are less predictable than ordinary hirelings. After a slave's initial loyalty is determined, roll *two* dice on the following table to determine a modifier for the slave's loyalty:

2-7 – No modifier.

8 – He was enslaved for some crime, and resents it. Reduce loyalty by 1.

9 – As above, but reduce loyalty by 2.

10 – His previous master was very cruel. If he is treated with kindness during the first week, his loyalty will increase by 2; otherwise, no change.

11 – He has a fanatic hatred of slavery. If he is treated well, he may like his masters as people, but will still escape as soon as possible. If treated badly (or even "average" for a slave) his loyalty drops to 6.

12 – He has a "slave mentality" and considers himself truly the property of his owner. His loyalty is automatically 20. You need never check loyalty; he will not demur even if he is given orders that condemn him to death.

Make loyalty checks for slaves as for any other hirelings. Modify loyalty by +1 or +2 if they are in a situation where they have nowhere to run!

Legal Complications

When slave-holding PCs enter an area where slavery is illegal, they must dispose of their slaves, or disguise the fact that they are slaves. Non-slave areas have different attitudes toward slavery. It may be: legal to own slaves, but not to buy or sell them locally; legal for non-citizens to own slaves while passing through, but illegal for permanent residents to own them; or illegal to own slaves at all.

A creative GM may impose other laws and customs regarding slavery. For instance, some races may be enslaved in a given area, while others may not. There may be ways for a slave to earn freedom. Slaves may even be permitted to own property and *buy* their freedom.

Job (Prerequisites), Monthly Income	Success Roll	Critical Failure
Poor Jobs		
Generic servant (no attribute below 7), $120	IQ	LJ/LJ, whipped, 2d
Thief* (at least 4 Thief skills at 13 +, or 2 at 16 +), $150	DX	3d/3d, caught and tried
Struggling Jobs		
Bravo*: low-class bodyguard, thug, fighter (ST 13 + and any Combat skill at 14+), $300	Best PR-2	2d/4d and jailed
Jongleur* (traveling entertainer). (Bard or Musical skill at 14+), $25 × skill, plus $5 × skill for each additional musical ability	PR-2	1d, audience throws tomatoes/2d, rocks!
Porter (ST 12+), $300	ST	1d, LJ/2d, LJ
Tenant farmer* (Agronomy 12+, ST 10+), $300	12	-1i/-2i, LJ
Average Jobs		
Artisan (any Craft skill at 14 +), $80× skill	Best PR-2	LJ/-2i, LJ
Free farmer* (Agronomy 12 +, ST 10 +, some land), $800	12	-1i/-3i, 2d
Guard or soldier (Combat skill levels totaling at least 40), $700	Best Weapon skill	2d/4d, C
Shopkeeper* (Merchant skill at 14+, $1,000 in goods), $80× skill	PR-1	-1i/bankrupt
Comfortable Jobs		
Master artisan* (any Craft skill at 20+), $170× skill	PR-4	LJ/LJ,-2i
Master Merchant* (Merchant skill at 16+, $10,000 in capital), $175× skill	PR	-2i/-6i
Military officer or knight (Weapon skill levels totaling at least 60; appropriate equipment: Strategy at 14+), $1,100	Best PR	-2i, -3d/-3i, -5d, LJ, . lose equipment
Wealthy Jobs		
Court noble/diplomat (Diplomacy 12 +, Politics 12 +, Savoir-Faire 14+), $100× PR total and up	PR-1	-1i/-2i, expelled from court
High church official (Administration 12 +, Theology 15 +; others depending upon specific creed), $5,000 and up	Best PR	-1i/-2i, LJ, declared heretic

* freelance jobs

HIRELINGS

A "hireling" is any non-player character employed by the adventurers. Hirelings are controlled by the GM; though the players can give any orders they like, the GM decides how they are followed.

A hireling provides an excellent way to add muscle or special talents to a party without bringing in more PCs. A party may have any number of hirelings. The number of important "personality" hirelings should be kept down to two or three at a time. The GM can manage any number of generic swordsmen – but keeping up with an important hireling, whose personality and record sheet are as detailed as any PC's, is challenging.

The GM keeps the record sheet for a hireling; the players may not see it. For unimportant hirelings, only a card or note is needed; important hirelings will require a full record sheet.

The GM may decide a hireling's attributes, appearance, skills, etc., in any way he likes. The Random Character Generation system is good for this.

Finding a Hireling

The players can't pull a hireling out of thin air. When they need to employ someone, they must search for a suitable person, just as in real life. They may not always get what they want. Of course, the GM can provide a hireling as part of a pre-planned adventure. He may do this overtly (the character approaches the party in a bar and asks for a job) or covertly (the players announce that they are looking for hirelings; the GM pretends to roll, but actually gives them a pre-planned character). To find a hireling of the desired type, a character makes an IQ roll. (Only one roll per hireling per party.) In a small town, a failed roll might mean that a hireling is just not available; in a city, the GM could allow another attempt in a week or even a day. The GM is also free to "load" the rolls. If he feels that they absolutely should have (or should not have) a hireling of a specific type, that is the way it will turn out.

Modifiers to your IQ when you search for a hireling:

City size. The bigger the city, the better your chance to find the particular type of hireling that you are looking for:

Under 99: .... -3	10,000 – 49,999: ....+1
100 – 999: ....-2	50,000 – 99,999:............... +2
1,000 – 4,999:............. -1	100,000 or more: .... +3
5,000 – 9,999: 0	

Scarcity. The pay a hireling can command depends on the scarcity of his abilities. If the best job he qualifies for (see p. 194) would be "poor," you are at +2 to find such a hireling. If it is "struggling," you are at +1. If "average," no modifier. -2 for "comfortable," -4 for "wealthy."

Advertising. +1 if you spend $30 to advertise, +2 for $300, +3 for $3,000, and so on. In a low-tech setting, "advertising" means posting handbills, hiring criers, etc.

Money offered. +1 if the pay is 20% over what the character should be able to command. +2 if it is 50% over. +3 if it is double what he should get.

Risk. -2 to find any non combat-type hireling for a job that involves obvious risk of combat. Combat-type hirelings will not be affected by this. The GM decides which potential hirelings are "combat-type."

Note that it is often impossible to find a highly-skilled hireling in a small village, and that even in a large city you may have to search for some time.

If the search is successful, the GM describes the potential hireling to the players, and can even take his part for an "interview." The players must then decide whether they actually want to hire that person. If they decide not to, they must start their search over again.

Loyalty of Hirelings

Since the hireling is an NPC controlled by the GM, he may not always act in the best interest of his employer. The GM is guided by the hireling's "loyalty rating." Unless this is pre-set for a reason, generate it by making a reaction roll (see p. 180) for "loyalty" when the hireling is first encountered. Thus, the GM can use it during the initial meeting or interview, to see whether the hireling lies about himself. Note that a very loyal potential hireling might exaggerate his abilities, out of desire to join the party!

RELIGION AND POLITICS

These vary so widely between game-worlds that no "generic" description is possible. Suffice it to say that these two forces are very powerful; they are usually interconnected; they are excellent "adventure hooks"; and they are also very dangerous hooks upon which the unwary adventurer can hang himself.

Loyalty Checks

A loyalty check is a roll *made by the GM*, usually in secret, to see how a hireling behaves in a given situation. It is made after the hireling's basic loyalty has been set. Check loyalty whenever a hireling is in mortal danger, or when violating his trust seems to be the wise, profitable or easy thing to do. A hireling with Loyalty 20+ passes all checks automatically.

The GM rolls 3 dice; if he rolls the hireling's loyalty or less, he "passed" the check and behaved loyally. If the GM rolls *over* the hireling's loyalty, he "failed" the check and served his own interests.

A failed check does *not* always mean total betrayal – it depends on the situation. It just means he let his employers down. He may repent and beg forgiveness; this is up to the whim (and dramatic ability) of the GM. If a hireling with a loyalty of 16+ is forgiven, with or without punishment, his base loyalty goes up by 1.

A loyalty check can be modified for special circumstances. A huge bribe from a foe, for instance, would give most hirelings a minus on their loyalty check.

It is always up to the GM to decide when a check is necessary. This depends on the hireling. For a veteran, "mortal danger" does not mean just any old combat. He would not fear an orc – or even a pack of them. But he might have to check loyalty if asked to battle a dragon!

Changes in Loyalty

Loyalty can be changed (temporarily or permanently) by several factors:

Higher pay. Add 1 to the hireling's loyalty for each 10% by which his pay exceeds his true worth, whether the increase in pay is from "salary" or a share in loot. Loyalty persists for a month after the extra pay ceases. (This factor also affects slaves, if they are allowed their own possessions.)

Great Danger. Whenever a noncombatant hireling is exposed to a combat situation, check loyalty. A failed check means his loyalty drops by 1 for a week. Repetitions may have permanent effect.

Rescue. If the PCs risk their lives (or the mission) to rescue the hireling, make a reaction roll at +3 or more, depending on the nature of the rescue. A successful roll means the hireling is grateful, and his loyalty is the result of the roll, or his original loyalty, whichever is higher.

Employers' Competence. Loyalty of a "continuing" hireling may change by 1 point at the end of an adventure, based on the performance of the party. A botched mission may caused loyalty to drop! Great success may increase loyalty.

Length of service. After each year, make a loyalty check. A pass means the hireling's loyalty goes up by 1. Thus, the best hirelings become better, but poor ones may not improve much.

Sooner or later, every GM wants to write his own adventures – or at least to modify store-bought ones to fit his own group. More power to you! Home-grown adventures can range from simple "dungeons" to entire worlds, intricately worked out over a period of years.

Dungeons

The term "dungeon" is often used for a simple fantasy adventure. In the typical dungeon, the players wander from room to room, killing monsters and grabbing treasure. There is often no rhyme or reason to the contents of the rooms – in children's fantasy games, every encounter may be rolled randomly!

But a dungeon setting is good for a beginning adventure; it teaches the basic game mechanics quickly. And an underground labyrinth does not *have* to be "kid stuff" – it can be part of a very realistic background.

A "dungeon" can also be a building, battleship, space station, etc. If the players are dropped into a limited area, with little or no goal except to grab what they can and get out alive, it's a "dungeon."

A dungeon is easy to map, since its area is limited. When players go too far, they just run into a blank wall and have to turn around. The typical dungeon is a collection of rooms, connected by corridors, shafts or tunnels.

Dungeon Inhabitants and Plot

The GM should populate his dungeon (or building, or whatever) with appropriate men, beasts and monsters. If you are just creating a "hack-and-slash" dungeon, you don't need to worry about what they are doing there, what they eat, why they attack the party, or anything else – just stock the rooms and go.

Likewise, the "plot of the story" for a hack-and-slash adventure will be very simple. "Joe the Barbarian, with his friends Ed the Barbarian and Marge the Barbarian, went down into a cave. They saw lots of monsters and killed them and took their treasure. A dragon ate Ed. Joe and Marge ran away. The End."

If you want to play on a more "mature" level, and create a situation that actually makes sense, you have advanced to the level of *adventure* design. Congratulations. Read on . . .

WHERE DO YOU GET YOUR IDEAS?

You can get ideas from commercially-produced supplements . . . from gaming magazines . . . from tournaments at game conventions . . . from other GMs . . . and from the players themselves. Whatever your source, you'll want to come up with enough new settings and "gimmicks" to keep your players (and yourself) interested.

Some GMs give their players a lot of voice in the type of adventures they will have. If the players want to hunt for treasure, the GM will come up with a treasure-hunting scenario. Other GMs see themselves as Blind Fate, and the characters never know what will happen next. It's all a matter of taste.

ADVENTURE DESIGN

When you design an adventure, you are writing the outline for a story. The full story will begin when the players' characters appear on the scene. To set the stage, you must prepare the plot, maps, character descriptions, etc. An adventure usually consists of a number of "encounters."

As the GM, you may buy adventure packages at the hobby shop – or make up your own. This section is intended for the GM who wants to write his own adventures or modify commercial ones.

Level of Difficulty

The first thing to decide is simply how "hard" your adventure is going to be. Are you planning an adventure for four beginning-level characters – or for a half-dozen experienced characters with point totals in the 150-to-200 range? You should also decide whether this adventure needs to fit into (or kick off) a campaign, or whether it is just a "one-shot."

The rewards should be appropriate to the risks. In a fantasy campaign, don't let your characters butcher two halflings and a senile goblin, and then rush back to town with a chest full of gold! (Or, if you do, have the king's tax man there to welcome them!) The real rewards in this game come in the form of bonus *character points* (p. 184). These are awarded for good roleplaying, and not the amount of wealth you drag home. But material things have their uses. Ask any fighter who couldn't afford to buy armor! Don't make wealth (or power, or fame) too easy to come by, or you will unbalance your campaign.

Of course, in a one-shot adventure, you have no future play balance to worry about. In one of the better *Fantasy Gamer* adventures, the players were faced with a knotty problem: the sun had gone out! If they failed in their quest, the world would end! On the other hand, if they *did* solve the problem, one of them would become the new God of the Sun. In a continuing campaign, either result would have caused difficulties. For a one-shot, it was fine!

Background

This is the setting of your story. In what game world does it take place, and where? What are the events leading up to your tale? Who are the important NPCs, and what are their motives? In short, what is happening behind the scenes, and what is the "big picture?" If this adventure is part of a campaign, a lot of the background is set. If it is a "one-shot," the background can be sketchy. But if you're starting a campaign, give the background a lot of thought.

Plot

The "plot" is your plan for the things that are supposed to happen during the adventure. In a simple adventure, the GM guides the characters from one "encounter," or scene, to the next. Each encounter starts when the characters arrive; then it is played out, and the next one can begin.

In a more sophisticated adventure, the GM will have planned for certain things to happen at certain times, regardless of the PCs' actions. If there is a murder to be solved, for instance, some clues may vanish if they are not found in time – and others may not exist yet if the characters come on the scene "too soon." The murders may even continue as the players investigate (that's one sure way to eliminate a suspect). Likewise, important NPCs may come and go with little regard for the players' wishes. There is no limit to what can happen "offstage" – war can be declared, gold can be discovered in Alaska, Martians can land in England. All these things will present new challenges . . .

This sort of plot is harder to write, and more demanding for the GM during play. But it will give the players a sense of urgency that is lacking in a plain straight-line adventure.

Introduction

The purpose of the introduction is to get the *players'* characters into *your* plot so that the game can begin. If the players are not familiar with your game world, you should tell them a little bit about it. If they know the game world (or are part of a continuing campaign), you can just set the scene with a few words and start the action. You should *not* give them the whole background. In a well-designed adventure, one of the players' objectives will be to find out "what is *really* going on." Don't give away all your secrets right at the beginning!

The most hackneyed introduction of all (but still one of the best) is the Old Man in the Tavern: "You are all strangers in town, looking for adventure. You are sitting in the local tavern when an old man comes up to you . . ." The old man can ask for help, order the PCs out of town, sell them a map, offer to guide them to fame and fortune . . . it doesn't matter. Whatever he does, he will provide a mouthpiece through which the GM can give the players a little background and start them off in the right direction. Some other good "mouthpiece" characters for an introductory encounter:

An officer briefing a group of military men, supers, troubleshooters or espionage agents to (perform a mission/deliver a message/steal a secret).

An injured stranger who staggers up and gasps a few cryptic last words.

A strange story in the news (the "mouthpiece" in this case is the person the PCs contact to ask about it – a reporter, a scientist, etc.). Or the GM could let the party *witness* the mysterious event themselves . . .

A storyteller, herald or town drunk, passing on an interesting rumor.

A wealthy person who offers to hire the party for a dangerous mission.

A retired adventurer telling about the treasure he couldn't quite get.

An angel or deity visiting the faithful (or fairly faithful) with commands – perhaps in a dream.

A villain's henchman, delivering a threat, ransom demand or boast.

A friend of one of the characters – or, for that matter, a total stranger rescued from immediate danger – who needs help.

A lawyer reading a will, which sends the party on a quest for an inheritance.

The "mouthpiece" NPC can end the introductory encounter by providing the maps, passwords or whatever the party needs to start the adventure.

Traps

Fantasy adventures traditionally feature a variety of traps. The novice designer can overdo this, with a crossbow behind every door and a pit in every corridor. If this doesn't kill the whole party, it will slow the game to a crawl as they check everything in sight for traps – and then check again, to make sure. But a few strategically-located traps can make an adventure more interesting.

This is true for adventures in non-fantasy genres as well! A criminal stronghold or millionaire's mansion may have unpleasant surprises for the intruder. Primitive natives encountered by explorers, whether in Africa, South America or Planet Zogbaum, may likewise have some upsettingly sophisticated defenses.

Some common types of traps include poison needles, hidden crossbows or other ranged weapons, hidden *giant* crossbows (or cannon, or antiaircraft missiles), pits (with spikes, snakes, or both), falling weights, rolling boulders, sliding walls (or descending roofs), explosives, chained beasts, slippery slides, poison gas, acid sprays and many more. Think of the last hundred adventure stories you read!

Not all traps are deadly. They can be designed to cripple, capture, annoy, embarass, or just frighten their victims. A burglar alarm is nothing more than a trap that produces only sound!

Traps, like rooms, should be shown on the map key – or a trap in a room can be part of the room's description. For each trap, the key should show:

(a) how hard the trap is to notice, and what skills can detect it

(b) how hard the trap is to disable (and/or set off harmlessly)

(c) what will set off the trap

(d) what happens if the trap is set off!

Some GMs delight in the invention of fiendish traps to test their players' wits. Such a "puzzle trap" can*not* be disabled by a simple Traps skill roll, or escaped by any simple skill roll. The players will have to think their way out! A *very* simple example might be a sliding-wall trap that will crush the strongest character to death . . . *unless* he opens the manhole in the floor. It's too small for him to fit into – but the lid is of such solid metal that, if held in place, it will block the closing walls!

Much more complex traps are possible. Have fun. "Puzzle" traps can add flavor to an adventure when simple deathtraps become boring.

Features of a Good Adventure

A good adventure (by the standards we use for our own publications) will include:

Lots of opportunities for the PCs to use their *non-combat* skills – including some difficult rolls, and some involving unusual skills (forcing the PCs to roll against defaults).

Contests of skill between PCs and NPCs, and possibly between PCs as well.

Situations where the players will have to think about the right thing to do . . . puzzles, moral choices, or both.

Situations where proper use of social skills, like Fast-Talk or Diplomacy, will avoid combat.

Situations where no possible use of social skills will avoid combat!

Interesting descriptions of people, places and things, to give the *players* the feeling that they are really there with their characters.

A clear introduction; a plotline which builds tension or mystery; and a clear conclusion.

Opportunity for roleplaying and character development. This should be present even if the adventure is the most light-hearted hack'n'slash imaginable! Fighters are interesting people, too – or they should be.

A reward for characters who complete the adventure successfully, and a consequence for characters who fail!

Sample Encounter Table

An encounter table can be used to provide extra interest in an adventure. Part of its value is that even the GM doesn't know what he's going to roll. An example:

Trivial Low-Tech Road Encounters: roll one die

1: A group of farmers (roll 2 dice for number)

2: One holy hermit

3: One not-so-holy beggar

4: One merchant with horse, wagon, and 1 to 3 guards

5: A single horseman

6: Nothing

Maps

As described under *Game Mastering,* p. 177, you will need a number of maps – one for every area you consider "important" to the adventure. Combat maps should be prepared in advance for any location where a fight is likely.

The experienced GM can save a lot of time by "recycling" maps. One house is a lot like another. One tavern is a lot like another. And so on. Of course, if you *always* use the same one, your players will kid you about it . . . "Aha, here we are, back in the Generic Tavern!"

Commercially-produced combat maps (from SJ Games, or any number of other companies) can also save time. And often an interesting map will suggest an appropriate encounter, helping you to design your adventure!

Characters (NPCs and Adversaries)

The non-player characters – the characters played by the GM and the Adversary – are vital to an adventure. Often, the whole adventure will be planned around two or three interesting NPCs, and what happens when the characters become involved with them.

The most important NPCs should be designed first, before you work out the encounters and the other details of the adventure. Their abilities, personalities, motivation and background will set the tone for the whole adventure, and give you ideas for encounters and lesser NPCs. These important NPCs should be worked out according to the *Character Creation* rules. You can start them off with 100 points, or even more. Make up a full-scale Character Sheet for each important NPC, and a brief character story – so you can roleplay him well.

Less important NPCs – spear-carriers, cannon fodder, minor encounters and the like – can be made up *after* the encounters are planned. You do not need complete stats or Character Sheets for these characters – just notes on their important stats. Some trivial characters will require no pre-planning at all – if you suddenly need to know (for instance) a Skill for one of them, you can just roll three dice and use the result.

You will also want to work out a few "generic" characters to use, as needed, in improvised or random encounters. For instance, in an adventure set in a fantasy city, you could prepare a few city guards, a couple of storekeepers, a couple of thieves, and maybe a strolling minstrel or wandering drunk. Then, if you need them, you have them. If you don't need them, you have them for next time. (And guards, like taverns, can be recycled over and over again). The pre-generated characters in this and other *GURPS* sets should be saved; they will come in very handy as instant NPCs.

Encounters

An "encounter" is a meeting with NPCs, animals, a trap or anything else the GM writes into his adventure. Encounters are of three kinds: *planned, improvised* and *random.* Ideally, as you run the game, your players should never know which kind is which!

Planned encounters are worked out in advance by the GM. He has already decided that when the characters come to *this* place, they will meet *these* people (or animals, or whatever). All the important encounters in your adventure should be planned.

Of course, few encounters will go *exactly* as planned. The GM should always be ready to adapt to the characters' actions. Suppose a planned encounter involves the bouncer at the "Blue Boar" – but the PCs don't go near there. You can drop a hint to send them there, of course – but it might be easier to change things a bit, and let the innkeeper at their rooming-house serve the same purpose. The more flexible you are, the more you can avoid the *appearance* of manipulating the players. And appearance is more important than reality!

Improvised encounters are "made up" by the GM in order to keep the adventure moving along planned lines. The simplest "improvised encounter" is the little old man

(looking a lot like the one you met at the tavern) who appears in your path and says, "Turn around! You're going the wrong way!"

Improvised encounters can provide extra clues, hints toward the "right path," etc. An improvised encounter can also be played out when the players think of something unusual to do. Let's say, for instance, that the PCs are hunting for a treasure buried 50 years ago by an old miser. Before the miser died, he endowed a university (the one generous act of his life). Now, as it happens, the university has nothing to do with the treasure, so no encounter at the university is planned. But the PCs decide to go there and hunt for clues. As the GM, you can just pass it off: "Okay, you went to the university and wasted a day. The people there were polite, but they knew nothing." However, it is more interesting – if you're up to it – to improvise and roleplay the encounter, taking the part of the doddering old Dean, somewhat hard of hearing . . . "We're hunting for buried treasure, sir." "A borrowed tea set? Thank you, young man, but we have our own china." If the players are polite and persistent, and you are feeling generous, you could reward them with some minor information after an encounter like this.

Random encounters are dictated by a random table. When the PCs are traveling along a road, the GM might roll once per hour on the table in the sidebar (p. 198) to see who they meet. Of course, this is a very simple table. Some commercial "adventures" consist mainly of random tables with many entries each, allowing play to proceed for hours with no previous planning at all! This is great for an quick game, but not in the same category with a "real" adventure.

However, if you don't let random encounters become a crutch, they can provide variety and free you from planning every single encounter. Some GMs like to invent a character on the spot, when the dice command it. But don't let the players know that you are rolling a totally random encounter. If they realize an encounter is not "part of the plot," they will act differently.

Finale

This is the climax of the adventure. Most adventures will have only one finale (unless the party gets killed along the way). As the GM, you should guide them, as subtly as you can, toward the "big ending" and resolution of the adventure.

The players' earlier actions affect the details of the finale, but its basic nature remains the same. If the players make "wrong" decisions along the way, it will take them longer to finish, and they should have a harder time dealing with the situation – but they *should* make it to the finale eventually. The exception might be a case where they have blundered *so* badly that the finale would certainly kill them all – in which case, the merciful GM will drop a hint that they are in over their heads, and let them give up and run for home.

A more sophisticated adventure will have several possible finales, depending on decisions made by the players during the adventure. This sort of "branching-path" adventure is harder to design, but sometimes easier for the GM to run – less improvisation is needed.

ORGANIZING A CONTINUING CAMPAIGN

Even more complex (and more interesting) than a full-scale adventure is a *series* of adventures involving the same characters. This is called a *campaign*. If a single adventure is the equivalent of a novel, then a campaign is an epic trilogy – the kind that is still going after seven books!

A large campaign can have dozens of players (not all playing at once!), several cooperating GMs, *planets* worth of mapped territory, and *hundreds* of significant NPCs, from kings and popes down to thieves and beggars.

Shared Campaigns and Travel Between Campaigns

Two or more GMs may agree to let players travel between their campaigns. In general this simply means that, at a pre-ordained time or place, one GM will replace another. The old GM may remove himself entirely, or introduce a character of his own and remain as a player.

The more similar the GMs' campaigns are, the more closely they can be connected. If the two campaigns operate in the same game world, and if the GMs interpret the rules in the same way and have the same "play style," then the boundary between their jurisdictions might be as trivial as a river-line or even a city boundary. This can also be considered a "shared" campaign.

One good system for GM co-operation involves (for instance) cities. A single "chief GM" is in charge of overall maintenance and development of the game world. A number of the campaign's players also have GM responsibilities of their own. Each such player designs and controls one city. All adventures within a city are refereed by the player controlling that city. Needless to say, that player's characters should take little part in the action there, even as NPCs. Even the best GM may become somewhat emotionally involved with the player-characters he has developed over a period of months! Adventures outside the players' cities are run by the chief GM. Thus, several players can have the fun of GM-ing an occasional adventure, while doing no more support work and world-building than they care to.

The same system will work in a space campaign, except that each player controls a whole solar system . . .

For this kind of campaign to work, the GMs must consult regularly. Minor "cultural" differences between cities or planets are acceptable – in fact, they're fun. But the GMs should agree among themselves about the overall nature and goals of the campaign, if players are allowed to move freely back and forth. If two or more GMs wish to "share" players and characters while maintaining significant differences between their worlds, a different procedure will be needed.

World-Building

A game world is a complete background setting for a game. It takes in *everything* described on p. 198 for adventures, and more. Creating an original, believable, interesting world is a real challenge. "World-building" can be the beginning of a campaign, but more often it's the *result* of a long and successful campaign. Designing an entire game world is complex and time-consuming. Many of the best game worlds started out as individual fantasies, and developed over a long period of time. Tékumel, the fictional creation of Professor M.A.R. Barker (***Empire of the Petal Throne***) is a perfect example.

To "design" a historical game world will require many hours of research. Worlds based on fiction (novels or TV series, for instance) require research too – to make sure every detail conforms to the source, and to fill in logically where the original story gave no information.

Some things you must consider when designing a game world are:

Cultures and Customs
Adventure Settings
Skills, Jobs and Professions
Monsters and Animals
Transportation
Medicine
Technology and Communications
Weapons and Combat
Special Advantages and Disadvantages
Maps
Politics and Religion

For examples, see any of the many game worlds already released by SJ Games. These are listed and described on p. 7.

We're Professionals (Don't Try This At Home)

Oh, never mind. Go ahead and try if you want to. We might even pay you for it! We've found that the people who enjoy our games are often the most creative, and the most likely to write good new material.

Steve Jackson Games is always interested in finding new writers of adventures or game worlds. We don't insist on previous experience. Send us a sample of your work; it will speak for itself.

But first, get our writer's guidelines. You can find them online at **sjgames.com/general/guidelines/authors**.

Or, if you want an easier way to break in, try submitting an article to *Pyramid* magazine. Review our online guidelines to get more details on how to do this: **sjgames.com/pyramid/writing.html**.

Warning: we're perfectionists. So be prepared – if you send us a manuscript, we'll nit-pick. Good luck.

DON'T PANIC. You don't have to do all this at once. Most campaigns just "grow," a bit at a time. One adventure leads to the next, and before you know it, you've been playing for a year, and you've got a campaign going. Much of the flavor of a good campaign will come from the players themselves. The PCs' patrons, dependents and enemies will become continuing NPCs . . . old foes will reappear when they are least wanted . . . maps will become more detailed each time you play. Players come and go, but the campaign goes on. And nobody learns to run a campaign by reading the rulebook. Experience is the best teacher.

A campaign consists of one adventure after another. Each adventure may consist of many sessions. The GM decides what goes on in the game world *in between* game sessions – and *especially* between adventures. The important NPCs will go about their own affairs. Wars, weather, politics and trade can go on in the "background" of the campaign, giving rise to new adventures. Your players will be a good source of suggestions . . . and they will be tremendously pleased if their adventures affect the "whole world" in some way, whether they turn aside a catastrophic war or simply find a cure for the Queen's wart.

TRAVEL BETWEEN GAME WORLDS

One of the chief purposes of the ***GURPS*** design is to let players move freely between different game worlds without learning a whole new set of rules each time. A player can participate in several different campaigns, each in a different place or time, and play a different character in each campaign. Each character stays in his own world. But the *characters* can also move from one game world to another. This can happen in two ways:

(1) A player can develop a character in one game world and then bring that character into another game world. An example might be a medieval wizard, hurled hundreds of years into the future by a magic spell, participating in a WWII adventure.

(2) An entire campaign can move from one game world to another. For example, suppose the party is the crew of an interstellar trading ship. They crash-land on a primitive planet. Until they can make their way to the spaceport, on the other side of the world, they have effectively been dropped into the 12th century!

Differences in Worlds

As a rule, the more different two worlds are, the harder it should be for PCs to move between them deliberately. Significant differences would include:

High-mana (magical) world vs. low-mana (technological) world.
Very low-tech world vs. very high-tech world, regardless of magic.
Largely-human or all-human world, vs. world with many races.
War-wracked, plague-ridden world, vs. peaceful, decadent world.
Fantasy world vs. strictly historical, "real" world.

Certainly any or all of these differences could exist on a single planet! But they would not be found next door to each other. Likewise, GMs should make travel between incompatible worlds *difficult*. This achieves an effect that is very rare in gaming; it improves both realism and playability. Players will appreciate the fact that "rule changes" come only with warning.

Possible obstacles to inter-world travel include all the standard geographical barriers: high mountain ranges, wide oceans, extensive deserts or badlands, swampy jungles, etc. Magical barriers are also a possibility, as are intervening hostile lands. GMs may also have their different worlds located, *literally, on different worlds*. The problems of interplanetary travel at low tech levels are not to be taken lightly, but powerful magic can do almost anything. Of course, such powerful magic is not likely to be within the PCs' own control . . .

CHARTS AND TABLES

RANGED WEAPON ATTACKS

When using a ranged weapon, figure your adjusted skill by:

(1) Taking your base skill with the weapon type. Add the bonus of the specific weapon's *accuracy* if you have taken at least 1 turn to aim. The Accuracy modifier cannot be more than your base skill.

(2) Modifying for *size of target*.

(3) Modifying for target's *range and speed*.

(4) Modifying for conditions (snap shot or aim, bracing, darkness, and so on) including any special conditions determined by the GM.

The result gives the attacker's *adjusted skill*. A roll of this number, or less, is a hit.

Size of Target

The larger the target, the easier it is to hit. Use its length (or its width, if width is less than $1/2$ of length). Round up to the next larger size, and read the modifier in the *second* column of the table. Objects larger than man-sized give a bonus to hit; smaller objects, a penalty.

Target's Speed and Range

The target's speed and range give a single modifier. The *sum of* range (in yards) and speed (in yards per second) gives a number from the table. This means that if the target is very fast, its distance becomes less important . . . or if it is very far away, its speed becomes less important. Round up to the next larger speed/range number. If the firer is moving, use the (apparent) *relative* speed.

RANGED ATTACK MODIFIERS

Aiming Time

Snap shot...................-4 unless adjusted skill ≥ weapon's SS number
One turn of aiming ....0 + Acc modifier
Two turns of aiming ....+1
Three turns of aiming ....+2
Four or more turns of aiming ....+3
Bracing a crossbow, rifle, pistol, etc...............+1 if time is taken to aim
Higher target ....+1 yd. to ranger per yd. higher
Long range...........................Double penalties if attacker is nearsighted
Opportunity fire (Includes snap-shot penalty)
Evaluating target before firing ....-2
One hex being watched ....-2
Two hexes being watched ....-4
Three or four hexes being watched ....-5
All hexes along a line being watched ....-5
Five or six hexes being watched ....-6
Seven to ten hexes being watched.................................-7
More than ten hexes being watched ....-8
Pop-up attack...-2, and -4 for snap shot; total -6
Rolling against wrong target ....Normal roll, max. 9
Shooting blind ....-10, or roll of 9, whichever is worse
Unfamiliar gun/beam weapon of known type ....-2
Unfamiliar type of weapon..-4
Unfamiliar vehicular aiming system ....-2
Weapon in bad repair ....-4 or more
Weapon as target: Most weapons...-4
Polearm, spear, rifle, greatsword................................-3
Knife, pistol, etc...-5
Target's Position
Prone behind minimum cover, head down.....................-7
Any position, only head exposed ....-5
Head and shoulders exposed ....-4
Behind someone else ....-4 for each intervening figure
Prone or crawling without cover ....-4
Body half exposed ....-3
Behind light cover ....-2
Crouching/sitting/kneeling without cover.......................-2

Yards per second is the Move score; it is also half the speed in miles per hour. Thus, 60 mph is the same as 30 yards per second. For very large or distant targets, the table gives a subsidiary column using *miles* and *miles per second*. If you use miles for the range, always use mps for the speed.

Examples: A target at 50 yards, with a speed of 30 yds/sec (60 mph) has a speed/range of 80 yards: modifier -10. A target at 5 yards, moving 1,000 yds/sec, has a speed/range of 1,005 yards: modifier -17.

SIZE AND SPEED/RANGE TABLE

Speed/ Range	Size	Linear Measurement (size or range/speed)		
+15	-15	$1/10$"		
+14	-14	$1/5$"		
+13	-13	$1/3$"		
+12	-12	$1/2$"		
+11	-11	$2/3$"		
+10	-10	1"		
+9	-9	$1 1/2$"		
+8	-8	2"		
+7	-7	3"		
+6	-6	6"		
+5	-5	12"		
+4	-4	$1 1/2$ ft	*Range/speed in miles*	
+3	-3	2 ft		
+2	-2	1 yd		2 mph
+1	-1	$1 1/2$ yd		3 mph
0	0	2 yd		4.5 mph
-1	+1	3 yd		7 mph
-2	+2	$4 1/2$ yd		10 mph
-3	+3	7 yd		15 mph
-4	+4	10 yd		20 mph
-5	+5	15 yd		30 mph
-6	+6	20 yd		45 mph
-7	+7	30 yd		70 mph
-8	+8	45 yd		100 mph
-9	+9	70 yd		150 mph
-10	+10	100 yd		200 mph
-11	+11	150 yd		300 mph
-12	+12	200 yd		450 mph
-13	+13	300 yd		700 mph
-14	+14	450 yd	$1/4$ mi	1,000 mph
-15	+15	700 yd	$2/5$ mi	1,500 mph
-16	+16	1,000 yd	$3/5$ mi	2,000 mph
-17	+17	1,500 yd	1 mi	3,000 mph
-18	+18	2,000 yd	$1 1/2$ mi	4,500 mph
-19	+19	3,000 yd	2 mi	7,000 mph
-20	+20	4,500 yd	3 mi	10,000 mph
-21	+21	7,000 yd	$4 1/2$ mi	15,000 mph
-22	+22	10,000 yd	7 mi	20,000 mph
-23	+23	10 mi		30,000 mph
-24	+24	15 mi		45,000 mph
-25	+25	20 mi	20 mps	70,000 mph
-31	+31	200 mi	200 mps	
-37	+37	2,000 mi	2,000 mps	
-43	+43	20,000 mi	20,000 mps	
-49	+49	200,000 mi	200,000 mps	

Example: The target is an automobile. It is 5 yards long (+3 to hit). It is 40 yards away, and moving 30 mph. 30 mph is 15 yards per second. 40 + 15 = 55; on the table above, 55 rounds up to 70, giving a speed/range modifier of -9. The cumulative modifier is -6 to hit, before the particular weapon is taken into account.

CRITICAL HIT TABLE

All doublings or triplings of normal damage refer to the basic die roll.

3 – If the blow hit the torso, it does normal damage and the foe is knocked unconscious. Roll vs. HT every 30 minutes to recover. Otherwise, it does triple damage.

4 – The blow *bypasses all armor* and does normal damage.

5 – The blow does triple normal damage.

6 – The blow does double normal damage.

7 – Normal damage only – *and* foe is *stunned* until he makes his HT roll.

8 – If blow hit an arm, leg, hand or foot, it does normal damage, and that body part is *crippled* regardless of the damage done. However, this is only a "funny-bone" injury, and will wear off in six turns. (Of course, if enough damage was done to cripple the limb anyway, it does not wear off!) Otherwise, the blow does normal damage.

9, 10, 11 – Normal damage only.

12 – As #8, above.

13 – The blow *bypasses all armor* and does normal damage.

14 – If the blow hit an arm, leg, hand or foot, it does normal damage, and that body part is *crippled* regardless of the amount of damage done. Otherwise, double normal damage.

15 – Enemy's weapon is dropped, *and* he takes normal damage.

16 – The blow does double normal damage.

17 – The blow does triple normal damage.

18 – If the blow hit the torso, it does normal damage and the foe is knocked unconscious. Roll vs. HT every 30 minutes to recover. Otherwise, triple normal damage.

CRITICAL MISS TABLE

3, 4 – Your weapon breaks and is useless. Exception: Certain weapons are resistant to breakage. These include *maces, flails, mauls, metal bars*, and other solid "crushing" weapons; *magic weapons*; and *finely-made* weapons. If you have a weapon like that, roll again. Only if you get a "broken weapon" result a second time does the weapon really break. If you get any other result, you drop the weapon instead. See *Broken Weapons*, p. 113.

5 – You managed to hit *yourself* in the arm or leg (50% chance each way). Exception: If this was an impaling or ranged attack, roll again. It's hard to stab yourself, but it can be done. If you get a "hit yourself" result a second time, count *that* result – half or full damage, as the case may be. If you get something other than "hit yourself," count that result.

6 – As above, but half damage only.

7 – You lost your balance. You can do nothing else until your next turn. All your active defenses are at -2 until your next turn.

8 – The weapon turns in your hand. Spend one extra turn to ready it before you use it again.

9, 10, 11 – You drop the weapon. Exception: A *cheap* weapon *breaks*. See p. 113 for dropped/broken weapons.

12 – The weapon turns in your hand. Spend one extra turn to ready it before you use it again.

13 – You lose your balance. You can do nothing else until your next turn. All your active defenses are at -2 until your next turn.

14 – Your weapon flies 1d yards from your hand – 50% chance straight forward or straight back. Anyone on the target spot must make their DX roll or take half damage from the falling weapon! Exception: If this was an impaling attack, you simply drop the weapon, as in #9 above. A missile weapon will not fly from your hand – it just drops.

15 – You strained your shoulder! Your weapon arm is "crippled" for the rest of the encounter. You do not have to drop your weapon, but you cannot use it, either to attack or defend, for 30 minutes.

16 – You fall down! (Ranged weapon users, see #7 instead.)

17, 18 – Your weapon breaks. See #3 above.

Unarmed fighters: Any "weapon breaks," "weapon drops," or "weapon turns in hand" result should be ignored. Instead, take 1d-3 damage to the hand or foot you were striking with.

CRITICAL SUCCESS AND FAILURE

A roll of 3 or 4 is always a critical success.

A roll of 5 is a critical success if your effective skill is 15+.

A roll of 6 is a critical success if your effective skill is 16+.

A roll of 18 is always a critical failure.

A roll of 17 is an ordinary failure if your effective skill is 16 or better, and a critical failure if your effective skill is under 16.

Any roll of 10 or greater than your effective skill is a critical failure. That is, 16 on a skill of 6, 15 on a skill of 5, and so on.

CRITICAL HEAD BLOW TABLE

Use this table only when a critical hit is rolled on a head blow.

3 – Foe is killed instantly!

4, 5 – Foe is knocked unconscious. Roll vs. HT every 30 minutes to recover.

6 – Foe is hit across both eyes and blinded. Use "crippling" rules to determine whether eyes can heal (roll separately for each). Foe is *stunned* and fights at -10 DX for the rest of the battle.

7 – Foe is blinded in one eye. Use "crippling" rules to determine if it heals. Foe is *stunned;* will fight at -2 DX for the rest of the battle.

8 – Foe is knocked off balance; he may defend normally next turn but may do nothing else. The blow also does normal head-blow damage.

9, 10, 11 – Normal head-blow damage only.

12 – If the attack was a crushing blow, it does normal head-blow damage *and* the foe will be deaf for 24 hours. If it was a cutting or impaling blow, it does only 1 hit damage, but the foe's face is scarred.

13 – If the attack was a crushing blow, it does normal head-blow damage *and* foe may be permanently deafened (use "crippling" rules to see if he recovers). If it was a cutting or impaling blow, it does only 2 hits damage, but the foe's face is badly scarred.

14 – Normal head-blow damage. Foe flinches and drops his weapon (if foe has two weapons, roll randomly to see which is dropped).

15-18 – Normal head-blow damage, *and* foe is *stunned*.

FIREARM CRITICAL MISS TABLE

3, 4 – The firearm breaks. It can be repaired (with the proper tools) in 1 to 6 hours (roll 1 die) with a successful Armoury roll. If the attack is with a grenade, it simply fails to go off.

5 – You managed to shoot yourself in the leg (50% chance, right or left), doing normal damage.

6 – As above, but you shot yourself in the foot.

7 – The weapon recoil knocks you off balance. You can do nothing until next turn, and all active defenses are at -2 until then. If the attack is with a grenade or a beam weapon, ignore this result.

8 – A dud. This shot simply doesn't go off (and the ammunition is wasted), but the weapon is not harmed.

9, 10, 11 – The weapon jams. It will require a successful skill roll (Guns-4, or Armoury) to unjam it. If the weapon is cheap, the skill is at a -3 penalty. If the attack is with a grenade, ignore this result and reroll.

12 – A dud, as #8 above.

13, 14 – You drop the weapon. A cheap weapon breaks (to fix it, see #3, 4 above). Otherwise, you must pick it up and ready it again. If the attack is with a grenade, place the activated grenade in an adjacent hex – and hope you set it for a long delay . . .

15 – The weapon recoil knocks you down. You are on the ground, sitting or lying (your choice). Make a DX roll to hold on to the weapon! If your ST is at least 5 more than the minimum ST for the weapon (or 12 and higher, in the case of weapons with no minimum ST rating), ignore this result, and use #7 above, instead. But if the weapon is *recoilless*, nothing happens.

16, 17 – The weapon breaks, as in #3, 4 above.

18 – The weapon explodes. You take the damage amount of the weapon in crushing damage, plus: If the Aim maneuver was taken before the shot was made, you are also blinded for five minutes. If the weapon was a grenade, it goes off in your hand, doing maximum damage to that hand, plus normal damage. If the weapon was a laser, blaster or flamethrower, you are also on fire.

MANEUVERS

Maneuver	Maximum move	Facing change (end of move)	Attack	Defense	Special Notes
Aim	1/2 move; max 2 after first turn of aiming.	may not change after first turn	+1 per turn aiming, after first turn	normal, but lose Aim benefits	+3 maximum bonus; ranged weapons lose Acc bonus without one turn of aiming.
Change Position	0	any	none	normal	See Table of Positions.
Step and Ready	1 hex	any	none	normal	Cannot parry without a ready weapon, or block without a ready shield.
Step and Attack	1 hex	any	normal	normal	
All-Out Attack	see special note	may not change	2 attacks, or 1 at +4 or feint and attack	passive only	Move up to half move.
Step and Feint	1 hex	any	quick contest (weapon vs. shield, weapon or DX)	normal	Win with successful roll: penalty to foe's active defense by that much next turn. Both weapons still ready.
Step and Concentrate	1 hex	any	none	any, but roll Will-3 or break concentration	Used with magic or psionics only.
Step and Wait	1 hex	any	normal, when foe comes in range	normal	If you didn't move on your turn, you can move 1 hex forward and attack.
All-Out Defense	1 hex	any	none	2 different defenses per attack	No more than 2 parries per weapon, and 2 blocks.
Move forward (cost 1) side or back (cost 2) change facing (1/hexside)	Up to Move score	Up to 1/2 Move: any facing. More than 1/2: change 1 hexside	wild swing only; penalties (see p. 105) for arming or firing ranged weapons	normal	See Tables of Positions for costs.

PARTS OF THE BODY

Random Location	Body Part	Hit Penalty (Subtract from Attack Skill)	Result of Major Damage
4 or less	Brain[4]	-7	See notes 1 and 4.
5	Head[4]	-5	No DR; no special damage to results, but critical hits go Critical Head Blow Table.
–	Eyes	-9	See note 2.
–	Eyes (through helm's eyeslits)	-10	As above. Armor does not protect! See note 2.
6	Shield (far) arm[3]	-4	Damage over HT/2 cripples arm. Excess damage is lost.
7	Hand (roll for left or right)	-4	Damage over HT/3 cripples hand. Excess damage is lost.
–	Shield (left) hand[3]	-8	As above.
8	Weapon (near) arm[3]	-2	As for shield arm.
9-11	Body (i.e., torso)	0	No special results.
12	Far leg[3]	-2	Damage over HT/2 cripples leg. Excess damage is lost.
13, 14	Near leg[3]	-2	As above.
15, 16	Foot (roll for left or right)	-4	Damage over HT/3 cripples foot. Excess damage is lost.
17 or more	Vital organs (in torso)[4]	-3	Impaling weapons that penetrate armor do triple damage, not double.
	Weapon (see attack mods)	-3 to -5	Weapon may fall or break.

Random location is used when a part of the body must be randomly targeted (for instance, by falling rocks or an arrow fired from far off). Roll 3 dice to see what was hit. Some parts are never hit randomly.

Hit penalty shows the subtraction to skill when attacking a part of the body. Note that armor may also give a body part extra *passive defense!*

Major damage shows the effect a serious wound has on a body part.

1. If the brain is hit, the skull provides a natural DR of 2. This is in addition to any armor, toughness, etc., the victim possesses. However, shooting for the eyes avoids this DR, and shooting for the eyeslits of a helm avoids both the helm's DR and the skull's DR! After skull's DR of 2 is subtracted, any hit does 4 times basic damage (regardless of weapon type). Victim is *stunned* on hits over HT/3, *knocked out* if over HT/2.

2. More than 2 hits of damage blinds the eye. An impaling or missile hit (if the missile is under 1" across) gives an automatic brain hit, as above; skull's DR does not protect! If the target is wearing a helm, only a missile or thrusting attack can hit the eye, and the attack is at -10.

3. The table is designed to distinguish between the arms of a shield-carrying man. If a shield is not present, and neither arm is nearer, the left arm/hand is no harder to hit than the right; roll randomly to determine which arm (or leg) is hit.

4. Any blow to the head or brain, or any crushing blow to the vitals requires the victim to make a roll against HT to avoid knockout (see *Knockout*, p. 127). Vitals may only be targeted by missile or thrusting attacks. If the brain, head or vitals are targeted, a roll that misses by only 1 gives a hit on the torso.

TABLE OF POSITIONS

Position	Attack	Defense or penalty	Movement
Standing	Normal	Normal	Normal; may sprint
Crouching	-2	Ranged weapons -2 to hit; normal vs. others	+1/2 cost per hex
Kneeling	-2	Ranged weapons -2 to hit; -2 to any active defense	+2 cost per hex
Crawling (2 hexes)	Only close attacks	Ranged weapons -4 to hit; -3 to any active defense	+2 cost per hex
Sitting	-2	As for kneeling	Cannot move!
Lying down (2 hexes)	-4 except w/crossbow or gun +1	As for crawling	Only 1 hex/turn

NPC REACTIONS

When the players meet an NPC whose reaction to them is not predetermined, the GM makes a "reaction roll" on 3 dice. The higher the roll, the better the reaction. The GM then follows the guidelines on the *Reaction Table*. For more on reaction rolls, see p. 180.

Many factors can influence a reaction roll. A reaction *bonus* is a factor which makes the NPCs *more* friendly, and a reaction *penalty* is something that will make them *less* friendly. Some common modifiers:

Personal appearance and behavior of the player characters – especially the one who does the talking! A good personal appearance will improve the roll. So will Charisma. In most situations, so will a high apparent social status.

Appropriate skills for the situation – e.g., Streetwise in an underworld situation. If the character has the skill at an "expert" level – 20 or better – it is more likely to help. Expert Diplomacy, for instance, is worth +2 on *any* reaction roll.

Racial or national biases between the NPCs and the character(s) in the party. These are usually penalties, and will be found in the appropriate game-world books.

Appropriate behavior by the players! A good approach should be worth a +1 modifier – maybe more! A wholly inappropriate approach should cost the party a -1 or -2 penalty on the reaction roll.

Remember: Reaction rolls are meant to flesh out a situation, NOT to control it! If an encounter is vital, the GM should decide in advance how he will play the NPCs. Only for less important situations, or for cases where the players must use their wits to negotiate, should reaction rolls be used. But the GM can always *pretend* to roll, so the players won't know for sure what is going on!

General Reactions

Make this roll to see, in general, how any NPC feels about the characters. When nothing else seems appropriate, make a general reaction roll and wing it! The GM can use any modifiers he thinks appropriate, especially those for personal appearance.

Potential Combat Situations (and Morale Checks)

Roll in any encounter where combat is possible but not *certain*. For a foe in a pitched battle, no roll is necessary. For a group of armed strangers on a wilderness trail, a reaction roll is appropriate unless the GM has predetermined their actions.

When the NPCs are losing a fight, a combat reaction roll can be made during the fight as a "morale check." "Good" or higher reactions indicate flight or surrender, as appropriate, and not sudden friendship.

Special Modifiers for Combat Reactions:

+1 to +5 if the party seems notably stronger than the NPC group.
-1 to -5 if the party seems to be notably *weaker* than the NPC group.
-2 if the party has no language in common with the NPCs.
-2 if the characters are intruders on the NPC's home turf.

Commercial Transactions

Roll when the PCs try to buy or sell goods, find a job, or hire someone. If no bargaining is involved, no roll is necessary – unless there is a chance that the merchant won't deal with the PCs at all.

As used below, "fair price" means the normal price, at that particular time and place, for the goods or services in question. The PCs can try to get a better price, at a -1 penalty for every 10% difference. Likewise, offering more than the fair price, or asking less than the fair price, will give a +1 bonus for every 10% difference. If players vary their offer, determine the NPC's counteroffer based on the proposed price instead of fair price if that is *less* favorable to the PCs. *Example:* If they ask 120% of fair price and get a "bad" reaction, the NPC will offer half of that, or 60%.

Bargaining will never reduce the price below 50% of "fair" unless the NPC has an ulterior motive!

Special Modifiers for Transactions

-1 for every 10% by which proposed price favors the PC, relative to the *fair* price.
+1 for every 10% by which proposed price favors the NPC.
+1 if the PC has the Merchant skill at *any* level.
+2 if the PC has the Merchant skill at expert level – 20 or better.

Requests for Aid

Roll when the PCs ask for any sort of help. (If appropriate, a roll for "potential combat" must be made first.) Examples would include an interview with a bureaucrat; an attempt to get a newspaper editor or police captain to listen to your story about the mad scientist's plot; or just a cry for help to the bystanders watching you get mugged!

Special Modifiers for Request for Aid:

+1 if the request is very simple.
-1 to -3 (or more) if the request is very complex or unreasonable.
-1 if the request would inconvenience the NPC or cost him money.
-2 or more if the NPC's job or social status would be endangered.
-1 or more if the request would physically endanger the NPC. This depends on the degree of the risk and the bravery of the NPC!

Requests for Information

Roll when the characters ask NPCs for directions, advice, "Have you seen this man?" etc. *Note:* If the NPC is a professional seller of information, it is a commercial transaction. If the NPC is being interrogated, the characters must use the Interrogation skill.

Remember that no NPC can tell more than he knows. Sometimes the NPC will tell the truth as he knows it . . . but be terribly mistaken! And certain NPCs may pretend to more knowledge than they have, in order to earn money or impress the characters.

If there is a question as to whether a given NPC (or player character, for that matter) knows some specific fact, roll against his intelligence, or against his score in the appropriate skill.

Special Modifiers for Information Requests:

-1 for a complex question; -2 for a *very* complex question.
-3 if the NPC thinks it's none of their business!
-3 or more if an answer would endanger the NPC.
+1 to +3 if a bribe is offered. To be effective, a bribe must be appropriate in size and *discreet*. Not everyone will take a cash payoff. You don't offer a newspaper reporter a $20 bill – he would be insulted – but buy him a good dinner and he'll appreciate it. GMs should reward intelligent use of disguised "bribes."
+2 to +4 if the NPC is a librarian, historian, scribe, teacher, etc. Such people are naturally disposed to help any seeker of knowledge.

Loyalty

When the PCs hire someone, the GM should determine his loyalty. This determines only the NPC's *attitude* – not his competence. If the NPC is important, the scenario (or the GM) will predetermine both his skills and his general attitude. Otherwise, a random roll is fine.

When the PCs take service with an employer, the GM should also determine (randomly or otherwise) how the employer feels about them.

Loyalty reactions are known to the GM, but not to the players (unless a successful use of Empathy is made). The GM should record each NPC's loyalty secretly, and let it guide him in determining all that NPC's later behavior. Note that loyalty can change. See p. 195.

Special Modifiers for Loyalty:

+1 for every 10% the PCs offer above the going pay rate.
-1 for every 10% the PCs offer below the going pay rate.
+2 or more if the PCs are serving a cause that the NPC believes in, or a leader to whom the NPC is very loyal.
+ or – as appropriate for the PCs' reputation in the area (if any).

REACTION TABLE

Roll 3 dice and apply modifiers described on p. 204.

0 or less: Disastrous.

General reaction: The NPC hates the characters and will act in their worst interest.

In a *potential combat situation*, the NPCs will attack viciously, asking no quarter and giving none.

Commercial transactions are doomed: The merchant will have nothing to do with you. Make a "potential combat" roll at -2.

Requests for aid are denied totally. Make a "potential combat" roll at -4. If combat is called for but not possible, the NPC will work against the PCs in any way possible.

Requests for information are met with anger. Make a "potential combat" reaction roll, at -2.

Loyalty: The NPC hates you or is in the pay of your enemies, and will take the first good chance to betray you.

1 to 3: Very Bad.

General reaction: The NPC dislikes the characters and will act against them if it's convenient to do so.

In a *potential combat situation*, the NPCs attack, and flee only if they see they have no chance. (A fight in progress will continue.)

Commercial transactions are next to impossible. The merchant asks three times the fair price, or offers 1/3 the fair price.

Requests for aid are denied. Make a "potential combat" roll; no reaction better than neutral is possible.

Requests for information are met with malicious lies.

Loyalty: The NPC dislikes you, and will leave your service (probably taking everything he can carry) or sell you out as soon as possible.

4 to 6: Bad.

General reaction: The NPC cares nothing for the characters and will act against them if he can profit by doing so.

In a *potential combat situation*, the NPCs will attack unless outnumbered. If they are outnumbered they will flee, possibly to attempt an ambush later. (A fight already in progress will continue.)

Commercial transactions go badly. The merchant asks twice the fair price, or offers half the fair price.

Requests for aid are denied. The NPCs go about their business, ignoring the player characters.

Requests for information are denied. NPCs will lie maliciously or demand payment for information. If paid, the NPC will give true, but incomplete, information.

Loyalty: The NPC has no respect for you. He will leave or betray you given even moderate temptation, and will be a sluggish worker.

7 to 9: Poor.

General reaction: The NPC is unimpressed. He may become hostile if there is much profit in it, or little danger.

In a *potential combat situation*, the NPCs will shout threats or insults. They will demand the PCs leave the area. If the PCs stick around, the NPCs will attack unless outnumbered, in which case they will flee. (If a fight is in progress, it will continue.)

Commercial transactions are unprofitable. The merchant asks 120% of the fair price , or offers 75% of the fair price.

Requests for aid are denied, but bribes, pleas, or threats might work. PCs may roll again, at -2.

Requests for information are unproductive. The NPCs will claim not to know, or will give incomplete data. A bribe may improve their memory; roll again if a bribe is offered.

Loyalty: The NPC is unimpressed with you and/or dislikes the job; he thinks he's overworked and underpaid. He'll probably betray you if offered enough, and would certainly take a "better" job if he thought he had one.

10 to 12: Neutral.

General reaction: The NPC ignores the characters as much as possible. He is totally uninterested.

In a *potential combat situation*, the NPCs are inclined to go their own way and let the PCs go theirs. (If a fight is already in progress, the NPCs will try to back off.)

Commercial transactions go routinely. The merchant will buy and sell at fair prices.

Requests for aid are granted – if they are simple. Complex requests are denied, but the PCs can try again at -2.

Requests for information will be successful. The NPC will give the information requested if it is simple. If the question is complex, the answer will be sketchy.

Loyalty: The NPC thinks you're just another boss, and this is just another job. He will work hard enough to keep you happy, but no harder. He will not leave unless he is sure the new job is better, and will not betray you unless the temptation is *very* strong.

13 to 15: Good.

General reaction: The NPC likes the characters and will be helpful within reasonable, everyday limits.

In a *potential combat situation*, the NPCs find the characters likeable, or else too formidable to attack. The characters may request aid or information – +1 on a second roll. (If a fight is in progress, the NPCs will flee.)

Commercial transactions go pleasantly. The merchant will buy and sell at fair prices, and will volunteer useful information or small bits of help if possible.

Requests for aid will be granted if the request is reasonable. The NPCs' attitude is helpful. Even if the request is silly and must be denied, they will offer helpful advice.

Requests for information will be successful. The question will be answered accurately.

Loyalty: The NPC likes you and/or the job. He will be loyal, work hard, and accept any reasonable hazard that you will accept.

16 to 18: Very Good.

General reaction: The NPC thinks highly of the characters and will be quite helpful and friendly.

In a *potential combat situation*, the NPCs are friendly. The PCs may ask for aid or information (+3 on a reaction roll). Even sworn foes will find an excuse to let the PCs go . . . for now. (If a fight has already started, the NPCs will flee if they can, or surrender otherwise.)

Commercial transactions will go very well. The merchant will accept your offer unless you tried to buy below 80% of the fair price or sell above 150% of the fair price. In that case, he will offer those rates. He will also offer help and advice.

Requests for aid are granted unless they are totally unreasonable. Any useful information NPCs have will be volunteered freely.

Requests for information will be successful. The NPC will answer in detail and volunteer any related information he has.

Loyalty: The NPC will work very hard, and risk his life if need be. Under most circumstances, he puts your interests ahead of his own.

19 or better: Excellent.

General reaction: The NPC is extremely impressed by the characters, and will act in their best interests at all times, within the limits of his own ability. Merchants will offer very good deals.

In a *potential combat situation*, the NPCs are extremely friendly. They may even join the party temporarily. The PCs may ask for aid or information: +5 on this reaction roll. (If the fight has already started, the NPCs will surrender.)

Commercial transactions will go extremely well. The merchant will accept your offer unless you tried to buy below 50% of fair price or sell above 200% of fair price. In that case, he will offer those rates. He will also offer help and advice.

Requests for aid will be granted. NPCs will help in every way within their power, offering extra aid.

Requests for information will be extremely successful. The question will be answered completely. If the NPC doesn't know everything you need, he will exert himself to find out. He may even offer to help; roll a request for aid (at +2), with no reaction worse than "poor" possible.

Loyalty: The NPC worships you (or your cause), will work incredibly hard, puts your interests ahead of his own at all times, and would even die for you.

ANCIENT/MEDIEVAL HAND WEAPON TABLE

Weapons are listed in groups, according to the skill required to use them. The skill's default level, and any defaults from other skills, are also shown. For swords, daggers, etc., the weight includes a good scabbard. Weapons which can be used in two ways have two separate lines – one for each type of attack. Some weapons can be used with two different *techniques*. These weapons are listed twice – one under each applicable skill.

Weapon	Type	Damage	Reach	Cost	Weight	Min ST	Special Notes
AXE/MACE (DX-5)†							
Hatchet	cut	sw	1	$40	2 lbs.	7	Throwable. 1 turn to ready.
Axe	cut	sw+2	1	$50	4 lbs.	12	1 turn to ready.
Throwing axe	cut	sw+2	1	$60	4 lbs.	12	Throwable. 1 turn to ready.
Small mace	cr	sw+2	1	$35	3 lbs.	11	1 turn to ready.
Mace	cr	sw+3	1	$50	5 lbs.	12	1 turn to ready.
Pick	imp	sw+1	1	$70	3 lbs.	11	1 turn to ready. May get *stuck*.
BLACKJACK (DX-4)							
Blackjack or sap	cr	thr	C	$20	1 lb.	7	May not parry
BROADSWORD (DX-5, Shortsword-2 or Force Sword -3)							
Broadsword	cut	sw+1	1	$500	3 lbs.	10	
	cr	thr+1	1				Standard broadsword has *blunt* point.
Thrusting "	cut	sw+1	1	$600	3 lbs.	10	More expensive because of sharp point.
	imp	thr+2	1				
Bastard sword	cut	sw+1	1, 2	$650	5 lbs.	11	1 turn to ready after swing.†
	cr	thr+1	2				Standard bastard sword has *blunt* point.
Thrusting "	cut	sw+1	1, 2	$750	5 lbs.	11	Same as above, with thrusting point.†
	imp	thr+2	2				
Light club	cr	sw+1	1	$10	3 lbs.	10	
FENCING (DX-5) *See p. 99 for fencing parry rules.*							
Smallsword	imp	thr+1	1	$400	1 lb.	–	Maximum damage 1d+1.
Rapier	imp	thr+1	1, 2	$500	1½ lbs.	–	Maximum damage 1d+1.
Saber	cut	sw	1	$700	2 lbs.	7	
	imp	thr+1	1				Thrust: maximum damage 1d+2.
FLAIL (DX-6) *Any attempt to **parry** a flail weapon is at a -4. Fencing weapons **cannot** parry flails.†*							
Morningstar	cr	sw+3	1	$80	6 lbs.	12	1 turn to ready.
Flail	cr	sw+4	1, 2*	$100	8 lbs.	13	2-handed. 1 turn to ready.
KNIFE (DX-4)							
Large knife	cut	sw-2	C, 1	$40	1 lb.	–	Maximum damage 1d+2.
	imp	thr	C				Throwable; Maximum damage 1d+2.
Small knife	cut	sw-3	C, 1	$30	½ lb.	–	Maximum damage 1d+1.
	imp	thr-1	C				Throwable; Maximum damage 1d+1.
Dagger	imp	thr-1	C	$20	¼ lb.	–	Throwable; Maximum damage 1d.
LANCE *(Spear-3 for those who have Riding 12+; DX-6 for others)*							
Lance	imp	thrust+3	4	$60	6 lbs.	12	May not parry. See p. 136 for readying.
POLEARM (DX-5) *All polearms require 2 hands.*							
Glaive	cut	sw+3	2, 3*	$100	8 lbs.	11	2 turns to ready.
	imp	thr+3	1-3*				1 turn to ready after thrust.
Poleaxe	cut *or* cr	sw+4	2, 3*	$120	10 lbs.	12	2 turns to ready after swing.
Halberd	cut	sw+5	2, 3*	$150	12 lbs.	13	2 turns to ready after swing.
	imp	sw+4	2, 3*				2 turns to ready after swing. May get *stuck*.
	imp	thr+3	1-3*				1 turn to ready after thrust.
SHORTSWORD (DX-5, Broadsword-2 or Force Sword-3)							
Shortsword	cut	sw	1	$400	2 lbs.	7	Sabers can be used w/Shortsword skill.
	imp	thr	1				
Baton	cr	sw	1	$20	1 lb.	7	A short, well-balanced club.
	cr	thr	1				
SPEAR (DX-5 or Staff-2)							
Javelin	imp	thr+1	1	$30	2 lbs.	–	Primarily for throwing.
Spear	imp	thr+2	1*	$40	4 lbs.	9	Used 1-handed. Throwable.
		thr+3	1, 2*				Same spear used 2-handed.
STAFF (DX-5 or Spear-2) *Requires two hands.*							
Quarterstaff	cr	sw+2	1, 2	$10	4 lbs.	6	Parry is ⅔ Staff skill.
	cr	thr+2	1, 2				
TWO-HANDED AXE/MACE (DX-5) *Requires two hands.†*							
Great axe	cut	sw+3	1, 2*	$100	8 lbs.	13	1 turn to ready.
Warhammer	imp	sw+3	1, 2*	$100	7 lbs.	13	1 turn to ready. May get *stuck*.
Maul	cr	sw+4	1, 2*	$80	12 lbs.	14	1 turn to ready.
Scythe	cut	sw+2	1	$15	5 lbs	12	2-handed. 1 turn to ready
	imp	sw	1		.	6	-2 to hit when impaling.

Weapon	Type	Damage	Reach	Cost	Weight	Min ST	Special Notes
TWO-HANDED SWORD (DX-5 or Force Sword -3) *Requires two hands.*							
Bastard sword	cut	sw+2	1, 2	$650	5 lbs.	10	Exactly as with Broadsword, but
	cr	thr+2	2				used two-handed.
Thrusting "	cut	sw+2	1, 2	$750	5 lbs.	10	As above, with thrusting point.
	imp	thr+3	2				
Greatsword	cut	sw+3	1, 2	$800	7 lbs.	12	Usually has *blunt* point.
	cr	thr+2	2				
Thrusting "	cut	sw+3	1, 2	$900	7 lbs.	12	As above, with thrusting point.
	imp	thr+3	2				
Quarterstaff	cr	sw+2	1, 2	$10	4 lbs.	9	Using sword technique with staff.
	cr	thr+1	2				
WHIP (No default)							
Whip	cr	sw-2	1-7	$20/yd	2 lbs./yd.	10	Max. dam. 1d-1; see p. 52.

* Must be *readied* for one turn to change from long to short grip or vice versa. †Becomes unready if used to parry.

ANCIENT/MEDIEVAL RANGED WEAPON TABLE

Weapons are listed in groups, according to the skill required to use them, along with skill defaults.

Weapon	Type	Damage	SS	Acc	Ranges ½D	Max.	Cost*	Weight†	Min ST	Special Notes
AXE THROWING (DX-4)										
Hatchet	cut	sw	11	1	ST×1½	ST×2½	$40	2 lbs.	7	
Throwing axe	cut	sw+2	10	2	ST	ST×1½	$60	4 lbs.	11	
BLOWPIPE (DX-6)										
Blowpipe	Special (p. 49)	–	10	1	–	ST×4	$30	1 lb.	–	See p. 49.
BOLAS (No default)										
Bolas	Special (p. 49)	thr-1	12	0	–	ST×3	$20	2 lbs.	–	See p. 49.
BOW (DX-6) *2 hands to fire. 2 turns to ready.*										
Short bow	imp	thr	12	1	ST×10	ST×15	$50/$2	2 lbs.	7	Max. dam. 1d+3.
Regular bow	imp	thr+1	13	2	ST×15	ST×20	$100/$2	2 lbs.	10	Max. dam. 1d+4.
Longbow	imp	thr+2	15	3	ST×15	ST×20	$200/$2	3 lbs.	11	Max. dam. 1d+4.
Composite bow	imp	thr+3	14	3	ST×20	ST×25	$900/$2	4 lbs.	10	Max. dam. 1d+4.
Quiver							$10	1/2 lb.		Holds 10 arrows/bolts.
CROSSBOW (DX-4) *2 hands to fire, 4 turns to ready (8 if ST is greater than yours).*										
Crossbow	imp	thr+4	12	4	ST×20	ST×25	$150/$2	6 lbs.	7	Max. dam. 3d.
Prodd	cr	thr+4	12	2	ST×20	ST×25	$150/$.10	6 lbs.	7	Fires lead pellets.
Goat's-foot	–	–			To cock crossbow		$50	2 lbs.	7	See p. 114.
KNIFE THROWING (DX-4)										
Large knife	imp	thr	12	0	ST-2	ST+5	$40	1 lb.	–	Max. dam. 1d+2.
Small knife	imp	thr-1	11	0	ST-5	ST	$30	1/2 lb.	–	Max dam. 1d+1.
Dagger	imp	thr-1	12	0	ST-5	ST	$20	1/4 lb.	–	Max. dam. 1d.
LASSO (No default)										
Lasso	Special	Special	16	0	–	–	$40	3 lbs.	–	See p. 51.
NET (No default)										
Large net	Special (p. 51)	–	13	1	–	ST/2 + Skill/5	$40	20 lbs.	–	See p. 51.
Melee net	Special (p. 51)	–	12	1	–	ST + Skill/5	$20	5 lbs.	–	See p. 51.
SLING (DX-6) *2 hands to load, 1 to fire. 2 turns to ready.*										
Sling	cr	sw	12	0	ST×6	ST×10	$10	1/2 lb.	–	Fires rocks.
Staff sling	cr	sw+1	14	1	ST×10	ST×15	$20	2 lbs.	–	Fires rocks.
SPEAR THROWER (DX-4 or Spear Throwing-4)										
Atlatl							$20	2 lbs.		
w/Dart	imp	sw-1	11	1	ST×3	ST×4	$20	1 lbs.	–	
w/Javelin	imp	sw+1	11	3	ST×2	ST×3	$30	2 lbs	7	
w/Spear	imp	sw+3	12	2	ST×1½	ST×2	$40	4 lbs.	9	
SPEAR THROWING (DX-4 or Spear Thrower-4)										
Javelin	imp	thr+1	10	3	ST×1½	ST×2½	$30	2 lbs.	7	
Spear	imp	thr+3	11	2	ST	ST×1½	$40	4 lbs.	9	
DX-3 or THROWING SKILL *(See p. 90)*										
Rock	cr	thr-1	12	0	ST×2	ST×3½	–	1 lb.	–	
Oil flask	fire	see p. 121	13	0	–	ST×3½	$50‡	1 lb.	–	

*Cost: The number after the slash is the cost per shot (arrow or other missile) for a missile weapon.
†An arrow weighs 2 oz.; a crossbow bolt, sling-stone or prodd pellet weigh 1 oz.   ‡Fantasy, or TL4; costs $1 at TL6+.

MODERN AND ULTRA-TECH WEAPONS

Weapons in the tables are described in the following format:

Weapon: Name of the manufacturer; most common name of the weapon and (for guns) the ammo caliber; date of introduction; nationality. Letters in parentheses indicate the skill to use: (**BP**) = Black Powder, (**BW**) = Beam Weapons. If no code is given, use Guns skill, or Throwing (or DX-3) for grenades.

Letter codes indicate the nationality of original manufacture: **AU** Austria, **BE** Belgium, **FR** France, **GE** Germany, **IS** Israel, **IT** Italy, **SF** science fiction, **UK** United Kingdom, **US** United States of America, **USSR** Union of Soviet Socialist Republics.

Type: The type of damage the weapon does.

Damage: The number of dice of damage the weapon does.

SS: This is the snap-shot number – the final to-hit number necessary to avoid a penalty of -4 on a snap-shot with the weapon.

Acc: The accuracy modifier of the weapon. See p. 115.

$^1/_2$D: The range at which the accuracy modifier of the weapon drops to zero and the damage done by the weapon is halved.

Max: The maximum range of the weapon. Maximum range as given here is the maximum range which the bullet can reach when the weapon is at the most efficient angle for the given combination of bullet and weapon under Earth-normal conditions.

Wt: The weight of the loaded weapon in pounds.

RoF: The rate of fire for the weapon. In some cases it is given as a combination. The number to the left of the slash is the number of shots the weapon can fire; the number to the right is the number of turns. If the number is greater than one, the weapon is capable of automatic fire, i.e., that many shots will be fired if the trigger is held down for the entire turn. A * indicates that it is capable of selective-fire, i.e., it may fire either automatic or semi-automatic. A ~ indicates that the weapon is not automatic, but can fire up to the indicated number of times each turn.

Shots: The number of shots that the weapon holds. A /B or /C refers to shots per *power cell* – see *Power Supplies*, p. 119.

ST: Minimum strength necessary to avoid an additional turn readying the weapon after it is fired, and extra recoil penalties.

Rcl: The recoil penalty of the weapon. See p. 120.

Cost: The retail price of the weapon when first introduced. Some weapons remain in use long after their introduction. To find the current price in an era with a different starting wealth, multiply the cost by the factor of different starting wealth (see p. 16). A .45 Auto that costs $30 in 1910 (starting wealth of $750) cost $600 in 1985 (starting wealth of $15,000).

TL: The tech level at which the weapon first appears.

Abbreviations: **ACP** Automatic Colt Pistol, **Br** British, **C** Colt, **CA** Charter Arms, **E** Enfield, **H&H** Holland & Holland, **H&K** Heckler & Koch, **IMI** Israeli Military Industries, **G** Gauge, **GN** Gauss needles, **L** Lebel, **LE** Lee Enfield, **LR** Long Rifle, **M** Magnum, **MH** Martini Henry, **Msr** Mauser, **N** Nitro, **Ne** needles, **P** Parabellum, **Pz** Polizei, **R** Russian, **Rem** Remington, **RP** Russian Pistol, **S** Short, **Sp** Special, **Spr** Springfield, **S&W** Smith & Wesson, **W** Webley, **Win** Winchester, **Wltr** Walther.

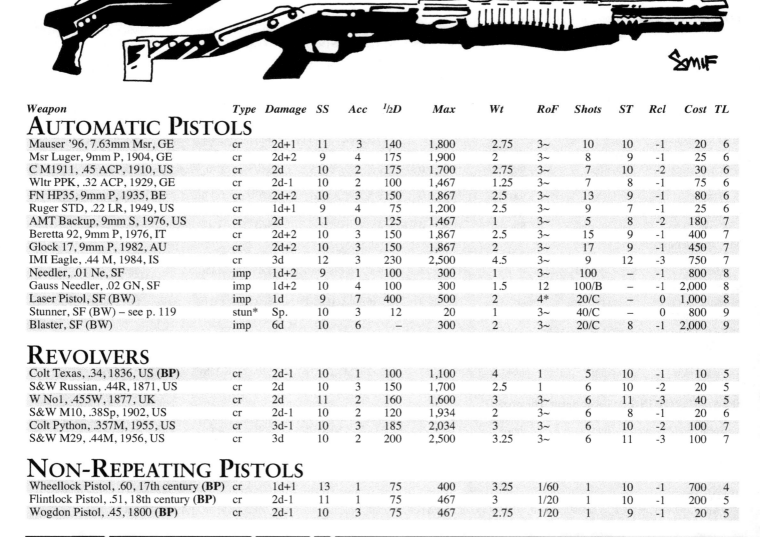

Weapon	Type	Damage	SS	Acc	$^1/_2$D	Max	Wt	RoF	Shots	ST	Rcl	Cost	TL
AUTOMATIC PISTOLS													
Mauser '96, 7.63mm Msr, GE	cr	2d+1	11	3	140	1,800	2.75	3~	10	10	-1	20	6
Msr Luger, 9mm P, 1904, GE	cr	2d+2	9	4	175	1,900	2	3~	8	9	-1	25	6
C M1911, .45 ACP, 1910, US	cr	2d	10	2	175	1,700	2.75	3~	7	10	-2	30	6
Wltr PPK, .32 ACP, 1929, GE	cr	2d-1	10	2	100	1,467	1.25	3~	7	8	-1	75	6
FN HP35, 9mm P, 1935, BE	cr	2d+2	10	3	150	1,867	2.5	3~	13	9	-1	80	6
Ruger STD, .22 LR, 1949, US	cr	1d+1	9	4	75	1,200	2.5	3~	9	7	-1	25	6
AMT Backup, 9mm S, 1976, US	cr	2d	11	0	125	1,467	1	3~	5	8	-2	180	7
Beretta 92, 9mm P, 1976, IT	cr	2d+2	10	3	150	1,867	2.5	3~	15	9	-1	400	7
Glock 17, 9mm P, 1982, AU	cr	2d+2	10	3	150	1,867	2	3~	17	9	-1	450	7
IMI Eagle, .44 M, 1984, IS	cr	3d	12	3	230	2,500	4.5	3~	9	12	-3	750	7
Needler, .01 Ne, SF	imp	1d+2	9	1	100	300	1	3~	100	–	-1	800	8
Gauss Needler, .02 GN, SF	imp	1d+2	10	4	100	300	1.5	12	100/B	–	-1	2,000	8
Laser Pistol, SF (BW)	imp	1d	9	7	400	500	2	4*	20/C	–	0	1,000	8
Stunner, SF (BW) – see p. 119	stun*	Sp.	10	3	12	20	1	3~	40/C	–	0	800	9
Blaster, SF (BW)	imp	6d	10	6	–	300	2	3~	20/C	8	-1	2,000	9
REVOLVERS													
Colt Texas, .34, 1836, US (**BP**)	cr	2d-1	10	1	100	1,100	4	1	5	10	-1	10	5
S&W Russian, .44R, 1871, US	cr	2d	10	3	150	1,700	2.5	1	6	10	-2	20	5
W No1, .455W, 1877, UK	cr	2d	11	2	160	1,600	3	3~	6	11	-3	40	5
S&W M10, .38Sp, 1902, US	cr	2d-1	10	2	120	1,934	2	3~	6	8	-1	20	6
Colt Python, .357M, 1955, US	cr	3d-1	10	3	185	2,034	3	3~	6	10	-2	100	7
S&W M29, .44M, 1956, US	cr	3d	10	2	200	2,500	3.25	3~	6	11	-3	100	7
NON-REPEATING PISTOLS													
Wheellock Pistol, .60, 17th century (**BP**)	cr	1d+1	13	1	75	400	3.25	1/60	1	10	-1	700	4
Flintlock Pistol, .51, 18th century (**BP**)	cr	2d-1	11	1	75	467	3	1/20	1	10	-1	200	5
Wogdon Pistol, .45, 1800 (**BP**)	cr	2d-1	10	3	75	467	2.75	1/20	1	9	-1	20	5

Shotguns

Weapon	Type	Damage	SS	Acc	1/2D	Max	Wt	RoF	Shots	ST	Rcl	Cost	TL
Blunderbuss 8G, 18th C, UK, (BP)	Cr.	5d	14	3	15	100	12	1/15	1	13	-4	$15	5
Ithaca 10G, 1900, US	Cr.	5d	12	5	25	150	10	2~	2	13	-4	$45	6
Rem M870, 12G, 1950, US	Cr.	4d	12	5	25	150	8	3~	5	12	-3	$235	7

Rifles

Weapon	Type	Damage	SS	Acc	1/2D	Max	Wt	RoF	Shots	ST	Rcl	Cost	TL
Cannon-lock, .90, 16th century (BP)	Cr.	2d	20	1	100	600	5	1/60	1	10	-3	$300	4
Matchlock Musket, .80, 17th century (BP)	Cr.	4d	18	2	100	600	20	1/60	1	12	-2	$400	4
Brown Bess, .75, 1720, UK (BP)	Cr.	3d	15	5	100	1,500	13	1/15	1	11	-3	$10	5
Kentucky Rifle, .45, 1750, US (BP)	Cr.	4d	15	7	400	3,700	6.75	1/20	1	10	-2	$40	5
Ferguson Rifle, .60, 1777, UK (BP)	Cr.	4d	14	7	400	3,700	7	1/10	1	10	-2	$60	5
Baker Rifle, .625, 1790, UK (BP)	Cr.	4d	15	7	300	2,500	9.25	1/20	1	12	-3	$20	5
E '53, .577 Br, 1853, UK (BP)	Cr.	3d	15	8	700	2,100	8.5	1/15	1	10	-2	$15	5
MH '71, .45 Br, 1871, UK	Cr.	4d	15	7	600	2,030	6.5	1/4	1	10	-2	$20	5
Rem Rifle, .45 C, 1871, US	Cr.	4d	15	8	700	2,100	9.25	1/4	1	10	-2	$55	5
Spr '73, .45-70, 1873, US	Cr.	4d	15	8	700	2,100	9	1/4	1	11	-2	$20	5
Win '73, .44-40 Win, 1873, US	Cr.	3d	13	7	300	2,200	7.1	2~	6	10	-2	$40	5
Lebel '86, 8mm L, 1886, FR	Cr.	6d+1	15	10	1,000	3,900	10	1/2	8	12	-3	$125	5
Sharps 50, .50-90, 1890, US	Cr.	6d	15	7	600	3,300	11	1/4	1	12	-3	$150	5
Win '94, .30-30 Win, 1894, US	Cr.	5d	13	8	450	3,011	7	2~	6	10	-1	$475	5
Msr '98k, 8mm Msr, 1898, GE	Cr.	7d	14	11	1,000	3,972	9.5	1/2	5	12	-3	$170	6
LE Mk3#1, .303 Br, 1903, UK	Cr.	6d+1	14	10	1,000	3,800	10.2	1	10	12	-2	$130	6
M1903A1, .30-06, 1906, US	Cr.	7d+1	14	11	1,000	3,710	9.5	1/2	5	12	-3	$135	6
H&H Express, .600 N, 1923, UK	Cr.	10d	16	7	1,500	5,063	16	2	2	13	-6	$200	6
M1 Garand, .30-06, 1936, US	Cr.	7d+1	14	11	1,000	3,710	10	3~	8	12	-3	$590	6
AK-47, 7.62mm R, 1949, SU	Cr.	5d+1	12	7	400	3,011	10.5	10*	30	10	-1	$290	7
FN-FAL, .308 Win, 1950, BE	Cr.	7d	14	11	1,000	4,655	11	11*	20	11	-2	$900	7
H&K G3, .308 Win, 1959, GE	Cr.	7d	14	10	1,000	4,655	11	10*	20	11	-2	$550	7
M16, .223 Rem, 1964, US	Cr.	5d	12	11	500	3,843	8	12*	20	9	-1	$540	7
AUG, .223 Rem, 1978, AU	Cr.	5d	11	10	500	3,843	9	11*	30	9	-1	$540	7
H&K PSG1, .308 Win, 1982, GE	Cr.	7d	15	13	1,200	4,655	11	3~	20	12	-2	$4,500	7
Needle Rifle, .01 Ne, SF	Imp.	2d	13	9	300	800	5	3~	100	8	-1	$1,200	8
Laser Rifle, SF (BW)	Imp.	2d	15	13	900	1,200	5	3~	12/C	–	0	$2,000	8
Military Laser Rifle, SF (BW)	Imp.	2d	12	15	1,500	2,000	9	8*	140/D	–	0	$4,000	8
Gauss Needle Rifle, .02 GN, SF	Imp.	2d+1	14	11	500	1,000	6	20*	100/B	9	-1	$2,500	8
Blast Rifle, SF (BW)	Imp.	12d	14	13	400	800	10	3~	12/C	9	-1	$3,000	9
Disruptor, SF (BW)	Imp.	6d	13	10	500	1,000	9	3~	20/C	–	0	$2,500	9
Stun Rifle, SF (BW) – see p. 119	Stun	Stun	12	10	300	1,000	4	3~	20/C	–	0	$1,000	9

Submachine Guns

Weapon	Type	Damage	SS	Acc	1/2D	Max	Wt	RoF	Shots	ST	Rcl	Cost	TL
Thompson, .45 ACP, 1922, US	Cr.	2d+1	11	7	190	1,750	12	20*	30	11	-3	120	6
MP40, 9mm P, 1940, GE	Cr.	3d-1	10	6	160	1,900	10.5	8	32	10	-1	70	6
PPSh41, 7.62 RP, 1941, USSR	Cr.	3d-1	10	6	160	1,900	12	16	71	10	-1	65	6
IMI Uzi, 9mm P, 1952, IS	Cr.	3d-1	10	7	160	1,900	9.5	10*	32	10	-1	150	7
H&K MP5, 9mm P, 1966, GE	Cr.	3d-1	10	8	160	1,900	7.25	10*	30	10	-1	340	7

Grenades

Weapon	Type	Dmg	Wt	Fuse	TL
US Mk 2 Defensive	Cr.	2d-1	1.5	3-5	6
US Mk 67 Defensive	Cr.	5d+2	1	4-5	7
US Mk 68 Defensive	Cr.	5d+2	1	impact	7
US AN-M8 Smoke	–	–	1.5	1-2	7
US M59 Offensive	Cr.	5d+2	1.5	impact	7
UK No. 36 Defensive	Cr.	2d-1	1.5	3-5	6
UK "jam tin"	Cr.	5d	1.5	0-8	6
GE "Potato masher"	Cr.	2d-2	1.3	2-4	6
USSR RGD-5 Defensive	Cr.	3d-1	.6	3-4	7

See p. 121 for grenade rules.

Ammunition

Name	DMG	Damage Mod.	Cost/100
TL5 and below	×1	×1.5	$2 (1850)
Most pistols at TL6+	×1	×1	$20 (1988)
Pistols, .40+ caliber	×1	×1.5	$40 (1988)
20th-century .22 LR	×1	×1	$2 (1988)
20th-century military rifles	×1	×1	$10 (1988)
Other 20th-century rifles	×1	×1	$30 (1988)
Armor Piercing	×2	×.5	×3
Hollow Point	×.5	×2	×1 1/2
Needles	×1	×1	$15 (TL8)
Gauss needles	×1	×1	$25 (TL8)

Note: The bullet, not the gun, determines damage. Changing the type of bullet can change the basic damage done by the gun. The Damage Modifier is applied to whatever damage gets through the target's DR.

ANCIENT/MEDIEVAL ARMOR

Use this table with the *Hit Location* rules when you want to buy armor piece by piece. To save space on your Character Sheet, list the pieces of armor on the back of the sheet rather than in the "Possessions" box. Note the PD and DR for each body part beside the character sketch on your record sheet. "Areas" refers to the parts of the body in relation to the die-roll numbers on the Parts of the Body table; see diagram, next page.

Headgear and Helmets

Cloth cap. A padded cloth cap. PD 1; DR 1. $5; weight negligible. Covers area 3-4.

Leather helm. Heavy leather with cloth padding. PD 2; DR 2. $20; .5 lb. Covers areas 3-4, 5

Chain coif. A chainmail hood, covering the head and shoulders. * $55; 4 lbs. Covers areas 3-4, 5.

Pot-helm. Steel; covers the top of the head. PD 3; DR 4. $100; 5 lbs. Covers areas 3-4.

Greathelm. Heavy steel; covers the entire head. All weapon skill rolls are at -1, and all IQ rolls to see, hear, etc., are at -3. PD 4; DR 7. $340; 10 lbs. Covers areas 3-4, 5.

Clothing and Torso Armor

If you are not using the "hit location" rules, the PD and DR of your torso armor are used against all attacks.

Ordinary clothing. Cost depends on quality. No PD or DR. Weight 1 lb.
  Peasant rags (random, dirty scraps): $2.
  Lower-class clothing (tunic and pants, indifferently clean): $10.
  Middle-class clothing (tunic and pants, or robe, decorated): $40.
  Upper-class clothing (various types, elaborately decorated): $200.
  Noble dress (various types, elaborately decorated and jeweled): $1,000 and up.

Winter clothing. As above, with no PD, but DR 1 due to thickness. Double above prices. Also covers arms and legs. 3 lbs. Covers areas 6, 8-14, 17-18.

Overcoat. Worn in addition to winter clothing in cold weather. No PD; DR 1. Adds its DR to clothing (or armor) over which it is worn, but *miserably hot* except in cold weather. Also covers arms and legs. $50 (or $100 and up for upper-class or better); 10 lbs. Covers areas 6, 8-14, 17-18.

Cloth armor. Padded cotton with leather straps. PD 1; DR 1. $30; 6 lbs. Covers areas 9-11, 17-18.

Leather armor. Heavy "boiled" leather. PD 2; DR 2. $100; 10 lbs. Covers areas 9-11, 17-18.

Leather jacket. Light, flexible leather. Also covers arms. PD 1; DR 1. $50; 4 lbs. Covers areas 6, 8-11, 17-18.

Chainmail. * $230; 25 lbs. Covers areas 9-11, 17-18.

Scale armor. Heavy leather armor, padded inside, with metal rings or scales attached. PD 3; DR 4. $420; 35 lbs. Covers areas 9-11, 17-18.

Breastplate. Covers neck to groin, but protects against blows from the front only. Bronze: PD 4; DR 4; $400; 20 lbs. Steel: PD 4; DR 5; $500; 18 lbs. Covers areas 9-11, 17-18.

Corselet. A custom-made plate-armor "back-and-breast" with leather straps. PD 4; DR 6. $1,300; 35 lbs. Covers areas 9-11, 17-18.

Heavy corselet. As above, but heavier and of better steel. PD 4; DR 7. $2,300; 45 lbs. Covers areas 9-11, 17-18.

Backpack. A full backpack protects against attacks from the rear only. PD 2; DR2. Cost and weight vary. Covers areas 9-10, 17-18.

Arms and Legs

Prices for arm (areas 6, 8) and leg (areas 12-14) armor are given in *pairs*. For one arm or leg, pay half the indicated cost and weight.

Cloth armor. Padded cotton with leather straps. PD 1; DR 1. Arms: $20; 2 lbs. Legs: $20; 2 lbs.

Leather armor. Strong "boiled" leather with articulated joints. PD 2; DR 2. Arms: $50; 2 lbs. Legs: $60; 4 lbs.

Chainmail. Standard "international" four-link mail shirt of steel wire. * Arms are added to a mail shirt to make it long-sleeved (add $70, 9 lbs.). Legs are usually laced to plate armor as part of a "half plate" outfit; $110; 15 lbs.

Scale armor. Padded leather with metal rings or scales. PD 3; DR 4. Arms: $210; 14 lbs. Legs: $250; 21 lbs.

Plate armor. Custom-made steel vambraces (forearms), greaves (leg pieces), etc., with articulated joints. PD 4; DR 6. Arms: $1,000; 15 lbs. Legs: $1,100; 20 lbs.

Heavy plate. As above, but heavier and of better steel. PD 4; DR 7. Arms: $1,500; 20 lbs. Legs: $1,600; 25 lbs.

Hands and Feet

Cloth gloves. Heavy canvas. PD 1; DR 1. $15; weight negligible. Covers area 7.

Leather gloves. Heavy leather with open palm to allow a better weapon grip. PD 2; DR 2. $30; weight negligible. Covers area 7.

Gauntlets. As above, but with steel plates riveted on for better protection. PD 3; DR 4. $100; 2 lbs. Covers area 7.

Sandals or slippers. Canvas, cloth, etc. No PD or DR. $10; 1 lb.

Shoes. Ordinary leather walking shoes. PD 1; DR 1. $40; 2 lbs. Covers areas 15-16.

Boots. Heavy leather boots, laced high. PD 2; DR 2. $80; 3 lbs. Covers areas 15-16.

Sollerets. Metal-plated boots, very uncomfortable except in combat. PD 3; DR 4. $150; 7 lbs. Covers areas 15-16.

*Normally, chainmail is worn *over* padded cloth armor. The combination has a PD of 3 and DR of 4. Exception: Against *impaling* weapons, it has PD 1 and DR 2. The cost and weight for a complete set of chainmail, as given in the *Equipment and Encumbrance* chapter (pp. 71-77), assume that padded cloth is included. Worn by itself, *without* cloth armor underneath, chainmail would have a PD of 3 and a DR of 3 (PD 0, DR 1 vs. impaling). Using chainmail this way is not efficient in terms of cost or weight!

MODERN AND ULTRA-TECH ARMOR

Most modern body armor covers only the torso and groin area. In the descriptions below, numbers (corresponding to the die roll numbers on the Parts of the Body table) are used to show the exact areas covered.

In the listing of helmets, most military helmets cover only the top of the head — the "brain" region. Riot helmets, used for police riot-control duty, cover the whole head.

Apply the following changes in protection to Kevlar vests whenever an impaling attack is made: PD 1, DR 2. This does *not* apply to areas protected by steel and ceramic inserts. In addition, when all of the damage in an attack is absorbed by the Kevlar, any rolls of 6 on any of the damage dice result in one point of crushing damage per 6 rolled being applied to the wearer.

Note: Areas 17 and 18 refer to the vitals. Area 11 is assumed to cover the groin. Area 10 is the abdomen and area·9 is the chest.

Headgear

1916 British "tin hat" (TL6). The first helmet issued to British soldiers in World War 1, this acquired a good deal of popularity among the troops, in part because of the broad brim which shielded one's face from the elements. PD 2, DR 4; 4 lbs., $70.

M1935 German helmet (TL6). The well-known German coal scuttle helmet. PD 4, DR 4; 5 lbs., $60.

US Army M1 helmet (TL6). The old GI steel pot, recently replaced by the PASGT helmet. PD 3, DR 4; 4 lbs., $30.

Police Riot helmet (TL7). A standard police issue item. The helmet comes with a visor that covers the face. Protection against crushing attacks is quite good, but less so against other attacks. The DR listed after the slash is that provided against cutting, impaling and bullet damage. PD 4, DR 5/2; 3 lbs., $75.

Gentex PASGT helmet (TL7). The current helmet used by the U.S. Army. PD 4, DR 5; 3 lbs., $125.

Combat Infantry Dress helmet (TL8). The helmet is normally worn with the rest of the CID. The helmet is a full-face, full-protection helmet. It fastens on to the attachment points of the hard torso armor to provide a complete seal. Two filtration units are built into the cheek pieces, and when swung down and locked in place, the visor provides a complete seal for operations on a hostile NBC battlefield. A voice-activated 128 channel radio is built in to the helmet, along with a targeting/rangefinding laser. A chin-activated thermal-imaging sight and optical rangefinder are also provided. A head-up display is projected and tied into all of the sensor/communications package by a 1M optical microprocessor. Connections are also provided for hookups to both backpack air units and vehicle systems. PD 4, DR 18 (visor is DR 10); 10 lbs., $300.

Body Armor

American Civil War era body armor (TL5). This was manufactured by a firm in New Haven, Connecticut in 1862, in the form of a breastplate of linked metal sections. It was designed to be worn under the uniform shirt. Areas covered are 9-11, but only from the front. PD 4, DR 10; 12 lbs., $18.

Flak jacket (TL6). Flak jackets have been around in many forms since before WWII. The intent of the flak jacket is not to stop bullets; rather, it is designed to protect the wearer from fragments delivered by grenades or artillery. This is not concealable. It is a heavy overgarment that protects areas 9-10, 17-18. It quickly becomes hot and uncomfortable to wear. PD 2, DR 4; 12 lbs., $150.

Gentex protective vest (TL7). The current U.S. military vest, intended for general issue. The purpose is to protect the wearer against fragments, but it has some utility against small arms. Kevlar protects areas 9-10, 17-18, and offers some protection to the throat/neck area as well. It is designed to be worn over the regulation shirt and field jacket. The vest also has two large pockets and attachment points, and comes in standard camouflage patterns. PD 2, DR 5; 5 lbs., $200.

EOD PS-820 (TL7). This Kevlar body suit is produced for the U.S. Army's Explosive Ordnance Disposal teams. Mobility is restricted (-3 DX). The listed protection is for areas 9-11, 17-18. Arms and legs and feet are DR 10. Head protection is DR 20; face is DR 10. The suit also has a layer of Nomex fire-retardant material. PD 3, DR 30; 35 lbs., $600.

Second Chance Hardcorps system (TL7). Exterior body armor designed specifically for military use. The basic Kevlar vest covers areas 9-11, 17-18 and is DR 16. Steel/ceramic inserts are available to cover areas 9-10, 17-18 at DR 35. There are separate inserts for front and back; each weighs 19 lbs. and costs $190. Basic vest is PD 2, DR 16; 6 lbs., $425.

Second Chance Standard (TL7). The manufacturer's most popular concealable Kevlar vest. Covers areas 9-10, 17-18. Side closure. PD 2, DR 14; 2½ lbs., $200.

Combat Infantry Dress (TL8). A chemically-coated and NBC-proofed jacket worn as an external garment. Steel plates inserted in a compound fiber mesh provide DR 40 over areas 9-11, 17-18. Plastic plates and compound fibers provide DR 12 over the arms and legs. A variety of attachment points and harnesses are provided. Boots are also similar. Jacket with gloves: PD 4, DR 40; 25 lbs., $300. Pants: PD 2, DR 12; 10 lbs., $140. Boots: PD 3, DR 15; 5 lbs., $70. See above for description of helmet.

Areas for Parts of the Body

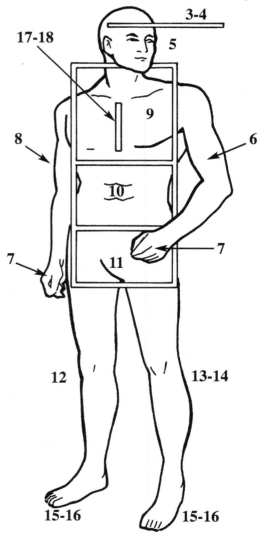

FANTASY/MEDIEVAL EQUIPMENT

The following equipment should be enough to outfit most parties. The GM is free to add items to this list. Note that weapons and armor are on separate tables (pp. 206, 207, 210).

All prices below assume that the item is of ordinary quality, and is neither common nor scarce at the time and place it is being bought.

PCs may buy food at any time they are in town, or passing through friendly farmland. In general, equipment is only available in towns; the GM may vary this as much as he wants.

Weapons and armor will not be freely available except in towns. You may encounter a farmer or wayfarer who will sell you a weapon, but he will probably want at least double the normal price for it!

Weight of money depends on the game world. In general fantasy/medieval settings a $ is a copper farthing; $1,000 in silver would weigh one pound. A gold coin is worth 20 silver coins of the same weight.

Food

Traveler's rations (one meal of dried meat and cheese) ....$\frac{1}{2}$ lb.,$2
Simple tavern meal (stew, fruit, vegetable, etc.) ....$2 to $4
Water (one quart) ....2 lbs., usually free
Wine (one quart) ....2 lbs., $2
Brandy (one quart) ....2 lbs., $15

Medical Gear

Simple first aid kit (adds 1 to First Aid skill) ....2 lbs., $30
"Crash kit" (adds 2 to First Aid skill) ....10 lbs., $100
Doctor's black bag (adds 2 to First Aid skill;
  -2 to Surgery skill without at least this much) ....15 lbs., $300

Equipment for Climbing, Breaking and Entering, etc.

Cord ($\frac{3}{16}$", supports 90 lbs.) ....10 yards: $\frac{1}{2}$ lb., $1
Rope ($\frac{3}{8}$", supports 300 lbs.) ....10 yards: $1\frac{1}{2}$ lbs., $5
Heavy Rope ($\frac{3}{4}$", supports 1,100 lbs.) ....10 yards: 5 lbs., $25
Cable ($1\frac{1}{2}$", supports 3,700 lbs.) ....10 yards: 17 lbs., $100
Iron spike or "piton" ....$\frac{1}{2}$ lb., $1
Light hooked grapnel (can support 300 lbs.) ....2 lbs., $20
Lockpicks (ordinary quality) ....Weight negligible; $30
Lockpicks (good quality: +1 on all attempts)....Weight negligible; $200

Tools

6-foot pole (for pitching tents or
touching questionable items) ....3 lbs., $5
Pick (for digging) ....8 lbs., $16
Shovel ....6 lbs., $30
Crowbar (5 feet long, iron) ....10 lbs., $8
Hammer (a small sledge, not a carpentry hammer) ....4 lbs., $12
Hatchet (for chopping wood, -1 to skill in combat) ....2 lbs., $20

Outdoor Equipment

Personal basics (the things nobody but an idiot leaves home without).
  -2 to any Survival roll if you're without them: Spoon, fork, and cup;
  flint and steel; towel; etc.....................................Weight negligible; $5
Group basics (a sturdy box with all the *ordinary* things a group of
  3 to 8 would take camping: cookpots, a bit of rope,
  hatchet, etc.) ....20 lbs., $50
Whetstone (for sharpening tools and
weapons; Armourer may *find* one after
an hour's search and a skill roll) ....1 lb., $5
Torch (will burn for one hour) ....1 lb., $3
Lantern ....2 lbs., $20
Oil for lantern (1 pint burns 24 hours) ....1 lb., $2
Tent (1 person). Includes ropes; no poles needed..................5 lbs., $50
Tent (2 people). Includes ropes; a 6-foot pole
  must be carried or improvised. ....12 lbs., $80
Tent (4 people). Includes ropes;
2 6-foot poles are required..30 lbs., $150
Tent (20 people). Includes ropes;
16 6-foot poles are required......................................100 lbs., $300
Blanket (heavy wool)..5 lbs., $20
Sleeping bag (for freezing weather)...............................15 lbs., $100
Fishing net ....10 lbs., $30
Small ceramic bottle (1 quart) ....1 lb., $3
Large ceramic bottle (1 gallon)....................................4 lbs., $5
Small wineskin (1 gallon) ....Weight negligible; $10
Large wineskin (5 gallons) ....1 lb., $30
Small pouch (will hold 3 lbs.) ....Weight negligible; $10
Large purse or pouch (will hold 10 lbs.)............................$\frac{1}{2}$ lb., $20
Small backpack (will hold 40 lbs. of gear) ....3 lbs., $60
Large backpack (with frame, will hold 100 lbs. of gear).....10 lbs., $100

Riding and Transportation

Riding animals: see *Animals*, p. 144.
Saddle, bit and bridle (for horse, mule, etc.)......................20 lbs., $150
One-horse wagon (carries up to 1 ton)............................300 lbs., $400
Two-horse wagon (carries up to 2 tons) ....500 lbs., $700
Four-horse wagon (carries up to 4 tons) ....800 lbs., $1,000
Ox team wagon (carries up to 10 tons).........................1,200 lbs., $1,500
Rowboat (carries up to 1,000 lbs., slowly) ....300 lbs., $500
Canoe (carries up to 600 lbs.) ....100 lbs., $300

MODERN EQUIPMENT

The following basic equipment is appropriate in any 20th-century campaign. The GM may add any item to the list – and, in general, PCs may buy anything that a store would actually carry, using the real price. Weapons and armor are on separate tables (see above).

All prices given here assume that the item is of ordinary quality, and is neither common nor scarce at the time or place it is being bought. Prices are based on U.S. prices circa 1985-1990; halve prices for 1960, divide by 4 for 1940. Also, adventurers buying equipment in Darkest Africa will face a limited selection and higher prices.

PCs may buy food anywhere, at least in civilized countries. Unusual equipment is available only in cities and towns, but any country convenience store will have tools, simple camping gear and clothing.

Guns are rarely for sale except in towns, though country stores will usually have ammo for common weapons (especially hunting rifles, .22s and shotguns). Body armor is only worn by the military and police, and can only be bought by civilians by mail order or at specialty stores in large cities.

Weight of money is usually negligible, since normal transactions use paper money, checks, or (in the last half of the century) credit cards.

Food

Low-quality meal	$3.50
Average-quality meal	$7.50
High-quality meal	$25
Bottle of cheap liquor	$10
Bottle of good liquor	$20
Concentrated rations (for one week)	2 lbs., $50

Medical Gear

Simple first aid kit (adds 1 to First Aid skill)	2 lbs., $30
"Crash kit" (adds 2 to First Aid skill)	10 lbs., $100
Doctor's black bag (adds 2 to First Aid or Surgery skill)	15 lbs., $300

Equipment for Climbing, Breaking and Entering, etc.

Cord (³⁄₁₆", supports 90 lbs.)	10 yards: ½ lb., $1
Rope (³⁄₈", supports 300 lbs.)	10 yards: 1½ lbs., $5
Heavy rope (¾", supports 1,100 lbs.)	10 yards: 5 lbs., $25
Cable (1½", supports 3,700 lbs.)	10 yards: 17 lbs., $100
High-quality cord/rope/cable available at 5 times the cost, holds twice the weight	
Iron spike or "piton"	½ lb., $1
Light hooked grapnel (can support 300 lbs.)	2 lbs., $20
Lockpicks (ordinary quality)	Weight negligible; $30
Lockpicks (good quality: +1 on all attempts)	Weight negligible; $200
Handcuffs	1 lb., $50

Tools

Crowbar (3 feet long, iron)	3 lbs., $8
Cutting torch	7 lbs., $75
Gass bottles (for cutting torch)	1 lb. per minute of cutting time; $1 per lb.
Hammer (a small sledge, not a carpentry hammer)	4 lbs., $12
Pick (for digging)	8 lbs., $16
Shovel	6 lbs., $12

Swiss Army knife (if this is the only tool a mechanic has, he rolls at -3 instead of -5) .... Weight negligible; $25
Tool kit (includes the basic equipment every mechanic needs) .... 40 lbs., $600

Outdoor Equipment

Personal basics (the things nobody but an idiot leaves home without). -2 to any Survival roll if you're withou them: Spoon, fork and cup; matches; towel; soap; toothbrush; etc. .... Weight negligible; $5
Group basics (sturdy box with all the ordinary things a group of 3 to 8 would take camping: cookpots, a bit of rope, hatchet, etc.) .... 20 lbs., $50

Axe	6 lbs., $15
Backpack (with frame – holds 100 lbs., of gear)	10 lbs., $100
Batteries	Weight negligible; $1 each
Binoculars (sports fan's set, 2.5× magnification)	2 lbs., $40

Binoculars (military issue; better view with rangefinder reticle – up to 2,000 yards – 7× magnification) .... 3 lbs., $400
Canteen (blanket-covered, holds one quart) .... 1 lb. (empty), 3 lbs. (full), $10

Electric lantern	2 lbs., $30
Fishing gear (rod, reel, tackle, etc.)	7 lbs., $25
Flashlight (requires 3 batteries)	1 lb., $10

Heavy flashlight (requires 3 batteries, acts as baton in combat) .... 3 lbs., $50
Gun cleaning kit (everything needed to keep a firearm clean in the field) .... 1 lb., $20

Hatchet	2 lbs., $7.50
Sleeping bag (for normal conditions)	7 lbs., $25
Sleeping bag (for freezing weather)	15 lbs., $100

Survival knife (large knife; handle contains variety of miniaturized survival equipment) .... 1½ lbs., $40

Tent (2 people). Includes ropes and poles	5 lbs., $80
Tent (4 people). Includes ropes and poles	12 lbs., $150
Watch	Weight negligible; $25 and up
Whetstone (for tools and weapons)	Weight negligible; $10

Transportation

Bicycle	$60 and up
Used car	$500 and up
New car	$6,000 and up
Fancy new car	$25,000 and up
Private prop-driven plane	$80,000 and up
Gasoline	$1 per gallon
New York to L.A., by plane, coach fare	$300
New York to L.A., by plane, first class	$600
Cab fare	$1.50 per mile
Bus fare	$.50 per trip

Communications

Walkie-talkie (range 2 miles)	Each unit – 3 lbs., $75
Headset communicators (as above, except worn on the head – range ¼ mile)	Each set – ½ lb., $20
Transistor radio (needs 1 battery)	½ lb., $15
Miniature shortwave radio (needs 3 batteries)	1 lb., $70
Miniature color TV (needs 6 batteries)	3 lbs., $200

GURPS®

CHARACTER SHEET

Name **DAI BLACKTHORN** Player _____

Appearance **5'6", 110 lbs., FAIR SKIN, DARK HAIR and EYES**

Character Story **STREET KID, THIEF**

Date Created	Sequence

Unspent Points	Point Total **100**

Pt. Cost		
-15	**ST**	**8**

FATIGUE

60	**DX**	**15**

BASIC DAMAGE

Thrust: 1d-3

Swing: 1d-2

20	**IQ**	**12**

HITS TAKEN

20	**HT**	**12**

Mvmt

BASIC SPEED	MOVE
6.75	6
(HT + DX)/4	Basic – Enc.

ENCUMBRANCE

None (0) = 2×ST	16
Light (1) = 4×ST	32
Med (2) = 6×ST	48
Hvy (3) = 12×ST	96
X-hvy (4) = 20×ST	160

PASSIVE DEFENSE

Armor: 1

Shield: _____

TOTAL **1**

ACTIVE DEFENSES

DODGE	PARRY	BLOCK
6	7	5
= Move	KNIFE Weapon/2	Shield/2

DAMAGE RESISTANCE

Armor **JACKET : 1**

:

:

TOTAL **1**

ADVANTAGES, DISADVANTAGES, QUIRKS

Pt. Cost	
5	ABSOLUTE DIRECTION
10	ACUTE HEARING (+5)
	Hears on 17
5	DOUBLE-JOINTED
15	DANGER SENSE
-15	ENEMY: Thieves' Guild
	roll of 6 or less
-10	OVERCONFIDENCE
-15	POOR
-1	SENSITIVE ABOUT HEIGHT
-1	AFRAID of DROWNING/dislikes lakes
-1	LOVES HIGH PLACES
-1	NO DRUGS OR ALCOHOL
-1	FLAMBOYANT SHOWOFF
0	CANNOT READ

REACTION +/- **NONE**

WEAPONS AND POSSESSIONS

Item	Damage Type	Amt.	Skill Level	$	Wt.
SMALL KNIFE	cut	1d-5	17	30	½
	imp	1d-4			
DAGGER	imp	1d-4	17	20	¼
LOCKPICKS				30	–
CLOTHES (low-class)				10	1
SHOES				40	2
LEATHER JACKET				50	4
RING				20	–
SILVER $				10	–

Totals: $ **200** Lbs. **7¾**

WEAPON RANGES

Weapon	SS	Acc	½D	Max
KNIFE	11	0	3	8
DAGGER	12	0	3	8

SKILLS

	Pt. Cost	Level
AREA KNOWLEDGE	2	13
CLIMBING	-	13
FAST-TALK	2	12
KNIFE	4	17
KNIFE THROWING	½	14
LOCKPICKING	4	13
PICKPOCKET	4	15
SHORTSWORD	4	16
STEALTH	2	15
STREETWISE	2	12
TRAPS (from lockpicking)	½	11

SUMMARY

	Point Total
Attributes	85
Advantages	35
Disadvantages	-40
Quirks	-5
Skills	25
TOTAL	100

GURPS®

CHARACTER SHEET

Name **ROBYN of the MEADOWS** Player _____

Appearance **5'6", 130 LBS., FAIR SKIN, RED HAIR**

Character Story **COUNTRY KID LOOKING FOR WEALTH IN THE BIG CITY.**

Date Created	Sequence

Unspent Points	Point Total
	100

Pt. Cost

10	**ST 11**
45	**DX 14**
30	**IQ 13**
10	**HT 11**

FATIGUE

BASIC DAMAGE

Thrust: _1d-1_

Swing: _1d+1_

HITS TAKEN

Mvmt

BASIC SPEED	MOVE
6.25	6
(HT+DX)/4	Basic – Enc.

ENCUMBRANCE

None (0) = 2×ST	22	
Light (1) = 4×ST	44	
Med (2) = 6×ST	66	
Hvy (3) = 12×ST	132	
X-hvy (4) = 20×ST	220	

PASSIVE DEFENSE

Armor: _____

Shield: _____

TOTAL **∅** SHOES 1

REACTION +/– _NONE_

ACTIVE DEFENSES

DODGE	PARRY	BLOCK
6	7	X
= Move	KNIFE Weapon/2	Shield/2

DAMAGE RESISTANCE

Armor ___(SHOES) : (1)___

: _____

: _____

TOTAL **∅** SHOES 1

ADVANTAGES, DISADVANTAGES, QUIRKS

Pt. Cost

10	ALERTNESS +2
10	NIGHT VISION
-10	PHOBIA – Insects
-10	STRUGGLING (½ normal wealth)
-15	GREEDY
-1	LOVES GEMS and JEWELS
-1	CLAIMS TO BE PART ELF
-1	DISLIKES AUTHORITY
-1	LIKES CATS
-1	DISLIKES CITY BUT FINDS IT FASCINATING
0	ILLITERATE!

WEAPONS AND POSSESSIONS

Item	Damage Type Amt.	Skill Level	$	Wt.
LARGE KNIFE	CUT 1d-1	16	40	1
	imp 1d-1			
DAGGERS (2)	imp 1d-2	16	20@	½
CLOTHES (middle-class)			40	1
SHOES			40	2
JEWELLED RINGS			200	–

At home:

TWO CHANGES of CLOTHING 80

BURIED SILVER 60

CATS

Totals: $ **500**   Lbs. **4½**

WEAPON RANGES

Weapon	SS	Acc	½D	Max
THROWN KNIFE	11	∅	9	16
THROWN DAGGER	11	∅	6	11

SKILLS

	Pt. Cost	Level
KNIFE	4	16
KNIFE THROWING	1	14
ACROBATICS	2	13
FAST-TALK	2	13
LOCKPICKING	2	13
PICKPOCKET	2	13
STEALTH	4	15
STREETWISE	4	14
JEWELER	2	12
MERCHANT	2	13

SUMMARY

	Point Total
Attributes	95
Advantages	20
Disadvantages	-35
Quirks	-5
Skills	25
TOTAL	100

GURPS®
CHARACTER SHEET

Name **KATRINA** Player _____
Appearance **5'9", 100 lbs., ATTRACTIVE**
Character Story **MERCENARY ARCHER WITH CHECKERED PAST**

Date Created	Sequence

Unspent Points	Point Total **100**

Pt. Cost		FATIGUE
20	**ST** 12	

		BASIC DAMAGE
30	**DX** 13	Thrust: 1d-1
20	**IQ** 12	Swing: 1d+2

		HITS TAKEN
10	**HT** 11	

Mvmt	BASIC SPEED 6 (HT+DX)/4	MOVE 6 Basic − Enc.

ENCUMBRANCE
		PASSIVE DEFENSE
None (0) = 2×ST	24	Armor: 1
Light (1) = 4×ST	48	Shield: ___
Med (2) = 6×ST	72	
Hvy (3) = 12×ST	144	TOTAL 1
X-hvy (4) = 20×ST	240	

ACTIVE DEFENSES
DODGE	PARRY	BLOCK
6 = Move	10 FENCING Weapon/2	X Shield/2

DAMAGE RESISTANCE
Armor	LIGHT LEATHER: 1	
	TOUGHNESS : 1	TOTAL 2
	:	

ADVANTAGES, DISADVANTAGES, QUIRKS
Pt. Cost	
5	ATTRACTIVE (+1 reaction)
10	TOUGHNESS-1
10	LITERATE
-5	SKINNY
-5	STUBBORN
-15	BERSERK
-15	ALCOHOLIC
-1	DISLIKES HEIGHTS
-1	SLEEPS OUTDOORS when possible
-1	PICKS FIGHTS FOR FUN
-1	FEMINIST - likes demonstrating she's "as good as any man"
-1	TALKS TO ANIMALS AND INANIMATE OBJECTS

REACTION +/− **+1 - GOOD LOOKS**

WEAPONS AND POSSESSIONS
Item	Damage Type	Amt.	Skill Level	$	Wt.
LONG BOW	imp	1d+1	14	200	3
QUIVER/10 ARROWS				30	1¾
SABER (CHEAP)	cut	1d+2	15	280	2
	imp	1d			
THROWING KNIVES(2)	cut	1d-1	13	60	1
	imp	1d-2			
LARGE KNIFE	cut	1d	13	40	1
	imp	1d-1			
LIGHT LEATHER ARMOR				210	10
GOLD and SILVER COINS				60	−
JEWELRY				120	

Totals: $ **1000**   Lbs. **18¾**

WEAPON RANGES
Weapon	SS	Acc	½D	Max
LONGBOW	15	3	180	240
THROWN KNIFE	11	0	7	12

SKILLS
	Pt. Cost	Level
BOW	8	14
FAST-DRAW ARROW	1	13
KNIFE	1	13
KNIFE-THROWING	1	13
FENCING	8	15
BRAWLING	1	13
ARMOURY	4	13
COOKING	½	11
GAMBLING	2	12
LEADERSHIP	2	12
SAVOIR-FAIRE	4	14
SCROUNGING	½	11
STEALTH	2	13
TACTICS	4	12
TRACKING	1	11

SUMMARY
	Point Total
Attributes	80
Advantages	25
Disadvantages	-40
Quirks	-5
Skills	40
TOTAL	100

GURPS®
CHARACTER SHEET

Name *CORWIN BEARCLAW* Player _____
Appearance *6'1" 180 lbs. TANNED, LIGHT BROWN HAIR*
Character Story *MERCENARY IN RANGER/SCOUT UNIT. EMPLOYER WENT BROKE, LEFT CORWIN BROKE AS WELL, AND FAR FROM HOME*

Date Created _____ Sequence _____
Unspent Points _____ Point Total **100**

Pt. Cost		
20	**ST**	*12*
20	**DX**	*12*
10	**IQ**	*11*
20	**HT**	*12*

FATIGUE

BASIC DAMAGE
Thrust: *1d-1*
Swing: *1d+2*

HITS TAKEN

Mvmt
BASIC SPEED **6** (HT + DX)/4
MOVE **4** Basic − Enc.

ENCUMBRANCE
None (0) = 2×ST *24*
Light (1) = 4×ST *48*
Med (2) = 6×ST *72*
Hvy (3) = 12×ST *144*
X-hvy (4) = 20×ST *240*

PASSIVE DEFENSE
Armor: *3/1*
Shield: *3*
TOTAL *6* *4 vs. impale*

ACTIVE DEFENSES
DODGE	PARRY	BLOCK
4	**7**	**6**
= Move	Weapon/2	Shield/2

DAMAGE RESISTANCE
Armor *CHAINMAIL : 4/2*
TOUGHNESS : 2
: _____
TOTAL **6** *2 vs. impale*

ADVANTAGES, DISADVANTAGES, QUIRKS
Pt. Cost
15	ALERTNESS +3
25	TOUGHNESS +2
-10	IMPULSIVE
-20	PHOBIA: reptiles (severe!)
-10	HONEST
0	ILLITERATE
-1	CONSIDERS GREEN HIS "Lucky color"
-1	LIKES GAMBLING
	(default skill is 6....)
-1	LIKES TO IMITATE PEOPLE
-1	OVERSLEEPS
1	SOFT TOUCH FOR BEGGERS, CHILDREN, ETC.

REACTION +/− _____

WEAPONS AND POSSESSIONS
Item	Damage Type	Amt.	Skill Level	$	Wt.
CHEAP SHORTSWORD	cut 1d+2		14	160	2
	imp. 1d-1				
LARGE KNIFE	cut 1d		12	40	1
	imp. 1d-1				
MEDIUM SHIELD	crush 1d+1		12	60	15
CHAINMAIL				550	45
SMALL BACKPACK, with				60	3
FIRST AID KIT (+1 to rolls)				30	2
BLANKET				20	5
PERSONAL CAMPING BASICS				5	−
GOLD and SILVER COINS				75	

Totals: $ **1000** Lbs. **63**

WEAPON RANGES
Weapon	SS	Acc	½D	Max

SKILLS
	Pt. Cost	Level
SHORTSWORD	8	14
FAST-DRAW SWORD	1	12
KNIFE	1	12
SHIELD	1	12
BROADSWORD (from Shortsword)	0	12
CROSSBOW	2	13
NATURALIST	14	16
SURVIVAL: ANY (from naturalist)	0	13
STEALTH	4	13
TRACKING (default)	0	11
TRAPS/TL 3	2	11
LANGUAGE (any one "average" language you choose)	1	10
FIRST AID	1	11
with Kit		12

NOTES:
(1) IF CORWIN DROPS HIS SHIELD, MOVE AND DODGE GO UP TO 5.

(2) THE BACKPACK WOULDN'T NORMALLY BE WORN IN COMBAT!

SUMMARY
	Point Total
Attributes	70
Advantages	40
Disadvantages	−40
Quirks	−5
Skills	35
TOTAL	100

ALL IN A NIGHT'S WORK
Introductory Solo Adventure

By Creede & Sharleen Lambard

Playtesters: Steve Jackson, Warren Spector, Mark Chandler, Norman Banduch, Monica Stephens, Rob Kirk, Michael Moe, Rod & Shanna Kurth, Allen Varney, C. Mara Lee, David Ladyman

This is a solo adventure – an adventure for a single character. No Game Master is required.

You can start playing right away – even if you don't know the *GURPS* rules yet. This solo adventure is designed to teach the rules as you go along. It's a lot more fun to play through and see how everything works, rather than reading 256 pages all at once . . .

In some places, page references are given to help you deal with new game mechanics. These italic references are *not* necessary to the adventure – they're just to provide clarification for players who are new to the system. At *any* time, you may mark your place and use the Index or Glossary to help clear up a question.

Getting Started

You will need a pencil, scratch paper and 3 six-sided dice. You should remove the game map from the *Instant Characters* booklet; you will be using the "indoor" side.

You will also need a character. There are four pregenerated characters on pp. 214-217. You should probably use one of the two thief-type characters (Dai or Robyn). You may photocopy the sheet for reference.

If you would rather create your own character using the rules in Chapters 1-8, go ahead. Remember that IQ and DX are very important to thieves; you should take some appropriate skills like Acrobatics, Pickpocket and Lockpicking. Stealth is *very* important!

Once your character is complete (make sure you have your weapons and equipment!) you can start the adventure. An important note: Burglars don't carry heavy equipment. You may not carry a shield, or any sort of bow or axe, or any sword larger than a short-sword or saber. If you use a pregenerated character with heavy weapons, leave them at home.

How to Play

The adventure is divided into numbered entries. *Do not read them in order – they will make no sense at all!* Instead, read entry #1 first, and then turn to the entry where it directs you.

Most entries will offer you at least two choices, and sometimes several. Sometimes you may choose freely; sometimes the entry you turn to will depend on a roll against one of your skills or attributes.

Occasionally you might go through a room more than once. If so, anything you took on a previous visit will be gone. Note also that if a particular room calls for a Vision roll to see something, or an IQ roll to figure something out, you may not come back for repeated attempts. Unless an entry specifies otherwise, you only get one try.

When you come across an object, you may drop it in your bag only if the instructions say you can take it. (With a GM to referee, of course, you could take *anything*.) When you take something, make a note on your Character Sheet. Note that your bag will only hold 50 pounds of loot! If at any time you want to get rid of something, just put it down and mark it off your Character Sheet.

You may want to map your progress as you travel. However, no map is *required* unless you get in a fight – and then only if you decide to use the Advanced Combat System (see below).

Combat

If you are already familiar with the *GURPS* combat system, you may want to use the "indoor" game map, and play out the combat when it occurs. Otherwise, you may find it easier to use the Basic Combat System – it's quicker and needs no map or figures.

Repeated Games

This adventure can be played over and over – with the same or different characters. (If you play with the same character, it's not fair to collect extra character points after *every* game!) Eventually you will learn the right decisions to make – but even so, if you don't have the right abilities and skills, you won't get all the loot.

Try different tactics. Whether you're using the adventure to learn the game, or just playing with it, you'll want to explore all the possibilities.

And try different sorts of characters. Taking a fighter can be interesting. You may miss most of the Stealth rolls, but when the guard shows up, you can handle him better!

Teaching Your Friends

Once you learn the system, you can use "All in a Night's Work" as a gamemastered adventure to teach other players. You can let them play through while you watch, help with the rules questions, and control the foes – or you can *read* them the entries, and let them choose what they want to do. You can also make any changes you want when you're the Game Master.

Another fun thing to do is to GM the adventure for a *group* of your friends. Let them work together to make the decisions for the thief. They'll be cooperating rather than competing, and they ought to have a great time!

---

it doesn't have to be fantasy

GURPS will work for any sort of background. This solo is written as a fantasy adventure. But if you want to GM it for your friends, a few minor alterations will change the genre! For example, to move the adventure to one of the Fortress Towns of *GURPS Autoduel*, just make the following changes. WARN-ING: Don't read any further before you first play the adventure as currently written, or some of your fun will be spoiled!

Character. The thief is now a "dreg" from outside the walls. He may carry no firearm heavier than a .22 pistol – if he can afford that!

25, 49, 67, 79, 117, 139, 149, and all other "sword" refer-ences. The guard's weapon is not a scimitar, but a 12-gauge shotgun! You cannot parry or block gunshots. Stats for the shotgun: 4 dice crushing damage. Acc 5, SS 12, ½D 25, Max 150. $125, 8 lbs., min. ST 12, Recoil -3. 8 shots.

36, 51, 59, 120. Instead of tapestries, there are paintings and posters. The smallest one is an antique Grateful Dead poster; an IQ-1 roll tells the thief it's valuable.

76. Instead of Broadsword-16 skill, the guard has Guns (Shotgun)-14, Karate-14, and Knife Throwing-14. Otherwise, he's the same.

98. There are a number of ceramic jars with screw-top lids.

140, 174. The jar has a chemical name on the lid. You must be literate and make your Physician roll to read the label and know that it's burn ointment!

Gunshots. If the player shoots at the guard, or vice versa, turn to 75 as soon as the fight is over. The "whistle" is now a loud intrusion alarm!

Of course, as GM, you can make any other changes you like: give Fatso a hideaway pistol, let the cops show up, add more rooms . . . it's up to you!

INTRODUCTION

You are a thief, and you're good at it. You specialize in robbing the rich – "Nothing noble about it," you laugh. "The poor folk don't have any money!"

Tonight you are prowling through an especially wealthy part of town. You don't often get in here; the neighborhood gates are usually well defended. But you saw your chance tonight when a watchman found the bottle of whiskey you left for him. You slipped by as soon as he had drunk himself to sleep.

It's a lovely night for a thief; the moonlight shines almost as bright as day. As you glide from shadow to shadow, you check the windows and doors. Soon you find a chest-level window that isn't barred.

You slip your knife-blade into the windowsill and undo the latch. Turn to Entry 1.

1 Take a moment for inventory. You have everything you nor-mally carry (it's all listed on your Character Sheet) and one other thing: a large canvas sack. This sack can carry up to 50 pounds of loot. Now you can slip through the window.

Make a Stealth roll as you come down. Check your Character Sheet to see if you have the Stealth skill. If you do, roll 3 dice. A result *less than or equal to* your skill means you succeeded; a roll higher than your skill means you failed. (Throughout this adven-ture, you will always roll 3 dice unless specifically told otherwise. All skill rolls, IQ rolls, etc. are made on 3 dice.)

If you do *not* have the Stealth skill listed on your sheet, make your "default" roll. This is a skill roll that shows your *untrained* ability. For Stealth, the default is *either* your DX-5 or your IQ-5 – whichever is better. So if you have no Stealth but an IQ of 12 and a DX of 14, you pick the better one: 14. 14 minus 5 is 9, so you roll against a 9.

For more on success rolls and "default" rolls, see p. 86. For details on the Stealth skill, see p. 67.

Now try your roll. If you succeed, turn to 128. If you fail, turn to 102.

2 If your clever idea involved cutting the bell-rope, you may attempt to do so as long as you have a knife or sword. If you want to do this, turn to 6. Otherwise, return to 110.

If you thought of something else . . . sorry about that! If you are playing with a Game Master, tell him your idea and see if he will let you try it. If you have no GM, you may attempt to cut the bell-rope anyway (turn to 6) or return to 110.

3 You light the candle from the embers. You may take the candle and candlestick if you wish. They weigh about a pound. Return to 128 and choose again.

4 The guard laughs. "Very well, my friend. I'll let you live." He puts his blade to your throat and backs you into the living room. He frisks you and takes everything of value – including your own possessions! Then he escorts you out the front door. Your adventure is over.

5 You notice that a plank in the pantry floor seems out of place. You move a barrel to investigate, and find a trap door built into the floor! You open the trap door and find it leads to a staircase. If you wish to go downstairs, turn to 71. If you want to look around some more, turn to 111. But you know this trap door is here; you may make a note of this entry and return here any time you are at 111.

6 Carefully, you reach for the bell-rope, gathering part of it in a loop in the hope of cutting it without accidentally pulling it. Roll vs. (DX+3). In other words, for this attempt only, your DX is considered to be 3 higher than normal . . . cutting a rope is not very difficult.

If your DX roll succeeds, turn to 55. If you fail, you pull on the rope while trying to cut it. Turn to 139.

7 Fatso is more interested in saving his life than in hanging on to his money. He reaches under his mattress and pulls out a bag. It is small – the weight is negligible – but it jingles very nicely! You may take the bag if you wish.

You don't have time to find out what's in the bag right now; someone is coming up the stairs.

If you want to pull on the bell-pull, turn to 78.

If you want to wait and see who enters the bedroom, turn to 49.

8 The key you took from around Fatso's neck works like a charm! Turn to 97.

9 You weren't fast enough. The spider bites you painfully. Your DX will be reduced by 1 for the rest of the adventure, and your hand will be very swollen and tender for several days.

If you still want to look at the jar, turn to 118.

If you want to look at something else, turn to 68.

10 You are in the guard's bedroom, with the guard hot on your heels. You don't have time to look around. This room opens out onto the great hall. Turn to 157.

11 Your clumsy blow merely awakens the giant, who snatches his scimitar (or his knife, if *you* have his scimitar) and rolls to the side. In your surprise, you let him reach his feet. You do have the initiative, though; you strike at him again, using the same weapon you tried before. Turn to 76.

12 As far as you can tell, these casks of ale are sitting here to age, and that's all there is to it. Return to 16 and choose again.

13 This jar is full of some kind of red powder. Make a Taste roll to identify it. This is a Sense roll; roll 3 dice vs. your IQ and add your bonus (if any) for the Acute Taste/Smell advantage. If you are successful, turn to 29. If you are not successful, turn to 137.

If you have the disadvantage of Anosmia (no sense of taste or smell), you don't even bother trying to smell the powder. In that case, return to 68.

14 You start back up the stairs to the pantry. Roll against your Stealth. If you make the roll, turn to 111. If you fail your roll, turn to 117.

15 This is your conscience speaking. You're a thief, not a murderer. Do you really want to do this? Even if you're willing to kill someone in cold blood, remember that the City Guard, and even the Thieves' Guild itself, will pay much more attention to murder than to an ordinary theft.

If you still want to try to kill the giant, turn to 21. (You *cannot* do this if you have the disadvantage of Pacifism.)

If you will just try to knock him out, instead, turn to 83.

If you would rather not attack him at all, turn to 149.

16 You are in the storage room underneath the pantry. A rack along one wall is filled with bottles of wine. There are perhaps two dozen casks stacked along another wall. A third wall holds a collection of random junk – boxes, statues, upended casks, et cetera.

You have many options in this room. When you return to this entry, remember that each of the options below can be chosen only once.

If you have the disadvantage of Alcoholism, turn to 116 immediately – don't read the other alternatives yet.

If you want to examine the wine rack, turn to 125.

If you want to examine the casks, turn to 94.

If you want to examine the junk along the wall, turn to 154.

If you want to leave the room, turn to 14.

17 Well, the statuettes seemed worthless, but you look at one last one, just in case – and it turns out to be hollow! Inside is an amulet on a chain. The amulet and chain look like they're solid gold – they weigh little, but are finely made. You may take them if you wish.

If you want to go over to the bed and investigate Fatso himself, turn to 52. If you go back downstairs, turn to 111.

18 You are at the top of a flight of stairs. There is only one door here, right at the top of the stairs. If you want to check out the door, turn to 64. If you want to go back down the stairs, turn to 111.

19 You break the seal and open the bag – and smoke pours out. Lots of smoke! Frantically, you try to close it, but it's too late. The smoke solidifies and reaches for you . . . Your adventure is over.

20 You look around for a few minutes, and give one or two of the statues a test-heft, but you don't find anything that looks both valuable and portable. As you search, you hear the fat man groan and mutter. You freeze – and he soon is snoring again.

If you want to take time for a careful search, turn to 43. If you would rather leave the room the way you came in, turn to 18.

21 It is easy to kill a sleeping man. Pick a weapon and roll against your DX. Only on a critical failure (see p. 86) will you miss your blow. On a critical failure, the giant takes 2 hits of damage, and you must turn to 11.

Otherwise, the giant is dead. Turn to 134.

22 You turn and run, hoping to dodge past the huge guard. Roll against your DX – but you'll have to be fast, so roll against DX-5. In other words, with a DX of 14, you would need a 9 or better to succeed. If you make your roll, turn to 63. If you fail, turn to 50.

23 You are in the kitchen, with the guard chasing you. If you want to go through the pantry, turn to 58.

If you want to dive through the window, turn to 113.

If you want to stand and fight, turn to 95.

24 You can't stifle a sharp cry as you feel the unexpected pain – and as you cry out you hear footsteps in one of the other rooms. Turn to 58.

25 The footsteps are coming closer – but you have the advantage. You will be able to surprise whoever is coming. Then you see him – a huge guard with a scimitar, filling the doorway!

If you want to try to fight, you have the initiative. Turn to 76.

If you want to try to talk him out of fighting, turn to 156.

26 You open the lid to find an oily white cream inside. You may take this if you wish. If you want to try some to see what it does, turn to 114. If not, return to 68.

27 You make your way through back alleys and deserted streets to your home. If you have no loot, your adventure is over. If you have something, turn to 185.

28 Roll one die. On a roll of 1-4, turn to 17. On a roll of 5 or 6, turn to 163.

29 It's a good thing you didn't taste very much of this. It's cayenne pepper! Pepper is rare and valuable! You may take the jar if you wish. Return to 68.

30 You carefully lift the scimitar; it is very heavy (5 lbs.), but you manage to keep it from scraping on the floor. You now have a scimitar. More importantly, the guard does *not* have a scimitar. If you face the guard later, he will be armed only with his knife. (He's brave and will attack you anyway.) If you decide you want to try to use the scimitar, treat it as a broadsword. If you don't have Broadsword skill, your default is DX-5, or Shortsword-2.

If you want to search the room further, turn to 132.

If you want to leave the room, turn to 59.

If you want to attack the guard, turn to 160.

31 A critical failure! You have fumbled badly. The trap door was in two parts – and you were standing on one part while you fooled with the other one. The door opens with a CREEEEK, and drops you through the floor. Turn to 139.

32 Make an IQ roll at -4. In other words, if your IQ is 12, you succeed only on an 8 or better! If you fail, then whatever idea you had wasn't clever enough. Return to 67 and make another choice.

If you succeed, you had a *brilliant* idea. Turn to 127.

33 You make it out the window just in time! You hear footsteps behind you, and see a man looking out the window. He doesn't see you, so he latches the window again.

If you want to try again in a half-hour or so, turn to 153. If you want to quit now and go home, turn to 27.

34 If you had not figured this out, someone will tell you when you try to fence it: this is burn ointment. There are ten doses; each dose will completely heal 1 hit of burn injury. A maximum of 3 hits' worth can be healed from any one burn. Now return to 185.

35 If you are literate, turn to 115. Otherwise, all you can tell is that the labeled jars contain various types of herbs and spices, and they are almost full! Turn to 42.

36 The tapestry is easy to remove from the wall. As you get ready to roll it up you notice an unusual mark in the lower right-hand corner.

Make your Merchant roll, at a +4. (So, if you don't have the skill, you are rolling at IQ-1 . . . a default of IQ-5, and a bonus of +4.) If you succeed, turn to 120. If you fail, turn to 41.

37 As you reach for the jar you notice some movement behind it. It's a huge, hairy spider, and it's right next to your hand!

If you happen to have a Phobia about insects, spiders, hairy things, or anything similar, turn to 173. If not, turn to 54.

To read about Phobias, see p. 35.

38 You cut the cord and carefully slide it out from under the fat man's neck. Now you have a key; what does it unlock? Nothing in here; you've already checked and you saw no keyhole. The key is far too small for the door locks; it looks like it opens a chest or drawer. You drop it into your pocket.

Fatso rolls and mutters in his sleep again. If you want to search further, turn to 53. If you want to leave the room, turn to 18.

39 After looking at the trap door and pushing on it once or twice, you realize that the bell-rope over Fatso's bed is the triggering mechanism. If you want to examine the device further, turn to 136. If you want to pull the bell-rope to see what happens, turn to 139. If you want to cut the rope, turn to 6.

40 The lid clatters, bangs and reseats itself on top of the pot. Now you've done it! Can you find somewhere to hide? Make your Stealth roll at -2. If you don't have Stealth, your usual default roll is IQ-5 or DX-5 – *but it is -7 in this case!*

If you make it, turn to 100. If you fail, turn to 93.

41 It comes down easily and you roll it up. You may take it; it weighs five pounds. Go back to 171.

42 You may take as many of the 36 labeled jars as you would like – write down how many you take. Each weighs about half a pound. They have well-fitted lids, so they won't come open in your bag.

If you want to check any of the five unlabeled jars, turn to 68. Or you may look around the pantry some more; turn to 176.

43 Make a Vision roll (roll against your IQ; if you have Alertness or Acute Vision, add the level of your advantage to your IQ). *For rules on Sense rolls (Vision, Hearing, etc.), see p. 92.* If you succeed, turn to 28.

If you fail, you didn't find anything. You decide there is nothing of value here. You can leave the room the way you came in; turn to 18. Or you can take a look at Fatso; turn to 52.

44 The casks come sliding right at you! Try your DX roll. If you fail, you are crushed beneath a pile of casks. You might have always wanted to die by drowning in ale, but certainly not *this* way. If this happens, your adventure is over.

If you make your roll, you manage to spring out of the way and up the stairs, but the casks make a LOT of noise. Turn to 117.

45 This is pretty good wine, but it takes its toll. For the rest of the adventure, your IQ and DX (and any skills based on them) are at -1. Return to 16 and choose again.

46 If you have the Common Sense advantage, make your IQ roll; if you succeed, turn to 60. Otherwise take a look at the three pillows and decide which one(s) you want to slit open.

If you open the red pillow, turn to 130.

If you open the yellow pillow, turn to 106.

If you open the blue pillow, turn to 87.

Return to 171 when you are finished here.

47 The porcelain tea set is very beautiful – and very fragile. The artist's markings on the bottom of the teapot show it to be at least 120 years old. It should be worth a lot of money – *if* you can get it to the fence intact.

Make an IQ roll. If you succeed, go directly to 73.

If you fail, you may put the porcelain in your bag if you wish; it is almost weightless. It has a DR of 0. Any hit to your body, while you are carrying it, will break it.

If you would like to examine the hookahs on the table, turn to 66. If you want to look elsewhere in the room, turn to 171.

48 You listen for several minutes, but you don't hear anything. You seem to have picked a house full of heavy sleepers. Turn to 128.

49 As you stand with your knife to Fatso's throat, the door opens behind you, and you turn to see a huge man filling the doorway. He is carrying a scimitar, and he looks angry. What do you do?

If you turn and knife Fatso, turn to 89.

If you want to fight the guard, turn to 76.

If you pull the bell-pull, turn to 78.

If you try to leave the room, turn to 63.

If you threaten Fatso, turn to 151.

50 With a desperate lunge, Fatso reaches the bell-pull. He yanks on the cord before you can run away. Beneath you, the floor gives way, and you go sliding down into darkness. Turn to 78.

51 There are five tapestries. Four of them are huge, but the fifth looks like it might be portable. Turn to 36 if you would like to try; otherwise go back to 171.

52 Fatso is wearing a number of rings and bracelets, but they are pressed so tightly into his flesh you wouldn't be able to remove them without taking off his fingers – which is *not* a good idea. As you check him out, he rolls over and groans loudly. You jump – but he's still asleep.

If you want to look further, turn to 180.

If you want to leave the room, turn to 18.

53 You pushed your luck a little too far! The fat man awakens and does what any normal person would do if he saw someone standing over him with a knife at his throat. He screams. Then he reaches up toward a bell-pull.

Roll a contest of DX (your DX vs. his DX of 11) to see if you can stop him from pulling that bell-pull. If you win the contest, turn to 162. If you lose or tie, turn to 144. *For more about Contests of Skill, see p. 87.*

54 You jerk your hand away from the spider. Make a DX roll. If you succeed, turn to 170. If you fail, turn to 9.

55 Gently, you saw on the rope. But your weapon seems to make little impression! The bell-rope is resisting your blade.

If you want to saw harder, turn to 91. If you abandon your attempt to cut the rope, return to 110.

56 This door leads outside. You take a quick look – nobody is watching! If you want to leave and head home, turn to 27. If you go back inside, return to 59.

57 You don't find anything of interest in the junk pile. Return to 16.

58 You are in the pantry. The guard is chasing you. Going up the stairs doesn't seem to be a good idea. If you want to go to the great hall, go to 157. If you want to go to the kitchen, turn to 23. If you want to try to fight, turn to 76.

59 You are in a great hall. The ceiling here is two stories tall, with vents in the eaves to let air in and out. There are also a number of windows, all fairly high on the walls.

Along one wall is a sofa with three pillows. There are also four statues, one against each wall. There are expensive-looking tapestries upon the walls. Other furnishings include a low table, a small bookcase, and a few hookahs. And finally, there are three doorways. One leads to the landing below a staircase. Another appears to lead into a bedroom, and a third is closed – but looks solid, as though it is an exit from the house.

If you want to go to the landing below the stairs, turn to 111.

If you want to go into the bedroom, turn to 149.

If you want to try the solid-looking door, turn to 56.

If you want to examine this room, turn to 171.

60 Your Common Sense prompts you to stop and think for a moment – do you really want to destroy those valuable pillows on the chance that something might be inside them? Return to 124.

61 You were sure there was a trap here, and you were right. At the first sound of sliding casks, you're out of there and up the stairs. The casks smash into the place where you were crouching, making a terrible noise. Turn to 117.

62 Most of the papers are worthless. But the bawdy limericks are a manuscript written in the hand of a famous poet who died some 250 years ago. The fence is delighted – "Some of these, I never even heard!" he says. He gives you $400 for them! Return to 185.

63 The guard fills the doorway, so you will have to Evade him. Roll a contest of the guard's DX (12) versus your DX (minus 5 because the guard is standing up). *For complete Evading rules, see p. 113.*

If you win or tie, turn to 142.

If you lose, you will have to fight the guard. Turn to 76.

64 Listening at the door, you hear only snoring. If you want to open the door, turn to 110. If you want to go back down the stairs, turn to 111.

65 The ointment feels good. In fact, your burn starts to heal immediately. Any penalties you had from the burn injury are totally gone! Now return to 114.

66 The hookahs have been heavily used; they are tarnished on the outside and have a heavy buildup of residue inside. To appraise them further, make an IQ roll.

If you fail, you didn't learn anything. You can take the hookahs if you wish. Go back to 129.

If you succeed, turn to 145.

67 AH-CHOO! You manage to recover from your sneezing fit – just as a huge man comes in, holding a scimitar. If you want to stand and fight, turn to 76.

If you want to retreat into the kitchen, turn to 23.

If you want to try to get past the guard, turn to 81.

If you have another idea, turn to 32.

68 Consider the jars as being labeled from 1 to 5, left to right. Decide which jars you want to examine. If you want to examine jar 1, turn to 13.

If you want to examine jar 2, turn to 182.

If you want to examine jar 3, turn to 77.

If you want to examine jar 4, turn to 37.

If you want to examine jar 5, turn to 140.

Turn to 176 when you are finished here.

69 The bag contains about a dozen glittering gems, each wrapped in paper! Make a Jeweler or a Merchant roll (default is IQ-5 for Merchant, IQ-6 for Jeweler); if you succeed, turn to 82.

If you don't succeed, you know nothing important about the gems, but they certainly look pretty! You may take them if you wish.

If you want to try to look through the papers you found in the safe, turn to 172. Otherwise, leave them and return to 16.

70 As you try to lift the sword it scrapes a little on the stone floor of the room. Instantly you feel a large hand around your wrist. "Now then, what might you be doing, borrowing my sword without my permission?" the man asks as he takes his scimitar from you.

You can either try to talk your way out of the situation (turn to 156) or Break Free. If you try to Break Free, roll a contest of your ST versus the guard's ST of 12 (he is only holding with one hand, so he gets no bonus). If you make it, turn to 105. If you fail, turn to 146.

71 Hey! It's dark down here! You go down the stairs and find yourself in almost complete blackness. If you have a lit torch, lantern or candle, or the Night Vision advantage, turn to 16.

If not, you can go back up the stairs (turn to 14) or grope around in the dark cellar (turn to 143).

72 It's only worth a few copper coins per bottle – not worth the trouble of stealing. If you want to drink a bottle, turn to 45. If not, turn to 16.

73 You have a brilliant idea – pack the porcelain in the pillows to keep it from breaking! (If you've already slit the pillows, you're out of luck. Return to 47.)

If you have the pillows, the porcelain will have a DR of 2 while it's in your bag. (If you take a body hit that does more than 2 points of damage, the porcelain breaks.) However, you must use all three pillows (a weight of six pounds) to achieve this. The porcelain itself is almost weightless.

If you would like to examine the hookahs on the table, turn to 66. If you want to look elsewhere in the room, turn to 171.

74 If you failed your Lockpicking roll by more than 10, or if you rolled a 17 or 18, turn to 90. Otherwise you may try to pick the lock again; turn to 122. But subtract 1 from your skill (this is cumulative – subtract 2 if you have already failed twice, and so on).

Or you can look around some more; turn to 16.

75 You have defeated the guard – but you hear a whistle blowing. The owner of the house, terrified by the ruckus, is signalling the watch. You dash out the front door and duck into an alley. Soon you're safe at home. Turn to 185.

76 This is it – the Big Fight Scene. The guard goes first unless you have been specifically told that *you* have the initiative. You can use the Basic Combat rules – or, if you prefer, you can use the Advanced Combat rules and the "indoor" hex map in the back of the book.

(You can drop your bag to lessen your encumbrance; if you do, the guard will not pick it up while the fight goes on. But if you have to flee, you must take a turn to pick it back up again, or flee without it!)

Combat goes like this: Suppose the guard goes first. He must roll his weapon skill or less on 3 dice. If he succeeds, he hit you – maybe. If he fails, his turn is over.

If the guard made his roll, you must *defend*. Add the total Passive Defense from your armor (and shield, if you've improvised one) to the Active Defense you choose. Your Character Sheet shows three defenses: Dodge, Parry, and (if you have a shield) Block. The total is your defense. Roll 3 dice; if you roll less than or equal to your defense, you are not hit.

If you *are* hit, the guard rolls damage. His character sheet shows he does 1d+3 damage. Roll 1 die, and add 3 to the result; this is how much basic damage he did.

Now subtract the DR (damage resistance) of your armor and Toughness, if any. The remainder of the damage actually affects you. But because you are being attacked by a cutting weapon, *add a 50% damage bonus* – round down.

Example: The guard rolls 2 for damage. 2+3 is 5; take 5 hits. Let's say that your armor is light leather (DR of 1). So 4 hits get through; increased by 50%, that's 6.

After the guard's attack, it is your turn to attack and his to defend. Follow the same procedure.

A character whose HT is reduced to 0 or less must roll against basic HT every turn before moving or attacking. A failed roll means that character falls unconscious.

This is only a very basic look at the combat system. For more detail, see Chapters 13 and 14 of the rules.

If you defeat the guard, turn to 75 if you were inside the house, or 185 if you had already escaped the house.

If the fight goes against you, you may try to flee. Turn to 81 if you are using only the Basic Combat rules, or 169 if you are using the Advanced Combat rules and the map.

If you are knocked unconscious, turn to 141.

77 This jar rattles when you shakes it. You open it to find a stash of small silver coins – about $20 worth.

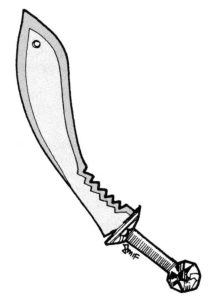

78 The last thing you see is the huge figure of Fatso's guard, scimitar upraised – then a trap door opens in the floor and you fall through. You take (3d-9) damage from the fall (roll 3 dice and subtract 9 to see how many hits you took [minimum 0]; a successful roll against your Acrobatics skill, or your default of DX-6, will keep you from taking any damage).

You land in a small room. The door is open, and through it you can see a door that looks like it might lead out of the house. Quickly you scramble to your feet. If you flee, turn to 10. If you want to wait here for the guard to come back, turn to 76.

79 AH-CHOO! This stuff is potent! You hear footsteps in the next room, and then see a huge shadow pass by. Moonlight glitters on an upraised sword. You feel another sneeze coming on!

Try another HT roll. If you succeed this time, you manage to avoid sneezing again, and you can run for the kitchen window. Turn to 23.

If you fail, you are overtaken by a fit of sneezing. Turn to 67.

80 You're blind! The ointment stings like fire. Make a HT roll. If you succeed, your vision clears enough to let you grope your way out the window and make your way home. You are all right the next day. Turn to 185.

If you fail, the pain makes you cry out. You blunder into the pantry shelves, knocking down several jars. It's almost a relief when the guard's fist sends you into oblivion. Turn to 141.

81 You try to duck past the guard. This is called Evading. Roll a Contest of DX. The guard's DX is 12; your own DX is at -5 because the guard is standing up. *For complete Evading rules, see p. 113.*

If you lose the contest (or tie), the guard got in your way and stopped you. You lost a turn; the guard may attack you again. Return to 76.

If you win you get past him, but he will chase you. Turn to 157.

82 The gems are worth a lot – probably around $7,500! Naturally, you pocket them! Their weight is negligible. If you want to try to look through the papers you found in the safe, turn to 172. Otherwise, leave them and return to 16.

Name: MAX the guard	Reaction +/-: −2 ordinarily / +1 in combat	Point Total: 75

Appearance: INCREDIBLY THREATENING

Advantages, Disadvantages, Quirks:
SENSE OF DUTY
GIGANTISM

12 ST Fatigue: _____

12 DX Basic Damage
Thrust: 1d-1
Swing: 1d+2

10 IQ

11 HT Hits Taken: _____

Skills: BROADSWORD - 16
KNIFE - 16

Basic Speed: 5.75 Move: 5
Encumbrance: NONE
Dodge: 5 Parry: 8 Block: 0

Weapons and Possessions:
SCIMITAR [Bastard sword] cut 1d+3 $650 5 lbs.
(2-hex reach) crush 1d
KNIFE (large) cut 1d $40 1 lb.
imp 1d-1

	Head	Body	Arms	Hands	Legs	Feet
PD	Ø	Ø	Ø	Ø	Ø	Ø
DR	(2)	Ø	Ø	Ø	Ø	Ø

Weapon Ranges:
KNIFE imp 1-1 SS:12 ACC:0 ½:10 Max:17

83 There is no "safe" way to knock someone out without hurting them – but a blow to the top of the head with a blunt instrument, if gauged properly, will usually have no permanent effects. You need something that does Crushing damage. A club, pair of brass knuckles, or frying pan would be ideal. If you have nothing else, you may use your fist (remember that your fist does "thrust-2" damage).

Pick your weapon and roll to hit your foe. A sleeping man is a very easy target, so any roll but a critical failure (a 17 or 18) will hit him squarely. On a 17 or 18, the giant takes no damage except to his pride, and awakens; turn immediately to 11.

Otherwise, you hit him. Roll your damage, according to the weapon you are using (see p. 100). The fact that this is a blow to the vulnerable part of the head (that is, the "brain") gives it special results, as described on p. 202. Start by subtracting 2 from the damage result (for the skull's Damage Resistance of 2).

Now multiply the remaining damage rolled by 4! If the result is over ⅓ the victim's HT, he is stunned. If it's over ½ his HT, he is knocked out. The giant's HT is 11, so if the original roll is 3, he will be stunned – turn to 164.

If the original roll is 4 to 7, he will be knocked unconscious for long enough to let you loot the house – turn to 134.

If the original roll did 8 or more points of damage, then at least 6 points get through the skull's protection. Multiplied by 4, this means the giant took enough hits to reduce his HT from 11 to -11 or less. It *might* kill him! For the purposes of this game, roll a die. On a result of 1 to 3, the giant is dead; on a 4 to 6, he's only knocked out. Either way, turn to 134.

84 The ointment feels good, but it doesn't do much of anything else. Return to 114.

85 As you case the kitchen you hear quiet footsteps in the next room. Someone is coming to check on the noise you made!

Make your Stealth roll at -2 (you're in a hurry). If you don't have the skill (what are you doing as a thief?), your default skill is either DX-5 or IQ-5, whichever is better, with that additional -2 because you're hurrying.

If you make the roll, turn to 100. If you fail, turn to 93.

86 You tiptoe over to the sword lying on the floor. You very gently take it by the grip, and . . . Roll against your DX, minus *six*. (Picking the sword up silently is hard, so there is a -6 penalty to your attempt.)

If you succeed, turn to 30. If you fail, turn to 70.

87 You slit the pillow open, and feathers fly everywhere – but you find nothing of value, except for about $1 worth of corroded copper coins you found on the sofa behind the pillow. The pillow is now worthless. Go back to 46.

88 The guard has you in his grip. You are now in Close Combat. You may try a Break Free maneuver. Roll a Quick Contest of ST. The guard has a ST of 12, and gets no bonus to his roll, because he is holding you with one hand; the other is holding his sword.

If you win the Contest of ST, you have broken free. You can run for the pantry (58) or try to go through the window (113).

If you lose or tie the Contest of ST, or if you want to fight anyway, turn to 76.

For more about Close Combat, see p. 111 of the rules.

89 You sink your knife into Fatso's wattled neck. He gurgles and sighs, then drops back – dead. But your triumph is short-lived; in the time it took to end Fatso's career, the guard has come up behind you. Time for combat. *The combat rules are explained in Chapters 13 and 14. If you're not already familiar with them, fight using the Basic Combat System – the die rolls you will need are explained below.*

The guard attacks first, rolling against his skill of 16. Roll for the guard. If he gets a 16 or less, he hit you!

If the guard hits, roll your defense. Your only defense is your "passive defense" (PD) from any armor you are wearing – he came up behind you, so you get no active defense at this time! A critical success on the defense roll will save you.

If you fail your defense roll, he hits you. Roll his damage: 1d+3. In other words, roll one die and add 3 to the result. This is the *basic damage* he does. Subtract the damage resistance (DR) of your armor, to find out how many hits you actually took. Then increase this number by 50% (the sword is a cutting weapon, and cutting damage that gets through the armor gets a 50% bonus). Subtract the total from your HT.

If your HT was not reduced below zero by the guard's attack, you may fight; turn to 76 *except* that the guard will now fight you to the death. Of course, if you die your adventure is over.

If you manage to defeat the guard you have the run of the house, starting with Fatso's bedroom. Ignore any references to people you see from now on. Do not turn to 75, even if you have already been instructed to do so. Turn to 110.

90 This was a "critical failure." You really messed up – you set off a trap! You hear a click, and the cask you were working on disappears into the floor. Then you hear a rumble as the casks start to shift.

Did you realize in advance that there might be a trap here? Roll against your Traps skill (it defaults to IQ-5, DX-5, or Lockpicking-3; choose the best one of these). If you have the Danger Sense advantage, you may *also* try a roll against your IQ to see if you sensed something was wrong.

If you succeed in either your Danger Sense or Traps roll, turn to 61. If you fail, turn to 44.

91 The cloth falls away, and you see that the rope has a core of woven metal, like very fine chainmail. You won't be able to cut it, after all.

Make another DX roll. If you succeed, turn to 110. If you fail, you pulled on the rope while trying to cut it. Turn to 139.

92 Oops. You should have known that pot was going to be hot. Now try a DX roll at -2 to see if you avoided being burned. If you make your roll, turn to 168. If you fail, turn to 138.

93 You look around frantically – and there seems to be nowhere for you to hide! You hear footsteps approaching from another room. If you can just get to the window, you might be safe . . .

Make a DX roll. If you make it, turn to 33. If you fail, or if you want to fight whoever is coming, turn to 25.

94 The casks smell faintly of ale. They are all corked and stamped with the Imperial tax seal. All of them seem to be full . . . but make an IQ roll, just in case. If you make your roll, turn to 177. If you fail, turn to 12.

95 The guard has caught up with you. He's angry and ready for a fight. Make an IQ roll at -2. If you succeed, turn to 123; if you fail, turn to 76.

96 Under the circumstances, Fatso complies quickly. The guard is surly, but obedient. He backs away. You realize that you've done all the burgling you will do tonight. With the master of the house as escort, you walk slowly toward the exit. At the front door, you release Fatso. With a mocking bow, you vanish into the night. Turn to 185.

97 The front of the cask swings open to reveal a stack of books and papers and a small bag. The bag has a greasy feel to it and is sealed with a lead seal. Inside you can feel small lumps and something that crackles.

If you want to look through the papers, turn to 172.

If you want to open the bag, turn to 69.

If you will leave them both, turn to 16.

If you take the bag without opening it, note it on your record sheet. Then turn to 172 (to look at the papers) or 16 (to go on).

98 On one of the shelves, you see many small apothecary's jars. Most of them are labeled. If you are literate, turn to 101 to see what they say.

If you are not literate, you have several choices:

You may leave the jars alone; turn to 176.

You may take some at random; turn to 42.

You may stop and open some of them; turn to 35.

99 Make a Vision roll. Your basic roll is your IQ; Alertness and Acute Vision bonuses will help here. If you make your roll, turn to 126. If not, turn to 128.

100 You manage to find a dark corner to hide in. It's a good thing, too, because a huge man enters the room to see what's going on. He looks around, but can't see you. After a few minutes he leaves.

After a few minutes you come out – but for the rest of the adventure all your Stealth rolls will be at -2 because you've alerted the guard. (This is cumulative.) Turn to 128.

101 Most of the labeled jars show the names of herbs and spices. Twelve of them show the names of common herbs and spices. Twenty of them show the names of moderately rare spices. Four show the names of very rare spices. Five are unlabeled.

If you want to take any or all of the jars, turn to 42.

If you want to open some of the jars, turn to 35.

If you ignore the jars, turn to 176.

102 As you climb through the window, you lose your balance for a second. One foot hits the floor rather hard, making a faint but audible noise. You think you hear something stirring in the house; it could be your imagination, or it might be someone moving. What do you do?

If you want to ignore the noise and go on, turn to 85.

If you want to stand still for a moment to see if the rustling stops, turn to 48.

103 After looking for a while you realize that all this junk is, indeed, junk. There is absolutely nothing worthwhile here, unless you come back in the morning and talk the lord of the house into paying you to take it all away – and that sounds too much like honest work. Return to 16.

104 You have three choices – think fast! If you want to fast-talk your way out of the situation, turn to 156. If you want to stand and fight, turn to 76.

If you want to try to run, turn to 81.

105 You manage to slip from your foe's grasp as he goes for his scimitar. Turn to 104.

106 You slit the pillow open and feathers fly everywhere – but there's nothing of value inside. The pillow is now worthless. Go back to 46.

107 Yeech!! This tastes *terrible*, and it nauseates you! Lose 1 hit point. Return to 114.

108 Carefully you grasp the key and ready your knife to cut the cord. Make a Pickpocket roll; if you haven't studied pocket-picking, use your default (DX-6). If you succeed, turn to 38. If you fail, turn to 53.

109 You are in the guard's bedroom. There is no furniture except the crude mattress on the floor. There is a closet under the stairway. There's only one exit, and the guard is standing in it, trapping you inside.

If you want to fight the guard, turn to 76.

If you want to try to duck past the guard, turn to 81.

110 You are in the master bedroom. There is only one person in here: a white-bearded, heavy-set man in loud silken pajamas. He is snoring loudly. Various statuettes and *objets d'art* adorn the bedroom. There is a bell-pull hanging from the ceiling beside the bed.

If you want to look for something to steal, turn to 20. If you would rather leave the way you came in, turn to 18. If you have another clever idea you want to try, make an IQ roll. If you succeed, turn to 2. If you fail, choose between searching and leaving.

111 You are at a little landing which leads into several areas. Facing the stairs and going clockwise, they are: stairs going up and to the left, a great hall, a kitchen, and a pantry.

If you want to check the pantry, turn to 159.

If you want to go to the kitchen, turn to 128.

If you want to go up the stairs to see where they lead, turn to 18.

If you want to go into the great hall, turn to 59.

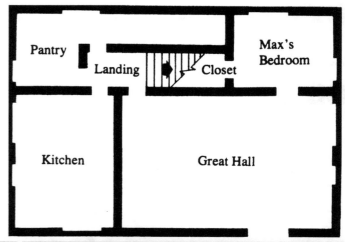

112 Hello. This is your conscience. Do you REALLY want to kill this man? You can get into trouble if you steal things; you can get *killed* if you commit murder. The Thieves' Guild and the City Watch will suddenly become very interested in you. Think fast, because someone is coming up the stairs.

You still have time to kill him, if that's what you want to do – *unless* you have the disadvantage of Pacifism. If you kill him, turn to 89.

If you wait to see who's coming up the stairs, turn to 49.

If you just try to bully Fatso out of his money, turn to 7.

113 Make an Acrobatics roll (defaults to DX-6). If you succeed you will be able to dive through the window and run before the guard can grab you. Proceed directly home, and from there to 185.

If you fail your roll, turn to 121.

114 What do you want to do with the oily white cream?

Test it on a cut? Turn to 131.

Try it on a burn? Turn to 65.

Rub it on uninjured skin? Turn to 84.

Taste it? Turn to 107.

Rub it in your eyes? Turn to 80.

None of the above? You may keep the jar if you wish. Return to 68.

115 You check several jars against their labels; all are accurate. Most of the jars are almost full. Turn to 42.

116 Make your IQ roll. For mental disadvantages like Alcoholism, any roll of 14 or more is an automatic failure. If you succeed, turn to 16 and choose freely.

If you fail your roll, you sample the wine and ale – extensively! For the rest of the adventure, each of your stats – ST, DX, IQ and HT – will be reduced by 1! This reduces all your skills by 1 for this adventure, as well. Now return to 16.

For more about Alcoholism, and mental disadvantages in general, see p. 30.

117 As you come up out of the cellar you see something that wasn't there before: a huge man with a scimitar. "I would give you five seconds to explain what you are doing here," the man bellows, "but I don't really care!" And he advances toward you.

If you want to try to talk your newfound friend out of slaughtering you, turn to 156.

If you want to stand and fight, turn to 76.

If you want to try to run past the guard, turn to 81.

118 The jar contains about $2 worth of small copper coins, weighing about a pound. You may take the jar and coins if you wish. Return to 68.

119 You may take the spoons if you like. Now make a Merchant roll (default IQ-5) as you study the china. If you make the roll, turn to 47.

If you fail, you decide that the china looks old, and you don't want to bother with something that fragile.

If you want to examine the hookahs, turn to 66.

If you want to look elsewhere in the room, turn to 171.

120 The mark is that of Jharno, a weaver whose work is in great demand. Once word gets around that this particular piece has been stolen it may be hard to sell it here, but your fence will almost certainly be able to find a buyer somewhere far enough away that it won't be recognized.

If you want to remove the tapestry from the wall, turn to 41.

If you want to try looking at something else, turn to 171.

121 The guard catches up with you and tries to Grapple. You are now in Close Combat. Roll a Quick Contest of DX. (He has a DX of 12, plus 3 because he is grappling.)

If you win or tie, you try again to get through the window. Turn to 113.

If you lose, the guard has caught you. Turn to 88.

For more about Close Combat, see p. 111 of the rules.

122 Roll against your Lockpicking skill – at a -5! (Whoever made this lock knew what he was doing.) If you don't have Lockpicking, your default for this lock is IQ-10. If you succeed, turn to 97. If you fail, turn to 74.

123 You're in the kitchen, remember? There are a lot of pots and pans here; some of them are very heavy and would be good weapons (treat as a club at -2 to your skill). You can easily grab one in a fight, if you need a better weapon than anything you have. Turn to 76.

124 There are three pillows. They are made of silk, with fine embroidery, and they look like they might be worth some money. They weigh about two pounds each. While you are checking them you feel a couple of lumps in the red pillow – like something might be hidden inside it.

If you want to try cutting the pillow open, turn to 46.

If you don't want to cut them open, you can put them in your bag, or leave them – whichever you choose. Return to 171.

125 Most of the wines are of a local vintage; stout, hearty and good for washing down meals. Make an IQ roll. If you succeed, turn to 175. If you fail, turn to 72.

126 You spot a heavy (10-pound) cast-iron skillet under the counter with some other cookware. You may take it if you wish. Good cooking utensils are in demand, and in a pinch you could use it as a weapon! (If used offensively, it counts as a mace; Mace skill defaults to DX-5. It does "swing+3" damage. You can also use it defensively as a small shield; Shield skill defaults to DX-4.) But, however you use it, you are at an extra -2 to your skill because it's so heavy and clumsy.

Return to 128 and choose again.

127 Holding your breath, you toss the entire jar of pepper at the guard's face. He stumbles back with a choked cry. Seizing the chance, you dodge past him. Above you a whistle has begun to blow; you know it's time you were leaving. Back to the kitchen and out the window you go. Turn to 148.

128 You are in the kitchen. A fire is dying in the fireplace; a heavy, lidded iron pot sits in the embers. Something in that pot smells very good! There is a candle in an ornate candleholder on the table near the fireplace.

If you want to search the kitchen, turn to 183.

If you want to open the pot, turn to 158.

If you want to light the candle, turn to 3.

If you want to go into the next room, turn to 111.

If you want to leave through the window and go home, turn to 27.

129 There is little in this room; just a low table with a tea service and three hookahs about it. The table is too big to consider stealing. The hookahs are ornate brass, and weigh some 10 lbs. each. The tea service looks very old and delicate.

If you want to look at the tea service, turn to 167.

If you want to appraise the hookahs, turn to 66.

If you are finished here, turn to 171.

130 You slit the pillow open and feathers fly every-where – but there's nothing of value inside. The pillow is now worthless. Turn to 46.

131 The ointment stings! Roll on your HT or IQ – whichever is better. If you have the advantage of Strong Will, you may add the level of your Strong Will to your HT or IQ.

If you make your roll, return to 114. If you fail, turn to 24.

132 Make an IQ roll. If you succeed, turn to 179. If you fail, turn to 155.

133 You dash through the door, slamming it behind you. You're outside! The closed door gives you a moment's head start on the guard. He has a Move of 5. If your own Move is greater, you can escape; turn to 185.

If your own Move is less than or equal to 5, try your Stealth roll (at -4 because you are running). If you don't make your Stealth roll and the guard manages to catch up with you, you will have to fight him. If this happens, turn to 76.

If you do make your Stealth roll, you manage to find a hiding place. The guard looks around for a few minutes; then he returns to the house, cursing under his breath. You sigh with relief and head for home. Turn to 27.

134 You may take the scimitar if you like. Searching the room, you find nothing else of any value whatever. Stepping over the motionless giant, you leave the room. For the rest of this adventure, you may ignore any references to the guard; you've defeated him without a fight. Make a note: if you read an entry that tells you the guard is after you, turn to 111 instead and pick another room to look at.

Now turn to 59.

135 The guard shouts with anger, raising his scimitar – and distracting you. The merchant seizes his chance. Grabbing your arm, he yanks the bell-pull. The floor opens beneath you, and you fall . . . with 250 pounds of angry fat man on top of you. Everything goes black. Turn to 141.

136 Further examination reveals nothing more. If you want to pull the bell-rope to see what happens, turn to 139. If you want to leave the room, turn to 18. If you want to take close look at Fatso himself, turn to 52.

137 You can't quite recognize the odor, so you try a bigger sniff. Then you know what it is – it's hot pepper! It's rare and valuable – and it's making you sneeze!

Make a HT roll to avoid sneezing. If you succeed, you may continue looking around. Turn to 68.

If you fail, you sneeze! Turn to 79.

138 *Ouch!* You managed to burn yourself. Take 1d-3 damage – that is, roll 1 die and subtract 3. This is how many hits you took from being burned (minimum of 1 in this case). You may choose which hand was burned. If you took more than ⅓ your HT in damage to that hand, it is crippled; otherwise, for this adventure, anything you do with that hand will be at a -1 because of the pain.

Now roll to see if you dropped the pan lid when you burned yourself. Roll your DX – *minus* the number of hits you took. If you fail your roll, turn to 40.

If you make your roll, you may eat some stew; turn to 168. Or you may look around some more; turn to 128.

139 A trap door opens beneath you! You fall into a room below the fat man's chambers. You take (3d-9) damage from the fall (a successful roll against your Acrobatics skill, or your default of DX-6, will keep you from taking any damage). *For more about Acrobatics skill, see p. 48. For more rules on falling, see p. 130.*

As you stand, you see a large man reaching for his scimitar. He will have it in hand before you can react. Turn to 104.

140 The jar has two marks inscribed on the lid. Make a Physician roll (default IQ-7) to recognize them; if you succeed, turn to 174. If not, the marks don't mean anything to you. Turn to 26.

141 You are lying unconscious on the floor. You wake up the next morning in a cold, dark prison cell. All your possessions are gone. Your adventure is over.

142 You dash past the guard and down the stairs. He charges after you, bellowing.

If you run for the great hall, turn to 157.

If you run for the pantry, turn to 58.

If you run for the kitchen, turn to 23.

143 You feel around the darkened walls. Evidently the cellar is full of junk. You feel the shape of a heavy box . . . then it starts to slide onto you! You try to catch it.

Roll against your ST. If you succeed, you catch the box; you are unhurt and you can put it down quietly.

If you fail your ST roll, the box falls to the floor, bruising your leg in the process. Take 2 hits of damage; DR (damage resistance) of armor or Toughness *will* protect.

It's too dark down here. You start back up the stairs. If you caught the box, turn to 14. If you failed and it hit you, turn to 117.

144 No bell rings. Instead, you hear a loud CREEEEK as the trap door beneath you opens. You find yourself falling, accompanied by a fat-man obbligato: "Get him, Max! Get him! He tried to kill me!" Turn to 139.

145 You recognize the mark of a local smith on the base of the hookahs. You can tell that the hookahs are too well-used to be valuable in and of themselves, and too recent to be antiques. You can take them if you wish, but they're probably not worth the effort to carry them home. Return to 129.

146 With his scimitar in one hand and you in the other, the guard hauls you into the pantry, opens the trap door, shoves you down the stairs and closes the door behind you. You hear him shoving a couple of flour barrels over the top of the trap door, making it too heavy for you to move. You can safely assume you will still be in the cellar when the guards arrive in the morning. Your adventure – and at least for the next few years, your career as a thief – is over.

147 NO! It's an AWFUL THING, and it TOUCHED you! You panic. Screaming, you run blindly for the exit . . . and slam into the doorframe, head first. Turn to 141.

148 Out the front door you dash – away from the house, and down an alley. You slow to a walk as you emerge into another street. Tipping your cap to the groggy watchman, you leave the fortified neighborhood and head toward your humble abode. Turn to 27.

149 You go through the doorway into a bedroom. You see a huge man, about seven feet tall, with a day's growth of beard. He is asleep on a crude mattress, snoring loudly. He is wearing a loincloth and nothing else. On the floor next to him is a scimitar.

If you want to look for valuables, turn to 132.

If you want to try to steal the sword, turn to 86.

If you want to attack the guard, turn to 160.

If you want to leave the room, turn to 59.

150 These papers are a mixed lot: old love letters, a pedigree for a canary, 100 shares in a corporation long dead, a collection of bawdy limericks, a good citizenship award, and so on and so forth. Some of these might be embarrassing to the owner, but none of them look important. You can take them if you like; they weigh about eight pounds.

If you have not opened the small bag and wish to do so, turn to 69. Otherwise, leave it and return to 16.

151 "Tell him to move away from the door!" you command Fatso. Make a reaction roll. This is a potential combat situation; under these circumstances, all your normal reaction modifiers apply. You can also use the Diplomacy skill (see p. 63) if you have it.

Roll 3 dice and add or subtract the reaction modifiers shown under your character's picture on the Character Sheet. Then consult the Reaction Table (*Charts and Tables* section).

If the adjusted reaction is Neutral or better (10 or up), go to 96. If it is Poor (7 to 9), turn to 50. If it is Bad or worse (6 or below), turn to 135.

152 The guard did not believe you in the slightest. If he was going to attack you, turn to 76.

If he already had you by the wrist, turn to 146.

153 Carefully, you re-enter the kitchen. The guard is gone – but he's been alerted. All your Stealth rolls will be at -2 for the rest of the adventure. (This is cumulative with any other penalties you may get.) Turn to 128.

154 This looks like the place where the owner of the house stores all the stuff he doesn't want any more. Make an IQ roll. If you succeed, turn to 103. If you fail, turn to 57.

155 This is obviously not a wealthy man. If he has any valuable possessions other than the scimitar, you can't find them. Return to 149 and make another choice.

156 You decide on a story to tell the guard – you are a world-class knife champion, you have seven starving children, whatever. Roll a Contest of Skills. The guard rolls against his IQ of 10. You can roll your Fast-Talk skill, or (if you're female) your Sex Appeal skill. If you have neither of these, Fast-Talk defaults to IQ-5, and Sex Appeal defaults to HT-3. You only get one try! (If you tie, roll again.)

If you win, you talked the guard out of attacking. Turn to 4.

If you lose, the guard laughs at you. Turn to 152.

For more about these skills, see p. 63 for Fast-Talk, and p. 64 for Sex Appeal.

157 You are in the great hall, being chased by the guard. You don't have time to look around. If you have Absolute Direction, turn to 161.

Otherwise you can go into a small room off to the side; turn to 109. You can go into a pantry; turn to 58. Or you can go through a door across from the guard's room; turn to 133.

158 You reach for the lid of the pot. Roll three dice against your IQ. If you succeed, you remembered to cover your hand with a towel. Turn to 168. If you fail, you forgot. Turn to 92.

159 You are in a pantry. There are shelves and shelves of goods here. Make a Vision roll (IQ plus Acute Vision and Alertness, if you have them). If you make your roll, turn to 98.

If you don't, you find nothing of value. You return to the landing to search somewhere else. Turn to 111.

160 Attacking someone this size, even while he's asleep, is risky. If you are Overconfident, this is right in character. Otherwise, you might want to think again.

If you want to reconsider, return to 149.

If you want to kill the giant (you must have a weapon), turn to 15.

If you want to try to knock the giant out, turn to 83.

161 You can tell the door opposite the guard's room leads out of the house. Turn to 133, if you want to leave. Otherwise, return to 157.

162 You manage to grab Fatso's arm before he can reach the bell-pull. You still have the knife at his throat.

You can cut Fatso's throat; turn to 112.

You can *threaten* to cut Fatso's throat in order to get him to tell you where he keeps his money; turn to 7.

Or you can flee; turn to 22.

163 As you check under Fatso's bed you notice something unusual – tapping the rug by the side of the bed reveals a hollow spot. You move the rug and see a trap door built into the floor.

Make a Mechanic (default IQ-5) or Traps (defaults to IQ-5, DX-5, or Lockpicking-3) roll. If you succeed, turn to 39. If you fail, turn to 136.

If you roll a "critical failure" (a 17 or 18, or any number at least 10 *over* the roll you needed), turn to 31. *Critical failures are explained on p. 86.*

164 Any head blow has a chance of knocking out the victim. Roll vs. the giant's HT of 12. On a failed roll, he falls unconscious; turn to 134.

If he makes the roll, your blow stunned the giant, but he's recovering quickly. If you want to hit him again, return to 83. If you want to flee from the house, you may do so before he gains his feet; if so, turn to 27.

165 A real prize! The gems are valuable, portable and anonymous – perfect loot. The fence pays you $3,000 and suggests you take a vacation. Return to 185.

166 "Do you know what you have here?" says the fence. You don't, of course. He chuckles, "The pedigree of a canary . . . some old love letters . . . and ten years of business records for a cesspool-cleaning service." He tosses the papers to the floor. Return to 185.

167 The tea service consists of four porcelain cups, a porcelain teapot, and four silver spoons. You study the spoons. Make a Merchant (defaults to IQ-5) or Jeweler (defaults to IQ-6) roll. If you have both skills, use whichever one is higher.

If you make your roll for the spoons, turn to 181. Otherwise, turn to 119.

168 It's a good stew! You may eat as much as you like. In fact, you may end up eating more than you should. If you have the disadvantage of Gluttony, make an IQ roll; anything over 13 automatically fails. Turn to 178 if you fail; otherwise, keep reading.

If you are Fatigued, eating some stew will reduce your Fatigue by 1 (but no more than 1).

When you are finished, turn to 128 if you want to look around the kitchen some more, or 111 if you want to leave the kitchen.

169 On the map, you must maneuver either to the kitchen window (where you came in) or the front door (which leads out of the Great Hall). If you get to the door, turn to 148.

If you make it to the window, and the guard is more than one turn's movement behind you, turn to 148. Otherwise, turn to 113.

170 You knocked the spider off onto the shelf. It scuttles behind a clutter of boxes and disappears.

If you want to look in the jar, turn to 118.

If you want to look at something else, turn to 68.

171 What will you do? If you want to examine the statues, turn to 184.

If you want to look at the pillows, turn to 124.

If you want to appraise the tapestries, turn to 51.

If you want to look at the other furnishings here, turn to 129.

If you are finished here, turn to 59.

172 If you are Literate, turn to 150 immediately. If not, the important-looking papers don't mean anything to you – but you may still take them if you wish. They weigh about eight pounds.

If you want to open the small bag, turn to 69. Otherwise, return to 16.

173 Make an IQ roll (at IQ-4 if your character sheet defines the phobia as "severe"). Remember that with a mental disadvantage, any roll over a 13 is an automatic failure! If you make your roll, turn to 54 – but the DX roll you make at that entry will be at a -2.

If you fail your roll, turn to 147.

174 The marks are Apothecaries' Guild symbols for "Ointment" and "Burn." Turn to 26.

175 One of the labels in the wine rack stands out. It's faded, but you can see the name written in gold leaf. Only very valuable wines are labeled in gold leaf; you should be able to fence it for at least a hundred dollars. You may take the wine if you wish; it adds three pounds to your encumbrance. None of the other bottles look unusual.

If you want to drink some of the wine (burgling is thirsty work), turn to 45. Otherwise, return to 16 and choose again.

176 Try another Vision roll – this one at -2. In other words, subtract 2 from your ordinary Vision roll. If you normally need a 13, you must roll 11 or less. If you succeed, turn to 5. Otherwise, you return to the landing to search somewhere else. Turn to 111.

177 You notice that the seal on one of the bungs on the bottom row isn't quite right. You pull on the bung and it comes out readily, disclosing a keyhole!

If you have picked up a key somewhere in the house, you may try to use it. Turn to 8.

If you want to try to pick the lock, turn to 122.

If you want to forget the casks, return to 16 and choose again.

178 The stew is delicious! You take several helpings. You can't eat the entire pot of stew, but you really try. Eventually, stuffed to the gills, you quit. Your IQ and HT are both reduced by 2 for the rest of the adventure, and your Move is reduced by 1. Go back to 128.

179 Turn to 155.

180 As you complete your perusal, you notice something unusual; a gold key on a silken cord around the fat man's neck. If you want to try to remove the key, turn to 108. If you want to leave the way you came in, turn to 18.

181 The spoons are hallmarked, indicating that they are silver and the work of a master smith. They weigh little and are worth $20 each. Turn to 119.

182 This jar feels like it might be empty, but when you open it – sure enough, it's empty! You may take the jar if you wish. Return to 68.

183 Whoever owns this house seems to have plenty of money. The huge pots and kettles here must have been very expensive. Unfortunately, they are also too large to fit comfortably into your bag.

If you want to look more closely, turn to 99.

Otherwise, return to 128 and choose again.

184 These statues are made of marble, life-size and VERY heavy. There is no way to take one with you. Return to 171.

185 When you get home, your adventure is over. Figure the worth of your loot, using the table below. The first column shows what you could buy the item for in the market. The second column shows what the fence will give you. Of course, you won't fence the coins – you'll spend them. And if you have a use for any of the items, you may keep them!

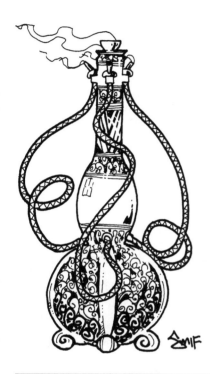

Item	Value	Fence will pay
Scimitar	$650	$400
Cast-iron skillet	$50	$20
Fatso's gold key	$20	$5
Amulet & chain	$400	$200
Bottle of rare wine	$100	$50
Jar of common herbs (12 of these)	$5 each	$2.50 each
Moderately rare herbs (20 of these)	$20 each	$10 each
Very rare spices (4 of these)	$100 each	$50 each
Jar of red pepper	$100	$50
Empty jar	$2	$0
Pillows (3 of these)	$50 each	$25 each
Tapestry	$2,000	$800
Porcelain tea service	$1,500	$600
Silver spoons (4 of these)	$20 each	$10 each
Hookahs (3 of these)	$40 each	$10 each
Bag of gems	Turn to 165 if you have this.	
Jar of white ointment	Turn to 34 if you have this.	
Fatso's bag of money	$500	
Silver coins	$20	
Jar of copper coins	$2	
Corroded coins	$1	

As for the sheaf of papers: The fence laughs uproariously when you take them in. "What's so funny?" you ask. He explains. If you are Literate, turn to 62. If not, turn to 166.

If you took some apothecary jars at random, use the table below to find out how much the jars you took were worth. Roll 1 die and use it to determine which column to use; roll another die for the row. Do this for each jar.

	1	2	3	4	5	6
1	20	5	20	100	20	20
2	100	20	5	20	20	5
3	20	5	20	5	5	20
4	4	20	100	20	20	5
5	20	20	20	5	5	20
6	20	5	20	5	20	100

These are the shop prices; the fence will give you *half* as much.

Experience

You will earn 1 character point just for surviving, plus 1 point for every $2,000 value of loot you stole (3 points maximum), plus 1 point if you fought the guard.

Lose 2 points for each person you killed. You're a thief, not a murderer. However, your score for the adventure can't go below zero.

APPENDIX
To the Third Edition Revised

After eight printings of the **GURPS Basic Set**, Third Edition, you'd think we had it just about right. Well, yes . . . and no.

As we went to press with what *started* as the ninth printing, we looked at the book and said, "Wait a minute! This is 1994!"

Since **GURPS** first came out, a number of really (pardon the expression) generic rules have appeared . . . rules that *should* be in the Basic Set. Most are for character creation – advantages, disadvantages and skills that would fit into almost any genre.

So, not without regret, we dropped the "Caravan from Ein Arris" group adventure. It's a good adventure, but face it – almost everybody who buys **GURPS** already knows what an adventure looks like. That gave us 18 pages, and here they are.

Organization

It would have been nice to put each of these new entries exactly where it belongs in the book – alphabetically, in the right section. But that would have been a *bad* idea, because there are more than a million **GURPS** books already out there, carefully cross-referenced to the page numbers in the existing **Basic Set.** Do we want to mess all that up? No, thank you.

So the new rules are all together, here in the Appendix, where they don't mess up the page numbering. The Index and Table of Contents have been updated; we hope you'll be able to find what you want.

What to Include?

Eighteen pages seemed like a lot when we started. But there's so much to choose from! The Mass Combat System would have been great, for instance – but it's 16 pages all by itself. There are a lot of interesting new advantages and disadvantages in **GURPS Space**, but most of them are *only* for outer-space campaigns. And so on. In the end, we tried to select those rules that were the most widely useful . . . the ones that *everybody* will end up playing with. These included a few advantages that may not be suitable for PCs in every genre, but make great special abilities for aliens, mutants, monsters or fantasy races.

Editing

All these have been gone over to check clarity, and edited where necessary to make them more generic and generally useful. These versions should be considered the definitive ones.

Significant changes were: First, the cost of the Contacts advantage was drastically lowered, thanks to feedback from many players.

The value of the worst version of Destiny was raised a great deal, to bring it into line with equivalent disadvantages like Terminally Ill.

Finally, Manic-Depressive had a new rule added; you can now switch phases because of an emergency.

And Yet More . . .

We have also released **GURPS Compendium I** and **II**. These are two *big* books of **GURPS** stuff. These books include *every* advantage, disadvantage and skill that we've ever published (expect those that are so closely tied to specific licensed worldbooks that there would be no point in it). Plus, finally, once and for all, the Mass Combat System, and a lot of other things that **GURPS** players kept asking us to repeat. Anything that's in the **Compendium** will *not* be repeated in later books, freeing up a lot more space for brand-new stuff.

The **Compendium** also include everything from this Appendix. If you have an old Third Edition, and the new **Compendium**, you'll have it all. Our purpose in publishing this revised edition is *not* to make anybody buy it again. It's just to make every new printing of the **Basic Set** the best possible introduction to **GURPS**. If you like it, great! If you don't, let us know, and we'll make the next one better. And, either way, thanks for playing **GURPS**.

– Steve Jackson

ADVANTAGES

Ally Group   *Variable*

You have a loyal group of followers. None of them has as high a point value as a normal PC, but together they are significant support for you. Noblemen, mercenary or bandit leaders, and similar characters are reasonable candidates to have Ally Groups.

Ally Groups are composed of NPCs, controlled by the GM. The point value of the Ally Group depends on its strength, modified by how frequently the group appears.

A small group (2 to 5 people) costs 10 points. Examples include an infantry squad or a small gang.

A medium-sized group (6 to 20 people) costs 20 points. Examples include a large gang, a small army of bodyguards, or a cavalry unit.

A large group (20 to 100 people) or a medium-sized group with some formidable individuals costs 30 points. Examples might include a whole barbarian army, or a small cadre of trained warriors with good equipment.

An entire government, a national army, or some similar group may be purchased as a Patron, but cannot be an Ally Group.

Point Level

The individuals in allied groups normally are 75-point characters. They may be increased to 100-point allies by raising the *base* cost of the group by 10 points. Allies of more than 100 points must be bought individually.

Frequency of Appearance

If the Ally Group appears almost all the time (roll of 15 or less): triple the listed value.

If the Ally Group appears quite often (roll of 12 or less): double the listed value.

If the Ally Group appears fairly often (roll of 9 or less): use the listed value.

If the Ally Group appears quite rarely (roll of 6 or less): halve the listed value (round up).

The player may choose the Ally Group when the character is created. With the GM's approval, a character may also acquire an Ally Group later. Either way, the GM may fill in the details of the group, including the circumstances under which the Ally Group may be available. The GM may also require the Unusual Background advantage to explain the ties between the character and the Ally Group.

If members of the Ally Group are lost during an adventure, they will be replaced . . . though, perhaps, not immediately. The details are up to the GM, and may be based on the circumstances in which the leader "acquired" the group.

A PC should get not character points for any game session in which he betrays or attacks his Ally Group. Leading a group into danger is all right – as long as the PC is a responsible leader. Any prolonged or severe mistreatment of the group, though, will break the ties; the Ally Group and points are lost.

If a PC and his Ally Group part ways amicably, the PC should not be penalized. The point cost of the Ally Group may buy another Ally Group met during roleplaying, or individual members of the group may continue as Allies (see p. 23). At the GM's discretion, remaining points may be traded in for money (see sidebar, p. 16), reflecting parting gifts.

Alternate Identity
15 or 5 points per identity

You have an extra identity, which to all appearances is legally established. Your fingerprints (and retina prints, if this is a common method of ID) are registered under two different names, you have two sets of licenses, passports, birth certificates, and so on. This can be extremely useful for anyone involved in illegal activities, or for anyone trying to conceal a super identity. This advantage may be purchased as many times as desired, giving another set of papers each time.

While the new identity may include credit cards and bank accounts, all money in these accounts must be supplied from the "real" character's bank account – it isn't included in the package.

If a law enforcement agency attempts to identify you from your prints, with no clues as to your name, there is an equal chance for each of your identities to come up. The search will stop at that point . . . unless they already have reason to believe you are a ringer. If the search continues, the second identity will, of course, surface, and you will be unmasked. At that point, once the agency determines who you *really* are, the alternate identity(s) are lost.

Alternate identities are illegal for ordinary people. If you are caught, you will face a stiff fine and possibly a jail sentence. An alternate identity can also be a "secret" identity, but it doesn't have to be!

Legal Alternate Identities: Certain PCs might have access to an Alternate Identity *legally.* An undercover FBI agent, for example, could have a complete set of papers, history, etc., in a fake name. Or a super-hero might have government help in creating a secret identity! A character must have at least 10 points of Legal Enforcement Powers (p. 21) to have a legal identity such as this – but the point cost of the Alternate Identity drops from 15 to 5 points. If a super has official permission to conceal his original name (to protect his family, etc.) and to hold property, etc., in his "super" name, that is a Legal Alternate Identity combined with a Secret Identity – see **GURPS Supers** (his real name is hidden).

"Weak" Identities: In many countries, including the U.S., it is legal to use false names for privacy, as long as you do not attempt to defraud or interfere with "public records." You can usually rent an apartment as "Mr. Smith," paying cash, without problems. But you can't get a driver's license, etc., legally. This sort of weak identity is worth no points.

Temporary Identity

You have obtained a set of identity papers, and had the appropriate records altered, to set up an Alternate Identity. However, the quality of the work is poor. The new identity will eventually be noticed and eliminated (and the user sought after!). Therefore, a Temporary Identity is not considered an "advantage," and costs no points. It is a convenience to be bought with cash.

A standard Temporary Identity is guaranteed to be good for one week. At the end of that week, a roll is made. On an 8 or less, the false records have been discovered. Each week an additional roll is made at a cumulative +1 (e.g., the discrepancies are discovered at the end of week 2 on a 9 or less, and at the end of week 3 on a 10 or less).

Cost of a temporary identity is negotiable, and depends entirely on the background. The cheaper the identity, the more often the GM will roll; a really cheap one might be good only for a day, with rolls every day! More expensive identities, lasting longer or starting at a lower number, might also be available.

In a high-tech background, where a temporary identity is a matter of tampering with computer files, the netrunner who builds the identity can put a "daemon" in the file. This will automatically place a warning phone call when the identity is blown! This will often be as expensive as the Temporary Identity itself.

Someone who has been Zeroed (p. 237) *can* use a Temporary Identity.

Blessed   Variable

You are in tune with some specific higher power. The simplest version of this advantage costs 10 points and grants the ability to use any one Divination spell at IQ level (see **GURPS Magic**, p. 55).

The type of Divination should match the "flavor" of the deity. The Blessed person (often a cleric) also gains a +1 reaction from any of the deity's followers who know him to be Blessed.

For 20 points, one can be Very Blessed, which confers a +5 bonus to Divination skill.

Any Blessed character must act in accordance with the rules or values associated with his deity, or the advantage will be lost.

A deity might also grant powers beyond Divination to especially Blessed characters. These powers must match the power or capability of the deity (a goddess of mercy and healing could grant healing gifts, for instance). These abilities come in many different forms, the exact cost of each depending on the ability granted. In addition, many of the standard advantages can be explained as divine gifts, at the GM's discretion. Some examples:

Immunity: Your blessing involves an immunity to (or protection from) certain substances, usually those associated with the deity granting the blessing. A fire god might, for example, bless his clerics with an immunity to fire damage. When determining the cost, the GM should keep in mind that these are powerful blessings, and *charge* accordingly. Costs for immunities in **GURPS Supers** are a good guide.

Aptitude: Your blessing gives you an added bonus to a particular skill. For Physical skills, the point cost for a +1 aptitude is equivalent to the cost (see p. 44) to learn the skill at DX level. The cost for a 2-point aptitude is equal to the cost for DX+1, and so on. For Mental skills, the cost for a +1 aptitude is equal to the cost of learning the skill at IQ level. A 2-point aptitude costs the same as learning it at IQ+1 and so on. The bonus applies to default skill levels as well as to those you have training in.

Magical Knack: Your blessing gives you the innate ability to do a particular magical spell. The cost is 2% of the price of a magic item that would be able to cast the same spell. See **GURPS Magic**.

Heroic Feats: 10 points. Your blessing gives you the innate ability to perform a particular heroic feat. Once per playing session you may add 1d to either ST, DX, or HT (the attribute is specified at the time of the blessing) for up to 3d seconds. At the end of this time, you revert to your normal attribute and must suffer all penalties amassed during the *heroic* period. (For instance, if you take more than 5 times your normal HT in damage during a time of raised HT, then without some sort of healing you will immediately die when the effects wear off.)

Other blessings can be defined at the GM's discretion.

Contacts   Variable

Note: The price of this advantage has been significantly reduced from that described in earlier books.

A Contact is an NPC, like an Ally or a Patron. However, the Contact only provides *information*. A Contact may be anything from a wino in the right gutter to the Chief of State of a country, depending on the character's background. The Contact has access to information, and he already knows the character and is likely to react favorably. Of course, offering a price, in cash or favors, is never a bad idea. The Contact is always played and controlled by the GM, and any price he asks will be set by the GM.

The GM may assume that a Contact is, in general, well-disposed toward the PC. However, the Contact is *not* an Ally or Patron, and is no more likely to give special help than any other generally friendly NPC!

A Contact doesn't have to be created when the PC is first developed. Contacts may be added later. When appropriate, the GM can turn an existing NPC into a Contact for one or more players, possibly in lieu of character points for the adventure in which the Contact was developed and encountered. For instance, the reward for an adventure in which the party helped solve a bank robbery might be a knowledgeable, reliable police contact, *shared by the whole party*. He's worth 18 points – more than any one character earned on the adventure, but a fair reward for the whole group.

Whatever the case, the Contact can provide information only about his own area of expertise. The technician at the forensics lab probably has no information about currency transfers, and the VP of the local bank probably can't do a ballistics comparison. The GM assigns a skill (Streetwise for a minor criminal, Forensics for a lab tech, etc.) to the Contact. All attempts to get information from him require a secret roll by the GM against the Contact's "effective" skill. Note that the effective skill is not necessarily the NPC's *actual* skill; the actual skill can be set by the GM if the NPC comes into regular play. For instance, the president of a local steel mill might actually have business-related skills of 16-18, but he has an *effective* skill of 21, making him worth 4 points, because he himself has good connections!

Point values for Contacts are based on the type of information and its effective skill, modified by the frequency with which they can provide information and the reliability of the information. Importance of information is relative and the list of possible Contacts is virtually endless; a few are listed below as a guide to help the GM determine value.

Type of Information

Street Contacts. These are minor criminals, derelicts, street thugs, gang members, small-time fences and other streetwise NPCs who provide information on illicit activities, local criminal gossip, upcoming crimes and so forth. Base cost is 1 point for "unconnected" Contacts (not part of the local criminal organization; Streetwise-12) and 2 points for "connected" Contacts (Streetwise-15). If the Contact is a major figure in a criminal organization (the Don, Clan Chief, or member of the "inner circle" of the Family; Streetwise-21), the cost doubles to 4 points.

Business Contacts. Executives, business owners, secretaries – even the mail room flunky – can provide information on businesses and business dealings. Base cost depends on how much the contact can be expected to know: 1 point for a mail boy or typist (effective skill 12), 2 points for the president's secretary (effective skill 15), 3 points for an accountant (effective skill 18) or 4 points for the president or Chairman of the Board (effective skill 21).

Police Contacts. This includes anyone connected with law enforcement and criminal investigations: beat cops, corporate security, government agents, forensics specialists, coroners, etc. Cost depends on access to information or services. Beat cops and regular private security officers are 1 point (effective skill 12); detectives, federal agents, or record clerks are 2 points (effective skill 15); administrators (lieutenants, captains, Special Agents in Charge, Heads of Departmental Security, etc.) are 3 points (effective skill of 18) and senior officers (sheriffs, chiefs of police, District Superintendents, Security Chiefs, etc.) are 4 points (effective skill 21).

Frequency of Assistance

Frequency refers to the chance that the Contact can be found when needed. When creating the character, the player must define the way the Contact is normally contacted! Regardless of the chosen frequency, a Contact cannot be reached if the PCs could not reasonably speak to him.

Available almost all of the time (roll of 15 or less): triple cost.

Available quite often (roll of 12 or less): double cost.

Available fairly often (roll of 9 or less): listed cost.

Available rarely (roll of 6 or less): half cost (round up; minimum cost is always 1).

During the adventure, if a PC wants to talk with his Contact, the GM rolls against the availability number for that Contact. A failed roll means the Contact is busy or cannot be located that day. If the Contact *is* available, then the GM must roll against the Contact's effective skill for each general piece of information the PC requests.

No Contact may be reached more than once per day, even if several PCs share the same Contact. If the PC has several questions to ask, he should have them all in mind when he first reaches his Contact. The Contact will answer the first question at his full effective skill, and each subsequent question at a cumulative -2. Don't overuse your Contacts!

A Contact can *never* supply information outside his particular area of knowledge. Use common sense. Likewise, the GM *must not* allow a Contact to give information that short-circuits the adventure or part of it!

If a PC gets a critical failure when trying to reach his Contact, that Contact can't be reached during that entire *adventure*.

Reliability of Information

Contacts are not guaranteed to know anything useful, and are not guaranteed to be truthful. Use the following modifiers (cumulative with frequency modifiers).

Completely reliable: Even on a critical failure, the worst response will be "I don't know." On an ordinary failure he can find information in 1d days. Triple cost.

Usually reliable: On a critical failure, the Contact will lie; on any other failure he "doesn't know now but check back in 1d days." Roll again at that time; a failure then means he can't find out at all. Double cost.

Somewhat reliable: On a failure, the Contact doesn't know and can't find out; on a critical failure he will lie; on a natural 18 he will let the opposition or authorities (whichever is appropriate) know who is asking questions. Listed cost.

Unreliable: Reduce effective skill by 2. On any failure he will lie; on a critical failure he will notify the enemy. Half cost (round up; minimum cost is always 1).

Money Talks

Bribery, whether cash or favors, motivates the Contact and increases his *reliability level*. Once reliability reaches "usually reliable," further levels of increase go to effective skill; bribery cannot make anyone totally reliable!

A cash bribe should be about equivalent to one day's income for a +1 bonus, one week's income for +2, one month's for +3 and one year's for +4. Favors should be of equivalent worth. The favor should always be something that the character actually performs in the game. The GM must maintain proper roleplaying – a diplomat might be insulted by a cash bribe, but welcome an introduction into the right social circle. A criminal may ask for cash, but settle for favors that will get the PCs in trouble. A police detective or wealthy executive might simply want the party to "owe him one" for later . . . which could set off a whole new adventure, somewhere down the road.

Dark Vision   25 points

This advantage is intended for nonhumans or supers; normal humans cannot have it without paying considerably more (GM's choice) for Unusual Background.

You can see in absolute darkness, using some means other than light, radar or sonar. The ability to detect *colors* in the darkness adds 5 points to the cost.

Destiny   Variable

Destiny is an irresistible force that can pull a hero's life this way and that, bringing good and bad luck by turns as it carries him blindly to his pre-ordained fate. One's destiny can be discovered by magical divination, the interpretation of omens, and similar magical techniques, but the true meaning of an omen is often not discovered until after the prophecy it revealed is fulfilled. A character with a Destiny is likely to become the subject of songs and stories for generations.

Destiny can be taken as an advantage or as a disadvantage, at a value of 15 to -15 points. When the player decides to take a Destiny, he tells the GM the point value he wants. The GM then secretly determines the nature of the character's Destiny, according to its value and the dictates of the campaign. Of course, the GM can change his mind later, as the campaign develops!

When a player chooses Destiny, he is giving the GM absolute license to meddle with his character's life. The more subtle the GM is, the better, but the GM *must* make the destiny work out. The point value of the Destiny determines the kind of impact it has on the hero's life, while the precise details are determined by the GM and the flow of the campaign. A hero should never know the nature of his Destiny, except through ambiguous omens or a supernatural agency.

Destiny taken as an advantage will work to the character's good in the end – although this may not always be clear, and is likely to be inconvenient at times. Destiny taken as a disadvantage leads to something bad – but perhaps not immediately, and not without a chance to gain honor by dealing with it well. A fated, tragic death can be an end worthy of a hero.

Great Advantage: 15 points. The character is fated to achieve greatness in his lifetime – in the end, everyone will know his name and praise it! Sooner or later a fortunate event will fulfill the character's fate. Note that this does not guarantee the "success" of the character. If he chooses to jump in front of an assassin's knife during the very next game session, the GM might just decide the destiny is fulfilled . . . he died a hero!

Major Advantage: 10 points. As above, but a lesser success. Alternatively, the character may be doomed to die in a particular place, or in a particular fashion: at sea, by the hand of an Emperor, underground, or whatever. Although he can be grievously wounded elsewhere and by other means, he will not die; all damage is applied normally, but he does not die. If he avoids the circumstances which would fulfill his Destiny, knowingly or otherwise, he may find that Fate has a few surprises. The sea may flood his home while he sleeps, the general against whom he marches may be the future Emperor, or Mt. Vesuvius may bury him under tons of ash. The GM may need to use these twists if a PC discovers that he has a Destiny of this kind.

Minor Advantage: 5 points. The character is fated to play a small part in a larger story, but this part will reflect to his credit. In game terms, he is guaranteed one significant victory.

Minor disadvantage: -5 points. Again, the character is fated to play a small part in a larger story, but this time he will not come off so well. He is guaranteed one tragic experience or one embarrassing failure. These things should not cause the fated character's death except in the most desperate and heroic of circumstances.

Major disadvantage: -10 points. The character is fated to play a key role in a sorry turn of events. For instance, he might arrive with a message which could have saved the day . . . but he came too late. Or he might have executed the only competent general in a threatened province, causing its loss to barbarian invaders. Still, the character will survive.

Great Disadvantage: -15 points. Death stalks the character. Something out there has his name on it, and it knows where he is, and it's getting closer all the time. He will either die, or be ruined, and his fall will have terrible repercussions for others. This level of Destiny is not suitable for every campaign! The GM does not have to allow it, and if he does, he should plan on letting the campaign take a radical turn, or simply end, when destiny is fulfilled.

Working out a good Destiny – and making sure it comes to pass – requires considerable ingenuity on the part of the GM. Before you decide on a Destiny, be sure that it won't drag the campaign off the rails.

If someone fulfills his Destiny and still lives, it is over – although its repercussions might haunt him for years to come. A disadvantageous Destiny must be bought off as soon as it is fulfilled . . . although this may be automatic, if the working-out of the Destiny costs the character riches or allies worth equivalent points.

If the character does not have enough points to buy off his Destiny at the time it is fulfilled, he gains the Unluckiness disadvantage, regardless of the level of the Destiny disadvantage (or, the GM might assign a new bad Destiny to the PC). The Unluckiness can then be bought off in the normal way. No extra character points are earned for fulfilling an advantageous Destiny.

Extra Fatigue   3/point

Your fatigue is higher than normal for your ST. You can run farther and fight longer than others, and you have more power available for powering magical spells. Extra fatigue goes into a separate pool that can be used to power super-powers, psionics, extra effort or magical spells. This pool recharges at the same rate as normal fatigue, but will only begin to regain points if regular fatigue (based on ST) has been completely regained first.

Extra Hit Points
5/point

You can take more damage than a normal human of your HT. Hit points are initially equal to HT, so a character with HT 14 could buy his hit point total up to 20 for 30 points. This would be written as HT 14/20. All rolls versus HT, Contests of HT, resistances, calculation of unconsciousness and survival rolls, and anything else involving HT would still be made against his health of 14. Only damage is subtracted from 20.

If the Stun Damage Only optional rule from **GURPS Supers** is in effect, stun is based on hit points, not basic HT.

Example: If a character has HT 14/20, he would have to roll to stay alive at -14 HT (and every -5 thereafter) rather than at -20.

Favor   Variable

You saved someone's life, kept silent at the right time, or otherwise did someone a good turn. Now they owe you one.

Think of a favor as a one-shot version of the Ally, Patron, or Contact advantages. You have one of these for one time only, for each time you buy the advantage. Work out the point cost for Favor exactly as you would the parent advantage, and divide the cost by 5. Round up to the nearest full point. Any time that you wish to "collect" on the Favor, the GM rolls against the "frequency" of the advantage. If it is successful, you get what you want, within the limits of the advantage. Remove the advantage from your character sheet unless you rolled a critical success; on a critical success, your "friend" still feels indebted to you.

If the roll is failed, you couldn't reach them in time, or they couldn't comply. You still have your favor coming. You may try again in another adventure.

Favors gained in play are treated as all other advantages, and should be paid for, but the GM may also wish to include a favor as part of the general reward for a successful adventure, in addition to earned points.

Fearlessness   2 points/level

Fearlessness is a special case of Strong Will (p. 23) that only applies to Fright Checks and attempts to intimidate (see p. 246).

Example: A PC has an IQ of 13, plus 2 levels of Strong Will and 3 levels of Fearlessness. He would make regular Will rolls at 15 (13 plus 2), but his Fright Checks would be at 18 (13 plus 3 plus 2). Any attempt to intimidate him would be at a -3 – if the intimidation is handled as a Contest of Wills, both his Will and Fearlessness would help him.

Hard to Kill   5 points/level

This is a "cinematic" advantage, and the GM is free to forbid it in a realistic campaign. On the other hand, the life expectancy of an adventurer in a fully realistic campaign can be depressingly short . . .

You are incredibly difficult to kill. Each level of this advantage confers a +1 on all HT rolls made for survival. If you miss your normal HT roll, but make it with your Hard to Kill bonus added in, you *appear* dead (a successful Diagnosis roll will reveal signs of life), but will come to in the normal 1 hour per point of negative HT.

Example: Bruno has HT 12 and 4 levels of Hard to Kill. He is hit by a LAW rocket doing 30 points damage, reducing his HT to -18. This will require him to make two HT rolls to stay alive (one at -12, then one at -17).

He rolls an 11 for the first one – no problem, still alive. On the second roll, he gets a 14. This is above his regular HT (12), but below his modified HT (12 + 4 levels of Hard to Kill). He passes out, and is left for dead by his foes. Roughly a day later, he'll regain consciousness – still injured, but not dead!

Healing   25 points

This advantage is intended for nonhumans or supers; normal humans cannot have it without paying considerably more (GM's choice) for Unusual Background.

You have the ability to heal others. You must be in physical contact with the subject. On a successful Healing roll, you can restore lost HT up to half your own health. Failure costs the healer 1d of Fatigue; critical failure also causes 1d damage. The Fatigue cost of successful healing is equal to twice the hits healed.

The Healing roll is at -2 when the victim is unconscious, and -2 or worse to cure disease. It can't restore a lost limb. Freshly broken limbs should be carefully set before healing is attempted, or the healing will result in a crippled limb. Crippled limbs are restored at a -6, and each healer only gets one try at any one limb. Healing cannot bring back the dead.

It is assumed that this power works on the user's own race and on all "similar" races. In a fantasy campaign, all the warm-blooded humanoid races (elves, dwarves, orcs, halflings, etc.) would be "similar."

Special Limitation: Works on user's own race only. -20%. This is not available in a campaign where there is onlyone intelligent race.

Special enhancement: Xenohealing. The user can heal creatures quite dissimilar from himself. Examples, assuming the healer is human: "All Mammals" (+20%), "All Earthly Life" (+40%), "All Carbon-Based Life" (+60%), "Anything Alive" (+80%), "Anything Animate" (including the undead, golems, etc.) (+100%).

Infravision   15 points

This advantage is intended for nonhumans or supers; normal humans cannot have it without paying considerably more (GM's choice) for Unusual Background.

Your vision extends into the infrared portion of the spectrum, allowing you to see varying degrees of heat. You can even see in absolute darkness if the temperature is above 70 degrees. No matter what the temperature, you suffer only a -1 when fighting at night, as long as your foe is someone or something that emits heat! You get +2 to see any living beings during daylight if you are scanning an area visually.

This advantage also allows you to follow a heat trail when tracking. Add +3 to any tracking rolls if the trail is no more than an hour old. A sudden flash of heat, such as an explosion, acts as a Flash spell (see p. 163) to anyone with Infravision.

Note: Infravision can be taken in conjunction with the Blindness disadvantage. Blind creatures with Infravision always operate as though at night. They can only track if the trail is less than one hour old.

Legal Immunity   5, 10, 15 or 20 points

You are a diplomat, a cleric, a privileged noble, or otherwise outside the traditional legal structures of your society. You cannot be arrested or charged with a crime by the "temporal authorities" – that is, by the normal government. Only your "own kind" – your own church, your own government, your own social class – can imprison or judge you.

Cost of this advantage depends on how sweeping the immunity is. For 5 points, the character is not subject to temporal authority, but the rules which govern his behavior are still strict, as determined by the GM. On the other hand, if the laws that apply to the character are less strict than the temporal ones, this is a 10-point advantage. And if the character can do pretty much what he pleases as long as he doesn't injure his own nation, church or organization, that is a 15-point advantage.

For an extra 5 points, you also have "diplomatic pouch" privileges. You can send or receive mail or objects that may not be stopped or examined by the temporal authorities.

20th-century diplomats have the full 20-point version of this advantage, as Diplomatic Immunity. Many medieval noblemen, and the very rich in some countries today, have this advantage at the 15-point level. Clerics will normally have this advantage only if their churches are so powerful that they have their own religious law outside the bounds of the state. The GM determines this when a religion is created, and may simply add the cost of this advantage to the value of the religion.

Multimillionaire   25 points/level

A character with the Filthy Rich advantage can buy additional levels of Wealth, at 25 character points per level. Each level of the Multimillionaire advantage increases total wealth by a factor of ten (the first level would increase total wealth to 1,000 times the average, two levels would increase this to 10,000 times the average, and so on). For every level of Multimillionaire, the character also gets a free level of Status, to a maximum bonus of +2 over the free level already given for high Wealth (see p. 18).

Perfect Balance   15 points

This advantage is intended for nonhumans or supers; normal humans cannot have it without paying considerably more (GM's choice) for Unusual Background.

You have no problem keeping your footing, no matter how narrow the walking surface, under normal conditions. You can walk on tightropes, ledges, tree limbs or any other anchored surface without having to make a DX roll. If the surface is wet, slippery or otherwise unstable, you are at +6 on all rolls to keep your feet. In combat, you get +4 to DX on any rolls to keep your feet or avoid being knocked down. This advantage adds +1 to the Piloting, Flight and Acrobatics skills.

Unfazeable   15 points,
or more by GM fiat

Nothing surprises you – at least, nothing that's not obviously a threat. The world is full of strange things, and as long as they don't bother you, you don't bother them. You are exempt from Fright Checks, and almost no reaction modifiers affect you, either way. You treat strangers with distant courtesy, no matter *how* strange they are, as long as they're well-behaved. You will have the normal reaction penalty toward anyone who does something rude or rowdy, but you will remain civil even if you are forced to violence. Intimidation (p. 246) just does not work on you.

This advantage is incompatible with all phobias. A character with this advantage is not emotionless – he just never displays strong feelings. The stereotypical Maine Yankee or English butler has this advantage. E.g., two fellows in rocking chairs on the porch of a general store:

Ed: "What'd that little feller with them orange tentacles on his head want?"

Burt: "Just another lost summer tourist. Took a wrong turn at Mars." (Looks up at the sky.) "Looks like it's gonna rain tomorra."

Ed: "Ayuh. Looks like."

This advantage must be roleplayed fully, or the GM can declare that it has been lost. In a campaign where Fright Checks are an hourly occurrence, the GM can charge 20 or more points, or disallow the advantage.

Zeroed   10 points

As computer information networks become more comprehensive, there are many times when it is an advantage to be an unknown. You are the sand in the gears, the wrench in the works.

Whether through an accident of birth, a recordkeeping foulup, a computer crash, or something else, the authorities (and their computer systems) know nothing about you. You do not officially exist. No records of you exist in any paper or computer files at the time play begins. Thus, you are immune to most varieties of government (or corporate) enforcement or harassment.

To maintain this status, you must deal strictly in cash or commodities. Any credit or bank accounts must be blind (the account isn't keyed to an individual, but to whoever knows a certain passcode) or set up through a Temporary Identity (see p. 233).

If you are investigated by the authorities, they will at first assume that there is a computer malfunction when they can't find you. They will become increasingly concerned over the next few days as no information can be found about your life. They will then try to pick you up. If they can't find you, they're likely to shrug and give up.

But if they apprehend you, you will be in for a long-drawn-out questioning session, possibly involving truth drugs and/or torture. After all, a non-person has no civil rights! Unless you have taken the right precautions in advance, no one can prove that you are being held, as you don't officially exist!

It is possible to *become* Zeroed, but it's not easy; the national databanks are well-guarded and multiply redundant. Treat cost and difficulty as to gain an Alternate Identity (p. 233).

DISADVANTAGES

SOCIAL DISADVANTAGES

Destiny — Variable

Destiny is described above, under *Advantages,* but can also be a disadvantage. See p. 235.

Duty (Involuntary) — An extra -5 points; see p. 39

Some duties are enforced by threats, by threats to loved ones, or by exotic methods of mind control. Such a forced duty can result in difficult decisions or surprising insights for the affected character. An involuntary duty would *not* include military service by draft (although service by impressment, as practiced by the British navy of the 18th century, would qualify), nor would any other "normal" service. Only cases where life or sanity are directly at stake qualify.

For instance, if the Flying Avocado's brain was taken over by Dr. Zod's Orbital Mind Control Laser, and the hero is now being forced to rob banks, he would have an involuntary duty bonus. If a duty is involuntary, add an additional -5 points to its value.

Secret — Variable

A Secret is some aspect of your life (or your past) that you must keep hidden. Were it made public, the information could harm your reputation, ruin your career, wreck your friendships, and possibly even threaten your life!

The point value of a Secret depends on the consequences if it is revealed. The worse the results, the higher the value, as follows:

Serious Embarrassment. If this information gets around, you can forget about ever getting a promotion, getting elected, or marrying well. Alternatively, your Secret could be one that will simply attract unwelcome public attention if it is known. *-5 points.*

Utter Rejection. If your Secret is discovered, your whole life will be changed. Perhaps you would lose your job and be rejected by friends and loved ones. Perhaps you will merely be harassed by admirers, cultists, long-lost relatives, or the press. *-10 points.*

Imprisonment or Exile. If the authorities uncover your Secret, you'll have to flee, or be imprisoned for a long time (GM's discretion). *-20 points.*

Possible Death. Your Secret is so terrible that you might be executed by the authorities, lynched by a mob, or assassinated by the Mafia (or the CIA) if it were ever revealed – you would be a hunted man. *-30 points.*

If a Secret is made public, there will be an immediate negative effect, as described above, ranging from embarrassment to possible death. There is a lasting effect – you suddenly acquire new, permanent disadvantages whose point value equals *twice* that of the Secret itself! The points from these new disadvantages go first to buy off the Secret, and may then (at the GM's option only) be used to buy off other disadvantages or (rarely) to buy new advantages. Any unused points are lost, and the character's point value is reduced.

The new disadvantages acquired must be appropriate to the Secret and should be determined (with the GM's assistance) when the character is created. Most Secrets turn into Enemies, Bad Reputations and Social Stigmas. They might also reduce your Status or Wealth – going from Filthy Rich to merely Very Wealthy is effectively a -10-point disadvantage. Some Secrets could even turn into mental or physical disadvantages, though this would be rare.

Similarly, if the GM allows you to buy off old disadvantages with the new points, these too must be appropriate to the Secret. The most common disadvantages that could be bought off are Duties and Dependents.

In general, a Secret appears in a particular game session if the GM rolls a 6 or less on three dice before the adventure begins. However, *as for all other disadvantages of this type,* the GM need not feel constrained by the appearance roll – if he thinks the Secret should come into play, it does!

When a Secret appears in play, it is not automatically made public. The character must have the chance to prevent the Secret from being revealed. This may require him to cave in to blackmail or extortion, to steal the incriminating documents, or even to silence the person who knows the Secret. Regardless of the solution, however, it's only temporary – the Secret will appear again and again until it is finally bought off. Secrets may be bought off either automatically through exposure (see above) or with earned character points over the course of play.

Weirdness Magnet   -15 points

Strange and bizarre things happen to you with alarming frequency. You are the one with whom demons will stop and chat. Magic items with disturbing properties will find their way to you. The only talking dog on 20th-century Earth will come to you with his problems. Dimensional gates sealed for centuries will crack open just so that you can be bathed in the energies released . . . or perhaps the entities on the other side will invite you to tea.

Nothing lethal will happen to you, at least not immediately, and occasionally some weirdness will be beneficial. But most of the time it will be terribly, terribly inconvenient. People who understand what a weirdness magnet is (and that you are one) will react to you at -2. The exceptions will be parapsychologists and thrill-seekers, who will follow you around!

PHYSICAL DISADVANTAGES

Terminally Ill   -50/-75/-100 points

You are going to die . . . soon. This could be due to some sort of nasty disease, an unremovable explosive device embedded in the base of your skull, a potent curse, an unbreakable suicide pact, or anything else that will result in your death.

Point cost is determined by the length of time remaining. One month (or less) is worth 100 points (and you'd better work fast!). More than one month but less than one year is worth 75 points, and from one to two years is worth 50 points. More than two years is worth nothing – anyone might be hit by a truck in two years!

If the GM is running a one-shot adventure where the characters aren't going to be reused, he should disallow this disadvantage as meaningless. If, during the course of a campaign, the character acquires a "miracle cure," has himself cloned or cyborged, or anything else that extends his life past his termination date, he must buy off the disadvantage. If he doesn't have enough points to buy it off, all earned character points should go to this purpose until he does.

This disadvantage is straight out of the "existential despair" school of literature. It is best fitted either to a character whose player really intends to roleplay a doomed man, or to a character who will struggle nobly to beat his fate, right up to the last minute.

MENTAL DISADVANTAGES

Amnesia   -10/-25 points

You've lost your memory – you can't remember any of your past life, including your name. There are two levels to this disadvantage: Partial and Total.

If you have Partial Amnesia, you can see your character sheet, but the GM may reserve up to 30 points for use as he sees fit for disadvantages. Other than these secret disadvantages, you know that you can do certain things and use certain skills, but have no idea where you learned how to do them. You are likely to have enemies – and possibly friends – that you can't remember. If you turn yourself in to the police, they can perform their standard ID checks . . . but you might turn out to be a wanted criminal. Even if you're an honest citizen, finding out your name won't restore your memory! Partial Amnesia is a -10-point disadvantage.

Total Amnesia (-25 points) is much more serious. Your physical skills are unaffected, but the GM makes all rolls for you (because you have no idea what you can do until you try it!). Likewise, the GM makes all of your Mental skill rolls, but at a -2 penalty. You have no idea what advantages, disadvantages and skills you have. If a player chooses to play a character with this disadvantage, the only things he can choose when designing it are those things that can be seen in a mirror. Everything else is assigned by the GM (and the GM holds on to the original character sheet until his memory is restored)!

If you are playing a character with Total Amnesia, the GM knows what your quirks and mental disadvantages are . . . *and you don't*. So, from time to time, he will overrule your statements about what you are doing. For instance, you won't know you have the Berserk disadvantage until you go berserk.

This disadvantage can only be bought off if there is some rationale for the victim recovering his memory. Meeting an old friend, reliving some fateful event, or the ever-popular blow-to-the-head are all reasonable. In most cases, the cure will be related to the cause of the memory loss.

Compulsive Carousing   -5 to -10 points

You cannot resist the urge to party! Tavern owners know you by name; taxi drivers have helped you home so many times they can do

it blindfolded. No offer of a social drink can be refused. This is not Alcoholism, though. You don't need to drink, really, as much as you need to be convivial. You must go in search of a social gathering at least once per day, and participate for at least an hour. The number of drinks you have is determined by economics – the more money you have, the more you'll spend. This disadvantage does not go well with Miserliness, demophobia or any introverted tendencies.

If a bar you enter is empty or nearly so, you'll seek out another. If the last tavern in town has only quiet folks present, you'll attempt to liven things up. If there's a party going that you should avoid for some reason, you must make an IQ roll to keep from joining in. Roll against IQ+2 if you would have to "crash" the party (a private party – you're not invited). Once you're in, though, you'll stay at least an hour – you may make an IQ roll every hour to be able to leave. If you keep failing the roll, you stay until forcibly evicted or the party drags to an end.

You get a +1 reaction (or more if you're very entertaining – see *Carousing*, p. 63) from like-minded extroverts, and a -1 or worse from sober-minded citizens. Puritans and other extreme Calvinists react at -4! This disadvantage is worth -10 points in campaigns set entirely in areas where such religions are in power. This includes England, 1650-1659, and the early Massachusetts colony. Otherwise, it is -5 points.

Compulsive Behavior (Generosity)   -5 points

You are just too open-handed. If a beggar asks you for cash, you have to make a Will roll *not* to put your hand in your pocket; where others will give a copper, you'll give silver. You will always listen to larger requests for financial aid, if they are even remotely plausible, and you need a Will roll to avoid falling for a good hard-luck story. (If you are flat out of cash when you are asked, you will apologize profusely.) You aren't a complete sucker; you just feel guilty about being better off than others. In a society with a lot of beggars around – such as most medieval towns – your living expenses are increased by 10%.

Note that this disadvantage is incompatible with Miserliness, but may earn you a +1 Reputation with pious Buddhists, Muslims and many varieties of Christian. If you yourself are poor, the reaction bonus will be even higher.

Compulsive Behavior (Spendthrift) -5, -10, or -15 points

Cash just runs through your fingers! You enjoy being seen as a big spender, you like luxury too much, or you just find the experience of buying to be fun – or perhaps all three. You aren't necessarily inept at *making* money – you may, in fact, have become good at it from sheer necessity – but you don't *keep* it. Unlike Compulsive Generosity, you don't simply *give* your money to anyone who asks; you *buy* goods and services, usually for yourself. This advantage is not limited to rich characters in rich worlds . . . a poor farmer in a low-tech world can be a spendthrift, wasting all his money at the local excuse for a tavern.

The point value varies with the intensity of your problem. At the 5-point ("Mild") level, you are simply careless about expenses. Your living costs are 10% above the standard for your social level, and any time you haggle over a purchase, your Merchant roll is at -1 for impatience.

At the 10-point ("Serious") level, you are noticeably casual with cash; the local merchants probably love you. Your living expenses are increased by 40%, and your rolls to haggle over a purchase are at -2. Furthermore, any time anyone offers you some luxury for sale that matches any of your quirks or known interests, and the cash in your pocket is more than twice the asking price, you must make a Will roll *not* to buy.

The 15-point ("Wastrel") version of this disadvantage really makes you a menace to yourself. Your living expenses are higher by one Status level or 80% – whichever is more. You haggle at -5 to your Merchant roll, and you have to make a Will roll *not* to buy something you like and can find the cash for. You must roleplay all this to the hilt.

Note that this disadvantage is incompatible with Miserliness (in fact, it's the opposite), but *can* be combined with Greed. You grab cash with one hand and spray it around with the other!

Curious -5, -10, or -15 points

You are naturally very inquisitive. When you are presented with an interesting item or situation, you must roll vs. IQ (*not* Will) to avoid examining it, even if you *know* it will be dangerous. Good roleplayers won't try to make this roll very often . . .

This is not the curiosity that affects *all* PCs ("What's in that cave? Where did the flying saucer come from?"), but the *real* thing ("What happens if I push *this* button?").

You will push buttons, pull levers, open doors, unwrap presents, and generally do everything in your power to investigate *any* situation with which you aren't 100% familiar. And, when faced with a *real* mystery, you simply may not turn your back on it.

You will rationalize your curiosity to others who try to talk you out of it. Common Sense won't help – you know you are taking a risk, but you're curious anyway!

Extremely Curious: -10 points. All IQ rolls to avoid overinquisitiveness are made at -2.

Insatiably Curious: -15 points. All IQ rolls to avoid overinquisitiveness are made at -5.

Cursed -75 points

Like Unluckiness, but worse. When anything goes wrong for your party, it happens to you, first and worst. If something goes right, it misses you. And any time the GM feels like hosing you, he

can, and you have no complaint coming, because you are cursed. You can't buy this off just by spending points – you must determine what has cursed you and deal with it, and *then* spend the points.

Flashbacks Variable

In a stressful situation, you may experience a *flashback*. These are vivid hallucinations, full-participation replays of memories, or any other similar phenomena. The player may choose, at the time of character creation, what *type* of flashback he will experience, but the content of each episode is up to the GM. Point value is determined according to the severity of the flashback.

Flashbacks are very appropriate as results from a failed Fright Check; if you have this disadvantage, roll for a Flashback *whenever* you miss a Fright Check, *or make the Fright roll exactly,* regardless of other results. In any other situation which the GM feels is stressful, he may roll 3 dice; on a 6 or less, you have a flashback.

-5 points: The flashback lasts only 2d seconds; attendant hallucinations do not seriously impair skills (-2 on all skill rolls), and accompanying delusions are minor – the victim realizes that he's having a flashback.

-10 points: Duration is 1d *minutes;* hallucinations seriously impair skills (-5 to all skills); the delusions *seem* real.

-20 points: Duration is 3d minutes; hallucinations are so severe that they preclude all skill use; the flashback seems completely, 100% real, and can be potentially fatal, as you are receiving *no* input from the real world.

Glory Hound -15 points

This is an advanced case of Overconfidence (p. 34); a character may not have *both* Glory Hound and Overconfidence. You will *always* take time to talk to the press, pose for photographs or sign an autograph. You insist on being in the limelight – you will always take the greatest risks, create complex plans that feature your abilities, lead the charge, etc.

You get a +1 reaction (at least publicly) from the press, small children, teenagers, etc., and a -1 reaction from co-workers, fellow heroes, etc. If the glory-hounding is successful, it can lead to an improved Reputation with the general public; buy this separately during character creation, or earn it free during the course of a campaign.

Incompetence -1 point

A character may be defined as *incompetent* in any one skill, for -1 character point. He cannot learn that skill, and any attempt at default use is at an extra -4.

An Incompetence is considered a mental disadvantage, even if the skill is physical. The character is simply inept, or has a mental block against learning this type of skill. You cannot be incompetent in a single specialization; if you are incompetent with Guns, for instance, you are incompetent with every type of gun.

No character should ever be allowed more than -5 points in Incompetences.

The GM may disallow any incompetence that seems silly or abusive in his particular campaign. Likewise, the GM can allow an incompetence or two to count as quirks, if a character is already at the maximum point value allowed for disadvantages.

Jinxed -20/-40/-60 points

A Jinxed character is to bad luck as a plague-carrier is to disease. It does not affect him, but it gets everyone else around him. If you are Jinxed, anyone in your immediate vicinity suffers a -1 through -3 penalty (depending on the severity of the jinx: -20 points per -1) on any roll that the GM makes for them. They have no penalty on rolls they make themselves. Thus, there is no way for the rest of the party to be sure that a jinx is present without keeping track of failed "sure-fire" attempts over a period of time.

A jinx gets everybody, friend or foe. Ulysses was a perfect example. He was tough, clever and determined, and he survived everything thrown at him, but none of his shipmates made it. Part of his own survival was due to the fact that when he was around, things went wrong for his foes as well. Polyphemus, for example, missed some easy IQ rolls when dealing with Ulysses.

Manic-Depressive   -20 points

Your moods are on a see-saw – you bounce back and forth between bubbling enthusiasm and morose withdrawal. At the beginning of each play session, roll 1 die. On a 1-3, you are in your manic phase; a 4-6 indicates depression. Every five hours of game-time thereafter, roll 3d. A 10 or less indicates that you begin a mood swing. Over the next hour, you will shift from your current phase into its opposite. You will remain in the new phase for at least five hours (after which you again roll 3d).

In the Manic phase, you suffer from Overconfidence (see p. 34). You will be friendly, outgoing and excited about whatever it is you're doing. In the Depressive phase, the Overconfidence is replaced with Absent-Mindedness (p. 30) and Laziness (p. 34). You will not be interested in doing anything other than lying in bed, sitting in a dark room and moping, or other equally exciting pastimes. If your companions force you to do something, you will be at a -5 on all skills.

A mood swing may also be caused by an emergency; in that case, the switch is immediate. On a roll of 10 or less on 3d, you change phases. This can be good (an emergency jars you into action) or bad (a problem triggers depression and you become worthless).

No Sense of Humor   -10 points

You never get any jokes – you think everyone is earnestly serious at all times. Likewise, you never joke, and you *are* earnestly serious at all times. Others react at -2 to you in any situation where this disadvantage becomes evident.

Obsession   -5 to -15 points

Your will is fixed upon a single goal. Everything you do is intended to further this goal. This differs from Compulsive Behavior in that it is not a daily habit, but an overpowering fixation which motivates all your actions. It differs from Fanaticism in that it does not necessarily imply a single belief or system of beliefs.

To play an obsessed character, you must be able to rationalize all of his actions as an attempt to reach his goal. A Will roll is required any time the character is requested (or forced) to do something that does not further the goal.

The point cost depends on how short-term or long-term the goal is. Assassinating someone or successfully seducing a particular person would be -5 points, while larger goals like getting to a hard-to-reach place or becoming President would merit higher point values. Some obsessions may cause others to react badly; if so, an Odious Personal Habit or Delusion may also be required (the Obsession cost only covers the obsessive behavior).

If and when the goal is reached, the character must substitute a new goal or buy off the Obsession.

On the Edge   -15 points

Sometimes you don't care whether you live or die. You are not actively suicidal, but you will take unreasonable risks in the face of mortal danger. When you face a life-threatening situation (piloting a burning vehicle, staring down an entire street gang while armed only with a toothbrush), you must make a successful IQ roll before you can retreat (attempt once per turn; 14 or higher fails automatically).

Each turn that you are in combat, make an IQ roll (again, 14+ fails) to avoid making an All-Out Attack (or the near-insane, suicidal behavior of your choice). Most sensible people avoid you (-2 reaction from anyone who realizes that you're crazy). Primitives and low-lifes will mistake your disregard for your own life for bravery, giving +2 reactions.

Trademark   Variable

Many heroes and villains, especially in cinematic campaigns, have a special symbol – a Trademark that they leave at the scene of action, as a way of "signing their work." Perhaps the classic fictional example is the carved initial Z of Zorro.

No character may have more than one Trademark. Multiple actions (e.g., binding your victims with purple phone wire, painting a frog on the wall *and* wrecking every computer in the building) simply makes your Trademark more distinctive – it is *not* multiple Trademarks.

-1 point: Your Trademark takes very little time to leave and cannot be used to trace your identity; it is essentially a Quirk. A typical example is something left at the scene – a playing card, a small stuffed animal, and so on – as long as it can't be traced and takes little time.

-5 points: Your Trademark is still simple, but you *absolutely* must leave it. You cannot leave the scene until you do, even if your enemies are breaking down the door.

-10 points: As above, but leaving your Trademark increases your chances of capture – initial carving, notes, traceable clues, and so on. Leaving this sort of Trademark takes a minimum of 30 seconds. Anyone searching the crime scene and examining your Trademark receives a +2 to their Criminology roll.

-15 points: Your Trademark is so elaborate – dousing the captured thugs with a certain cologne, painting the entire crime scene pink, writing a long poem to the police – that it virtually assures your eventual capture (with this disadvantage, the GM may give clues *without* a successful Criminology roll).

Remember that a Trademark is an action separate from capturing the crooks or committing a crime. It's the particular *way* that it is done. Destroying files on a computer is not a Trademark; trashing them by substituting a "7" for each "5," is.

SKILLS

ARTISTIC SKILLS

Video Production/TL (Mental/Average)
Defaults to IQ-6
or any Performance skill -4

You are familiar with video production equipment, and can competently direct a show (TV, holovid, movie, etc.). This can be a very useful skill in a modern or post-modern campaign, letting you deal with a world of rock videos, politicians-as-performers and mass media. Note that if you're using the skill by default, technical problems with the equipment are almost a certainty, even if you roll well and know exactly what *effect* you want.

ATHLETIC SKILLS

Body Sense (Physical/Hard)　Defaults to DX-6 or Acrobatics-3

This is the ability to adjust quickly after teleporting or any similar sort of magical or psionic "instant movement." Roll at -2 if you are changing facing, -5 if you are going from vertical to horizontal or vice versa. Note that you cannot change physical *position* during a teleport – only orientation.

A successful roll allows you to act normally on your next turn. A failed roll means disorientation – no actions except defense are possible for 1 turn. A critical failure means you fall down, physically stunned.

Modifiers: +3 for Absolute Direction.

Flight (Physical/Average) Defaults to DX-4

This is the skill to use a non-technological Flight power *well*, for acrobatics, tight turns, and so on. It's the same skill, whether the flight is magical or psionic.

For a naturally winged creature, Flight skill defaults to DX rather than DX-4, but can still be improved as a normal P/A skill.

COMBAT/WEAPON SKILLS

Boxing (Physical/Average)　No default

Although not considered a martial art by the average Westerner, boxing is a scientific unarmed combat technique. Boxing falls somewhere between Brawling and Karate in terms of precision and finesse.

Boxing punches add ⅕ of the character's Boxing skill to damage. There is no similar bonus for kicks. In fact, the Boxing skill does not teach one how to kick; use DX-2 or Brawling-2 instead. Parries are ⅔ of the skill, at -3 against weapons other than thrusting attacks, and at -2 against kicks (boxing does not train to specifically defend against kicks).

Where Boxing does excel, however, is in teaching fighters how to dodge, by reading the foe's body language before a punch is thrown. Against bare-handed or thrusting attacks, a boxer gets a Dodge bonus equal to ⅛ his skill (rounding down). This Dodge bonus does not count against swinging or ranged attacks.

In a *GURPS Martial Arts* cinematic campaign, Boxers get the same extra attack bonuses as martial artists (see *GURPS Martial Arts*, p. 47). They cannot have the Trained by a Master advantage, however, so they cannot make Chambara attacks.

Note that some Asian styles have incorporated Western boxing or very similar techniques.

Cloak (Physical/Average)
Defaults to DX-5, Buckler-4 or Shield-4

This is the skill of using a cloak or cape, both offensively and defensively. Treat a cloak in close combat as if it were a shield (see sidebar, p. 114).

There are two types of cloaks used in combat: a large, heavy, hooded full-length cloak, and the smaller, light-weight, torso-length dress cloak that most supers wear as a cape.

Heavy Cloak

The heavy cloak is used as a shield; treat the defensive maneuver as a Block, figured at half cloak skill with PD 2.

The offensive maneuver with a heavy cloak is to attempt to envelop the opponent. The cloak is treated as a thrown weapon (SS 12, Acc 1, Max 2, no half damage). The maximum aiming bonus is +1. A thrown heavy cloak may be Dodged or Blocked, and Parried by a weapon of 2 lbs. or more. A heavy cloak weighs 5 lbs.

At a 1-yard range, the attacker may hold on to the heavy cloak while throwing it. If the throw misses or the defense is successful, one turn is needed to ready it again for offensive or defensive use. If the throw is successful, the attacker may attempt to pull his opponent off-balance. Roll a Quick Contest of ST; the attacker is at +2. If the defender loses the contest, he is at -2 DX the next turn. If he loses by 5 or more, he is pulled off his feet onto his knees. On a critical failure, the defender falls down. It takes a successful DX roll and one turn to remove the cloak. In the meantime, the cloak blinds the defender and prevents any attack or active defense.

Light Cloak

The light cloak is more versatile. Although it only has PD 1 when used as a shield, it can be used more creatively as an attack weapon. A light cloak weighs 2 lbs. As a weapon, it can:

　Be thrown over the opponent's head.
　Entangle the opponent's weapon or arm.
　Be snapped at the opponent's face.

Throwing the light cloak is similar to throwing the heavy cloak (same range modifiers), but it cannot be held on to, can be parried by *any* readied weapon, and requires no DX roll to remove. The opponent is blinded until he takes a turn to remove the cloak.

Entangling the opponent's weapon allows the cloak-wielder to retain his grip on the cloak. Roll a Quick Contest of the attacker's Cloak skill (minus any penalty to hit – see *Striking at Weapons*, pp. 110-111) and the defender's Weapon skill (or DX if carrying a ranged weapon). If a melee weapon is entangled, the defender must win a Contest of weapon skills before he can use his weapon again. Each such attempt counts as an action. If the cloak-user wishes to attack with another weapon, he is at -2 (in addition to any off-hand penalties) if he retains his hold on the entangling cloak. The defender may fire an entangled gun, but the shot is at an addition -6 to hit, and no aim bonuses may be taken. A successful contest of DX vs. Cloak skill is required to free a missile weapon.

Entangling the arm is a Quick Contest of Cloak-2 (the -2 is for aiming at the arm) versus the defender's DX. If the defender is holding a melee weapon in either hand, he has the opportunity to Parry the cloak before the Quick Contest. The defender must win a Contest of ST to free an entangled arm. Weapon fire from an entangled arm is treated as above.

Snapping the light cloak in the opponent's face is done at Cloak-5. If the attack is successful, the attacker may be blinded for a turn. Any defense may be used against this attack. Critical success on the Cloak skill roll does 1 point of damage to one eye (roll randomly to determine which one), blinds the opponent for 1 second and mentally stuns him. If the attacker makes the attack roll by less than 5 and the defender fails the defense roll, the defender's DX is reduced by 1 for the next turn only.

Damage to cloaks is handled by the rules in the sidebar on p. 120. A cloak (heavy or light) has DR 1, and can only be destroyed by 5 points or more of *cutting* damage (3 points for a light cloak).

Forward Observer/TL (Mental/Average) Defaults to IQ-5

This is the skill of directing fire from artillery or aircraft onto the target. It includes the use of map, compass and terrain features to locate targets and the tactical skill of matching ordnance to target for best effect.

Modifiers to the roll are -1 if no binoculars are available, -3 if no map is available, -5 for neither map nor binoculars, and -1 for each 500 yards from the target (-3 per 500 yards without binoculars). Failures miss the desired target without harming the enemy; critical failures do something embarrassing or dangerous. The very worst critical failures (GM's choice) drop the fire on the observer's own position. An Air Force trained observer has +1 to skill when directing air strikes and -1 to skill when directing artillery fire.

A more detailed treatment of air and artillery observation is found in *GURPS High-Tech,* Second Edition, pp. 79-85 and 87-90.

No-Landing Extraction (Mental/Average) Defaults to IQ-6

This is the skill of getting things from the ground into or onto flying aircraft without requiring a landing. There are several systems; they all require considerable preparation and equipment by the ground element (GM's decision or 2d hours to get everything ready for the pickup). Failures result in no pickup, or damage to the cargo or passenger (GM's decision). A critical failure always causes cargo loss, or passenger death or critical injury.

Note that it is not necessary that the person to be picked up have the No-Landing Extraction skill . . . as long as someone in the ground element *does* have that skill.

Nuclear-Biological-Chemical Warfare/TL (Mental/Average) Defaults to IQ-5

This is the ability to operate in a nuclear, biological, or chemical warfare environment with appropriate protective gear. Without this skill, one runs a considerable risk of misusing the protective gear andbeing exposed to contamination.

This skill requires access to the proper equipment; improvisations are possible (if the GM consents) but at -5 to -15. Note that even so, a person with good NBC skill is far more likely to improvise successfully; the difference between high skill, and IQ-5, will probably be the difference between life and death. However, when an improvisation is rolled, use the highest skill in the whole party.

Throwing Stick (Physical/Easy) Defaults to DX-4

This is the ability to throw a carefully-balanced and shaped throwing stick, such as a boomerang. This type of throwing stick does *not* return to the user.

A throwing stick has the following stats: swing+1 crushing damage, SS 11, Acc 2, ½ Damage range ST×6, maximum range ST×10, weight 1, minimum ST 7.

Wrestling (Physical/Average) Defaults to DX-5

This is a Western sport that can also be useful in combat. Wrestling teaches how to take down opponents, pin them and to apply some holds and locks. While not as effective as Judo, this skill gives its user an edge in Close Combat.

You can use your Wrestling skill to replace DX in Close Combat, just as for Judo. You also add ⅛ of your skill to your effective ST to attempt a Takedown or a Pin, to Grapple, to use an Arm Lock (see *GURPS Martial Arts*) or to Break Free (see p. 112). This bonus does not apply to defaults.

HOBBY SKILLS

Games (Mental/Easy) Defaults to IQ-5

In a campaign where detailed roleplaying is important, a character may also be a gamer. The Vikings and Celts, for instance, were very fond of boardgames like hnefatafl, nine men's morris, and Fox and Geese, and there have been many archaeological finds of boards and pieces. Chess reached Europe from India via Arab traders, and chess-like games are common to many cultures.

Ancient Africans played mankala, and variations of Go are found throughout Oriental history. Modern miniatures gaming dates to the 18th century, when toy soldiers were used both as a military training aid and as a social pastime.

Each game must be acquired as a separate skill. Most cultures regard an ability to play one or more games well as a worthwhile social accomplishment.

In the campaign, vast sums might be staked on a game, or a hero might be forced to game against a powerful monster or wizard, with the lives of his companions at stake. Sometimes a game might be played to settle a dispute, as a kind of bloodless duel.

MAGICAL SKILLS

Flight (Physical/Average)   Defaults to DX-4
See p. 242 under *Athletic Skills*.

Spell Throwing (Physical/Easy) Defaults to DX-3, Throwing, or Spell Throwing (other spell)-2
This is the skill used to hit a target with a missile spell after it has been created (see p. 150). All normal ranged weapon rules and modifiers apply. Each missile spell uses a different skill, except for Fireball/Explosive Fireball, which are both thrown with the Fireball Throwing skill, and Stone Missile/Ice Sphere, which are the same. Note that "throwing" is not an entirely accurate name for this skill. The missile spells fly under their own power when released, regardless of the caster's ST; the Spell Throwing skill helps the caster *direct* the missile.

OUTDOOR SKILLS

Hard-Hat Diving/TL (Mental/Average) Defaults to Scuba-2
This is the skill of diving with helmet, weights and (usually) full diving dress. Most hard-hat diving is with lines and hoses attached to a surface air supply; hard-hat equipment can be used with a rebreather or from a submarine, but these are uncommon techniques. See *GURPS High-Tech*, *Second Edition*, pp. 90-91.

Hiking (Physical/Average)   No default
This skill is based on HT, not DX. It represents training for endurance walking, hiking, marching, etc. It also includes knowledge of how best to carry a pack, how to pace yourself, and so on. Roll vs. Hiking before each half-day's march; on a successful roll, increase distance traveled (see p. 187) by 20% before calculating terrain effects. If a party is traveling together, all must make the Hiking roll in order to get the increased distance.

The GM may allow bonuses for good maps and good walking shoes, but not for terrain; effects of terrain on distance are covered on pp. 187-188.

Orienteering (Mental/Average) Defaults to IQ-5
This is the ability to locate oneself with respect to terrain (the U.S. military calls this "land navigation"). Orienteering rolls are -1 to -10 (GM's discretion) for being in an unfamiliar area. It is much harder to locate oneself in the Arctic barrens than in downtown Cleveland!

Modifiers: Orienteering rolls are +1 for an accurate map, a compass or clear view of the sun or stars and at least one hour to make observations (these bonuses are not cumulative).

PROFESSIONAL SKILLS

Nuclear-Biological-Chemical Warfare/TL (Mental/Average)   Defaults to IQ-5
See p. 243 under *Combat/Weapon Skills*.

Video Production/TL (Mental/Average) Defaults to IQ-6 or any Performance Skill -4
See p. 242 under *Artistic Skills*.

PSIONIC SKILLS

Mind Block (Mental/Average) Defaults to Will-4
Although listed under Psionic Skills for organizational purposes, this skill does *not* require psionic ability. Mind Block is the technique of creating a non-psionic mental block to prevent psis from listening in on thoughts or emotions with Telereceive or Emotion Sense skills (only).

An example of a mental block might be doing complicated mathematical calculations, or repeating poetry over and over again. Anyone can do this for a short time (roll vs. IQ or Will+4), but maintaining a deliberate mental block while doing something else, under stress, or for more than a minute, requires skill.

The GM may require a Mind Block roll whenever a question arises about whether someone is or is not thinking about something important. This procedure is useful even for those who don't have the skill – roll against the default value. A new roll may be required each minute that the person does nothing, or each turn in combat or stressful situations (e.g., when someone is *trying* hard not to think about something that concerns him a lot).

If this skill is used, roll a Contest of Skills between Mind Block and Telereceive, once per minute. This is separate from any other roll required to make the skill work or to get through a Mind Shield. If the subject wins, the peeper will get nothing but poetry or the multiplication tables. If he loses, he is not successfully blocking.

A successful Telereceive will discover part or all of whatever he is thinking.

If the Mind Blocker rolls a critical failure, *he thought about it* – in detail – right there in the forefront of his mind!

If someone is doing *nothing* but concentrating on blocking, he gets a +2. Someone who is mentally or physically stunned rolls at -3. Rolls to hide *emotions* rather than thoughts are harder, and should be made at -2 or more depending on how strong the GM rules the emotions are. GMs may impose additional penalties for other circumstances, e.g., trying to mind block your emotions while sneaking up on your most hated enemy.

Flight (Physical/Average) Defaults to DX-4
See p. 242 under *Athletic Skills*.

SCIENTIFIC SKILLS

Computer Hacking/TL (Mental/Very Hard) Defaults to Computer Operation-8 or Computer Programming-4
This skill is used to "hack" into a computer system. No cyberdeck is needed – only a regular terminal with access to the system (whether directly or through a communications network). However, the skill *can* be used in conjunction with a cyberdeck, in campaigns where such equipment is available. See Chapter 4 of **GURPS Cyberpunk** for more details.

Cryptanalysis/TL (Mental/Hard)   Special default; see below
This skill allows one to invent and break codes. It may be used in wartime, in espionage, or simply in high-stakes business dealings. It can involve anything from state-of-the-art tactical encryption systems to unsophisticated ciphers.

There is no default when dealing with modern high-tech encryption, but pre-20th-century ciphers were much simpler. Even in present-day and future campaigns, simple ciphers can be encountered. Terrorists seldom have access to good encoding equipment. And professional spies often lack the equipment and training of modern cryptanalysis. Therefore, agents may encounter the same symbol codes, substitution ciphers and other basic deceptions used throughout history. When using these simple codes, characters may attempt default rolls, to Mathematics-3 or IQ-5. Alternatively, the GM can actually hand out coded messages and let the players try to solve them.

Cryptanalysts may also attempt to devise codes and ciphers of their own. When they create a hasty cipher, note the amount by which they succeed on their Cryptanalysis roll. This equals the penalty applied to rolls by enemy cryptanalysts trying to read the message. By rolling at a -2 penalty to Cryptanalysis, one can try to devise a code that appears to be innocent conversation, thereby avoiding attention from eavesdroppers.

Those with access to a computer gain a bonus of from +1 to +5 when using cryptology. A home computer confers +1, a mini-computer confers +2, a mainframe confers +3 or +4 and a supercomputer offers a +5. One must have a trained programmer or a Computer Operations skill of 15+ to effectively use a computer in cryptanalysis. Appropriate software is also required.

When decoding, a sample of the code (with translation) gives a +5. If the message to be decoded is shorter than 25 words, roll at -5. Anyone with the Mathematical Ability advantage may apply it to Cryptanalysis rolls.

Cryptanalytical training requires a Top Secret/Special Compartmentalized Intelligence Clearance in the U.S., and similar clearance in other armies. Therefore, those whose disadvantages pose a security risk may not learn this skill through normal channels. Furthermore, agents with this skill become targets for enemy spies. Superiors may be quite reluctant to let a trained cryptanalyst go on risky missions. But spies and criminals may find their way around the restrictions. A spy agency with powerful connections might arrange to have some of its members trained through unofficial channels. Foreign cryptographers may find themselves forced into spying by defection.

Planetology/TL (Mental/Average) Defaults to IQ-5, Geology-4, Meteorology-4, other Planetology-3
This Scientific skill is the overall study of planetary makeup and conditions – geological, meteorological, climatic, atmospheric, hydrographic and ecologic – of one general planetary type. Pick one skill:

Rock/Ice Worlds: Mercury, Pluto types (also most moons, asteroids and other small, airless planets).

Earthlike: Essentially, all habitable worlds.

Hostile Terrestrial: Titan types.

Gas Giants: Jupiter, Uranus types.

Planetology can be used in place of several other skills. Geology and Meteorology default to it at -3; Botany, Ecology, and Zoology at -4; Survival in that world's major terrain(s) at -5. For detailed information about a world, consult an expert in the pertinent scientific skill – Geology, Meteorology and so on. GM may assess penalties for worlds that differ greatly from the norm for their type.

Philosophy (Mental/Hard) Defaults to IQ-6
This is the study of a body of beliefs similar to Theology (p. 62). Each different philosophy is a specialization. A student of philosophy does not necessarily believe in the principles he studies, or, if he believes, does not necessarily think they are divinely ordained. The beliefs of Philosophy are not necessarily related to a religious or supernatural concept.

This skill is particularly appropriate for a martial-arts campaign in which the character knows combat skills with different (and even antagonistic) spiritual teachings; by adopting both schools' *philosophical* teachings, they may be combined without conflict (note that in Asia many people combine opposing religions matter-of-factly, despite blatant contradictions between them).

If, during an adventure, a philosophical PC is dubious about the rightness of a course of action, the GM should let him roll against his Theology or Philosophy (Buddhism, Shinto, Taoism or other specialized religion). On a successful roll, and depending on how good the roll was, the GM can "enlighten" the PC, if possible with a clever phrase or even a parable. The GM should not tell the player what to do, but should instead indicate to him how a person with the character's background would feel.

A successful Philosophy roll can also be used to predict the behavior of other characters who are ruled by that philosophy.

Xenobiology/TL (Mental/Average)
No default

This is the overall study of life of all kinds, native to any one general planetary type. Pick one skill:

Terrestrial: Earthlike planets.
Hostile Terrestrial: Titan types.
Gas Giants: Jupiter, Uranus types.

Xenobiology can be used in place of several other skills. Zoology, Ecology and Botany default to it at -3; Genetics, Biochemistry and Physiology at -4. For detailed information about a life form, consult an expert in the pertinent biological skill. GM may assess penalties for worlds that differ greatly from the norm for their type.

Xenology/TL (Mental/Hard)
Defaults to IQ-6

This is an overall knowledge of the major alien races in the known universe, their cultures, lifestyles, mores, societies and psychology. It identifies an alien's race, and gives information about its culture, physical makeup, attributes and possible behavior patterns once identified; it provides *very basic* information about aliens of new races. It would also be useful in a fantasy campaign in which the world is largely unknown and contains dozens of different races.

A successful Xenology roll is required before use of Diplomacy with aliens; for very alien races, even Merchant, Tactics, etc., will be different and will require a Xenology roll first. If the Xenology roll fails, the actual skill being attempted is at a -4.

Modifiers: +1 or more for familiar races; -1 to -6 for "very alien" races. Difficult questions should carry an appropriate penalty. Prolonged observation should give a bonus, especially for new races. A xenologist may specialize in a particular alien race, getting a +5 on rolls for that race and a -1 on all others.

"Depth" of a xenologist's knowledge will also depend on the number of races known to science: -1 for 5-10 races, -2 for 11-50, -3 for 51-100, -4 for more than 100. This applies only to remembering facts about an already-known race. When contacting new races, experience with a wide variety of aliens is an advantage: +1 if 11-50 races are already known, +2 if more than 50 are known.

SOCIAL SKILLS

Intimidation (Mental/Average)
Defaults to ST-5 or Acting-3

This is the skill of hostile persuasion. The essence of intimidation is to convince the subject that you are able and willing, and perhaps eager, to do something awful to him.

Intimidation may be substituted for a reaction roll in any situation, though it is at a -3 penalty when used in a request for aid. A successful Intimidation roll gives a Good (though usually not friendly) reaction. A failed roll gives a Bad reaction. On a critical success, the subject must make a Fright Check at -10!

The exact result of a successful roll depends on the target. An honest citizen will probably cooperate, sullenly or with false cheer. A low-life may lick your boots (even becoming genuinely loyal). A really tough sort may not be frightened, but may react well anyway: "You're my kind of scum!" The GM decides, and roleplays it.

When Intimidation is used against a PC (or, at the GM's option, against an NPC), this can also be rolled as a Contest of Intimidation skill vs. Will. See *Influence Rolls,* sidebar, p. 93.

Modifiers: Up to +2 for displays of strength or bloodthirstiness, or +3 for superhuman strength or inhuman bloodthirstiness. The GM may give a further +1 bonus for witty or frightening dialogue, but should apply a penalty if the attempt is clumsy or inappropriate. The GM may apply *any* level of penalty if the PCs are attempting to intimidate somebody who, in his opinion, just can't be intimidated. This includes anyone with the Unfazeable advantage (p. 237).

Specious intimidation: If the PC can make both a Fast-Talk and an Intimidation roll, and roleplays it well, he can appear to be intimidating even when he can't back it up. This is the only way to intimidate some people (martial-arts masters, world leaders, bellicose drunks). Success on both rolls gives a Very Good reaction. Success on one and failure on the other gives a Poor reaction. Failure on both gives a Very Bad reaction.

Note that Interrogation skill can default to Intimidation-3. It will not help you tell a good answer from a bad one, but it can get people to talk.

THIEF/SPY SKILLS

Computer Hacking/TL (Mental/Very Hard)
Defaults to Computer Operation-8 or
Computer Programming-4
See p. 245 under *Scientific Skills*.

Cryptanalysis/TL (Mental/Hard)No default
See p. 245 under *Scientific Skills*.

Intimidation (Mental/Average)
Defaults to ST-5 or Acting-3
See p. 246 under *Social Skills*.

No-Landing Extraction (Mental/Average)
Defaults to IQ-6
See p. 243 under *Combat/Weapon Skills*.

VEHICLE SKILLS

Exoskeleton/TL (Physical/Avg.) Defaults to
IQ-6, DX-6 or Battlesuit-2
This is the ability to use powered exoskeletons, from the personal, nonaugmenting walkers that enable humans to move in very high gravity (see **GURPS Space**) to the large cargo exoskeletons that take the place of forklifts in high-tech societies. Unfamiliar units are operated at a penalty, as in Driving skill (p. 68).

For any ordinary DX roll, an exo wearer rolls on the lower of Exoskeleton skill or DX. For DX-based skills, he rolls on the lower of (skill-1) or (Exoskeleton-1). The GM may assess penalties for actions that should be especially difficult in a suit, such as Acrobatics. However, most exoskeletons (or "exosuits") have removable gauntlets so the wearer can do delicate work.

OTHER RULES

POWER CELLS

At tech level 8 and above, most equipment runs on standardized *power cells*. Their technology is up to the GM. The costs and times given below assume that power cells use plutonium, antimatter, or something equally esoteric, can't be recharged, and can't be discharged quickly enough to explode. Assume that a cell will store indefinitely if not in use, and is good for two years of continuous use unless otherwise specified.

Cells might also be simple high-capacity storage batteries. In that case, they last only half as long, but can be recharged at any power plant, including that of a spaceship, in about a day. And they *might* explode if short-circuited . . .

Power cells are heavy for their size. The consequences of breaking a cell depend on what is in it; the more destructive the contents, the harder they are to break. Antimatter or plutonium cells will *not* be fragile.

Types of Cells

There are six sizes of power cells, designated by letter from AA (the smallest) to E (the largest). Power cells increase in power exponentially. An A cell is ten times as powerful as an AA cell, a B cell has ten times the power of an A cell, and so on.

AA cell: This cell is a disk the size of a pinhead, 1/16" in diameter and 1/32" thick. AA cells are used in brain implants, calculators, etc. They cost $2; 500 AA cells weigh 1 ounce.

A cell: An A cell is a cylinder 1/4" in diameter and 1/8" tall. They are used to power small radios and similar devices. An A cell costs $10; 25 weigh 1 ounce.

B cell: B cells are cylinders 1/2" in diameter and 1/2" tall. They are used to power various sorts of hand-held equipment, including small weapons. B cells cost $30; 20 weigh 1 pound.

C cell: This is a 1" diameter by 2" tall cylinder. C cells are the most common power source for personal weapons, tools and equipment. C cells cost $100 and weigh 1/2 pound each.

D cell: A D cell is a cylinder 2" in diameter and 4" tall. D cells power military weapons and heavy equipment. Each D cell costs $500 and weighs 5 pounds.

E cell: Each E cell is a cylinder 4" in diameter and 6" tall. E cells power vehicles, support weapons and other power-intensive systems. An E cell costs $2,000 and weighs 20 pounds. Large vehicles, etc., may use banks of dozens of E cells.

Replacing Power Cells

It takes three seconds to replace an A, B, C or D cell with a new one, or six seconds to replace a tiny AA or large E cell. Speed-Load (Power Cell) skill (see p. B52) applies to B and C cells being reloaded into weapons. Successful use of this skill reduces the time to one second. Life-support systems, and other items that cannot afford power interruptions, have two or more cells, so that if one is drained another takes over immediately. They are also usually equipped with a warning system to notify the user that one cell has been expended.. This allows a vehicle's cell to be changed in flight, or a robot to change its own cells.

Jury-Rigging

In an emergency, wrong-sized cells can be used. This requires an Electronics-2 roll and 3d+10 minutes of work; a failure means the gadget doesn't work, and a critical failure damages the gadget. A larger cell can be substituted for a smaller, lasting no more than twice as long. A set of 10 smaller cells can be substituted for the next larger size, usually lasting only a short time (details are up to the GM, depending on the Electronics skill of the tinkerer; on a good roll, the GM warns the technician what to expect from his jury-rig).

The GM may also rule that different star systems or nations use different voltages or sizes for their power cells. This means an Electronics roll, of difficulty set by the GM, will be required to use your own power cells in strange equipment or vice versa.

VITAL ORGANS

These are optional rules for players who want more detail in combat. Certain parts of the body are more susceptible to damage than others. Below are the effects of successful attacks on them, in addition to normal damage effects.

Groin

The groin is area 11 on the Parts of the Body Table on p. 203 and 211. It has a -3 penalty to hit; a miss by 1 hits the body or the leg (roll a die). On human males, this is excruciatingly painful; on a hit, the target must make a HT roll, at -1 for every point of damage, or be physically stunned. If an unmodified HT roll is missed, the victim falls unconscious (see p. 127). High Pain Threshold gives a +5 to the roll. Low Pain Threshold *doubles* the penalties.

Jaw

The jaw is at -6 to hit; if the attack misses by 1, the face is hit. The victim must roll against HT-2 or HT minus damage taken (whichever is *less*) or be physically stunned.

Kidneys

The kidneys can only be targeted on an attack to the victim's back. They are at -4 to hit (Hit Location-1); a miss by 1 indicates a hit to the body. Crushing attacks do 1.5× damage; other types do damage like an ordinary hit to the vitals (see p. 203).

Nose

The nose is targeted at Skill-6; missing by 1 hits the face. Movies and pulp novels to the contrary, it is almost impossible to kill a person by driving nose splinters into the brain. A blow to the nose is extremely painful, however. The victim must make a HT-1 roll (HT+4 if he has High Pain Threshold, -1 per point of damage if he has Low Pain Threshold) or be physically stunned.

Throat

Attacks on the neck can be lethal. The throat is at -5 to hit; a miss by 1 hits the body. Crushing attacks do 1.5× damage; cutting and impaling attacks both do double damage. The victim is stunned if he takes total hits over 1/3 HT to the neck. If the neck takes full hit point damage from an edged weapon, a successful HT roll is necessary to avoid decapitation!

SUPER-STRENGTH

Even outside the *Supers* genre, some characters – and a lot of monsters! – have superhuman strength.

This table shows the basic damage done by strengths above 20.

ST	Thrust	Swing	ST	Thrust	Swing
21	2d	4d-1	39	4d+1	7d-1
22	2d	4d	40	4d+1	7d-1
23	2d+1	4d+1	45	5d	7d+1
24	2d+1	4d+2	50	5d+2	8d-1
25	2d+2	5d-1	55	6d	8d+1
26	2d+2	5d	60	7d-1	9d
27	3d-1	5d+1	65	7d+1	9d+2
28	3d-1	5d+1	70	8d	10d
29	3d	5d+2	75	8d+2	10d+2
30	3d	5d+2	80	9d	11d
31	3d+1	6d-1	85	9d+2	11d+2
32	3d+1	6d-1	90	10d	12d
33	3d+2	6d	95	10d+2	12d+2
34	3d+2	6d	100	11d	13d
35	4d-1	6d+1	110	12d	14d
36	4d-1	6d+1	120	13d	15d
37	4d	6d+2	and so on: +1d for each full
38	4d	6d+2	10 points of added ST.

Example 1: You have ST 14 and need to throw a 120-lb. body over a 6' pit. Divide 120/14 = 8.571. Looking at the Ratio column, this rounds up to 10.000. The Distance Modifier is .1×.

.1 × 14 = 1.4 yards. Oooops. The body just hit the bottom of the pit.

Example 2: You have ST 80 and want to throw a 50-lb. bag of cement at a foe. 50/80 = .625 which rounds up to .750. The multiplier is 1.0×, so you could throw the bag 1.0 × 80 = 80 yards. Thunk.

Throwing Damage Table

Object Weight	Damage
Less than 2 lbs.	thrust-2 per die
2 lbs. to 5 lbs.	thrust-1 per die
5 lbs. to ST lbs.	thrust
ST to 3×ST lbs.	thrust+1 per die
3×ST to 7×ST lbs.	thrust
7×ST to 11×ST lbs.	thrust-1/2 per die
Over 11×ST lbs.	thrust-1 per die

Example 1: You hit your foe with that 50-lb. bag of cement thrown with your ST 80. It is between 5 lbs. and (your ST) lbs. As shown on the table above, it does straight thrust damage. Now check the table in the column to the left (or refer to your character sheet!). Thrust damage for ST 80 is 9d damage, so you do 9 dice with the cement bag.

Example 2: You throw a 750-lb. motorcycle with your ST 80. On the table above, 750 lbs. is between 7 and 11 times your ST, so it does (thrust-1/2 per die) damage. You would do 9d minus 4.5 damage with it, which rounds to 9d-4. The motorcycle actually does less damage than the bag of cement; it's too heavy for you to throw with your maximum effectiveness.

Throwing Distance Table

Ratio	Distance Modifier	Ratio	Distance Modifier
.100	3.5×	2.000	0.6×
.125	3.0×	2.500	0.5×
.200	2.5×	3.000	0.4×
.300	1.9×	4.000	0.3×
.400	1.5×	5.000	0.25×
.500	1.2×	6.000	0.2×
.750	1.0×	8.000	0.15×
1.000	0.8×	10.000	0.1×
1.500	0.7×	20.000+	.05×

SOCIETY CONTROL RATINGS

The Control Rating (CR) is a general measure of the control which a government exercises. The lower the CR, the more freedom the people have and the less restrictive the government is. Government type does not *absolutely* determine CR; it is possible (and interesting) to have a very free monarchy, or an Athenian democracy where the voters have saddled themselves with thousands of strict rules. The GM can assign the CR as he pleases, or just roll 1 die.

CR also affects what weapons can be carried (see below), but especially violent or nonviolent societies will have a separate, modified CR for weapon laws.

If any question of legality arises, or to determine how severely the government will check and harass newcomers, roll 1 die. If the result is lower than the CR, the act is illegal or the PCs are harassed, delayed or even arrested. If it is higher, they escape trouble, either because the act is legal or the authorities overlook it. If the CR is rolled exactly, the situation could go either way; play out an encounter or make a reaction roll.

Control Ratings are as follows:

0. Anarchy. There are no laws or taxes.

1. Very free. Nothing is illegal except (perhaps) use of force or intimidation against other citizens. Ownership of all but military weapons is unrestricted. Taxes are light or voluntary.

2. Free. Some laws exist; most benefit the individual. Hunting weaponry is legal. Taxes are light.

3. Moderate. There are many laws, but most benefit the individual. Hunting weaponry is allowed by registration. Taxes are moderate and fair.

4. Controlled. Many laws exist; most are for the convenience of the state. Only light weaponry may be owned, and licenses are required. Broadcast communications are regulated; private broadcasts (like CB) and printing may be restricted. Taxation is often heavy and sometimes unfair.

5. Repressive. There are many laws and regulations, strictly enforced. Taxation is heavy and often unfair. What civilian weapons are allowed are strictly controlled and licensed and may not be carried in public. There is strict regulation of home computers, photocopiers, broadcasters and other means of information distribution and access.

6. Total control. Laws are numerous and complex. Taxation is crushing, taking most of an ordinary citizen's income. Censorship is common. The individual exists to serve the state. Private ownership of weaponry, broadcasting or duplication equipment is prohibited. The death penalty is common for offenses, and trials – if conducted at all – are a mockery.

Weapon Legality

Some cultures are very permissive about weapons; others regulate them tightly. Adventurers entering a new society often ask, "What weapons can we carry?" If they *don't* ask that, they may be in for a surprise.

Each weapon has a *Legality* class. In general, the more lethal the weapon, the lower the Legality.

Class 6: Wholly nonlethal items, like short-range stunners.

Class 5: More powerful nonlethal weapons, like stun rifles, and low-tech armor.

Class 4: Hunting weapons, like single-shot laser rifles. Knives and other low-tech weapons.

Class 3: Light concealable weapons, like most pistols, and light body armor.

Class 2: Medium weapons, such as single-shot elephant guns or disruptors.

Class 1: Military hand weapons like automatic rifles.

Class 0: Heavy personal weapons like hand grenades, and squad-level military weapons.

The class of weapons and armor that will be *legal* in any given locale will generally depend on the local government's Control Rating (see above). However, effective Control Rating for weaponry may be reduced in some societies (e.g., 20th-century USA) where the citizens insist on the right to bear arms. It may be increased in others (e.g., 20th-century England, where the cop on the beat isn't allowed a gun). The effective CR determines who will be allowed to have what kind of weapon. A very violent society may have a *negative* CR with respect to weapons!

Note also that airline or starship passengers aren't likely to be permitted any weapons at all.

Legality = CR+2 or more: Any citizen may carry the item.

Legality = CR+1: May be carried by anyone except a convicted criminal or the equivalent. Registration is required, but there is no permit fee.

Legality = CR: A license is required to own or carry the item. To get a license, one must show a legitimate need. Generally, a license costs 1d×10% of the price of the item itself.

Legality = CR-1: Prohibited except to government agents, police, and bonded security troops.

Legality = CR-2: Prohibited except to police SWAT teams, military units, and perhaps secret intelligence agencies.

Legality = CR-3 or worse: Only permitted to the military.

So, for instance, in a futuristic society with Control Rating 4, anybody could carry a stun pistol (Legality 6); registration would be required for a stun rifle (Legality 5); permits would be required for hunting weapons (Legality 4); and ordinary citizens could own nothing heavier.

GLOSSARY

Most of these terms will be familiar to roleplaying gamers. In some cases, *GURPS* introduces a new term, or uses a familiar one in a slightly different way. Most definitions are followed by a page reference for a more complete explanation.

For a glossary of magic terms, see p. 148.

For a glossary of psi terms, see p. 168.

AC: See "adversary character."

active defense: An action (dodging, blocking or parrying) that defends against an attack, but requires special effort on the part of the defender. *Pp. 98, 108.*

advantage: An inborn ability; something a character is created with. *P. 19.*

adventure: The basic "unit" of play in a roleplaying game. A roleplaying game is never over until the players want to end it, but a single adventure will have a beginning and an end. It may last through several sessions of play, or be finished in a single day. An adventure may be a published booklet, or it may be created by the GM. *P. 8.*

adversary character: Any character played by the Adversary. *P. 180.*

Adversary: An "assistant GM" who plays the "enemy" characters. The Adversary knows only as much about the game world and the player characters as the GM tells him. Therefore, the players are not at an unfair disadvantage when fighting him, as they might be if the GM controlled the enemies. *P. 180.*

attack roll: A success roll made against your weapon skill, to see if you can use it well enough to hit the foe. *Pp. 97, 108.*

attributes: The most basic statistics that describe a character. In *GURPS*, the attributes are Strength, Dexterity, Intelligence and Health. A score of 10 in each attribute represents "average" for humans; higher is better. *P. 13.*

block: Use of a shield as an active defense. *Pp. 98, 108.*

buy off: To pay character points, earned during play, to get rid of a disadvantage that your character started with. *Pp. 26, 82.*

campaign: A continuing series of adventures. A campaign will usually have a continuing cast of player characters, and the same GM (or team of GMs). A campaign may move from one game world to another, with a logical reason ("We found this time machine, and the next thing we knew, we were in 1492.") *Pp. 177, 199.*

character: Any being (person, animal, etc.) played by the GM, Adversary or a player in a roleplaying game. *P. 10.*

character points: The points used to buy attributes, skills, etc., when creating a character. Extra character points can be used to buy off disadvantages or to increase characters' skills, wealth or attributes. *Pp. 9, 10.*

character sheet: A written description (possibly including a picture) of a character. Only important characters are worth a full character sheet; less-important characters can be described by a few statistics on an index card. *Pp. 12, 78-80.*

character story: A character's background; the fictional history of the character's whole life, invented by the person playing that character. *P. 80.*

close combat: Combat between characters in the same hex (not used in the Basic Combat System). Unarmed combat (fists, judo or karate) is not necessarily "close," because the fighters do not have to be in the same hex. *Pp. 111-114.*

combat map: A map used as a gameboard for combat. See "room map." *P. 178.*

contest of skill: A competition between two characters in which each tries to make his success roll, to see who wins a fight, argument, etc. *P. 87.*

Control Rating (CR): A general measure of control which the government exercises. *P. 249.*

cripple: To hit a foe on the hand, foot, arm or leg and do enough damage that the limb cannot be used. This may be temporary or permanent. *Pp. 110, 127.*

critical failure: A skill roll missed so badly that something disastrous happens to the character who tried the roll. *P. 86.*

critical hit: A blow so well struck that the foe does not get to make a defense roll. It may also do special and unusual damage — e.g., a broken arm, a broken weapon or instant unconsciousness. *Pp. 86, 202.*

critical miss: An attack which fails so badly that the attacker is hurt, drops his weapon, etc. *Pp. 86, 202.*

critical success: A skill roll which succeeds so well that the character has an extra or unusual degree of success. *P. 86.*

damage: The *amount* and *type* of injury a weapon causes. *Pp. 9, 73.*

damage amount: The effectiveness of a weapon. The better a weapon is, the higher its damage number will be. Damage is measured in "dice plus adds." For a "3d+2" weapon, roll 3 dice and add 2 to the total. *Pp. 9, 74.*

damage roll: A die roll made to see how much injury you do when you hit with your weapon. *P. 9.*

damage type: The *kind* of injury (crushing, cutting or impaling) a weapon causes. *P. 74.*

default: If a character has no training in a skill, but tries to use that skill anyway, a "default" roll is made instead of a regular success roll. This default roll may be to some other skill, or to one of the character's four basic attributes. For example, Lock-picking "defaults" to IQ-5. If you have never studied Lockpicking, your skill equals your IQ score, minus 5. *Pp. 44-46.*

defense roll: A die roll made after your foe's *attack* roll succeeds, to see if you can avoid being hit. *P. 98.*

dependent: An NPC for whom your character is responsible in some way. *P. 38.*

Dexterity (DX): A measure of a character's agility and coordination. *P. 13.*

disadvantage: An inborn handicap, something a character is created with. A character may also acquire a disadvantage by being injured during play. *P. 26.*

dodge: The "active defense" of ducking or evading an attack. *Pp. 98, 108.*

DR: Damage Resistance. The DR of your skin and/or armor are subtracted from the damage you take from a blow. *P. 71.*

dungeon: An underground fantasy game world. *P. 196.*

DX: Dexterity (see above).

effective skill: Your basic score in a given skill, modified (up or down) for a particular situation. *P. 86.*

encounter: One "scene" of an adventure. A meeting between the PCs and one or more animals, monsters or NPCs. *P. 198.*

encumbrance: The weight of all objects carried by a character. The greater the encumbrance, the slower your movement will be. *Pp. 76-77.*

enemy: An NPC, created when a character is created, as that character's particular foe and antagonist. *P. 39.*

fatigue: Points marked off your ST due to exhaustion in the same way that "hits" (below) are marked off your HT. *P. 134.*

Fright Check: A Will roll (see below) made specifically to see how a character reacts to a frightening situation. *Pp. 93, 94.*

Game Master: The referee, who chooses the adventure, talks the players through it, judges the results, and gives out character points. *P. 177.*

game time: Time that passes in the game world. *P. 183.*

game world: A background for play; the setting for a game adventure. The Civil War, a GM's own fantasy creation, or a science-fiction novel could each provide a "game world." *GURPS* is designed to work in any game world, and to allow characters to move from one game world to another. *Pp. 6, 185-195, 200.*

GM: See "Game Master."

hand weapon: A weapon that strikes the foe directly — not thrown, or used to fire a missile. Opposite of "ranged weapon."

Health (HT): A measure of a character's energy and vitality. *P. 13.*

hex: A hexagonal space on a game map. Different maps have different scales. A hex on the combat map is one yard across. *Pp. 7, 177-178.*

hireling: An NPC who is a member of the party. The players can give the hireling orders, but the hireling remains the GM's character, and the GM always has the last word on what the hireling decides to do in a pinch. *Pp. 194-195.*

hits: A measure of damage taken by a character or object. The more damage something (or someone) incurs, the more "hits" it takes. Each hit subtracts 1 from your HT until it is healed. *P. 13.*

HT: Health (see above).

influence roll: A skill-vs.-IQ contest made to see if a character (PC or NPC) is affected by any of several skills intended to influence others, such as Fast-Talk and Sex Appeal. Reaction modifiers always apply to influence rolls. *P. 93.*

initiative: In combat, the side that "has the initiative" may act first. Initiative is gained by surprising the foe, or by thinking more quickly. *P. 122.*

Intelligence (IQ): A measure of a character's brainpower, alertness and adaptability. *P. 13.*

IQ: Intelligence (see above).

magery (magical aptitude): Special talent for magic. *P. 21.*

maneuver: One of ten possible "moves" a character can choose in combat. A maneuver may consist of a movement, an attack or defense, some other action, or a combination. *Pp. 95, 105.*

modifier: A number that is added or subtracted to a success roll or attribute roll, in order to allow for a specific situation. *P. 86.*

morale check: A reaction roll, made during combat, to see whether NPCs will continue to fight in the face of discouraging events such as the death of their leader. *Pp. 204-205.*

Move: A score, computed from Speed and Encumbrance, that tells how fast you can move in combat, in hexes (yards) per turn (second). *P. 77.*

non-player character: Any character played by the GM. An "adversary character" is a special type of NPC. *P. 179.*

NPC: See "non-player character."

opportunity fire: A pre-planned attack (or other action) made "out of turn," as soon as a target presents itself. *P. 104.*

parry: Use of your weapon as an active defense to ward off an attack. *Pp. 99, 108.*

party: A group of PCs taking part in the adventure.

passive defense: A defensive factor (like armor) that wards off blows, giving protection with no effort on the character's part. This is not the same as damage resistance. Passive defense makes it less likely that you will be hit; damage resistance protects you if you *are* hit. *Pp. 71-72.*

patron: An NPC who employs, watches over and/or commands your character. *P. 24.*

PC: See "player character."

PD: See "passive defense."

player character: Any character created and played by one of the players, as opposed to an "NPC" — a character played by the GM or Adversary. *P. 10.*

prerequisite: A skill or spell which a character *must* know at level 12 or higher in order to take some other skill or spell. For instance, the Chemistry skill is a prerequisite for the Biochemistry skill. *P. 43.*

programmed adventure: One in which the player(s) use a book of numbered paragraphs to play. Reading about a situation in one paragraph, they make decisions which send them to one of several numbered choices. See "solo."

quirk: A minor (1-point) disadvantage taken to flesh out a character and improve roleplaying. Not necessarily a "real" disadvantage at all. "Likes children" and "Hates children" would both be permissible quirks. *P. 41.*

ranged weapon: A thrown or missile weapon; a weapon used at a distance. *Pp. 100, 114.*

reach: The distance at which a hand weapon can strike — from "close" (same hex only) to 3 (or occasionally more) hexes. Reach is governed by a weapon's length. *P. 102.*

reaction modifier: A penalty or bonus to all reaction rolls (see below). If a character has a reaction bonus, he is especially likeable. A reaction penalty means a character is unattractive or obnoxious. *P. 180.*

reaction roll: A die roll made by the GM to determine the NPCs' reaction to a request or proposal made by the player characters. *P. 180.*

ready weapon: The weapon your character has in hand and ready to use. You can't strike with it unless it is "ready." *Pp. 95, 97.*

real time: The time that passes in the real world, as opposed to "game time."

roleplaying game: A game in which players take on the personalities of imaginary individuals, or "characters," in a fictional or historical setting, and try to act as those characters would.

room map: A map in 50mm scale (1" = 3 feet), used to play out combats. The GM may prepare maps in advance, or draw each room as needed. Miniatures can be used on the map to show characters' locations. *P. 178.*

scenario: See "adventure."

score: A general term for an attribute or skill number. *P. 13.*

sense roll: A roll against IQ, with bonuses or penalties for Alertness or strong or weak senses, made to determine whether a character sees (or hears, or smells) something. *P. 92.*

skill: A number defining a character's ability at some specific thing. *P. 42.*

solo: A "solo" adventure is one designed to be played by one person, without a GM. It is usually, but not always, a "programmed" adventure. *P. 218.*

sourcebook: A game supplement giving background material — e.g., a collection of weapons, a collection of animals and so on.

Speed: A score computed from HT and DX, indicating how fast your character can run without encumbrance. *P. 14.*

ST: Strength (see below).

statistics: (stats) The numbers and other factors that describe a character. *P. 13.*

Strength (ST): A measure of a character's "brawn," or physical muscle. *P. 13.*

stunning: A character can be stunned by an enemy blow or by surprise. He defends at -4, and can initiate no maneuvers until he recovers. *P. 127.*

success roll: A die roll (3 six-sided dice) made when a character attempts to do something, to determine whether he succeeds. *P. 86.*

supplement: Anything designed to add to the basic *GURPS* rules; types include *adventure, sourcebook* and *worldbook.*

TL: Tech level. A number indicating a culture's level of technological development, where 0 is no technology and the present day is 7. *P. 185.*

weapon table: A listing of weapons for a particular adventure or game world, giving cost, weight, damage and other statistics for each weapon. *Pp. 206-209.*

will roll: A roll against IQ, plus or minus Strong or Weak Will if applicable, made to determine whether a character has the "willpower" to do (or not do) something. The total of IQ and Strong/Weak Will is also called "Will." *P. 93.*

worldbook: A game supplement which gives a detailed background for a particular game world, and gives rules for the special situations, abilities, hazards, rewards, etc., found there.

INDEX

INSTANT CHARACTERS

This quick reference sheet will allow fast creation of characters by players who are already familiar with the system. For details, refer back to Chapters 1-9. See also the diagram on p. 12.

Starting Point Total

The starting character points depend on your campaign. 100 points is the usual starting amount for a heroic character. A "normal" would be about 25.

Selection of Attributes

An attribute score of 10 represents the general adult human average. For children under 16, see p. 14.

Level	Point Cost	Level	Point Cost	Level	Point Cost
1	-80	8	-15	15	60
2	-70	9	-10	16	80
3	-60	10	0	17	100
4	-50	11	10	18	125
5	-40	12	20	19	150
6	-30	13	30	20	175
7	-20	14	45	then 25 pts./level	

Speed

Your Speed score is equal to (HT + DX) ÷ 4.

Advantages

All advantages from the Basic Set are listed on p. 3 of this reference.

Disadvantages

All disadvantages from the Basic Set are listed on p. 3 of this reference. Unless the GM rules otherwise, you are limited to disadvantages totalling 40 bonus points or less, or a single disadvantage of any point value. An attribute level of 7 or less counts as a disadvantage here.

Quirks

You may take five "quirks" (see p. 41) at -1 point each. These do not count against your 40 points of disadvantages, but you must roleplay them.

Physical Appearance

You may set this as you please. Outstanding good looks are an advantage; outstanding bad looks are a disadvantage (see p. 15). Anything else is up to you. Use the tables below only if you want a randomly generated appearance.

Height and Weight

You are free to choose any height and weight for your characters, within reason (whatever you think that is). Or you can roll the dice. The tables below can be used to determine "average" height and weight, and to provide a slight random variation if desired. Average height is based on your ST score, as follows:

ST	Height	Weight	ST	Height	Weight
≤ 5'2"		120 lbs.	10	5'9"	150 lbs.
	5'3"	130 lbs.	11	5'10"	155 lbs.
≤ 5	5'4"	130 lbs.	12	5'11"	160 lbs.
6	5'5"	135 lbs.	13	6 feet	165 lbs.
7	5'6"	135 lbs.	14	6'1"	170 lbs.
8	5'7"	140 lbs.	15	6'2"	180 lbs.
9	5'8"	145 lbs.	≥ 16	6'3"	190 lbs.

For each inch over 6'3", add 10 lbs. to average weight.

Modifications

If you don't want a character of exactly average height or weight, roll 3 dice and consult the following table. Determine modified (i.e., true) height before determining weight – then determine weight based on your true height, and use the modification table again to determine true weight.

Die roll of		
3: -6" or -40 lbs.	12: +1" or +5 lbs.	
4: -5" or -30 lbs.	13: +2" or +5 lbs.	
5: -4" or -20 lbs.	14: +3" or +10 lbs.	
6: -3" or -10 lbs.	15: +4" or +20 lbs.	
7: -2" or -5 lbs.	16: +5" or +30 lbs.	
8: -1" or -5 lbs.	17: +6" or +40 lbs.	
9, 10, 11: no modifications	18: +6" or +50 lbs.	

These tables assume the character is a 20th-century male. For a female, subtract 2" from average height and 10 lbs. from average weight. For a historically accurate pre-19th-century character, subtract 3" from average height. Weight is determined *after* height.

To determine skin, hair and eye color, refer to pp. 84-85.

Skills

All skills from the Basic Set are listed on pp. 2 and 3 of this reference. Unless the GM rules otherwise, the maximum number of points a beginning PC can spend on skills is equal to twice his age. Point costs for skills levels are figured as follows:

Physical Skills

Your Final Skill Level	Difficulty of Skill		
	Easy	Average	Hard
DX-3	–	–	½ point
DX-2	–	½ point	1 point
DX-1	½ point	1 point	2 points
DX	1 point	2 points	4 points
DX+1	2 points	4 points	8 points
DX+2	4 points	8 points	16 points
DX+3	8 points	16 points	24 points
DX+4	16 points	24 points	32 points
DX+5	24 points	32 points	40 points

Mental Skills

Your Final Skill Level	Difficulty of Skill			
	Easy	Average	Hard	Very Hard
IQ-4	–	–	–	½ point
IQ-3	–	–	½ point	1 point
IQ-2	–	½ point	1 point·	2 points
IQ-1	½ point	1 point	2 points	4 points
IQ	1 point	2 points	4 points	8 points
IQ+1	2 points	4 points	6 points	12 points
IQ+2	4 points	6 points	8 points	16 points
IQ+3	6 points	8 points	10 points	20 points
IQ+4	8 points	10 points	12 points	24 points
IQ+5	10 points	12 points	14 points	28 points

Advantages

Advantage	Cost	Page
Absolute Direction	5	19
Absolute Timing	5	19
Acute Hearing	2 per +1	19
Acute Taste & Smell	2 per +1	19
Acute Vision	2 per +1	19
Alertness	5 per +1	19
Allies	variable	23
Ally Group	variable	232
Alternate Identity	15 or 5/identity	233
Ambidexterity	10	19
Animal Empathy	5	19
Appearance: Attractive (+1)	5	15
Handsome/Beautiful (+2/+4)	15	
Very Handsome/Very Beautiful (+2/+6)	25	
Blessed	variable	233
Charisma	5 per +1	19
Clerical Investment	5 or more	19
Combat Reflexes	15	20
Common Sense	10	20
Contacts	variable	234
Danger Sense	15	20
Dark Vision	25	235
Destiny	variable	235
Double-Jointed	5	20
Eidetic Memory	30/60	20
Empathy	15	20
Extra Fatigue	3 per point	236
Extra Hit Points	5 per point	236
Favor	variable	236
Fearlessness	2 per level	236
Hard to Kill	5 per level	236
Healing	25	237
High Pain Threshold	10	20
Immunity to Disease	10	20
Infravision	15	237
Intuition	15	20
Language Talent	2 per +1	20
Legal Enforcement Powers	5/10/15	21
Legal Immunity	5/10/15/20	237
Lightning Calculator	5	21
Literacy	10 (TL4-)	21
Longevity	5	21
Luck	15/30	21
Magical Aptitude (Magery)	15/25/35	21
Magical Resistance	2 per +1	21
Mathematical Ability	10	22
Military Rank	5 per rank (max. 40)	22
Musical Ability	1 per +1	22
Night Vision	10	22
Patrons	variable	24
Perfect Balance	15	237
Peripheral Vision	15	22
Psionic Resistance	2 per level	22
Rapid Healing	5	22
Reputation	5 per +1 (max. 20)	17
Status	5 per level (max. 40)	18
Strong Will	4/+1	23
Toughness	10 (DR1)/25 (DR2)	23
Unfazeable	15 or more	237
Unusual Background	10 or more	23
Voice	10	23
Wealth: Comfortable (×2)	10	16
Wealthy (×5)	20	
Very Wealthy (×20)	30	
Filthy Rich (×100)	50	
Multimillionaire	25/level	237
Zeroed	10	237

Disadvantages

Disadvantage	Cost	Page
Absent-Mindedness	-15	30
Addiction	variable	30
Age	-3 per year over 50	27
Albinism	-10	27
Alcoholism	-15/-20	30
Amnesia	-10/-25	239
Appearance:		15
Unattractive (-1)	-5	
Ugly (-2)	-10	
Hideous (-4)	-20	
Bad Sight	-10/-25	27
Bad Temper	-10	31
Berserk	-15	31
Blindness	-50	27
Bloodlust	-10	31
Bully	-10	31
Code of Honor	-5 to -15	31
Color Blindness	-10	28
Combat Paralysis	-15	32
Compulsive Behavior	-5 to -15	32
Generosity	-5	239
Spendthrift	-5/-10/-15	240
Compulsive Carousing	-5 to -10	239
Compulsive Lying	-15	32
Cowardice	-10	32
Curious	-5/-10/-15	240
Cursed	-75	240
Deafness	-20	28
Delusions	-1/-5/-10/-15	32
Dependents	variable	38
Destiny	variable	238
Duties	variable	39
Duty (Involuntary)	extra -5	
Dwarfism	-15	28
Dyslexia	-5/-15	33
Enemies	variable	39
Epilepsy	-30	28
Eunuch	-5	28
Fanaticism	-15	33
Fat	-10/-20	28
Flashbacks	variable	240
Gigantism	-10	28
Glory Hound	-15	240
Gluttony	-5	33
Greed	-15	33
Gullibility	-10	33
Hard of Hearing	-10	28
Hemophilia	-30	28
Honesty	-10	33
Illiteracy	-10 (TL5+)	33
Impulsiveness	-10	33
Incompetence	-1	240
Intolerance	-5/-10	34
Jealousy	-10	34
Jinxed	-20/-40/-60	240
Kleptomania	-15	34
Lame: Crippled Leg	-15	29
One leg	-25	
Legless	-35	
Laziness	-10	34
Lecherousness	-15	34
Low Pain Threshold	-10	29
Megalomania	-10	34
Manic-Depressive	-20	241
Miserliness	-10	34
Mute	-25	29
No Sense of Humor	-10	241
No Sense of Smell/Taste	-5	29
Obsession	-5 to -15	241
Odious Personal Habits	-5/-10/-15	26
On the Edge	-15	241
One Arm	-20	29
One Eye	-15	29
One Hand	-15	29
Overconfidence	-10	34
Overweight	-5	29
Pacifism	-15/-30	35
Paranoia	-10	35
Phobias	variable	35
Poverty: Struggling (×1/2)	-10	16
Poor (×1/5)	-15	
Dead Broke (×0)	-25	
Primitive	5 per TL level	26
Pyromania	-5	36
Quirk	-1	41
Reputation	-5/-1 (max. -20)	17
Sadism	-15	36
Secret	variable	238
Sense of Duty	-5/-10/-15/-20	39
Shyness	-5, -10, -15	37
Skinny	-5	29
Social Stigma	-5/-10/-15/-20	27
Split Personality	-10/-15	37
Status	-5 per level (max. -20)	18
Stubbornness	-5	37
Stuttering	-10	37
Terminally Ill	-50/-75/-100	239
Trademark	variable	241
Truthfulness	-5	37
Unluckiness	-10	37
Vow	-1, -5, -10, -15	37
Weak Will	-8 per -1	37
Weirdness Magnet	-15	239
Youth	-2 per year (max. -6)	29

Skills

Skill	Type/Level	Default	Page
Accounting	M/H	IQ-10, Merchant-5 or Mathematics-5; *Prereq.*	58
Acting	M/A	IQ-5, Bard-5 or Performance-2	62
Acrobatics	P/H	DX-6	48
Administration	M/A	IQ-6 or Merchant-3	62
Agronomy/TL	M/A	IQ-5	59
Alchemy/TL	M/VH	None	59
Animal Handling	M/H	IQ-6	46
Anthropology	M/H	IQ-6	59
Area Knowledge (type)	M/E	IQ-4	62
Archaeology	M/H	IQ-6	59
Architecture/TL	M/A	IQ-5	59
Armoury/TL (type)	M/A	IQ-5, Weapon skill-6 (for that weapon only) or Blacksmith-3 at TL4 and below	53
Artist	M/H	IQ-6	47
Astrogation	M/A	Navigation-5, Astronomy-4 or Mathematics-4	59
Astronomy/TL	M/H	IQ-6	60
Axe/Mace	P/A	DX-5	49
Axe Throwing	P/E	DX-4	49
Bard	M/A	IQ-5 or Performance-2	47
Battlesuit/TL	M/A	IQ-5, DX-5 or Vacc Suit-3	49
Beam Weapons/TL (type)	P/E	DX-4 or (other Beam Weapon)-4	49
Bicycling	P/E	DX-4 or Motorcycle	68
Biochemistry/TL	M/VH	Chemistry-5; *Prereq.*	60
Biology		*This is not an individual skill.* See p. 60	
Blackjack	P/E	DX-4	49
Black Powder Weapons/TL (type)	P/E	DX-4	49
Blacksmith/TL	M/A	IQ-5 or Jeweler-4	53
Blowpipe	P/H	DX-6	49
Boating	P/A	IQ-5, DX-5 or Powerboat-3	68
Body Sense	P/H	DX-6 or Acrobatics-3	242
Bolas	P/A	None	49
Botany/TL	M/H	IQ-6 or Agronomy-5	60
Bow	P/H	DX-6	50
Boxing	P/A	None	242
Brawling	P/E	None	50
Breath Control	M/VH	None	48
Broadsword	P/A	DX-5, Shortsword-2 or Force Sword-3	50
Buckler	P/E	DX-4 or Shield-2	50
Calligraphy	P/A	Artist-2 or DX-5; *Prereq.*	47
Camouflage	M/E	IQ-4 or Survival-2	65
Carousing	P/A	HT-4; based on *HT*	63
Carpentry	M/E	IQ-4 or DX-4	53
Chemistry/TL	M/H	IQ-6	60
Climbing	P/A	DX-5 or ST-5	57
Cloak	P/A	DX-5, Buckler-4 or Shield-4	242
Computer Hacking	M/VH	Computer Operation-8 or Computer Programming-4	245
Computer Operation/TL	M/E	IQ-4 (TL7+ only)	58

Skill	Type/Level	Default	Page
Computer Programming/TL	M/H	None; *Prereq.*	60
Cooking	M/E	IQ-4	53
Criminology/TL	M/A	IQ-4	60
Crossbow	P/E	DX-4	50
Cryptanalysis/TL	M/H	special	245
Dancing	P/A	DX-5	47
Demolition/TL	M/A	IQ-5 or Engineer-3	65
Detect Lies	M/H	IQ-6 or Psychology-4	65
Diagnosis/TL	M/H	IQ-6, First Aid-8, Vet-5 or Physician-4	56
Diplomacy	M/H	IQ-6	63
Disguise	M/A	IQ-5	65
Driving/TL	P/A	IQ-5 or DX-5	68
Ecology/TL	M/H	IQ-6 or Naturalist-3	60
Economics	M/H	IQ-6 or Merchant-6	60
Electronics/TL (type)	M/H	Other Electronics-4; *Prereq.*	60
Electronics Operation/TL (type)	M/A	IQ-5 or Electronics-3	58
Engineer/TL (type)	M/H	Mechanic-6; *Prereq.*	60
Escape	P/H	DX-6	65
Exoskeleton	P/A	IQ-6, DX-6 or Battlesuit-2	247
Falconry	M/A	IQ-5	46
Fast-Draw (type)	P/E	None	50
Fast-Talk	M/A	IQ-5 or Acting-5	63
Fencing	P/A	DX-5	50
First Aid/TL	M/E	Physician, IQ-5, Vet-5 or Physiology-5	56
Fishing	M/E	IQ-4	57
Flail	P/H	DX-6	50
Flight	P/A	DX-4	242
Force Shield	P/E	DX-4	50
Force Sword	P/A	DX-5 or (other Sword skill)-3	50
Forensics/TL	M/H	Criminology-4	61
Forgery/TL	M/H	IQ-6, DX-8 or Artist-5	65
Forward Observer/TL	M/A	IQ-5	243
Free Fall	P/A	DX-5 or HT-5	48
Freight Handling	M/A	IQ-5	46
Gambling	M/A	IQ-5 or Mathematics-5	63
Games (type)	M/E	IQ-5	243
Genetics/TL	M/VH	Biochemistry-5 or Physiology-5	61
Geology/TL	M/H	IQ-6 or Prospecting-4	61
Gesture	M/E	IQ-4 or Sign Language	55
Gunner/TL (type)	P/A	DX-5 or (other Gunner skill)-4	50
Guns/TL (type)	P/E	DX-4 or (other Gun skill)-4	51
Hard-Hat Diving	M/A	Scuba-2	244
Heraldry	M/A	IQ-5 or Savoir-Faire-3	58
Hiking	P/A	None	244
History	M/H	IQ-6 or Archaeology-6	61
Holdout	M/A	IQ-5 or Sleight of Hand-3	66
Hunting		See *Tracking*, p. 57	
Hypnotism	M/H	None	56
Intelligence Analysis	M/H	IQ-6	66
Interrogation	M/A	IQ-5 or Intimidation-3	66
Intimidation	M/A	ST-5 or Acting-3	246
Jeweler/TL	M/H	IQ-6 or Blacksmith-4	53
Judo	P/H	None	51
Jumping	P/E	None	48
Karate	P/H	None	51
Knife	P/E	DX-4	51
Knife Throwing	P/E	DX-4	51
Lance	P/A	Spear-3 (with Riding 12+) or DX-6 for others; *Prereq.*	51
Languages	M/varies	IQ for native language	54
Lasso	P/A	None	51
Law	M/H	IQ-6	58
Leadership	M/A	ST-5	63
Leatherworking	M/E	IQ-4 or DX-5	53
Linguistics	M/VH	None	61
Lip Reading	M/A	Vision-10	66
Literacy		*This is not considered a skill.* See pp. 17, 21, 33	
Literature	M/H	IQ-6	61
Lockpicking/TL	M/A	IQ-5	67
Mathematics	M/H	IQ-6	61
Mechanic/TL (type)	M/A	IQ-5, Engineer-4, others	54
Merchant	M/A	IQ-5	64
Metallurgy/TL	M/H	Blacksmith-8, Jeweler-8, Armoury-8 or Chemistry-5	61
Meteorology/TL	M/A	IQ-5	61
Mind Block	M/A	Will-4	244
Motorcycle	P/E	DX-5, IQ-5 or Bicycling-5	69
Musical Instrument	M/H	Any *similar* instrument-3	47
Naturalist	M/H	IQ-6	57
Navigation/TL	M/H	Astronomy-5 or Seamanship-5	57
Net	P/H	None	51
No-Land Extraction	IQ-6	243	
Nuclear Physics/TL	M/VH	None; *Prereq.*	61
Nuclear-Biological-Chemical Warfare/TL	M/A	IQ-5	243
Occultism	M/A	IQ-6	61
Orienteering	M/A	IQ-5	244
Packing	M/H	Animal Handling-6 or IQ-6; *Prereq.*	46

Skill	Type/Level	Default	Page
Parachuting	P/E	DX-4 or IQ-6	48
Performance	M/A	IQ-5, Acting-2 or Bard-2	64
Philosophy	M/H	IQ-6	245
Photography/TL	M/A	IQ-5	47
Physician/TL	M/H	Vet-5, First Aid-11 or IQ-7	56
Physics/TL	M/H	IQ-6	61
Physiology/TL (race)	M/VH	IQ-7 or any Medical skill-5	61
Pickpocket	P/H	DX-6 or Sleight of Hand-4	67
Piloting/TL	P/A	IQ-6	69
Planetology	M/A	IQ-5, Geology-4, Meteorology-4 or other Planetology-3	245
Poetry	M/A	IQ-5 or Language-5	47
Poisons	M/H	IQ-6, Chemistry-5, Physician-3, others	67
Polearm	P/A	DX-5	51
Politics	M/A	IQ-5 or Diplomacy-5	64
Pottery	M/A	IQ-5	54
Powerboat	P/A	IQ-5, DX-5 or Boating-3	69
Prospecting	M/A	IQ-5 or Geology-4	62
Psionics		*See pp. 165-176*	
Psychology	M/H	IQ-6	62
Public Speaking		See *Bard*, p. 36	
Research	M/A	IQ-5 or Writing-3	62
Riding (type)	P/A	Animal Handling-3 or DX-5	46
Running	P/H	None; based on *HT*	48
Savoir-Faire	M/E	IQ-4	64
Scrounging	M/E	IQ-4	67
Scuba	M/A	IQ-5 or Swimming-5	48
Sculpting	P/A	DX-5 or IQ-5	47
Seamanship/TL	M/E	IQ-4	57
Sex Appeal	M/A	HT-3; based on *HT*	64
Shadowing	M/A	IQ-6 or Stealth-4 (on foot)	67
Shield	P/E	DX-4 or Buckler-2	52
Shipbuilding/TL	M/H	IQ-6	54
Shortsword	P/A	DX-5, Broadsword-2 or Force Sword-3	52
Sign Language (type)	M/A	None	55
Singing	P/E	HT-4	48
Skiing	P/H	DX-6	49
Sleight of Hand	P/H	None	67
Sling	P/H	DX-6	52
Spear	P/A	DX-5 or Staff-2	52
Spear Thrower	P/A	DX-4 or Spear Throwing-4	52
Spear Throwing	P/E	DX-4 or Spear Thrower-4	52
Speed-Load (type)	P/E	None	52
Spell Throwing	P/E	DX-3, Throwing or Spell Throwing (other spell)-2	244
Spells		*See pp. 155-164*	
Sports (type)	P/A	DX-5; very rough sports also default to ST-5	49
Staff	P/H	DX-5 or Spear-2	52
Stealth	P/A	IQ-5 or DX-5	67
Strategy (type)	M/H	IQ-6, Tactics-6 or (other Strategy)-4	64
Streetwise	M/A	IQ-5	68
Surgery/TL	M/VH	Vet-5, Physician-5, Physiology-8 or First Aid-12. *Prereq.*	56
Survival (by type)	M/A	IQ-5, Naturalist-3 or Survival (other area type)-3	57
Swimming	P/E	ST-5 or DX-4	49
Tactics	M/H	IQ-6 or Strategy-6	64
Teaching	M/A	IQ-5	64
Teamster (type)	M/A	Animal Handling-4 or Riding-2; *Prereq.*	47
Telegraphy	M/E	None	55
Theology	M/H	IQ-6	62
Throwing	P/H	None	49
Throwing Stick	P/E	DX-4	243
Thrown Weapon (type)	P/E	DX-4	52
Tracking	M/A	IQ-5 or Naturalist-5	57
Traps/TL	M/A	IQ-5, DX-5 or Lockpicking-3	68
Two-Handed Axe/Mace	P/A	DX-5	52
Two-Handed Sword	P/A	DX-5 or Force Sword-3	52
Underwater Demolition/TL	M/A	Demolition-2; *Prereq.*	68
Vacc Suit/TL	M/A	IQ-6 (TL7+ only)	69
Ventriloquism	M/H	None	68
Veterinary/TL	M/H	Any appropriate Medical skill-5, or Animal Handling-5	47
Video Production	M/A	IQ-6, or Performance-4	242
Whip	P/A	None	52
Woodworking	P/A	DX-5 or Carpentry-3	54
Wrestling	P/A	DX-5	243
Writing	M/A	IQ-5 or Language-5	48
Xenobiology	M/A	None	246
Xenology	M/H	IQ-6	246
Zoology	M/H	IQ-6 or any Animal skill-6	62

Equipment

Before buying equipment, determine how much *money* you have. This is $1,000 unless (a) the GM or scenario says otherwise, or (b) you chose some level of Wealth as an advantage or Poverty as a disadvantage. This is the total value of your savings and belongings.

Choosing Weapons

Refer to the *Weapon Table* appropriate for the scenario or time period in which you are playing.

To determine the damage that *you* do with any low-tech weapon, take the appropriate type of Basic Weapon Damage (swinging or thrusting) for your own ST. Add or subtract the damage modifier given on the Weapon Table for that weapon.

The basic damage you do with each type of atttack is determined by your ST.

Basic Weapon Damage

ST	Thrust	Swing	ST	Thrust	Swing
4	0	0	13	1d	2d-1
5	1d-5	1d-5	14	1d	2d
6	1d-4	1d-4	15	1d+1	2d+1
7	1d-3	1d-3	16	1d+1	2d+2
8	1d-3	1d-2	17	1d+2	3d-1
9	1d-2	1d-1	18	1d+2	3d
10	1d-2	1d	19	2d-1	3d+1
11	1d-1	1d+1	20	2d-1	3d+2
12	1d-1	1d+2			

For strengths over 20, follow the same progression.

Choosing a Shield

In a fantasy, medieval or other low-tech game (TL4 and below) you may want a shield. In a higher-tech situation, don't bother . . . unless you are at TL11+ , when you can get a Force Shield!

Type	Passive Defense	Cost	Weight	Hits
Improvised	1 or 2	–	varies	varies
Buckler	1	$25	2 lbs.	5/20
Small	2	$40	8 lbs.	5/30
Medium	3	$60	15 lbs.	7/40
Large	4	$90	25 lbs.	9/60
Force (TL11+)	4	$1,500	½ lb.	–

Remember that your effective weapon skill is at -2 if you have a large shield.

Choosing Armor

In a low-tech game (TL4 and below) you will want armor if you expect to be in combat. In some high-tech situations, armor is also appropriate. If you are using the Advanced Combat System and selecting armor part by part, refer to the separate Armor Table. Otherwise, choose armor from the table below. "TL" indicates the tech level at which that type of armor is usual. Each set of armor includes light clothing to wear underneath.

Type	TL	PD	DR	Cost	Weight
Summer clothing	any	0	0	$20	2
Winter clothing	any	0	1	$60	5
Padded cloth armor	1-4	1	1	$180	14
Light leather armor	1-4	1	1	$210	10
Heavy leather armor	1-4	2	2	$350	20
Chainmail	3-4	3[1]	4[2]	$550	45
Scale armor	2-4	3	4	$750	50
Half plate[3]	2-4	4	5	$2000	70
Light plate[3]	3-4	4	6	$4000	90
Heavy plate[3]	3-4	4	7	$6000	110
Flak jacket[4]	6	2	3	$220	17
Kevlar (light)[4]	7	2[1]	4[2]	$220	5
Kevlar (heavy)[4]	7	2[1]	12[2]	$420	9
Light body armor	7+	4	15	$270	22
Reflec[5]	8-9	6	2	$320	4
Medium body armor	8+	6	25	$1,520	32
Heavy combat armor	9+	6	50	$2,520	52

[1] 1 vs. impaling [2] 2 vs. impaling [3] all combat skills at -1 [4] protects torso only [5] against lasers only. PD3, DR 0 against sonics. No protection vs. other weapons.

Defenses

Passive Defenses: total PD from armor, shield, etc.
Dodge: equal to your Move score.
Block: ½ your Shield skill, rounded down.
Parry: ½ your skill for the hand weapon you are using, rounded down.
Damage Resistance: total DR from armor, Toughness, etc.

Your "Move" Score

Subtract the "movement penalty" for your encumbrance level (below) from your Basic Speed. Round fractions down. The result is your Move score.

Completing Your Character

Double-check point totals and fill in the character sketch. Your character is now complete.

Encumbrance

Total the weight of everything you are carrying.

Weight up to *twice* ST: no encumbrance. You have no penalty.

Weight up to *four times* ST: light encumbrance. Movement penalty of 1.

Weight up to *six times* ST: medium encumbrance. Movement penalty of 2.

Weight up to *12 times* ST: heavy encumbrance. Movement penalty of 3.

Weight up to *20 times* ST: extra-heavy encumbrance. Movement penalty of 4.

Weight up to *30 times* ST: absolute *most* you can carry! Move only 1 hex per turn, and take one point of *fatigue* each turn.

Encumbrance Levels

ST	None (0)	Light (1)	Medium (2)	Heavy (3)	Extra-Heavy (4)
6	12 lbs.	24 lbs.	36 lbs.	72 lbs.	120 lbs.
7	14 lbs.	28 lbs.	42 lbs.	84 lbs.	140 lbs.
8	16 lbs.	32 lbs.	48 lbs.	96 lbs.	160 lbs.
9	18 lbs.	36 lbs.	54 lbs.	108 lbs.	180 lbs.
10	20 lbs.	40 lbs.	60 lbs.	120 lbs.	200 lbs.
11	22 lbs.	44 lbs.	66 lbs.	132 lbs.	220 lbs.
12	24 lbs.	48 lbs.	72 lbs.	144 lbs.	240 lbs.
13	26 lbs.	52 lbs.	78 lbs.	156 lbs.	260 lbs.
14	28 lbs.	56 lbs.	84 lbs.	168 lbs.	280 lbs.
15	30 lbs.	60 lbs.	90 lbs.	180 lbs.	300 lbs.
16	32 lbs.	64 lbs.	96 lbs.	192 lbs.	320 lbs.
17	34 lbs.	68 lbs.	102 lbs.	204 lbs.	340 lbs.
18	36 lbs.	72 lbs.	108 lbs.	216 lbs.	360 lbs.
19	38 lbs.	76 lbs.	114 lbs.	228 lbs.	380 lbs.
20	40 lbs.	80 lbs.	120 lbs.	240 lbs.	400 lbs.

GURPS®
CHARACTER
SHEET

Name _____ Player _____

Appearance _____

_____

Date Created	Sequence
Unspent Points	Point Total

Pt. Cost

ST

DX

IQ

HT

Mvmt

FATIGUE

DAMAGE

Thrust: _____

Swing: _____

Kick: _____

____: _____

HITS TAKEN

BASIC SPEED	MOVE
(HT+DX)/4	Round off

SWIM

ENCUMBRANCE   **MOVE**

None (0) = 2×ST _____ _____
Light (1) = 4×ST _____ _____
Med (2) = 6×ST _____ _____
Hvy (3) = 12×ST _____ _____
X-hvy (4) = 20×ST _____ _____

BODY PROTECTION

Head Body Arms Legs Hands Feet ALL

	Head	Body	Arms	Legs	Hands	Feet	ALL
PD							
DR							

ACTIVE DEFENSES

DODGE	PARRY	BLOCK
= Move	Weapon/2	Shield/2

OTHER PD
Shield: _____

OTHER DR

Pt. Cost

ADVANTAGES, DISADVANTAGES AND QUIRKS

SKILLS   Pt. Cost   Level

SUMMARY   Point Total

Attributes _____

Advantages _____

Disadvantages _____

Quirks _____

Skills _____

TOTAL

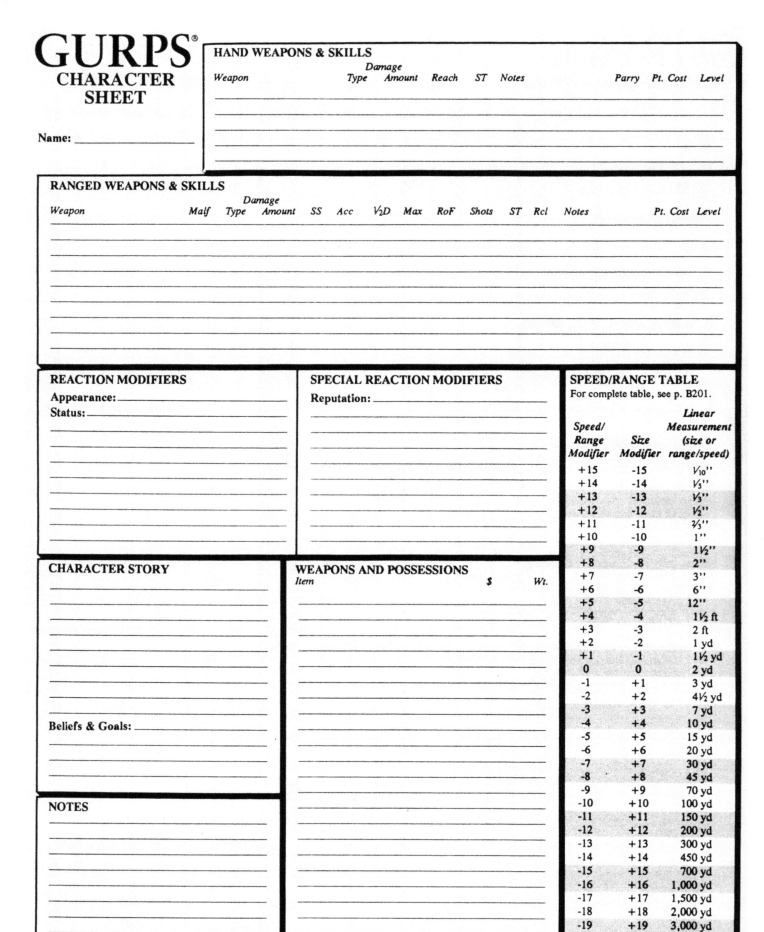

GURPS®
CHARACTER
SHEET

Name _____ Player _____

Appearance _____
_____

Date Created	Sequence
Unspent Points	Point Total

Pt. Cost

ST

DX

IQ

HT

Mvmt

FATIGUE

DAMAGE
Thrust: _____
Swing: _____
Kick: _____
_____: _____

HITS TAKEN

BASIC SPEED	MOVE
(HT+DX)/4	Round off

SWIM

ENCUMBRANCE — **MOVE**

None (0) = 2×ST _____ _____
Light (1) = 4×ST _____ _____
Med (2) = 6×ST _____ _____
Hvy (3) = 12×ST _____ _____
X-hvy (4) = 20×ST _____ _____

ACTIVE DEFENSES

DODGE	PARRY	BLOCK
= Move	Weapon/2	Shield/2

BODY PROTECTION

	Head	Body	Arms	Legs	Hands	Feet	ALL
PD							
DR							

OTHER PD
Shield: _____

OTHER DR

SKILLS — Pt. Cost — Level

_____

Pt. Cost — ADVANTAGES, DISADVANTAGES AND QUIRKS

SUMMARY	Point Total
Attributes	_____
Advantages	_____
Disadvantages	_____
Quirks	_____
Skills	_____
TOTAL	

GURPS®
CHARACTER SHEET

Name: _____

HAND WEAPONS & SKILLS

Weapon	Damage Type	Damage Amount	Reach	ST	Notes	Parry	Pt. Cost	Level

RANGED WEAPONS & SKILLS

Weapon	Malf	Damage Type	Damage Amount	SS	Acc	½D	Max	RoF	Shots	ST	Rcl	Notes	Pt. Cost	Level

REACTION MODIFIERS

Appearance: _____
Status: _____
_____
_____
_____
_____
_____
_____

SPECIAL REACTION MODIFIERS

Reputation: _____
_____
_____
_____
_____
_____
_____
_____

SPEED/RANGE TABLE

For complete table, see p. B201.

Speed/ Range Modifier	Size Modifier	Linear Measurement (size or range/speed)
+15	-15	⅒"
+14	-14	⅕"
+13	-13	⅓"
+12	-12	½"
+11	-11	⅔"
+10	-10	1"
+9	-9	1½"
+8	-8	2"
+7	-7	3"
+6	-6	6"
+5	-5	12"
+4	-4	1½ ft
+3	-3	2 ft
+2	-2	1 yd
+1	-1	1½ yd
0	0	2 yd
-1	+1	3 yd
-2	+2	4½ yd
-3	+3	7 yd
-4	+4	10 yd
-5	+5	15 yd
-6	+6	20 yd
-7	+7	30 yd
-8	+8	45 yd
-9	+9	70 yd
-10	+10	100 yd
-11	+11	150 yd
-12	+12	200 yd
-13	+13	300 yd
-14	+14	450 yd
-15	+15	700 yd
-16	+16	1,000 yd
-17	+17	1,500 yd
-18	+18	2,000 yd
-19	+19	3,000 yd
-20	+20	4,500 yd
-21	+21	7,000 yd
-22	+22	10,000 yd

CHARACTER STORY

_____
_____
_____
_____
_____
_____
_____
_____
_____

Beliefs & Goals: _____
_____
_____
_____

WEAPONS AND POSSESSIONS

Item	$	Wt.
Totals: $		Lbs.

NOTES

_____
_____
_____
_____
_____
_____
_____
_____

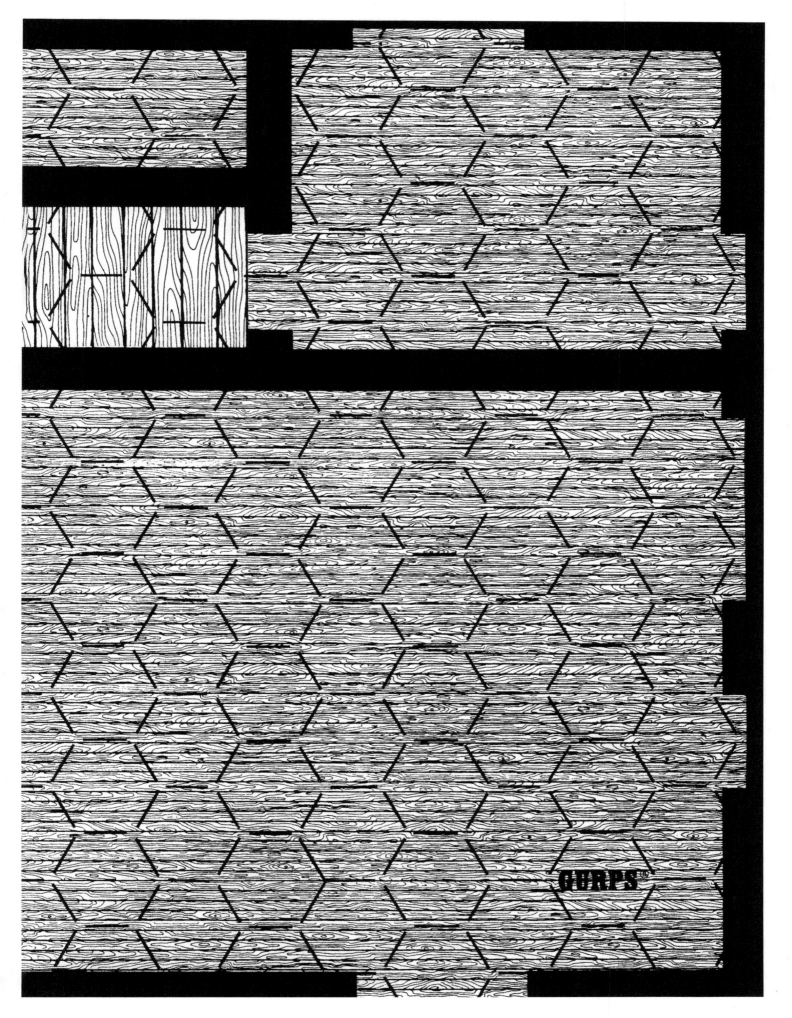

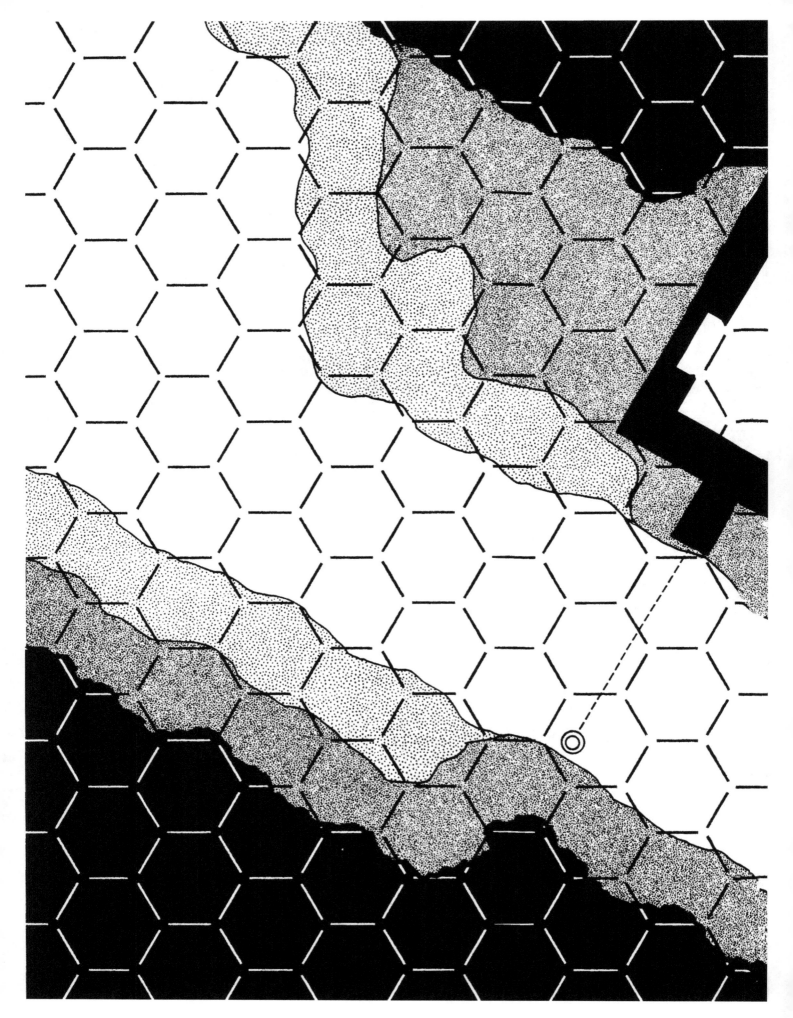

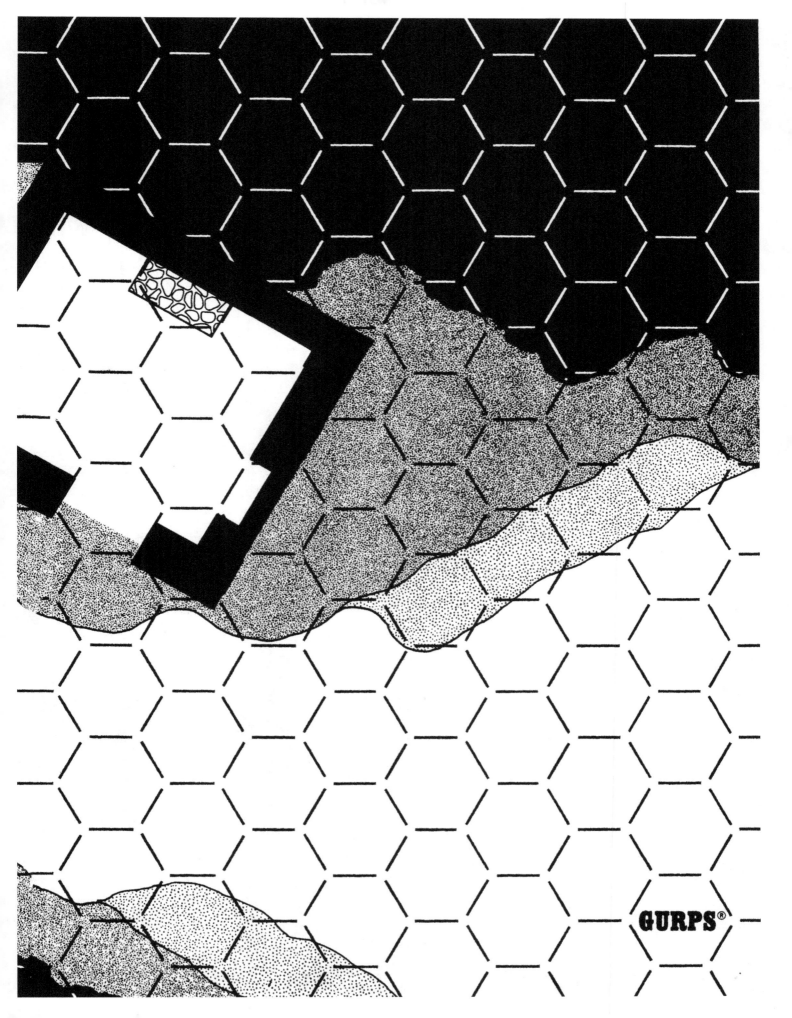

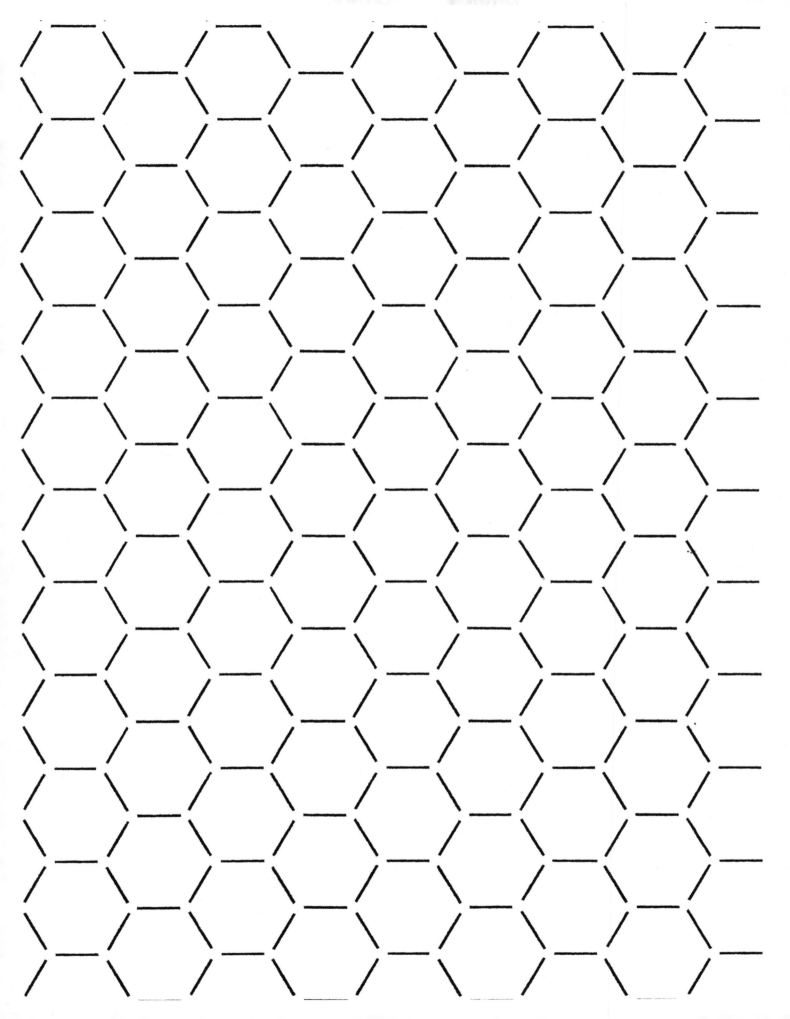

GM CONTROL SHEET

CHARACTERS and NPCs

Character Name and Player	Reaction + or –	ST	DX	IQ	HT	Speed: SPD	MOV	Passive Defense Armor	Shield	DR	Hits Taken

SPECIAL ABILITIES

Character   Abilities

REQUIRED ROLLS

Character   Roll   To Avoid

Time Use Form

Character _____ Played by _____

Period of time covered _____

Time use:

Sleep: 56 hrs/week (70 if you are Lazy) ....

Meals, personal care, etc. 20

Job: time spent depends on job or Wealth level ....

Travel (depends on adventure and situation) ....

Religious observances, etc. ....

Entertainment ....

Study of _____ skill ....

Study of _____ skill ....

Study of _____ skill ....

Study of _____ skill ....

Study of _____ skill ....

Study of _____ skill ....

Other: ....

TOTAL: per week .... 168 hours

Automatic language study: If you are in a foreign country, or if you are for any reason speaking a foreign language exclusively, this counts as an automatic 4 hours per day of language practice. Language skill gained with "automatic" practice cannot exceed your IQ.
Hours of automatic language study: (4/day): _____

Automatic study on the job: If your job involves a skill (and most do) you can count ¼ of the time spent on the job as "study." This time may be split between two skills if both are job related.
Hours of automatic job study (¼ time spent at work): _____

Study bonuses for magical intervention, mechanical education, etc.:

Skill: _____ Study equivalent (hours): _____

Skill: _____ Study equivalent (hours): _____

Skill: _____ Study equivalent (hours): _____

Skill: _____ Study equivalent (hours): _____

Other notes:

Character Record (blank card)

Name: _____ Reaction +/-: _____ Point Total: _____

Appearance: _____ Advantages, Disadvantages, Quirks:

ST _____ Fatigue: _____

DX _____ Basic Damage

IQ _____ Thrust: _____

HT _____ Swing: _____

Hits Taken: _____ Skills:

Basic Speed: _____ Move: _____

Encumbrance: _____

Dodge: _____ Parry: _____ Block: _____

Weapons and Possessions:

	Head	Body	Arms	Hands	Legs	Feet
PD						
DR						

Weapon Ranges:

NPC Record Card

To make it easy to keep track of NPCs, all necessary data can be kept on a 3" × 5" card. A boxful of foes is easy to use; you can even use a paper clip to fasten the appropriate *Cardboard Heroes* figures to each card.

Name: MAX *the guard* Reaction +/-: *-2 ordinarily* *+1 in combat* Point Total: 75

Appearance: INCREDIBLY THREATENING Advantages, Disadvantages, Quirks:

SENSE OF DUTY

GIGANTISM

12 ST Fatigue:

12 DX Basic Damage

10 IQ Thrust: 1d-1

11 HT Swing: 1d+2

Hits Taken:

Skills: BROADSWORD-16

KNIFE-16

Basic Speed: 5.75 Move: 5

Encumbrance: NONE

Dodge: 5 Parry: 8 Block: 0

Weapons and Possessions:

SCIMITAR [Bastard sword] cut 1d+3 $650 5 lbs

(2-hex reach) crush 1d

KNIFE (large) cut 1d $40 1 lb.

imp 1d-1

	Head	Body	Arms	Hands	Legs	Feet
PD	0	0	0	0	0	0
DR	(2)	0	0	0	0	0

Weapon Ranges:

KNIFE imp 1-1 SS:12 ACC:0 ½:10 Max:17

Where the world is round, but also flat!

GURPS Fourth Edition

DISCWORLD
ROLEPLAYING GAME

By Terry Pratchett and Phil Masters
Illustrated by Paul Kidby and Sean Murray

STEVE JACKSON GAMES

Journey through the mind of Terry Pratchett . . .
Find it at your friendly local game store today!
Or order at warehouse23.com.

STEVE JACKSON GAMES

sjgames.com
#PlaySJGames

DUNGEON FANTASY™

POWERED BY GURPS®

AVAILABLE NOW

DungeonFantasy.SJGames.com

Storm Dungeons, Slay Monsters, Seize Treasure

A fun hack 'n' slash campaign challenges unique heroes with clever dungeons. To get the most out of your fantasy adventures, you need a game that lets you customize and perfect characters, monsters, treasures, and traps.

That's where the ready-to-play *Dungeon Fantasy Roleplaying Game* comes in. It harnesses the customizing power of the award-winning *Generic Universal RolePlaying System* (*GURPS*), and streamlines it so you have exactly what you need to take fully realized characters on fantastic adventures.

Choose from 11 classic professions and nine races. Tailor your hero using quick-start templates and the time-tested *GURPS* point-build system. Gear up with a massive list of customizable armor and weapons. Pick from over 400 spells. Then battle foes chosen from more than 80 monsters.

All this power guarantees epic games in no time . . . starting with the new adventure that comes in the box!

STEVE JACKSON GAMES

CPSIA information can be obtained
at www.ICGtesting.com
Printed in the USA
LVHW05s1225080718
583079LV00005B/256/P